CAMBRIDGE SOUTH ASIAN STUDIES

GANDHI'S RISE TO POWER

CAMBRIDGE SOUTH ASIAN STUDIES

These monographs are published by the Syndics of Cambridge University Press in association with the Cambridge University Centre for South Asian Studies. The following books have been published in this series:

1 S. GOPAL: *British Policy in India, 1858–1905*
2 J. A. B. PALMER: *The Mutiny Outbreak at Meerut in 1857*
3 A. DAS GUPTA: *Malabar in Asian Trade, 1740–1800*
4 G. OBEYESEKERE: *Land Tenure in a Village in Ceylon*
5 H. L. ERDMAN: *The Swatantra Party and Indian Conservatism*
6 S. N. MUKHERJEE: *Sir William Jones: A Study in Eighteenth-Century British Attitudes to India*
7 ABDUL MAJED KHAN: *The Transition in Bengal, 1756–1775: A Study of Saiyid Muhammad Reza Khan*
8 RADHE SHYAM RUNGTA: *The Rise of Business Corporations in India, 1851–1900*
9 PAMELA NIGHTINGALE: *Trade and Empire in Western India, 1784–1806*
10 AMIYA KUMAR BAGCHI: *Private Investment in India, 1900–1939*

GANDHI'S RISE TO POWER

Indian Politics 1915-1922

JUDITH M. BROWN

Lecturer in History, University of Manchester

CAMBRIDGE

AT THE UNIVERSITY PRESS

1972

Published by the Syndics of the Cambridge University Press
Bentley House, 200 Euston Road, London NW1 2DB
American Branch: 32 East 57th Street, New York, N.Y.10022

Library of Congress Catalogue Card Number: 71-171674

ISBN: 0 521 08353 2

Printed in Great Britain by
Alden & Mowbray Ltd at the Alden Press, Oxford

In Memory of My Father

CONTENTS

PREFACE

My interest in modern India grew into something deeper than curiosity about the country where I was born when I returned there to teach in 1962 before going to university. Post-graduate work provided the opportunity to develop this interest, just at the time when new work on Gandhi as a central figure in the politics of Indian nationalism seemed both necessary and possible as a result of the opening of new source material in England and India. I began my study of Gandhi's early Indian career for a Cambridge Ph.D. thesis and continued it during the tenure of an Ivy Buchler Research Fellowship at Girton College. I would like to express my gratitude to those who helped me during my research, in particular to my college for its generosity to me as a student and fellow, to the Managers of the Smuts Memorial Fund for a research and travel grant, to Dr Anil Seal, my former supervisor, and to the numerous friends in India who welcomed me into their homes and assisted my archival forays during two visits to the subcontinent in 1966–7 and 1969–70.

Details of the sources on which this book is based are in the bibliography: my thanks are due to the libraries and archives listed there for permission to consult the papers deposited with them, to the Government of India for permission to work on its Home Department records, and to the Government of Maharashtra for access to the Bombay Police Abstracts of 1915–22. I am particularly indebted for their friendly assistance to the staff of the Cambridge University Library; the Centre of South Asian Studies, Cambridge; the India Office Library; the National Archives of India; the History of the Freedom Movement Unit, Bombay; the Harijan Ashram, Ahmedabad; and the Nehru Memorial Museum and Library.

While I was writing this book I received generous help from many people. I owe special thanks to my colleague and former teacher, Mrs Margaret Bowker, and to Professors Jack Gallagher, Anthony Low and Eric Stokes, all of whom read parts of the manuscript and made valuable suggestions and criticisms. However, Swaraj obtains in scholarship as well as in the South Asian subcontinent, and the faults that remain are mine. Christopher Bayly, Gordon Johnson and Francis Robinson have also contributed to this book in many informal discussions and with their related studies.

I am grateful to the Committee of Management of the Centre of South Asian Studies, for including my book in this series; and to the staff of the Cambridge University Press for their courtesy and expertise. I also wish to record my deep thanks to Mrs Dusha Bateson who read the whole manuscript, and to my brother and sister-in-law, Peter and Kathy Brown, who helped in preparing it for the press. My greatest debt of gratitude is to my parents, whose constant encouragement and generosity made this book possible, though my father never saw it completed.

JUDITH M. BROWN

Cambridge
March, 1971

ABBREVIATIONS

A.I.C.C.	All-India Congress Committee
C.P.	Central Provinces
D.C.C.	District Congress Committee
D.C.I.	Director of Central Intelligence
E.N.	Report on English Newspapers
Home Pol.	Political Files of Home Department of Government of India
I.N.C.	Indian National Congress
I.O.L.	India Office Library
K.-W.	Keep-With (papers to be kept with a government file)
Mss.	Manuscripts
N.A.I.	National Archives of India
N.N.	Report on Native Newspapers
N.-W.F.P.	North-West Frontier Province
P.C.C.	Provincial Congress Committee
Rs.	Rupees
S.I.S.	Servants of India Society
S.P.	Papers of V. S. S. Srinivasa Sastri
U.P.	United Provinces of Agra and Oudh

INTRODUCTION

'Honest, but a Bolshevik & for that reason very dangerous' – so was Gandhi described in 1918 by Lord Willingdon, Governor of Bombay. His fumbling for an epithet which would accurately describe M. K. Gandhi was symptomatic of the confusion contemporaries felt when confronted by this new figure in Indian public life. Here was a man who announced that he wished to live the life of a Hindu ascetic, yet plunged into politics and parleyed with Viceroys. Here was an Indian who castigated his compatriots as unfit for Home Rule because of their moral and social failings, yet presented them with a novel technique of revolution with which to undermine the might of the British raj. Here was a nationalist who preached love of the imperial opponent. In the face of this phenomenon both rulers and ruled were at a loss. They had only a dim idea of Gandhi's ultimate goal, and consequently were often unable to understand or anticipate the steps he took towards that goal. Among his fellow countrymen his public image ranged from 'not only the greatest Indian living, but perhaps the saintliest human being now alive in any part of the world,' to 'this unsafe shepherd who is bringing the country on the very brink of chaos and anarchy.' The Viceroy, Lord Reading, thought Gandhi's 'religious and moral views...admirable' but found it difficult 'to understand his practice of them in politics'; while a few weeks later a provincial governor described Gandhi as 'a clear enemy of the British, swollen with vanity.' One police report even suggested that the Mahatma was 'a medical case of a peculiar psychological nature.'[1]

Similar confusion coupled with a compulsion to describe and understand a character so enigmatic and yet so important in his country's history remains nearly half a century after Gandhi returned to live in his native land. His admirers and detractors have continued to produce a steady stream of literature about him, and any addition to this array needs stringent justification and a firm delimitation of the problems to be discussed if it is to make real contribution to Gandhian studies. My present work is based on the belief that the usefulness of most earlier work on Gandhi to the historian concerned with Indian politics has been limited in one or both of two ways, by archival restrictions and by the approach of the authors. The fifty-year rule barring access to government archives closed many of the original sources for a study of Gandhi's Indian career until

[1] These impressions of Gandhi in the order quoted come from Willingdon to Sir H. Butler, 5 May 1918, I.O.L., Harcourt Butler Papers, Mss. EUR. F. 116 (53); *The Bengalee*, 19 March 1922, Bengal E.P., No. 12 of 1922; Sir D. E. Wacha to G. A. Natesan, 6 October 1920, Nehru Memorial Museum and Library, G. A. Natesan Papers; Reading to E. S. Montagu, 19 May 1921, I.O.L., Reading Papers, Mss. EUR. E. 238 (3); Sir H. Butler to his mother, 23 June 1921, Mss. EUR. F. 116 (12); Bombay Police Abstract, 1921, par. 399 (1).

that rule was relaxed to thirty years in 1966. Among the closed documents were the records of the Government of India and the private papers of the Viceroys, Hardinge, Chelmsford and Reading, and the Secretary of State for India, E. S. Montagu. Without access to these sources the scholarly value of the best biographies of Gandhi, D. G. Tendulkar's *Mahatma* and B. R. Nanda's *Mahatma Gandhi*, was considerably reduced. These papers are now open, and there has been a similar increase in private source material from the Indian side, with the collection of Gandhi's private papers at Sabarmati *ashram*, Ahmedabad, and the continuing publication of *The Collected Works Of Mahatma Gandhi* by the Government of India. Consequently the way is now open for work from new sources on Gandhi in India in the second and third decades of this century. The other major restriction on previous literature about Gandhi has lain in the approach of the authors. Most of them set out to produce straight biographies, psychological studies, or assessments of Gandhi as moralist, political philosopher, social worker, exponent of passive resistance and the like. Few analysed Gandhi's role in Indian politics or explored the actual mechanisms whereby he emerged from obscurity to a dramatic assertion of power in 1920, and thereafter to leadership of the nationalist struggle against the raj.

I try to overcome these two limitations in my study of Gandhi in India between 1915 and 1922. Using the newly available evidence I trace Gandhi's emergence as a leader step by step from his return from South Africa to his remarkable triumphs at the Calcutta and Nagpur Congresses of 1920, through his transition from a little known philanthropist to a political leader imprisoned for launching an all-India civil disobedience movement against the British. By 1922 the man who had received an official decoration on his return to his homeland was lodged in one of His Majesty's gaols: he who had looked like an ordinary Gujarati trader was now the 'naked fakir' who was to lead the Indian nationalist movement. Changes as striking as these in Gandhi's personal life had also taken place in Indian politics. In 1915 nationalist politics were essentially the preserve of a few high caste, western educated Hindus whose political techniques were as restricted as their demands and the range of their audience. By 1922 many of these restrictions had disappeared – in the number and character of the participants, the demands made and the techniques employed. The essential problem is to relate changes in Gandhi's life to changes in the nature and tempo of nationalist politics, to analyse Gandhi's role in politics and to see what forces of change he was either creating or exploiting.

Because confusion and sometimes inaccuracy have so often accompanied accounts of Gandhi's career it has seemed to me particularly important to plot the course of the Mahatma's rise to power as precisely as the evidence now permits, to investigate exactly what he did, with whom he made contact, and the nature of his strength. If this seems a somewhat pedestrian task or if the supporting evidence on occasion seems too bulky I hope I will be excused, in the recognition that it is only on the basis of such a description that we can begin to analyse Gandhi's place in the complexities of Indian politics and appreciate the stature of the man. New evidence and the passing of a generation since the nationalist movement and the opposing passions it aroused have made possible this groundwork on which a new assessment of the Mahatma can rest. If Gandhi's actions have often been ill documented, his intentions have suffered still more from conjecture based on inadequate evidence. Contemporaries and later commentators have understandably devoted much attention to the driving forces behind such an enigmatic figure, and no one who studies Gandhi can evade the problem of his aims and aspirations, and the balance within him of the religious seeker after truth for himself and his country and the politician out for power.

The historian who attempts to fathom Gandhi's intentions meets two major obstacles. First, although there are private papers of Gandhi's in plenty, none of these is private in the sense that it reveals the innermost thoughts of the 'real' Gandhi which he showed only to his intimate friends. Gandhi was one of the most public of public men. He lived his life in full view of friends and followers, indulged in didactic self-examination through an autobiography and the columns of the press, and kept a mound of papers and correspondence, knowing that these would probably be made public. (On the rare occasions when he wanted some exchange to be private he had the letters destroyed.) It was part of his ideology that an exponent of *satyagraha* or 'truth-force' should make the reasons for his actions transparently clear so that they should not be open to misinterpretation. Little can be done to overcome this problem of 'private' sources intended for public consumption except to collate evidence from as many different sources as possible and with the Mahatma's own explanations of his actions try to build up a picture of Gandhi caught in the strains and stresses of public life. The second obstacle is the fact that Gandhi did not express his ideology within the framework of English or any of the Indian languages at his disposal. His ideas broke through such confines, demanding a new vocabulary and a redefinition of some existing words. For this reason I have on occasion kept extensive quotations in the text. Description and interpretation of the ideology there must be, but I hope that by letting the Mahatma speak for himself the 'flavour' of his ideas and his distinctive mode of reasoning will become clear, and that a living picture will emerge of the man, his hopes and his fears.

This is not a biography. Consequently areas of Gandhi's life which though important do not impinge heavily on the main theme, like his life in his *ashram*, will only be touched on briefly. Nor is this a detailed survey of Indian politics between 1915 and 1922. Modern Indian history is expanding extremely rapidly as a subject for study since it has become evident that in order to see the driving forces behind political activity and political change we must not stop at the obviously political world of councils and congresses, but must go to the localities and investigate the positions and aspirations of local groups and leaders. In the present state of the subject I could not hope to make a definitive analysis even of such a limited period, though I have of course used detailed studies of particular groups and areas where these are available to supplement my own research. I have deliberately taken Gandhi as my angle of approach since he was manifestly a central figure in the political changes of those years. Because of his position in public life a study of him is a fruitful way of investigating the nature of Indian politics and drawing together some of the particular studies which have recently been made. Some assumptions about the nature and structure of Indian politics will inevitably emerge in the course of this work. They are not previous constructs of how politics work in non-European societies under colonial rule, though I am indebted to the work of several political scientists for their analyses of and generalizations about roles and relationships in such politics. My assumptions and interpretations have been forced on me by the evidence uncovered by my research. I started with Gandhi, but to understand his power I had to look at him in his environment; and a study of the leader became also a study of change in Indian politics.

CHAPTER I

SOUTH AFRICAN PRELUDE: THE CREATION OF A LEADER AND IDEALIST

Mohandas Karamchand Gandhi returned to India in 1915 at the age of forty-six after twenty years in South Africa. Unlike other Indian nationalist leaders Gandhi did not grow to maturity through experience of public life in his own country, but laid the spiritual and political foundations of his leadership in a foreign land. South Africa taught him the techniques with which he was to combat the might of British imperialism in India, but he envisaged his future in India in these words: 'For me there can be no deliverance from this earthly life except in India. Anyone who seeks such deliverance...must go to the sacred soil of India. For me, as for everyone else, the land of India is the "refuge of the afflicted".'[1] This hope echoed the traditional Hindu belief in a life cycle which gave a man the time to mature as a father and a householder and then pass on to a state of deliverance, detachment from worldly concerns, in which state he would be free to meditate on eternal truths and strive for *moksha*, or salvation.

In practice South Africa spoiled Gandhi for such a transition from involvement to detachment. It had created in him a deep concern for his fellow men which tied him to their service and compromised any ideal pattern of detachment from their concerns in later life. As he wrote to one of his nephews,

> The real secret of life seems to consist in so living in the world as it is, without being attached to it, that *moksha* might become easy of attainment to us and to others. This will include service of self, the family, the community, and the State. We should not stop till we reach that stage.[2]

Gandhi's friends anticipated the lengths to which such a belief might lead him in his native land and he had hastened to assure one of them, 'Please do not think that I shall incur the sin of falling into the delusion that I should serve the entire world. I well realize that my work can only be in India and that in Gujarat, rather in Kathiawad.'[3] Nevertheless on his

[1] *Indian Opinion*, 15 July 1914, *The Collected Works Of Mahatma Gandhi*, vol. 12, p. 455. (*The Collected Works*, in process of publication in Delhi, are hereafter cited as *C.W.*)

[2] Gandhi to Chhaganlal Gandhi, 11 March 1914, *ibid.* p. 382.

[3] Gandhi to Pranjivan Mehta, 10 October 1911, *C.W.*, vol. 11, p. 166. Kathiawad or Kathiawar was the part of Gujarat in western India from which Gandhi's family came.

return to India his friend and adviser, or *guru*, in political matters, the Bombay politician, G. K. Gokhale, felt that Gandhi would be a liability in Indian public life; and to soften the impact of his ideals and his passion for service he imposed on Gandhi a year's silence on political matters.[1]

Gokhale's fears indicated that a leader of disturbing quality was returning to India in 1915. Nobody could have foreseen this in 1888 when Gandhi's despairing family sent him to England in the hope that an English legal qualification would salvage some future for this diligent but unsuccessful student who had had to leave an Indian college because his English was not fluent enough to follow the lectures. In the intervening years Gandhi's interests, ambitions and capacity for public action were transformed. The scene of the transformation was South Africa where Gandhi went in 1893, two years after returning from his studies in England. His years in England had given him a taste for the fashions of late Victorian London: in the words of a contemporary who encountered him in Piccadilly Circus, he was 'a nut, a masher, a blood – a student more interested in fashion and frivolities than in his studies'.[2] When he eventually applied himself to his studies he gained a London matriculation and was called to the Bar; but these qualifications did not bring him the position or prosperity in India which he and his family had anticipated. He failed as a lawyer and a teacher in metropolitan Bombay and was earning his living as a petition writer in his native Gujarat when an opportunity came in the form of an invitation to South Africa as junior legal assistant to an Indian trading firm. His contract was for a year only; but its expiry coincided with a proposed bill in the Natal Legislature to disenfranchise Indian settlers, and his compatriots in Natal persuaded him to stay on and help them fight the bill. So South Africa became Gandhi's training ground for leadership. Barred by his own inadequacies from the more orthodox entry into Indian public life through legal practice and local political associations, Gandhi entered through the back door. Whereas in India he had been a total failure, in South Africa he became a respected householder and prosperous lawyer, and found a situation which forced him into leadership of men.

Gandhi's work in South Africa was a campaign to stem the tide of racial discrimination which threatened to engulf the Indian community – discrimination expressed by the white population in laws and social conventions which reflected the degree to which they felt themselves threatened by the Indian immigrants.[3] For twenty years he campaigned against re-

[1] Gandhi to G. K. Gokhale, 27 February 1914, *C.W.*, vol. 12, pp. 360–1.

[2] Quoted in B. R. Nanda, *Mahatma Gandhi* (Boston, 1958), p. 28.

[3] The precise provisions of these laws varied in the four provinces of South Africa in relation to the size and character of the Indian community. For the relative strength of the Indian and white communities in the four provinces, see W. K. Hancock, *Survey of British Commonwealth Affairs. Volume 1. Problems of Nationality 1918–1936* (Oxford, 1937), p. 244. For the provisions of anti-Indian legislation, see R. A. Huttenback, 'Indians In South Africa, 1860–1914: the

strictions on franchise, property holding, living areas and immigration, and kindred regulations which made the Indians less than citizens. He organized the previously quiescent Indian community, contacted officials as high-ranking as General Smuts in South Africa and Lord Hardinge, Viceroy of India; travelled to India and England to rally support; and from 1907 resorted to passive resistance when constitutional action failed him. So successful was he in rousing South African Indians and creating indignation abroad that in 1914 the South African government agreed to a compromise package deal with the Indian community and viewed Gandhi's departure for India with considerable relief. The Secretary of State for the Colonies, who had been holding the ring for the contending parties, wrote in near desperation:

> The best possible outcome will be if Gandhi will return to his native land. He is a quite astonishingly hopeless and impracticable person for any kind of deal, but with a sort of ardent, though restrained, honesty which becomes the most pig-headed obstinacy at the critical moment.[1]

'The saint has left our shores,' wrote Smuts five months later, 'I sincerely hope for ever.'[2] The contest wore down the government but it created Gandhi the leader and armed him with a battery of weapons for political warfare. South Africa was the forge where he beat out his ideals and his techniques of leadership. There he gained the experience which was critical for his later career in India and the explosive effect he was to have in Indian politics.

Most political leaders have opportunities to learn from seasoned campaigners. Gandhi's school of politics was rough and ready because there was none to help him, and he was pushed into action by the pressures of the situation in which he found himself. The techniques he evolved were those of the pragmatist; in particular he was limited by the people he had to organize, the audience at which he aimed, and the nature of the issues at stake.

British Imperial Philosophy on Trial', *The English Historical Review*, LXXXI (April 1966), 273–91.

1 Crewe to Hardinge, 26 March 1914, Cambridge U.L., Hardinge Mss. (120). Accounts of Gandhi's work in South Africa and the background to the struggle are available in Nanda, *op. cit.* pp. 37–125; D. G. Tendulkar, *Mahatma*, vol. I (revised edition, Delhi, 1960), pp. 36–151; M. K. Gandhi, *Satyagraha In South Africa* (revised 2nd edition, Ahmedabad, 1961); M. K. Gandhi, *An Autobiography. The Story Of My Experiments With Truth* (paperback edition, London, 1966), pp. 85–289; Hancock, *op. cit.* pp. 187–202; W. K. Hancock, *Four Studies Of War And Peace In This Century* (Cambridge, 1961), pp. 59–92; M. Palmer, *The History Of The Indians In Natal* (Cape Town, 1957), pp. 1–75; Huttenback, *E.H.R.*, LXXXI, 273–91.

2 Smuts to Sir Benjamin Robertson, 21 August 1914, Smuts Archive, vol. 12, no. 139, quoted in W. K. Hancock, *Smuts. The Sanguine Years 1870–1919* (Cambridge, 1962), p. 345. For an account of Gandhi's career in South Africa with particular reference to his relationship with Smuts, see *ibid.* pp. 321–47.

Before 1906 Gandhi's main concern was the complex of disabilities and discourtesies suffered by the so-called 'Arabs', the small group of prosperous traders, mostly Muslims from western India, who came to South Africa as birds of passage, making their money and returning home. Such Indians had just enough education, prosperity and expectations to feel sharply restrictions on franchise, landholding and trading: they were also the people who stood to suffer from violent or unconstitutional forms of protest as they themselves made clear to Gandhi. They enabled Gandhi to stay in South Africa by giving him retaining fees. On the proceeds he moved into a fashionable house in Durban where his wife and family joined him from Gujarat, and he began to build up a thriving legal practice. Wearing European dress, making friends among whites and Indians alike, he did his best to prove that the 'Arabs' were in no way inferior to other British subjects. As he put it,

> part of the expense was solely for the sake of prestige. I thought it necessary to have a household in keeping with my position as an Indian barrister in Natal and as a representative. So I had a nice little house in a prominent locality. It was also suitably furnished. Food was simple, but as I used to invite English friends and Indian co-workers, the housekeeping bills were always fairly high.[1]

When Gandhi became champion of the 'Arabs' he took his stand on the assumption that their position was difficult merely because the white population was not true to the principles of justice which he believed were enshrined in British law and the British constitution. As there was no written British constitution to which he could appeal he used as a symbol of it the Royal Proclamation issued in 1858 after the Indian Mutiny, which laid down that there should be no discrimination among British subjects on grounds of colour, race or religion. To this Proclamation he harked back continuously, making it the spring-board for his political demands. He wrote in 1903,

> It is superfluous to refer to the numerous occasions on which it has been referred to as the document giving the people of India full privileges and rights of British subjects. Viceroys after Viceroys have repeated the same thing...
>
> Is it, then, any wonder that the British Indians, no matter where they go, invoke the aid of that Proclamation in their favour whenever any attempt is made to curtail their liberties or their rights as British subjects ?[2]

Gandhi directed his appeals for the enactment of the British constitution to a very restricted audience – to the white community in South Africa,

[1] Gandhi, *An Autobiography*, p. 134.

[2] *Indian Opinion*, 9 July 1903, *C.W.*, vol. 3, pp. 357–8. For the relevant section of the Royal Proclamation of 1 November 1858, see C. H. Philips (ed.), *The Evolution Of India And Pakistan 1858 to 1947 Select Documents* (London, 1962), p. 11.

and to governments in Africa, India and England – in fact to those who were most likely to respond to appeals couched in these terms and had actual influence on affairs in South Africa. Because his audience, his aims and his followers were so limited, so were his political techniques.

By the hard method of trial and error Gandhi learnt to draft and organize petitions, to draw together his 'Arab' compatriots in political associations like the Natal Indian Congress; and – most significant of all – he taught himself the craft of journalism. His chief mouthpiece was *Indian Opinion*, which he founded in June 1903, the first in a sequence of papers which channelled to the public the continual literary flow by which he spread his personal views and influence from then until his death. Through *Indian Opinion* he endeavoured to educate Indians in matters as diverse as European history and public health, and when he began to organize passive resistance it was the medium through which he issued instructions about tactics. Because it was so important to him as a political weapon rather than a commercial enterprise he kept tight control over its policy and poured nearly all his savings into it, at one point paying out £75 a month.[1] While his main journalistic efforts were concentrated on *Indian Opinion* he also produced leaflets for the public in India, describing the plight of their compatriots in South Africa, and he kept a list of 'friendly' papers in England.[2] Press contacts with England showed his appreciation of newspapers as political weapons. They also indicated the value he placed on an English audience, as did his idea of establishing an English committee to concentrate the efforts of well-disposed Englishmen – an idea which came to fruition in 1906 in the South African British Indian Committee.[3]

Such tactics could only succeed if the white community and the governments they manned in South Africa were amenable to reasoned petitions or if the British government had some lever of influence on South Africa's internal policy which it was willing to use in the Indians' favour. However in the last decade of the nineteenth century and the first decade of the twentieth economic and political factors worked to entrench the white settlers in their position and to weaken the influence the British government had over them. In such circumstances the Liberal government which came to power in Britain in 1905 declined to make unpopular use of the slender constitutional threads of power left to it, preferring to keep the loyalty of the South African whites, which was critical for the security of the sea route to India, by the methods of conciliation and friendship. In

1 Gandhi, *An Autobiography*, p. 238.

2 List of 'friendly' people and papers in England, undated, Sabarmati Sangrahalaya Collection, Ahmedabad, No. 3727. (Collection hereafter cited as S.N.)

3 Provisional Draft Constitution of the Committee, November 1906, S.N. No. 4576. Gandhi first mooted the idea in a letter to D. Naoroji, 16 November 1906, *C.W.*, vol. 6, p. 164.

other words Gandhi found that the British audience was growing increasingly deaf to his pleas.[1] The growing strength of the white communities in South Africa was demonstrated by new forms of discrimination which touched far more Indians than the small group of 'Arabs'. In 1906 the Transvaal passed a law that Indians must register themselves and carry passes. This was followed in 1913 by the Union government's decision not to rescind the £3 tax imposed by Natal on indentured labourers who wished to remain in South Africa after their contracts of indenture had expired, and in 1913 by a court ruling known as the Searle Judgement, which touched all Indians, even the women, by threatening to invalidate all non-Christian Indian marriages.

It became clear that Gandhi, the lawyer, the lover of the British constitution, the loyal political leader with decorous political methods, could no longer hope to gain redress for his compatriots. As the circumstances and the grievances changed so did Gandhi's political tactics; and from 1907 when he realized that the Imperial government would not help South African Indians he played what was always thereafter to be his trump card – passive resistance. It was a weapon suitable now that he was fighting on issues which concerned a far larger section of the Indian community, and the poorer and less educated at that, people who had nothing to lose and all to gain by abandoning the politics of restraint. It was a means of direct action where indirect pressure had failed, a technique with which to appeal to a much larger audience, a way of playing to the gallery which in this case included the watching ranks of the public in India.

The ideology behind Gandhian passive resistance was a blend of the Hindu Vaishnava tradition of *ahimsa*, non-violence, and a belief in suffering rather than fighting to overcome an opponent. Brought up in Gujarat, an area steeped in the Vaishnava tradition, Gandhi had been deeply influenced in childhood by literature expounding belief in the power of suffering. He built on these early foundations as he read both the Bhagavad Gita and the New Testament for the first time when he was a student in London, and during his first year in South Africa when he plunged into Tolstoy's writings.[2] However, when Indians in South Africa resorted to passive resistance they did so as the natural reaction to their situation of a

[1] For British reluctance to interfere in South Africa, see R. Hyam, *Elgin and Churchill at the Colonial Office 1905–1908. The Watershed of the Empire–Commonwealth* (London, 1968), pp. 55–193, 237–88. For the variations in the constitutional connection of the four provinces with Britain during these two decades, see Huttenback, *E.H.R.*, LXXXI, 273–91. The crisis of authority faced by the British government in South Africa is also discussed in R. Robinson and J. Gallagher, *Africa and the Victorians. The Official Mind of Imperialism* (paperback edition, London, 1965), pp. 410–61.

[2] Gandhi wrote of his early days in South Africa, 'I made...an intensive study of Tolstoy's books. *The Gospels in Brief*, *What to do?* and other books made a deep impression on me. I began to realize more and more the infinite possibilities of universal love.' Gandhi, *An Autobiography*, p. 133.

weak group without other forms of leverage, rather than as the direct result of any of the ideas Gandhi had been studying or of his personal contacts with contemporary exponents of passive resistance. Gandhi's correspondence with Tolstoy, for example, only started after passive resistance had begun, and he only read Thoreau's essay on civil disobedience when he was in prison for that very offence.[1]

Having embarked on passive resistance as a pragmatist Gandhi began to consider it as an idealist, and drew for inspiration on his earlier experiences and reading. He formulated sets of circumstances in which it was applicable, laid down the type of person who could use it, and invested it with his own meaning, distinguishing it very sharply from the pragmatic political weapon which he found it was in the mind of English-speakers. In his words,

> When in a meeting of Europeans I found that the term 'passive resistance' was too narrowly construed, that it was supposed to be a weapon of the weak, that it could be characterized by hatred, and that it could finally manifest itself as violence, I had to demur to all these statements and explain the real nature of the Indian movement. It was clear that a new word must be coined by the Indians to designate their struggle.[2]

The new word chosen after a competition to find the fittest description was *satyagraha*, meaning 'truth-force'. Behind this redefinition of passive resistance lay a total philosophy of life and action. At the heart of Gandhi's new commitment to satyagraha was his belief that the goal of human life should be the search for truth, but that since no one could know ultimate truth and could only search for it the methods employed in human action and particularly in conflict between people should never attack another's integrity or prevent another's search for truth. Hence the methods and the goal were to Gandhi equally important. Only non-violence and suffering willingly accepted in the search for truth could guarantee the integrity of both parties in a relationship and their right to seek truth according to their own lights without hindrance. Only those of iron will, self-forgetfulness and tolerant disposition would stay the course and not revert to varieties of

[1] L. Fischer, *The Life of Mahatma Gandhi* (London, 1951), pp. 103–4, 114–17. Gandhi's brief correspondence with Tolstoy was cut short by Tolstoy's death in 1910. Gandhi sent Tolstoy some of his writings, including *Hind Swaraj*, and explained the situation in South Africa. Tolstoy expressed sympathy and interest in Gandhi's work. His last letter to Gandhi was a long exposition of his belief in 'non-resistance' which he described as 'in reality nothing else but the discipline of love undeformed by false interpretation.' See Gandhi to Tolstoy, 1 October 1909, *C.W.*, vol. 9, pp. 444–6; Tolstoy to Gandhi, 7 October 1909, *ibid.* p. 593; Gandhi to Tolstoy, 4 April 1910, *C.W.*, vol. 10, p. 210; Tolstoy to Gandhi, 8 May 1910, *ibid.* p. 505; Gandhi to Tolstoy, 15 August 1910, *ibid.* pp. 306–7; Tolstoy to Gandhi, 7 September 1910, *ibid.* pp. 512–14.

[2] Gandhi, *An Autobiography*, p. 266.

violence in thought and action.[1] Despite Gandhi's redefinition of passive resistance as satyagraha, with its ideological implications, for most of Gandhi's followers satyagraha was nothing more than passive resistance in thin disguise, as his detractors did not hesitate to say and as was indicated by the recurrent outbreaks of violence which accompanied his satyagraha campaigns.

Satyagraha became Gandhi's most powerful weapon in the South African struggle, and he resorted to it intermittently from 1907 to 1914, when the Union government agreed to a compromise settlement. Its strength was its simplicity and adaptability. In practice it took various forms, depending on the issue at stake, and ranged from burning registration certificates to mass marches across provincial borders in order to court imprisonment for breaking immigration laws. Total numbers involved are not readily available, but between 60 and 160 Indians actually went to gaol in 1908, while in 1913 Gandhi led across the Transvaal border a column of satyagrahis (the name given to exponents of satyagraha) consisting of 2,037 men, 127 women and 57 children.[2] Although satyagraha was so important there is surprisingly little evidence of the way in which Gandhi actually organized it. The pages of *Indian Opinion*, mass meetings and the Transvaal British Indian Association, which Gandhi had helped to create, were all used at one time or another; but the paucity of evidence suggests that Gandhi rarely delegated responsibility for the organization and preferred to rely on his own influence and actions. This is borne out by a later complaint from an Indian merchant who said, 'I am afraid you make the same mistake as in S. Africa, and attempt to do too much yourself whilst not organizing a staff of assistants.'[3] Similar complaints about Gandhi's dictatorial methods were to be made after his return to India.

Whatever his critics said, South Africa had transformed Gandhi from a shy and youthful pleader with no experience of public life into a mature idealist and leader. By 1915 he had become a skilled political mobilizer and had evolved a political technique of superb flexibility which was to be his hall-mark when he returned to India. Another part of the equipment he imported to his native land was his experience of organizing a wide range of people, and the attitudes he developed towards them in the process.

1 For a detailed study of satyagraha as a concept and technique, see J. V. Bondurant, *Conquest of Violence. The Gandhian Philosophy of Conflict* (Princeton, 1958); see also E. Erikson, *Gandhi's Truth. On the Origins of Militant Nonviolence* (London, 1970).

2 Palmer, *The History Of The Indians In Natal*, p. 67; Gandhi, *Satyagraha In South Africa*, pp. 220, 300.

3 Parsee Rustomjee to Gandhi, 5 March 1921, S.N. No. 7497. Rustomjee added, 'It seems to me very important that you have an efficient staff to keep proper accounts etc, and not allow things to be muddled like the Passive Resistance here.'

During his first decade in South Africa his followers were mostly 'Arabs': some non-'Arab' Indians even made public their sense of grievance that Gandhi seemed to pay disproportionate attention to 'Arab' problems. As one who called himself 'Colonial Born Indian' wrote to the press in 1897,

> The petitions sent to the Govt. are mostly signed by Arabs, rather than Hindoos and Madrasees, or colonial-born Indians... When Mr. Gandhi left India, the promise he made there was, that he would do everything he could on behalf of the Indians in Natal, but I find our Indian barrister (Mr. Gandhi Sahib) doing more to his countrymen (Arabs) than to others. A colonial-born Indian thinks that Mr. Gandhi should help colonial-born Indians more than those who come from India, Natal being their native land.[1]

Because the 'Arab' traders were Muslims Gandhi found himself in effect a Muslim leader. South Africa could scarcely have been a better place for a Hindu to work with and lead Muslims had he chosen it for that purpose. He campaigned on their behalf on the general questions of trade licences and immigration restrictions, and at times on questions which interested them specifically as Muslims rather than as traders – for example, the plight of Muslim prisoners in the Transvaal who did not have facilities to observe the Ramzan fast, and the Muslims in Pietermaritzburg who could not get a maulvi for their mosque because the maulvi knew no European language and was therefore a prohibited immigrant.[2]

As a result of his association with Muslims Gandhi developed a horror of communal strife between Hindus and Muslims. In 1909 he asserted that his life was 'devoted to demonstrating that cooperation between the two is an indispensable condition of the salvation of India.'[3] Applying to India the lessons of his South African experience he affirmed what was to be one of his deepest convictions for the next four decades.

> India cannot cease to be one nation because people belonging to different religions live in it. In reality, there are as many religions as there are individuals; but those who are conscious of the spirit of nationality do not interfere with one another's religion. If they do, they are not fit to be considered a nation. The Hindus, the Mahomedans, the Parsis and the Christians who have made India their country are fellow countrymen, and they will have to live in unity, if only for their own interest. In no part of the world are one nationality and one religion synonymous terms; nor has it ever been so in India.[4]

1 Letter to editor of *The Natal Advertiser*, 31 March 1897, S.N. No. 2198.
2 Gandhi to Private Secretary to Secretary of State for India, 18 September 1909, S.N. No. 5083; Gandhi to A. Ali, 27 September 1909, S.N. No. 5096. Gandhi's Muslim interests in fact aroused opposition in South Africa from some Hindus. They considered that in the Natal Indian Congress too much attention was paid to Muslim grievances and that too many Muslims held posts in the Congress. S. R. Pather to Gandhi, 31 July 1912, S.N. No. 5679.
3 Gandhi to A. Ali, 6 September 1909, S.N. No. 5055.
4 Extract from *Hind Swaraj*, *C.W.*, vol. 10, p. 29.

Gandhi reached this conviction by working in a community partially united by fear of a common enemy; that their unity was only partial 'Colonial Born Indian' had made clear. In India Gandhi would find a plural society where religion was one of the most divisive forces at work and where loyalty to community overrode fear of a common enemy. Because the comparative unity of Muslims and Hindus in South Africa did not reflect their relationship in India Gandhi's experience was not typical of that which helped to mould other Indian leaders in their homeland.[1] Consequently he was to find that his principle of communal tolerance, reached in African conditions, was not readily acceptable to many of his compatriots in India.

In the latter part of his South African career Gandhi deliberately appealed to wider groups than the 'Arabs', in particular to the large number of indentured labourers who had come to Natal to work in mines and plantations and were now subject to taxation if they wished to stay on as free Indians, and also to women who found the validity of their marriages threatened by the Searle Judgement. The indentured and ex-indentured labourers were mostly poor Hindus of low caste, and as Gandhi organized them for satyagraha he was forced to develop his own attitude to caste distinctions just as he had developed a belief in communal tolerance by working among Muslims. Although Gandhi proclaimed that he was a believing and practising Hindu and considered caste, the traditional fourfold division of Hindu society, a 'perfectly natural institution' to be revered,[2] he condemned categorically the practice of treating some people as apart from and defiling to the rest of the community because of their caste ranking. As early as 1907 he wrote to one of his nephews, 'Do not allow the useless and wicked superstitions about untouchability to come in your way': he had already nearly thrown his wife physically out of their house in Durban because she clung to the 'useless and wicked superstitions'. Like her husband she was a Bania, a trading caste of comparatively high standing, and she cried when he forced her to clean the chamber pot of a Christian clerk who was staying in their house. This was a job which in traditional Hindu society would have been done by an untouchable, and was made doubly defiling to her because the Christian clerk was an outcaste. Shortly after his return to India Gandhi declared his loathing of untouchability outside the privacy of his family circle, insisting, 'if it were proved to me that this is an essential part of Hinduism, I for one would declare myself an open rebel against Hinduism itself...'[3] Similarly his

[1] For the harmonious relationship between the two communities in South Africa compared with India, see report by W. Pearson enclosed in letter from C. F. Andrews to Sir James DuBoulay, 14 May 1914, Hardinge Mss. (87).

[2] *Bharat Sevak*, October 1916, *C.W.*, vol. 13, p. 301.

[3] Gandhi, *An Autobiography*, pp. 231–2; Gandhi to Chhaganlal Gandhi, 21 April 1907, *C.W.*, vol. 6, p. 435; speech by Gandhi on 1 May 1915, *The Hindu*, 3 May 1915, *C.W.*, vol. 13, p. 69.

work among women made him consider their status. He deplored the tendency in Indian public life to leave women out of account or to treat them as second class citizens, and he deliberately involved them in satyagraha on equal terms with men. However, just as he retained a belief in the concept of caste while condemning its abuses so he did not throw overboard the traditional Hindu beliefs about the woman's role in society and the sanctity of a woman's relationship to one husband, and he was consequently no advocate of widow marriage.

By working among businessmen, Muslims, low caste Hindus and women because they were the only human material to hand Gandhi was in fact investing in political capital which was to pay handsome dividends on his return to India. Necessity had taught him to mobilize people who in their native land had no voice in politics because they were unable to organize themselves or because no politician found it worthwhile to champion their interests. But this experience, novel by the standards of other Indian leaders, also created considerable problems for Gandhi as there was no guarantee that the diverse groups he attempted to lead would have compatible interests as they had had in South Africa. Although South Africa opened Gandhi's eyes to the potential of all his fellow countrymen it also blinded him to their different interests in their motherland, and made some of them for their part doubt whether he was a leader they could trust.

Gandhi's twenty years in South Africa were not just his apprenticeship as a political mobilizer. They also provided the time and circumstances in which he formulated his attitude to India and the West; and this, far more than his political capacity and experience, was to mark him out on his return to India. In South Africa Gandhi underwent a deep disillusionment in his attitude to western civilization. His early enchantment with western fashions and styles of living exerted a strong pull over him for nearly two decades after his student life in London. Although even in 1894 there were signs that he was not satisfied by 'the dazzling and bright surface of modern civilization',[1] it was not until 1909 that he returned from a visit to London with a very different impression from his enjoyment of 1892, an impression undoubtedly coloured by his reading during the intervening years when his thoughts on satyagraha had been maturing. As he wrote in *Indian Opinion*,

> Looking at this land [England], I at any rate have grown disillusioned with Western civilization. The people whom you meet on the way seem half-crazy. They spend their days in luxury or in making a bare living and retire at night thoroughly exhausted. In this state of affairs, I cannot understand when they can devote themselves to prayers... While Western civilization is still young, we find things have come to such a pass that,

1 Gandhi to editor, 26 November 1894, *The Natal Mercury*, 3 December 1894, *C.W.*, vol. 1, p. 140.

> unless its whole machinery is thrown overboard, people will destroy themselves like so many moths.[1]

Gandhi advised people not to go to England where they would be contaminated by this civilization; though he made it clear that what he condemned was not England or Europe but modern civilization itself, which meant to him that way of life springing from the industrial revolution, whose standards were purely material, weighing men down with false ideals of gain, wealth and success.

The cream of Gandhi's ideas on this subject were set out in *Hind Swaraj*, a booklet written in 1909, whose title meant 'Indian Self Rule'. The main theme was that modern, materialistic civilization gripped England and, as a result of the British raj and Indian acquiescence in it, was luring India into its stranglehold. Indians educated in western style, particularly lawyers, doctors, teachers and industrialists, were undermining India's ancient heritage by insidiously spreading modern ways. Swaraj was the Hindustani word later used to translate the English phrase 'Home Rule'. But for Gandhi Swaraj was not a question of who held the reins of government; he saw Swaraj, self rule, as a quality or state of life which could only exist where Indians followed their traditional civilization, uncorrupted by modern innovations. In his view the task for Indians was the regeneration of their own lives and through them of India as a country. The means to this end was 'truth-force', satyagraha, available to those who trained themselves in self-control and self-reliance by practising poverty, chastity and fearlessness. *Hind Swaraj* showed plainly how satyagraha was for Gandhi not a mere political tactic but part of a total philosophy of life and ideology of action, and why he felt that to call it passive resistance was a misnomer bordering on blasphemy. By 1914 these convictions were even stronger than in 1909, and in a new edition of the booklet he described himself as 'an uncompromising enemy of the present-day civilization of Europe.'[2]

Several years before Gandhi delivered his theoretical broadside against western civilization in *Hind Swaraj* he had begun to shed the conventions of a western style of life and to experiment with simpler modes of living. The practical difficulties of leading a western life were partly responsible for this: he found, for example, that laundry bills were inordinately heavy, and that the washerman was so unpunctual that he had to keep a running stock of two to three dozen shirts and collars! So he took to doing his own laundry.[3] Gradually a deeper conviction that simplicity was necessary for self rule and self-reliance, which enabled the search for truth, moved him to abandon his old home and in 1904 to set up a community known as Phoenix, near Durban. There he housed the press for *Indian Opinion* and

[1] *Indian Opinion*, 2 October 1909, *C.W.*, vol. 9, p. 389.

[2] *Indian Opinion*, 29 April 1914, *C.W.*, vol. 12, p. 412. The full text of *Hind Swaraj* is in *C.W.*, vol. 10, pp. 6–68.

[3] Gandhi, *An Autobiography*, p. 177.

began an experiment in simple communal living which he continued later at Tolstoy Farm near Johannesburg. This experiment extended to children's education, hygiene, nature cures, basic cookery and the practice of celibacy, all of which Gandhi came to see as aids along the road to truth. Non-violence was the rule for relations between the members of the communities, and was even extended in Tolstoy Farm to snakes which infested the land. Gandhi believed so passionately that Phoenix was a training ground for satyagrahis, 'right men' and 'right Indians',[1] that he controlled every aspect of its life, even when he was absent or in the throes of a political campaign. In 1905, for example, he chided his nephew, Chhaganlal, for suffering from boils which seemed to him clear evidence of wrong diet;[2] he even sent him detailed instruction on cooking.

> If you cannot make the cake properly, it must be the fault of the oven, or you do not add sufficient ghee. You will remember that the meal must be kept soaked in cold water for nearly three hours. When you make your cake the ghee should be added first and thoroughly mixed with the flour before you pour water over it, and it should be well kneaded.[3]

For Gandhi this was not an irrelevant departure into culinary faddism. Just as much as doing his own washing it was part and parcel of his belief in self-reliance and self-control, a practical way of shedding the encumbrances of western civilization and producing men equipped by satyagraha for the search for truth.

Parallel to disillusion with western civilization Gandhi felt an increasing disenchantment with the British Empire in political terms because of its manifest impotence to help Indians in South Africa although they were British subjects, and its consequent failure to enact what he believed were the ideals of the British constitution. His early faith in British justice would have been appropriate to any Victorian patriot in Britain: it shone out of all the petitions he drafted and prompted him to lead an Indian Ambulance Corps in the service of the Empire during the Boer War. But rebuff after rebuff over Indian grievances forced him to think that though the theory of British justice and equality for all subjects within the Empire was a fine one, its practical implications for Indians were minimal. In 1903 he drew attention to the difficulties Indians were having over the possession of a mosque because of their nationality.

> It is a pretty outlook for people living under the British flag, which takes under its protecting fold all the religions. We may, therefore, well ask, what are Indians coming to in the Transvaal? Is the British Constitution going to be revised at Pretoria? Or will justice ultimately triumph?[4]

1 Gandhi to H. Polak, undated, probably 1909, S.N. No. 5042.
2 Gandhi to Chhanganlal Gandhi, 6 May 1905, S.N. No. 4236.
3 Gandhi to Chhanganlal Gandhi, 19 April 1905, S.N. No. 4233.
4 *Indian Opinion*, 27 August 1903, *C.W.*, vol. 3, p. 426.

Reluctantly he came to the conclusion that justice would not triumph for Indians unless they took the law into their own hands. Whereas in 1896 he had said that 'British love of justice and fair play' was 'the sheet-anchor of the Indian's hope', in 1910 he had moved so far as to rewrite the phrase as 'the sheet-anchor of our hope lies not in the uncertainty of law suits but in the certainty of passive resistance.'[1] In the same year he advised Indians to express their disillusion by declining to take part in the official welcome to the visiting Duke of Connaught. This did not mean a total break in his loyalty to the Empire, and he retained a personal notion of loyalty, based on the hope that one day Britain might enact the principles he believed she upheld in theory.[2]

Such changes in outlook naturally affected Gandhi's attitude to the British raj in India. But would disillusionment with the West inspire him to lead a movement to throw the British bag and baggage out of the homeland where he hoped his ideals would be enacted? In his early days as a public figure Gandhi predictably accepted British rule in India without criticism, and in 1895 wrote, 'It is true England "wafts her sceptre" over India. The Indians are not ashamed of that fact. They are proud to be under the British Crown, because they think England will prove India's deliverer.'[3] He justified the raj on the grounds of British ability and character, and the weakness of Indians, principally their lack of unity and public spirit: in this he expounded what amounted to a law of karma for nations – nations have the rulers they deserve and only by building up their strength of character can they expect to have strong rulers of their own in future generations. In 1907 he stated that he had no quarrel with British rule as it afforded India much protection, though in the following year he did say that Indians would have to rebel against the raj if it were proved that India was a subject country within the Empire and that there was no possibility of equality for her under its flag.[4] Even after Gandhi made public his total rejection of western civilization and his disgust that the Empire was of no avail to Indians in South Africa, he did not turn against the raj as such. Rather he saw India as crushed not by Britain but by modern civilization, and he even pitied Britain for suffering under the same oppression. In his opinion if the British were expelled from India then India would only suffer an indigenous version of the same evil.

> If British rule was replaced by Indian rule based on modern methods, India would be no better, except that she would be able then to retain some

[1] Gandhi to editor, 15 November 1897, *The Natal Mercury*, 17 November 1897, *C.W.*, vol. 2, p. 365; *Indian Opinion*, 30 July 1910, *C.W.*, vol. 10, p. 299.

[2] *Indian Opinion*, 2 April 1910, *ibid.* p. 189.

[3] Pamphlet written by Gandhi, 16 December 1895, *C.W.*, vol. 1, pp. 284–5.

[4] *Indian Opinion*, 1 June 1907, *C.W.*, vol. 7, pp. 6–7; *Indian Opinion*, 4 April 1908, *C.W.*, vol. 8, p. 169.

> of the money that is drained away to England; but, then, Indians would only become a second or fifth edition of Europe or America.[1]

This statement was firmly grounded on Gandhi's own interpretation of Swaraj. For him this was not merely a political issue of who governed the country; for him Swaraj was self rule, which had to be achieved at a personal level before it could be extended to politics. So far as he could see the British raj provided a favourable environment for those who wished to follow these ideals through the practice of satyagraha because it gave them free scope for the exercise of their energies as directed by their consciences. On these grounds he publicly proclaimed his loyalty to the British at a Madras Law Dinner three months after his return to India.[2]

South Africa had cast Gandhi, the leader and the idealist, in a distinctive mould, and the Gandhi who returned home in 1915 was a curious combination of attitudes. Committed to the rejection of western civilization he still affirmed loyalty to the government which upheld that civilization: idealizing the land of his birth he decried its current state. Even so India was still for him 'the land of deliverance', the one place where he could attain salvation through service of his fellow men. However, Gokhale's insistence that Gandhi should keep silent for a year on political matters suggested that the Bombay veteran felt that Gandhi was out of touch with his native land and would be something of a misfit in Indian politics. It therefore seems important to pause and look at the political scene which faced Gandhi when he stepped off the boat in Bombay in 1915, before investigating the way in which he became part of that scene when the weapons forged on the South African anvil were put to the test and the ideals created in South Africa clashed, coincided or compromised with the realities of Indian politics.

[1] Gandhi to H. Polak, 14 October 1909, *C.W.*, vol. 9, p. 479.
[2] *The Hindu*, 26 April 1915, *C.W.*, vol. 13, pp. 59–60.

CHAPTER 2

GANDHI AND INDIAN NATIONALIST POLITICS, 1915–16

(I) THE POLITICAL NATION

When Gandhi returned home in 1915 the India of his dreams, if indeed it had ever existed, was fast disappearing under the influence of the British raj. There had been no regeneration of oriental society as envisaged by British reformers in the early nineteenth century; but though the Utilitarian and Evangelical prophets of progress were sadly disillusioned in their lifetime there occurred during the century that followed a slow and piecemeal erosion of traditional Indian values and customs. Change came not in the form of dramatic transformation but of continuous adaptation, as traditional institutions and groups of people encountered the new, choosing out those novel elements which seemed most profitable and moulding them for their own ends.[1] The interplay of internal tensions and external pressures began to create the India of the twentieth century.

The main external pressures were ones deliberately exerted by the new rulers. Foreign rule was not strange to India – the British were the last in a long succession of foreign conquerors; but they were the first who were able to a very great extent to resist absorption into the Indian scene. The reason for their stouter resistance lay in the timing of their arrival: for they acquired territorial control in India on the flood tide of nineteenth century European technological power and ideological exuberance. Where earlier conquerors had tended to be the objects of change, the British became the agents of change. Their land settlements, often twisted by local conditions out of all recognition from the original blueprints, helped to redistribute power in society and create some degree of social mobility. Their systems of law, administration, and modern communications began to create one country where before there had been only an unstable federation of separate regions. Their presence as a maritime power opened the door to new industries and world-wide markets, bringing new importance to the coastal areas to the detriment of the heartland of the subcontinent, which was the hub of earlier networks of imperial power. But the most powerful agent of change which the British imported was western education. To an extent far greater than even T. B. Macaulay or C. E. Trevelyan

[1] This theme is worked out with specific examples in L. I. & S. H. Rudolph, *The Modernity Of Tradition. Political Development in India* (Chicago & London, 1967).

had prophesied,[1] English-medium higher education was critical for the development of modern India. Its effects were far reaching not just because of its intellectual content but because the British made western education the entrance to place and power in administration and law. It became a most tempting path to success under the new dispensation, but only for a few.

By the end of the nineteenth century the spread of western education had created a new social group with its particular style of life and values, its own means of subsistence, and its own avenues of recruitment. The western educated, those educated either in the West or in western-style institutions in India, were a new elite. Among them were men like Surendranath Bannerjee, Pherozeshah Mehta and Motilal Nehru, lawyers of all-India fame who mixed with the rulers on nearly equal terms, as well as a host of lesser folk, pleaders, teachers, doctors, clerks, who for all their different gradations of income and influence shared the heritage of western education. Although this group was a new social phenomenon its members were not all 'new men' in terms of power. Precisely who they were differed from region to region. In some places they were men who were already powerful locally, and now bolstered their existing power in a new way. The Brahmins of Madras and Maharashtra are a case in point. Elsewhere they might be high status groups clutching at new means of actual influence to reinforce their ritual authority, like the *bhadralok*, the higher castes of Bengal who were finding it increasingly difficult to live off their incomes from land. What was critical for the future of India was not just the spread of western education but the uneven extent of its penetration among different groups and in different areas. English-medium schools and colleges mushroomed, but only in certain places: they attracted large numbers of scholars, but only from certain groups. Regions, and caste, religious and occupational groups within regions, were influenced in widely differing degrees by the new education. The main group to take advantage of it were high caste Hindus in the three Presidencies of Bengal, Bombay and Madras. In contrast to them lower castes in the Presidencies lagged behind in registers of students and lists of degrees gained. In the heartland of India and in the north-west, the Cinderella areas of the subcontinent in the new era where western penetration had been late and slight, whole regions were backward in opportunities for western education; and all castes and communities in those regions had low educational standards as a result. One curious result of this pattern of penetration was the low educational achievement of the Muslim community when viewed on an all-India scale: for the Muslims clustered at the core of the former

IMP.

[1] Macaulay's hopes for the regeneration of India through western educated Indian 'interpreters' was clear in his minute of 2 February 1835 on Indian education, G. M. Young (ed.), *Macaulay. Prose And Poetry* (London, 1952), pp. 719–30; see also C. E. Trevelyan, *On the education of the people of India* (London, 1838).

Mughal empire, where there were few opportunities for western schooling, and in the one Presidency where they lived in large numbers they were converts to Islam from low Hindu castes, and kept the style of life of their former caste brethren, a style of life which had little room for English schools and colleges.[1]

It was India's western educated who evolved a new form of public activity which was recognizably political to western observers accustomed to patterns of political awareness and action which had developed in the particular circumstances of nineteenth century Europe. Before the British penetration into India there had of course been varieties of politics, since the essence of politics lies not in particular institutions and organizations but in the aspiration to exercise power within the community and the development of techniques to that end. Princes and their courtiers had intrigued in palace politics for power over tracts of Indian territory; literate groups accustomed to administration in the service of the ruling power competed for the privilege; landlords and their tenants manoeuvred for positions from which to profit from the land; wealthy merchants and moneylenders built up networks of clientage to control the profits of urban and business life; castes jostled against each other and factions within castes vied for power in the realm of ritual authority. There was no one mode of politics since there was no single struggle for power, but rather a variety of political modes reflecting a variety of struggles for different sources of power within the community. The British changed the situation in the later nineteenth century by adding to the existing sources of influence in society as they devolved power in the local and central administration into Indian hands. By employing Indians in the lower reaches of the civil service, by extending municipal self-government and by admitting Indians, however few in number, to the councils of the Viceroy and the provincial governors, they hoped to solve the problems of financing their imperial administration and of attracting the collaboration of Indians with their raj.[2] They did not destroy the older political modes because they left intact many of the sources of influence which the older modes of politics were designed to capture: but by holding out a new source of power they

1 For an analysis of the uneven spread of education in different areas and among different groups see A. Seal, *The Emergence Of Indian Nationalism. Competition and Collaboration in the Later Nineteenth Century* (Cambridge, 1968).

2 For the government's hope that the extension of municipal self-government would help to solve its financial problems, see Government of India Resolution on the Municipalities, 31 August 1864, Philips (ed.), *The Evolution Of India And Pakistan 1858 to 1947 Select Documents*, pp. 43–4. The subsequent major steps in the devolution of power before 1915 as a way of attracting Indian cooperation were the extension of local self-government in 1882, the admission of more Indians to the central and provincial legislative councils with enlarged powers through the 1892 Councils Act and the 1909 Indian Councils Act (the Morley–Minto Reforms); *ibid.* pp. 50–6, 66–7, 88–90.

provided the incentive for Indians to develop a new political style designed to capture that power.[1]

The older tendency to write Indian history in terms of the initiatives of the imperial government has rightly yielded to an emphasis on initiatives from within Indian society, on the indigenous forces pushing men into public action. However the balance of emphasis can swing so far in that direction that it is possible to underestimate the raj as a vital component of Indian public life and a constituent element of Indian society. It held the arena of public life and its actions, directly or indirectly, were the cause of much public activity by Indians. In one area of public life particularly, the new style of politics, it created the objects and to a very large extent decided the rules of the political game.

The correlation between the new style of institutional politics and the spread of western education was striking[2] and understandable because the western educated were those whose new skills enabled them to take up the opportunities offered by the raj in administrative posts and in seats on district boards and in the legislative councils. Men from the Presidencies were the first to meet in social and educational societies from which the new political activity emerged; they created the Indian National Congress to consolidate the efforts of their local associations, and they became the backbone of its strength for the first thirty years of its existence. Between 1885 and 1909 there were 19,605 delegates to Congress sessions. Of these Bengal produced 3,905, Bombay 4,857 and Madras 4,062; while the whole of the rest of India produced only 6,740.[3] Contemporaries were quick to comment on the backwardness of other provinces in this respect. *The Hindustan* noted in 1916:

> For the past ten years the Punjab has been locked in deep slumber. From the political point of view this province is so inactive that while the public men of all other provinces have expressed their opinions regarding the operation of the Press Act, the public of this province has shown no activity, except in publishing a few articles on the subject. Then again, when other provinces are preparing for the coming session of the Indian National Congress nothing is being done in the Punjab, where the Provincial Congress Committee wakes up only once a year, when nearly a dozen

1 For a study of the older political styles in an Indian town and the way these overlapped with newer styles, see C. A. Bayly, 'The Development Of Political Organisation In The Allahabad Locality, 1880–1925' (D.Phil. thesis, Oxford, 1970), particularly pp. 206–71. When the words politics and politicians are used hereafter they denote the activities of and participants in the new style of politics which were focussed on the institutions of councils, municipalities and Indian associations such as Congress.

2 See B. T. McCully, *English Education And The Origins Of Indian Nationalism* (New York, 1940), and Seal, *op. cit.*

3 P. C. Ghosh, *The Development Of The Indian National Congress 1892–1909* (Calcutta, 1960), pp. 25–6.

> residents of Lahore meet and reluctantly perform the duty of electing two or three delegates to the Congress.[1]

The following year a Lahore paper reported that still 'the Punjab considers it an act of heresy to take part in politics. The province has, therefore, neither had a conference, nor is any important question discussed here.'[2] A distinguished Bombay politician, D. E. Wacha, commented in similar fashion on the state of the United Provinces. 'My countrymen in the backward provinces have got to learn the fundamental essentials of public life and even of organization and procedure.'[3] The 'backward provinces' included Bihar and Orissa, Central Provinces and Berar as well as U.P. and the Punjab, and even regions within the Presidencies, like Gujarat and Sind in Bombay.

Not only regions which were backward in institutional politics, but whole religious, caste and occupational groups, whether in the Presidencies or in the obviously backward areas, showed distinct reluctance to join Congress and its local associations; and they were just those groups who had barely felt the effects of western education. Muslims, for example, provided only 912 delegates to Congress between 1892 and 1909. Those of the community who had some western style education, as in the U.P., preferred to gather at sessions of the Muslim League, which despite its grand title was a weak and sickly body, poorly supported and generally divided against itself. Lower caste Hindus were equally unpractised in politics, if attendance at Congress is taken as a measure of their activities. So were the landholders, large and small, landless peasants, and commercial men of various kinds.[4] The rulers took comfort from the fact that lawyers and lecturers from the Presidencies ran Congress virtually as a closed shop; and many officials taunted western educated Indians on being a microscopic minority, totally unrepresentative of the aspirations and activities of the rest of their countrymen. Indian politicians stoutly denied this charge, except in rare moments of candour like that shown by a writer in *Mahratta* in 1891.

> We fear even the fringe of Indian society has not yet been touched. It is the towns that have been reached if at all. The vast numbers of rural India have yet to know what Congress is like. They do not know what we have been doing. They do not know that we are speaking in the name of the

[1] *The Hindustan*, 28 June 1916, A. Husain, *Fazl-i-Husain. A Political Biography* (Bombay, 1946), p. 82.

[2] *The Virat*, 30 April 1917, *ibid.* p. 82.

[3] D. E. Wacha to Sir James Meston, 1 November 1915, I.O.L., Meston Papers, Mss. EUR. F. 136 (4).

[4] Figures for delegates to Congress by religion, caste and occupation are in Ghosh, *op. cit.* pp. 23–4. A case study of one commercial group and its indifference to politics is A. P. Kannangara, 'Indian Millowners And Indian Nationalism Before 1914', *Past And Present*, no. 40 (July 1968), pp. 147–64.

whole nation without knowing ourselves if what we have been saying is likely to be approved by those in whose name we are speaking.[1]

Early Indian politics were limited, not merely in the number and character of the participants but in their demands and techniques and the audience to which the politicians played. Resolutions passed at annual Congress sessions are a convenient index of the early politicians' demands. They harped on several constant and restricted themes – the admission of Indians to the provincial legislative councils and the executive councils of provincial governors, Viceroy and Secretary of State, the employment of more Indians at all levels of the administration, the abolition of all regulations which, like the Arms Act of 1878, appeared to suggest that Indians were inferior to the British, and the poverty of India under foreign rule. At heart all these demands reflected the ambitions of the western educated for place and power, and their aspirations for recognized equality with the rulers whose educational qualifications they could now equal. The point had been reached where there was conflict between the interests of the rulers and the group they had deliberately created by their educational policy. Even the resolutions protesting that Britain was draining wealth from India, which at first sight appear to have been prompted by a wider concern, were geared to the concerns of this tiny group because they recommended a drastic reduction in the number of foreigners in the administration – a remedy which dovetailed neatly with their own wish for more jobs in government service.[2]

Congress demands if granted promised few benefits to those who had not the educational qualifications to take advantage of them; these included lower caste Hindus, Muslims and the backward areas of India. In some cases Congress demands even posed a threat to those outside the circle of the western educated. For example, if Congress pleas for more posts in the administration were granted it would mean more jobs for the Bengali *bhadralok* and the Brahmins of Madras and Maharashtra, not for areas and communities which had few educated men. This sharpened the bitter feeling which already existed in areas like Bihar that the Presidency men were gaining too much power at the expense of local people. Congress was a closed shop. Like most closed shops its strength lay in its isolation and internal solidarity. What was more, its members realized this very early on, and deliberately damped down the divisions which might threaten them if they extended the range of their demands. After 1888 Congress refused to discuss all religious and communal issues unless the community concerned was virtually unanimous in wanting such a discussion; and for similar reasons it steered clear of the thorny and divisive question of social reform. If once

1 *Mahratta,* 15 November 1891, G. Johnson, 'Indian Politics 1888–1908' (Ph.D. thesis, Cambridge, 1967), p. 129, fn. 2.

2 For Congress demands see *ibid.* pp. 428–59.

Congressmen embarked on such topics outside their limited range of demands their unity would be shattered, and with it much of their strength.

The corollary of limited demands was a limited audience. Early Indian politicians played not to the gallery of the Indian public but to the select audience of the British rulers, and behind the hierarchy of the raj to the British public which had final if remote control of Indian affairs through Parliament.[1] The British alone could grant the concessions the politicians wanted; therefore at the British the politicians aimed their appeals. Precisely for this reason the politicians restricted the type of technique they used. They made speeches in legislative councils when they were eventually admitted to them; they agitated in decorous fashion through local associations and Congress; they conducted orderly campaigns in the press, through public meetings and petitions to the raj; they even had a committee of British M.P.s and an English paper to voice their claims in England. As the British alone could concede their demands those early politicians had a vested interest in studied moderation. They kept to the style of politics to which the British could be expected to respond favourably, partly because it did not threaten them, and partly because it closely resembled the political activity they indulged in at home. A. O. Hume, who had helped to found Congress, put it this way, 'Every adherent of the Congress, however noisy in declamations, however bitter in speech, is safe from burning bungalows and murdering Europeans, and the like. His hopes are based upon the British nation, and he will do nothing to invalidate these hopes and anger that nation.'[2]

There was another reason for the limitation of political techniques. Just as Congressmen dared not alienate the raj, they dared not extend their range beyond their own limited circle for fear of letting loose the diverse ambitions and interests which motivated their less educated countrymen and their compatriots from outside the Presidencies. Rarely did they have access to networks of local power or resources for leadership which would have enabled them to mobilize wider sections of society: even if they had, this would have been a course fraught with danger for them in their position of isolated success. The one great occasion when the educated did attempt to organize wide-scale political agitation showed them exactly how dangerous it could be. After Curzon's partition of Bengal the *bhadralok* flirted for a brief period with the techniques of a wider politics, hoping to rouse such wide support for a passive resistance campaign that the raj would be forced to take them seriously. But they found that they lost control of

[1] The importance of the British audience is clearly shown in M. Cumpston, 'Some early Indian Nationalists and their allies in the British Parliament, 1851–1906' *The English Historical Review*, LXXVI (April 1961), 279–97.

[2] A. O. Hume to Lord Lansdowne, 5 March 1891, I.O.L., Mss. D. 558, Part 1, No. 230, pp. 201–2, quoted in S. A. Wolpert, *Tilak And Gokhale: Revolution and Reform in the Making of Modern India* (Berkeley & Los Angeles, 1962), p. 59.

their own group and aroused hostility from the mass of the population, who in Bengal were Muslim peasants and low caste Hindus, people concerned not with places for the educated but with the tensions of village life and the constant battle against poverty.[1] Even worse, the *bhadralok* let loose the fiends of communal violence and invited the heavy hand of the raj to suppress violence and disorder. It was a warning to them that the politics of limitation best suited their interests.

By 1915 the western educated, particularly from the Presidencies, were the political nation in relation to the new style of institutional politics, but within their ranks there was an infinite variety of groupings. None of these was a political party by the canons of European politics: they had no firm creeds, no organized methods of recruitment, no party funds or ties. Rather, they were personal networks of loyalty around prominent leaders, related to each other by shifting alliances, sometimes within a region and sometimes across regional borders. The fundamental aim of all those who led or joined these networks was the pursuit of influence and place in their own locality, whether in local colleges, legal, educational or political associations or in council chambers. All had to bear in mind not just their local competitors; they also had to keep an eye to the government, the source of many of the concessions they desired, and, if they were Hindus, to their own position in Congress. Although Congress, two decades after its foundation, was still little more than an annual gathering of local leaders, its organization in the localities was becoming sufficiently important for men to think it worth capturing, and its annual sessions were vital arenas for men who wanted local and all-India power. Congress reflected the position of groups within the provinces, but success in Congress also influenced the relation and relative power of groups within provinces. Because the politicians had to face in so many directions their alliances and groupings became at times bewildering. However, in 1915–16 an outsider or returning exile like Gandhi would at once have seen three major types of political alliance or foci for political activity – the Congress, the Home Rule Leagues and the Muslim League.

Congress was the apex of institutional politics. However much Curzon as Viceroy had hoped at the turn of the century 'to assist it to a peaceful demise',[2] by 1915 both raj and politicians recognized that it was the main mouthpiece of Indian political demand. Rulers had to listen to it: politicians aspired to control it. But not all the politicians had a place within it. There were the 'ins' and 'outs', a split dating back to 1907 when at the Surat session two groups of politicians had gone their separate ways, one group

1 This aberration from the political norm is discussed in J. H. Broomfield, *Elite Conflict in a Plural Society: Twentieth-Century Bengal* (Berkeley & Los Angeles, 1968), pp. 29–34.

2 Lord Curzon to Lord Hamilton, 18 November 1900, Philips (ed.), *The Evolution Of India And Pakistan 1858 to 1947 Select Documents*, pp. 150–1.

led by B. G. Tilak, out into the wilderness, excluded by the others under Pherozeshah Mehta and G. K. Gokhale, who firmly grasped control of the organization.

This split has been seen both by later commentators and by contemporary participants in the controversy as a deep ideological one between politicians of an 'Extremist' and a 'Moderate' hue, the former advocating a more overt Hindu form of nationalism, relying less on the ideology of the West, willing to resort to unconstitutional and even violent methods if necessary to obtain major concessions from the British, the latter demanding less from the raj, more willing to accept western ideals, and rejecting all but the most moderate methods of political action. Although many of the speeches and writings of contemporaries support this view, and were indeed designed to argue this distinction in order to rally support,[1] when the groups involved are analysed in detail this distinction is very hard to maintain. Both 'Moderates' and 'Extremists' shared far more than they cared to admit at the time, since all owed their current position and future prospects to the raj, and since all faced equal danger from less educated groups if they abandoned the politics of limitation. The discord of 1907 was part of a continuing debate common to the western educated of any colonial territory emerging into the modern world under foreign rule, but the rift occurred when it did so sharply because ideology cloaked what was also a phase in a battle between personal groupings – Tilak and his Poona henchmen allying with some Bengali politicians in an attempt to seize control of Congress from Gokhale and his allies based on Bombay.[2]

That this split was not fundamental became clear in 1915–16 when negotiations began for the reunification of Congress. By this time Tilak had cooled his heels for some years in Mandalay jail, and he and his fellow 'outs' realized that now it was worth their while to join the ranks of the 'ins'. Without a base in the Congress organization their local power was limited. Furthermore, the British, now involved in the First World War, were in dire need of collaboration from Indian leaders and consequently were more sensitive to the demands of the politicians;[3] and if a united

[1] See, for example, Aurobindo Ghose's condemnation of the 'false political ideal and equally futile methods' of the 'Moderates', *Bande Mataram*, 8 November 1907, quoted in H. & U. Mukherjee, *Sri Aurobindo And The New Thought In Indian Politics* (Calcutta, 1964), p. 215. Copious quotations from the writings of 'Moderates' and 'Extremists' are given in Wolpert, *Tilak And Gokhale: Revolution and Reform in the Making of Modern India.*

[2] For the conventional division of Indian politicians into 'Moderates' and 'Extremists' see D. Argov, 'Moderates and Extremists: two attitudes towards British rule in India', S. N. Mukherjee (ed.), *St. Anthony's Papers. Number 18 South Asian Affairs Number Two* (Oxford, 1966), pp. 19–33; and an extended study in D. Argov, *Moderates And Extremists In The Indian Nationalist Movement, 1883–1920* (London, 1967). A detailed analysis of the political situation from 1904 to the Surat Congress is in Johnson, 'Indian Politics, 1888–1908', pp. 467–548.

[3] For the effect of the war on British policy see below, pp. 124–6.

Congress put sufficient pressure on them substantial concessions might well be forthcoming. Put at its crudest, Tilak and his men wanted to be in at the kill. Late in 1914 the Congress General Secretary and Annie Besant, the theosophist politician from Madras, made attempts to patch up an agreement between Gokhale and the Bombay men on the one hand, and Tilak's men on the other. These attempts failed, largely because the Bombay men were reluctant to give their local opponents any base from which to regain power in western India and in Congress. Tilak for his part recognized that it was not fundamental beliefs which kept them apart.

> The...question of importance is the character of a clique now imposed on the Congress by restricting the right of electing delegates only to the Committees recognized by the Moderates. If they are prepared to yield on this point and keep the doors of election open to all, I think we may accept the proposal of inviting all the parties in the Congress this year.[1]

Twelve months later it looked as if the Bombay men were still obdurate. A deputation of Poona men in favour of readmitting Tilak sounded out the views of their counterparts in Bombay, but the latter said quite frankly that they could not hope to retain their power once they let Tilak in; 'his was a catching propaganda, and it was not easy to resist it; let those therefore who were in possession of the national organisation be firm.'[2] But by this date Pherozeshah Mehta and Gokhale were both dead, and consequently in the Congress of 1915 the views they represented carried less weight than before. At that meeting permission to elect delegates was granted to a wider range of political associations, and the door was opened to Tilak's men. He weighed up the advantages of entering through a small hole and fighting from within to capture the whole organization, against those which might accrue if they stayed outside Congress longer and fought for a compromise which entirely suited them: and under his direction the 'outs' in western India decided in April 1916 to accept the offered compromise.[3] The prospect of the 1916 Congress when the results of this compromise would become apparent produced dire misgivings not only in some Bombay men. Men in other provinces saw that it was not just a Bombay matter; the influx of Tilakites would have repercussions outside that Presidency because it would boost the position of groups in other areas whose views were akin to those of Tilak. D. E. Wacha voiced acute fears about the repercussions on the U.P.

1 B. G. Tilak to G. S. Khaparde, 22 November 1914, Khaparde Record I, pp. 58–9.

2 S. G. Vaze to V. S. S. Sastri, 16 December 1915, N.A.I., Sastri Papers, Correspondence File 1915, Letters to & from Sastri, No. 162. (The Sastri Papers are hereafter cited as S.P.)

3 B. G. Tilak to B. S. Moonje, 8 January 1916, M. D. Vidwans (ed.), *Letters Of Lokamanya Tilak* (Poona, 1966), pp. 276–7; Report of meeting of Bombay Provincial Conference at Belgaum on 29 April 1916, Weekly report of D.C.I., 16 May 1916, Proceeding No. 579 of Home Pol., B, May 1916, Nos. 577–580.

I have never known in my public life of 40 years here such a volcanic agitation and eruption as has been going on in the United Provinces for the last two years. I suppose this is the "new spirit" which is the forerunner of the "Home Rule" of the Besantine order which has been temporarily hypnotising the unthinking flock of sheep of which the United Provinces is the stronghold. Anyhow, my flesh creeps as I daily read the bombarding organs of opinion. And heaven knows to what heights abysmal, or rather *depths*, speaking correctly, these will reach at Lucknow during the Christmas week. I had an inclination to attend the Congress, but I have finally determined to hold aloof from it, as I foresee the storm which is threatened by the united phalanx of the Besantines and Tilakites. The so-called "compromise" of last year, in which I took *no part*,...is now doing all the mischief which I had forecast. I am quite sure that all this babbling and bubbling, with all its political hysteria, would receive its own quietus with the safe internment for some years of the pretentious leaders of the movement.[1]

A precisely similar assessment of the balance between various provincial groups prompted leaders like Annie Besant to take an interest in the 'compromise'. Seeing the position exactly as Wacha saw it, but from the other side of the fence, she realized that the arrival of Tilak's men in Congress would strengthen her own position in that gathering and would consequently increase her power in Madras. In the event the Lucknow Congress of 1916 was a dramatic success for Tilak and his allies outside Bombay. He was able to secure the election of all fifteen of his adherents to the Bombay delegation to the subjects committee; and the Lieutenant-Governor of the U.P. reported that the session 'was a great personal triumph for Tilak, and his enormous popularity was apparent at every turn.'[2]

Tilak and his allies were convinced that while Britain was at war the time was ripe for them to press the government for substantial political concessions and from the Lucknow Congress emerged a resolution demanding self-government at an early date.[3] One way of putting pressure on the raj was the very 'unification' of the politicians under the Congress banner, since the rulers would then find it harder to play off one group against another and so shelve the issue of reform. Another was to found organizations outside Congress designed specifically to spread the idea of Home Rule and to generate a country-wide demand for it. This was the course Tilak and Annie Besant followed in 1916, when they divided the country between them and established two complementary Home Rule Leagues. By going out into the highways and byways of India and collecting support

[1] Sir D. E. Wacha to Sir James Meston, 4 December 1916, Mss. EUR. F. 136 (4).

[2] Sir James Meston to Lord Chelmsford, I.O.L., Chelmsford Papers, Mss. EUR. E. 264 (18); Fortnightly report from Bombay, 31 December 1916, Home Pol., Deposit, January 1917, No. 45.

[3] *Report of the Thirty-first Indian National Congress held at Lucknow on the 26th, 28th, 29th and 30th December, 1916* (Allahabad, 1917), pp. 70–1.

wherever they could, they hoped to goad the government into concessions and simultaneously to strengthen their own political positions both locally and in Congress by their access to new networks of support.

Eighteen months after Gandhi's return to India these two leagues were critical factors in the political scene. Their significance lay not just in the new doctrines they were spreading, but in the range of people whom they were attracting. By the end of 1917 their joint membership numbered about 60,000. Clearly this was nothing approaching a mass political organization. But the size was impressive when compared with the numbers of delegates to Congress in earlier years.[1] What was more important was the fact that many of these members came from areas, castes and occupations which had previously been barely touched by Congress politics. Tilak's league had considerable appeal in C.P. and Berar, though its main strength lay in the Karnatak, Maharashtra and Bombay: of these areas only the last two had taken an active part in Congress affairs. Though the league tended to be controlled by experienced Brahmin politicians there is evidence of support from lower castes as well. In Khandesh district, for example, there were significant minorities of Gujar and Maratha members, who taken together outnumbered Brahmin members: in Poona and Nasik districts Brahmins were in a large majority but there were also considerable numbers of Gujarati, Marwari and Maratha members, who were probably traders and agriculturalists. Annie Besant's league had the additional advantage of drawing on those who had previously been attracted to Theosophy. It had notable success in Sind among the Amil trading caste, and in Gujarat among the Bania traders. Both Sind and Gujarat were notorious backwaters as far as institutional politics were concerned. Numerous branches of her league also mushroomed in Bihar and the U.P.; again regions with comparatively few western educated men, and consequently comparatively little influence in Congress.[2]

Reports from Madras, C.P. and Bombay during 1916 and 1917 showed that local governments were becoming distinctly worried by the increased range of the politicians' appeal, an appeal which was now directed at students, schoolboys, lesser government servants and even ordinary villagers. In the words of a report from Madras,

> While Mrs. Besant and her lieutenants pay particular attention to the student class, there are indications of the initiation of a special campaign for village work based mainly on the distribution of vernacular pamphlets

1 See above, p. 19

2 For an account of the foundation and development of the Home Rule Leagues see H. F. Owen, 'Towards Nation-Wide Agitation And Organisation: The Home Rule Leagues, 1915–18', D. A. Low (ed.), *Soundings In Modern South Asian History* (London, 1968), pp. 159–195. The Poona records of Tilak's Home Rule League in the Nehru Memorial Museum and Library, New Delhi, contain two volumes of registers, 1916–18, which also give members' castes.

> and the itineration of Home Rule preachers. Hitherto the district reports have for the most part pictured the Home Rule movement as confined to younger vakils and students in central towns, but in the report from the Guntur district for the past fortnight the Collector lays stress upon the activities of the League in the delta villages of the Tesali taluk. *New India*, he writes, owing largely to its cheapness, has a very wide circulation in rural areas generally and the fact, in his opinion, is giving the Home Rule movement a marked impetus among English-knowing people of all classes; the paper has a specially large circulation in the lower ranks of Government service.[1]

As this report indicated, once the politicians decided to extend their appeal they had to use a variety of new political techniques; and there is evidence of the growing importance of cheap newspapers like *New India*, vernacular pamphlets, posters, illustrated postcards, missionary preachers, *kirtans* (religious songs adapted for political propaganda) and even a drama society, as well as the traditional type of mass meeting with speeches.

The Home Rule Leagues began in halting fashion what Gandhi was later to do boldly and with far greater success. They formulated techniques which he developed, and began to till the ground in areas where he was to reap a great harvest of support. Their activities were a hint that there might soon be an end to the politics of studied limitation. Some of the politicians at least had realized that if they were to succeed in gaining the raj's consent to anything beyond the very limited demands they had so far made they would have to expand their range of support, and in order to do so would have to evolve a new political style. Some Congressmen had even earlier temporarily enlisted in their ranks as local allies men who had made contact with wider groups in society on issues such as cow-protection, temperance and religious reform.[2] But such alliances only lasted while the interests of the different groups of leaders coincided. Temporary alliances were no longer enough, but the limited extension of the politicians' range of support through the Home Rule Leagues suggests that the established political leaders were often not the right men to replace such temporary alliances with more lasting bonds. Many of the politicians refused to be involved in the attempt, while those who did in effect came up against the same barriers which had limited the Bengali politicians' room to manoeuvre during their agitation against the partition of their province.

In the circumstances of Indian society if the politicians were to mobilize support from outside their own elite group they needed powerful networks of linkage with wider social groups, or a compelling appeal which would override the need for such channels of influence. Such networks were

[1] Fortnightly report from Madras, 18 December 1916, Home Pol., Deposit, January 1917, No. 44.

[2] See, for example, such temporary alliances in the U.P., Bayly, 'The Development Of Political Organisation In The Allahabad Locality, 1880–1925', pp. 206–71, 314–34.

generally only created through caste solidarity or the relationship of patrons to clients, while appeals to the less educated would have to be couched in religious or economic terms. Lacking this type of network or rallying cry the politicians would have to gain the support of men who in their turn could mobilize wider groups in their localities by virtue of their appeals or local webs of influence. In the second decade of this century the western educated could rarely mobilize for themselves outside their own circle or rely on the services of intermediate leaders who could act as their subcontractors in the work of political construction. They were hamstrung by the very fact that they were an elite. Consequently the Home Rule Leagues in the light of Gandhi's later success look more like the death throes of the politics of limitation than the infant steps of a new political style.

The desire to put pressure on the government made the politicians stretch tentatively outside their existing circle of supporters and join hands among themselves in Congress. It even prompted them to patch up an agreement with the Muslim League. Negotiations for an inter-communal alliance went on throughout 1915, and came to fruition at Lucknow in 1916 when League and Congress met simultaneously and produced a united demand for constitutional reform. To an outsider like Gandhi this new alliance would have been one of the most striking developments on the political scene. Muslims had so far not joined Congress in any numbers. In areas like Bengal and the Punjab where they were a local majority they were generally ill-educated peasants, not the sort of people who were interested or welcome in Congress politics. In areas like the U.P. where they were an influential and educated minority they had just as little incentive to join the Congress. In western U.P., for example, economic circumstances pushed them into competition with those Hindus who gravitated into Congress, while in eastern U.P., as landlords and government servants, they were doing well out of the politics of loyal collaboration and were therefore hesitant to join in any political demand which might endanger their position.[1]

The Muslims' attitude dated back to the 1880s and the policy of the great Muslim leader, Sir Syed Ahmed Khan, who warned his co-religionists that whatever the variations in their regional standing they were in the country as a whole a minority community, backward in education and underrepresented in government service. He feared that if the government granted the concessions the Congressmen wanted they would bring no benefits to Muslims but only to educated Hindus; and consequently he advised Muslims to attend to education, to be scrupulously loyal to their rulers, and to shun 'friendship with the Bengalis in their mischievous

[1] For the status and subsequent politics of different groups of U.P. Muslims see F. C. R. Robinson, 'The Politics Of U.P. Muslims 1906–1922' (Ph.D. thesis, Cambridge, 1970).

political proposals.'[1] Where Muslims had sufficient western education to develop an interest in institutional politics, primarily in the U.P., their loyalty focussed on the Muslim League, which was founded in 1906 to protect the community in the face of proposals for constitutional reform. Its founders realized that if politics became a matter of counting heads rather than interests their community would be swamped, and they pressed successfully for the permanent protection of their 'interest' through the mechanism of communal representation. The League's founders also realized that the political tactics of cooperation with the government were increasingly suspect in the eyes of the so-called 'Young Party' Muslims who were tempted by the Hindu example to feel that agitation was a more productive tactic: consequently the foundation of the League was also an attempt to channel the energies of this restless group.

Ten years later contemporaries were treated to the spectacle of the League actually uniting with the Congress in a demand for constitutional reform. The terms of that unity were carefully calculated agreements that Muslims should have separate electorates under the proposed scheme of reform, and that in each area they should have a fixed proportion of seats in the legislative council: where they were in a minority they would be given 'weightage' to safeguard their interests, and where Hindus were in a minority they in turn would have the protection of 'weightage'.[2]

However, this alliance was not built on any deep foundations of unity. Rather it was engineered by politicians on both sides in whose interests it was to paper over the cracks between the two communities and present a united front to the government. The League itself was not representative of the whole Muslim community: indeed it could scarcely have been so because that community was as deeply divided, as were the Hindus, by regional differences, and, like the Hindus, the Muslims' interests depended mainly on their standing in their own localities. Between 1915 and 1916 the League probably only had between 500 and 800 members, provincial leagues existed only on paper, and the Council of the League, though theoretically made up of 300 members, was in practice a small group of autocrats. The negotiations with Congress carried on during 1915 by this so-called representative Muslim body were in fact dominated by a clique from the U.P., Bihar and Bengal, led by representatives of the U.P. 'Young Party' who, far from being subdued by the Muslim League as its founders had hoped, now controlled it and were bent on using it for the politics of agitation.[3]

[1] Speech by Sir Syed Ahmed Khan, 14 March 1888, Philips (ed.), *The Evolution Of India And Pakistan 1858 to 1947 Select Documents*, p. 189.

[2] The terms of the agreement, known as the Lucknow Pact, are set out in *ibid.* pp. 171–3.

[3] A crucial analysis of the strength, standing, and inner workings of the Muslim League is a note by Biggane of the U.P. C.I.D., 12 March 1919, U.P. General Administration Dept., File 423/1918. (I owe this reference to Mrs Gail Graham.)

Regional reactions to the Lucknow Pact showed just how unrepresentative the League was, and how divided the Muslim community. In Bombay (excepting Sind) the Muslims were a commercial minority, but factions and divisions of sect among them were reflected in the strife which broke out between M. A. Jinnah, a Khoja Muslim, Secretary of the Muslim League and a main organizer of the Lucknow Pact, and Sirdar Saheb Sulleman Cassim Mitha, Vice-President of the provincial branch of the League. Mitha, supported by the local Sunnis, felt that any alliance with their Hindu competitors would do irreparable harm to their position. Such was the bitterness between different groups of Muslims that in 1915 a meeting of the League in Bombay broke up in confusion, and, according to one observer, affairs were 'in such a mess now that to keep the League from dissolution has become the prime consideration just now.'[1] Bengali Muslims were equally divided, in this case between a few like Fazlul Haq whose background of education made them more like their Hindu counterparts, the *bhadralok* politicians, and therefore more willing to work with them, and the more traditional who felt that an ill-educated, rural community could do better by collaboration with the raj rather than alliance with urban Hindus. When the terms of the Lucknow Pact were announced the latter realized that because they were locally a majority the principle of 'weightage' would be brought into play against them, and in protest many of them resigned from the local branch of the League.[2] In the Punjab, where Muslims were also a peasant majority, they like the Bengalis disagreed among themselves over the terms of the Pact, which proposed that they should have only half the elected seats in the local legislative council. Those who opposed the Pact as undermining the Muslim position took their stand beside M. M. Shafi, the Secretary of the provincial league; and the upshot of this local division was a split in the provincial league. During 1916 there were two Punjab branches of the Muslim League, though Shafi's branch was disaffiliated at the League's Lucknow meeting in December that year.[3]

In Madras Muslims were a minority divided among themselves into three language groups, Tamil, Urdu and Telugu speakers. Only the Urdu speakers had taken much interest in institutional politics by 1916. As descendants of foreign conquerors they retained a sense of separation from

For a detailed account of the way in which the U.P. 'Young Party' Muslims engineered the alliance and pushed it through the League, see Robinson, 'The Politics Of U.P. Muslims 1906–1922', pp. 256–63.

1 Gulam Husein in Bombay to Mahomed Ali, 28 December 1915, Jamia Millia Islamia, Ali Papers. For the December 1915 meeting of the League and the divisions which disrupted it see Report by L. Robertson, Secretary to Govt. of Bombay, Judicial Dept., Home Pol., A, February 1916, Nos. 425–8.

2 Broomfield, *Elite Conflict in a Plural Society*, pp. 113–17.

3 P. C. Bamford, *History of the Non-Co-operation and Khilafat Movements* (Delhi, 1925), p. 122. (This is a confidential printed report in the I.O.L.)

their Hindu neighbours: as deposed rulers their position was deteriorating under British rule. Consequently they supported the Lucknow Pact with its promise of reform and its safeguard of 'weightage' for them as a minority. However the Pact received no support from their Tamil-speaking co-religionists, and in time even some Urdu Muslims began to feel that too close cooperation with Hindus was no good thing.[1]

In the U.P. and Bihar Muslims were just as divided. In both provinces they were an urban based minority with more local influence than their numbers would have suggested, because they retained some of the status they had enjoyed in the heyday of Mughal rule. But whereas the sprinkling of great landlords and the older educated men clung to the traditions of politics initiated by Sir Syed, the younger educated, particularly lawyers and journalists, with a rowdy following in the towns of U.P. and Bihar, had decided to search for power in company with Congress rather than in the government's train. One of the old school, Nawab Fateh Ali Khan, toured the U.P. in March and April 1914 in the hope of rallying like-minded Muslims,

> to checkmate the Muslim extreme political movement engineered by people like Messrs Mazharul-Haq and Muhammed Ali Jinha, Barristers, and Abul Kalam Azad and Muhammad Ali, Editors, and patronised by men like Raja of Mahmudabad as being dangerous to the country and to the community no less than to the Government and especially to the aristocracy whom they are trying to trample under foot and bring down to the level of the common people.[2]

But the Editors and the Barristers triumphed at Lucknow. They obtained considerable 'weightage' for the U.P. Muslims, while the older men who disapproved of the whole alliance muttered of schism and stayed away from the meeting on pretexts such as the Educational Conference at Aligarh.[3] Clearly the Muslim League was no more representative of all Muslims than was Congress of all Hindus.

However, activities which were recognizable as the politics of nationalism to western observers were only one facet or layer of Indian public life. To focus on them and merely to describe the political nation which participated in them is to limit too strictly the bounds of the arena which Gandhi entered on his return to India. Obviously it is impossible here to paint a total picture of Indian public life in 1915; the canvas would have to be vast and detailed. But it is possible to sketch briefly some of the stirrings in public life which were to have a bearing on the new style of institutional politics, to hint at movements which had political potential and might in

[1] For Madras Muslims and their politics see K. McPherson, 'The Political Development of the Urdu- and Tamil-speaking Muslims of the Madras Presidency 1901 to 1937' (M.A. thesis, University of Western Australia, 1968), pp. 26–74.

[2] Extract from journal of Nawab Fateh Ali Khan during his tour of U.P., March and April 1914, Mss. EUR. F. 136 (6).

[3] Sir James Meston to Chelmsford, 11 January 1917, Mss. EUR. E. 264 (18).

time throw up groups interested in reacting strongly in favour of or in opposition to the influence of a man like Gandhi. What makes Gandhi's career so worthy of note is that he is for the historian a way into the complexities of Indian public life. Just because his range and interests were not those of the recognized politicians a study of his activities must also include those jostlings and strivings in the community which to politicians and government alike certainly appeared sub-political, and sometimes were even subterranean.

It is clear that by the end of the nineteenth century the influence of the West was modifying Indian public life most profoundly. One of its most important effects was the creation of western educated groups which varied in strength and size from area to area. Just as its educational impact was uneven, differing in different parts of the subcontinent, so its economic, political and administrative penetration varied in depth in different regions. A result of this unevenness was that public life differed radically from province to province as old and new reacted on each other to produce power structures peculiar to the circumstances of each locality. Another result was the triggering of a host of subreactions in society which the raj, as the herald of the West, never intended or could have anticipated. External influence and internal tension crossed to produce undreamed-of mutations in society. Sometimes these external influences created new divisions, sometimes they merely exacerbated old ones. In the case of western education it provided new paths to influence and success in public life for those who took the opportunities it proffered: to those who lagged behind it held out new threats of failure and declining influence and prestige. As public life changed at a rate greater than ever before under the impact of the West, groups in society began to reassess their positions, to realign themselves, and to make provision for their future. Concern about changes in the locus and balance of power in society was manifested in various ways and by various mechanisms, some of them recognizably political, some not so, with a host of gradations in between. All these were part of the fabric of public life to which Gandhi returned in 1915.

One outstanding example was the phenomenon of whole areas becoming aware that change was occurring in society to their detriment. Areas which had felt only lightly the influence of western education and produced few western educated men began to feel that the changing environment was hostile to them, and their interests were being ignored. They could produce few men to fill government posts and professional appointments; they could send comparatively few representatives to voice their claims in councils and congresses where only the educated knew the ropes. In contrast to their plight they saw that areas which could produce numbers of western educated were gaining influence throughout the subcontinent, not just in their own areas but, by a process of overspill, in the territories of their less educated neighbours as well. Their anxiety about change focussed on the one thing which held together diverse groups within each area – language. As a result by the end of the nineteenth century the mechanism by which such areas responded to the changing situation was a combination of conscious linguistic revival and the cry for linguistic provinces.

The Andhra region of Madras Presidency was a prominent example. Following the late nineteenth century renaissance of Telugu, Telugu speakers resented the dominance of Tamil speakers in education and government service in the Presidency. In 1912 the idea of a separate Andhra province was first mooted – unsuccessfully: but from 1913 onwards an Andhra Conference met annually and called for an Andhra province. As the Conference secretaries wrote in 1917:

> The recent awakening of national consciousness in India has set the Andhras to enquire about their own conditions of life and their position amongst the peoples and communities in the land. It has enabled them to discover that they had fallen behind in the race for progress, and that their backwardness is due to want of opportunities and facilities for development. They have therefore been agitating for some years past for the constitution of the eleven northern districts of the Madras Presidency into a separate province.[1]

Similarly Oriya speakers resented their linguistic area being administered by three different local governments staffed by Bengali, Hindi and Telugu speakers respectively. Their self-assertion was first evident in the Oriya linguistic revival which began in the 1870s, and from 1903 onwards spilled over into an overtly political demand for a separate Oriya province.[2] By the second decade of this century the Sindhis, too, were fretting at their subjection to the influence of Bombay men, while Kannada speakers likewise staked claims to separate identity and position in the changing circumstances, claims which were couched in terms of a Kannada 'nationalism'.

> We have seriously realised that we have fallen behind in the race for political progress by reason of unequal competition with more advanced peoples. We are of opinion that the creation of a Kannada Provincial Congress circle will ensure our progress enabling us to develop on lines

[1] Letter from Andhra Conference Committee to Joint Secretaries of A.I.C.C., 11 September 1917, Adyar Archives, Annie Besant Papers. For a detailed account of the Andhra movement see J. G. Leonard, 'Politics And Social Change In South India: A Study Of The Andhra Movement', *Journal of Commonwealth Political Studies*, v, 1 (March 1967), 60–77.

[2] For example, the demand for a separate Oriya province voiced at the 12th session of the Utkal Conference, 29–30 December 1916, at Balasore, *The Amrita Bazar Patrika*, 4 January 1917. For a detailed history of the Oriya Movement and the arguments advanced by its protagonists see Two Bachelors of Arts, *The Oriya Movement* (Aska, 1919).

most congenial to our self-expression and to the preservation of the individuality of our race.[1]

Language areas were not alone in feeling the pinch in a changing India. Religious groups which failed to produce enough western educated men adequately to represent their interests in the new India, or which for one reason or another felt that their interests were being threatened locally, reacted in a whole gamut of ways ranging from the most sophisticated to the virtually incoherent. The Punjab was one area where this happened most obviously. For reasons which have yet to be studied in great depth, the impact of western rule and education on the Punjabis was such that from the end of the nineteenth century they tended to align according to community, Sikhs, Hindus and Muslims all fearing each other and calculating that they were losing out in the new era. At its most primitive this fear and communal alignment showed itself in periodic outbursts of communal rioting on the question of cow-killing. At a less rustic level the same motivation led to the foundation of communal associations which advocated religious purity, social improvement and educational reform. Sikhs joined Singh Sabhas, Muslims joined *anjumans*, or religious associations, while Hindus flocked to the Arya Samaj. All had the same end in view – to define the identity of their community and to safeguard its local position in a changing situation.[2] This intensely communal reaction to change became overtly political when the British by their proposed measure of constitutional reform in 1909 introduced even greater opportunities for shifts in the local balance of power. The cultural and educational associations of the three communities became agencies for demands for communal representation, as Muslims feared they would lose out because they were an ill-educated minority in the subcontinent, while Hindus and Sikhs felt the threat of the local Muslim majority and hastened to claim special protection.[3]

Similar reactions occurred in other areas where religious groups felt that their interests were being threatened. In the U.P. the Muslim minority reacted strongly as western penetration seemed to undermine their traditionally influential status and boost the influence of their Hindu neighbours. As in neighbouring Punjab their reaction took place at various levels, ranging from cow-killing riots, through a bitter campaign against the adoption of Hindi instead of Urdu as the language of local administration,

[1] Undated circular to all members of A.I.C.C., Nehru Memorial Museum and Library, A.I.C.C. Files, 1917, No. 1.

[2] N. G. Barrier, 'The Punjab Government and Communal Politics, 1870–1908', *The Journal Of Asian Studies*, XXVII, 3 (May 1968), 523–39. K. W. Jones, 'Communalism in the Punjab. The Arya Samaj Contribution', *The Journal Of Asian Studies*, XXVIII, 1 (November 1968), 39–45.

[3] Johnson, 'Indian Politics 1888–1908', pp. 372–4; the Muslim view was explained by M. M. Shafi to Dunlop Smith in a letter dated 13 January 1909, M. Gilbert, *Servant of India* (London, 1966), pp. 181–2.

to a severe local fracas about the representation of the two communities on municipal councils. Similarly in Madras the Urdu-speaking Muslims, once a dominant minority by virtue of their local connection with the ruling power, particularly the Nizams of Hyderabad and the Nawabs of the Karnatak, began to lose local influence when the British gained power. They failed to learn the techniques of the new administration, or to take advantage of western education; but, in belated recognition of their deteriorating situation, by the turn of the century they began to join forces in the Southern Indian Muhammedan Educational Association and in various *anjumans*, to define themselves as a separate community and to retrieve their social position. Their claims to local status were not made through political channels until the promise of constitutional reform between 1906 and 1909, which to them was no promise but a threat of submergence by the Hindu majority unless they could procure special protection through separate representation.

Certain caste groups also began to feel that they were joining the ranks of the backward as new opportunities for influence in public life opened up around them and their members seemed unable to take advantage of them. Until late 1917 it was rare for caste fears and aspirations to find expression in overt politics. It only occurred before that date in two areas, where caste feeling was particularly bitter and western education specially deep-rooted among the higher castes, enabling them and them alone to take advantage of government proposals for constitutional reform. These two areas were Madras and Maharashtra.[1] In Madras this sort of comment was being freely circulated:

> Political Home Rule without Social Home Rule will land us in a Home Rule which will be a euphemism for the tyrannising of the minority by the majority, of the poor by the wealthy, of the ignorant by the intelligent, of the low caste and the no caste by the high caste.[2]

The result of such fears was the foundation of the South Indian Liberal Federation in 1916, later the Justice Party, designed to ensure that under any scheme of reform the Brahmins would not walk away with all the plums because of their high standards of western education.[3] In Maha-

[1] Professor D. A. Low suggested to me that the bitterness of inter-caste hostility in Madras and Maharashtra was partly due to the absence in those areas of large groups of Kshatriyas and Vanias who might have acted as a middle or buffer social group. The contrast is clear with Gujarat, where the trading castes were numerous and well educated in the vernacular while the Brahmins were comparatively ill educated and aroused little hostility from the lower castes. For the spread of education in Gujarat, see below, pp. 89–90.

[2] *The Social Reform Advocate*, 17 June 1916.

[3] For non-Brahmin unrest in Madras and the foundation of the Justice Party see E. F. Irschick, *Politics And Social Conflict In South India. The Non-Brahman Movement and Tamil Separatism, 1916–1929* (Berkeley & Los Angeles, 1969), pp. 41–54.

rashtra Tilak's Home Rule campaign frightened some of the lower and less educated castes into downright opposition to the idea of Home Rule, and prompted the foundation of the Belgaum Lingayat Association in 1916 'to promote, by strictly lawful means, the interests of the Lingayat Community in all matters affecting it.'[1]

Far more often, however, caste reactions to the changing environment came within the purview of the anthropologist or local census and gazetteer compiler rather than the western style politician. Many castes outside the range of the western educated realized that as society changed around them, turning the tables against the ill-educated, they were losing local prestige and power. Their response was twofold – to try to claim prestige in the traditional terms of ritual purity, and simultaneously to increase their actual power by improving their educational and economic standing. The result was a curious blend of the traditional and the modern, both in aim and technique. Local reports showed castes apeing the customs of higher castes, hoping thereby to improve their standing according to traditional criteria and by thoroughly traditional means.[2] At the same time they used the modern instrument of the census report to reach the same goal, much to the embarrassment of local officials. As one noted in 1911:

> No part of the census aroused so much excitement as the return of castes. There was a general idea in Bengal that the object of the census is not to show the number of persons belonging to each caste, but to fix the relative status of different castes and to deal with questions of superiority. Some frankly regarded the census as an opportunity that might fairly be taken to obliterate caste distinctions. The feeling on the subject was very largely the result of castes being classified in the last census report in order of social precedence. This "warrant of precedence" gave rise to considerable agitation at the time and proved a legacy of trouble. The agitation was renewed when the census operations of 1911 were instituted. Hundreds of petitions were received from different castes – their weight alone amounts to 1½ maunds – requesting that they might be known by new names, be placed higher in the order of precedence, be recognised as Kshattriyas, Vaisyas, etc.[3]

Some castes also brought into play another very modern technique, the voluntary, secular association, in their attempt to acquire a mixture of old prestige and new power. These caste *sabhas* or associations called on their members to reform their social habits in deference to ancient standards of ritual purity, claimed exalted origin and high social status for their members; while urging on them a reduction of marriage expenses to improve their economic position, and adopting measures to spread education so that

[1] Bombay Police Abstract, 1916, par. 1019.

[2] This phenomenon, known as 'sanskritization' is discussed in M. N. Srinivas, *Social Change In Modern India* (Berkeley & Los Angeles, 1966), pp. 1–45.

[3] *Census Of India, 1911. Volume V. Bengal, Bihar And Orissa And Sikkim. Part I. Report* (Calcutta, 1913), p. 440.

their members might be equipped to take advantage of modern opportunities. Among these *sabhas*, to name only a few, were the Ahir Sabha which claimed Kshatriya origin for its members across northern India, the Mehra Rajput Sabha of the Punjab which claimed Rajput status for the Mehra caste, and the Qaum Sudhar Sabha of Punjabi barbers who tried to pass as Kshatriyas. As yet these associations were pursuing aims which were by no stretch of the imagination political, according to the standards of institutional politics. But having got as far as organization and appeal to the government there was a likelihood that they would use the same mechanism for overt politics if they thought this an appropriate way of bettering their position.[1]

Finally there were distinct economic groups who were subject to severe pressure as India changed around them. Prominent among them were the great landowners in those areas where land had not been settled with individual peasant proprietors or village communities in the nineteenth century, in U.P., Bihar and parts of Madras and the Punjab, for example. Until the twentieth century they had built their very great social power on a traditional foundation – land; and like the Princes, encouraged by the British as 'breakwaters in the storm' after the Mutiny, had buttressed this power by judicious collaboration with the raj. For them there was no need of institutional politics, as their interests were well catered for under the existing regime. Writing of the U.P. in 1916 the Lieutenant-Governor, Sir James Meston described

> the very limited spread of the political sense among the people of this province. The big landlord or the yeoman farmer is particularly defective in it. He has not been educated, and is not educating his sons, as the townsmen are. The only politics he knows is the constant struggle between landholder and tenant. The only legislation which interests him is the long series of land laws, in regard to which the fear that Government will side against him makes him unwilling to burn his fingers in ordinary public affairs. Almost his only distraction is endless litigation with his tenants, his co-sharers and his relatives, which make him dread and dislike the lawyer as a class. The consequence of all this is that he cannot and will not face the modern methods of a contested election, the facile speech-making, the obloquy of the press, or the heckling which cuts his dignity like a lash. In small constituencies...or among his own class, he will occasionally stand, confining himself to writing a few letters and sending round his estate-agent to canvass for him: but with large mixed constituencies this would be impossible and he would be wiped out.[2]

[1] This was precisely the pattern followed by the Bengal Namasudras, whose caste association founded in 1912 was by 1918 taking part in institutional politics in opposition to the Montagu–Chelmsford Reforms. For a discussion of the political potential of these associations see L. I. & S. H. Rudolph, 'The Political Role of India's Caste Associations', *Pacific Affairs*, XXXIII, 1 (March 1960), 5–22.

[2] Sir James Meston to Chelmsford, 19 August 1916, Mss. EUR. F. 136 (1).

The large landholders lived in a totally different world from the politicians, pursuing quite different sorts of influence; but that other urban, political world was rapidly impinging on the landholders, and they found themselves threatened in their own localities by men who were deriving power from other sources, the professions, government administration and business. Nor were they unaware of this challenge. One of Bihar's largest landholders, the Maharajah of Darbhanga, complained bitterly to Sir James Meston that local politicians like Madan Mohan Malaviya were dominating the affairs of Benares Hindu University and that the landed aristocracy were being pushed out of all public movements. He wanted to know what the government intended to do for its old friends in their hour of need.[1] Change in government and society hit the old aristocrats hard, and as yet they did not know what to do about it.

At the other end of the rural scale there were in some areas small landholders and tenant cultivators who felt as keenly changes which followed on the heels of western penetration. Their difficulties sprang not from western educated competitors for power but from economic change; and the ways in which they responded varied enormously in their sophistication. Peasants in Bihar, for example, were virtually forced to grow indigo by European planters who found it a highly lucrative industry. When the pressure grew too great the peasants rioted.[2] This was the traditional expression of rural discontent, the only means of protest open to an illiterate peasantry, and was repeated at countless times and in countless places in the subcontinent. By contrast, prosperous Punjabi peasant proprietors in the canal colonies reacted in 1906 to increased water rates and government plans to tighten conditions of landholding with a systematic agitation which looked almost political in western terms, though it was not in fact led by urban politicians.[3] These were the two ends of the spectrum. Between the actions of the Bihari and Punjabi cultivators there was a variety of mechanisms by which lowlier country-folk tried to make known their distress in the face of social and economic change – mechanisms which reached the notice of the local C.I.D. but did not rouse the interests of the politicians except on rare occasions.

The common element in these diverse strivings by occupational and religious groups, castes and linguistic areas was that all were reactions to a changing environment, as India was laid open to the influence of the West

[1] Sir James Meston to Chelmsford, 4 September 1916, Mss. EUR. E. 264 (17). M. M. Shafi had made a similar complaint in relation to the effects of the 1909 reforms on Punjabi landowners, M. M. Shafi to Dunlop Smith, 13 January 1909, Gilbert, *Servant of India*, p. 182.

[2] One of the worst outbreaks of rural rioting is described in B. B. Kling, *The Blue Mutiny. The Indigo Disturbances in Bengal 1859–1862* (Philadelphia, 1966).

[3] N. G. Barrier, 'The Punjab Disturbances of 1907: the response of the British Government in India to Agrarian unrest', *Modern Asian Studies*, 1, 4 (October 1967), 353–83.

for an increasing length of time. Economic change was critical for some groups; but for many others the aspect of change which pushed them into new forms of public activity was that precipitated by western education, in particular the dividends the new education paid to those who acquired it, in terms of employment and public influence. They were dividends likely to be more valuable still as the raj took its first hesitant steps in devolving some of its power through the administration and new provincial councils.

Clearly no one pattern of reaction to change occurred in the subcontinent. Rather, each area produced its particular pattern, dependent on the local power structure in indigenous society, the nature and timing of the western impact, and the interaction of the two. Sometimes groups traditionally influential found new ways of increasing their strength, sometimes they found themselves losing ground most lamentably in the new era. Sometimes groups who for decades had been weak and ineffectual in a locality found new routes to prosperity and power; and at other times and in other places such groups merely lapsed further into the slough of poverty and subjection. But throughout the country there were stirrings and strivings in society which were the response to change, and in very many cases the groups involved had interests which were not registered in institutional politics, or only peripherally so. Either their interests were not within the politicians' scope, like those of the Bihari peasants or the aspirant castes of north India; or they were diametrically opposed to the interests voiced in Congress, as in the case of the great landlords or the restless non-Brahmins of Madras. Although they were outside the range of the politicians the crucial thing about these groups was that they were a reservoir of latent political material. In a situation of rapid change and with the right leadership these groups might find it profitable and possible to register their interests in institutional politics, and perhaps to challenge the sitting tenants in Congress, if not to oust them completely. 'Latency' was the reverse side of the coin of 'limitation' in a political situation where only a few were equipped by training and ideology to manipulate the new mechanisms of influence in public life provided by the institutional politics of nationalism.[1]

(II) GANDHI AND THE POLITICAL NATION

When Gandhi is compared with the early Indian nationalist politicians the similarities between them during the first phase of his South African career are striking. He used similar techniques and appealed to a similar audience; but there is no evidence that he modelled himself on them. He became like the Indian politicians because his situation was similar to theirs. He, like

[1] I owe this concept of 'latency' to G. M. Kahin, G. J. Pauker and L. W. Pye, 'Comparative Politics Of Non-Western Countries', *The American Political Science Review*, XLIX, 4 (December 1955), 1022–41.

them, was a child of English education, with its examples of political ideology and practice. He, like them, organized a limited and comparatively privileged group within the community; and just as much as they, he had a supreme interest in retaining the sympathy of the British in the hope that they would intervene to change the Indians' position. Neither Gandhi nor the politicians demanded a revolution: rather they wanted adjustment of position within an existing framework – hence their profuse declarations of loyalty to the Crown and their studied moderation.

However, this similarity did not last. As Gandhi's ideas changed and as the situation in Africa altered, so he drew away from the style and ideals of the Presidency politicians, and it became clear that on his return he would not fit easily into the Indian scene as one of them. He began to work with Muslims, with low caste Hindus, with commercial men – just the groups who found no place in Congress politics because their interests were not those of the educated few. He gradually abandoned his old political techniques in favour of satyagraha, whereas the politicians clung to their moderate methods, and hastily drew back from their experiment with passive resistance in Bengal.

When Gandhi returned to India, satyagraha was not his sole technique at the expense of all others. He still used what weapon seemed most appropriate for the particular situation, though the development of his ideals was swinging the balance in favour of a more constant resort to satyagraha. But it was clear that he had none of the inhibitions of the Indian leaders, and that though they were timid he would not hesitate to use a technique which could mobilize a wider following if he thought it desirable.

At first, however, there was no occasion for a clash between Gandhi and the western educated on political matters. Keeping his vow of a year's silence on political topics Gandhi spent 1915 and much of 1916 touring India, visiting places as far apart as Sind and Rangoon, Benares and Madras, in order to get to know his homeland. He was feted at receptions to welcome him to India, he attended political meetings as an honoured but generally silent observer, he spoke at colleges and conferences on his experiences in South Africa and the ideals he had formulated there, and he visited Hindu communities like Rabindranath Tagore's Shantiniketan and Mahatma Munshiram's Gurukul at Hardwar.[1] His main concern at this time, with Gokhale's blessing, was to continue the experiment he had started at Phoenix and Tolstoy Farm to train Indians 'for long service to the Motherland';[2] and his only major deviation from this programme of observation and experimentation was his campaign for the abolition of the

[1] For Gandhi's programme and itinerary during 1915 and 1916, see *C.W.*, vol. 13, pp. 607–16.

[2] Interview given by Gandhi to the press on his future plans, *The Madras Mail*, 23 April 1915, *ibid.* pp. 54–6. For the foundation of the *ashram* at Sabarmati to continue this experiment, see below, pp. 42–3.

practice of recruiting indentured labourers in India for work abroad.[1] When asked in April 1915 what he thought about contemporary nationalist politics, Gandhi made it clear that he was not interested in such agitation. The surprised representative of *The Madras Mail*

> gathered that Mr. Gandhi does not lay so much store by agitation for obtaining concessions from the Government as by working for the moral, material and economic regeneration of his countrymen, for he is of the opinion that once people make themselves fit by their character and capacity, the grant of privileges will follow as a matter of course – in fact, there will be no need for people to ask for concessions, and what is granted will be no concessions, for people will have grown into them. Mr. Gandhi implicitly believes that no agitation for concessions will do any service to the country without reform coming from within, at the same time. Mr. Gandhi prefers to be judged by his conduct rather than by the words he utters, words spoken under the limitations of an interview not being, in his opinion, capable of expressing all that the person interviewed might like to say on the subjects discussed.[2]

Such a pronouncement was no immediate challenge to the power of the politicians; but the differences between Gandhi and India's western educated, whose representatives the politicians were, became obvious when he returned to India and actually confronted them with his philosophy and in particular with his attitude to the West. Within days of his arrival they were commenting on his odd habits and noting how unlike their ideas of an educated leader he was. One of the earliest reactions was that of V. S. Srinivasa Sastri who wrote:

> Queer food he eats; only fruit and nuts. No salt: milk, ghee, etc. being animal products, avoided religiously. No fire should be necessary in the making of the food, fire being unnatural...
>
> The odd thing is he was dressed quite like a *bania*: no one could mark the slightest difference. He had a big sandal mark on his forehead and a kunkum dot besides.[3]

The first occasion for an overt confrontation was the foundation of the Sabarmati *ashram* at Ahmedabad in May 1915. There Gandhi hoped to

1 For example, his demand for the abolition of the system of indentured labour made in Bombay on 28 October 1915 at a meeting held under the auspices of the District Congress Committee, *The Bombay Chronicle*, 29 October 1915, *C.W.*, vol. 13, pp. 130–4. Indentured labour was stopped by regulation in India in 1917. For a brief sketch of the system from its initiation in the 1840s see Hancock, *Survey Of British Commonwealth Affairs. Volume 1. Problems Of Nationality 1918–1936*, pp. 178–81.

2 Interview given by Gandhi to the press on his future plans, *The Madras Mail*, 23 April 1915, *C.W.*, vol. 13, pp. 55–6.

3 V. S. S. Sastri to V. S. R. Sastri, 10 January 1915, T. N. Jagadisan (ed.), *Letters Of The Right Honourable V. S. Srinivasa Sastri P.C., C.H., Ll.D., D.Litt.* (2nd edition, Bombay, 1963), p. 41.

create in a religious community on the traditional Hindu pattern an environment where he could obtain the spiritual 'deliverance' he sought in his homeland. But his ideal of service to widening circles of his fellow men compromised his withdrawal from the concerns of the world which should in conventional Hindu thought have been the precondition for 'deliverance'. It twisted the traditional pattern of an *ashram* and made the Sabarmati *ashram* not so much a spiritual retreat as a factory for what Gandhi considered to be ideal Indians for the service of their motherland. He planned for the inmates utter simplicity of life, manual labour, hand spinning, and the use only of Indian products, backed by vows typical of his philosophy of life and action, among them vows of truth, non-violence and celibacy.[1] Indian reaction to this varied. Some praised it unreservedly like the *sadhu* who wrote from Hrishikesh, or the correspondent from Madras who welcomed the *ashram* as embodying the spirit of *aryavarta*, the land of the Aryans. Others criticized it on grounds ranging from wonder at the harshness of the life and bewilderment at the vow of celibacy, to anger that Gandhi should discard obvious benefits of western knowledge.[2]

These different responses were symptomatic of the attitude of the educated towards India and the West. Among them there was a wide range of reactions to the West, and endless combinations of western and Indian habits. All of them had been forced to come to terms with some western innovations, although uncritical acceptance of the West was no longer in vogue as it had been in the late nineteenth century. Gandhi's hope of reconstructing traditional Indian life commended him to the more traditional, but it found an echo in nearly all the obviously 'westernized'. One of the severest critics of Gandhi's attitude to civilization was the Bombay journalist, K. Natrajan, who edited *The Indian Social Reformer*. Even he was clearly torn between criticism and admiration.

> May I take the liberty of saying that no one thinks or says that any Civilisation – least of all Western Civilisation – is without faults ? So long as there is so much of brute in the vast mass of us, Civilisation cannot but consist of a large proportion of savagery. You may not agree with us that Western Civilisation, taken as a whole, *tends* more strongly to justice for all than any other Civilisation. But what I wish to tell you with sincere respect is this: Condemn by all means as strongly as you like every *feature* of Western Civilisation which merits condemnation. You will not find many of us dissenting from you. Where we find, to our great regret, that we cannot follow you, is in your generalisation against modern civilisation as such. Your career and character is such a vast public asset that one feels

[1] Draft constitution for the *ashram*, *C.W.*, vol. 13, pp. 91–8. An *ashram* is the home of a Hindu religious community.

[2] Varied reactions to the *ashram* are in letters to Gandhi from S. Subramanium, Madras, 6 August 1915, S.N. No. 6219; Sadhu Magalnath, Hrishikesh, 2 September 1915, S.N. No. 6228; S. Rudra, Simla, 2 July 1915, S.N. No. 6201; S. G. Ranade, Bournemouth, 25 August 1915, S.N. No. 6226.

> that it is a pity it should be rendered less useful than it might and should be...by this prejudice, as I must hold it to be, against modernity as such.[1]

The cultural rift between Gandhi and his educated compatriots was deepest when they dealt with education itself. It was not surprising that the subject of western education should be the most acute area of conflict between them, because this was the main channel through which western civilization was flowing into India. Moreover, the western educated owed their status in society and their livelihood to it, while Gandhi, true to the views he had expounded in *Hind Swaraj*, proclaimed that 'to be a voluntary victim of this system of education is to betray one's duty to one's mother.'[2] He admitted that the western educated had done much for India, but he thought the system enslaved and corrupted the country. According to him its literary bias and foreign medium had dried up Indian nationality, separated the educated from the masses, and turned the educated into an army of scribbling clerks and office seekers. His remedy was national education as in his *ashram*, through vernacular media, stressing religious instruction and practical knowledge of agriculture and weaving, as well as more customary academic subjects.[3]

Gandhi's national education had a precursor in the Bengali national education movement, which accompanied the agitation against the partition of Bengal. But this was basically a political movement, and when the political fire died down the educational work was also reduced to ashes, particularly when students from 'national' institutions found that employers would not accept their qualifications.[4] As in the case of passive resistance, Indian leaders drew back when they saw the danger to their own position. The educated found much of Gandhi's educational theory unacceptable, their main disagreement concerning the content rather than the media of education. All agreed on the importance of primary instruction in the vernacular, though most realized that in higher education English was essential at least for a long time to come. Similarly most thought that western knowledge was unavoidable and beneficial, and it was here that Gandhi disagreed with them most passionately as he envisaged a syllabus on more traditional Indian lines. In stark contrast to his condemnation of a western type of syllabus, Gokhale had proclaimed

> the greatest work of Western education in the present state of India is...

1 K. Natrajan to Gandhi, 26 May 1915, S.N. No. 6195.

2 Speech by Gandhi at 2nd Gujarat Educational Conference, 20 October 1917, *C.W.*, vol. 14, p. 16.

3 Circular letter appealing for funds for the *ashram*, July 1917, *C.W.*, vol. 13, p. 462.

4 For a survey of the Bengali National Education Movement see H. & U. Mukherjee, *The Origins Of The National Education Movement (1905–1910)* (Calcutta, 1957). The main difference between Gandhi and the Bengali National Educationalists was the latter's desire to assimilate western scientific techniques, while Gandhi shunned these and advocated cottage industries.

> the liberation of the Indian mind from the thraldom of old-world ideas and the assimilation of all that is highest and best in the life and thought of the West. For this purpose not only the highest but *all* Western education is useful.[1]

Even those who did not share Gokhale's exuberance realized that for practical purposes western education had come to stay, because it was the key to material advancement for its recipients. In attacking western education and castigating lawyers and doctors, Gandhi was challenging the vested interests of his educated contemporaries, the very people who were the heart of the new politics and controlled the Congress. It was hardly likely that they would find such an opponent congenial company. Where they campaigned for more jobs and over the years evolved a demand for eventual Home Rule, Gandhi cast such mundane considerations aside. On the lines laid down in *Hind Swaraj* he publicly proclaimed that he 'did not ask for self-government or Home Rule, but he urged his listeners to regenerate themselves.'[2]

There were other issues on which Gandhi held equally firm views; but none of these roused quite as strong a reaction as his views on education and the West. His economic ideas were just as strange and emphatic, for he advocated swadeshi, the use of things belonging to one's own country, particularly stressing the replacement of foreign machine-made cloth with Indian hand-made cloth. This was his solution to the poverty of peasants who could spin at home to supplement their incomes, his cure for the alleged drain of money to Manchester in payment for imported cloth, and an integral part of his exaltation of traditional civilization.[3] But on this issue he did not clash too fiercely with the educated because swadeshi did not endanger their vested interests, since they were not an economic class supported by manufacture and trade. Indeed they had already learnt to use swadeshi as a method of political protest against the raj at the time of the partition of Bengal. Much of Indian industry was still in British hands; while Indian industrialists found Gandhi's attitude to products made in Indian factories sufficiently lenient for them to be able to support him and even display their products in a patriotic light.

Similarly Gandhi's attitude to such thorny topics as caste, untouchability and the status of women did not provoke total opposition from the educated, because he preached a discreet blend of the reformist and the orthodox. His attitude towards caste was a case in point. Though he con-

[1] Speech by Gokhale in Imperial Legislative Council, 18 December 1903, D. G. Karve and D. V. Ambekar (ed.), *Speeches and Writings of Gopal Krishna Gokhale. Volume Three: Educational* (Poona, 1967), p. 11.

[2] Report of speech by Gandhi at Kangri, 16 March 1916, Bombay Police Abstract, par. 469.

[3] An exposition of some of Gandhi's economic ideas is found in the report of his speech on 22 December 1916 to the Economic Society of Muir College, Allahabad, *The Leader*, 25 December 1916, *C.W.*, vol. 13, pp. 310–17.

demned the practice of untouchability without equivocation he still upheld the theoretical fourfold division of Hindu society and condemned any marriage which broke through the division.[1] More important still, when he urged Indians to reform their social habits he insisted that they should do so according to the tenets of a pure and ancient Hinduism.[2] This approach meant that he could support certain reforms without appearing iconoclastic towards Hinduism as such. Combined with his traditional image as an austere Mahatma living in an *ashram*, this made it clear that whatever his quirks and peculiarities he was thoroughly Indian, a crucial aspect of his appeal both to the educated as they grew more disgruntled with the raj, and to the uneducated who saw him as a type of leader familiar from tradition. The social reform movement of the nineteenth century had been disorganized and diffuse, including within its spectrum all shades of opinion from the most timid to the most radical.[3] Consequently it was possible for Gandhi's contemporaries to find precedents for every reform he advocated, and for most of them to feel sympathy with some of his convictions. He appealed to few wholly, but to many partially. Though his estrangement from the western educated was deep on certain issues it was not yet a complete divorce.

However, Gandhi was not just a social worker and religious reformer, whose activities the western educated could afford to tolerate if they disapproved of them. He was also a public figure of note,[4] a man with considerable political experience who might prove to be a powerful ally or a dangerous opponent, a potential politician with whom the politicians would have to come to terms if he chose to try to implement his ideals through the methods of politics. For Gandhi's part the role of the lone wolf and the political outsider would probably not suffice for long if he wished to gain support for his ideals, though it was appropriate while he observed his country and tested out the feelings of influential men.

On Gandhi's return the main channels through which the western educated pressed their political aspirations upon his notice were the Congress, the Muslim League and the Home Rule Leagues. It is debatable how far Gandhi was on his return actually aware of the complexities and hosts of

1 *Bharat Sevak*, October 1916, *ibid.* pp. 301–3; article dated 15 February 1919, describing Gandhi's attitude to a current Inter-Caste Marriage Bill, *The Bombay Chronicle*, 20 February 1919.

2 The grounds for reform of the status of women are set out in a speech by Gandhi to the Bhagini Samaj, Bombay, 20 February 1918, *C.W.*, vol. 14, p. 204.

3 For a survey of the social reform movement see C. H. Heimsath, *Indian Nationalism And Hindu Social Reform* (Princeton, 1964).

4 In 1915 Gandhi was awarded the Kaiser-i-Hind Gold Medal (ironically in company with Lady Willingdon, the wife of one who was to be one of his firmest opponents within five years!). His recommendation described him as 'The well-known South African leader, who has now returned to India, where he is regarded almost as a saint.' Hardinge to Crewe, 21 April 1915, Hardinge Mss. (121).

conflicting interests behind these apparently solid fronts, and the challenge these conflicts presented to his ideal of a united Indian nation evolved in the special circumstances of the Indian community in South Africa. The nearest to an answer the historian can get is to trace Gandhi's initial involvement with particular groups of politicians. The details of these early contacts also show how in practice he came to a working relationship with the political representatives of the western educated during his first months back in India.

Indian Muslims were one of Gandhi's particular concerns. He returned to India with the specific intention of working with and for them, as he had done in Africa. He said later, 'With that object I came to India. My first duty was, when I came to India, to find out such Moslem brethren who would give their lives for truth and for unity between Hindus and Mussalmans.'[1] Evidence is meagre about contacts between Gandhi and 'Moslem brethren' at this time. Early in 1916 he attempted to see two Muslim journalists, Mahomed and Shaukat Ali, who were interned for their sympathy with Turkey during the war, but he was stopped by the government.[2] In March 1916 he visited a Sind Muslim leader, the Pir of Luwari, whose 200,000 followers believed him to be the Mahdi. The police immediately took an interest in this visit, but it produced no particular results and it appeared that the reason for it was a totally innocent one – Gandhi had worked with some of the Pir's followers in South Africa and had promised to visit their leader if he was in Sind.[3] In December that year he went to the Lucknow meeting of the Muslim League, where he was given 'a great reception', and was invited to speak. He did so, pointing out that any concessions which Indians had gained in South Africa had depended on cooperation between Hindus and Muslims, and that India would only gain self-government if the two communities worked together.[4]

Another indication that he was popular among some Muslims was the public praise given to him by two Muslim members of the Bombay Legislative Council, though this did not go unchallenged. One Muslim paper commented that it could not see why Gandhi deserved an ovation: 'we do not know what he has done in India to deserve the great position of leadership which is assigned to him, and to the Muhammadan Community he has been a total stranger.'[5] Despite this assertion Gandhi was

1 Report of speech by Gandhi in Bombay, 9 May 1919, Bombay Police Abstract, 1919, par. 665.

2 See below, p. 152.

3 Weekly report of D.C.I., 14 March 1916, Proceeding No. 669 of Home Pol., B, March 1916, Nos. 667–70; Memorandum from Political Department Officer of the Commissioner in Sind, Proceeding No. 194 of Home Pol., A, September 1916, Nos. 193–4 & K.-W.

4 Bombay Police Abstract, 1917, par. 139.

5 *Islamic Mail*, 12 March 1916, English edition, Bombay N.N., No. 12 of 1916, pp. 12–13.

clearly keeping up the links between himself and Muslims which he had forged in Africa; at this point they did not look particularly strong ones, but they were crucial for his own future. There is no evidence that he was aware of the differences among Muslims in status and interests; he tended to treat their community as a monolithic and united one, as it had been in South Africa. This, too, was to have a bearing on his future attitude to Muslims and his decision to lead the Khilafat movement in their name.

However, as far as Congress was concerned, Gandhi was more aware of the wheeling and dealing which went on behind the bland facade, and he appears deliberately to have steered clear of it all. In South Africa he had preached admiration for the Congress, and urged it to champion the cause of Indians abroad: but Congress replied by doing very little positive for that cause, though it officially recognized Gandhi's services to his compatriots. This inaction made him feel that Congress was too sedentary and cerebral a body for his own liking, and after his return to India he remained somewhat aloof from its activities. The vow of silence on political matters of course bound him for the whole of 1915 and contributed to his isolation. In 1915 he attended Congress and was a member of the subjects committee, nominated by the President rather than elected to represent any particular province. He spoke on the resolution about India and the colonies, but not on the self-government resolution.[1] Four months later he attended the conference at Belgaum when Tilak and those who had been excluded from Congress met to decide whether they should re-enter on the terms offered to them. Gandhi supported the resolution in favour of a united Congress, but insisted that he himself was an outsider who did not belong to any party, and was merely present because he thought it was his duty as a servant of his country.[2] When he went to the first reunited Congress in 1916 he was received with loud cheers, but he still refused to speak on issues which would have meant aligning with particular groups, and reserved his fire for a resolution condemning the recruitment of indentured labourers.[3]

Gandhi's isolation at the centre of institutional politics was repeated in his relations with particular groups of politicians in the localities, and he refused to become enmeshed in any of their alliance networks. As far as the remaining evidence shows, Gandhi had little contact with these networks outside western India. Based on Gujarat, his political relations did not spread far beyond the bounds of the Bombay Presidency and were limited to the Servants of India Society and the groups bound by loyalty to Tilak and Annie Besant.

During his Africa days Gandhi had virtually no direct contact with

[1] *Report of the Thirtieth Indian National Congress held at Bombay on the 27th, 28th and 29th December, 1915* (Bombay, 1916), pp. 62–4.

[2] Bombay Police Abstract, 1916, par. 757.

[3] *31st I.N.C. Report*, pp. 62–3.

Annie Besant, though he had firm views on the Theosophical Society headquarters near Madras, condemning them as a hotbed of fraud. He felt that Annie Besant herself was honest but credulous.[1] In 1915 she approached Gandhi and invited him to join in founding a Home Rule League, an invitation he refused on the grounds that he did not wish to embarrass the British during the war.[2] This difference of approach degenerated into overt antipathy after an incident at Benares on 6 February 1916 when Gandhi spoke at the opening of the Hindu University. In the course of his speech he touched on the problem of bomb throwing and political assassination, and though he condemned such actions he said he sympathized with the patriotism and bravery which prompted them. Mrs Besant interrupted and stopped his speech, later maintaining that he had encouraged anarchy and violence and should not even have spoken in a non-political meeting of the possibility of the British being driven out of India. Gandhi for his part asserted that but for her ill-advised interruption his meaning would have been perfectly clear.[3] After this incident the chance of cooperation between the two of them in political work became very remote. Whereas Gandhi looked back on it as 'one of the proud events of my life', she announced that though she would 'honour and venerate him for his life and lofty ideals' she considered 'his politics – if we so name them – as impracticable, and even as a hindrance in the path of constitutional change'.[4]

There was even less chance that Gandhi would align with Tilak and his group based on Poona. While in South Africa Gandhi had praised Tilak for his patriotism, but, thinking that his object was to incite Indians against British rule, he had condemned Tilak's political views.[5] After his return Gandhi tried to act as mediator between Tilak and his opponents who had excluded him from Congress, though he assured Tilak that he did this merely as a go-between, not as a supporter or representative of those who controlled Congress. But his approach was not well received.[6] Apart from that interchange the only contact between the two men from 1915 to 1917 for which evidence remains was the occasion of the Bombay election to the

1 Gandhi to Pranjivan Mehta, 8 May 1911, *C.W.*, vol. 11, pp. 64–5.

2 K. Dwarkadas, *Gandhiji Through My Diary Leaves. 1915–1948* (Bombay, 1950), pp. 10–11.

3 Speech by Gandhi at Benares, 6 February 1916, *C.W.*, vol. 13, pp. 210–16; Mrs Besant's justification of her action, *New India*, 17 February 1916, Bombay Police Abstract, 1915, par. 218; Gandhi's defence, *The Bombay Chronicle*, 10 February 1916, *C.W.*, vol. 13, pp. 217–18.

4 Gandhi to Sri Prakasa, 2 October 1928, Nehru Memorial Museum and Library, Sri Prakasa Papers; Statement by Annie Besant, *New India*, 19 February 1916, *C.W.*, vol. 13, p. 566.

5 *Indian Opinion*, 1 August 1908, *C.W.*, vol. 8, pp. 418–19.

6 Account by Tilak of conversation with Gandhi, undated, sent to Gandhi in July 1915, Vidwans, *Letters Of Lokamanya Tilak*, pp. 266–9; Gandhi to Tilak, 27 July 1915, *C.W.*, vol. 13, p. 121.

Congress subjects committee in 1916, when Tilak's men rejected Gandhi because he would not publicly support their Home Rule League.[1]

It might have been expected that Gandhi would have found a political home in the Servants of India Society, founded by his *guru*, G. K. Gokhale, in 1905 to educate the backward and to organize political work. But even in South Africa Gandhi had feared that the society was just an indifferent imitation of the West, and both he and Gokhale had had doubts about each other's attitudes and methods. Gandhi did envisage working with Gokhale and the S.I.S. on his return; but on 19 February 1915 Gokhale died, depriving Gandhi of his closest ally. Thereafter Gandhi's relationship with the S.I.S. deteriorated.[2] Differences between them caused open discord just days after Gokhale died. V. S. Srinivasa Sastri, who succeeded Gokhale as President of the society, noted in his diary that there was a 'scene' at a meeting of the society with Gandhi. The police reported that the clash concerned basic attitudes: Gandhi advocated the ideals which inspired his *ashram*, while the object of the S.I.S. was 'to equip men to take part in every movement of modern life, educational, political and economic.' However, the discord was smoothed over temporarily, and it was agreed that Gandhi should study Indian conditions for a year before a final decision was made about his future.[3] When that year was up Gandhi realized that many S.I.S. members still opposed his entry, and he decided not to press the matter. As he explained to Sastri,

> Whilst there is possibility of co-operation when we are working independently, I can see that I would, as a member, become a disturbing factor. The methods of the Society as such are so totally different from mine in many respects. Our common discipleship would constitute an indissoluble bond though we would be following out Mr. Gokhale's work from different view-points.[4]

The society accepted Gandhi's decision with considerable relief and let the whole question subside without public announcement. As a result Gandhi's isolation in institutional politics was complete. None of the contacts which were his stepping-stones from African to Indian politics led to a permanent road; and by the beginning of 1917 he was still more of a freelance preacher and social worker than a recognized politician.

However, in retrospect this isolation appears to have been the foundation of much of his later strength. Limited politics had reached something of an

1 Fortnightly report from Bombay, 31 December 1916, Home Pol., Deposit, January 1917, No. 45.

2 For Gandhi's early relationship with Gokhale and the S.I.S. see J. M. Brown, 'Gandhi In India, 1915–20: his emergence as a leader and the transformation of politics' (Ph.D. thesis, Cambridge, 1968), pp. 60–3, 100.

3 Diary of V. S. S. Sastri, 13 February 1915, S.I.S., Madras; Bombay Police Abstract, 1915, par. 186.

4 Gandhi to V. S. S. Sastri, 13 January 1916, *C.W.*, vol. 13, p. 200.

impasse by 1915–17, and when Gandhi encountered the established politicians they had come to a point where they had very little room to manoeuvre, as the fate of the Home Rule Leagues showed. But Gandhi was not subject to their limitations. There is no evidence that he was aware of many of the stirrings and strivings in Indian society created by the pressures of changing circumstances which were not registered in nationalist politics; nor is it at all clear that he had any intention of championing such strivings at the expense of the existing political leaders. He was committed to the ideal of a united India, which the diversities of a plural society threatened: but it is equally clear from an analysis of his attitudes and his relationship with the politicians that he had no vested interest in the political status quo and that he would indeed have welcomed a shift of power over the country's future from the hands of the western educated.

Moreover South Africa had accustomed him to working with people outside the ranks of the western educated, and had given him an interest in problems outside the scope of their activities. Labourers' grievances, communal tensions, caste activities were within the scope of his public work and were to him far more important than constitutional schemes and the provision of jobs in the administration. His ideal of service to those in need made it likely that he would only participate in politics when he felt that by so doing he could right 'wrongs' which people were suffering; but he, if any one, had the potential for reaching out to those beyond the political camp, to make the new style of institutional politics burst out of its early limitations, and to create a larger political nation. What was more, in satyagraha he had a technique ideally suited to work among those who were unaccustomed to institutional politics. It was a simple technique of direct action, open to literate and illiterate, appropriate to a wide variety of occasions, a means of demanding redress for almost any grievance.

What Gandhi was to make of this potential was only clear after 1916. By then his period of silence and observation was over and he was ready to launch himself in public life. To see the unfolding of this potential the historian must turn to Gandhi's activities at a local level: for the localities with their particular power structures, their diverse tensions and problems, produced the driving forces behind all public activity, whether obviously political or not. It was in the localities that Gandhi was to find occasion and scope for his personal style of action and leadership.

CHAPTER 3

SATYAGRAHA, 1917–18

Gandhi's entry into Indian politics occurred almost fortuitously in 1917 and 1918 when he became involved in three local disputes: with peasants against landlords in Champaran, Bihar, farmers against revenue officials in Kaira, Gujarat, and mill-workers against their employers in Ahmedabad, the capital of Gujarat. Such disputes would have been considered outside the normal range of political activity, in areas notorious for their backwardness in the politics of nationalism; but Gandhi chose to deploy his technique of satyagraha in each case, and by so doing made his debut as an influential actor on the Indian political stage.

(I) CHAMPARAN

Champaran district, in the Tirhut Division of North Bihar, was in 1917 one of those rural fastnesses beloved by officers of the raj as the 'real India', in contrast to the noisy development of the maritime towns. Part of the district was uncultivable hillside, part was grazing land, and part only was suitable for cultivation; though after the opening of the first part of the Tribeni Canal in 1909 there was no reason why cultivation should not expand if only the scourge of malaria could be eradicated. Champaran was potentially prosperous; the cultivable land was good, the holdings were generally an economic size, while rents were fair in relation to the produce of the soil, and population pressure was not heavy. In fact it was the district with the lowest population density in the province of Bihar and Orissa, having 940,841 inhabitants in 1921, scattered over its 3,531 square miles. The vast majority of the inhabitants were part or full time agricultural workers. Like the rest of North Bihar Champaran was an area of large villages but few towns: its two towns, Motihari and Bettiah, were small and decreasing in size. In 1911 Motihari had only 14,876 inhabitants, and ten years later had lost 7% of those, while Bettiah with 25,793 in 1911 lost 5.8% over the decade.[1]

[1] *Census Of India, 1921. Volume VII. Bihar And Orissa. Part I. Report* (Patna, 1923), pp. 10, 23, 24, 83. Settlement Officer, North Bihar, to District Officer, Champaran, 2 July 1917, B. B. Misra (ed.), *Select Documents on Mahatma Gandhi's Movement in Champaran 1917–18* (Patna, 1963), p. 263. *Champaran. District Gazetteer. Statistics, 1900–01–1910–11* (Patna, 1914), p. 2 (hereafter cited as *Champaran Gazetteer Statistics*).

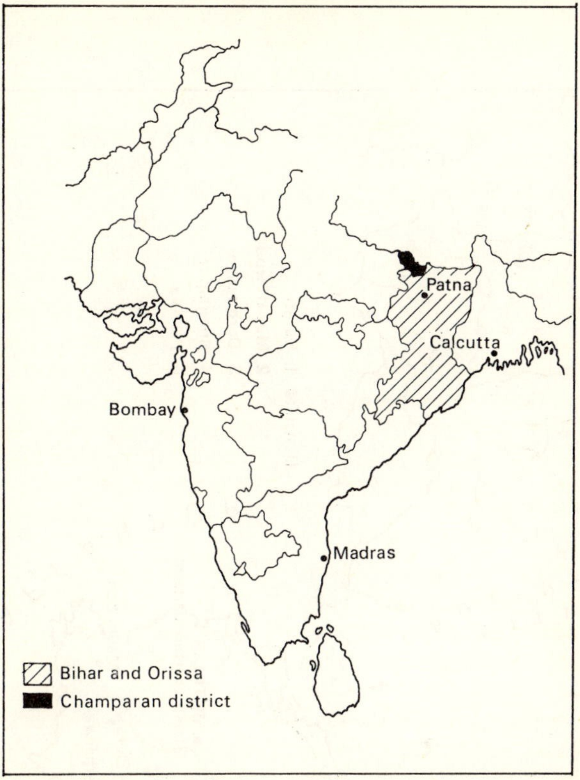

Such a rural area was unlikely to feel the pressure which pushed the townsmen of the Presidencies into institutional politics; and there was scarcely any mobility of population to bring the political 'infection' from other provinces. In 1921 nearly 99% of the inhabitants of Bihar and Orissa had been born in that province, 95.7% in the district where they still lived; and what movement of population there was was largely temporary, related to the agricultural seasons. In North Bihar most railway tickets were bought in November, that being the beginning of the slack season between winter and spring crops when agricultural labourers tended to leave home in search of temporary work.[1] As Champaran was so rural it did not even suffer the Bengali inroads into government service and the law courts which angered more urban Biharis and interested them in Congress politics to a limited extent in self-defence.

The major communities in Champaran were the Hindus and the Muslims, with a couple of thousand Christians and a sprinkling of people

[1] *Census Of India, 1921. Vol. VII. Part I*, pp. 103, 109.

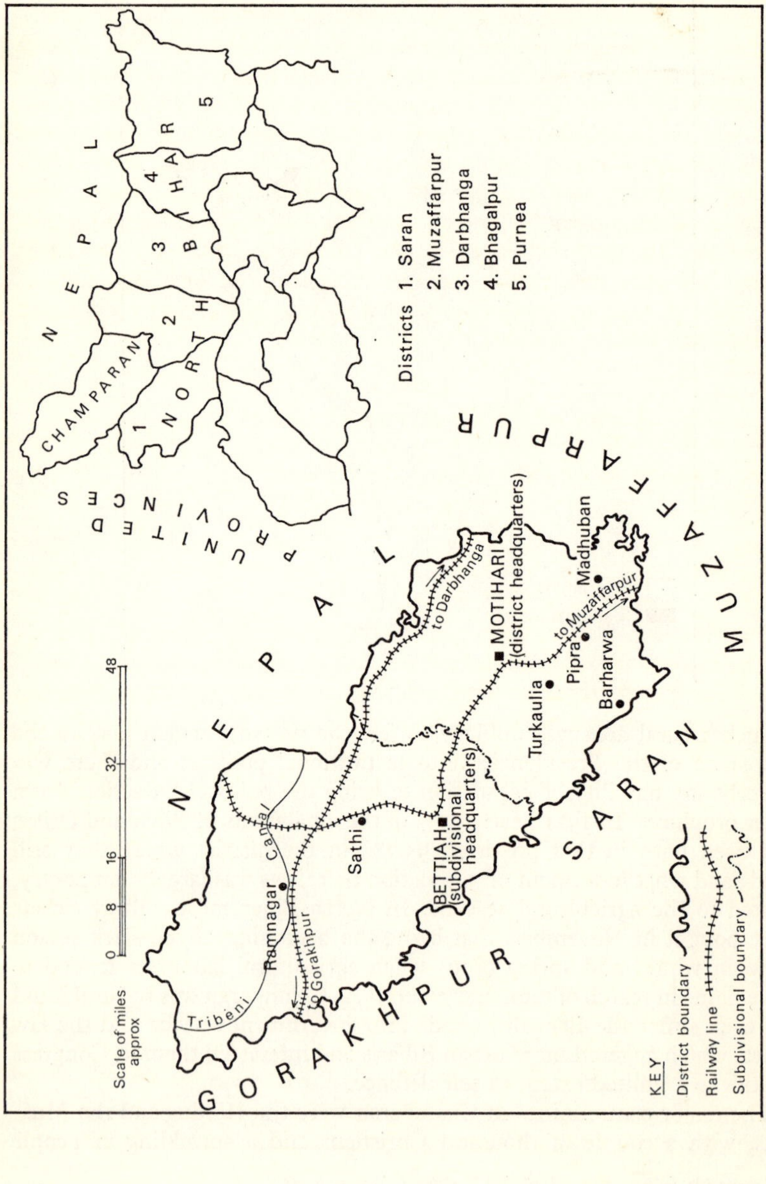

Map of North Bihar showing Champaran District

classified by the census as 'others' making up the remainder. In 1921 15.6% of the population were Muslim, all of whom were Sunnis.[1] Although the province as a whole, like neighbouring U.P., had a turbulent record of Hindu–Muslim tension, in Champaran itself there was very little evidence of communal feeling. In 1893–5 there was an outburst of anti-cow-killing agitation, particularly in the villages bordering on Muzaffarpur, which led to the looting and burning of one village; but otherwise there was no indication that communal strife was pushing Champaran people into any form of public activity. Rather the reverse: both communities suffered similar economic disabilities, and when they were moved to public outburst it was on the same side of the fence and not as antagonists. In 1907 for example Muslim raiyats (peasants) at Sathi erupted into open disturbances because of their dislike of indigo cultivation, while in 1914 and 1916 Bhumihar Brahmins of Pipra and Turkaulia became turbulent for precisely the same reason.[2]

Table 1

Castes among Champaran Hindus in 1914

Babhan (Bhumihar Brahmin)	55,152	Koiri	105,739
Brahmin	85,941	Kurmi	95,767
Chamar	133,167	Mallah	57,335
Dosadh	85,973	Naniya	59,035
Goala (Ahir)	196,410	Rajput (Chhatri)	82,844
Kandu	70,336	Teli or Tili	63,189

The large castes among Champaran Hindus were as shown in Table 1.[3] The Babhans or Bhumihar Brahmins, though comparatively few in number, were one of the most influential castes in the district, producing tenants of all grades as well as some of the biggest Bihar landowners, including the Maharajah of Bettiah and the Rajkumar Babu of Madhuban. Locally they were not fully accepted as Brahmins, though they claimed to keep higher standards of ritual purity than the Rajputs. Champaran had a far smaller Brahmin population than the neighbouring districts of Muzaffarpur, Darbhanga and Saran, and those there were were supported by agriculture. The much smaller group of Kayasths (27,274), though traditionally the writer caste, had also secured a strong place in the local pattern of landholding, and they ranked ritually in public esteem beneath the Babhans and Rajputs. The Rajputs clung to their former prestige as landowners and warriors, and were in some cases still zamindars, village headmen or tenants claiming remission of rent by virtue of their caste. But their fortunes were declining as they dropped back in education, finding them-

[1] *Ibid.* pp. 134, 140.

[2] *Bihar and Orissa District Gazetteers. Champaran* (1907 edition revised 1932, Patna, 1938), pp. 82–6.

[3] *Champaran Gazetteer Statistics*, pp. 5–6.

selves unable to adapt to the new requirements for success in a changing India. By contrast the Telis and Goalas had done well out of the changing environment. Traditionally an oil-pressing and trading caste the Telis had branched out into general trading and banking, and by the beginning of this century were taking steps to better their ritual status to keep pace with their new prosperity. The Goalas also responded to changes around them with a judicious combination of modern caste organization and sanskritization of their social customs. At the bottom of the ritual scale came the Chamars and Dosadhs, while in a respectable middle position were the agricultural castes of Kandus, Koiris and Kurmis.[1]

Caste was not a critical factor in shaping the structure of power in Champaran. It did not produce a particular dominant group; nor did the balance of power between caste groups in ritual and practical terms, and changes in that balance, produce the bitter rivalries which in some parts of India became the incentive to new forms of public action. The reason for this was basically that the stakes in the local power game were not high enough; to put it another way, caste groups did not become antagonistic because they were not competitors for profit but fellow-sufferers in deprivation.[2] In Champaran the higher castes as well as the lower depended on agriculture for their livelihood, since few other opportunities were open. Whereas in Bihar as a whole some members of powerful castes were landlords and tended to provoke considerable feeling against themselves from their lower caste tenants, in Champaran, because of the peculiar structure of landholding, many members of influential castes were tenants of European landlords right outside the caste hierarchy, and shared with lower caste Hindus common grievances against those landlords.

In areas where caste rivalries did become acute, as in Madras and Maharashtra, one of the main contributory factors was the initial spread of western education and its fruits to the high castes. In Champaran the familiar pattern of high caste predominance in education occurred, though to a very limited extent. In North Bihar as a whole the Kayasths, true to their clerkly traditions, were the best educated, with a literacy rate of 33%. Brahmins followed with a figure of 13.4%, and the Babhans came next with 12.7%. Other castes, including the Rajputs and the Goalas, came nowhere near this standard. Hindus were slightly ahead of Muslims in vernacular literacy, but Muslims just beat Hindus in the number of English literates they produced.

1 For details of the various castes see the alphabetical entries in H. H. Risley, *The Tribes and Castes of Bengal. Ethnographic Glossary* (Calcutta, 1891). Further information about Champaran Brahmins is in *1932 Revised Champaran Gazetteer*, p. 43.

2 The social aspirations of the Goalas led to initial resistance from Rajputs and Babhans, but there is no evidence that this had any bearing on the situation in Champaran as Gandhi found it in 1917. For the Goalas' aspirations and rebuffs see *Census Of India, 1921. Vol. VII. Part I*, pp. 236–7.

Within agrarian Champaran these educational inequalities were not an important element in the local balance of power and caused practically no friction because the actual extent of education was minimal and because there were so few opportunities for the educated in their home district. In 1921 only 4.22% of the population of Champaran aged over twenty could read and write in the vernacular, and only 0.273% in English.[1] Bihar and Orissa was the fifth Indian province in descending order by educational standards,[2] and Champaran was very near the tail within Bihar and Orissa. The government had produced schemes in the 1870s for encouraging vernacular education in Champaran, but these had evoked little Indian response, mainly because those in a position to cooperate with the government either failed to realize the importance of education at all or were nervous lest it should create competition for their own positions. As an official reported at the time,

> Anything like systematic education is quite unknown in these parts; and the new system is not only not viewed with favour by the people but has been passively resisted as much as possible. The *patwari* class oppose it especially because they fear that an extended system of education will afford too great facilities to aspirants for their particular business. The zamindar class has also failed to give that assistance which in other and more enlightened districts has been willingly afforded. This arises very much from the fact that there are very few resident members of this class, who are themselves sufficiently intelligent to comprehend the utility of an extended system of education among the masses, and to take an active interest in its promotion.[3]

Nevertheless, the number of schools and the number of literates was on the increase by the time Gandhi reached Champaran. In 1914–15 there were 1,138 schools of various sorts teaching 27,513 pupils, compared with 943 schools in 1908 attended by 21,268 pupils. But most of these schools were primary: only 1,124 pupils were receiving secondary education locally in 1907, and there was no college in the district. Even in 1929–30 there were

1 Percentages calculated from figures given in *Census Of India, 1921. Volume VII. Bihar And Orissa. Part II. Tables* (Patna, 1923), pp. 47–8, 56–9.

2

Province:	*Percentages of literates of the population aged 5+*:
Burma	31.4
Bengal	10.4
Madras	9.8
Bombay	8.3
Bihar and Orissa	5.1
Punjab	4.5
C.P.	4.3
U.P.	4.2

Source: Census Of India, 1921. Vol. VII. Part I, p. 196.

3 *1932 Revised Champaran Gazetteer*, p. 129.

only about five and a half thousand pupils receiving secondary education locally.[1]

It was predictable that with such an educational background Champaran men would not have participated in institutional politics. They shared no interests with the educated elite, and were ignorant of the techniques of manoeuvre and manipulation in the political world of the educated, as Gandhi remarked after his arrival in the district.

> The peasants were all ignorant. Champaran, being far up north of the Ganges, and right at the foot of the Himalayas in close proximity to Nepal, was cut off from the rest of India. The Congress was practically unknown in those parts. Even those who had heard the name of the Congress shrank from joining it or even mentioning it.[2]

Congress organization had reached Patna, the capital of Bihar, when in 1908 a provincial Congress was founded and a provincial Conference was held. The local leaders in this development in provincial public life were Nawab Sarfraz Husain Khan Bahadur, Sir Ali Imam, Mazharul Haq and Sachchidananda Sinha – all men trained in the new political style by practice in the local courts or seats in the provincial legislative council. In 1916 the same group founded a Bihar branch of the Home Rule League at Bankipur, but it was not until two years later that the League decided on a deliberate campaign to educate villagers in their style of politics.[3] What really broke Champaran's isolation in 1917 was not a downward reach from the Patna politicians nor even an upward thrust by local men searching for more effective methods of publicly expressing their grievances or ambitions. It was rather the presence of a new leader at a time of chronic rural unrest produced by the interaction of economic changes and the local pattern of landholding. This pattern of landholding was the most critical factor in Champaran's power structure.

Champaran was an area of large estates. This was no new phenomenon, because when the district was permanently settled in 1793 the men who emerged as proprietors were not, as in Bengal, men who had risen to prominence through the rent-collector's office, but petty rajas 'whose ancestors had for generations past exercised the powers of semi-independent chiefs ruling over a large extent of territory.'[4] By 1916–17 more than three-quarters of the district was held by three proprietors, the Bettiah, Ramnagar and Madhuban Estates; Bettiah, the largest, consisted of well over one and a half thousand villages. What was new was the fact that most of the villages were not managed directly by the landlords but were leased out to *thikadars*, or temporary tenure-holders, of whom the most in-

[1] *Ibid.* pp. 129, 130.
[2] Gandhi, *An Autobiography*, p. 343.
[3] R. R. Diwarkar, *Bihar Through The Ages* (Calcutta, 1959), pp. 652–3.
[4] *1932 Revised Champaran Gazetteer*, p. 108.

fluential group were European indigo planters. The first indigo factory was founded in the district in 1813, but after 1850 the industry really boomed, and by the time Gandhi reached Champaran approximately half the district was leased out to European *thikadars*.[1] *Thikadars* either cultivated their land directly (*zirat* cultivation) or leased it to peasant tenants; but whatever mode of cultivation they employed the net result was a virtual planter raj. As Gandhi described it,

> The permanent settlement of Bengal has brought little permanence to the raiyats amongst whom the vast permanent holdings are parcelled out. In Champaran, the majority of permanent holders are European planters. They are like Rajas: although they are not clothed by law with any civil or criminal jurisdiction over the *raiyats* – their tenants – they succeed in exercising practically both jurisdictions over the abjectly helpless tenantry of Champaran.[2]

Local officials hesitated at Gandhi's description of the raiyats as abjectly helpless, but they recognized that in many cases their position was one of 'tutelage and dependence'. It could hardly be otherwise because the planters were not only landlords but members of the District Board, Assessors and Pound-keepers, since there was no intermediate group of small, independent proprietors to do these jobs.[3]

What produced distress in 1917 was not just the pattern of landholding, but economic changes which underlined the power of the planters and the weakness of the raiyats, and threw the contrast in dramatic relief on to the public screen. Gandhi's satyagraha campaign and the subsequent official enquiry rightly publicized the faults of the indigo planters and the problems of indigo production, but indigo was one of the smaller crops grown, though one of the most lucrative. The main food crops were rice, sugar cane, maize, barley, wheat and lentil.[4] Economic change and pressure touched these crops as well as indigo, and the state of harvests and markets of these was an important factor in the situation: this tended to be forgotten by those involved in discussing the more obvious pressures of the indigo industry.[5]

Crop prices were supremely important to a wholly agricultural area like

[1] Report of the Champaran Agrarian Enquiry Committee, 3 October 1917, *C.W.*, vol. 13, p. 582.

[2] *Young India*, 27 August 1919, *C.W.*, vol. 16, p. 64.

[3] Subdivisional Officer, Bettiah, to District Magistrate, Motihari, 1 June 1917, Misra, *Select Documents*, pp. 186–7.

[4] *1932 Revised Champaran Gazetteer*, pp. 57–8. In 1892–9 98,000 acres, 6.63% of the net cropped area, were under indigo; in 1916 the figure for indigo was 21,900 acres, Report of the Champaran Agrarian Enquiry Committee, 3 October 1917, *C.W.*, vol. 13, p. 583.

[5] The fate of crops other than indigo is not discussed in the most recent study of the background to the Champaran satyagraha, G. Mishra, 'Socio-Economic Background of Gandhi's Champaran Movement', *The Indian Economic And Social History Review*, v, 3 (September 1968), 245–75.

Champaran. All the inhabitants, whether directly engaged in agriculture or not, depended on the harvest for their food. Paradoxically non-agriculturalists and those living on wages suffered most when prices were high because they, unlike the farmers, made no profit from high prices; while in a season of low prices the farmers made little profit, could buy little above their basic needs, and consequently the whole district felt a slump in commerce. Understandably officials kept an eagle eye on price levels as the single most important factor making for unrest or tranquillity in their districts. In 1917 the effect of the World War on prices was becoming very marked. If 100 is taken as the base in 1873, the index of all prices rose as follows:[1]

1913:	143	1916:	184
1914:	147	1917:	196
1915:	152	1918:	225

By 1917 only about one-fifth of India's rolling stock was available for ordinary rail traffic, and this hit a district like Champaran particularly hard because it produced little except food and indigo, and depended on the two railway lines which crossed the district for the export of its surplus food to other parts of India in return for necessities of life produced elsewhere. As a result of the shortage of railway waggons goods imported into Champaran, such as cloth, salt, and kerosene, soared in price, while produce normally exported, principally rice, was jammed up in the district and dropped sharply in price. Between mid-1916 and 1918 the price of rice fell suddenly, dipping dramatically to its lowest point during just the months when Gandhi was active in Champaran (see Fig. 1). Other food grains dropped in price in the period 1915–18, and as one official put it, 'Everything the cultivator had to sell, rice oil-seeds or *gur*, had either fallen or at least not risen in price, while everything he had to buy, cloths, salt, kerosene, had become extremely expensive.'[2] This meant serious shortage of money among cultivators, causing hardship and unrest, particularly among the middle group who were accustomed to buying products imported into Champaran with the profit from the small surplus they grew over and above their own immediate needs. The local government was well aware of this hardship and the fact that local traders and dealers tended to exploit it, and its officials intervened to control some prices, as in the case of salt.[3]

[1] *Statistical Abstract For British India 1917–18 to 1926–27* (London, 1929), Cmd. 3291, Table 297, p. 628.

[2] *Report On The Administration Of Bihar And Orissa 1917–1918* (Patna, 1919), p. ii. For the price of food grains other than rice, see *Census Of India, 1921. Vol. VII. Part I*, pp. 18–19. In January 1918 the average cost of an ordinary pair of *dhotis* (a man's ordinary dress, like a loin cloth) was Rs. 5.8.0 – Rs. 6, compared with Rs. 1.12.0. in 1911, *ibid.* p. 19.

[3] For a survey of economic conditions in Champaran and the resulting hardship, see *ibid.* p. 12; *Report On The Administration Of Bihar And Orissa 1917–1918*, pp. i–ii.

Fig. 1. Average Price of Rice in Bihar and Orissa, 1911–20

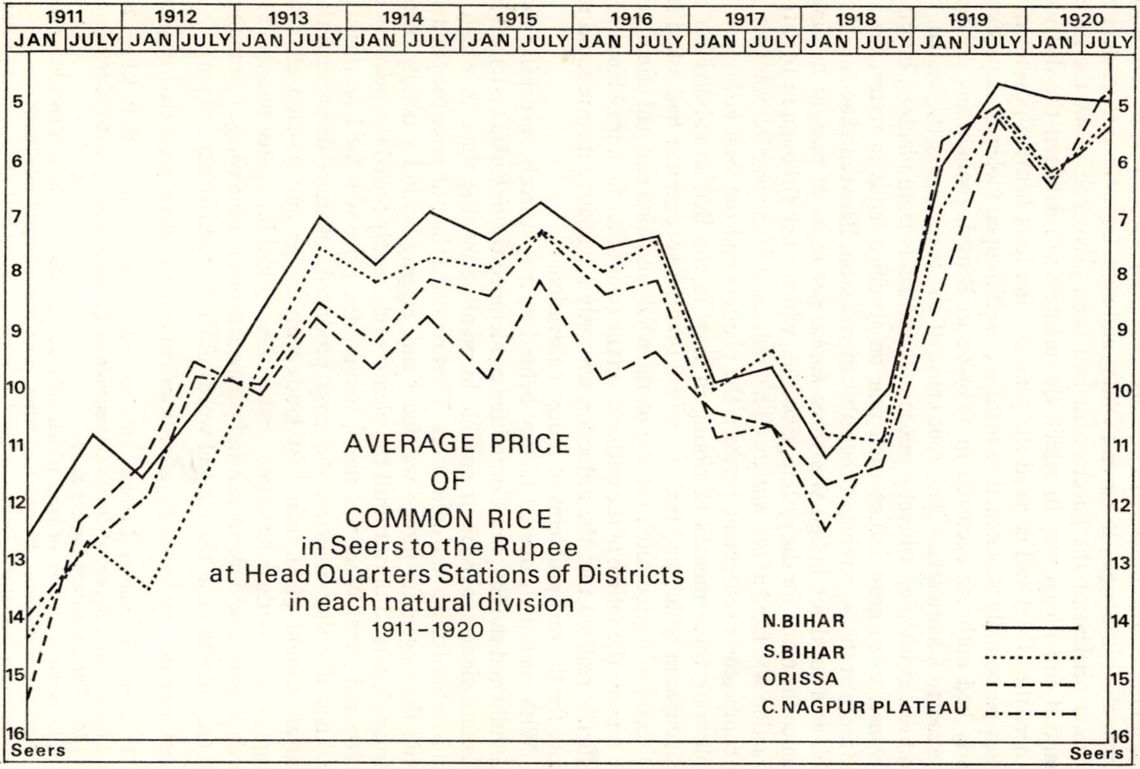

Source: *Census Of India, 1921, Volume VII. Part 1*, p. 17.

Quite apart from this general economic pressure Champaran cultivators also suffered specific difficulties as a result of indigo production. From the beginning of the nineteenth century European planters had established themselves in Bengal, Bihar and Oudh; and right from the earliest days of planter settlement the government had been perturbed about the high-handed and illegal way in which the planters virtually ran the districts where they lived and coerced the peasants, not least because peasant distress perpetually threatened to manifest itself in open violence. A particularly bad outbreak occurred in 1859–62 in Bengal, though this did not spread to Champaran.[1] The root cause of the trouble was the system of indirect cultivation whereby peasants leased lands from planters, binding themselves to grow indigo each year on specified lands in return for an advance at the beginning of the cultivation season. Between 1860 and 1910 the area fixed for indigo was three *kathas* per *bigha* of peasant holding, hence the name for the system, *tinkathia*, which stuck although in 1910 the fraction was fixed at two *kathas*.[2] This reduction of the fraction was part of a compromise settlement between the planters and the local government, following three months of rioting in 1908 in the Bettiah subdivision of Champaran which had been so severe that the government had asked its Director of Agriculture to report on the whole situation and had attempted to remove the source of the outbreak on the basis of his findings.[3] However, officials realized that the reduction was only a palliative measure and no cure for the real problems of indigo cultivation.

With such a chequered history behind it, it is scarcely surprising that Gandhi and the Enquiry Committee condemned the *tinkathia* system. The Commissioners were most specific in pointing out the ways in which it caused hardship to the cultivators. They reported that the price the planters paid the raiyats for indigo was fixed and, lagging behind generally rising prices, it caused unrest until the planters reluctantly raised the price, as in 1869 and 1877. What was more, because the price was fixed on the area cultivated rather than on the crop produced, planters demanded that raiyats should plant their best lands with indigo and insisted on close supervision by their henchmen, who often turned into petty tyrants. The web of economic dependence and personal control in the village community is only hinted at in the clinical words of the Commissioners' report.

supervision undoubtedly affords an opportunity for a great deal of petty

[1] P. Spear, *The Nabobs* (London, 1963 revised edition), pp. 91–2; B. B. Kling, *The Blue Mutiny; Report of Indigo Commission and Papers relating to that Commission, 1861*. Parliamentary Papers XLIV.

[2] The *bigha* is an area of land which differs from place to place. The Champaran *bigha* was between 1.16 and 1.40 acres. Two *kathas* equal one tenth.

[3] Officiating Secretary, Revenue Dept., Govt. of Bihar and Orissa, to Secretary, Govt. of India, Dept. of Revenue & Agriculture, 23 March 1918, Home Pol., B, August 1918, No. 207.

> tyranny, and the cultivator resents being compelled to carry out the various cultivation processes not at the time most convenient to himself, but at the time when the work is considered necessary by factory subordinates. The system gives opportunities to the factory servants to harass cultivators against whom they may have a grudge; or to exact payment as the price of their favour.[1]

This inequitable system of producing indigo by itself caused unrest; but the situation was made worse at the beginning of the twentieth century by the severe pressure on planters and peasants which resulted from Indian indigo's position in the world market. In the mid-1890s Germany began to manufacture synthetic indigo, and undercut the price of natural indigo so successfully that in 1912–13 Indian indigo fetched a mere Rs. 130 per factory-maund compared with Rs. 232 at the turn of the century.[2] After trying to salvage their position by reducing costs and introducing a new indigo plant from Java, most Champaran planters realized that indigo cultivation was no longer a paying proposition. As a result the area sown with indigo dropped from 98,000 acres in 1892–9, to 52,600 in 1907, and down to 8,100 in 1914; though there was a temporary boom during the war, when German indigo was cut off just when there was a need for it to dye khaki uniforms, and Champaran sowed 21,900 acres to meet the demand.[3] Unhappily for the raiyats the planters saved their own position by making their tenants bear the burden of their losses. Most planters took to commuting the indigo agreements into money payments. Commutation took the form either of enhanced rents (*sharabeshi*) or a lump sum (*tawan*). The Enquiry Committee reckoned that 40,000 acres of *tinkathia* land was freed from the indigo obligation, 18,000 by the mechanism of *tawan* and 22,000 by *sharabeshi*. The average enhancement of rent in the *sharabeshi* cases was 50–60% of previous rents, while *tawan* was taken at Rs. 50–60 per acre of indigo grown, which worked out at about Rs. 7.8.0. to Rs. 9 per acre of actual peasant holding.[4] Gandhi argued that these commutations had been forced on the cultivators; but the Settlement Officer challenged this allegation, saying that if there had been compulsion on a massive scale there would surely have been serious disturbances, and that wherever pleas of compulsion had been raised revenue officials had investigated with particular care. He thought it far more probable that the cultivators had felt the tide of economic change and were glad of a chance to free themselves from the indigo obligation. But his comments showed how powerful the

1 Report of the Champaran Agrarian Enquiry Committee, 3 October 1917, *C.W.*, vol. 13, pp. 583–6; Gandhi's report on conditions in Champaran in letter to Chief Secretary, Govt. of Bihar and Orissa, 13 May 1917, Misra, *Select Documents*, pp. 127–8.

2 *1932 Revised Champaran Gazetteer*, p. 82.

3 Report of the Champaran Agrarian Enquiry Committee, 3 October 1917, *C.W.*, vol. 13, p. 583.

4 *Ibid.* p. 588.

planters were in practice, though they might not be technically guilty of compulsion.

> A much more reasonable ground to take than that of compulsion would be that of undue influence, but I am afraid that if the theory of undue influence were applied to the relations between landlords and tenants, there would be no contract in the Tenancy Law for this province.[1]

Other issues which came up at the time and were noted by Gandhi and the Commissioners highlighted this picture of planter raj. Raiyats claimed that questions of grazing and tree felling rights, and contracts for the hire of labour and carts were always decided in the planters' favour; and it is quite clear that planters were not above using their minor rights, such as management of pounds or ploughing of waste land, in such a way as to coerce raiyats. In one case of ploughing up roads in 1913 the Motihari District Magistrate said he could see no other motive on the part of the offending planters 'than the intention of making the existence of...[those who] have not agreed to pay indigo *tawan* intolerable in the village.'[2] Planters who did not have indigo contracts on their hands also did some profiteering, mainly by making a variety of illegal levies, or *abwabs*. These levies, such as *Painkharcha*, a water tax, and *Bapahi putahi*, an inheritance tax, had been declared illegal in 1793, 1859 and 1885. Local officials still fought a running battle against them, and the Committee of Enquiry had no doubt that they were still prevalent, particularly on the Ramnagar Estate.[3]

The net result of these social and economic pressures by the second decade of this century was an extremely disturbed district. Between 1914 and 1916 the record of rights was attested in Bettiah and Motihari and the cultivators, particularly Bhumihar Brahmins from Pipra and Turkaulia, seized on the opportunity to question the legality of their landlords' actions and threatened non-payment of rent. Their discontent was fanned by a circular from the *Pratap* Press in Cawnpore which was busy collecting evidence for a volume to be entitled 'The Oppression of the Indigo Planters of Champaran'.[4] Although Champaran was ripe for public agitation when

1 Settlement Officer, North Bihar, to District Officer, Champaran, 2 July 1917, Misra, *Select Documents*, p. 256. In this letter the Settlement Officer said he thought enhanced rents had not in practice placed the peasants in an uneconomic position as their earlier rents were low, but he reported that the payment of lump sums in commutation led to grave peasant indebtedness. Gandhi's allegation about compulsion was in his letter to the Chief Secretary, Govt. of Bihar and Orissa, 13 May 1917, Misra, *Select Documents*, p. 127.

2 *Biharee*, 6 July 1913, quoted in Rajendra Prasad, *Satyagraha In Champaran* (2nd revised edition, Ahmedabad, 1949), p. 77.

3 Report of the Champaran Agrarian Enquiry Committee, 3 October 1917, *C.W.*, vol. 13, pp. 593–4; *Report On The Land Revenue Administration Of The Province Of Bihar And Orissa For The Year 1916–1917* (Patna, 1917), p. 15.

4 Fortnightly reports from Bihar and Orissa, 16 & 28 February 1916, Home Pol., Deposit, March 1916, Nos. 49 & 50; for a general survey of disturbances in Champaran, 1907–17, see *1932 Revised Champaran Gazetteer*, pp. 82–6.

Gandhi went there in 1917, there were no indications that agitation would be anything more than a recrudescence of rural rioting of the type which had been endemic for at least a century. With the exception of one local man there was nobody who appeared to aspire to more sophisticated ways of expressing peasant grievances: nor was there any Bihar politician who thought it worth while to investigate the Champaran situation at all deeply. What actually occurred was the result of Gandhi's intervention, with his very personal range of interests and type of leadership.

Champaran was in fact Gandhi's least anticipated satyagraha. In 1915 he had not expected to use this weapon for at least five years, and even early in 1917 he knew nothing about Champaran, not even its name or geographical position, let alone the economics of indigo planting.[1] However, in March 1916 the Champaran police heard rumours that Gandhi was coming to their district 'to deliver lectures'; though it was not until December that year at the Lucknow Congress that Gandhi was invited to investigate the plight of Champaran raiyats by Raj Kumar Shukla, son of a prosperous Brahmin cultivator in Champaran. Even then Shukla had to trail after Gandhi from Lucknow to Cawnpore, to Ahmedabad and thence to Calcutta before he could prevail on him to visit Champaran.[2] Gandhi eventually reached north Bihar in early April, having suffered various vicissitudes on the way as a result of Shukla's inefficiency and the fact that, since strict caste distinctions were observed locally, nobody was willing to show him hospitality, not knowing to what caste he belonged. His impending visitation perturbed the Champaran police who were already dealing with an extremely inflammable situation; and they enquired of their superiors what the official line should be. They received the forthright reply:

> We quite agree with you that his mere presence in Champaran is most undesirable. Unfortunately this gentleman has in the past been allowed to speak pretty freely in other provinces on the question of indentured labour for the abolition of which he is a champion. He is not on any list of agitators ...He has a biggish following and one needs to be very careful in dealing with men of his notoriety.[3]

Gandhi meanwhile began to spy out the land. He met the Secretary to the Bihar Planters' Association, he conferred with a group of Indian lawyers in Muzaffarpur, and finally on 13 April he met L. F. Morshead, Commissioner of the Tirhut Division. Morshead assured Gandhi that all the government's administrative resources were actually being used to rectify

[1] Gandhi, *An Autobiography*, pp. 319, 337.

[2] Bihar and Orissa Police Abstract, 1916, par. 401, Misra, *Select Documents*, p. 51; Gandhi, *An Autobiography*, pp. 337–8.

[3] Special Assistant to D.I.-G., Crime and Railway, Bihar Special Branch, to Champaran Superintendent of Police, 12 April 1917, Misra, *Select Documents*, pp. 56–7; in reply to letter from Champaran Superintendent of Police to Bihar Special Branch, 10 April 1917, *ibid.* pp. 55–6.

peasant grievances, but Gandhi refused this official assurance and informed Morshead that he had decided to investigate in person. 'I am anxious to test the accuracy of the statements made to me by various friends regarding indigo matters and to find out for myself whether I can render useful assistance. My mission is that of making peace with honour.'[1] Privately he acknowledged that this seemed to be just the sort of wrong or grievance which was within his scope of action: he suspected that the situation might be worse than in Fiji and Natal, where were employed the indentured labourers whose cause he championed, and he hinted that he might be gaoled for investigating.[2]

The day after this was written the Champaran District Magistrate, W. B. Heycock, served Gandhi with an order to quit Champaran as he was a danger to the public peace; this order was the result of a recommendation from Morshead, who since his interview with Gandhi had been informed that Gandhi's object was likely to be agitation rather than a genuine search for knowledge.[3] Gandhi decided to commit satyagraha, and disobey the order 'out of a sense of public responsibility', firmly denying Morshead's interpretation of his motive. At the same time as he informed Heycock of his intention he wrote to the Viceroy's Private Secretary, describing his motive as 'national service' and asking for an independent enquiry into the cultivators' condition. The same night he wrote out detailed instructions for investigations in Champaran in case he was removed from the scene and prevented from leading an investigation himself.[4] His fears in this respect were not unfounded: even before he appeared in court to explain his disobedience, Morshead asked the local government for power to extern him from Tirhut Division under the Defence of India Rules on grounds of public safety.

> It is not, in my opinion, advisable to wait to see if Mr. Gandhi's enquiry actually provokes disturbances, because he may be presumed to be clever enough to guard against this happening whilst he is on the spot; and the mischief will reveal itself later. In my opinion, it is unsafe to let him intrigue in the district at all...[5]

On 18 April Gandhi appeared in the Champaran District Magistrate's court to answer for his action, and he explained that he felt civil dis-

1 Gandhi to L. F. Morshead, 13 April 1917, *C.W.*, vol. 13, pp. 362–3; note of interview between Gandhi and Morshead, 13 April 1917, recorded by Morshead, Misra, *Select Documents*, pp. 58–9.

2 Gandhi to Maganlal Gandhi, 15 April 1917, *C.W.*, vol. 13, p. 363.

3 Order under section 144 Cr. P.C., 16 April 1917, *C.W.*, vol. 13 p. 570; L. F. Morshead to W. B. Heycock, 13 April 1917, Misra, *Select Documents*, pp. 61–2.

4 Gandhi to W. B. Heycock, 16 April 1917, *C.W.*, vol. 13, p. 367; Gandhi to J. L. Maffey, Private Secretary to Viceroy, 16 April 1917, *ibid.* p. 368; Gandhi's instructions for workers, 16 April 1917, *ibid.* pp. 369–70.

5 L. F. Morshead to Chief Secretary, Govt. of Bihar and Orissa, 16/17 April 1917, Misra, *Select Documents*, p. 66.

obedience was the only honourable course open to him. Such an event was far outside the normal routine of such a court, and the perplexed Magistrate postponed judgement, pending consultation with the local government; while Gandhi for his part made things easier by promising not to go into the villages or start a public agitation until the government attitude was known.[1]

When the Government of Bihar did reply it was quite clear that it disapproved strongly of the Commissioner's action. Refusing categorically his request for extra powers against Gandhi, it instructed by wire both Commissioner and District Magistrate to withdraw Heycock's order and grant to Gandhi facilities for investigation, providing that he was warned not to stir up trouble. The Bihar government followed up its telegram to Morshead with an extremely sharp letter to him, condemning his action as taken without sufficient evidence that Gandhi was a public menace and without consultation with the government straight away. It considered that the externment order was of dubious legality, as Gandhi had shown no signs of disturbing the area; and besides creating a very delicate position for the government it was just the thing to play into Gandhi's hands.

> Mr. Gandhi is doubtless eager to adopt the role of martyr which as you know he has already played in South Africa, and nothing perhaps would suit him better than to undergo a term of imprisonment at the hands of an "unjust" magistracy. This was a development which, knowing Mr. Gandhi's record, you might have anticipated.[2]

The government's fears that Gandhi would turn Champaran into a *cause célèbre* were well justified; and, though it saved itself from the critical step of externing or gaoling Gandhi, it still had to face muted hunting cries from the bloodhounds of the Indian press. Papers from the Bombay Presidency, *Message*, *Dnyan Prakash*, *Indian Social Reformer* and others, all complained that the order against Gandhi was completely undeserved, and an example of the bludgeoning authority of the magistracy; while the Bengali paper, *The Amrita Bazar Patrika* hailed Gandhi as a hero.

> So Mr. Gandhi has gained his point. The part which he has played in this sensational matter is no less important than what he did when he started his passive resistance campaign in South Africa. There he braved jail and the displeasure of the authorities in the cause of suffering humanity; here also he did the same...
>
> God bless Mr. Gandhi and his work. How we wish we had only half a dozen Gandhis in India to teach our people self-abnegation and selfless patriotism.[3]

[1] Gandhi to Maganlal Gandhi, telegram, 18 April 1917, *C.W.*, vol. 13, p. 376.

[2] Chief Secretary, Govt. of Bihar and Orissa, to L. F. Morshead, 20 April 1917, Misra, *Select Documents*, pp. 75–8; the earlier wires to L. F. Morshead and W. B. Heycock, both dated 19 April, are in *ibid.* pp. 73–4.

[3] *The Amrita Bazar Patrika*, 23 April 1917; extracts from the Bombay papers on this issue are in Bombay N.N., No. 16 of 1917, pp. 1–2.

Such praises were only pale reflections of the adulation which greeted Gandhi in Champaran. Once the order against him was withdrawn he set to work investigating the condition of the raiyats, taking statements from them, and contacting members of the planting community. As he and his helpers toured the countryside where no earlier leaders had penetrated he found himself becoming a rural hero and saviour. He was exhibited at specified hours to *darshan*-seekers, and had to have a gate keeper to protect him from his admirers.[1] W. H. Lewis, the Subdivisional Officer for Bettiah, caught the local atmosphere of exhilaration when he reported that Gandhi had captured the raiyats' loyalty and virtually superseded established local authority.

> We may look on Mr. Gandhi as an idealist, a fanatic or a revolutionary according to our particular opinions. But to the raiyats he is their liberator, and they credit him with extraordinary powers. He moves about in the villages, asking them to lay their grievances before him, and he is daily transfiguring the imaginations of masses of ignorant men with visions of an early millennium.[2]

For the first time in India Gandhi was displaying that magnetic personality which was to draw multitudes to him, and to earn him the title of Mahatma or 'Great Soul' and the nickname of Bapu or 'Father'. His appeal lay partly in his simplicity and undoubted humour, to which contemporaries bore witness: but it was as much due to his ability to make ordinary people feel that he appreciated and cared about their particular problems, however local and insignificant these might have seemed in the rarefied atmosphere of Congress debates. In stark practice, trudging round on foot or trundling in a bullock cart, Gandhi came where ordinary people lived, and talked about their concerns in the language they understood. Far from reaching down with political ideas like the Home Rulers, Gandhi started at the bottom with the issues at stake in local society.

In spite of public acclaim Gandhi found his position in Champaran increasingly difficult, as local officials mistrusted his group of helpers and their motives, though they reluctantly agreed that Gandhi's own sincerity was above dispute. Lewis reported that rumours of Gandhi's intentions were flying about, such as one that he intended to break all the planters by mid-May; and he said he was sure Gandhi could not control the tongues of his followers. One member of the Bihar Executive Council actually suggested that Gandhi should dispense with the services of his helpers, much to his distress.[3] The planters understandably objected vociferously to

1 Gandhi, *An Autobiography*, pp. 348–9. *Darshan* means a sight or view, but is generally used to mean that quality which emanates from a particularly good or holy man on to those who see him.

2 W. H. Lewis to W. B. Heycock, 29 April 1917, Appendix D to Proceeding No. 323 of Home Pol., A, July 1917, Nos. 314–40.

3 W. H. Lewis to W. B. Heycock, 29 April 1917, *ibid.*; note by W. Maude, 10 May

Gandhi, and to 'the band of disloyal and seditious agitators...in his train.' However much Gandhi protested that he was not stirring up an anti-European movement, they refused to believe him, and even after the agitation was over affirmed that 'the agrarian issues were merely a very transparent cloak to the real and far more serious object of the agitation, the raising of an anti-European feeling among the royats...'[1] When two fires broke out in the district, Gandhi's position became even more delicate. One of the fires, at an outwork of the Turkaulia indigo factory, could not be traced directly to the influence of Gandhi or any of his close assistants, but, as that factory had recently been the victor in a big test case about cultivators' obligation to grow indigo, those responsible for law and order in the district could not help concluding that the fire was an indirect result of Gandhi's investigations into indigo culture.[2]

Gandhi's original intention was to come to some sort of private agreement with the planters, but as his enquiries progressed he became convinced that the planters were too powerful for any private agreement to be feasible. By mid-May he reported to the government that the courts were insufficient protection for the peasants, and the current settlement operations too cumbersome for such an emergency: in his view only government action would be an effective remedy.[3] To his followers he said that even the appointment of a commission of enquiry, such as he had demanded of the Viceroy on his arrival in Champaran, could only help the raiyats and be acceptable to him if *sharabeshi*, *tinkathia* and illegal exactions were stopped first; otherwise it would merely delay any real solution of raiyat grievances.[4] From the government's point of view the local situation was getting out of hand. Gandhi, the planters and local officials all clamoured with different voices and violence was dangerously near the surface.

At the end of May the government took action and summoned Gandhi to Ranchi in somewhat forbidding tones:

> In the circumstances the Lieutenant-Governor in Council is compelled to consider very seriously the question of your continued presence in the district, but before taking any definite action in the matter, he desires to

1917, Misra, *Select Documents*, pp. 123–4; for information on Gandhi's helpers see below, pp. 76–8.

[1] Hon. Secretary, Bihar Planters' Association (Champaran), to L. F. Morshead, 28 April 1917, Misra, *Select Documents*, p. 96; General Secretary, Bihar Planters' Association, to Secretary, Home Dept., Govt. of India, 26 April 1919, *The Pioneer*, 1 May 1919, S.N. No. 6578.

[2] Fortnightly report from Bihar and Orissa, 16 May 1917, Home Pol., Deposit, June 1917, No. 68.

[3] Gandhi's report on conditions in Champaran to Chief Secretary, Govt. of Bihar and Orissa, 13 May 1917, Misra, *Select Documents*, pp. 126–31; Gandhi to Chief Secretary, Govt. of Bihar and Orissa, 25 May 1917, *C.W.*, vol. 13, pp. 416–17.

[4] Gandhi's notes on the situation in Champaran, 20/21 May 1917, S.N. No. 6352.

have the advantage of personal conversation with you regarding this matter and the general situation in Champaran.[1]

Gandhi feared that this heralded his expulsion from Champaran, but when he met the Lieutenant-Governor, Sir Edward Gait, and members of the Executive Council he was told that the government was appointing a Committee of Enquiry. He asked Sir Edward if certain abuses like the levy of *abwabs* could be stopped immediately, but received the answer that this would imply that government had prejudged these issues. Instead the Lieutenant-Governor and Gandhi came to an agreement that local officials should stop abuses wherever they came to light, while the planter member of the Committee should be asked to point out to his fellow planters the harm such actions did: Gandhi and his assistants for their part would stop taking evidence and would not go into the Champaran countryside. After this discussion Gandhi accepted an invitation to sit on the Committee which was formally constituted by a government resolution on 10 June.[2]

While Gandhi parleyed with Sir Edward Gait, intergovernmental negotiations were going on behind the scenes which determined what was done. Gandhi was unaware of this inner power battle, but the records make it clear that the Government of India intervened, putting pressure on the Government of Bihar, just as the latter had intervened to stop the action of its local Commissioner. One reason for Gandhi's considerable triumph in Champaran was this fact, hidden at the time. Unlike South Africa, there was in Champaran a higher authority possessing reserve powers and willing to use them for reasons of its own. The Bihar government was subject to pressure from above and below to set up an official enquiry into the state of Champaran.

From Champaran came a plea by Morshead: now his initial tactic of excluding Gandhi had been dished he hoped to checkmate Gandhi another way. He wrote, 'If the relations of planters and *raiyats* are to be placed under searching scrutiny, it is essential that the scrutiny should be applied by a reasonable body capable of weighing evidence.' His proposal was rejected on the grounds that it could serve no useful purpose while settlement officers were gradually dealing with the matter.[3] The Bihar government gave a similar reply to the Government of India when the

[1] Chief Secretary, Govt. of Bihar, to Gandhi, 27 May 1917, Misra, *Select Documents*, p. 170.

[2] Gandhi's wire accepting seat on Committee, to Chief Secretary, Govt. of Bihar, 7 June 1917, *ibid.* p. 207; note on interview between Gandhi and Gait, written by Gait and assented to by Gandhi, 5 June 1917, *ibid.* pp. 203–6. There is evidence that both sides kept the bargain made between Gandhi and Gait.

[3] L. F. Morshead to Chief Secretary, Govt. of Bihar, 1 May 1917, Misra, *Select Documents*, p. 106; Chief Secretary, Govt. of Bihar, to L. F. Morshead, 4 May 1917, extract quoted in letter from Chief Secretary, Govt. of Bihar, Political Dept., to Secretary to Govt. of India, Home Dept., 23 May 1917, Proceeding No. 23 of Home Pol., A, July 1917, Nos. 314–40.

latter also began to press for an enquiry. In explanatory letters to Sir William Vincent, Home Member of the Government of India, and to Lord Chelmsford, the Viceroy, Sir Edward Gait said that the main reasons for his government's reluctance to appoint an enquiry were that they were already collecting information on the whole problem through their settlement officers, that it would look like a device for 'heading off' Gandhi, and that it would mean going back on a rejection of a similar proposal for an enquiry made in the Bihar Legislative Council two years previously.

On the same day, 21 May, the Bihar government made a formal request to the central government for further powers to deal with Gandhi should he refuse to leave Champaran. Ironically the local government was now hankering after the Defence of India Rules just as the Tirhut Commissioner had done: this time the Viceroy himself refused the request, and instead urged Sir Edward Gait seriously to consider appointing a commission of enquiry. Two days later Sir Edward informed the Viceroy that his government was preparing for a commission in deference to superior orders; while on the same day Chelmsford held a consultation with his Council, after which a wire was sent to Bihar definitely requesting the appointment of a commission which should include Gandhi. Bihar gave its grudging acquiescence in a telegram on 27 May, and on 2 June the central government clinched the matter with a firm order to appoint the commission as soon as possible.[1]

The Viceroy was well aware that his insistence had disturbed the Bihar government, and he hastened to explain in a personal letter to Sir Edward that no criticism of his government was intended, and that it was a case where all-India considerations weighed against local convenience.

> I realise that the force of circumstances has carried you along a road which you were not particularly anxious to follow;...We all felt – and this was dealt with as a Council and not merely as a Home Department matter – that it would be inexpedient and impolitic at the present time to risk raising a storm over the question, particularly as it is not denied that

[1] The sources for this description of inter-governmental negotiations are: Home Dept., Govt. of India, to Govt. of Bihar and Orissa, telegram, 17 May 1917, Proceeding No. 319 of Home Pol., A, July 1917, Nos. 314–40; Govt. of Bihar and Orissa to Govt. of India, Home Dept., telegram, 19 May 1917, Proceeding No. 320, *ibid*; Sir Edward Gait to Sir William Vincent, 20 May 1917, Misra, *Select Documents*, pp. 138–40; Sir Edward Gait to Chelmsford, 21 May 1917, Mss. EUR. E. 264 (18); Chief Secretary, Govt. of Bihar and Orissa, to Home Dept., Govt. of India, telegram, 21 May 1917, Misra, *Select Documents*, pp. 152–3; Chelmsford to Sir Edward Gait, telegram, 22 May 1917, Mss. EUR. E. 264 (18); Sir Edward Gait to Chelmsford, telegram, 24 May 1917, *ibid*; Home Dept., Govt. of India, to Chief Secretary, Govt. of Bihar and Orissa, telegram, 24 May 1917, Proceeding No. 322 of Home Pol., A, July 1917, Nos. 314–40; Chief Secretary, Govt. of Bihar and Orissa, to Home Dept., Govt. of India, telegram, 27 May 1917, Proceeding No. 324 of *ibid*; Home Dept., Govt. of India, to Govt. of Bihar and Orissa, telegram, 2 June 1917, Proceeding No. 325 of *ibid*.

> Gandhi's enquiry was inspired by substantial grievances. In appointing a Commission, to use your phrase, we are "heading off" Gandhi, but in doing so we avoid giving the appearance of shirking our responsibilities. We feel that it is more expedient to head him off than to lay him by the heels and thus give a handle to the suggestion that we are burking the whole enquiry.[1]

The record of these negotiations makes it quite clear that when Gandhi was summoned to Ranchi on 27 May the Bihar government had already been refused power to deport him and had been told to give him a seat on the forthcoming commission.

The Committee of Enquiry held its preliminary meeting on 11 July and signed its report on 3 October. Gandhi spent only part of these months in Champaran, finding time to travel to Ahmedabad, Bombay, Poona and Madras. He supervised the choice of the raiyats' representatives to give evidence before the Committee, and though his choice was not entirely judicious – one of the chosen being a dismissed factory servant, for example – he himself impressed the Chairman of the Committee with his personal sincerity and freedom from racial bias.[2] The main recommendations of the Committee were included in the Champaran Agrarian Act of 1917, by which the *tinkathia* system was abolished, and enhanced rents fixed at a reduction of 20% or 26% according to the indigo factory concerned. The Committee's lesser recommendations, as for example the repayment of *tawan*, were enforced by executive orders.[3] The reduction of enhanced rents in the act was the ratification of an agreement between Gandhi and the planters, signed on 29 September[4] at the instigation of the Committee, which thought an immediate settlement preferable to the delays involved in special legislation or expensive law suits.

Some of Gandhi's helpers were surprised that he agreed to a compromise and did not press for a return to the original rent in such cases: but quite apart from the planters' refusal to give up more, Gandhi felt that their prestige had been damaged sufficiently and that as peasants and planters had still to live together in the future a compromise was the best foundation for better relations. Even so, the planters were enraged at the Committee's findings and fought the bill both in the Legislative Council and by memorial to the government, insisting that they had been sacrificed to appease Gandhi and other political agitators. Reports from Champaran in 1918 showed that relations between the two groups were by no means har-

[1] Chelmsford to Sir Edward Gait, 8 June 1917, Mss. EUR. E. 264 (18).

[2] Sir Edward Gait to Chelmsford, 23 August 1917, *ibid.*; Gandhi's selection of witnesses was reported in Fortnightly report from Bihar and Orissa, 30 July 1917, Home Pol., Deposit, August 1917, No. 3.

[3] Report of the Champaran Agrarian Enquiry Committee, 3 October 1917, *C.W.*, vol. 13, pp. 578–600; text of Champaran Agrarian Bill, 1917, Misra, *Select Documents*, pp. 518–20.

[4] Text of agreement, 29 September 1917, *ibid.* pp. 267–8.

monious. On their side the planters still levied *abwabs* where they could, while the cultivators terrorized planters' servants, looted factory crops and grazed down their crops grown under factory contract.[1]

These disquieting accounts only confirmed Gandhi's conviction that the long term solution to Champaran's problems was the education of the raiyats and a constant process of mediation between them and the planters. In a situation where the latter were so powerful and the former so abject and ignorant, legislative and administrative action could only deal with symptoms and could never reach the core of the problem. His own attempt to reach the core and transform local society was the creation of a band of about fifteen volunteers to do this work of education and mediation. By late 1917 local officials were commenting somewhat sourly that Gandhi had left behind 'two standing camps to which malcontents and litigants resort to the detriment of the prestige of the district authorities',[2] although there is also evidence that these groups of workers were in fact doing the work Gandhi had intended for them. They reported to him that their schools had an average daily attendance of over sixty, they had formed a Hindu–Muslim committee in Barhawa to organize village health and education, they planned to teach hygiene via weekly religious meetings held by Muslims and Hindus, and they had been making strenuous efforts to clean up village water supplies. Here were Gandhi's dreams of true Home Rule in action: but by May 1918 the groups of helpers were disintegrating and only three people remained.[3]

In retrospect Gandhi's satyagraha in Champaran can be called successful because it precipitated a committee of enquiry to deal with peasant distress, though he himself would have maintained that this success was limited because Champaran society was not transformed by his efforts. Quite apart from the actual results of the satyagraha, Champaran was of immense significance in Gandhi's career. Before 1917 his reaction to Indian problems had been largely theoretical, and it was these Bihar raiyats who brought him to grips with India's people and government. By championing them Gandhi began to clothe with flesh and blood the figure which had hitherto been only a shadowy contender in the arena of Indian public life.

Gandhi's first step in this direction was a reaffirmation that he was not

[1] Examples of the planters' opposition to the bill are in Home Pol., B, August 1918, No. 207; evidence of the disturbed state of Champaran in 1918 comes from Rajendra Prasad to Gandhi, 23 August 1918, S.N. No. 6420, and Weekly report of D.C.I., 5 January 1918, Proceeding No. 488 of Home Pol., B, January 1918, Nos. 487–90.

[2] Weekly report of D.C.I., 22 September 1917, Proceeding No. 242 of Home Pol., B, September 1917, Nos. 239–43. Official government policy towards Gandhi's schools was one of 'benevolent neutrality', Order in Council by Sir Edward Gait, 3 December 1917, Misra, *Select Documents*, p. 457.

[3] Weekly report of D.C.I., 18 May 1918, Proceeding No. 583 of Home Pol., B, May 1918, Nos 581–4; Baban Gokhalay to Gandhi, 6 December 1917, Misra, *Select Documents*, pp. 457–8.

aligned with any particular political group. He refused to link the Champaran struggle with conventional politics, though this restraint was difficult for his more educated followers. As Rajendra Prasad remembered,

> We used to read reports in the papers how many of our friends and co-workers in other districts were busy going about holding meetings and delivering lectures, and sometimes felt tempted to follow the same course in Champaran also. But Mahatmaji had sealed his own as well as our lips and we were not permitted to deliver public speeches either on the Champaran situation or in connection with the Home Rule movement. We expressed our desire to take part in the movement. . . He used to tell us that by our very silence we were doing the highest kind of Home Rule work. After all, it was work among the masses that would bring Home Rule, especially work of the nature we were engaged in at the time.[1]

There were good reasons for Gandhi's self-denying ordinance. If he threw in his lot with a particular political group he would be sucked into the vortex of political alliances, and his independence would vanish. As he had made clear before 1917, he felt his ideals differed from those of every existing political group, and he prized his independence as the safeguard of his personal integrity. Moreover, he had no wish to embarrass a government which in this matter was his friend. Because the peasants had clear economic grievances already officially recognized, Gandhi could appeal over the planters' heads to the local government, and even beyond that to the Government of India. The technique which foundered on the rocks of British security in South Africa was a consummate success in Champaran, since here the superior government was able and willing to act on his behalf.

His determination to guide the Champaran struggle independently was reflected in his decision not to make any general appeal for funds.[2] He was only prepared to appeal to wealthy Biharis, and in emergency to an old friend and financial supporter, Dr Pranjivan Mehta, and the Imperial Citizenship Association, a body founded in 1915 to protect Indians outside India, which had received some of the surplus from Gandhi's South African satyagraha fund. It is quite clear that sufficient funds were raised in Bihar for the campaign. About Rs. 10,000 were collected in Champaran before Gandhi ever arrived; and when he actually appealed for Rs. 1,500 for necessary expenses after receiving permission to investigate, the Bihari politician, Hasan Imam, gave him Rs. 1,000 and friends including Sachchidananda Sinha, Mazharul Haq and Krishna Sahay planned to raise at

1 Rajendra Prasad, *Mahatma Gandhi And Bihar. Some Reminiscences* (Bombay, 1949), p. 19.

2 'I was. . . determined not to appeal to the country at large for funds to conduct this inquiry. For that was likely to give it an all-India and political aspect. Friends from Bombay offered Rs. 15,000, but I declined the offer with thanks.' Gandhi, *An Autobiography*, p. 347.

least Rs. 15,000 to finance the enquiry and the publication of evidence. There were also some indications that whatever Gandhi's intentions funds were coming from outside Bihar. In June 1917, for example, a C.I.D. officer reported meeting two men in a train between Chapra and Muzaffarpur who were carrying Rs. 4,000 to Gandhi from a U.P. merchant who had apparently allotted a lakh of rupees to finance Gandhi's enquiries in Champaran.[1] Gandhi later calculated that about Rs. 3,000 were actually spent during the agitation; but what was done with the surplus is impossible to discover. What is quite obvious, however, is that even at this early stage in his public career, though he was not tapping any obviously political network for funds, he had no problem in finding financial backers.

Gandhi maintained his political isolation by restricting his use of the press as well as his sources of finance. Whereas he was vociferous on the problems of indentured labourers and Indians in South Africa, on the Champaran issue he damped down publicity, sending little to the press for release and actively discouraging reporters. His motive in this was quite clear. Once the political press got hold of the story, highly coloured versions would spread around, strong feeling would be aroused, people would take sides, and Gandhi would be unable to play the game his own way – the way of adamant resistance judiciously mixed with conciliation. However when Gandhi did choose publicity he was most proficient in promoting it. For example, he distributed to the press copies of his statement in court; and copies of his telegram to his *ashram* announcing that he was allowed to investigate were freely distributed in Ahmedabad city. The police even called the Champaran episode 'a revival of his old "passive resistance" game with improved methods in the publicity department.'[2]

Although Gandhi denied himself the help of practised politicians he gathered other assistants around him. Evidence about them shows very precisely the groups with whom Gandhi worked, and where he found a foothold in the local power structure. Taking a bird's eye view of Bihar, and leaving aside the European population, it is possible to describe public life and political awareness in the province in three tiers. At the top were the wealthiest and most successful of Bihar's professional and business men; but this group was small because Bihar was backward in education and, as an agrarian region, had few avenues to wealth and advancement outside agriculture. From this group came a handful of semi-professional politicians, often Patna lawyers like Mazharul Haq, who had some all-India affiliations through the Congress. At the same level of influence in

[1] Evidence of financial aid is in note by the Tirhut Commissioner's Personal Assistant, 23 April 1917, Misra, *Select Documents*, pp. 84–5; Weekly report of D.C.I., 19 May 1917, Proceeding No. 447 of Home Pol., B, May 1917, Nos. 445–8; Bihar and Orissa Police Abstract, 2 June 1917, par. 595, quoted in Bombay Police Abstract, 1917, par. 706.

[2] Bombay Police Abstract, 1917, par. 486.

public life were the larger landowners like the Maharajah of Darbhanga, who were skilled in the arts of social and political collaboration with the rulers and had little need of Congress politics. Indeed they often mistrusted the Congress wallahs because these men with their new education and legal skills seemed to be stealing power from those who had traditionally wielded paramount influence in the province.

Beneath the landlords and the tiny professional elite were lesser folk, resident in small provincial towns, minor pleaders, merchants and money lenders, who sometimes had political experience but tended to be interested in politics only because of its effects on their business or professions, rather than for the sake of power in the all-India political world. No hard and fast distinction can be made between the professional politicians and these local men, as the careers of two of Gandhi's helpers showed. Rajendra Prasad was a small town lawyer with peripheral political interests, who after Champaran rose to the status of a professional, all-India politician; while Braj Kishore Prasad operated in Congress and at the level of local interests. Beneath these two tiers there were the villagers with their own networks of influence and their own leaders, whose public awareness as yet barely stretched beyond the boundaries of their fields and caste groups.

During the Champaran struggle Gandhi had very little contact with the highest tier of Bihar society. Except in the matter of finance he deliberately avoided cooperation with professional politicians inside and outside the province: the exception to this was Mazharul Haq, who had known Gandhi since his student days in London and now kept in touch with his friend's activities. He welcomed Gandhi to Bihar, advised him on tactics and became one of his pool of helpers, available when necessary and always making a point of visiting Champaran once or twice a month.[1] Since Champaran's landlords were mostly European the question of Gandhi's relations with Indian landholders hardly arose. There is slight evidence that he would have liked to investigate their activities too, but was restrained by the politicians for whom it would have created considerable embarrassment. As one Indian onlooker reported,

> "I am told that Mr. Gandhi was at one time anxious to extend his investigations to the whole field of relations between the zemindars and their tenants. It is well-known that the disabilities of the tenants are by no means confined to the indigo plantations owned by Europeans. But the local politicians cannot afford to set the zemindar party against themselves, and that is the reason why Mr. Gandhi's investigations are so much restricted."[2]

[1] Gandhi, *An Autobiography*, p. 349. From outside Bihar Gandhi considered M. M. Malaviya and V. S. Srinivasa Sastri as possible leaders of the struggle if he were gaoled, and he corresponded with both of them while he was in Champaran.

[2] Quoted in Weekly report of D.C.I., 9 June 1917, Proceeding No. 439 of Home

The limitations of the earlier politicians were apparent; and even at this early stage Gandhi's novel activities posed a threat to their position in public life.

Gandhi's main assistants in Champaran came from the middle tier of Bihari society and were professional and business men from small provincial towns. He used as his spearhead a small group of local lawyers: Braj Kishore Prasad, vakil from Darbhanga who had the most political experience of the group, having piloted the Champaran cause in Congress and the Bihar Legislative Council, and who was marked out to direct the collection of evidence should Gandhi be gaoled; Rajendra Prasad, a lawyer from Chapra, for whom the Champaran episode was the door to all-India eminence as one of Gandhi's closest supporters; Dharanidhar, a Darbhanga pleader; Gorakh Prasad, a Motihari pleader; Ramnawami Prasad, a Muzaffarpur lawyer; and two more lawyers, Sambhusaran and Anugrah Narain Sinha.[1] Kripalani, one time Professor of the Muzaffarpur Government College, also helped. These were the men who conferred with Gandhi when he first came to the area; they were the volunteers who manned two posts at Motihari and Bettiah, taking down over 4,000 statements of peasant distress. In the eyes of local officials they were the assistants least open to suspicion.

> Mr. Gandhi while conducting his enquiries was accompanied by a number of men for whose honesty he was prepared to vouch, and for whose actions he was prepared to accept all responsibility...All these men would under Mr. Gandhi's instruction be careful or guarded in anything they actually said... [they] were probably sincere in thinking some matters up here were not right and satisfied themselves that they were undertaking an urgent and pressing public duty in the interests of their own countrymen. Their work also of course had the attraction of political advancement for themselves.[2]

But there were others from a similar urban background whose motives and activities were less scrupulous – 'Local agitators with interested motives, ...Mahajans whose business has been opposed by factories, lawyers whose employment will increase, and any others who will gain in one way or another by the weakening of factory influence.'[3] Most prominent among this type was Pir Muhammed, a Muslim convert who lived in Bettiah and

Pol., B, June 1917, Nos. 438–41. Gandhi's only reference to Indian landlords in Champaran was a brief request that where they, too, were guilty of the practices noted in the case of the European planters, their tenants should obtain relief. Gandhi to Chief Secretary, Govt. of Bihar and Orissa, 13 May 1917, Misra, *Select Documents*, p. 129.

1 Gandhi's notes on the position in Champaran, 14 May 1917, S.N. No. 6352.

2 Undated letter from W. H. Lewis to L. F. Morshead, Misra, *Select Documents*, p. 339.

3 Note on the situation in Champaran submitted by L. F. Morshead to the Chief Secretary, Govt. of Bihar and Orissa, 23 September 1917, *ibid.* p. 347.

worked for the *Pratap*, a paper distinguished for its anti-planter attitude; he had once taught in the Bettiah Raj school but had been dismissed for publishing virulent attacks on its management. In the same category came the Bettiah Marwaris who considered themselves as Gandhi's hosts, but had a keen eye to their future prospects should the power of the indigo planters be permanently undermined. Pir Muhammed was the link between these interested townsfolk and the true peasant leaders.[1] Gandhi obviously was a leader of an entirely different order compared with such men, but he was forced to make use of them. Neither he nor his group of lawyers had sufficient local knowledge or influence to do without them: in order to do the job they set themselves they had to come to terms with those who had that knowledge and expertise, however dubious their motives.

Gandhi himself emphasized his close contact with the lowest tier of Bihar society, the raiyats. It is true that he toured the villages taking statements, and that he became a hero figure for many of them: but when it came to actual organization he had to work through the few who understood that something more concrete was required than mere adulation. These few were Khenda Rai of Lankaria, Sita Ram Tavari and Saying Upadhyay of Dhokraha, Deonandan Rai of Singa, Chapra, and foremost of them all Raj Kumar Shukla, whose persistence had brought Gandhi to Champaran.[2] He, like Khenda Rai, had personal grievances against the planters from whom he rented his land, but he was the only raiyat leader with a vision of any way of gaining redress more sophisticated than law suits and, failing them, violent outbreaks. Shukla had tried the law suit, and when that failed him he left his rural fastness and moved resolutions about indigo plantations at the 1915 Bihar Provincial Conference and the 1916 Congress. The other raiyats had to wait until Gandhi's presence and leadership provided them with a new weapon against the planters.

Champaran provides not just a case study of inhabitants of a 'backward' area arising from former lethargy and stretching out to grasp new styles of public action. It also shows how Gandhi, previously unknown in Bihar, was able to turn the province into a power base for himself. The pattern of his leadership is clear. Leaving aside the recognized politicians, he went into the villages dressed in the sort of clothes villagers wore, speaking the vernacular, espousing causes which concerned his rustic audience: while doing so he drew in the local business and educated men who had had little interest or influence in the Congress style of politics. He acted as go-

[1] Undated letter from W. H. Lewis to L. F. Morshead, *ibid.* pp. 340–1. Marwaris were a trading community who originated in Marwar, western India, and had fanned out over north and central India, forming prosperous, tight-knit trading and money-lending groups wherever they went.

[2] Undated letter from W. H. Lewis to L. F. Morshead, Misra, *Select Documents*, p. 341.

between for these different groups, mediating between two tiers of public life, and in return secured a powerful provincial following. He succeeded where earlier politicians had failed or had not even attempted to mobilize support because he had assets which were liabilities in their sort of politics. He was deeply concerned with issues which were of little importance to them, and he wielded a weapon which they hesitated to use, because it was so patently disturbing and its range of use so much wider than their own limited political nation. Despite his success in Champaran, the aftermath of the struggle showed that even he had not claimed the total loyalty of Bihar and broken the regional barriers which confined the influence of earlier politicians to their home regions. Biharis rallied to Gandhi while his agitation served their own ends, but when it came to educating peasants and cleaning up villages they were less than enthusiastic. Eventually only five Biharis volunteered as teachers, and Gandhi had to fall back on twenty-one volunteers from the Bombay Presidency, ten of whom came from his own *ashram* at Ahmedabad.[1]

Even though Gandhi had not in 1917 moved entirely beyond the confines of regional loyalties, Champaran did give him an all-India public reputation. After his exploits there men from outside the Bombay Presidency might still be reluctant to follow him, but at least a very great number of them now knew who he was and how he worked. The growth of a public image is difficult to assess under the most favourable circumstances where there is much trustworthy evidence available: it is the more difficult in Gandhi's case because a majority of the population were illiterate and the written records left behind reflect only the reactions of the literate few and the impressions of literate observers who may have been heavily biassed in one direction or another. But for several reasons it seems worth investigating whatever scraps of evidence do exist about the way people thought of Gandhi. For him, as for every public leader, his public image became a weapon in its own right, the more particularly in his case because he appears to have created an impression far greater in range and intensity than any leader before him. As a result much has been written about his 'charismatic' leadership; and the temptation is to take refuge in that concept as an explanation of his influence, rather than looking behind the vague phrase to the records of people's actual attitudes and how these were created.[2]

Gandhi's reputation was critical not just as one way of mobilizing support; it also determined to a very large extent the policy of the government towards him. The raj had to walk the tightrope of collaboration at all times,

[1] List of volunteers from the Bombay Presidency, Rajendra Prasad, *Satyagraha In Champaran*, p. 219; names of teachers in Gandhi's schools are given in two police reports, 15 April 1918, Misra, *Select Documents*, pp. 534–7, 542–7.

[2] For a recent consideration of the concept of charismatic leadership and some of the literature on the topic see P. Worsley, *The Trumpet Shall Sound. A Study of 'Cargo' Cults in Melanesia* (2nd edition, London, 1968), pp. ix–xxi.

but increasingly as autocratic power was being tempered by schemes of constitutional reform, and public opinion in England would not tolerate repression where conciliation was possible.[1] In such circumstances the rulers had to weigh up the advantages and disadvantages of having Gandhi with or against them, and their decision depended primarily on their assessment of his following. As a result Gandhi's public image became a pawn in politics.

The records show that Gandhi's public image was no monolithic one, but varied among different groups in different places and at different times. Before 1917 his idiosyncrasies had begun to undermine the favourable impression he made on the educated Indian public as a result of his activities in Africa, but the news of the Champaran satyagraha and the withdrawal of the externment order against him reversed this trend. From Ahmedabad came the following report:

> One local effect of these events has been the rehabilitation of Gandhi's reputation as a patriot of the first order, which has been threatened with partial eclipse as the result of a movement which was gaining headway here to disparage him on account of his primitive manners and ways of life and mode of dress and his insistence of vernaculars to the exclusion of English in ordinary intercourse and as the vehicle of education.[2]

Outside his home region of Gujarat his success in Champaran gave a similar boost to his reputation among the educated. In Aligarh in November 1917 he was received cordially, more because of his Champaran exploits than his speeches about Hindu–Muslim unity. A month later in Bengal he was given a great ovation at Congress, though Tilak outstripped him in the amount of applause he gained. Although he was still a lesser public figure his reception marked something of a watershed for his standing in Congress. Jawaharlal Nehru explained the feelings of his contemporaries at the time:

> My first meeting with Gandhiji was about the time of the Lucknow Congress during Christmas 1916. All of us admired him for his heroic fight in South Africa, but he seemed very distant and different and unpolitical to many of us young men. He refused to take part in Congress or national politics then and confined himself to the South African Indian question. Soon afterwards his adventures and victory in Champaran...filled us with enthusiasm. We saw that he was prepared to apply his methods in India also and they promised success.[3]

[1] See below, pp. 124–6.

[2] Bombay Police Abstract, 1917, par. 733.

[3] J. Nehru, *An Autobiography* (London, 1936), p. 35; reports on Gandhi's reception in Aligarh and at Congress are in Fortnightly report from U.P., 18 December 1917, Home Pol., Deposit, January 1918, No. 59, and Bengal Police Abstract, 1918, par. 267 quoted in Bombay Police Abstract, 1918, par. 128 (a). There was also a rumour abroad that Bengali politicians were to invite Gandhi to enquire

Even so, many sophisticated urban Indians found Gandhi strange company. He stayed in Ranchi in June 1917, but when a meeting was convened in his honour he refused to speak and sat on the floor, explaining that he was one of the poor public! His behaviour was not understood at all and caused considerable amusement.[1]

Similar differences of opinion emerged from the Indian-owned press, the voice of the educated public. Whereas most took the line of criticizing the government's initial externment order, and by implication pictured Gandhi as the innocent victim and public hero, a few launched into overt criticism of him. The *Islamic Mail* commented,

> We have every sympathy with our great patriot Mr. Gandhi and would have been much pained if any untoward incident had happened to him. But the defiance of law and authority and the baneful effect it has upon the impressionable people of India is not conducive to public peace or to good government, and put it whatever way you like, Mr. Gandhi's action amounts to that.

A less charitable critic in the *Political Bhomiyo*, published by an Ahmedabad Muslim, advised Gandhi to give up dabbling in political matters and instead of dashing off to Bihar to tackle social problems nearer home.[2]

If the educated were divided and not a little mystified by Gandhi, Champaran's peasants were whole-hearted in their enthusiasm, at least temporarily. His perambulations through the district brought peasants flocking to him, and roused the whole area to a pitch of feverish excitement and anticipation. Here clearly Gandhi's leadership had qualities of charisma: here he appealed in almost messianic terms to those at the very bottom of society. But how deep and long lasting the effects of such leadership would be remained in doubt. Late in 1917 peasant enthusiasm had waned, raiyats openly disobeyed Gandhi and refused to pay the reduced *sharabeshi* agreed to by him as their representative.[3] Charisma might produce temporary pageants of loyalty, but the less dramatic allegiance of men like Rajendra Prasad was the solid foundation of Gandhi's influence.

Officialdom, too, began to rethink its picture of Gandhi as a result of his exploits in Champaran. Within the ranks of the rulers just as among Gandhi's compatriots, views about him varied from person to person and from group to group. On this occasion the Bihar government was the most seriously embarrassed by Gandhi's presence, and its reaction was the

into the grievances of Bengal colliery workers as a result of his success in Champaran, but nothing seems to have come of this. Weekly report of D.C.I., June 1917, Proceeding No. 439 of Home Pol., B, June 1917, Nos. 438–41.

1 Bombay Police Abstract, 1917, par. 733.

2 *Political Bhomiyo*, 4 May 1917, *Islamic Mail*, 13 May 1917, Bombay N.N., No. 18 of 1917, p. 11, No. 20 of 1917, p. 4.

3 J. T. Whitty, Manager of Bettiah Raj, to L. F. Morshead, 17 November 1917, Misra, *Select Documents*, p. 427.

strongest. Having first defended Gandhi from its district officials the provincial government found itself stuck with him at the behest of the government of India. One member of the Bihar Executive Council protested that Gandhi was completely and unjustly prejudiced against the planters; though the Lieutenant-Governor was somewhat milder in his assessment.

> Mr Gandhi is a philanthropic enthusiast, but I regard him as perfectly honest; and he was quite reasonable in his discussions with us. He has very strong views regarding the state of things in Champaran, but I am hopeful that he may modify them when he comes to examine the situation in a less biassed environment than that of the pleader clique with which he has hitherto been associated.[1]

By November 1917 it was clear that the Committee of Enquiry and the enforcement of its recommendations had brought little respite to Champaran; and once again the provincial government toyed with the idea of getting Gandhi to leave the district alone, as his presence appeared to aggravate a situation already tense as a result of communal feeling and Home Rule propaganda in neighbouring districts. One official said he thought the only remedy was for Gandhi to leave Champaran for six months to a year: 'As long as his name and personality keep bobbing up there is no chance of things settling.'[2] To the local government's relief Gandhi transferred his attentions to Kaira district in Gujarat in the new year: but their experiences of 1917 convinced Bihar officials that the spinning Mahatma was at best a crank who was being used by unscrupulous people, and at worst a potential demagogue with an anti-European bias.

By contrast the Government of India viewed Champaran from a distance. Taking into account the all-India implications of action against Gandhi it decided that Bihar must put up with discomfort for the sake of peace in the subcontinent. The Viceroy was not unaware of the embarrassment Gandhi could cause. Sir Benjamin Robertson, Chief Commissioner of C.P., who had encountered Gandhi in South Africa, told him so in no uncertain terms, though he, like several other high officials, bore witness to Gandhi's personal honesty and idealism.[3] However, since the raj was involved in a

1 Sir Edward Gait to Chelmsford, 8 June 1917, Mss. EUR. E. 264 (18); *cf.* the attitude of Sir E. V. Levinge, Member of Executive Council of Bihar, in note dated 3 June 1917, Misra, *Select Documents*, p. 193.

2 Note by W. Maude, 27 November 1917, *ibid.* p. 436.

3 Robertson said that although Gandhi was extremely difficult to deal with he was 'an extraordinary person, thoroughly earnest and, I believe, straight and honest.' Sir B. Robertson to Chelmsford, 11 June 1917, Mss. EUR. E. 264 (18). The Lt.-Governor of the U.P. earlier reported that following the Benares incident Gandhi's future visits to the U.P. would be watched and steps taken 'to prevent him from again becoming publicly intoxicated by his own verbosity', though he regretted that this should be so as he gathered that Gandhi was 'a man of personal probity and high ideals.' Report by U.P. Govt.'s Chief Secretary, 23 March 1916, Home Pol., Deposit, July 1916, No. 23. For the Benares incident in 1916 see above, p. 49.

World War and in dire need of acquiescence if not concrete help from Indian leaders it would not pay to act against such a leader as Gandhi, who had an undoubted following and a reputation of extreme moral rectitude. The storm which hit Champaran with full fury and disturbed Simla with less intensity was the merest ruffle of a breeze by the time it reached Whitehall. The further away from Champaran the easier officials found it to be appreciative of Gandhi; and when the Secretary of State eventually met him later that year he described him as 'the renowned Gandhi.'

> He is a social reformer, he has a real desire to find grievances and to cure them, not for any reasons of self-advertisement, but to improve the conditions of his fellow men. He is the real hero of the settlement of the Indian question in South Africa, where he suffered imprisonment. He has just been helping the Government to find a solution for the grievances of the indigo labour in Bihar.[1]

However, Gandhi's next satyagraha involved the government's authority so closely that its officers could no longer afford to describe his activities in such charitable terms.

(II) KAIRA

The scene of Gandhi's second Indian satyagraha was much nearer his home, the Gujarat district of Kaira in the Northern Division of the Bombay Presidency. Kaira was less than half the size of Champaran, only 1,596 square miles in area; but unlike the Bihar district with its arid and hilly tracts, most of Kaira was fertile plain fit for cultivation, as it had an adequate water supply from wells, ponds and the rivers Mahi and Sabarmati. By 1918 most of Kaira bore the marks of irrigation and good agriculture, but particularly prosperous was the centre of the district known as the Charotar, famous for its good crops, its clumps of trees, and its well-built villages behind high hedges. In 1921 Kaira's population was 710,982. This was smaller than Champaran's and smaller, too, than in the last decades of the nineteenth century in Kaira itself, the drop in numbers being due to the great famine of 1899–1901.[2] Despite the disaster of famine and the invasion of locusts and rats which hit the district then, Kaira picked up its prosperity again by growing small quantities of valuable products like tobacco, and large amounts of food and cotton for

[1] E. S. Montagu, *An Indian Diary* (London, 1930), p. 58.

[2] *Population of Kaira*:

1872	782,938	1901	716,332
1881	805,005	1911	691,744
1891	871,794	1921	710,982

Source: *Census Of India, 1921. Volume VIII. Bombay Presidency. Part I. General Report* (Bombay, 1922), p. 8.

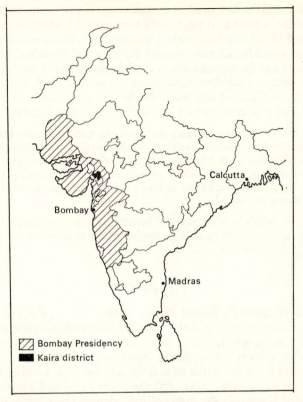

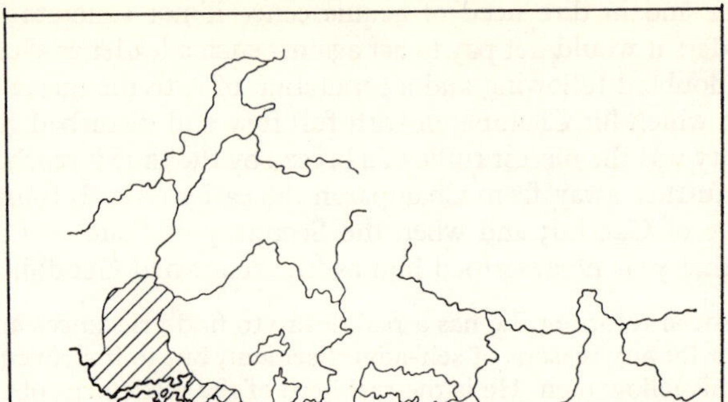

which Ahmedabad provided a convenient and sizeable market.[1] The exception to this pattern of growth was the rice tract of Matar and Mehmadabad talukas and the north-west strip of Nadiad, which could not like the rest of Kaira switch to growing more cotton than rice after the famine at the turn of the century.[2]

Most Kaira people lived in the countryside; but the district was less rural than Champaran, which had only two towns to its name compared

[1] Descriptions of the district and its crops are in *Gazetteer Of The Bombay Presidency. Volume III. Kaira And Panch Mahals* (Bombay, 1879); *Gazetteer Of The Bombay Presidency. Volume III-B. Kaira And Panch Mahals* (Bombay, 1914). The growing prosperity of Gujarat as a whole is analysed in J. M. Mehta, *A Study Of Rural Economy Of Gujarat Containing Possibilities of Reconstruction* (Baroda, 1930). For a description of modern Kaira see K. Nair, *Blossoms In The Dust. The Human Element in Indian Development* (London, 1961), pp. 170–8. By the time this was written the prosperity of Kaira compared with Champaran was very much more marked than in the second decade of the century, when the full impact of modern farming methods had not been felt.

[2] *Census Of India, 1921. Vol. VIII. Part I*, p. xxix.

with Kaira's ten. Of these ten the largest were Nadiad, with 27,145 inhabitants in 1911, Umreth with 13,651 and Kapadvanj with 13,126.[1] Of course the smallest of these towns were little more than overgrown villages compared with places like Ahmedabad. Nadiad was a good example of the gradual urban development which was taking place in western India: in 1886 it had not gained a place in the *Imperial Gazetteer*, but by 1911 it was Kaira's largest town. The old trading traditions of Gujarat assisted this slow process of urbanization, but simultaneously brought wealth into the families of many cultivators; and agriculture still remained the primary occupation of the district. 71.9% of Kaira's people were supported by agriculture in 1921, compared with 60.1% of the population of Gujarat as a whole; while only 9.7% were supported by industry and 4.4% by commerce in Kaira compared with 15.9% and 8.2% in Gujarat.[2] With the exception of the Panch Mahals district Kaira was the most agricultural part of Gujarat, and the actual process of cultivation touched the lives of nearly all its people, not just the traditional cultivating castes like the Kunbis and Kolis. Some Brahmins cultivated land; so did Dheds and weavers when not at their looms, and even urban artisans eked out their living with agricultural sidelines. The Vania traders alone were not involved.[3]

Although Kaira and Champaran shared the importance of agriculture, the way this was translated into terms of actual power was markedly different in the two areas. Where Champaran was a district of large estates, Kaira was a district of sizeable smallholdings. Between 1861 and 1867 average holdings of land by acre in Kaira were as follows:[4]

Borsad—$10\frac{4}{40}$	Kapadvanj —$9\frac{23}{40}$
Anand — $7\frac{12}{40}$	Mehmadabad—$7\frac{2}{40}$
Matar — $6\frac{25}{40}$	Thasra —$6\frac{21}{40}$
Nadiad— $5\frac{35}{40}$	

This pattern of landholding dated from the settlement of the area when the British hoped to create a class of thriving, independent yeomen farmers, compared with their earlier ideal of setting up an improving landlord class in Bihar and Bengal. The implications in social power and public influence were obvious. Here was no powerful group of zamindars lording it over a restless tenantry, nor was there a peasant population trying to eke out a living on patches of land not economically viable. Rather there was a group of tough and prosperous peasant proprietors, cultivating their own lands with the assistance of landless labourers who lived on the outskirts

1 *Kaira Gazetteer. Vol. III-B*, p. 8.

2 *Census Of India, 1921. Vol. VIII. Part I*, pp. 238–9.

3 *Kaira Gazetteer. Vol. III*, p. 56.

4 *Ibid.* p. 44. An economically viable holding, capable of supporting a family, was 3 acres of garden, or 5 acres of rice land, or 8 acres of dry crops.

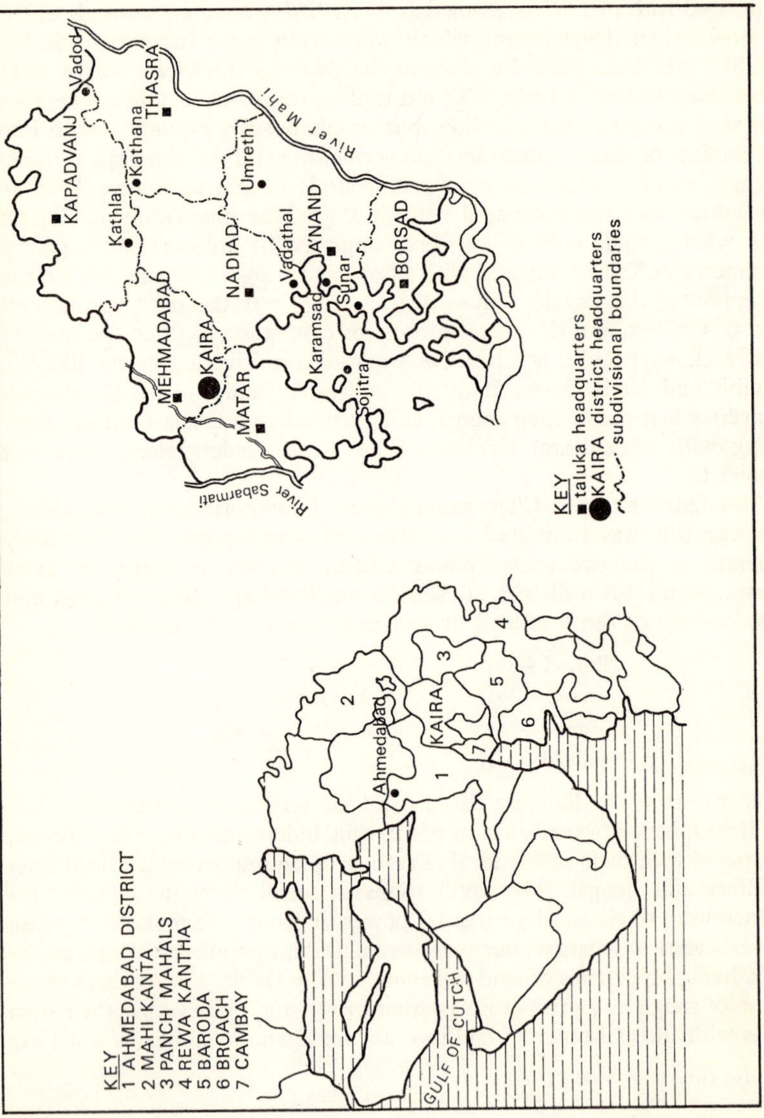

Map of Gujarat showing Kaira District

of the villages within which the proprietors held sway. These proprietors might not be powerful as individuals, but if they chose to act together as a cohesive group they were potentially very strong.

Kaira was, like Champaran, a predominantly Hindu district. In 1911 about 86.5% of the population were Hindus, just over 9% were Muslims, nearly 1% Jains, while the remaining few were Christians and Parsis.[1] But the balance of power between various groups was in marked contrast to the situation in Champaran, and the whole feel of the district was consequently different.

Table 2

Principal castes in Kaira, 1914

Hindus			
Bhangi or Halalkor	12,770	Kunbi	107,805
Bhoi	10,064	Mahar, Holiyar or Dhed	18,085
Brahmin	30,581	Rajput	28,382
Chamar or Mochi	10,642	Vaghri	14,179
Koli	266,665	Vani	18,929
Muslims			
Bohoras	11,158		

The main castes in Kaira were as shown in Table 2.[2] Bhangis, Bhois, Chamars and Vaghris were service castes of low standing, often employed in various types of casual labour. Brahmins, at the other end of the ritual scale, did not have in Gujarat the actual dominance in local affairs which their ritual status suggested, and which their caste fellows did possess elsewhere in western India. Such indeed was the distinction between the 'degenerate' Brahmins of Gujarat and the dominant Brahmins of the Deccan, for example, in dress, customs and language, that groups of the latter living in Gujarat tended to hold aloof from their Gujarati counterparts, preferring to keep up social and religious links with Brahmins in the Deccan and in Baroda. Whereas the Deccani Brahmins had secured a hold on administrative office in their home region, in Kaira most Gujarati Brahmins lived on alms, except for the small groups of Nagar and Khedaval Brahmins who were merchants, money-lenders, pleaders and government servants.[3]

The Kolis, Kaira's largest caste, were cultivators. Those with social and economic aspirations tended to prohibit widow marriage in imitation of

[1] *Census Of India, 1911. Volume VII. Bombay. Part I. Report* (Bombay, 1912), p. 71.

[2] *Kaira Gazetteer. Vol. III-B*, p. 9. For details of the various castes see the alphabetical entries in R. E. Enthoven, *The Tribes And Castes of Bombay* (Bombay, 1920–2).

[3] *Gazetteer Of The Bombay Presidency. Volume IV. Ahmedabad* (Bombay, 1879), p. 35; *Kaira Gazetteer. Vol. III*, pp. 29–30. The Nagar and Khedaval Brahmins were respectively 4.17% and 22.9% of Kaira's Brahmin population.

Rajput customs, and to better their status by marrying their daughters to Rajputs; for it was Rajputs rather than Brahmins who provided the local standard for sanskritization. However the Rajputs, hereditary landlords and soldiers in Gujarat, were themselves losing influence in practical terms. Far more important in Champaran were the trading castes who prospered as agriculture throve, taking their cut from the prosperity produced by cash crops, good transport and convenient markets. Vanias (of whom Gandhi was one) were Gujarat's main trading caste. Their Muslim counterparts were the Shia Bohoras, who traded abroad and locally, and were the richest and best organized, though the most scattered, of Gujarati Muslims. By contrast Sunni Bohoras were mainly landholders and cultivators.

The crucial aspect of Kaira's caste structure, and that which distinguished it most sharply from Champaran's, was the importance of the Patidars, who were more influential than local Brahmins, and over a period of two hundred years had usurped the traditional power of the Rajputs. Patidars were originally a few families of the Kunbi cultivating caste, who acquired the name Patidar as revenue farmers, responsible to the Mughals and then to the Marathas for the village tax. From this office and their cultivation of indigo, cotton and tobacco they acquired considerable wealth, while the prosperity of the other wealthy group in Gujarat, the Vanias, was undermined for a time by the turmoil under the Maratha princes, and by the silting up of the port of Cambay. Although the Patidars' power over taxes ended with the advent of the British raj, their landholding rights were endorsed, and they benefited under the new regime from land drainage schemes, improved agriculture, the growth of a money economy, and the development of Ahmedabad as a market for their produce. As a close-knit social and commercial group, clustering in the talukas of Anand, Borsad and Nadiad, they became extremely prosperous.

To trace the progress of the Patidars is to uncover one of the success stories of modernizing India: they were unfailing opportunists, a group who responded eagerly to every change in their environment. Even the great famine of 1899–1901 did not stop them, and many went to Africa to trade, returning later to Gujarat with their accumulated wealth which they ploughed back into their ancestral villages, thus creating no dichotomy between landed and commercial wealth. From Sunar alone, a poor mud-walled village at the time of the famine, members of at least three hundred Patidar families went to Africa; and the post-independence prosperity of the village rests largely on the profits of their trade.[1] Agricultural improvements at the beginning of the twentieth century, particularly the development of tobacco as a cash crop, as well as the profits of the African trade, benefited the whole Kunbi caste, preventing its fission into Patidars and non-Patidars. Instead the whole caste adopted the name Patidar in 1931.

[1] Nair, *Blossoms In The Dust*, p. 173.

Whereas in the early nineteenth century they were locally ranked as Sudras, they now stood with the Vanias in ritual status, and reinforced their economic success with those signs of ritual purity, like the prohibition of widow marriage, essential to a caste claiming high status.[1]

Caste, land and wealth were not the only determinants of local patterns of power. Education was a vital factor too, either as an avenue to power for previously powerless groups, or as a buttress to existing strength, depending on who took advantage of it. The difference between Kaira and Champaran in patterns of education was as marked as their differences in the realm of caste. Bombay Presidency had a higher standard of education than Bihar and Orissa; and while Champaran sank perilously near the bottom in Bihar, Gujarat was the best educated area in the Presidency, its success being mainly in primary, vernacular education. In 1921 15.6% of Gujaratis over five were literate, compared with 7.1% in Konkan, 7.2% in the Deccan, 8.6% in the Karnatak and 6.2% in Sind.[2] Kaira shared the general Gujarat pattern of a good primary base, with a smaller though increasing secondary superstructure. Surprisingly Champaran had more schools than Kaira, but Kaira had far more pupils. In 1912–13 evidence from the government run or aided establishments showed 42,650 pupils in Kaira attending five high schools, twelve vernacular middle schools, 523 primary schools, one normal college, and five technical and special schools.[3] In contrast to the urban heart of the Presidency, with its long tradition of English-medium higher education, improvement in educational standards in rustic Kaira was a humble and comparatively recent phenomenon.[4]

The influence of education lay in the groups who took advantage of it as much as in the actual numbers of pupils: this was as true for each locality as for the subcontinent as a whole. Kaira's educated were spread between the different religious communities in the following percentages of literates to the local strength of their community:[5]

Hindus	9%	Jains	42%
Muslims	10%	All religions	10%

[1] For the rise of the Patidars see the following: Enthoven, *op. cit.* vol. 2, p. 149; Nair, *op. cit.* pp. 170–8; Srinivas, *Social Change In Modern India*, p. 38; K. L. Gillion, *Ahmedabad. A Study in Indian Urban History* (Berkeley & Los Angeles, 1968), pp. 27, 160–3; D. Pocock, 'The Movement of Castes', no. 79, *Man*, LV (May 1955), 71–2; D. Pocock, 'Inclusion And Exclusion: A Process In The Caste System Of Gujarat', *Southwestern Journal of Anthropology*, 13 (1957), 19–31.

[2] *Census Of India, 1921. Vol. VIII. Part I*, p. 147. Of Gujarat's male population 7.2% were in primary school, compared with 4.9% in the Deccan and Konkan, 5.2% in the Karnatak, and 3.5% in Sind. Gujarat and Deccan with Konkan came first in the Presidency in secondary education with 0.8% of their male populations at secondary school. *Report Of The Director Of Public Instruction In The Bombay Presidency 1912–13–1916–17* (Bombay, 1917), pp. 35, 56.

[3] *Kaira Gazetteer. Vol. III-B*, p. 30.

[4] In 1877 there had been only 13,168 pupils in government schools in Kaira. *Kaira Gazetteer. Vol. III*, p. 135.

[5] *Kaira Gazetteer. Vol. III-B*, p. 28.

The outstanding performance of the Jains is understandable because they were a small, wealthy, urban group. Muslim literacy reflected the wealth of Muslim traders, in comparison with the Hindus, of whom the majority were cultivators. Unfortunately, there are no accurate figures for education by caste in Kaira. It is therefore impossible to trace precisely the differential spread of education among the Hindus; but what concrete evidence there is suggests that traders, shopkeepers and prosperous cultivators took advantage of the new educational opportunities, while Brahmins did not on anything like the same scale as their Deccani caste fellows. In the words of one contemporary, 'With a few exceptions Gujarat Brahmins have no claim to learning. The religious training of family and village priests does not go beyond the learning by rote of the ritual required at the every-day ceremonies.'[1]

An investigation of the sources and distribution of power in local society makes it clear why Kaira men had little to do with institutional politics before the second decade of this century. There was little communal rivalry or tension making Hindus and Muslims compete and barter for place, as in the U.P. Brahmins did not have sufficient power to raise up a low caste movement against themselves, as in Madras and parts of Maharashtra. Education was widely spread, mainly primary and vernacular and tended to reinforce existing social patterns rather than throwing up a new elite or dramatically extending the power of an old one. Its beneficiaries were generally well established in agriculture or trade, and the fruit of literacy was increased efficiency in those occupations, rather than increasing unemployment and a growing discontent capable of generating political demand in the style of Calcutta, Madras and Bombay. Contemporaries from the Presidencies commented how backward Gujarat was in their kind of politics. Tilak, writing in *Mahratta* in 1895, asserted that Gujarat was completely indifferent to Congress; while a decade later another Congressman encountered ridicule as well as indifference when he tried to organize Congress in Bardoli district.

> The objects in view of the Congress and Conferences they take to be impossibilities so far that I am sometimes laughed out and hence my inconveniences are very great. When this part of Gujarat which is most prominent in Gujarat as regards enlightenment is so backward in seeking rights other parts of the same must be in total darkness about the persevering attempts of our Congress.[2]

[1] *Gazetteer Of The Bombay Presidency. Volume IX. Part I. Gujarat Population: Hindus* (Bombay, 1901), p. 31. Of the pupils attending government schools in Kaira in 1877, 36.67% were from cultivating castes, 20.86% were from castes of traders and shopkeepers, 22.60% were Brahmins and 9.45% were Muslims. *Kaira Gazetteer. Vol. III*, p. 135.

[2] P. H. Shastri to D. Naoroji, 21 December 1906, Naoroji Papers, Johnson,

In this 'total darkness' Kaira and Champaran were alike, though the reasons for it were somewhat different. Although the wealth and education of Gujarat did not appear to have immediate implications in the world of institutional politics, the existence of a prosperous trading community and the rural Patidar elite meant that Gujarat would be an area to be reckoned with should circumstances turn the energies of these groups in the direction of such politics. As their position depended on their economic success, it was likely that economic change would be the decisive factor in determining their attitude. This factor was provided by war-time trading difficulties and the economic situation in 1917–19; also present was Gandhi, a leader able to articulate their discontent and harness this new force to political ends.

Although Congress politics barely touched Gujarat before the First World War, the region did not lack public awareness. It was just that to the Gujaratis other forms of public activity appeared more appropriate to their particular situation: change there was in their environment, but they found they could adjust to change most profitably without recourse to the techniques and demands of institutional politics. Their adjustment to change was demonstrated in claims to higher ritual status by castes whose social power and aspirations began to outstrip their traditional ranking. It was also clear in the vigorous social reform movement which developed in the 1830s and found expression through the beginnings of a vernacular press and various voluntary, secular associations. Among these were the Gujarat Vernacular Society, founded in Ahmedabad in 1848, which worked to reform the Gujarati language, to spread female education and to improve the position of women in society, and the Gujarat Hindu Social Reform Association of the 1880s, one of the earliest legally incorporated social reform organizations in India, which campaigned against child marriage.[1] The leaders of this reform movement were a tiny group of Nagar Brahmins and Jains. They were a minority: the majority of Gujarat's influential people were businessmen or Seths in local parlance, based in Ahmedabad, who tended to be too engrossed with the new mill industry to concern themselves with issues wider than their profits, and for many of whom even municipal improvement was too novel for their support.

During the century a small group of western educated men began to emerge, but when they did found two associations to represent 'the wants of the people' – the Ahmedabad Association (1872) and the Gujarat Sabha (1885) – they, too, were crassly conservative and contented themselves

'Indian Politics 1888–1908', p. 394, fn. 1; *Mahratta*, 27 October 1895, G. Johnson, 'Maharashtrian Politics And Indian Nationalism 1880–1920' (unpublished Thirlwall Prize Essay, Cambridge, 1969), p. 94. Compare Bardoli district in 1921, see below, pp. 321–2.

1 Gillion, *op. cit.* pp. 63–9; Heimsath, *Indian Nationalism And Hindu Social Reform*, pp. 100–2, 234.

with complaints about increased municipal taxation.[1] No ripples of this reached the more rural districts, and Gujaratis continued to display the greatest reluctance to have any dealings with Congress and its politics.

However, they could not resist the blandishments of the Presidency politicians indefinitely; and as literacy spread it opened the door to political ideas which were increasingly being disseminated through Bombay if the publication of books on political matters can be taken as a rough measure.[2] What finally broke Gujarat's isolation was not literature but the Home Rule League organization. Tilak set to work in 1917 to rouse Gujarat to nationalist politics, and considered his efforts 'very successful. Gujarat is now entirely different from what it was in 1907.'[3] Though he was right in seeing that a partial cure had been found for Gujarat's political lethargy, the physician who actually administered the dose was Annie Besant. Most Gujarati Home Rulers belonged to her League, which received a tremendous boost when she was interned in 1917 and great public lamentation was made on her behalf. Spreading from Ahmedabad, where a branch was founded in 1916, her League's tentacles reached Kaira district in 1917, and a branch was established in Nadiad in July, which kept in close touch with the Bombay League. Meetings were held in Nadiad town and Home Rulers toured the villages, some of these perambulating lecturers coming from as far afield as Ahmedabad and Bombay. Within a short time eighty-six active branches had been founded in Kaira district.[4]

Gandhi was himself instrumental in opening Gujarat to new forms of public activity, even before he led the Kaira satyagraha; though at this stage he was not an associate of either Tilak or Annie Besant, and had motives different from both of them. In 1917 he acquired his first footing in a political institution in Gujarat when he was elected President of the Gujarat Sabha. Immediately he galvanized the Sabha into organizing a monster petition in support of the Congress and Muslim League scheme of constitutional reform, not so much because he was enthusiastic about the scheme itself, but because this seemed a splendid opportunity to reach out into the villages and give the educated a chance to come into contact with the illiterate. As he wrote privately at the time, 'For me the value of it lies in the education that the masses will receive and the opportunity that the educated men and women will have of coming in close touch with the people.'[5]

1 For municipal reform and the attitude of businessmen and the educated see Gillion, *op. cit.* pp. 118–42.

2 Publication of books on political subjects in the Bombay Presidency jumped from 2 in 1911, to 11 in 1916, 35 in 1917 and 63 in 1918, *Census Of India, 1921. Vol. VIII. Part I*, p. xxv.

3 B. G. Tilak to G. S. Khaparde, 23 September 1917, Khaparde Record 1, p. 74.

4 Special Department File No. 521 (3A), *Source Material for a History of the Freedom Movement in India. (Collected from Bombay Government Records.) Vol. II. 1885–1920* (Bombay, 1958), pp. 729–30; Gillion, *op. cit.* pp. 163–4.

5 Gandhi to V. S. Srinivasa Sastri, 30 September 1917, *C.W.*, vol. 13, p. 559.

For him the gravest ill in contemporary India was the great divorce between the educated and the masses, and here was a bridging device to hand.

Another such device was offered later the same year, and again Gandhi seized it. Several pleaders from Godhra, particularly W. S. Mukadam, D. L. Shah and G. C. Sariya, decided to organize a Gujarat Political Conference, partly prompted by Home Rule ideas but doubtless also by awareness that this would bring them considerable public recognition. They needed a popular public figure to preside, and for this purpose approached Gandhi. He did not initiate this political venture, but when brought in because of his provincial reputation he made sure that it served his purpose of linking the educated to their compatriots. When the Conference met at Godhra in November 1917, over 9,000 people were reported to have attended on the first day, and at Gandhi's insistence Gujarati was the language used, so that those outside the ranks of the English educated could also participate. Moreover the outcaste Dhed community at Godhra was induced to hold a conference at the same time.[1]

What the Home Rule Leagues had tentatively begun in Gujarat Gandhi extended dramatically. Reaching out into the villages, paying special attention to the ill-educated and outcaste, he brought politics to people who had probably never heard a political speech before. His appeal was not that of the Presidency politicians, just as his aims differed from theirs: the politics he preached were moulded to suit the real interests of the people in the streets and villages, as his satyagrahas of 1918 showed. The established politicians had meagre success in Gujarat, because their plans and aspirations had little relevance to Gujarati life. It was the economic situation which touched the lives of Gujaratis most deeply, whether they were Ahmedabad Seths or mill-workers, or Patidars from Kaira: and economic change thrust Kaira into political activity, incidentally giving Gandhi the opportunity to build up a solid base of support for himself.

In Kaira the state of the crops during the 1917–18 season was the immediate issue at stake in the agitation Gandhi led, though, as in the case of the indigo issue in Champaran, it needs to be set in the context of war-time change and distress if its full impact is to be realized. Officials described 1916–17 as an excellent season, 1917–18 as fair, and 1918–19 as very bad. In 1917 throughout Gujarat excessive rain considerably damaged the *kharif* crop, sown after the rains break in June–July and harvested in the autumn, though the *rabi* crops, sown after the rains and harvested in the spring, went a long way to offset the earlier damage by their good yield and the high prices they fetched. As the largest part of Kaira's cultivated land was given over to *kharif* crops, farmers did not get as much benefit from the good *rabi* crops as in other areas, and were understandably nervous before they knew the spring harvest would be a good one. Sick-

[1] Bombay Police Abstract, 1917, par. 1041, 1224 (r), 1247; *The Bombay Chronicle*, 18 November 1918.

ness also hit the district. Gujarat as a whole suffered a severe epidemic of plague in 1918, and in Kaira alone 16,740 people died from it, quite apart from a mild form of cholera which also broke out locally.[1]

The fortunes of the *kharif* crop were reflected in a sharp rise in the price of food; and this rise was aggravated by the difficulty of importing food from other areas because of the war-time shortage of railway waggons. Both Kaira and Champaran suffered because railway traffic was so restricted, although the actual effects on the price of food were diametrically opposite in the two districts. Throughout Gujarat other prices jumped too; as one Collector reported, the price of salt had doubled, the price of food had gone up in leaps and bounds, and not even government controlled imports of rice had steadied the price of rice permanently, while cloth had become uncomfortably expensive. The people who made a profit from this situation were businessmen, particularly Ahmedabad millowners and middlemen, who rode to fortune on the rising price of cotton. What profit went to farmers as they sold their food crops tended to be swallowed up by the rising cost of living. The people hardest hit were landless labourers whose wages did not keep pace with rising costs, and those in professions and administration who had to live on fixed incomes.[2] Clearly there was economic hardship throughout Gujarat by the beginning of 1918, particularly in Kaira, where there were the added pressures of bad health and bad harvests: but whether the participants in the Kaira satyagraha were those worst hit was open to debate.

Gandhi and the Bombay government disagreed over the way the Kaira agitation started. Gandhi insisted that the cultivators themselves first raised the question of possible relief from the land revenue demand because of economic hardship.

> This struggle was not started by outsiders. Nobody instigated the Kheda [Kaira] public to launch it. There is no political motive behind it. It did

1 *Land Revenue Administration Report, Part I, of The Bombay Presidency, Including Sind, – For The Year 1917–18* (Bombay, 1919), p. 3; *Census Of India, 1921. Vol. VIII. Part I*, p. 11.

2 *Land Revenue Administration Report, Part II, of The Bombay Presidency, Including Sind, – For The Year 1917–18* (Bombay, 1919), pp. 11, 13. The following table shows three examples of the rising price of food in the Ahmedabad area of Gujarat. Bajra, one of the worst affected, was one of Bombay Presidency's main foods. The base = 100 in 1873.

	Common Rice	*Wheat*	*Bajra* (spiked millet)
1914	172	166	220
1915	178	186	210
1916	197	169	190
1917	208	179	150
1918	233	259	410

Source: *Statistical Abstract For British India 1917–18 to 1926–27*, Table 295, pp. 618, 620, 624.

> not originate with the Home Rulers or with any barristers or lawyers as some people allege...It was started by the tillers themselves. After the Political Conference at Godhra, some agriculturalists in Kheda decided to request the Government for relief in view of the excessive rains. They wrote to me, informing me that they were legally entitled to relief and asking me whether I could help.[1]

However the fact that Gandhi told the Gujarat Sabha to show publicly and conclusively that farmers started the agitation and that the Sabha only took it up at their request indicates that the farmers' request was not immediately obvious.[2] Local government officials thought that the agitation was not a spontaneous expression of peasant discontent, but was started by local Home Rulers and then taken up by the Gujarat Sabha. The Commissioner for the Northern Division of the Presidency described it as 'undoubtedly a political agitation worked from outside.' The Collector of Kaira named Mohanlal Kameshwar Pandya, of Kathlal in Kapadvanj taluka, as one of the leading Home Rulers involved: Pandya was a Bachelor of Agriculture and consequently felt entitled to a hearing on matters agricultural! This impression was confirmed by a series of reports from the local police that Pandya was speaking at Home Rule meetings on the condition of the crops, and advocating the suspension of land revenue.[3]

Precise details of the earliest stage of the agitation are hard to find. A later government report noted:

> Mr. Somabhai Kashibhai of Nadiad who is called 'African' first began to agitate, and printed applications dated 15th November 1917 praying for total remission of land revenue for the year began to pour in. Subsequently at a mass meeting held at Nadiad on 25th November 1917 it was resolved that the Honourable Messrs. Gokuldas Kahandas Parekh and Vithalbhai Jhaverbai Patel and others should go in a deputation before the Collector (Mr. Namjoshi). These gentlemen had an interview with the Collector at Thasra in the middle of December 1917, and the Collector promised to give the matter his best attention.

At the time the police did not hesitate to call the mass meeting on 25 November a Home Rule meeting, and they named an Ahmedabad politician, Maganbhai Chaturbhai Patel, as the main exponent of the draft resolution calling on the government to remit the assessment.[4] The two

[1] Speech by Gandhi at public meeting in Bombay, 23 April 1918, *C.W.*, vol. 14, p. 369. I have not been able to trace any letter sent after the conference requesting Gandhi's help in Kaira.

[2] Gandhi to Gujarat Sabha, undated telegram, *C.W.*, vol. 14, p. 155.

[3] Fortnightly report from Bombay, 18–21 January 1918, Home Pol., Deposit, March 1918, No. 38; Report by Collector of Kaira, *1917–18 Bombay Land Revenue Administration Report, Part 2*, p. 2; Bombay Police Abstract, 1918, par. 64.

[4] Special Department File No. 521, Part (3A), *Source Material for a History of the Freedom Movement in India, vol. 2*, pp. 730–1; Bombay Police Abstract, 1917, par.

Bombay barristers, G. K. Parekh and V. J. Patel, 'invited and assisted by the Gujarat Sabha' according to Gandhi, visited Kaira on 12 December and reported their findings to the Sabha. Subsequently they put the case in writing to the Collector of Kaira on 15 December, and saw him on the same day.

The Sabha as a body appealed direct to the Bombay government on 1 January, urging exemption from land revenue in some cases and postponement in others.[1] Gandhi, as President, convened a meeting of the Sabha on 7 January, at which Kaira was discussed; and three days later the Sabha's secretaries saw F. G. Pratt, Commissioner of the Northern Division. Having received from him an unfavourable reply the Sabha publicly advised Kaira cultivators not to pay their land revenue – a declaration for which Gandhi assumed total responsibility. At the same time Gujarat Home Rulers, led by M. C. Patel, held their own meeting to protest against the government's attitude to the farmers' demands.[2] Clearly if the Gujarat Sabha and the Home Rulers did not actually start the hare they went hot foot on the trail immediately it was started, and it is obvious why the local government held them responsible.

The Kaira agitation happened in two phases: the period of appeal to the government (15 December 1917 – 22 March 1918) and the actual satyagraha (22 March – 6 June 1918). The period of appeal degenerated into a verbal battle, in which each side repeated its own argument without entering into genuine discussion with its opponent. It therefore seems most convenient to summarize the arguments used by each side before giving an account of the struggle.

The local government took its stand on the Bombay Land Revenue Code of 1879, and subsequent administrative decisions which affected the revenue rules.

> The rules in force for the suspension of land revenue provide that when the Collector has ascertained by local inquiries that owing to a partial or total failure or destruction of the crops throughout any tract on account of drought or any other cause, it will be necessary to suspend the collection of revenue in any area, he is authorized, especially when the tract is

1261 (g). There is no more evidence available about Somabhai Kashibhai; presumably the nickname 'African' meant that he was a Patidar or other trader returned from Africa.

1 Statement to press by Gandhi, 28 March 1918, *The Hindu*, 1 April 1918, *C.W.*, vol. 14, p. 289; printed copies of deputation and letter from Parekh and Patel to the Collector, 15 December 1917, S.N. No. 9845. The Sabha's appeal is not available but it is referred to in the Bombay Government Press Note, No. 498, 16 January 1918, S.N. No. 9845.

2 Bombay Police Abstract, 1918, par. 204; speech by Gandhi in Bombay, 4 February 1918, *The Bombay Chronicle*, 5 February 1918, *C.W.*, vol. 14, p. 182; details of the interview with Pratt were given by Gandhi in a letter to 'a public worker', undated, *C.W.*, vol. 14, p. 144.

already impoverished or the previous harvests have been poor, to grant suspension.[1]

After enquiry into the state of the crops in Kaira the Collector decided that there was no justification for the remission of land revenue, though he thought certain areas merited suspension of revenue – forty villages in Nadiad taluka, thirty-four in Kapadvanj, and thirty in Mehmadabad. He was also prepared to deal separately, under the 'local calamities' section of the revenue rules, with seven villages in Matar taluka which had been flooded.[2] The government believed that the amount of revenue actually collected justified the assessment in retrospect: by 12 May not less than 80% of the revenue had been paid, by 22 May 93% of the total demand was in, and by the end of July 98.5% had been collected. Officialdom contended not merely that its assessment was correct, but that as a matter of principle suspension of revenue was not by right but by grace, at the discretion of the Collector, whose judgement could not be challenged. Members of the Government of India discussed Kaira in April and felt that the independence of the local government was an important principle to defend. As one of them put it, 'I...strongly deprecate any interference. We have for years now left questions of remission and suspension of land revenue to local Govts.'[3]

Gandhi, however, maintained that officials had over-valued the crops and that cultivators were entitled to suspension as a legal right, not as a concession by grace. He stated this on 28 March in a press release, and suggested that since both sides thought they were in the right, 'if the Government have any regard for popular opinion they should appoint an impartial committee of inquiry with the cultivators' representatives upon it, or gracefully accept the popular view.' The Revenue Member of the Government of India considered and dismissed this suggestion, deciding that the situation in no way resembled Champaran, where the Government of India had pressed for an enquiry; in this case he preferred to trust local officials. Gandhi believed that the government attitude raised a question of supreme constitutional importance, which was the real issue at stake in the agitation.

> It is contended on behalf of the Ryots that, where there are, in matters of administrative orders, sharp differences of opinion between local officials and them, the points of differences are and ought to be referred to an

[1] Description by Collector of Kaira of revenue rules in force, *1917–18 Bombay Land Revenue Administration Report, Part 2*, p. 1. The revenue rules also laid down a scale for suspensions.

[2] Bombay Government Press Note, No. 498, 16 January 1918, S.N. No. 9845.

[3] Handwritten note, 6 April 1918, in file relating to Gandhi's activities in Kaira, Home Pol., Deposit, May 1918, No. 18. The government's attitude was set out in Note by Bombay Government on Kaira, Enclosure C in letter from Chelmsford to E. S. Montagu, 20 March 1919, Mss. EUR. E. 264 (5).

impartial committee of inquiry. This, it is held, constitutes the strength of the British Constitution. The Commissioner has on principle rejected this position and invited a crisis.[1]

The first skirmish in the battle occurred on 15 December 1917, when Parekh and Patel confronted Namjoshi, the Collector of Kaira, before he had passed his formal orders about the revenue collection. They argued that the crops had been almost entirely devastated, and plague and high prices made the situation even worse: Namjoshi in return assured them that the government had no wish to over-assess crops, and although he could not remit the revenue demand he would suspend the whole or part in cases which merited it. After an enquiry into actual conditions he passed his formal orders.[2] The Gujarat Sabha, having failed to get a more satisfactory reply, even after going to the Commissioner, decided to advise Kaira farmers not to pay their land revenue. The local government retaliated with a press note on 16 January, supporting the Collector's decision; whereupon Gandhi immediately took up the cudgels. He urged the Sabha to press for an independent investigation and to show that it and the two lawyers had intervened at the farmers' request, and recommended that people who would have to borrow money or sell cattle to pay their revenue should be advised not to do so. Parekh and Patel reiterated their position on 24 January, condemning the Collector's suspensions as totally inadequate and criticizing the government method of valuing crops; they refused to defend the Gujarat Sabha against the insinuations of the government note, pointing to the anxious crowds which met them in Kaira as proof that this was not an outside agitation.[3]

At this point the Servants of India Society intervened. Three of its members, Deodhar, Joshi and Thakkar, took it upon themselves to start an enquiry in the Matar taluka on 24 January. They came to the conclusion that in some cases government valuation of the crops had been too high, and recommended some areas for total suspension and some for half suspension of the land revenue. Their overall picture of this, by common consent the worst-hit area, was far less gloomy than that painted by the Sabha of Kaira as a whole.

[1] Gandhi to editor, 15 April 1918, *The Bombay Chronicle*, 17 April 1918. Gandhi's earlier statement to the press, 28 March 1918, was published in *The Hindu*, 1 April 1918, *C.W.*, vol. 14, p. 290. The Revenue Member's decision is given in typed summary of papers on Kaira, Home Pol., Deposit, May 1918, No. 18.

[2] See above, p. 97.

[3] The documents on which this paragraph is based are printed copies of letter and deputation of Parekh and Patel to Collector of Kaira, 15 December 1918, S.N. No. 9845; Bombay Government Press Note, No. 498, 16 January 1918, S.N. No. 9845; Gandhi to Gujarat Sabha, undated telegram in reply to 16 January government press note, *C.W.*, vol. 14, p. 155; reply to government press note by Parekh and Patel, 24 January 1918, S.N. No. 9846.

> This inquiry has led us to believe that though there is no famine or acute distress in this Taluka at present there are strong grounds for showing real and tangible sympathy with the condition of the people, whose anxiety and trouble caused by the failure of the last Kharif have been considerably aggravated...by additional disturbing and unfortunate factors such as (1) the high prices, (2) the prevalence of plague in the villages and (3) the dread that rats and frost might cause damage to the standing crop which is generally admitted to be fairly good even by the agriculturalists themselves.[1]

Gandhi was clearly annoyed by this poaching on his territory, and even more by the contents of the report. In a touchy letter to Deodhar he disputed the S.I.S. valuation, remarked that Deodhar had unconsciously let himself be a tool in the hands of the Commissioner, and asked why they had not consulted him before publishing their report.[2]

Meanwhile he had returned from Bihar to Gujarat and became personally involved in the interchanges with the government. On 4 February, at a public meeting in Bombay, he mentioned the possibility of satyagraha in Kaira; and the next day, in company with Parekh, Patel and D. E. Wacha, he saw the Governor of Bombay, Lord Willingdon. After the interview he wrote to press home the request he had made for an independent enquiry, preferably with Parekh and Patel on it; but he received the reply that since the Governor did not think local officials had been harsh he could see no point in authorizing an enquiry.[3] Having tried his hand in Bombay without success, Gandhi returned to Ahmedabad and there devoted his attention to local officials. On 7 February he complained to F. G. Pratt, the Commissioner, that the *mamlatdar*[4] of Kapadvanj had threatened to confiscate land if revenue was not paid, a threat bound to provoke bitterness locally. Pratt replied tersely that officials only acted according to the law, and therefore he could not see why Gandhi called such action irritating or conducive to bitterness. Gandhi then found further cause for complaint in a notice issued over the Collector's signature, which he considered insulting to the Gujarat Sabha. He sent it to Pratt, who found 'no reasonable basis' for complaint.[5] Having run across a clearly obdurate

[1] Summary of S.I.S. members' report, *The Bombay Chronicle*, 25 February 1918. It is impossible to find any solid grounds for judgement between the various attempts to value crops by the contending parties; valuation was at best a tricky operation as *kharif* and *rabi* crops were assessed together, and at the time of assessment the *rabi* crops were not fully grown.

[2] Gandhi to G. K. Deodhar, 26 February 1918, *C.W.*, vol. 14, pp. 212–13.

[3] Speech by Gandhi in Bombay, 4 February 1918, *The Bombay Chronicle*, 5 February 1918, *C.W.*, vol. 14, pp. 182–4; Gandhi to Governor of Bombay, 5 February 1918, *ibid.* p. 184; Secretary to Governor of Bombay to Gandhi, 9 February 1918, *ibid.* p. 184, fn. 3.

[4] The *mamlatdar* was the chief Indian revenue official in a taluka: the title was used mainly in western India.

[5] Gandhi to F. G. Pratt, 7 February 1918, *C.W.*, vol. 14, p. 185; Pratt to Gandhi,

Commissioner, Gandhi decided to go to Kaira, and announced his intention to Pratt.

> I would like to reassure you that it is not my intention just to start an agitation or to encourage a futile agitation. I am going to Kheda district in search of truth. I see that, until the reports of your local officers are proved to be incorrect, you will not pay any attention to our representations. Although, therefore, I have full assurance of reputable leaders of the district, I feel it my duty to verify the facts for myself. If you are able to postpone the land revenue recovery work until my inquiry is completed, it will help a great deal in reducing the discontent that has now spread among the people.

Not unnaturally Pratt refused the last request but did say that the Collector would probably help if Gandhi asked him.[1]

During the following weeks Gandhi divided his attention between Kaira and Ahmedabad, where he was organizing satyagraha among the millhands. As in Champaran so in Kaira, he and a group of assistants collected statements in the district; and on the basis of these enquiries he again requested the postponement of revenue collection and the establishment of an independent enquiry if the government would not accept his findings. He sent the request to the Collector of Kaira and to the Governor of the Presidency, but the latter replied that he had been kept fully informed of the situation in Kaira and thought that though local officials were acting in strict accordance with the revenue rules they were concerned for the welfare of the people.[2] Here Willingdon was falling back on the old argument of the raj against the complaints of the educated, maintaining that the government was the protector of the poor, and the District Officer was the *ma-bap*, or mother and father, of the people in his district.

Despite a final plea to the Commissioner, Gandhi was told on 20 March that no modifications could be made in the Collector's orders; and the next day he presided at a meeting of the Gujarat Sabha where the die was cast and the decision taken to resort to satyagraha as the only course left.[3] Gandhi inaugurated satyagraha at a meeting of Kaira men in Nadiad,

10 February 1918, *ibid.* p. 185, fn. 2; Gandhi to Pratt, undated, *ibid.* pp. 187–8; Pratt to Gandhi, 16 February 1918, *ibid.* p. 188, fn. 2. Confiscation as a possible penalty for non-payment of land revenue was authorized in the Bombay Land Revenue Code.

[1] Gandhi to F. G. Pratt, undated, probably 15 February 1918, *C.W.*, vol. 14, p. 195; Pratt to Gandhi, undated, probably 15 February 1918, *ibid.* p. 195, fn. 1.

[2] Gandhi to Collector of Kaira, 26 February 1918, *C.W.*, vol. 14, pp. 215–16; Gandhi to Governor of Bombay, undated, *ibid.* pp. 259–60; Governor of Bombay to Gandhi, 17 March 1918, *ibid.* p. 260, fn. 1.

[3] Gandhi to F. G. Pratt, undated, *C.W.*, vol. 14, p. 275; Note by Bombay Government on Kaira, Enclosure C in letter from Chelmsford to E. S. Montagu, 20 March 1919, Mss. EUR. E. 264 (5).

urging them to take a sacred pledge not to pay their land revenue. The crucial part of the pledge was:

> We the undersigned...solemnly declare that we shall not pay the assessment for the year whether it be wholly or in part; we shall leave it to the Government to take any legal steps they choose to enforce recovery of the same and we shall undergo all the sufferings that this may involve. We shall also allow our lands to be confiscated should they do so. But we shall not by voluntary payment allow ourselves to be regarded as liars and thus lose our self-respect.[1]

Satyagraha lasted from 22 March until 6 June. According to the press the peak was reached by 21 April, when there were 2,337 signatories to the pledge.[2] Gandhi himself worked on two main lines, external publicity and internal consolidation. As far as the rest of India was concerned he did his utmost to capture public sympathy, writing to friends, speaking in Bombay, and courting the press, as he had refused to do in Champaran, with letters to editors and numerous public statements. In his own words, 'It is not money they want so much as the voice of a strong, unanimous and emphatic public opinion.'[3]

Within Kaira he toured the villages, speaking in place after place, encouraging satyagrahis to stand by their pledge. Sometimes his presence alone seemed to be the only thing which could keep the satyagraha going.

> "In Kathana in Kapadwanj Taluka many people who had signed the pledge began to pay up. This made Mr. Gandhi's followers send for him post haste. When Mr. Gandhi turned up he persuaded the few who were going to pay but had not actually paid up to allow distraint of ornaments, etc., and these were bought back by the people.[4]

Gandhi's main concern was not to help the farmers financially, but to give them moral support in refusing to pay revenue, and to take away their cringing fear of government authority. He likened peasants confronted by the government to a bullock sweating and crying for fear at the approach of a motor car! To give them an object lesson in courage he advised Mohanlal Pandya, who had been in the agitation from the start, to remove a standing crop of onions which had been attached in lieu of revenue. Pandya and his fellow 'thieves' were subsequently imprisoned, and like local heroes were escorted to gaol by a procession of admirers.[5]

1 Satyagraha pledge published in *Young India*, 12 June 1918, *C.W.*, vol. 14, p. 279.

2 Note by Bombay Government on Kaira, Enclosure C in letter from Chelmsford to E. S. Montagu, 20 March 1919, Mss. EUR. E. 264 (5).

3 Statement to press by Gandhi, 29 March 1918, *The Hindu*, 1 April 1918, *C.W.*, vol. 14, p. 292.

4 Report by Kaira District Magistrate, 6 April 1918, quoted in Weekly report of D.C.I., 20 April 1918, Proceeding No. 25 of Home Pol., B, May 1918, Nos. 23–6.

5 Speech by Gandhi at Vadod village, 11 April 1918, *C.W.*, vol. 14, p. 329; Gandhi, *An Autobiography*, p. 365.

Just as Champaran was temporarily roused to great heights of expectation and enthusiasm by Gandhi's activities, so Kaira seemed to be in the hands of this most unconventional leader. The Collector described what it was like to be there at the time.

> "The mainstay of the movement was a pratidnya, or sacred vow which all were invited to take, whether able to pay or not, that they would not pay the revenue, and many copies of this were circulated in the villages and signatures obtained. Every method of obstruction was adopted; even the boycott of those who paid was advocated and enforced in several villages, and Government servants engaged in the work of collection were subjected to all kinds of petty annoyance and sometimes even insult. Not only were the usual services and courtesies withheld, but the purchase of supplies was frequently prevented and in some cases Mamlatdars themselves had difficulty in procuring water from the village well. A movement of this kind was naturally likely to degenerate from passive to active resistance and there were a few cases of forcible obstruction to distraint, but this was no part of Mr. Gandhi's policy and his influence was strongly exercised on the side of peaceful methods."[1]

Government policy appeared to ease very slightly on 24 April, when Pratt pointed out to the Collector of Kaira that in view of the Viceroy's recent appeal to the country to sink differences and work together to win the war they should be willing to make concessions, provided these did not sacrifice the essential rights of the state. He ordered that no land should be forfeited to cover arrears, that no fine should be exacted if revenue was not paid in full, that recovery of revenue should preferably be by distraint of moveable property, that lands already forfeit could be handed back if arrears were paid, and that arrears could be carried forward to the next year's account. He also ordered that *mamlatdars* should not put pressure on those too poor to pay. Despite this slight change of attitude the government still stuck to its refusal to grant Gandhi's request for an independent enquiry. On 22 May the Collector of Kaira repeated to the *mamlatdars* the Commissioner's orders not to put pressure on poor defaulters, as it was clear that these local officials were reluctant to remove the heavy hand of authority. Eventually the Nadiad *mamlatdar* issued an order to this effect on 3 June; and when Gandhi was assured that this policy held good for the whole district he called off the satyagraha on 6 June.[2] Later he recorded that he had been 'casting about for some graceful way of terminating the struggle', and the Nadiad *mamlatdar's* order provided him with the occasion as it fulfilled the satyagraha pledge. He lamented that this satyagraha gave him no happiness, and lacked the essentials of a complete satyagraha

[1] Report by Collector of Kaira quoted in *1917–18 Bombay Land Revenue Administration Report, Part 2*, p. 2.

[2] Letter of Gandhi and Vallabhbhai Patel to people of Kaira, 6 June 1918, *Young India*, 12 June 1918, *C.W.*, vol. 14, pp. 416–19.

triumph, since it did not leave the satyagrahis 'stronger and more spirited' than they were before.[1]

However, one may with justice query Gandhi's assessment of the satyagraha's effect in Kaira: later events proved that it was immensely significant in the public life of Gujarat, and in his own development as a leader. Most obviously it brought him a step nearer deliberate political activity. Whereas he had tended to see Champaran primarily as a humanitarian issue, he acknowledged that Kaira raised major political issues, in particular that of government by consent.

> I venture to suggest that the Commissioner's attitude constitutes a peril far greater than the German peril, and I am serving the Empire in trying to deliver it from this peril from within. There is no mistaking the fact that India is waking up from its long sleep. The Ryots do not need to be literate to appreciate their rights and their duties. They have but to realise their invulnerable power and no Government, however strong, can stand against their will. The Kaira Ryots are solving an Imperial problem of the first magnitude in India. They will show that it is impossible to govern men without their consent.[2]

Although this sounded like a democratic Home Ruler pronouncing on people's rights, Gandhi was still outside the mainstream of Indian political thought. He declared to a Kaira audience that his real aim was 'to bring back the olden days in India'; and he told an old acquaintance that he believed autocracy was the best form of government, and that he only supported the Home Rule movement as a temporary measure, since he felt India must pass through the throes of parliamentary government before attaining her true destiny, and because he hoped that through the movement he might popularize some of the principles of true Swaraj.[3]

In practice as in theory it was clear that Gandhi was a political outsider for he declined to join any group of politicians and campaigned on issues outside their normal range. In the light of this isolation the Kaira satyagraha was the more important for Gandhi, as it helped to create a place for him in the ranks of the politicians. The political nature of the Kaira agitation was reflected in Gandhi's use of weapons which were part of the conventional armoury of political protagonists – the petition, the mass meeting, the

[1] Gandhi, *An Autobiography*, pp. 365–6. When Gandhi said that the *mamlatdar's* order fulfilled the pledge he presumably meant the part which read, 'If the Government would graciously postpone for all the remaining villages collection of the balance of the revenue, we, who can afford it, would be prepared to pay up revenue, whether it be in full or in part. The reason why the well-to-do amongst us would not pay is that, if they do, the needy ones would, out of fright, sell their chattels or incur debts and pay the revenue and thus suffer.'

[2] Gandhi to editor, 15 April 1918, *The Bombay Chronicle*, 17 April 1918.

[3] Speech by Gandhi at Vadathal village, 5 April 1918, *C.W.*, vol. 14, p. 311; Gandhi to Florence Winterbottom, 21 February 1918, *ibid.* p. 210.

public speech and the press. In spite of the political interest these actions aroused, no major politician was called in to assist.

Most of the funds for the satyagraha came from Bombay merchants, many of whom were Gujarati by origin; and when the Bombay Home Rule League decided to collect five lakhs of rupees for a Kaira Distress Relief Fund it turned to the Bombay cloth merchants for two-fifths of the amount.[1] But these donations were not just businessmen's charity with no political strings attached. Since many of the Bombay merchants, particularly those based on the Mulji Jetha Cloth Market, were noted for their Home Rule tendencies, Gandhi found himself drawn into the world of politics by relying on their funds. Contemporary records make it quite clear that the National Union and the Home Rule League of Bombay worked in close collaboration with the Gujarat Sabha in connection with Kaira. The League was a source of material support; apart from donations it opened a number of shops in Kaira, and one of its members, Mavjee Govindjee, made arrangements to bring grain to the district from the Central Provinces.[2]

Although the Kaira agitation had its more conventional political facet, Gandhi also used two techniques which were to become peculiarly his own and the hallmarks of his campaigns. One was a tightly knit band of associates who formed the spearhead of his advance. In Kaira, as in Champaran, he graced these associates with the title of 'public worker'. There were precedents for perambulating philanthropists, in Tilak's earlier 'famine workers' and in the members of the Servants of India Society; but Gandhi was the first to use them consistently, because he was the first leader to make more than tentative sorties outside the citadels of the educated, and consequently to need bridging devices between the worlds of the literate and illiterate. He maintained that public workers were responsible citizens who were impartial, and more considerate of people's rights than were government officials, and he used this argument as a passport to interference in local affairs, challenging government decisions in the process, and claiming what amounted to a miniature diplomatic immunity.[3] In Kaira Mohanlal Pandya was Gandhi's main associate from

[1] Gandhi, *An Autobiography*, p. 364; Fortnightly report from Bombay, 18 February 1918, Home Pol., Deposit, March 1918, No. 40.

[2] A Report from the Commissioner of Police Bombay to the Government of Bombay (1919) Concerning Political Developments before and during 1919. South Asian Studies Centre, Cambridge, Papers of J. C. Curry. Although Gandhi drew very heavily on the support of the Indian mercantile community he was not the first or the only leader to do so. M. M. Malaviya was reported to have received about two lakhs of rupees from the Marwari community, and Tilak tapped the same source when the Bombay Marwari Association gave him Rs. 15,000 in March 1918; Weekly report of D.C.I., 20 October 1917, Proceeding No. 45 of Home Pol., B, November 1917, Nos. 43–5; Diary of G. S. Khaparde, 24 March 1918, Khaparde Papers.

[3] Before Gandhi descended on Kaira he wrote to the Commissioner on 15 February

the ranks of the local farmers. The police reported others from further afield:

> Valabhai J. Patel and Kalidas Jeskaram Vakil of Ahmedabad, Deoshankar Dave of Umreth, Raojibhai Patel of Sojitra, Haribhai J. Patel of Broach and Mahadev Desai of Surat have been active in connection with the Assessment Agitation.

Anasuya Sarabhai, sister of a prominent Ahmedabad millowner, also came up to Kaira at least once to help; and Gandhi added two Bombay newspaper and business men, Indulal Yajnik and Shankarlal Banker, to the list.[1] He gave pride of place as his deputy commander to Vallabhbhai Patel, brother of the Vithalbhai Patel who had carried the initial appeal from Kaira farmers to the government. A Patidar from Karamsad who was also an Ahmedabad lawyer and a municipal commissioner, a peasant who had reached out and plucked the fruits of western education, Vallabhbhai Patel was an ideal link-man in Gandhi's attempt to bridge the gap between the educated and the villagers, although at first Gandhi had been somewhat dubious about him.

> 'I must admit when I met him first, I could not help wondering who this stiff-looking person was and whether he would be able to do what I wanted. But the more I came to know him the more I realised that I must secure his help. If it were not for his assistance, I must admit that this campaign would not have been carried through so successfully.'[2]

Patel in turn had been sceptical about this preaching Mahatma who had inserted himself into the public life of Ahmedabad, and even dared to expound his ideals in the garden of the Ahmedabad Club to the discomfort of its members. The events of 1918 cured this scepticism and Patel became for Gujarat what Rajendra Prasad was for Bihar. In both Gandhi gained allies who helped to swing their provinces, once so 'backward', into the forefront of nationalist politics committed to the Mahatma's cause.

The second hallmark of Gandhi's campaigns was satyagraha itself. As in South Africa and Champaran he resorted to it when other methods of protest failed; but in Kaira it led neither to an independent enquiry nor to the suspension of revenue he had first demanded. The failure of satyagraha in Kaira was due to the combined hostility to his cause of the local and central governments. In this case there was no higher authority

1918, 'I shall be glad if you will instruct the Collector to give me, as a public worker, as much assistance as he can.' *C.W.*, vol. 14, p. 195. For Gandhi's theory of the 'public worker' see Gandhi to G. V. Mavlankar, 27 January 1918, *ibid.* p. 176.

1 Bombay Police Abstract, 1918, par. 315; Gandhi, *An Autobiography*, p. 363.

2 Quoted in K. L. Panjabi, *The Indomitable Sardar* (Bombay, 1964), p. 27. Patel's initial reaction to Gandhi is described in D. V. Tahmankar, *Sardar Patel* (London, 1970), pp. 15–16.

to intervene on his behalf and embarrass the local government once Delhi had decided to back Bombay. As one member of the Government of India put it, 'We should only be justified in taking action if we had reason to believe that the situation resembled in its general features those which characterized Champaran last year. I have every reason to believe that this is not the case.'[1] Although satyagraha failed in Kaira, in that it did not procure the objects for which it had been initiated, it showed its true colours as a very powerful weapon because it was so simple and so versatile. Kaira hammered home the lesson of Champaran that satyagraha could be used in virtually any situation of conflict, by literate and illiterate. It was a weapon for all seasons, and in Gandhi's hands, directed by his personal ideology, it gave him the edge over conventional politicians with their techniques of petitions, public speeches and debates, which were more suitable for the educated.

The new pattern of leadership which Gandhi developed in conjunction with the new weapon was clear in Kaira. The pattern was similar to that in Champaran, though the degree of public awareness and sophistication was markedly different in the two districts. In both Gandhi took up an issue which was comprehensible and important to peasant cultivators, basing his campaign of support in the villages, while articulating rural discontent through the better educated urban groups, who had some overt political awareness and expertise. His strength lay in being the mediator between these groups.

The Gujarat urban group of lawyers, teachers and tradesmen, though tiny by comparison with similar groups in the Presidency towns, was larger and more politically conscious than its counterpart in Bihar. The number of political bodies from which Gandhi drew support showed this. Of these the Gujarat Sabha has already been noted; so has the local Home Rule League, which collected funds and held meetings, and whose members, according to the District Magistrate, were 'busy touring about the district preaching Gandhi's advice not to pay but to suffer in patience.'[2] Gandhi also used the executive body of the First Gujarat Political Conference. Just as later he insisted that the Congress should have a full time executive to carry on Congress work throughout the year, so in Gujarat in 1917 he had made sure that the provincial conference set up a strong executive to put its resolutions into action. As a contemporary reported,

> It is well-known that Mr. Gandhi is a man of action. He does not believe in merely passing resolutions or delivering lectures. Action must follow. So, he plainly told the Conference last year after they had passed their resolutions that men must be found to devote time to the questions that were taken up by the Conference. Mr. Gandhi's insistence upon this aspect

1 Handwritten note, 9 April 1918, in file relating to Gandhi's activities in Kaira, Home Pol., Deposit, May 1918, No. 18.

2 Bombay Police Abstract, 1918, par. 380.

of the Conference was great. And as a result, much practical work has been accomplished by the executive body of the Conference. During the year information was collected on such varied subjects as the mahura flower, grazing ground in villages, and other questions respecting which the people may have to put up a tough fight...But for the Kaira Passive Resistance struggle which taxed the energies of the whole executive body of the Conference, its activities would have embraced many other questions.[1]

This tally of local associations sounds impressive, but their membership probably overlapped to a considerable extent, which meant that Gandhi was effectively drawing on a small section of politically aware who joined whatever association was going. He had, however, clearly secured an established position of local leadership by the time of the Kaira satyagraha. The educated had enlisted Gandhi because they needed the strength of his prestige as a public figure famed for social and religious work: now they found themselves swept along in his wake into waters unfamiliar and uncharted.

The base of the Kaira agitation were the two thousand and more who signed the satyagraha pledge. There is practically no evidence about individual signatories, but the wording of the vow indicates that richer farmers who could have paid were the ones who refused, the theory being that if the wealthy took a stand the poorer would not be frightened into selling goods and cattle or borrowing money to pay their revenue. Kaira's wealthiest farmers were Patidars, and it is logical to assume that it was they who were the core of the satyagraha. Certainly Gandhi thought so, writing later, 'For the Patidar farmers, too, the fight was quite a new thing.' So did officials like Pratt, who said publicly that he would 'be very sorry to see the lands of good Patidars confiscated.'[2] By working with the educated and the Patidars and mediating between them, Gandhi gave the Patidars a more sophisticated way of expressing their concerns and the urban educated the solid backing of a tough, rural elite. He introduced the former to politics of a kind, and began to educate the latter to be his 'subcontractors' in the process of reaching down through society to groups the more conventional politicians had hardly touched.

This pattern of leadership was no accident. Gandhi issued detailed instructions to his volunteers, teaching them how to preach satyagraha in the villages with courtesy, adapting themselves to village conditions as much as possible by going on foot and eating only the simplest food.[3] Nor was he unaware of the significance of his action. As he wrote later,

Dr. Besant's brilliant Home Rule agitation had certainly touched the peasants, but it was the Kheda campaign that compelled the educated

[1] *The Bombay Chronicle*, 18 November 1918.

[2] Gandhi, *An Autobiography*, p. 364; speech by F. G. Pratt, 12 April 1918, *C.W.*, vol. 14, p. 551.

[3] Gandhi's instructions to volunteers, 17 April 1918, *C.W.*, vol. 14, pp. 350–1.

public workers to establish contact with the actual life of the peasants. They learnt to identify themselves with the latter. They found their proper sphere of work, their capacity for sacrifice increased. That Vallabhbhai found himself during this campaign was by itself no small achievement. We could realize its measure during the flood relief operations last year and the Bardoli *Satyagraha* this year. Public life in Gujarat became instinct with a new energy and a new vigour. The Patidar peasant came to an unforgettable consciousness of his strength.[1]

In 1918 Gandhi was sowing the seeds: he was to reap the harvest of this new pattern of leadership later when Gujarat entered Indian politics as an area both solidly loyal to him and differing in composition and interests from the regions which had thrown up the early political elites.

Like Champaran, Kaira was also important in Gandhi's career for its effect on his public image. The Gujarat satyagraha gives us another opportunity to look at this image in some detail and to trace the elements, charismatic and otherwise, which were part of it. By this time Gandhi himself was clearly worried about his reputation. In Kaira he cautioned one of his audiences against setting him up as a *guru*. He said that he himself was in search of a *guru*, having lost Gokhale, his political *guru*, and that he could not guide others because he was 'still a child in matters of politics.'[2] We have no evidence of how the really poor and illiterate viewed Gandhi. There was no local official who described public reaction at the lowest levels of society as there was in Champaran; this is a very great gap because if Gandhi was exercising a charismatic leadership it is at such levels that we would expect to see it in action, for really lowly folk had virtually no other type of linkage with leaders from outside their village networks of power and influence. What evidence is left from the villages of Kaira is evidence about the reaction of a rural elite, the Patidars. Among them Gandhi appears to have aroused a very real personal devotion. The following spring when he was arrested on his way to the Punjab, it was villages with Patidars in them which shut up shop in mourning; and the police noted that Nadiad and Anand talukas, where the Patidars clustered most thickly, were particularly disturbed. In spite of their personal loyalty to Gandhi many ex-satyagrahis had found their faith in him strained to breaking point when he decided in the summer of 1918 to go on a recruiting drive in Gujarat.[3]

1 Gandhi, *An Autobiography*, pp. 366–7.

2 Speech by Gandhi at Kathlal village, 28 June 1918, *C.W.*, vol. 14, p. 458.

3 Bombay Police Abstract, 1918, par. 910; 1919, par. 625. It is necessary to stress that the Patidars were a rural elite as it is often assumed that Gandhi roused personal loyalty among the 'masses'. The elite nature of support for him and subsequently for Congress in Kaira was demonstrated in the 1960s when the 'masses' of Kaira, the non-Patidar castes, began to feel that Congress was Patidar-dominated, and defeated it by giving their votes to the Swatantra Party. See M. Weiner, *Party Building In A New Nation. The Indian National Congress* (Chicago & London, 1967), pp. 69–110.

Among urban, educated Indians the public reaction to Gandhi's activities in Kaira was very varied. Some papers were enthusiastic about passive resistance, like Bombay's *Gujarati*, which proclaimed that a nation whose cultivators 'are prepared to make such a stand is sure to prosper.' The police reported that many people in Bombay 'regard him as saint and approve of his method of passive resistance', while Annie Besant was becoming jealous as Gandhi's popularity increased among Bombay Home Rulers and her own waned. The activities of the Bombay Home Rule League in support of him showed that her jealousy was not misplaced. Moreover, there was a movement afoot among members of the Bombay Presidency Association to honour Gandhi publicly for his Kaira satyagraha.[1] In Ahmedabad the Kaira campaign considerably enhanced Gandhi's reputation, and people were beginning to feel that his power was virtually unlimited. Against this, however, must be set the evidence that even in Ahmedabad and Bombay, the places where he was regarded most highly by the educated, they were also torn by his aloofness from the Home Rule League and by his decision to recruit soldiers for the service of the raj.[2] Such was the impact of Kaira on the educated that its effects were felt beyond the politicians of the Bombay Presidency, and some political leaders in C.P. attempted to follow Gandhi and work up an agitation there for remission of revenue.[3]

However, from some educated Indians, even in the Bombay Presidency, Gandhi received open criticism on the Kaira issue. *Dnyan Prakash*, an Anglo-Gujarati fortnightly published in Gandhi's native Rajkot, urged that passive resistance should only be used in cases of dire need, as it involved a breach of the law; it thought that Kaira was not such a case, and that as a result of this example people might resort to it over trifling matters. *Kaiser-i-Hind*, an Anglo-Gujarati weekly published by a Bombay Parsi, professed respect for 'the great man of Gujarat' but criticized his unconstitutional behaviour and his championship of a 'band' of richer land holders rather than individuals suffering real hardship.[4] The Bombay Commissioner of Police noted:

"The Passive Resistance Movement in Kaira is causing much comment amongst educated and thoughtful Indians in Bombay, who express surprise at the latitude given to the handful of Home Rulers who have made it

1 Evidence of Gandhi's public image in Bombay comes from *Gujarati*, 7 April 1918, Bombay N.N., No. 15 of 1918, p. 13; Bombay Police Abstract, 1918, par. 619; Fortnightly report from Bombay, 16/18 June 1918, Home Pol., Deposit, August 1918, No. 30.

2 Bombay Police Abstract, 1918, par. 419, 1132 (d), (m).

3 Fortnightly report from C.P., 2 March 1918, Home Pol., Deposit, March 1918, No. 41. This is particularly interesting in the light of C.P.'s response to Gandhi in 1920. See below, pp. 226–7, 256, 270, 282–3, 292.

4 *Dnyan Prakash*, 10 April 1918, Bombay N.N., No. 15 of 1918, pp. 13–14; *Kaiser-i-Hind*, 19 May 1918, Bombay N.N., No. 20 of 1918, p. 15.

> their business to intervene in matters which do not concern them and adopt such obstructive tactics in war time...The movement is regarded by many as a direct incitement to lawlessness."

An Indian contemporary commented on the same type of feeling in the Presidency, despite the high personal esteem Gandhi enjoyed; he added that outside the Presidency many people thought the satyagraha 'most inopportune, undesirable and mischievous.'[1] Already people had begun to fear that satyagraha would lead to lawlessness, a fear which was to recur whenever Gandhi advocated it. Despite its avowed non-violence mass satyagraha, like terrorism, cut at the heart of the established political elite, with its implicit assumption that reform should come by constitutional means within a limited political arena for a limited number of people.

The more ardently constitutional men were, the fiercer was their opposition to satyagraha. The *Indian Social Reformer*, for example, condemned satyagraha as virtually seeking to overthrow a system which gave peasants greater security and freedom than ever before, and, moreover, as undermining the possibility that constitutional procedures could ever be effective. 'If the people are to be advised, whenever they think that the officials are in error, to abstain from obeying the law, all hope of improvement of an existing system by constitutional means should be abandoned.'[2] The Servants of India Society opposed Gandhi on similar grounds. Its official line was that passive resistance was a legitimate weapon only under certain conditions, and those conditions were not present in Kaira, particularly during the war and when reforms were imminent.

> The very grave war situation...renders the carrying on of a passive resistance movement at this juncture particularly inexpedient; and we make an earnest appeal to Mr. Gandhi, to whom considerations of chivalry appeal as to no other, to suspend his movement as he did in South Africa when the situation was complicated by labour strikes.[3]

It is almost unnecessary to add that Gandhi was fast expending what credit he had with the raj. The shine of the Kaiser-i-Hind Gold Medal which he had received in 1915 was tarnished by Champaran; Kaira virtually obliterated it. Even before Kaira the Bombay police were taking the precaution of watching the people who came and went at Gandhi's *ashram*; but Bombay's staunch stand over Kaira and Delhi's concurrence in this showed that government patience was wearing very thin. As one mem-

[1] Weekly reports of D.C.I., 13 & 27 April 1918, Proceedings No. 24 & 26 of Home Pol., B, May 1918, Nos. 23–6.

[2] *Indian Social Reformer*, 7 April 1918, in file relating to Gandhi's activities in Kaira, Home Pol., Deposit, May 1918, No. 18.

[3] Article by V. S. S. Satri, 'The Situation In Kaira', *The Servant of India*, 25 April 1918, S.P., file containing articles 1903–1946, No. 16. Sastri wrote this appeal thinking that Gandhi might be 'glad of some way of getting out of a tight place.' V. S. S. Sastri to S. G. Vaze, 14 March 1918, S.P., Correspondence File 1918, Letters to & from Sastri, No. 208.

ber of the Government of India put it, 'Mr. Gandhi is, this time, on a thoroughly bad wicket.'[1] Lord Willingdon, the Governor in whose province the satyagraha took place, described Gandhi even more forthrightly as 'honest, but a Bolshevik & for that reason very dangerous.'[2] When the satyagraha had run its course he minced his words even less.

> He [Gandhi] has taken a bad fall over the Kaira business. We had collected 93 per cent of the assessment, and, when he saw the game was up, he and Patel ! issued a joint manifesto to say that Government had given a concession and so the passive resistance movement might cease. We gave *no* concession and my Commissioner tells me that Gandhi's assertion that he knew nothing of our orders to the Mamlatdars in April and May is a barefaced lie.[3]

Whatever the justice of Willingdon's outburst, it was a clear indication that Kaira had pushed Gandhi further into the raj's category of political agitator, rather than harmless crank or enthusiastic philanthropist.

(III) AHMEDABAD

Satyagraha in Gujarat in 1918 was not confined to Kaira. Gandhi organized a similar campaign in Ahmedabad, which received less publicity because it was directed against Indian employers, not government officials. Ahmedabad, in contrast to Champaran and Kaira, was an urban setting. With a population of about 274,000 in 1921 it was India's eighth largest city, and the second largest in the Bombay Presidency.[4] It was a long established commercial centre and had experienced various changes of fortune through the centuries until, with the new political tranquility under the British raj, it throve on a growing cotton industry and expanding markets. Castes with old trading traditions took up the opportunities the new era offered and, building on old foundations, turned Ahmedabad into a modern, industrial city, equipped to prosper in the twentieth century. Natural fortune favoured the efforts of men, and in the later decades of the nineteenth century no epidemic or plague undermined the steady growth in the city's population.[5] The rise in population reflected the rapid industrialization of the city; so did the growing disproportion of men in the community.

[1] Handwritten note, 9 April 1918, in file relating to Gandhi's activities in Kaira, Home Pol., Deposit, May 1918, No. 18.

[2] Willingdon to Sir Harcourt Butler, 5 May 1918, I.O.L., Harcourt Butler Papers, Mss. EUR. F. 116 (53).

[3] Willingdon to Chelmsford, 11/12 June 1918, I.O.L., Willingdon Papers, Mss. EUR. F. 93 (1).

[4] In 1921 Bombay had 1,175,914 inhabitants, Ahmedabad 274,007, Karachi 216,883, Poona 214,796, Surat 117,434, and Sholapur 119,581. *Census Of India, 1921. Vol. VIII. Part I*, p. 51.

[5] Ahmedabad had 128,505 inhabitants in 1872 and the number rose steadily thereafter, *idem.* For a general description of Ahmedabad and its development see Gillion, *Ahmedabad. A Study in Indian Urban History.*

The normal ratio between the sexes for this part of Gujarat was 905 women to every 1,000 men; in 1881 Ahmedabad's ratio was 1,010 : 1,000, but by 1921 it had dropped to 765 : 1,000. At that date over fifty per cent of the city's population were engaged in industry of some kind, and of these almost one-third were supported by the cotton industry, many of them actually working in the city's forty-eight cotton weaving establishments. Even so, Ahmedabad was not as industrial as Bombay; nor was it as cosmopolitan, since it drew over seventy per cent of its inhabitants from Ahmedabad district and neighbouring Baroda State.[1]

Ahmedabad's population was divided by religion by the percentages given in Table 3.

Table 3
Population of Ahmedabad by religion in 1921

	Hindu	Muslim	Jain	Parsi	Christian	Other
Whole city	72.5	19.6	6.3	0.6	0.9	0.1
Municipality	72.5	19.6	6.4	0.6	0.8	0.1
Cantonment	70.9	19.3	0.9	0.2	8.7	–

Jains and Parsis, clustering in the commercial area, were exceptionally well-to-do. They, with some Vania families, were millowners, industrialists, financiers and traders, and held the reins of real power in the city. Other Hindu castes held a middle place in the prosperity ladder, while the city Christians, compared with their co-religionists in the cantonment who were mostly Europeans, came right at the bottom. Muslims, with the exception of those who went into the army and the Bohora traders, were losing out in the new era. Those who had been government officials lost their posts when the British came to power, and the community as a whole had no trading or business traditions on which to build a new prosperity in an industrial age. By the beginning of the twentieth century there were no Muslim millowners, only one Muslim industrialist, while the majority of the community were weavers.[2]

Of the indigenous religions Jains were by far the best educated community, and Muslims the worst. Whereas 47.1% of school age boys of all religions were actually at school, with 13.1% of school age girls, only 25.9% of Muslim children of school age were being educated.[3] Educationally

1 *Census Of India, 1921. Volume IX. Cities Of The Bombay Presidency. Part I. Report* (Poona, 1922), pp. 65, 68; *Census Of India, 1921. Volume IX. Cities Of The Bombay Presidency. Part II. Tables* (Bombay, 1922), p. ccxlviii.

2 *Census of India, 1921. Vol. IX. Part I*, p. 64 and Part B, p. xxii; Gillion, *op. cit.* pp. 54–6, 60, 85–90. The figure for Muslims in the Cantonment is given as 29.3 in the Census at the place cited, but is clearly a misprint for 19.3 when checked against the actual figures for population given in the companion volume of tables.

3 *Gazetteer Of The Bombay Presidency. Volume IV-B. Ahmedabad* (Bombay, 1913), p. 25; table of literacy by community, *Census Of India, 1921. Vol. IX. Part I*, p. 64.

Ahmedabad city beat Ahmedabad district easily, having 24.2% of its population literate, compared with 10.3% in the district: but opportunities for education were always better in Indian towns. There are no separate figures for schools in the city as opposed to the district, but taking the two together there were in 1910–11 494 educational institutions, educating 36,523 pupils: these institutions included one arts college and seven high schools aided by government. Clearly Ahmedabad shared the Gujarat pattern of good primary education, developing secondary education, but few local facilities for study at college level, even though it was the capital of the area.[1]

As the city's population was more literate than that of the rural districts, so its interest was stronger in some of the broader issues at stake in the public life of the Bombay Presidency. By 1918 Ahmedabad was much more alive politically than the country areas of Gujarat, and the initial conservatism of its few western educated men was gradually being eroded. A branch of the Home Rule League was active there from 1916, its founder members being two local barristers, Maganbhai Chaturbhai Patel and Jivanlal Varajrai Desai. These two men were obvious leaders of local political activity, Patel taking most of the limelight (we have already seen his connection with the Kaira satyagraha), but Desai doing most of the organization.

The city had been host to a provincial conference late in 1916, and afterwards the local politicians made a deliberate attempt to broaden their political circle, particularly by trying to persuade members of the business community to join them. Sheth Mangaldas Girdhardas, a prominent millowner, after being made chairman of the reception committee of the conference, was invited to take office in the Gujarat Sabha. Special invitations were sent to traders to attend a meeting of the Home Rule League, which had so far only gained support from Brahma-Kshatriyas. Moreover, the Gujarat Sabha made sure that it elected nearly all the prominent millowners, and even the wives of some, as Ahmedabad delegates to the Congress. Many of these millowner delegates had not angled for election, and had neither wish to attend Congress nor any intention of doing so.[2]

Whatever inducements the barristers and students might hold out, millowners and other commercial people were not easily tempted out of their shells when war conditions favoured them by raising prices and stimulating business; and the rest of the population were tolerant of the politicians rather than enthusiastic. The Collector of Ahmedabad described the situation as he saw it:

"As regards political ideas and ambitions, a few are found in the larger

[1] *Census Of India, 1921. Vol. VIII. Part I*, p. 140; *Ahmedabad Gazetteer. Vol. IV-B*, p. 25.

[2] Gillion, *op. cit.* pp. 163–4; Bombay Police Abstract, 1917, par. 132.

towns who are interested in Home Rule; but...they are mostly to be found in Ahmedabad. Here the active Home Rulers are not very numerous but make a considerable show. The bulk of the population are well disposed towards them but inclined to take things very much as they find them. In fact, the population of the City as of the district is timid, easy going and inert. The Home Rulers at their meetings adopt a fairly moderate tone. At the same time there is a spirit of unrest and uncertainty about the future which manifests itself in many different ways now by insistence on cash payments or discounting of Government notes, now by strikes and undisciplined behaviour amongst employees."[1]

This indicates that there were strains and stresses in the public life of Ahmedabad. As in Champaran and Kaira, it was economic strain in particular which produced a situation where Gandhi could use satyagraha and build up an even firmer base for himself in Gujarat. The war was a boon to Ahmedabad. European countries at war produced fewer consumer goods for export as they diverted their resources and shipping to the war effort, and Indian industrialists seized their opportunity, trying to compensate for the decline of imports into India by stepping into the breach with Indian goods. Cloth producers even opened up new foreign markets for themselves in Mesopotamia, Iraq, Persia, Asiatic Turkey, the Straits Settlements, Aden, Africa, Ceylon, Japan and China. The Ahmedabad textile industry was geared rather more to a local market, and, freed from Lancashire's competition, it extended its grip at home, to such an extent that its cloth production rose from 250 million yards in 1913–14 to 392 million yards in 1916–17, though dropping to 332 million yards in 1918–19.[2]

Millowners could only make the most of their new opportunities if there was sufficient labour to work their mills; and as labour was scarce in Gujarat they had to pay high wages to attract enough millhands. Late in 1917 plague made the labour shortage more acute because it drove workers out of the cities back to the villages in the hope of avoiding infection. To keep them at work millowners paid a plague bonus which was sometimes as high as 75% of their normal pay, and helped to offset the war-time rise in the cost of living which affected Ahmedabad as much as Kaira.[3]

The mills were in dire danger of industrial unrest if anything should break this equilibrium of good profits and good wages. The crack came when the millowners announced at the end of January 1918 that as the

[1] Report by Collector of Ahmedabad quoted in *1917–18 Bombay Land Revenue Administration Report, Part 2*, p. 17.

[2] Gillion, *op. cit.* pp. 153–4; R. J. Soman, *Peaceful Industrial Relations. Their Science And Technique* (Ahmedabad, 1957), pp. 209–10.

[3] *1917–18 Bombay Land Revenue Administration Report, Part 2*, p. 14; Fortnightly report from Bombay, 1 March 1918, Home Pol., Deposit, March 1918, No. 41. For the all-India price index and for the prices of food in the Ahmedabad area of Gujarat, see above, pp. 60, 94.

plague was over they intended to stop the bonus from 15 February.[1] Workers throughout the Presidency were feeling the pinch of continually rising prices, and there were rumblings of discontent among millhands, even in places like Sholapur where there was not the added irritant of the cancelled plague bonus.[2] However, the Ahmedabad millowners were prepared to fly in the face of discontent and risk their labour supply, because at the turn of the year they found themselves embarrassingly short of coal to power their mills. Fuel was a constant worry to them as the only local source was wood, and from the beginning of this century nearly all the Ahmedabad mills had turned over to coal, which had to be brought by rail either from the port where it had been imported, or from Bengal and Central India. War-time restrictions on railway traffic consequently hit them very hard, their effect really being felt by the beginning of 1918, when it was predicted that 100 collieries would stop supply from 1 January because of waggon shortages. The Ahmedabad District Magistrate commented wryly during the lock-out of workers which followed the withdrawal of the plague bonus, 'the shortage of coal makes it very convenient to close down the mill just at present.'[3]

The first indication that Gandhi was interested in the Ahmedabad mills was a letter he wrote while he was in Champaran to Ambalal Sarabhai. Sarabhai was a prominent Ahmedabad millowner and personal friend of Gandhi: he had in fact saved Gandhi's *ashram* when it was in financial difficulties in its early days by an 'anonymous' gift of Rs. 13,000. His sister, Anasuya, visited Kaira during Gandhi's satyagraha there, and even before Gandhi took up the cause of the millworkers she had taken an interest in them and started a night school for them. Gandhi was moved to write the letter to Sarabhai by information he had received about the workers' conditions from one of the secretaries of the Gujarat Sabha. He asked Sarabhai to give his workers higher wages because they needed them, and also for the sake of his sister, who would be hurt if their conditions were not improved. After this written request he met Sarabhai in person in Bombay on 2 February 1918, and as a result of their discussion decided to intervene in the dispute.[4]

The question at issue was the plague bonus, which the millowners had decided to stop on 15 February. Their employees demanded a rise of 50% in their wages, because the bonus would no longer cushion them from high prices; but the owners would only give 20%. Neither side was organized for conflict. The Millowners' Association was at sixes and sevens internally,

[1] Fortnightly report from Bombay, 1 March 1918, Home Pol., Deposit, March 1918, No. 41.

[2] *1917–18 Bombay Land Revenue Administration Report, Part 2*, p. 8.

[3] Bombay Police Abstract, 1918, par. 293; article entitled 'Coal Famine', *The Bombay Chronicle*, 1 January 1918.

[4] Gandhi to Ambalal Sarabhai, 21 December 1917, *C.W.*, vol. 14, p. 115; M. H. Desai, *A Righteous Struggle* (Ahmedabad, 1951), p. 4.

and the millworkers had no definite leaders, though they tended to look to Gandhi for guidance. Despite the protests of some of the workers that Gandhi could do little for them, he was invited to preside at a meeting on 8 February which about 3,000 of them attended. At this meeting Gandhi appealed to the men to search for a solution which would not create bitterness between the opposing parties. He suggested that they should write to the owners about their grievances, but not demand an immediate wage increase of 50–60%, and that if their appeal failed they should resort to arbitration.[1]

At first some millowners refused to treat with Gandhi, considering him to be an interloper in mill affairs; but when they realized that he was the only possible person with whom to parley as the workers' representative they agreed to refer the matter to a board of arbitration under the chairmanship of the Collector of Ahmedabad. This board was set up on 14 February, with Gandhi, Shankarlal Banker and Vallabhbhai Patel representing the workers, and Ambalal Sarabhai, Jagabhai Dalpatbhai and Chandulal representing the owners.[2] But arbitration did not work. Gandhi could not control all the workers, some of whom struck in mill after mill; and a group of owners, deciding on a common policy, locked out the weavers, offering, however, to support those who accepted their terms. They withdrew from arbitration on the grounds that Gandhi had no real authority or mandate from the weavers and that there was no guarantee that weavers would accept an arbitration award, even though Gandhi pleaded with them to cooperate lest their employees should lose faith in the principle of arbitration.[3] The owners held to their decision, and the lock-out began on 22 February.

Thereafter a curious situation developed: only weavers, a small minority of the millhands, were locked out and the owners still paid them part wages on 'some very fluctuating and loosely defined conditions.'[4] Gandhi, having studied as best he could the financial state of the mills and compared their wage rates with those in Bombay, advised the weavers that a 35% increase on their July wages was justified, and henceforth they took their stand on a demand for a 35% instead of a 50% increase.

As in Kaira, so in Ahmedabad, Gandhi prepared a pledge for the

[1] Fortnightly report from Bombay, 1 March 1918, Home Pol., Deposit, March 1918, No. 41; Bombay Police Abstract, 1918, par. 235; speech by Gandhi on 8 February 1918, *Gujarati*, 17 February 1918, *C.W.*, vol. 14, pp. 185–6.

[2] Fortnightly report from Bombay, 1 March 1918, Home Pol., Deposit, March 1918, No. 41; Desai, *A Righteous Struggle*, p. 38.

[3] Report by the District Magistrate quoted in Bombay Police Abstract, 1918, par. 293; Gandhi to Gordhandas Patel, Secretary of the Millowners' Association, 21 February 1918, *C.W.*, vol. 14, pp. 211–12.

[4] Bombay Police Abstract, 1918, par. 293. Many of the weavers were Muslims and this seems to be another occasion when Gandhi quite fortuitously found himself in the role of a Muslim leader. No contemporary seems to have commented on this.

satyagrahis, the Ahmedabad pledge stating that they would not resume work without a 35% increase and that they would remain law-abiding during the lock-out. This was the anchor of the satyagraha, but its strength depended on the daily mass meetings Gandhi began to hold for the weavers, at which he gave a daily discourse and issued a series of leaflets on the situation. There were seventeen of these leaflets, published between 26 February and 19 March; one was written by Shankarlal Banker and the rest by Gandhi, though they were issued in Anasuya Sarabhai's name. Their purpose was the same as that of *Indian Opinion* in South Africa, to educate the satyagrahis in the principles of satyagraha and to give them instructions on how to act in the specific satyagraha in hand. Gandhi incidentally used these leaflets to expound his ideal of industrial relations.[1]

While he concentrated on consolidation as far as the weavers were concerned, he also appealed to the employers. He reasoned with Sarabhai that a victory for the millowners would have dire consequences for society as it would increase 'the arrogance of money'.

> If you succeed, the poor, already suppressed, will be suppressed still more, will be more abject than ever and the impression will have been confirmed that money can subdue everyone. If, despite your efforts, the workers succeed in securing the increase, you, and others with you, will regard the result as your failure...Do you not see that in your failure lies your success, that your success is fraught with danger for you?...Do you not see that your success will have serious consequences for the whole society?[2]

His pleas fell on deaf ears and on 12 March the lock-out ended when the millowners announced they would take back those who accepted a 20% increase. As a result the weavers' refusal to work became a genuine strike. Gandhi continued to hold daily mass meetings, but now he moved the time from the evening to the morning, just when the mills opened, to stiffen the resolve of the strikers. Those present repeated the satyagraha pledge before him each day, and he went on issuing leaflets, urging the men to keep the pledge taken at the beginning of the lock-out.

> The workers have considered all things before taking the pledge and now they cannot resume work without securing a 35 per cent increase, whatever may be the temptation or the misery they may have to encounter. Herein lies their honesty. If you weigh a pledge against *lakhs* of rupees, the weight of the pledge will be greater. We are sure that the workers will never forget this.[3]

The moral pressure of such statements on potential blacklegs and the force of the dramatic public gatherings worried the owners, and Sarabhai

[1] Text of workers' pledge, Desai, *A Righteous Struggle*, p. 39; text of leaflets, *ibid.* pp. 38–70.

[2] Gandhi to Ambalal Sarabhai, 1 March 1918, *C.W.*, vol. 14, pp. 229–30.

[3] Leaflet No. 12, Desai, *A Righteous Struggle*, p. 57.

appears to have challenged Gandhi with this. In reply Gandhi assured him that he would not countenance any pressure being put on weavers who wanted to work, even promising to escort to the mill any such. By 'pressure' he presumably meant physical force, because he did picket the mills to 'dissuade' those who were beginning to return to work.[1]

Relations with the millowners reached a crisis on 15 March, when Gandhi announced his intention of fasting until a settlement was reached or all the workers left the mills. Various interpretations exist of the reasoning behind his decision. Later Gandhi himself said that his motive was to rally the strikers who seemed to be giving in despite their pledge. His leaflet issued during the fast announced that he was showing how greatly he valued the pledge and was prepared to undergo suffering similar to that which strikers might have to endure in keeping their pledge; it denied that the fast was intended to put pressure on the millowners.[2] Attendance at his meetings was dwindling and workers were drifting back to the mills, and in view of this the police dismissed the fast as 'merely a typical theatrical finale when he knew a settlement was inevitable.'[3] The District Magistrate, however, after a conversation with Sarabhai on 4 April, concluded that criticism by the workers was at the back of Gandhi's fast.

> "The weavers assailed him bitterly for being a friend of the millowners, riding in their motor cars and eating sumptuously with them, while the weavers were starving. It was at this point and when stung by these taunts that Gandhi took his vow that he would eat no food until the weavers' terms were granted by the millowners."[4]

The Magistrate's impression, taken with Gandhi's own accounts, probably gives a fair picture of his state of mind at the time.

Whatever Gandhi's motives, the fast created a tremendous flurry in Ahmedabad. Frightened that Gujarat's most popular public figure would fast to death, the millowners agreed to negotiate and a solution was reached on 18 March. On their first day back at work, 20 March, the weavers would receive a 35% increase, in keeping with their pledge. On the second day they would receive the 20% offered by the millowners. From the third day until the date of an award by an arbitrator they would split the difference and receive a $27\frac{1}{2}$% increase. The arbitrator selected was Professor Dhruva, Vice-Principal of Gujarat College, Ahmedabad; and on 10 August he awarded a 35% increase in wages, commenting that in the majority of

[1] Bombay Police Abstract, 1918, par. 423; Gandhi to Ambalal Sarabhai, 12 March 1918, *C.W., vol.* 14, p. 250. (Gandhi destroyed this letter, not wanting a copy to remain, but he gave Mahadev Desai permission to record the substance of it, and it is this summary which is quoted in *C.W.*)

[2] Gandhi, *An Autobiography*, p. 359; Leaflet No. 15, Desai, *A Righteous Struggle*, pp. 62–4.

[3] Bombay Police Abstract, 1918, par. 386.

[4] Report by the District Magistrate quoted in *ibid.* par. 423.

mills this was already being given, and in some cases as much as a 50% increase.[1] Although the settlement saved face for both parties Gandhi was dissatisfied because his fast had put pressure on the millowners, contrary to the principles of satyagraha. As he said to people in his *ashram*, 'My weak condition left the mill-owners no freedom. It is against the principles of justice to get anything in writing from a person or make him agree to any conditions or obtain anything whatever under duress. A satyagrahi will never do so.'[2]

The Ahmedabad satyagraha was the first occasion when Gandhi participated in a purely industrial dispute; in 1913 he had called miners out on strike in South Africa, but that was for political reasons. Now in Ahmedabad the idealist of *Hind Swaraj* who condemned industrial civilization faced the realities of Indian industrialization, and had to adopt a practical attitude to industrial relations. Gandhi told the secretary to the Ahmedabad Millowners' Association that he could never think of harming the city's industry, and that he did not champion workers as workers, but justice, on whichever side it might be. He believed that Indian capital and labour were interdependent and that their relationship should be one of mutual regard, employers and employed united with 'the silken thread of love.'[3] This ideal was somewhat utopian. In practice Gandhi advocated strong trade unions, and helped to found the Ahmedabad Textile Labour Association in 1920. He insisted that the purpose of unions was to protect workers, not to coerce employers, and he urged that strikes should take place only with union consent and after attempts at negotiation and arbitration had failed.[4]

This industrial satyagraha was not a backwater in Gandhi's experience as a leader, merely contributing to his theory of industrial relations. Despite the parochial nature of the dispute and the fact that it did not involve conflict with the government, it was highly significant in Gandhi's political development. In the realm of political technique this was Gandhi's first fast intended to influence public events, and was the forerunner of his hunger-strikes in all-India politics. Within his theory of satyagraha as a means of resolving conflict there was a place for fasting, as part of the self-purification and suffering which were intended to win over the opponent. Inevitably fasting by such a public figure brought to bear pressure of the kind he himself decried in 1918; and the arguments which raged around his decision to fast in Ahmedabad were repeated more bitterly in wider circles

[1] Gandhi's speech announcing settlement to millhands, Desai, *A Righteous Struggle*, pp. 33–4; text of arbitrator's decision, 10 August 1918, *ibid.* pp. 90–1.

[2] Speech by Gandhi, 18 March 1918, *C.W.*, vol. 14, pp. 265–6 (this quotation is in italics in the text).

[3] Gandhi to Ambalal Sarabhai, 21 December 1917, *C.W.*, vol. 14, p. 115; Gandhi to Gordhandas Patel, 21 February 1918, *ibid.* p. 211.

[4] *Navajivan*, 8 & 29 February 1920, *C.W.*, vol. 17, pp. 19, 49.

when he used the fast in larger arenas, as at the time of the Communal Award in 1932.

In the wider pattern of leadership the weavers' grievances gave Gandhi the opportunity to organize industrial workers, and to build up both an urban and a rural base in Gujarat. As Kaira drew Gandhi into the villages and fields of Gujarat, so Ahmedabad drew him into the towns and factories, distinguishing him even more clearly from the older political leaders in the scope of his interests and the character of his following. Evidence about the real attitude of the factory workers to Gandhi is sparse. We know from contemporary accounts that thousands flocked to his meetings, but that when hardship bit deep they trailed away in search of employment, rather like those Kaira Patidars who morosely left recruiting meetings organized by their former hero. Although satyagraha flagged, Gandhi's popularity in Ahmedabad was not ephemeral. A year later news of his detention led to mob violence in the city, to killings and the burning of jail, telegraph office and Collector's offices: this demonstrated something of Gandhi's popularity among the mass of the city's population, though not the permeation of his doctrine of non-violence.

As significant as factory level support, and partly dependent on it, was Gandhi's hold over the business community in Ahmedabad. Economic pressures worked to throw employees against Indian employers, a situation like that which might have arisen in Bihar had Gandhi included the Indian zamindars in the scope of his investigations. In spite of the potential embarrassment of such a situation it was resolved in a way that was most advantageous for Gandhi's own standing. Bluntly put, Gandhi acquired the support of the millowners because he held the loyalty of the workers who were the key to their prosperity. During the satyagraha the owners had been afraid of Gandhi and hoped to break his power;[1] but having failed to beat him they joined him, though some hesitation still remained about the wisdom of his activities. Their alliance had a solid foundation of mutual convenience, but it was undoubtedly strengthened by the more gracious ties of personal friendship, a common loyalty to Gujarat and a common concern for Ahmedabad's prosperity.[2] The city's politicians had angled for such an alliance with the businessmen. When Gandhi succeeded where they failed they had even more reason for giving him their loyalty, since he freed them from the possibility of a clash between the interests of the local commercial and professional elites. Before 1918 Gandhi had been a popular preacher and humanitarian in Gujarat, with only a footing in local politics. By mid-May, when the Ahmedabad satyagraha drove home the implications of the Kaira campaign, Gandhi was the most powerful leader

1 Report by the District Magistrate quoted in Bombay Police Abstract, 1918, par. 293.

2 For the alliance between Gandhi and the Ahmedabad industrialists see Gillion, *op. cit.* pp. 158–9, 169–71.

in the region's public life, though he had attained that position by activities outside the normal scope of nationalist politicians.

Detailed investigation of satyagraha in Champaran, Kaira and Ahmedabad brings to light a clear, almost day-to-day picture of Gandhi at work after the end of his silent observation of Indian public life. He stands out as a figure quite distinct from the established political leaders. Before 1917 that distinction had been one of ideology, reinforced by voluntary isolation from the political scene; now Gandhi's actions in public as well as his beliefs set him apart. He worked in two regions notoriously backward according to the standards of the political leaders, and attracted large followings precisely because he took up issues which were outside their range of interests, and provided his adherents with a technique of action appropriate to their needs but which the politicians feared to use. Though much has been made of Gandhi's charismatic appeal, it becomes clear that in Gujarat and Bihar his public image was no simple or single one. He appealed to different groups for different reasons and in different ways, and the pattern of his leadership was far more complicated than the manipulation of an adulatory audience. In certain areas where he was personally known, his appeal to the lowest groups in society was temporarily charismatic, as he became virtually a local messiah; but for his real work he relied on small groups of influential local men whom he educated to be his 'subcontractors' in rallying support and organizing his campaigns. Such men followed him for a variety of reasons – personal attraction, religious conviction, the prospect of economic gain or increased local prestige, or for lack of anyone else.

Like any other leader Gandhi had to gain access to local networks of power and loyalty, to create such networks for himself, or to manage a combination of the two. In Bihar and Gujarat he succeeded because he campaigned on specific local issues which had obvious bearing on the fortunes of local men. This loyalty had not yet been exposed to the strains which would be involved if Gandhi began to consider wider issues in public life and took to less local forms of public action: whether it would stand firm only time would tell. Nor was it at all certain whether this pattern of leadership could be repeated in regions where Gandhi had not taken up local issues, thereby inserting himself into local public life. Whatever the doubts about his future, by mid-1918 he had manifestly established strong local positions for himself in Gujarat, and outside his home region in Bihar; these were potential power bases if he chose to spring from local action there to a wider range of public activity.

These local satyagrahas also indicate some reasons for backwardness in institutional politics and hint at some of the pressures which pushed backward areas at least to the verge of such politics. Where there was little western education there was little incentive for local men to participate in the politics of Congress: landed or commercial groups rather than western educated men held the reins of local power, and tended to find other ways more effective for buttressing or extending their positions. However, external pressure could alter local power structures, throwing up newly influential groups or impinging so acutely on existing groups that local men found it attractive to follow a leader who made possible for them new forms of public action. In 1917 and 1918 Bihar and Gujarat were both experiencing such pressures, and Gandhi's ideology and experience were at hand to channel the aspirations and fears of those who felt the pinch of change. The differences between Champaran, Kaira and Ahmedabad are a warning not to expect any one pressure for change. Just as local power structures varied so did local strains and stresses; and in other backward areas these might produce people who would not find in Gandhi a leader who could represent their interests, nor even in institutional politics an arena where they could forward those interests. By mid-1918 Gandhi was walking on the verges of institutional politics, still isolated from the politicians, though widely known as a powerful and original leader of men. It was not yet clear whether he would make a sortie into their world, or whether he would be content with his role as preacher and humanitarian righter of wrongs.

CHAPTER 4

GANDHI, THE POLITICIANS AND THE RAJ, 1917–18

The First World War transformed Gandhi into a political leader in his native land. If India had not felt the repercussions of the European conflict it is possible that Gandhi would have remained a public worker in the small world of the district and the market town, only occasionally participating in the activities of the political nation. But the war was a watershed in Gandhi's own career and in Indian politics.

Change in society was the driving force behind developments in Indian politics, and the trigger of diverse stirrings at less articulate levels of public life; therefore it is not surprising that the war years saw a rapid upsurge in political activity in India. The war acted directly as an agent of change by its economic impact on the subcontinent. It forced up prices, caused economic dislocation and precipitated government controls on trade and prices, thereby creating a situation where people outside the political nation felt the pinch of hardship and the hand of the raj, and became in consequence more willing to participate in new forms of public activity to protect themselves in the changing environment. Indirectly the war caused deeper changes in society by its pressure on the raj. The British, attacked in Europe, needed to secure India as the back door of their empire and a major source of troops. To do so they planned a further devolution of power to contain growing public discontent and to attract collaborators who would form a stable foundation for their rule, thus consciously altering the locus of power in society and initiating political change.

This was the situation in which Gandhi felt forced into public action; but he was no politician in the ordinary sense of the word. He seems to have had no clear plan for a career or ambition for power, but to have visualized himself as a religious devotee and a public worker, whose duty it was to forward his ideal of Swaraj wherever possible and to right obvious wrongs wherever such came to light. So far he had only been able to pursue his ideal of Swaraj in his *ashram* and through the constructive work of his assistants in Champaran; while the 'wrongs' he had discovered were local ones, felt more sharply because of the economic effects of the war. The incentive to work on a larger scale, and so to come face to face with the politicians and the raj in the political arena, only came when 'wrongs' occurred which were not confined to a particular locality and yet appeared to be within his compass, or when opportunity offered to spread his vision of true Swaraj before a wider audience. This incentive was provided by the relationship between the raj at war and the members of the political nation.

(I) WAR: THE RAJ AND THE POLITICAL NATION

All governments, imperial or otherwise, have to work a judicious combination of conciliation and assertion of power. In India in the nineteenth century the British olive branch of conciliation and the search for Indian collaborators had tempered the early idealism of government sponsored social reform, made the native states 'breakwaters in the storm' after the Mutiny, and turned the conservative landholders into welcome bulwarks of British dominion. In the twentieth century the same search led the British down the paths of constitutional reform in the hope of rallying to their side the western educated, now that such men were as much a power in the land as the great landholders and princes had been in the previous century. Having helped to alter the locus of power in society, the British reluctantly had to employ new mechanisms for attracting allies from among the newly powerful and containing their discontents. The Morley–Minto Reforms of 1909 were a step in this direction; but as it became increasingly clear that no reform the rulers were prepared to grant could satisfy all the politicians, the British worked on the theory that they must at any rate 'rally the Moderates'. The labels 'Moderate' and 'Extremist' which were bandied about after the split among the politicians at Surat confused the issue. The politicians the British wooed with reform were not just those who were labelled 'Moderate' at the time, but all those who would cooperate in planned constitutional advance and not countenance or resort to violent political techniques. When in 1916 the question of announcing the goal of British policy came up the Secretary of State, Austen Chamberlain, saw it as a plank to be thrown to the Moderates, while Sir James Meston wrote:

> The vital question for us is, will the Moderates rally to the side of Government and show some political courage and power of resistance, if Government does disclose a policy which can be weighed, article for article, against the manifestos of the Extremists?[1]

Under the pressure of war British policy evolved rapidly to keep pace with the demands of their intended collaborators. Whereas before 1914 the Viceroy, Lord Hardinge, had dismissed as 'ridiculous and absurd' the idea that India might evolve towards some form of colonial self-government, by 1915 he was saying, 'India after the war will be a very complex question... The old regime *must* be changed, and the people must have more to say to their own administration.'[2] Chelmsford succeeded Hardinge in April 1916

[1] Sir James Meston to Chelmsford, 11 January 1917, Mss. EUR. E. 264 (18); Austen Chamberlain to Chelmsford, 27 November 1916, Mss. EUR. E. 264 (2).

[2] Hardinge to Sir Walter Lawrence, 29 July 1915, Hardinge Mss. (94); for his

and almost immediately the idea was mooted that there should be a declaration of the goal of British policy towards India. In fact the British had their backs to the wall. On the home front in India they were caught in a spiral of rising prices (see Table 4) which was a recognized danger signal for discontent and disorder: simultaneously they were faced with the uniting of the politicians of both major communities in the demand for constitutional reform, and the emergence of the Home Rule Leagues whose avowed aim was to spread the political virus as wide as possible. Abroad the capture of Kut by the Turks in April 1916 discredited the management of the Mesopotamia campaign and led to the resignation of the Secretary of State for India, while the horrors of the Somme made it clear that no quick victory lay ahead. To hold their Indian dominion under such internal and external pressure they had only a drastically depleted establishment of British troops;[1] and some new policy departure was urgently needed to ensure the stability of India.

Table 4

Prices in India, 1913–1923

1913	143	1919	276
1914	147	1920	281
1915	152	1921	236
1916	184	1922	232
1917	196	1923	215
1918	225		

1873 = 100

Source: Statistical Abstract For British India 1917–18 to 1926–27, p. 628, table no. 297.

Discussions with provincial governors and in the Viceroy's Council eventually produced a despatch in November 1916, which argued that in recognition of India's services during the war an announcement should be made about the goal of British policy and steps taken towards that goal.[2] This despatch was subjected to lengthy consideration by an India Office Committee and then by the Cabinet, although the scheme only came to fruition after Austen Chamberlain had been succeeded as Secretary of State for India by E. S. Montagu. Montagu, known to be liberal on Indian

earlier attitude, see Hardinge to Lord Sanderson, 25 July 1912, Hardinge Mss. (92).

1 At one time the garrison of British soldiers in India was only 15,000. E. Thompson and G. T. Garratt, *Rise And Fulfilment Of British Rule In India* (London, 1935), p. 600. Even in 1914 Hardinge spoke of the very considerable risks he was running 'in denuding India of troops', and described the British position in India as 'a bit of a gamble'. Hardinge to Sir Valentine Chirol, 19 November 1914, Hardinge Mss. (93).

2 Despatch to His Majesty's Secretary of State for India, no. 17, 24 November 1916, Home Pol., A, December 1916, No. 358.

affairs, took over where Chamberlain had been forced to leave off, and on 14 August extracted a decision from the Cabinet. On 20 August he announced in Parliament that the goal of British policy was 'increasing association of Indians in every branch of the administration, and the gradual development of self-governing institutions, with a view to the progressive realisation of responsible government in India as an integral part of the British Empire.'[1] There was criticism of this in England from conservatives who opposed any relaxation of imperial control over India; but among the ranks of the rulers in India only the Government of Madras felt that the search for Indian allies had gone too far. In a fruitless plea to Montagu it condemned the announcement 'unanimously and in strongest terms...as most inopportune and unwise'.[2]

Montagu toured India in the cold weather after his declaration, and the following July he and Chelmsford published their report on the precise form they thought the reforms should take to implement the declaration. They intended the declaration to be the beginning of a new epoch and they planned to found India's government 'on the co-operation of her people, and make such changes in the existing order as will meet the needs of the more spacious days to come.'[3] For the next eighteen months their proposals were discussed in Parliament and considered by a Franchise and Functions Committee which toured India. What emerged at the end of 1919 was an act enlarging the legislative councils at the centre and in the provinces and freeing them from the restraining hand of an official majority, though the Viceroy and Governors kept reserve powers for emergency use if deadlock should occur between the legislative and executive branches of government. There was to be no radical change in the central administration, but in the provinces a system known as dyarchy was introduced, giving control of 'transferred' subjects to ministers responsible to their electorate, while 'reserved' subjects were dealt with directly by the Governor and his council. The provinces were freed from some central control in that they received some sources of revenue solely for their use, while certain topics came completely under their legislative control. The franchise was thoroughly overhauled and enlarged, and special and general constituencies were created, continuing the principle of communal representation set out in the Morley–Minto Reforms of 1909.

1 Announcement by the Secretary of State for India, 20 August 1917, *The Parliamentary Debates, 5th Series, Volume 97, House of Commons*, cols. 1695–6. For detailed accounts of the events leading up to the announcement and the way the announcement was finally worded see S. R. Mehrotra, 'The Politics Behind The Montagu Declaration Of 1917', C. H. Philips (ed.), *Politics And Society In India* (London, 1963), pp. 71–96; R. Danzig, 'The Announcement of August 20th, 1917', *The Journal Of Asian Studies*, XXVIII, 1 (November 1968), 19–37.

2 Governor of Madras to Secretary of State for India, telegram, 19 August 1917, quoted in E. S. Montagu to Chelmsford, 24 August 1917, Mss. EUR. E. 264 (3).

3 *Report On Indian Constitutional Reforms* (London, 1918), Cd. 9109, p. 4.

While the reforms were under consideration Montagu and Chelmsford became disillusioned by the effects their announcement produced on Indian public life. Where they looked for collaborators they found a motley crew of suppliants. *Jagrak*, a non-Brahmin paper from Poona, had anticipated this with some satisfaction.

> It welcomed the announcement of Mr. Montagu's visit to India as it believed that it would enable him to see for himself how sharply divided the several classes in India are and that he would also find that the class which is foremost in political agitation and will benefit most by the reforms is numerically very small and that its interests clash with those of the majority.[1]

Together Chelmsford and Montagu visited Delhi, Calcutta and Madras before writing their report, and at each place they were besieged by petitioners. The diverse elements in Indian public life saw that there was to be a redivision of the spoils of administration, and an extension of Indian power via legislation over a wider range of matters, and they rushed to stake their claims. Some had interests to safeguard, others merely wanted public recognition that they ought to be heard in public life, using Montagu in politics as aspiring castes used the census to legitimize social claims. Montagu's tour demonstrated not so much the support which the raj could enjoy but the deep divisions in public life which became apparent whenever there were hints of change in the balance of power in India.

Some of Montagu's petitioners represented religious bodies. In Delhi he received, to name only a few, the Punjab Hindu Sabha and five U.P. Muslim deputations, including the provincial branch of the Muslim League and a deputation of maulvis, all requesting their own variant of communal representation in the enlarged councils.[2] In Madras similar petitions came from League and non-League Muslims, while local ulema said bluntly that they did not want Home Rule. In every province where they were a minority community Hindus and Muslims began to wonder if the Lucknow Pact was sufficient protection for them, and they took the opportunity of Montagu's visit to state their fears and claims more explicitly. The divisiveness of reform was brought home to Montagu particularly in Calcutta where even Indian Christians asked for communal representation, though they had a high standard of literacy and were well able to take care of themselves under the new dispensation. In Calcutta the Jains, too, met and demanded special representation in the new legislative councils, as they were an 'important minority'.[3]

1 Fortnightly report from Bombay for first half of September 1917, Home Pol., Deposit, November 1917, No. 6.

2 For these and other petitioners see Montagu, *An Indian Diary; Addresses Presented In India To His Excellency The Viceroy And The Right Honourable The Secretary Of State For India* (London, 1918), Cd. 9178.

3 Secretary of Jain Provincial Conference, Calcutta, to Annie Besant, President of Congress, 28 December 1917, A.I.C.C. Files, 1917, No. 1.

Economic groups also presented memorials to Montagu. Among them were large landholders who feared that constitutional reforms with even a faint democratic tinge would undermine their power, and European business firms which had similar apprehensions. All hoped to gain from Montagu a promise of some bulwark in an era of change; in Montagu's own words, one group, the Zemindars of Agra and Talukdars of Oudh, 'frankly put before us, with unblushing effrontery, a desire for land-lord Raj.'[1] Of the social groups who memorialized Montagu the bitterest were those motivated by caste rivalry, among them the Madras non-Brahmins, the Deccan ryots and the Depressed Classes of Bombay, all clamouring for separate representation because they feared that reform would merely give more power to Brahmins, who were better educated and better equipped to take advantage of any devolution of power to Indian hands. A Kunbi from Bombay (a member of a prosperous agricultural caste) wrote to *The Times of India* explaining their motives.

> The daily unfolding of the political panorama, whether in the press or in the Legislative Councils, has produced a sudden awakening of the masses. The mere idea that the direct British control over the administration is jeopardized has unsettled the minds and it is but natural that we, Kunbis, should try to protect our legitimate interests. Every blessed community is up and in arms. And why? Is it because they have more confidence in the even-handed justice of the Government? What greater compliment can we poor masses ever pay to the British mode of administration? And the least hint that all this is going to be changed for an oligarchy formed of sacerdotal classes has turned the usually quiet Kunbi into one, going in for meetings and speechifying.[2]

Three regions, Andhra, Sind and Berar, were also fearful lest reform should mean subjection, in their case to men of other languages rather than specific caste groups. They, too, came to Montagu and asked for protection, in the form of separate administrations for their linguistic areas.

Most of these petitioners subsided from active politics once Montagu had gone away. Under pressure of impending reform, with the probability that the British would devolve extensive power over a wider area of public

1 Montagu, *An Indian Diary*, p. 41. The background to many of these memorials is shown in a letter from Sir James Meston to the Nawab of Rampur, 12 November 1917, Mss. EUR. F. 136 (4). 'It is perfectly pathetic the way in which the landed classes and the more conservative Muhammadans are waking up now to the danger of their position, at the very last moment. They are surrounding me with applications for advice and help in presenting their case to Mr. Montagu;... I am doing my best to assist both classes in getting ready their memorials.'

2 Letter from a Kunbi, Bombay, to editor, 8 November 1917, *The Times of India*, 9 November 1917. Kunbis' fears were expressed in the demand for separate representation by the Deccan Ryots' Association. For this and the social development which was the background to their demand see R. Kumar, *Western India In The Nineteenth Century. A Study in the Social History of Maharashtra* (London & Toronto, 1968), pp. 313–16, 332.

life to Indians, they had felt that they must make their interests known in public. For many of them, like the Kunbis of Bombay or the U.P. maulvis, it was their first attempt to register their interests through the mechanisms of institutional politics, but the prospect of reform made the stakes in such politics so high that they began to realize that they could not afford to be left out if they were to hold their own in public life. Latent groups erupted into the world of limited politics – but only temporarily. Their fears and aspirations remained only a potential source of power in politics because they lacked the organization for sustained agitation, the major exception to this being the non-Brahmins of Madras.[1]

Rumblings of discontent continued to be heard sporadically from some low caste and Muslim groups throughout the subcontinent, but the group equipped for agitation were the professional politicians. Assuming that they would be the beneficiaries of any scheme to extend Indian participation in government, they carried on public discussion about the proposed reforms until the Reform Act was passed in December 1919. They failed to see that a wider franchise would unleash forces which, if channelled by appropriate leadership into politics, might wreck the glass house they had constructed for themselves. Their politics worked mainly by personal manipulation within their own restricted group; they had never needed to woo constituents from a wider social range, and had rarely adopted methods suitable to areas wider than their own cities.[2] Now they seemed unaware of the simmerings of dissatisfaction and fear among the very people whose support they would need in the future if they were to stay as elected representatives in positions of power. As one Indian contemporary observed,

> "The opposition to Home Rule among the landholders, Muhammadans, Non-Brahmans and the upper middle class is increasing greatly and the impression is becoming increasingly general among the people that the effect of the proposals made by the Congress and other political organisations in the country will be to transfer power and authority from European hands to those of the Hindu pleaders and this is a contingency which the people at large view with disapproval and even dismay."[3]

When confronted with such criticisms the politicians hedged. Mrs Besant, as President-elect of Congress, was faced with a deputation of backward castes in Bombay who asked her to secure seats in the local legislative council for Marathas, Kolis, Agris, Bhandaris, Telegus, Malis,

1 For the efforts of the Justice Party in Madras to extract the best conditions for non-Brahmins from the reforms, see Irschick, *Politics And Social Conflict In South India*, pp. 54–170.

2 For the politicians' failure to capture the loyalty of even the limited electorate under the Morley–Minto Reforms, see a case study from Bengal, J. H. Broomfield, 'The Vote and the Transfer of Power: a Study of the Bengal General Election, 1912–1913', *The Journal Of Asian Studies*, XXI, 2 (February 1962), 163–81.

3 Weekly report of D.C.I., 5 January 1918, Proceeding No. 488 of Home Pol., B, January 1918, Nos. 487–90.

Shimpis and Bhoyees! She gave no definite reply and, as the government rightly commented,

> it is difficult to see what line her party can take. If they give guarantees to the numerous important and unimportant communities which ask for representation, they will make themselves and their own scheme ridiculous. On the other hand, a refusal might unite the "non-Brahman" multitudes against them. They will presumably continue to temporise and, as at present, to ride off attacks by accusing the bureaucrats of attempting to stir up discord between Hindu and Mahomedan and between Brahman and non-Brahman.[1]

From 1917 to 1919, between Montagu's announcement and the passage of the Reform Act, the politicians carried on their old style of politics; but now their united front, patched up in 1916, was shattered by bickering over anticipated spoils. Although they and the raj still referred to different groups among them as 'Moderates' and 'Extremists', for lack of better labels, these titles pointed to no fundamental distinctions of ideology or method. Their aim, colonial self-government, was identical and had even been endorsed by the raj: their methods were similar, as it was clear that violent rebellion was unprofitable if not impossible.[2] Moreover, often there were several groups of 'Moderates' and of 'Extremists' within each province, who agreed neither with each other nor with their ostensible namesakes in other provinces. Politicians moved through different positions, and at any one time it was hard to tell where an individual stood. For example, in August 1918 nobody knew whether Madan Mohan Malaviya was one of the 'Extremists' or the 'Moderates': the former hoped he might be a bridge between them and the latter, but the latter repudiated his overtures.[3] Personal loyalty to such leaders as Tilak, Annie Besant or Surendranath Bannerjee was often more important than political principle in determining a man's affiliations. As one observer commented, 'The general opinion in the country is that there are really no differences of principles and convictions between the extremists and the moderates and that their bickerings are due to causes mainly, if not wholly, personal.'[4] Moreover, the factor which generally determined whether a political group was 'Moderate' or 'Extremist' towards a particular issue was its members' position in their own locality, their choice falling on whichever attitude

[1] Fortnightly report from Bombay for second half of October 1917, Home Pol., Deposit, November 1917, No. 30.

[2] Letter to editor, 7 October 1917, *The Times of India* (undated cutting).

[3] For the case of Malaviya see Weekly report of D.C.I., 7 September 1918, Proceeding No. 191 of Home Pol., B, October 1918, Nos. 191–4. For divisions among Bengali 'Moderates' and their inability to agree with 'Moderates' from other provinces see Weekly report of D.C.I., 14 December 1918, Proceeding No. 94 of Home Pol., B, January 1919, Nos. 93–5.

[4] Weekly report of D.C.I., 12 October 1918, Proceeding No. 203 of Home Pol., B, November 1918, Nos. 202–4.

seemed likely to emphasize their identity and influence in local public life. Therefore the only practical use for the terms 'Moderate' and 'Extremist' during the years 1917–19 is to describe two temporary all-India alliances which emerged in reaction to the projected reforms among groups who often disagreed with each other but were placed in sufficiently similar positions in their own localities to find it profitable to work together on this issue. Of course it suited them to explain their alliances in terms of ideology and method, in order to strengthen their tenuous links with each other and to rally support: and so the myth of a fundamental division among the politicians was perpetuated.

Chelmsford's disappointment at the political effect of Montagu's announcement showed how little there was to choose between the 'Moderates' and the 'Extremists' in principle.

> If moderate opinion is worth anything, our announcement should have rallied it...Perhaps it has to be a small extent in some quarters, but on the whole this body of moderate opinion, which we are so often called upon to placate, has so far shown itself to be utterly unreliable, inert and invertebrate, and we have still to find a stimulant which will rally this poor ghost. Outside official interviews, its voice is not heard in the land to any practical purpose.[1]

The politicians assembled at the 1917 session of Congress and received Montagu's announcement with 'grateful satisfaction', though they asked for responsible government at an early and stated date, with their own Congress–League scheme as the first step.[2] However, differences of opinion soon appeared, particularly after the Montagu–Chelmsford Report was published, as local groups began to size up where they would stand under the new regime.

In Bombay the press opposing the report included *Kesari*, *Mahratta*, *Home Ruler* and *Young India*, which complained that 'behind clever and soothing words in the document, there is the iron fist of the bureaucrats who are not prepared to give up materially any fraction of the power which they have enjoyed.' This was the voice of the most vociferous Home Rulers, who judged that they had much to gain and nothing to lose by pitching their demands as high as possible. By contrast there were some who were well established in the local legislative council and hoped that this would be a base for further power under the reforms. *Servant of India* expressed their views when it appealed to Sir Dinshaw Wacha, Surendranath Bannerjee and Madan Mohan Malaviya to organize those

[1] Chelmsford to Willingdon, 8 November 1917, Mss. EUR. E. 264 (19).

[2] *Report of the XXXII Session of the Indian National Congress. Held at Calcutta on 26th, 28th & 29th December, 1917* (Calcutta, 1918), p. 90. The Congress–League scheme, containing the Lucknow Pact, proposed complete autonomy in the provinces and increasing Indianization of the central government. For details of the scheme see Philips, *Select Documents*, pp. 171–3.

who wished to save the reforms 'from being wrecked by the fierce opposition of the Anglo-Indians from the one side and the violent denunciation of irreconcilable Indian critics from the other'.[1]

In the U.P. the local politicians, who were mainly gathered in Allahabad, were caught between fear lest extravagant demands should result in small concessions, and the knowledge that only 'extreme' views would attract large scale support and a wide circulation for their press. *The Leader* opted for caution, though it had previously been the most important provincial Congress paper; but a special provincial conference held on 11 August 1918 condemned the Montagu–Chelmsford proposals 'as not affording in their present form even that substantial step towards responsible government which was promised in the declaration of August 20, 1917, and which the necessities of the present situation imperatively demand.'[2] In neighbouring Bihar a similar tension emerged between the politicians' desire not to wreck the reforms with undue criticism, and their local manoeuvring so that they could claim to be the leaders of provincial opinion. Hasan Imam and P. N. Sinha told the officiating Commissioner of Patna that they had no intention of doing anything which might lead to the final rejection of the reforms, but when it came to the Bihar Provincial Conference on 4 August 1918, they did little to defend the Montagu–Chelmsford proposals, and the Conference rejected them as failing to give substantial steps in the direction of self-government.[3]

In Bengal most obviously the reception given to the reform proposals depended on the state of local politics more than on major considerations of principle. The so-called local 'Moderates', Surendranath Bannerjee and his allies, had maintained a consistent policy of collaboration with the raj in the Bengal Legislative Council, combined with a demand for further constitutional reform. Now was their chance to vindicate their past stand and to secure their local position for the future. The so-called 'Extremists', mostly younger men and comparative newcomers to politics without established positions, like C. R. Das and B. Chakravarti, had nothing to lose by denouncing the reforms, and feared that they would look like their opponents if they welcomed them. They won the day by mobilizing a wider range of supporters than the 'Moderates', and at a provincial conference on 14 July the Montagu–Chelmsford proposals were denounced.[4]

1 *Home Ruler*, 13 July 1918, *Mahratta*, 21 July 1918, *Young India*, 17 July 1918, Bombay N.N., No. 29 of 1918, pp. 1, 2, 3, 6; *Servant of India*, 1 August 1918, Bombay N.N., No. 31 of 1918, p. 6.

2 Resolutions passed at U.P. Special Provincial Conference at Lucknow on 11 August 1918, A.I.C.C. Files, 1918, No. 2, Part V; *Report on the Administration of the United Provinces Of Agra And Oudh, 1917–1918* (Allahabad, 1919), p. 56.

3 Fortnightly report from Bihar and Orissa, 16 August 1918, Home Pol., Deposit, September 1918, No. 40.

4 The details of this local rivalry are in Broomfield, *Elite Conflict in a Plural Society*, pp. 134–40.

The Madras Provincial Conference on 3/4 August also condemned the reforms as unsatisfactory. One of the most vehement speakers was Annie Besant, who said they would lead to 'a perpetual slavery which can only be broken by revolution'. She, like C.R. Das, was making a public claim for provincial recognition as a prominent leader; though for her the problem was not that she was a newcomer, but a veteran whose influence was on the wane compared with the halcyon days of her internment, when men all over India had flocked to her support.[1] Opposed to her now were 'Moderates' led by Sir P. S. Sivaswami Aiyer, lately of the Madras Executive Council, G. A. Natesan and others, who had been staunch Home Rulers but now judged that such criticism of the reforms was suicidal.[2] They could not have helped calculating that rejection would play into the hands of the non-Brahmins who were clamouring for special protection, while modified approval would strengthen the hands of the governors against such pleas.

In the Punjab the divisions occurred along communal lines. At the end of 1917 of the most prominent local papers eighteen supported the Congress–League scheme, and these were almost all Hindu papers. Eleven, all Muslim, opposed that scheme, while twelve remained neutral, some of these being Sikh organs, which welcomed reform provided Sikhs acquired a substantial number of seats.[3]

These local differences crystallized at the all-India level when a Special Congress was held in August 1918 in Bombay to discuss the reforms. Prominent 'Moderate' leaders who judged that acceptance of the reforms would be the most profitable tactic refused to attend, fearing that Congress would decide to reject the reforms; and they held to this position in spite of a twenty-four hour postponement of the start while Madan Mohan Malaviya appealed for unity.[4] That this was a question of tactics and not of principle was clear from the dilemma obviously felt by a 'Moderate' such as Srinivasa Sastri. He believed that weighty support should be given in India to the reforms lest they should be dropped by the British; and, unlike his 'Moderate' friends, who thought they had no chance of a hearing in Congress, he would have liked to take a chance in the session. As these friends, Sir Dinshaw Wacha, Surendranath Bannerjee, T. B. Sapru and Y. Chintamini, had decided to stay away, he felt he had no option but to align

[1] See below, p. 141.

[2] Fortnightly report from Madras, 1 August 1918, Home Pol., Deposit, September 1918, No. 20; Fortnightly report from Madras, 20 August 1918, Home Pol., Deposit, September 1918, No. 40.

[3] Fortnightly report from Punjab for first half of November 1917, Home Pol., January 1918, No. 1.

[4] Surendranath Bannerjee to Annie Besant, telegram, 24 August 1918, A.I.C.C. to various 'Moderate' leaders, including T. B. Sapru and Y. Chintamini, telegram, 27 August 1918, A.I.C.C. Files, 1918, No. 2. Part IV; Diary of G. S. Khaparde, 27 & 28 August 1918, Khaparde Papers.

himself with them.[1] The complexion of the Congress was determined by a massive majority of Bombay delegates – nearly 4,000 out of an attendance of over 5,000. Hasan Imam as President led the way, by describing the reforms as a great disappointment because they conceded Indian demands in theory but not in practice. He singled out for criticism the facts that no real responsibility was introduced into the Government of India and that there seemed no immediate prospect of 'reserved' subjects in the provinces coming under popular control. Eventually the session pronounced the reforms disappointing and unsatisfactory, though it was willing to accept dyarchy for a limited period, demanding full responsible government in fifteen years, and at a provincial level in six years.[2]

The abstainers from Congress met in Bombay on 1/2 November, a thousand strong, under the presidency of Surendranath Bannerjee. They approved of the reforms as a substantial step towards the realization of responsible government, though they suggested certain modifications, including fiscal freedom for India and some element of responsibility to an electorate in the central government. The essential difference between this and the Congress resolution was the 'Moderate' desire to work the reforms, whatever their hesitations, while Congress appeared to rule out the possibility of such cooperation, so fierce was their denunciation of the Montagu–Chelmsford scheme. As Bannerjee said, epitomizing the 'Moderate' attitude,

> "if unfortunately no advance is made (I trust this will not be the case), even then we shall be ready to accept the scheme as an improvement upon the existing state of things and an advance (it may be only a small advance) towards responsible government."[3]

The contrast between this and official Congress policy became clearer after the regular session of Congress at Delhi in December 1918. There the Bengali group headed by C. R. Das and B. Chakravarti obviously carried weight, and those 'Moderates' like Srinivasa Sastri who plucked up sufficient courage to attend found themselves ruled out of court. The delegates went further than the Bombay Special Congress, and demanded full responsible government in the provinces immediately.[4] It is worthy of note

1 V. S. S. Sastri to G. A. Natesan, 14 August 1918, S.P. Correspondence File 1918, Letters to & from Sastri, No. 242.

2 Report of Bombay P.C.C. for 1918, and Syed Hasan Imam's Presidential Speech, 28 August 1917, Jayakar Papers, Correspondence File No. 478; L. F. Rushbrook Williams, *India In The Years 1917–18* (Calcutta, 1919), p. 58.

3 Extract from Surendranath Bannerjee's Presidential Speech at All-India Moderates' Conference in Bombay, 1/2 November 1918 in Weekly report of D.C.I., 9 November 1918, Proceeding No. 158 of Home Pol., B, December 1918, Nos. 158–9; Bombay Police Abstract, 1918, par. 1636.

4 Weekly report of D.C.I., 11 January 1919, Proceeding No. 161 of Home Pol., B, January 1919, Nos. 160–3; *Report of the Thirty-third session of the Indian National Congress held at Delhi on the 26th, 28th, 30th, 31st December, 1918* (Delhi, 1919), p. ii.

that, in their efforts to distinguish themselves from the 'Moderates' and to strengthen their hand in discussion of the reforms, Congress leaders, particularly Madan Mohan Malaviya, rallied a group of about 700 peasant delegates from areas near Delhi like Rohtak, Karnal and Gurgaon, paying all their expenses to attract them to the Congress meeting.[1]

Whatever the tirades of the 'Extremists', the politicians' discussions indicated that the British had succeeded in their war-time search for collaborators. Their offer had been large enough to draw the sting from the Home Rule movement. By making reform an immediate certainty instead of a distant possibility, it opened up the cracks which the politicians had tried to paper over in 1916, and so gave back to the rulers considerable leverage in the political situation. Discussion and petition diverted the politicians during the remaining years of the war; and once the war was over the raj was assured of sufficient allies from their ranks to work the reforms. But conciliation was only one side of the coin of British policy. Its reverse side was the determination to keep a firm hand on any whose discontents could not be contained or appeased with conciliation, particularly if, in an attempt to create a following, they seemed likely to exploit the hardship felt by the public as a result of the war. The British had limited resources for repression, and the iron fist could only be used if the majority of the political nation were amenable to the gestures of the velvet glove. But during the First World War the balance was in favour of the British, and they were able to work a judicious combination of the stern and the conciliatory.

Annie Besant was one of the few major political leaders to feel the iron fist. After at least eighteen months of restraint,[2] the government interned her and two of her assistants on 16 June 1917 at Ootacamund in the Nilgiri Hills. The raj found this ageing English Theosophist a constant source of embarrassment, but when she took to violent speeches in the course of her Home Rule campaign during the war she became in official eyes a sufficient menace to warrant internment under the Defence of India rules. The Madras government, to whose lot it fell to deal with her, maintained that it had no wish to stifle constitutional agitation but felt bound to act against someone whose inflammatory activities exceeded the bounds of honest criticism.[3]

[1] Weekly reports of D.C.I. 4 & 11 January 1919, Proceeding Nos. 160 & 161 of Home Pol., B, January 1919, Nos. 160–3.

[2] As early as December 1915 Hardinge wrote: 'We have discussed the question of prohibiting Mrs. Besant from speaking at Bombay, and we think it best to let her speak this time, and if she offends, to take action against her under the Defence of India Act. By speaking she is more likely to do harm to the cause she has espoused than by posing as a martyr.' Hardinge to Willingdon, 16 December 1915, Hardinge Mss. (90).

[3] Govt. of Madras, Public Dept., to Govt. of India, Home Dept., Letter No. 836, Proceeding No. 92 of Home Pol., A, August 1917, Nos. 86–106.

Far more dangerous in the eyes of the rulers were the Muslim journalist brothers, Mahomed and Shaukat Ali, who publicized the ideal of Pan-Islam, with its possible implication for Indian Muslims of loyalty to the Sultan of Turkey, who was currently an ally of the Germans and so at war with the British. Consequently in 1915 the Alis were placed under house arrest. As the Viceroy explained,

> I am a little doubtful at present as to the attitude of the Mahomedans. They are undoubtedly sulky and carefully watching affairs in the Dardanelles. If we get a big and early success there, I anticipate no more trouble; but if the reverse, the result might really be serious. In order to take every precaution, and to put an end to their unwholesome activities, we have interned Mahomed Ali and his brother, Shaukat Ali.[1]

Officials of the raj rightly saw that the spread of Pan-Islamic beliefs in India might have a critical influence on the loyalty of their Muslim subjects and threaten the foundations of their rule. Pan-Islam was an ideal with many facets and many modes of expression; but at its core lay the Muslim belief in the brotherhood of all believers and the organization of society for the practice of the faith, under a Khalifah or successor of the Prophet. One Muslim polity under a Khalifah was early shattered, but the title of Khalifah remained as a constant reminder of the ideal, although each Muslim state had its own temporal ruler. In the course of the nineteenth century most Indian Muslims came to accept a working alliance with the British raj, although it was an infidel raj, on the grounds that it provided an environment where Islam could be freely lived and taught. However, by the end of the century there was a distinct revival of interest in Turkey and the person of the Sultan, the Khalifah; and he began to be remembered in the Friday congregational prayers of Indian Muslims, an honour previously reserved for the Khalifah in areas where he was actually the temporal ruler.[2]

At about the same time changes in the attitudes of some Indian Muslims towards western knowledge lent added weight to this concern for Turkey and its Sultan, because they tended to stress the historical source and continuity of Islam. Whereas Sir Syed Ahmed Khan's great Muslim university at Aligarh had tried to demonstrate that Islam was compatible with liberal western ideas, the newer interpretation saw Islam as the source of

1 Hardinge to Sir V. Chirol, 13 May 1915, Hardinge Mss. (94).

2 Ishtiaq Husain Qureshi, *The Muslim Community Of The Indo-Pakistan Subcontinent (610–1947)* (The Hague, 1962), pp. 270–2. Qureshi thinks this was a highly significant development with political implications, but at the time Nawab Mohsin-ul-Mulk, Hon. Secretary of the Mahomedan Anglo-Oriental Club at Aligarh, said that the practice only implied honour to the Sultan and was 'on no account to be taken to mean that Indian Muslims regard him as their ruler in any way, or consider his orders binding on them.' V. Chirol, 'Pan-Islamism', *The National Review*, XLVII (December 1906), 647.

such ideas, emphasizing the religious and historical foundations of the faith compared with the secular 'modernity' of Aligarh. Typical of this way of thought was the Calcutta journalist, Abul Kalam Azad.[1] His vehement opposition to Aligarh's approach to the West naturally led him to give great value to the common bonds between Muslims of different nationalities and their focus in the Middle East as the homeland of their faith. As he wrote soon after founding his paper, *Al-Hilal*, in 1912,

> Aligarh movement has paralysed the Muslims. The real aim is the promotion of Pan-Islam, which is the true foundation and link for the progress and reform of Islam, and for this there will never be a better opportunity than we have now. Today no local or national movement can benefit the Muslims, even if it be the tall talk of the [Aligarh] University. So long as the whole world of Islam does not come together in an international and universal alliance, how can small tracts help the forty crores of Muslims.[2]

Such religious and philosophical emphasis on the geographical centre of a world-wide Muslim community could easily spill over into something approaching political loyalty, and in the first decade of the twentieth century events inside and outside India produced just such a development. The Turkish Sultan, Abdul Hamid, deliberately fostered the ideal of Pan-Islam, and as relations between Great Britain and Turkey deteriorated it became all too easy for Indian Muslims to see Britain as a partner in an international spoliation of Islam. British neutrality when Italy fought Turkey over Tunis and her neutrality in the Balkan War, combined with Indian Muslim grievances over the Cawnpore Mosque affair and the reunification of Bengal, all compromised the position of the British raj and began to shift the foundations of that working arrangement which the Muslims had evolved with the raj on the basis of British sympathy towards Islam. When the British began to fail them they turned towards Turkey as their prop in a faithless world. This was evident in the 1912 All-India Medical Mission to Turkey, the foundation in 1913 of the Anjuman Khuddam-i-Ka'bah whose aim was to unite Muslims to save their sanctuaries of Mecca, Medina and Jerusalem from falling into non-Muslim hands, and in the cult of Turkey which was expressed in a flowering of historical political poetry and only driven underground on the outbreak of the 1914–18 War.[3] As early as 1912 Sir Valentine Chirol, a British journalist

[1] This general trend is described in W. Cantwell Smith, *Modern Islam In India. A Social Analysis* (reprint of 1946 London edition, Lahore, 1963), pp. 44–103; for the thought of A. K. Azad see A. Ahmad, *Islamic Modernism In India And Pakistan* (London, 1967), pp. 175–85.

[2] Quoted in Waheed-uz-Zaman, *Towards Pakistan* (Lahore, 1964), pp. 19–20.

[3] For the growing importance of historical–political poetry, see Ahmad, *Islamic Modernism In India And Pakistan*, pp. 97–102; for the Medical Mission and the Anjuman Khuddam-i-Ka'bah, see *A History Of The Freedom Movement. Volume III. 1906–1936. Part I* (Karachi, 1961), pp. 154–5, 208–9; for Britain's changing

with particular interest in India and the Middle East, warned the Viceroy of the trouble the raj was storing up for itself.

> I think it extremely important that you should keep in close touch with Mahomedan opinion, & not in connection only with the re-partition of Bengal. I am very much concerned at the tone of several letters I have received by the last mail from Indian Mah^ns^ who took the opportunity...to express, almost in menacing tones, their resentment of British indifference, if not complicity, in the "spoilation" of Islam which is going on all over the world. Even the Aga Khan tells me that the bitterness produced by Morocco, Persia & Tripoli, is driving the Indian Mah^n^ into the arms of the Hindus, & that all he & moderate men of his way of thinking can hope to do is to try & prevent their co-religionists from joining hands with the more extreme Congress party. I can't help thinking that it would be worth our while to take a little more trouble to enlighten Mah^n^ leaders as to the true inwardness & purpose of Brit. policy.[1]

It is almost impossible to generalize about Indian Muslim feeling, because the Muslims were such a diverse community. There were the divisions of sect, the divisions of region, and the divisions created by economic interest, all of which were clear at the time of the Lucknow Pact. Even among the ulema, the Muslim clerisy, there were distinctions springing from standards of learning and from schools of thought. In the U.P. alone, for example, there were the different currents of thought expounded at the seminaries of Ferangi Mahal and Nadwat al-'Ulama, both in Lucknow, and at Deoband.[2] Amidst such diversity it is difficult to trace precisely who was affected by Pan-Islamic ideas by the second decade of this century. According to the assessments of contemporary observers, most Urdu-speaking Muslims felt a certain historical and cultural pull towards Turkey, and shared anxiety about that country's fate in a changing Europe.

Those who felt this particularly poignantly and were ready to act on it were some younger Muslims, mostly in northern India, whose reaction against the assumptions of the Aligarh school of thought was mingled with a growing disillusion with the politics of collaboration, initiated in the previous generation by Sir Syed Ahmed Khan. Such men found ready allies among some ulema, whose motives were variously personal ambition, religious scruple, and the fear that the ulema as a whole were losing their

relationship with Turkey, see A. Cunningham, 'The Wrong Horse? – A Study Of Anglo-Turkish Relations Before The First World War' in A. Hourani (ed.), *St. Anthony's Papers. Number 17. Middle Eastern Affairs. Number Four* (Oxford, 1965), pp. 56–76.

1 Sir V. Chirol to Hardinge, 24 January 1912, Hardinge Mss. (70).

2 For diversity of opinion among the ulema see Ahmad, *Islamic Modernism In India And Pakistan*, pp. 103–22; P. Hardy, 'The 'Ulama In British India' (unpublished paper presented to seminar at the School of Oriental and African Studies, London, 10 February 1969).

power over Muslims in an increasingly secular society.[1] U.P. was the critical area in this development, but its Lieutenant-Governor anticipated no wholesale Muslim disturbance, since only a small group seemed to be moved by the ideal of Pan-Islam.

> Speaking broadly, we have to reckon only with the younger educated men and one section of the priests. The old men as a whole are sound. They have experience and nearly always a sense of humour. They dislike the vapourings of the noisy party and think them undignified. They know that, if they lost us, the Hindus would eat them up.[2]

The 'younger educated men', typified by Mahomed and Shaukat Ali, could not fail to see that the politics of agitation had paid substantial dividends to their educated Hindu counterparts. Consequently they decided that they must take to agitation to define and safeguard the position of the Indian Muslim community – hence their alliance with Congress on the basis of the Lucknow Pact.[3] This was only one side of their activity: another was their struggle at Aligarh to oust the secular modernists and the European members of staff.[4] Both were facets of their determination to steer their community on a course different from that plotted by Sir Syed Ahmed Khan.

However, the reactions of different groups of Muslims to the position of Indian and international Islam made it plain that the issue at stake was not only that position but also the relative strength of different groups and leaders within the Indian Muslim community. Just as the Montagu–Chelmsford scheme of reform was dragged into local and all-India faction struggles among politicians jostling for place, so the ideal of Pan-Islam and the future of Aligarh became pawns in the hands of men who were bidding for leadership in their community. S. H. Freemantle, Magistrate and Collector of Allahabad, hinted at this after he met the Ali brothers in 1915 and noticed that they were both wearing Turkish half-moons in their grey caps and Khuddam-i-Ka'bah badges, compared with their European style of dress in previous years. Once before Mahomed Ali had told him that he thought it was a pity that India had no really professional politicians and Freemantle now commented, 'He has since that time become what he desired then to be a professional politician and there is not the slightest

1 For the concern of some ulema for their declining power as government interfered with Muslim personal law, mosques, schools etc., and as the Muslim community was increasingly represented by 'secular' Muslims in the legislative councils, and their consequent willingness to ally with some of the younger Muslim politicians, see Robinson, 'The Politics Of U.P. Muslims 1906–1922', pp. 301–26.

2 Sir James Meston to Hardinge, 25 March 1915, Hardinge Mss. (64).

3 See above, pp. 29–30.

4 Sir James Meston to J. Ramsay MacDonald, 11 September 1913, Mss. EUR. F. 136 (3); M. Ali to Mas'ud, grandson of Sir Syed Ahmed Khan, 18 March 1919, Ali Papers.

doubt that the religious role has been adopted by the two brothers in order to impress the minds of the lower orders of Muhammadans.'[1]

The main instruments through which Mahomed Ali spread his Pan-Islamic doctrines were his new papers, *Comrade* and *Hamdard*; these were accompanied by Hasrat Mohani's *Urdu-'i-Mu'alla*, Wahiduddin Salim's *Muslim Gazette*, Zafar Ali Khan's *Zamindar* and A. K. Azad's *Al-Hilal*. These all maintained that Pan-Islam was a Koranic ideal invested with new political meaning by the current danger to Muslim countries and to the very integrity of Islam. The aim of Pan-Islam was the defence of Turkey, the sole remaining bulwark for Indian Muslims, 'whose political extinction means their own annihilation.'[2] However, defence of Turkey could divide the loyalty of Indian Muslims should Turkey and Britain ever be at war: and the test came in the First World War. Abdul Bari of Ferangi Mahal, the Alis' spiritual adviser, asked the Sultan to support Britain or remain neutral. Mahomed Ali in his notorious article, 'The Choice of the Turks', in September 1914, likewise proclaimed the hope that the Khalifah would stay out of the war and so save Indian Muslims from a conflict of loyalties.[3] The rest of this article was obviously sympathetic to the German cause; and it was this type of journalism which eventually landed the Alis and A. K. Azad in internment. The raj at war with Turkey could do little to conciliate the Pan-Islamists among its subjects; therefore it took the only other course open to it. It tried to contain the spread of Pan-Islamic beliefs by the harsh method of interning editors and gagging the press, trusting that the prospect of reform accompanied by communal representation would soothe most of the politically aware among the Muslims and give them sufficient influence to hold their co-religionists loyal to the raj.

(II) GANDHI, THE PART-TIME POLITICAL PROTAGONIST

War-time threats to British security in India and the policy of balance between conciliation and repression which the raj evolved in response were of fundamental importance to the development of Indian politics and the course of Gandhi's career. They determined the pattern of Indian government for at least the next fifteen years, and forced Gandhi to take a stand in the all-India political arena. However, even in the last two years of the war

[1] Extract from note by S. H. Freemantle on his meeting with the Alis on 21 November 1915, Home Pol., Deposit, December 1915, No. 6. (I owe this reference to Mrs Gail Graham.)

[2] Z. A. Khan, 'Indian Mussalmans And Pan-Islamism', *Comrade*, 14 June 1913, R. A. J. Nadvi (ed.), *Selections From Mohammad Ali's Comrade* (Lahore, 1965), pp. 297–9.

[3] Abdul Bari to Sultan of Turkey, telegram, 31 August 1914, Ferangi Mahal, Lucknow, Abdul Bari Papers (I owe this reference to Mrs Gail Graham); M. Ali, 'The Choice of the Turks', *Comrade*, 26 September 1914, Appendix I of Home Pol., A, January 1915, Nos. 76–97.

Gandhi was never a full-time politician or a predictable one. He pursued no obvious political ends and appeared to care little for political power as understood by his contemporaries. The focus of his life and work was still his *ashram* at Ahmedabad, and he only participated in politics when he thought he saw a 'wrong' which could be righted by his particular techniques, or when he saw an opportunity to display and forward his vision of true Swaraj. As a result neither the politicians nor the government quite knew where they were in relation to him: they could not predict when he would venture into their world, what stand he would take, or whom he would support.

Annie Besant's internment was the first 'wrong' Gandhi took up which had India-wide appeal to the political nation. Many politically minded Indians saw this official action against a Home Ruler as action against the idea of Home Rule, and whether or not they belonged to her League they sprang to defend one of their own kind. T. B. Sapru, one of the most constitutional of Indian politicians, was an example. Though he shunned her methods of agitation he wrote to Sita Ram, a colleague in the U.P.,

> So the campaign of repression has begun in right earnest. I am afraid the political atmosphere has never been more gloomy or threatening than it is at present...I think we must stand by...Mrs. Besant who had fought for us & worked for us so bravely. I personally am not one of her chelas but I feel that she has been very unjustly and harshly dealt with. The Govt. men say in private that they are not opposed to Self-govt or Home Rule as an ideal but they object to its immediate grant & to strong speeches & writings. What is the good of their platonic love for the ideal, when they don't indicate any intention to give us even a decent instalment of reforms.[1]

Sapru also asked why Sita Ram did not establish a branch of the Home Rule League. He himself joined her League at this point, in company with so many others that the League's membership doubled.[2]

Prompted by a feeling of frustration and hoping to make some impression on the bureaucratic hide, some politicians mooted the idea of passive resistance on her behalf. Madan Mohan Malaviya began sounding out opinion on the matter, while a group of Bombay men, feeling that something practical ought to be done, began circulating a passive resistance manifesto for signatures. Annie Besant heard and approved of these proposals.[3] At this point Gandhi came to the fore. Passive resistance was not unknown in India before Gandhi's return from South Africa,[4] but he had the reputa-

[1] T. B. Sapru to Sita Ram, 30 June 1917, N.A.I., Sita Ram Papers, File No. 29 B.

[2] Low (ed.), *Soundings In Modern South Asian History*, p. 176.

[3] Bombay Police Abstract, 1917, par. 785 (n); B. G. Horniman to J. Nehru, 1 July 1917, J. Nehru, *A Bunch of Old Letters* (2nd edition, Bombay, 1966), pp. 1–2; July 7th, typed copy of Mrs Besant's Internment Diary, Besant Papers.

[4] See above, pp. 22–3. For the theoretical differences between Gandhi and earlier Bengali advocates of passive resistance and for other instances of pre-Gandhian passive resistance in India, see Brown, 'Gandhi In India, 1915–20', pp. 243–5.

tion of being its most practised exponent and people began to turn to him as an authority in the matter. Several Bombay men, Umar Sobhani, Shankarlal Banker, Indulal Yajnik and the brothers Jamnadas and Kanji Dwarkadas, were among the earliest to approach him, but he perplexed them by suggesting that they should collect 100 volunteers to walk from Bombay to her place of internment in protest.[1]

It was not inevitable that Gandhi would champion Annie Besant, particularly in view of the frigid truce which existed between them after their clash at Benares in 1916. However in July 1917 he took up the 'wrong' done to her and wrote to the Viceroy to tell him so. He asked that the government should acknowledge its 'big blunder' and revoke the internment order, as he feared that violence might break out in support of Mrs Besant; and he explained that precisely in order to prevent violence he was 'asking the leaders to adopt this method [passive resistance] fully and boldly at this critical juncture.' But he made it clear that he was no ally of Mrs Besant on other issues. 'I myself do not like much in Mrs. Besant's method. I have not liked the idea of the political propaganda being carried on during the War. In my opinion, our restraint will have been the best propaganda. But the whole country was against me.'[2] Throughout the summer of 1917 Gandhi reiterated his advice on passive resistance. Umar Sobhani and Shankarlal Banker published a letter from him to Banker, urging that those who found the internment 'unendurable' should resort to passive resistance, unless Mrs Besant was released by the time E. S. Montagu visited the country in the late autumn to discuss the proposed constitutional reform.[3] At about the same time, in August, Gandhi met some leading Biharis informally at Hasan Imam's house and talked to them about satyagraha in South Africa. He suggested that the joint meeting of the A.I.C.C. and the Muslim League Council planned for October in Allahabad should give the government a deadline when passive resistance would begin if Mrs Besant had not been released. One of the forms of passive resistance he contemplated was a protest march to the place of internment.[4]

1 K. Dwarkadas, *Gandhiji Through My Diary Leaves*, p. 12. Less prominent people also asked advice from Gandhi as the acknowledged exponent of passive resistance. For example, K. Sadashiv Rao, a High Court vakil from Mangalore, wrote to him on 26 August 1917, having heard that Bombay politicians were in touch with him on the subject and that S.I.S. members in Poona were saying that Gandhi was prepared to lead passive resistance against Mrs Besant's internment if there was enough support for it. Rao thought Gandhi should lead India 'in this glorious struggle for freedom'. S.N. No. 6386.

2 Draft letter from Gandhi to J. L. Maffey, Viceroy's Private Secretary, 7 July 1917, S.N. No. 6372.

3 Leaflet entitled 'Satyagraha', 31 August 1917, Besant Papers; the letter was also published in *Gujarati*, 2 September 1917, *C.W.*, vol. 13, pp. 519–20.

4 Weekly report of D.C.I., 1 September 1917, Proceeding No. 239 of Home Pol., B, September 1917, Nos. 239–43.

These, however, were Gandhi's private views, and the meeting of the A.I.C.C. and the Muslim League Council in Bombay on 28/29 July had decided to gather local opinion before reaching a final decision. The meeting was a stormy one: although men from the U.P. and a majority of those from Madras and Calcutta were in favour of passive resistance, some elder statesmen, like Sir Narayan Chandarvarkar, Sir Dinshaw Wacha, Chimanlal Setalvad and Surendranath Bannerjee, were firmly opposed. At one point several of them left the discussion to the cries of 'shame', 'traitors', and eventually the issue was shelved to prevent a more serious split.[1] Local discussions in P.C.C.s produced equally diverse opinions. Berar considered passive resistance advisable, while Burma and the Punjab favoured its postponement in view of Montagu's impending visit. Bihar thought the government should be asked to release Mrs Besant by a certain date, and if no release was forthcoming passive resistance should be preached. U.P.'s P.C.C. opposed the idea, despite the attitude of the U.P. men at the tense Bombay meeting and despite Malaviya's earlier manoeuvring.[2] Bengal held no special meeting to discuss the question: in fact its inaction had already roused the feelings of men from other provinces, like Sapru, who wrote,

> only Bengal is giving us half-hearted support. The fact is that in Bengal the old leaders can't bring themselves in to line with new developments & the younger men don't believe in constitutional agitation. Besides, it is characteristic of Bengal, that unless it is directly touched by anything it does not move.[3]

The deepest divisions occurred in Madras and Bombay. The Madras P.C.C. discussed the question of passive resistance at three meetings, amid stormy scenes and against the background of a blasting manifesto published by seven of its members who urged 'the grave inexpediency of passive resistance in the present situation' when Montagu was about to arrive. Among the signatories was V. S. Srinivasa Sastri, who explained privately that he opposed passive resistance because all other constitutional measures had not been tried, because it would embarrass the government during the war and because it would alienate the sympathy of English friends and the Prime Minister. Although he was willing to use passive resistance if the government denied them the elementary rights of free speech and assembly, he did not approve of its use as a protest against a wrong or in order to obtain political concessions. Eventually the P.C.C. agreed to defer

[1] Bombay Police Abstract, 1917, par. 859 (n); S. Banerjea, *A Nation In Making* (Calcutta, 1963 reprint of 1925 edition), pp. 223–4.

[2] B. P. Sitaramayya, *The History Of The Indian National Congress. Volume 1 (1885–1935)* (Bombay, 1935), p. 133; printed notices announcing decisions of Burma and Bihar and Orissa P.C.C.s, Besant Papers; Fortnightly report from U.P., 4 September 1917, Home Pol., Deposit, September 1917, No. 6.

[3] T. B. Sapru to Sita Ram, 30 June 1917, Sita Ram Papers, File No. 29 B.

the whole question.[1] In Bombay the local press was divided on the subject; so was the P.C.C., which met on 12 August and appointed a subcommittee to report back to it. Although Gandhi was not a member of this sub-committee, he was allowed to attend its meeting and explain his views.

> Mr. M. K. Gandhi in explaining his views, observed *inter alia* that it was a mistake to have referred the subject to the Provincial Congress Committees, that "passive resistance" was not a proper expression, that what was meant to be conveyed by that expression was "soul-force," which eluded definition, that the resort to the exercise of that "soul-force" was purely a matter of individual conscience and that being so, the Congress as a body could not and should not adopt the policy of "passive resistance." He was of opinion that the subject should not be considered at all by the Congress Committees or by the Congress.[2]

When the P.C.C. met to receive the report of the sub-committee it was again divided, and like Madras decided to shelve the question in anticipation of Montagu's visit.[3]

The results of these local discussions were brought to the joint meeting of the A.I.C.C. and the Council of the Muslim League on 6 October in Allahabad, and there the whole question of passive resistance was dropped in view of the changed political situation, by the unanimous decision of all provinces.[4] This 'changed political situation' was the impending visit of Montagu and the fact that Mrs Besant had been released in the middle of September. Against the judgement of the Madras government, the Government of India procured her release at the prompting of Montagu, who had an eye to his forthcoming tour. As the Viceroy put it, 'We had to get a calm atmosphere for Montagu's visit. We had to be sure that when he came out people would come and lay their views before us, otherwise we should have found ourselves in the ridiculous position of having got the Secretary of State out and of everyone refusing to meet him.'[5]

So was the occasion for passive resistance removed. However it seems unlikely that a concerted passive resistance movement would have taken place even if the government had not released Mrs Besant. The politicians

[1] Sitaramayya, *op. cit.* p. 133; Fortnightly report from Madras, 1 September 1917 Home Pol., Deposit, September 1917, No. 6; Weekly report of D.C.I., 1 September 1917, Proceeding No. 239 of Home Pol., B, September 1917, Nos. 239–43; V. S. S. Sastri to S. G. Vaze, 16 August 1917, S.P. Correspondence File 1917, Letters to & from Sastri, No. 180.

[2] Report of meeting on 26 August 1917 of sub-committee of Bombay P.C.C., N.A.I., Jayakar Papers, correspondence file No. 478.

[3] Bombay Police Abstract, 1917, par. 949 (1).

[4] *The Bombay Chronicle*, 8 October 1917.

[5] Chelmsford to Austen Chamberlain, 14 December 1917, Mss. EUR. E. 264 (15). For the interchanges between the Viceroy and the Government of Madras in the first fortnight of September see Mss. EUR. E. 264 (19).

were divided, and some at least were restive at her pretensions to leadership. M. A. Jinnah told the Home Member of the Government of India 'that he and his colleagues were heartily sick of the old lady; that her internment put them in a difficult position, and that, if she were released and then again indulged in violence, they would accept her reinternment and give her up.'[1] This was one reason why the government was willing to risk her release. It also had convincing evidence from the provinces that, however great the hue and cry had been at the time of her internment, there was hardly any feeling for her outside the ranks of the regular politicians.[2]

Although it passed so quickly, this episode showed where Gandhi stood when he turned outwards from the tiny worlds of particular districts and took up 'wrongs' which had all-India implications. He was still an outsider in institutional politics, though an acknowledged authority on one particular political technique. This was made clear when he was not given a seat on the Bombay sub-committee on passive resistance but only called in as an expert. He did not make his acceptance in the political world easier by his stand at that sub-committee, when he was obviously determined to keep satyagraha above the level of political decision-making to prevent its degeneration from 'soul force' into 'passive resistance'. Moreover, his public pronouncements on the matter were inconsistent: what he said to the Bombay sub-committee was the opposite of his advice to the Biharis in the same month. He was still feeling his way in politics, experimenting in a new sphere. As yet he was unable to play the political game with a steady hand, because he lacked both the necessary experience and sense of direction. More significant for the future was the evidence that when satyagraha was mooted it created deep divisions and intense feelings among the political elite. A few politicians genuinely welcomed it, some acquiesced because they did not want the reputation of being backward,[3] and many opposed it vigorously. It was clear that if Gandhi ever launched satyagraha he could expect diverse and often hostile reactions, because satyagraha was a fundamental challenge to the ethos and conventions of limited politics. It was equally plain during these months that Gandhi's relationship with the raj was a curious one. Just at the time when he was sitting on a government commission in Champaran he was planning to embarrass the raj and break its laws. On the one hand he saw the raj as a benevolent benefactor of the poor: on the other, he accused it of imprisoning and molesting the innocent.

The ambivalence of Gandhi's relationship with the rulers and of his role among the politicians was demonstrated more forcibly when Gandhi took a

[1] Chelmsford to Austen Chamberlain, 8 September 1917, Mss. EUR. E. 264 (15).

[2] Fortnightly reports from the provinces for first half of July 1917, Home. Pol., Deposit, August 1917, No. 2.

[3] Fortnightly report from Bihar and Orissa for first half of July 1917, *ibid.*

stand on another all-India issue precipitated by the war – whether or not to help the raj in its war effort. In 1917 he had told the Viceroy that he was out of line with most of his countrymen on this question, but he stuck to his convictions. While he was actually leading satyagraha against the government in Kaira he lamented that he was not helping that same government in the war. 'I seem to be ever worrying the administrators in the country when as a responsible citizen of the Empire I should be taking my share in the war...I feel ashamed that since my arrival in India I can show no war work record in the conventional sense of the term.'[1] The Government of India immediately took him up on this and, assessing him as a public figure who carried weight among ordinary people, invited him to attend a war conference at Delhi on 27/29 April 1918. At first he refused to attend because those who he thought carried most weight with the Indian public, Annie Besant, Tilak and the Alis, had been excluded, and because he had read a press report that Britain had signed a secret treaty whereby Constantinople would be ceded to Russia after the war. After an interview with the Viceroy on 27 April he changed his mind and attended the conference.[2] Although Tilak was not present at the conference some of his Home Rule henchmen were, led by G. S. Khaparde, who attempted to get through a resolution proposing that, if the raj wished to mobilize Indian manpower and resources, it should introduce a bill in Parliament to grant responsible government to India within a reasonable time. Gandhi fought this in the manpower sub-committee, to Khaparde's disgust and discomfort, and merely supported the resolution on recruiting with a single Hindi sentence to the effect that he understood it and agreed with it whole-heartedly.[3] His objection to Khaparde's stance was that it made help conditional on concessions. Though he would have wished for concessions himself, in Kaira for example, his own help was not conditional, and this he made plain when he placed his services at the disposal of the government. His only caveat was that he personally would not fight or encourage financial contributions as he thought India had donated enough money already.[4]

However, at a Bombay provincial war conference on 10 June Gandhi was less cooperative, and appeared to have moved nearer to the local Home Rulers. Willingdon, Governor of Bombay, saw the reason. 'Gandhi came to see me in the morning before the meeting and said he didn't want to speak. I realise his difficulty for the Home Rule Leaguers have been very

1 Gandhi to J. L. Maffey, 10 April 1918, *C.W.*, vol. 14, p. 321.

2 Gandhi to Sir Claude Hill, 26 April 1918, *ibid.* pp. 371–3; Gandhi to J. L. Maffey, 27 April 1918, *ibid.* p. 374. For Gandhi's relations with the Ali brothers see below, pp. 152–6.

3 28 April 1918, Diary of G. S. Khaparde, Khaparde Papers; speech by Gandhi at war conference, 28 April 1918, *C.W.*, vol. 14, p. 375.

4 Draft letter from Gandhi to J. L. Maffey, 29 April 1918, S.N. No. 9838; draft letter from Gandhi to Viceroy, 29 April 1918, S.N. No. 9834.

busy helping him in Kaira and he has since he has been down here, been in constant communication with Tilak.'[1] Gandhi pressed the Bombay government to include Tilak on the manpower committee if it wanted a national response.[2] However, in spite of his pleas for cooperation between the government and the local Home Rulers, the conference degenerated into a public clash between the two sides. Tilak and several of his supporters left the conference, when Willingdon interrupted their speeches on the grounds that they were introducing political discussion under the cloak of the loyalty resolution and imposing conditions for their cooperation in the war effort.[3] Gandhi immediately wrote to Willingdon, criticizing his action as 'a serious blunder' likely to be interpreted by the growing Home Rule party as an insult, and to become the cause of anti-government agitation. In this he was repeating almost exactly the arguments he had used to the raj about Mrs Besant's internment. On this occasion too, he was not a simple ally of the Home Rulers he defended. As President of a Bombay protest meeting on 16 June he criticized the insult to Tilak, to the Home Rule organization and by implication to India, but said he personally felt that Tilak should have preserved a dignified silence, and that the quickest way to Home Rule was full cooperation with the government in the war. Privately he explained his views to Shankarlal Banker:

> In my view it is the duty of members of the League all over India to plunge into this work [of recruiting]. Simultaneously, you may carry on any agitation that you want to against the misdeeds of the Government. By following this course, you will have served both ends. The Home Rule League will suffer a serious set-back if it does nothing to help recruitment.[4]

Practising what he preached, throughout the summer of 1918 Gandhi conducted a personal recruiting campaign – a strange phenomenon in one who preached non-violence. He justified his action on the grounds that Indians must help in the war if they wished to enjoy the benefits of the state under whose protection they lived, that those who wanted freedom in their own country must assist in a war being fought for freedom's sake, and that Indians would never be independent of British help or even partners in the British Empire unless they learned to defend themselves.[5] Gandhi's call to his countrymen to display their courage and their ability to help

[1] Willingdon to Chelmsford, 11/12 June 1918, Mss. EUR. F. 93 (1).

[2] Gandhi to L. Robertson, Secretary to Govt. of Bombay, Political Dept., 9 June 1918, *C.W.*, vol. 14, p. 422.

[3] Fortnightly report from Bombay, 16/18 June 1918, Home Pol., Deposit, August 1918, No. 30; Willingdon to E. S. Montagu, 16 June 1918, Mss. EUR. F. 93 (3).

[4] Gandhi to Willingdon, 11 June 1918, *C.W.*, vol. 14, p. 423; speech by Gandhi in Bombay, 16 June 1918, *The Bombay Chronicle*, 17 June 1918, *ibid.* pp. 425–31; Gandhi to S. Banker, 16 June 1918, *ibid.* p. 431.

[5] Gandhi to Esther Faering, 30 June 1918, *ibid.* pp. 462–3; leaflet by Gandhi appealing for enlistment in Kaira, 22 June 1918, *ibid.* p. 440; Gandhi to V. S. S. Sastri, 18 July 1918, *The Bombay Chronicle*, 19 July 1918.

themselves was the key to his attitude to war work. Courage and self-help were indispensable qualities for a people who wished to gain Swaraj and in the circumstances provided by the war Gandhi saw an opportunity for his compatriots to train themselves for their future. As he wrote to an old friend, 'You must be watching my work of recruitment. Of all my activities, I regard this as the most difficult and the most important. If I succeed in it, genuine swaraj is assured.'[1]

Gandhi's main recruiting centres were Bihar and Gujarat: but even in those areas where he might have seemed assured of popular support because of his local satyagrahas he met with severe rebuffs. In Patna many people left a meeting when he broached the subject of recruits. In Kaira he had difficulty in rallying volunteers and even in hiring transport for his recruiting drive, and his exhortations dismayed ex-satyagrahis. By 15 July the Nadiad Sub-Inspector of Police could only report about 120 recruits as a result of Gandhi's campaign.[2]

It was hardly surprising that people were reluctant to become cannon fodder in the service of a government which Gandhi himself had taught them to resist. The politicians too were seriously embarrassed by Gandhi's campaign, as he proposed for them the role of recruiting officers. Few shared his attitude, but none dared lead an anti-recruiting drive and risk being labelled disloyal in war time. Consequently they compromised, making their support conditional on the grant of post-war reforms and the right of Indians to carry arms and hold commissions in the army. The official A.I.C.C. line was to support recruiting, provided that recruits could serve under Indian officers. Tilak said he could only encourage recruitment to an army where equal opportunities were open for Indians and Europeans, and Annie Besant would only support recruitment to a citizen army, not to the regular army.[3] Gandhi's isolation from current political opinion on this matter was apparent even in Bombay and Ahmedabad, where the educated had been longest exposed to his ways of reasoning and action: in both places the politicians were reported to be nonplussed and annoyed at his unconditional recruiting drive.[4]

When Gandhi turned his attention to all-India issues neither the raj nor the politicians knew what to make of him. However, in retrospect his sorties into politics do not look as haphazard or as inconsistent as they appeared at the time. He became a political protagonist only when he saw

[1] Gandhi to Pranjivan Mehta, 2 July 1918, *C.W.*, vol. 14, p. 468.

[2] Bombay Police Abstract, 1918, par. 810, 910, 1049; Gandhi, *An Autobiography*, p. 371.

[3] Report of A.I.C.C. meeting on 3 May 1918, *The Bombay Chronicle*, 4 May 1918; Tilak to Gandhi, 19 June 1918, *The Bombay Chronicle*, 3 August 1918; report of Mrs Besant's speech at Madras Provincial Conference on 9/10/11 May 1918, Weekly report of D.C.I., 25 May 1918, Proceeding No. 584 of Home Pol., B, May 1918, Nos. 581–4.

[4] Bombay Police Abstract, 1918, par. 1132 (d), (m).

a 'wrong' he thought he could right, or when he saw an opportunity to promote his ideal of Swaraj. But on no occasion was he prepared to sacrifice his personal beliefs, either for the sake of implicit loyalty to the raj, or for full alliance with any group of politicians.

Gandhi's political isolation and his peripheral concern for ordinary political activity were clearest when the question of constitutional reform was under discussion. A public figure of his stature could not avoid taking some stand on a development in public life as momentous as the reform scheme. However, there is very little record of his reaction to the host of demands for special protection which greeted the prospect of reform. Whether this is because he deliberately avoided making pronouncements on the question, or because he was seldom faced with it, since he was not a leading politician, is impossible to tell. We do know that in April 1916 he spoke at a meeting after a Jain had said that Home Rule would bring advantages for Brahmins only and would keep the backward classes in a state of servitude. His reply accorded well with his views on caste, but it did not face the political issue squarely.

> Home Rule must be granted to India and all classes should present a united front in demanding it. If Home Rule should be granted, no particular class would dominate, otherwise it would not be Home Rule. He for one would oppose any party or class that wanted to set itself above the others. He made no distinction between the higher and the lower classes and did not look with disdain upon a man simply because he was a sweeper or a barber, nor did he look up to anyone merely because he was a Brahmin. His religion taught him to consider all men alike, without distinction of class or creed. Home Rule would not be granted so long as there were differences between them. He promised to do all in his power to remove their disabilities.[1]

Clearly Gandhi did not mean what the politicians meant by Home Rule, if he could assert that it 'would not be granted so long as there were differences between them.' This difference in meaning had been clear in theory from the time when Gandhi wrote in *Hind Swaraj* that Home Rule was self-rule; but now the definite promise of reform made the difference one of practical politics. Soon after Montagu's announcement, Gandhi told the Gujarat Political Conference that he wanted Home Rule as much as anybody, but only when they were fit for it and had sufficient self-control to curb the racial, religious and caste differences which had become so evident among them. This embarrassed the Bombay Home Rulers considerably, and since in his case they could not denounce him as a traitor to the motherland they attempted to forget the speech altogether, and *The Bombay Chronicle*, one of the most prominent Home Rule papers, did not even summarize it or refer to it in its editorial columns.[2]

[1] Bombay Police Abstract, 1916, par. 610 (d).

[2] Fortnightly report from Bombay, 16 November 1917, Home Pol., Deposit,

Although Gandhi was aware of the difference between his interpretation of Home Rule and that of the politicians, he was willing to participate in their Home Rule demands, as a way of publicizing and realizing his own aims. Consequently he accompanied the Congress deputation to Montagu in support of the Congress–League scheme of reform; but when Montagu dismissed him as 'a pure visionary' who did not understand the details of constitutional schemes he misjudged him.[1] Gandhi was a trained lawyer and could understand such details well enough when he wished, as at the 1917 session of Congress, when he and Tilak championed the Congress–League scheme in the face of some Bengalis' wishes for more extensive demands.[2]

After the Montagu–Chelmsford Report was published Srinivasa Sastri pressed Gandhi publicly to state his views. In his reply, which was widely published, Gandhi pointed out that he was not a keen politician and had not studied the proposals in great detail, and therefore hesitated to give an opinion on them. On balance he felt that they deserved 'sympathetic handling rather than a summary rejection', though they fell short of the Congress–League scheme. He hoped for a frank recognition that British interests should be subservient to Indian interests, and for this reason thought that dyarchy in the provinces should be rejected, military expenditure dramatically cut, the British element in the administration reduced to a minimum, local industries protected and taxes decreased. He still maintained, however, that Indian freedom would not emerge from such schemes concocted in Whitehall and Delhi, but from the battle fields of France which he hoped to 'crowd...with an indomitable army of Home Rulers'.[3]

When the approach of the Special Congress to discuss reforms made divisions among the politicians an important public issue, Gandhi advised that there should be 'no patched-up truce between the so-called extremists and the so-called moderates'. In his opinion each group should declare its policy, and those who made out the best case by argument and agitation would carry the day before the House of Commons.[4] His own position was clear: he belonged neither with Congress nor with the abstainers from Congress and preferred to bide his time, ploughing a solitary furrow. As he told Tilak,

January 1918, No. 1; Gandhi's Presidential Address at Gujarat Political Conference, 3 November 1917, *C.W.*, vol. 14, pp. 48–66.

1 Montagu, *An Indian Diary*, pp. 56, 58.

2 Weekly report of D.C.I., 12 January 1918, Proceeding No. 488 of Home Pol., B, January 1918, Nos. 487–90.

3 Gandhi to V. S. Srinivasa Sastri, 18 July 1918, *The Leader*, 24 July 1918, *C.W.*, vol. 14, pp. 486–9 (also published in *The Bombay Chronicle*, 19 July 1918). The police reported at this time that Tilak had asked Gandhi to start passive resistance over the Montagu–Chelmsford proposals, and Gandhi replied that he would do so if Tilak and his men would take up recruiting; this they refused to do. Bombay Police Abstract, 1918, par. 1180 (d).

4 Gandhi to Surendranath Bannerjee, 10 August 1918, *C.W.*, vol. 15, p. 15.

I do not propose to attend the Congress or the Moderates' Conference either. I see that my views are different from those of either...My view is that if all of us take up the work of recruitment for the war and enlist hundreds of thousands of recruits we can render a very great service to India. I know that Mrs. Besant and you do not share this view. The Moderates also will not take up the work earnestly. This is one thing. My other point is that we accept the substance of the Montagu–Chelmsford Scheme, explain clearly the improvements that we wish to be made in it and fight till death to have the improvements accepted. That the Moderates will not accept this is clear enough. Even if Mrs. Besant and you accept it, you will certainly not fight in the way I wish to fight. Mrs. Besant has declared that she is not a satyagrahi. You recognize satyagraha as [only] a weapon of the weak. I do not wish to get caught in this false position. And I do not wish to carry on an agitation in the Congress in opposition to you both. I have unshakable faith in my own formula.[1]

Gandhi's correspondence with prominent politicians shows how much they valued his approval and angled for his support on the reforms question; but his persistent refusal to be enmeshed in their shifting alliances perplexed them. As one of Tilak's men commented, 'Mahatma Gandhi [is] very estimable and good & yet in quantity so uncertain that you cannot count upon [him] for any particular purpose.'[2] Gandhi chose to be an isolated and part-time protagonist in the political field because his ambitions were not those of the other politicians. His choice became necessity after the Special Congress, because from August 1918 to January 1919 he was seriously ill. Sickness prevented him from making a public stand at the December session of Congress, and thereby possibly saved his reputation from further tarnishing in the eyes of the politicians.

Although Gandhi held his fire on most political issues during 1917 and 1918, there was one cause for which he made an all-out political offensive – the interned Ali brothers. Their fate, part of the war-time balance between conciliation and repression worked out by the raj, became Gandhi's springboard into overt political action; but because they were Muslims and so much his personal cause he was still able to keep clear of entanglements with Hindu politicians. Little was done for them until Gandhi became their spokesman. The reasoning behind his action was clear. To him their internment was not a legitimate action for the raj, even though it was at war; rather, it was a 'wrong' inflicted on members of a community whose interests he had become accustomed to championing in South Africa, a 'wrong' which he felt constrained to try to rectify. Moreover, an agita-

[1] Gandhi to B. G. Tilak, 25 August 1918, *ibid.* p. 31.

[2] G. S. Khaparde to J. Nehru, 4 November 1918, Nehru Memorial Museum and Library, New Delhi, J. Nehru Papers, File No. K. 78. In spite of this Gandhi was elected as one of the Bombay members of the A.I.C.C. at the end of 1918; he gained as many votes as M. A. Jinnah and two more than B. G. Tilak. *The Bombay Chronicle*, 23 December 1918.

tion to obtain their release was a means to the end he had in view, Swaraj. As he wrote to Mahomed Ali, 'my interest in your release is quite selfish. We have a common goal and I want to utilise your services to the uttermost, in order to reach that goal. In the proper solution of the Mahomedan question lies the realisation of Swarajya.'[1] Gandhi appears to have assumed that the Alis were representative of Muslim opinion and therefore an ideal instrument in his hand for creating a Hindu–Muslim alliance with the aim of obtaining Swaraj. Because to Gandhi Swaraj meant not just political Home Rule but a state of communal harmony, the brothers were valuable to him both as an issue on which to cement a communal alliance, and also because he thought they were splendid examples of that mingling of Hindu and Muslim culture which had occurred in the U.P.

However, his relationship with them was scarcely harmonious, as he had allied with men as strong-willed as himself. He therefore found himself forced to fight a battle on two fronts, demanding their release from the government while simultaneously trying to restrain their wilder demands which would dash any hopes of their release and alienate the Hindu community.

Gandhi first contacted the Alis early in 1916. At the 1915 Congress he was able to get their address and promptly wrote to ask if he could be of any service and said, 'I wanted to write to you to say how much my heart went out to you in your troubles.'[2] He was forbidden by the government to visit them in internment, and decided that the only thing he could do 'as a passive resister...in circumstances such as this' was 'to bow to the decision of the Govt of India.'[3] The earliest signs that he proposed to be their champion came nearly two years later when at the First Gujarat Political Conference he called for their release, and at a meeting of the Muslim League urged Hindus and Muslims to appeal to the government on their behalf, assuring his Muslim audience, amid loud cheers, that the Hindus were with them to a man.[4]

He was not alone in his interest in the Alis. Politicians as different as Annie Besant and Dr B. S. Moonje (a Tilakite from C.P. who was later a leading figure in the Hindu Mahasabha) expressed concern about their internment; and in some areas Home Rulers took up their cause as a counterweight to Muslim hesitations about Home Rule propaganda. Gandhi, however, was the one leader who consistently stood out as the Alis' champion, and he dated his alliance with them from the 1917 meeting

1 Gandhi to M. Ali, November 1918, Home Pol., Deposit, December 1918, No. 3. (Dated as 18 November in *C.W.*, vol. 15, pp. 63–4.)

2 Gandhi to M. Ali, 9 January 1916, Ali Papers, quoted in Robinson, 'The Politics Of U.P. Muslims 1906–1922', p. 351.

3 Gandhi to M. Ali, 14 April 1916, Ali Papers.

4 Speech by Gandhi at First Gujarat Political Conference, 3 November 1917, *C.W.*, vol. 14, p. 51; speech by Gandhi at Muslim League meeting, Calcutta, 31 December 1917, *The Bombay Chronicle*, 1 January 1918, *ibid.* p. 120.

of the Muslim League, maintaining that from that date they 'implicitly accepted the advice' he gave them.[1]

Gandhi envisaged 'a battle royal' over the Alis' internment and as a precaution he instructed his nephew, Maganlal Gandhi, to transfer all the money received for the *ashram* into his (Maganlal's) name, so that it would be safe in the event of a government campaign against him.[2] The first volley in the battle was a letter from Gandhi to the Viceroy's Private Secretary on 1 January 1918 in which he argued that the Alis were loyal to the British government and that their internment was causing great bitterness in India among both Hindus and Muslims. He asked permission to visit them and obtain a public declaration of their loyalty. The visit was not permitted but Mahomed Ali wrote to him 'I declare for myself and my brother that you are at liberty to state publicly, if need be, that both of us ... believe in the British connection and consider ourselves perfectly loyal citizens of the Empire.' He explained that during his internment he had for the first time been able to read the Koran right through, and as a result had experienced a kind of conversion. He now believed that the whole aim of life was to serve God. The only reservation in his loyalty to the British was that obedience to God took first place, and for a Muslim this meant resisting any encroachment on Muslim sanctuaries or on the spiritual position of the Khalifah.[3]

However genuine this conversion may or may not have been, this was a line of reasoning guaranteed to appeal to the Mahatma; and in March Gandhi visited the Viceroy's Private Secretary, putting their case again by word of mouth and in writing. To the arguments that their internment was unjust and was generating much bitterness he added the suggestion that their release would make Abdul Bari, their spiritual adviser, a staunch government supporter. Gandhi thought that Bari had thousands of Muslim followers and he was in effect offering the raj the bait of sure collaborators according to his calculations![4]

When appeals for the Alis' release fell on deaf ears, Gandhi altered his tactics and throughout the summer of 1918 corresponded with the Home Member of the Government of India in an attempt to secure an enquiry into the Alis' case. In his own words, 'Before throwing the country in a very

[1] Gandhi to J. L. Maffey, 20 February 1919, Home Pol., A, July 1919, No. 1 & K.-W. For the interest of other politicians and Home Rulers in the Alis see the following: A. Besant to M. Ali, 29 October 1915, Ali Papers; B. S. Moonje to Mr Dhok, 28 September 1917, Ali Papers; Fortnightly reports from Bombay and Madras for first half of October 1917, Home Pol., Deposit, November 1917, No. 29.

[2] Gandhi to Maganlal Gandhi, 20 January 1918, *C.W.*, vol. 14, p. 160.

[3] Gandhi to J. L. Maffey, 1 January 1918, *ibid.* pp. 141–2; M. Ali to Gandhi, 20 February 1918, Ali Papers (this appears to have got through the censorship of the Alis' post though I can find no trace of it in Gandhi's papers).

[4] Gandhi to J. L. Maffey, 25 March 1918, *C.W.*, vol. 14, pp. 280–1.

big agitation I want to give the Government every opportunity of a proper and decent retreat.'[1] The government eventually appointed a committee of enquiry, but to the Alis' fury Gandhi was not allowed to visit and advise them on their submissions to the committee. They complained bitterly about this, describing Gandhi as their 'trusted friend and advisor' and as one of the Indians in whom they placed the most confidence, who had been interested in their cause for a long time.

> We regard the refusal to receive a visit from one whose name we had deliberately put at the head of the list that we had been asked to submit as a wholly unmeritted hardship; what Mr. Gandhi who has so often been refused permission feels on the subject we need not say; but we feel certain that it would be regarded by the entire public as a slur on one of the noblest men in India.[2]

For his part Gandhi treated with disdain the indictment of the Alis put before the committee, because he thought it was so weak. He wrote to Mahomed Ali,

> Any way we can now contemplate the findings of the Committee with complete indifference. Your defence is so overwhelmingly strong that if the Committee's finding is hostile an agitation can be raised which will make India resound with indignation over the monstrous injustice under which you have laboured so long and so patiently.[3]

The committee recommended the brothers' release because peace had come by the time it reported and there was little it thought the brothers could do to harm Anglo-Turkish relations, although it carefully justified their war-time internment. The government, however, felt that it could not act on this recommendation because the committee 'were not in a position to appreciate the political situation in all its bearings, or the difficulties arising out of the fact that there has been no change whatever in the attitude of the brothers'.[4]

Gandhi continued to complain that the charges against the Alis were unwarrantable and to press for their release; but now the real battle began against the brothers' violent impatience at the government's refusal to release them. Whereas in November 1918 Gandhi had talked of making India resound with indignation, March 1919 saw him immersed in pre-

1 Gandhi to O. S. Ghate, the Alis' legal adviser, 6 August 1918, *C.W.*, vol. 15, p. 5. The whole of the correspondence between Gandhi and the Home Member is not available but is referred to in this letter to Ghate, and in a letter from Gandhi to J. L. Maffey, 20 February 1919, *C.W.*, vol. 15, p. 94.

2 M. & S. Ali to S. R. Pandit, 30 September 1918, Ali Papers.

3 Gandhi to M. Ali, November 1918, Home Pol., Deposit, December 1918, No. 3.

4 Proposed government answer to question in Imperial Legislative Council, Home Pol., A, July 1919, No. 1 & K.-W. The committee consisted of Mr B. Lindsay, Judicial Commissioner of Oudh, and Abdur Rauf, late officiating judge of Allahabad High Court.

paration for satyagraha on a far wider topic – the Rowlatt bills – and he decided to play down the Alis' plight for the time being, proposing to bring it up as an issue later in the struggle if it seemed appropriate.[1]

When Gandhi was restricted to Bombay in the course of the Rowlatt satyagraha, he felt the time was ripe for action and sent the Alis a verbal message advising them to break their own restriction order after sending the Viceroy a temperate letter detailing Muslim grievances.[2] The brothers followed Gandhi's advice, but the letter they sent to the Viceroy on 24 April was scarcely temperate. They denounced the war against Turkey and the committee which studied their case, they complained that they were interned for an article of their faith, namely sympathy with Turkey, and they made extreme claims for the international protection of Islam, with emphasis on the integrity of the Khalifah's empire and his control of the Muslim holy places. In conclusion they announced that their patience having ended, they would resort to civil disobedience. This letter was printed at the Nimroz Press, Bombay; a few copies were circulated by Umar Sobhani in Bombay, Calcutta and the U.P., and about 900 were sent to Shaukat Ali's son in Chhindwara, where the brothers were interned. The remaining 4,000 copies appear to have been burnt by Sobhani and Jamnadas Dwarkadas when the government forfeited the letter and the press's security money.[3] Undeterred, the day after the letter was forfeited the Alis announced their intention of breaking their internment order, telling Gandhi and other friends that they were tired of waiting, whatever restraint their advisers argued.[4]

Gandhi reacted strongly to the brothers' letter to the Viceroy. He told them and their legal adviser that he thought their language was undignified and inflammatory, and that they had made an exaggerated statement of Muslim claims, by raising questions which had been settled before the war. He had sent them a further message from Bombay when he was released, advising them not to break their own internment order; he did not know whether this had ever reached them, but now he suggested that they

1 Gandhi to O. S. Ghate, 25 March 1919, *C.W.*, vol. 15, p. 151. For the Rowlatt bills and Gandhi's satyagraha against them, see below, pp. 160–89.

2 Fortnightly report from Bombay, 16/19 May 1919, Home Pol., Deposit, July 1919, No. 48. The idea of a letter to the Viceroy and some form of passive resistance by the Alis had been mooted in a letter to Gandhi, 14 March 1919, Ali Papers. This may have been sent by Ghate, but as it also appears in the Abdul Bari Papers at Ferangi Mahal, Lucknow, it may have been sent by Bari.

3 M. & S. Ali to Viceroy, 24 April 1919, Ali Papers; note by W. S. Marris, 29 May 1919, Home Pol., A, July 1919, Nos. 2–32; Fortnightly report from Bombay, 16/19 May 1919, Home Pol., Deposit, July 1919, No. 48.

4 M. & S. Ali to Chief Commissioner of C.P., 9 May 1919, S.N. No. 6602, also in Home Pol., A, July 1919, Nos. 2–32; letters from M. & S. Ali to Gandhi, 9 May 1919, S.N. No. 6601; M. Ali to M. A. Ansari, 12 May 1919 (intercepted), Weekly report of D.C.I., 19 May 1919, Proceeding No. 496 of Home Pol., B, June 1919, Nos. 494–7.

should 'summon up the courage to recall the notice of disobedience and tell the Viceroy that upon maturer consideration and for the sake of the cause for which you stand you have decided not to disobey the order for the time being.'[1] He was also reported to be irate with Umar Sobhani and Jamnadas Dwarkadas for their action in helping with the distribution of the letter. This was understandable: both of them were prominent Bombay leaders in his satyagraha against the Rowlatt bills and here they were, compromising his campaign on a far more important issue by circulating inflammatory literature.[2]

In June Gandhi was still at loggerheads with the Alis over this letter, but admitted, 'I quite agree with you that so long as I can not convince you you must act as you feel right.'[3] At this point the Government of India intervened and imprisoned the brothers. Before, as internees in a private house rather than prisoners in gaol, they had had considerable liberty of movement and correspondence: now their freedom to choose their own course of action was drastically curtailed and they fell back again on Gandhi's direction. Abdul Bari also said he would do nothing without Gandhi's advice, although the brothers were becoming extremely restive, as nothing seemed to be done on their behalf. To him and the prisoners Gandhi replied that it was best that they should keep completely quiet and that no agitation should be started on their behalf.[4] In the event they had to wait until the government released them of its own accord in December 1919, under the amnesty for political prisoners which accompanied the inauguration of the Montagu–Chelmsford Reforms.

By 1919 Gandhi was fishing in the far deeper waters of the Rowlatt satyagraha and the Khilafat agitation, and the Ali brothers had to take a back place in his plans. However, his early championship of them had prepared him for the all-India role he was to play; and as their mentor he had entered the political arena as a serious protagonist, whereas on other political issues he was still the part-time amateur. At the end of 1918 he was recognized as a spokesman for Muslims and as one who could initiate and control action among some members of the Muslim community. Dr Ansari, a prominent Delhi Muslim who chaired the reception committee of the 1918 Muslim League meeting, called him 'that dauntless champion

1 Gandhi to M. & S. Ali, 23 May 1919, S.N. No. 6622. See also Gandhi to O. S. Ghate, 8 May 1919, *C.W.*, vol. 15, p. 290.

2 Fortnightly report from Bombay, 16/19 May 1919, Home Pol., Deposit, July 1919, No. 48.

3 Gandhi to M. & S. Ali, 5 June 1919, S.N. No. 11700.

4 A. Bari to Gandhi, 16 June, 4 August 1919, S.N. Nos. 6663 & 6788; Gandhi to Bari, 20 June 1919, reported in Bombay Police Abstract, 1919, par. 901 (g); Gandhi to Bari, 27 August 1919, Abdul Bari Papers, Ferangi Mahal, Lucknow (I owe this reference to Mrs Gail Graham); Gandhi to M. Ali, 29 June 1919, S.N. 6657 (this letter is not dated in the Sabarmati collection but *C.W.*, vol. 15, p. 404 dates it as 29 July 1919 from a Home Pol. source).

of our rights' and thanked him as 'that acknowledged intrepid leader of India...who is never afraid to speak out the truth and who has, by his noble actions, endeared himself, as much to Musalmans as to Hindus.'[1]

Despite Ansari's acclamation of Gandhi as a friend of Muslims, the Mahatma had only allied with a small group in the Muslim community. Most Muslims felt that the war was a grievous strain on their community with its dual sympathy for the British and the Turks, but by no means all of them supported the openly Pan-Islamist propagandists,[2] particularly since such propagandists wanted to change the whole political direction of Indian Islam towards agitation in alliance with Congress. The differences of opinion which split the community and its political body, the Muslim League, when the Lucknow Pact raised the issue continued through 1917 and 1918. During those years the League was controlled by U.P.'s Rajah of Mahmudabad and his henchman, the Hon'ble Syed Wazir Hassan, members of the 'Young Party' but increasingly moderate by contrast with the Pan-Islamists. Consequently the League was caught in the cross-fire of recrimination: the Pan-Islamists criticized it as inactive and moribund, while those who still favoured the tactics of collaboration with the raj opposed it because of its compromise with Congress at Lucknow.[3]

The fate of the League was decided at its session in Delhi on 30/31 December 1918, when Mahmudabad and Hassan resigned from office and the Pan-Islamists took over in force. Fazlul Haq from Bengal presided, and Dr Ansari made a powerful speech criticizing the internment of the Ali brothers and demanding that the Sultan of Turkey should continue to control Muslim sanctuaries and a wide empire including Arabia, Palestine and Mesopotamia, because he was 'the only Muhammadan who could possibly be capable of successfully combating the intrigues and secret machinations of non-Muslim governments.'[4] Ansari insisted that a good Muslim was also a good nationalist and would fight for the rights of Hindus and Muslims at the same time as he strove to maintain his own position. To prove the point he launched into adulation of Gandhi, while the League took up the same position by echoing the demands of the simultaneous Congress session about the reforms.

[1] Speech by M. A. Ansari in Delhi at Muslim League meeting, 30 December 1918, Besant Papers.

[2] Not even the ulema could agree on the precise religious implications of the war or the degree to which it was legitimate to embarrass the British raj by agitation in support of the Khalifah. See Weekly report of D.C.I., 2 February 1915, Proceeding No. 777 of Home Pol., B, February 1915, Nos. 777–80; Fortnightly report from U.P., 17 August 1916, Home Pol., Deposit, September 1916, No. 17.

[3] Weekly report of D.C.I., 9 June 1917, Proceeding No. 439 of Home Pol., B, June 1917, Nos. 438–41; Weekly report of D.C.I., 9 November 1918, Proceeding No. 158 of Home Pol., B, December 1918, Nos. 158–9.

[4] Weekly report of D.C.I., 18 January 1919, Proceeding No. 162 of Home Pol., B, January 1919, Nos. 160–3; speech by M. A. Ansari in Delhi at Muslim League meeting, 30 December 1918, Besant Papers.

The opposition of many Muslims to the Lucknow Pact and the reforms made Ansari's claim a highly dubious one, but he, like Gandhi, either failed to see or chose to ignore the ambiguity of the Muslim position in relation to the nationalist movement. However, the vacillations of those Muslims who opposed the Pan-Islamists and their lack of organization gave the Pan-Islamists their chance to seize control of the League, and Gandhi his opportunity to ally with the most vociferous and skilled political agitators the community could produce.

As momentous for Muslim politics and for Gandhi's political standing as the takeover of the League's organization by the Pan-Islamists was the entry into politics of a group of ulema at this session of the League. The 'Editors and Barristers' who so frightened the older generation of Muslim politicians brought their priestly allies with them. A group of ulema met at the Fatehpuri Mosque in Delhi the day the session opened and passed a resolution reminding the government of the sanctity of Jerusalem and other Muslim shrines. The next day ten of them, including Abdul Bari, took this resolution to the League meeting and declared that if Jerusalem was not evacuated they would not answer for the loyalty of Indian Muslims. In reply to a resolution welcoming them at the League their spokesman 'repudiated the charge that they considered religion and politics were two separate things. No doubt they had left politics to the League in the past, but when the call went out, they were only too glad to join in the political body.'[1] The potential of this alliance between the politician and the priest was clear to contemporaries. In the words of one official:

> If the *ulemas*, with their power to arouse the fanaticism of the ignorant masses, become the tools of the extremists of the Muslim League, the danger to the tranquility of India is obvious. It is doubtful, however, if their adhesion to the League will be permanent. For the moment, the international situation excites the apprehension of both political and religious leaders, but when the crisis is over it seems improbable that the *ulemas* will use their influence in favour of Congress–League politics.[2]

Just as the Congressmen who were furthest from accepting the reforms roped in peasant delegates to support their claims, so the Muslim politicians who opted for agitation rather than collaboration with the raj spread their net outside the normal range of the politically active to gain support. In both cases policies produced by the pressures of the war helped to widen the span of participation in institutional politics; and by the end of 1918 Gandhi was in a position where he might be able to exploit at least the new network of support which the ulema opened up, because he had cemented an alliance with the politicians who worked with them

1 Bamford, *Histories of the Non-Co-operation and Khilafat Movements*, p. 133.

2 Weekly report of D.C.I., 18 January 1919, Proceeding No. 162 of Home Pol., B, January 1919, Nos. 160–3.

through his political offensive on behalf of the Ali brothers. His Muslim allies might be a minority in their community, but they were strategically placed to arouse far deeper and wider support than the older politicians of either community had been able to muster.

Compared with the man who had merely been called in to advise on passive resistance in 1917, the Gandhi who got up from a sick bed to fight the Rowlatt bills at the beginning of 1919 was an all-India figure of considerable stature. The policies of the raj at war had forced him out of the restricted world of local grievances into the all-India political arena. The government had created certain issues on a far wider scale than particular localities, which Gandhi considered to be 'wrongs' which he was in conscience bound to try to redress: but it had also attracted his cooperation in the matter of recruiting and constitutional reform. Consequently it was not possible for contemporaries to say exactly where Gandhi stood in relation to the raj. His was a loyalty punctuated with much criticism on specific issues where he felt the British were not implementing the ideals of the constitution which was the basis of his allegiance to their rule.

A similar ambivalence was apparent in his relationship with the politicians. He fitted into no one political group because of his singular ideology and method of work, and he was not prepared to challenge the politicians on their own ground. Yet they dared not discount him, because by working in his own ways he had become a recognized leader with some powerful local followings and a hold over those Muslim leaders who were skilled at agitation and might arouse widespread Muslim concern with the cry of 'Islam in danger'. The potential for a new leadership in the world of politics was there, if Gandhi chose to enter that world more permanently, although it was impossible to know whether the networks of support he had created or tapped for specific causes would hold firm on more general issues. So far he had shown no signs of wanting to conduct a country-wide satyagraha or to try to supersede the established political leaders. Whether or not he would depended on external circumstances, in particular on the actions of the raj.

CHAPTER 5

THE ROWLATT SATYAGRAHA

Before 1919 Gandhi was only a peripheral figure in the politics of nationalism. He joined the ranks of the politicians to forward a few well-defined causes, and because he was not prompted by any conventional political ambition he was content with local and sectional leadership and made no attempt to challenge the existing political leaders when he disagreed with them. However, by mid-1919 the Mahatma had broken out of these limits. He had made a bid for all-India leadership in the teeth of much opposition, and had declared that occasional participation in politics was no longer adequate for the ends he had in mind. He described how he saw his role in July 1919:

> My bent is not political but religious and I take part in politics because I feel that there is no department of life which can be divorced from religion and because politics touch the vital being of India almost at every point. It is therefore absolutely necessary that the political relation between Englishmen and ourselves should be put on a sound basis. I am endeavouring to the best of my ability to assist in the process.[1]

The occasion for this transition from peripheral to committed participation in politics, from local to continental leadership, was satyagraha against the Rowlatt bills. At first sight it is particularly curious that this should have been so, because the Rowlatt Report and the bills which incorporated its recommendations concerned governmental power to deal with sedition and conspiracy – an issue with very limited political appeal, which disturbed the politicians but barely impinged on the lives of ordinary people. Few causes could have been further from those for which Gandhi had launched satyagraha in 1917 and 1918, and on the surface it seemed an improbable foundation on which to try to build a broadly based, continental leadership.

The Rowlatt bills were the postscript to the policy of balance between conciliation and repression which the British had evolved during the war. Even while the rulers wooed collaborators with reforms they feared the loss of coercive power against 'conspiracy and political outrage' when the Defence of India Act lapsed after the war.[2] A committee was therefore

1 Gandhi to G. Arundale, 4 July 1919, *The Bombay Chronicle*, 12 August 1919.

2 Secretary of State to Governor-General in Council, Judicial Despatch No. 1 (Secret), 13 October 1916, Proceeding No. 230 of Home Pol., A, August 1917, Nos. 225–32.

appointed in December 1917, headed by Mr Justice Rowlatt, to review the situation. Its report, published on 19 July 1918, described as centres of dangerous conspiracy Bengal, plagued by 'a long series of murders and robberies' prompted by the 'elaborate, persistent and ingenious' propaganda of 'young men belonging to the educated middle classes', Bombay Presidency, where Chitpavan Brahmins fostered Mahratta nationalism, and the Punjab, disturbed by emigrants returned from America.[1]

In the light of this the committee recommended that the government should have emergency powers to deal with any area officially proclaimed subversive. Among the powers it suggested were the trial of seditious crimes by benches of three judges, sitting *in camera* if necessary, without juries, who might be subject to terrorism and would certainly be influenced by public discussion, the power to demand security from suspects, to restrict places of residence, to require abstention from certain activities, and to arrest and imprison in non-penal custody.

To the Secretary of State many of these recommendations were 'most repugnant' and he told the Viceroy,

> I do most awfully want to help you to stamp out rebellion and revolution, but I loathe the suggestion at first sight of preserving the Defence of India Act in peace time to such an extent as Rowlatt and his friends think necessary. Why cannot these things be done by normal, or even exceptional processes of law? (I hate to give the Pentlands of this world or the O'Dwyers the chance of locking a man up without trial.)[2]

He sanctioned the bills with obvious reluctance, after the Viceroy had said he thought it impossible for his government to do otherwise than produce legislation enacting the committee's recommendations,[3] and they were introduced into the Imperial Legislative Council in February 1919. There they were opposed by every Indian member: as one member commented, 'In the life of this council this was the first instance on which all the Indians voted one way.'[4] The Viceroy spoke publicly of his government's 'very deepest regret' at having to differ from its 'non-official Indian friends', but as he and the Home Member explained in Council, they felt they must press on to avoid any gap between the new legislation and the lapse of war-

[1] *Report Of Committee Appointed To Investigate Revolutionary Conspiracies In India* (London, 1918), Cd. 9190, p. 75. The other members of the committee were Sir Basil Scott, Chief Justice of Bombay, C. V. Kumaraswami Sastri, Madras High Court Judge, Sir Verney Lovett, member of U.P. Board of Revenue, and P. C. Mitter, additional member of Bengal Legislative Council.

[2] E. S. Montagu to Chelmsford, 10 October 1918, Mss. EUR. E. 264 (4). Pentland was the Governor of Madras who so reluctantly released Annie Besant and protested against Montagu's declaration in August 1917. Sir Michael O'Dwyer was the Lieutenant-Governor of the Punjab, for whose policy see below, p. 231.

[3] Chelmsford to E. S. Montagu, 19 November 1918, E. S. Montagu to Chelmsford, 23 December 1918, Mss. EUR. E. 264 (4).

[4] 7 February 1919, Diary of G. S. Khaparde, Khaparde Papers.

time regulations.[1] The bill as it finally emerged from committee and Council gave the government the proposed powers, but it was only to last for three years and could only be used 'for the purpose of dealing with anarchical and revolutionary movements'. Chelmsford assented to the bill on 21 March 1919, despite the ominous fact that the government had to force it through Council with its official majority, with the result that voting was on purely racial lines, 35 for and 20 against.[2] At least one Indian member, Pandit B. D. Shukul, representing landholders from C.P., resigned his seat in protest because he thought the Indian voice carried no weight in Council.[3]

Politicians of all shades of opinion saw this as a blow to their type of politics. What worth had reforms if the government could retain autocratic powers? What chances had they with the electorate if they could take news only of repressive legislation to their constituencies, branding their politics as powerless before a determined government?[4] There were dire misgivings in Indian political circles about the Rowlatt Committee before its report was published, and N. C. Kelkar, one of Tilak's Chitpavan Brahmin lieutenants, suggested that Indians might have to resort to passive resistance if unjust laws and orders were the result.[5] In Bombay after the report was published every paper except *The Indian Social Reformer* opposed it, and even that lone voice became hostile when the report's suggestions were turned into bills. 'If constitutional reforms cannot be had but at such a price, we do not want them. What will it profit India if it have the beginnings of responsible government if the liberties of the Indian people are carefully consigned beforehand to the keeping of the irresponsible part of the Executive?'[6]

Similar reactions came from all over India. The political press in U.P., C.P. and Berar chorussed protest, and one Bengali paper was so hostile on the subject that its security was forfeited. Annie Besant's *New India* con-

[1] Speech by Sir W. Vincent in the Imperial Legislative Council, *The Times of India*, 17 March 1919; speech by Chelmsford in Imperial Legislative Council, 21 March 1919, Mss. EUR. E. 264 (28).

[2] Home Pol., B, June 1919, No. 82. A copy of the Rowlatt Act, Act No. XI of 1919 is also in that file. The other proposed Rowlatt bill, which would have altered the Indian Penal Code and the Code of Criminal Procedure, was dropped because public opinion was hostile, official opinion was divided, and the government did not want another battle in the Imperial Legislative Council, Home Pol., Deposit, May 1921, No. 43.

[3] Letter, 7 June 1919, from some landholders in C.P. to B. D. Shukul, asking him to stand for re-election, and Shukul's reply, *The Bombay Chronicle*, 13 June 1919.

[4] The prevalence of this feeling was described by the editor of *The Times of India*, Sir Stanley Reed, in his *The India I Knew. 1897–1947* (London, 1952), pp. 72–3.

[5] *Mahratta*, 17 February 1918, Bombay N.N., No. 7 of 1918, p. 4.

[6] Quoted in *The Times of India*, 12 February 1919; report on reactions to the Rowlatt Report in Bombay in Fortnightly report from Bombay, 3 August 1918, Home Pol., Deposit, September 1918, No. 20.

demned the report's proposals and the bills as vitiating the reforms and placing India under a regime more coercive than the Irish government in the nineteenth century, while *The Tribune* from the Punjab declared, 'These Bills and the manner in which the bureaucracy is carrying and is likely to carry them through contain in a nutshell the whole of the Indian case for self-government'.[1] The politicians held protest meetings, but their wrath spilled over and touched people who were certainly not part of the political nation, as one politician noted in Delhi. 'I went to the Secretariat in a hired Tonga', he wrote in his diary, '& was very much surprized [sic] to see that the driver who was an illiterate Mahomedan spoke of the Rowlatt bills & objected to them very strongly.'[2]

Once the bill became law verbal protest was useless and the politicians' unanimity disintegrated. The episode had showed up the poverty of their limited politics, built on the assumption that the raj and the politicians could best serve their own interests by coming to a mutually acceptable agreement about the division of power. On the rare occasions such as this when the raj was adamant, the politicians had no leverage, and they were at a loss to know what to do. Protest in Council and public meetings had got them nowhere, and they could not take to violence, even if they had countenanced such methods, without inviting more repression and proving to the government that the Rowlatt legislation was indeed necessary. They had reached a political impasse, and the man who stepped forward to offer them a way out was Gandhi.

Illness prevented Gandhi from participating in the early discussions on the Rowlatt recommendations, but once the bills came before the Imperial Legislative Council he began to campaign from his bed. Early in February he told Srinivasa Sastri that he thought the bills were not just 'a stray example of lapse of righteousness and justice' but 'evidence of a determined policy of repression', and consequently he was considering the possibility of passive resistance if they became law. 'For myself if the Bills were to be proceeded with, I feel I can no longer render peaceful obedience to the laws of a power that is capable of such a piece of devilish legislation as these two Bills, and I would not hesitate to invite those who think with me to join me in the struggle.'[3]

1 *The Tribune*, 28 February 1919; *New India*, 11 October 1918, 30 January 1919; *Report on the Administration of Bengal, 1918–1919* (Calcutta, 1921), p. ii; *Report on the Administration of the Central Provinces & Berar for the year 1918–19* (Nagpur, 1920), p. xv; *Report on the Administration of the United Provinces Of Agra And Oudh, 1918–1919* (Allahabad, 1920), p. 64.

2 6 March 1919, Diary of G. S. Khaparde, Khaparde Papers. Report of meeting of protest against the bills in Madras on 30 January 1919, at which Kasturi Ranga Iyengar presided, *The Bombay Chronicle*, 1 February 1919; report of Bombay meeting of protest against the bills, where M. M. Malaviya presided, *The Times of India*, 3 February 1919.

3 Gandhi to V. S. S. Sastri, 9 February 1919, *C.W.*, vol. 15, pp. 87–8. Gandhi wrote to Pandit Malaviya similarly on 8 February 1919, *ibid.* p. 86.

Gandhi opposed the bills for several reasons. He believed that the proposed powers were out of all proportion to the danger, particularly when the Viceroy possessed emergency powers of legislation by ordinance, and he thought that they were instruments of distrust and repression, nullifying the proposed reforms. Moreover he opposed not just the content of the bills, but also the manner in which they were foisted on the country without regard to public opinion.[1] He justified resistance to the government on the grounds that it was taking away from the people their God-given rights: since in his view the government only held power by the will of God it ceased to command obedience when it disobeyed the fundamental laws of God.[2]

Gandhi's entry into the political arena was novel only in its scale and the scope of his intentions. It was consistent with his earlier incursions into politics, but now he saw a national 'wrong' which could possibly be righted only by his methods, and a way of bringing the whole of India nearer to his ideal of Swaraj through the technique of satyagraha. He saw what he had seen in Kaira, a total disregard by the government for the wishes of the people, but this time on a far wider stage. Echoing what he had said then, he told the Secretary of State, 'This retention of Rowlatt legislation in the teeth of universal opposition is an *affront* to the nation. Its repeal is necessary to appease national honour.'[3] The remedy he proposed to his compatriots, as in Kaira, was satyagraha. Not only was it for him the sole means which by its effect on its exponents could bring about the end he had in view, true Swaraj;[4] it was also in utilitarian terms a way out of the politicians' impasse, since it avoided violence but liberated them from their dependence on petition and negotiation. As he explained to one of the veterans of limited politics, 'I think the growing generation will not be satisfied with petitions, etc. We must give them something effective. Satyagraha is the only way, it seems to me, to stop terrorism.'[5]

The first phase of the Rowlatt satyagraha – the phase of deliberation and preparation – lasted from February to the observance of hartal at the beginning of April. The heart of the movement was the Bombay Presidency, in particular Bombay city and Ahmedabad. On 24 February, the

1 Evidence by Gandhi before the Hunter Committee at Ahmedabad, reported in *The Bombay Chronicle*, 20 January 1920; message sent by Gandhi to Madras meeting, *The Bombay Chronicle*, 4 April 1919; message sent by Gandhi to Madras meeting, *The Bombay Chronicle*, 22 March 1919.

2 J. Dwarkadas to A. Besant, 27 February 1919, Besant Papers.

3 Draft letter in Gandhi's handwriting to E. S. Montagu, 14 June 1919, S.N. No. 6658. For Gandhi's attitude towards government by consent in Kaira, see above, p. 103.

4 Gandhi believed that satyagraha over the Rowlatt bills would 'purify the atmosphere and bring in real swaraj.' Gandhi to C. F. Andrews, 25 February 1919, *C.W.*, vol. 15, p. 104.

5 Gandhi to Sir D. E. Wacha, 25 February 1919, *C.W.*, vol. 15, p. 107.

day after a meeting of the Ahmedabad branch of the Home Rule League to protest against the Rowlatt bills, there was a gathering of Ahmedabad and Bombay Home Rulers at Gandhi's *ashram*. From Ahmedabad came Vallabhbhai Patel, Chandulal Desai, K. Thakoor, Anasuya Sarabhai and others, and they were joined by Jamnadas Dwarkadas, Sarojini Naidu, B. G. Horniman, editor of *The Bombay Chronicle*, and Umar Sobhani from Bombay. Already familiar with Gandhi's doctrines and methods from the Kaira and Ahmedabad satyagrahas, they now looked to Gandhi for guidance on an overt and national political issue. Gandhi himself was uncertain what to do, but the last word rested with him, and from the meeting there emerged a Satyagraha Sabha and a manifesto containing a satyagraha pledge for its members.[1] The pledge ran,

> Being conscientiously of the opinion that the Rowlatt Bills...are unjust, subversive of the principle of liberty and justice, and destructive of the elementary rights of individuals on which the safety of the community as a whole and the State itself is based, we solemnly affirm that, in the event of these Bills becoming law and until they are withdrawn, we shall refuse civilly to obey these laws and such other laws as a Committee to be hereafter appointed may think fit and we further affirm that in this struggle we will faithfully follow truth and refrain from violence to life, person or property.[2]

The same day, 24 February, Gandhi informed the Viceroy that if the government would not reconsider its position over the bills he would have to publish the pledge and invite further signatures to it.[3]

To have given this small breathing space to the raj apparently salved Gandhi's conscience. 'I am now quite at peace with myself', he wrote, 'The telegram to the Viceroy eased me considerably. He has the warning. He can stop what bids fare to become a mighty conflagration. If it comes, and if the satyagrahis remain true to their pledge, it can but purify the atmosphere and bring in real swaraj.'[4] Immediately he plunged into a publicity campaign on a greater scale than he had attempted before. He wrote letters to politicians and editors whom he knew would probably disapprove of his actions, in order to explain his real intentions.[5] The committee of the Satyagraha Sabha published detailed instructions to volunteers who were collecting signatures to the pledge to ensure that the news of the

1 Gandhi to C. F. Andrews, 25 February 1919, *ibid.* p. 104; *Report Of The Committee Appointed By The Government Of India To Investigate Disturbances In The Punjab, Etc.* (London, 1920), Cd. 681, p. 9. (Henceforth, *Hunter Report.*)

2 Satyagraha Pledge, 24 February 1919, *New India*, 3 March 1919, *C.W.*, vol. 15, pp. 101–2.

3 Gandhi to the Viceroy, telegram, 24 February 1919, S.N. No. 6434.

4 Gandhi to C. F. Andrews, 25 February 1919, *C.W.*, vol. 15, p. 104.

5 For example, Gandhi to Sir D. E. Wacha, Sir S. Reed, editor of *The Times of India*, and K. Natrajan, editor of *The Indian Social Reformer*, all 25 February 1919, *ibid.* pp. 107, 106, 105–6.

Rowlatt bills was spread far and wide, and Gandhi himself wrote an open letter to the press explaining the pledge.[1]

His main henchmen were the Home Rulers. When the police watched him in Bombay they noted that Home Rulers were constantly visiting him. They dominated the Executive Committee of the Satyagraha Sabha, they took signatures to the pledge, and their local branches held meetings in support of satyagraha in provincial towns and villages.[2] From the beginning of 1919 Jamnadas Dwarkadas, B. G. Horniman, Anasuya Sarabhai and others had interested themselves in the problems of the Bombay mill-workers, though they found this was a section of the city's population which they could not control; and when they organized a meeting and procession in the mill area as part of their protests against the Rowlatt bills they met with little success.[3] Outside the overtly political circle in Bombay the campaign appealed to young people and to the cloth merchants. The Mulji Jetha Cloth Market, where support for the Kaira satyagraha had been marked, even observed a hartal of its own on 21 March to mark the passage of the Rowlatt Act, and two other Bombay markets followed suit.[4] By mid-March between 600 and 800 people had actually signed the satyagraha pledge in the Bombay Presidency.[5]

Bombay and Gujarat were the core of the movement. This was what Gandhi intended, according to Jamnadas Dwarkadas, because only in those areas did he and his followers who had first signed the pledge know the conditions and the people, and therefore only there could they hope to keep the movement on the right lines.[6] Other parts of India produced only a half-hearted response. In Madras a branch of the Satyagraha Sabha was founded on 22 March with Gandhi as its President, Kasturi Ranga Iyengar as its Vice-President and C. Vijiaraghavachariar as one of its Secretaries. In spite of this only about 120 people signed the pledge. In Bengal the movement made no headway outside Calcutta. Although a group of

1 Instructions to volunteers, 26 February 1919, *The Bombay Chronicle* and *Young India*, 12 March 1919, Gandhi's letter to the press on satyagraha pledge, 26 February 1919, *ibid.* pp. 118–20, 120–2.

2 Bombay Police Abstract, 1919, par. 378 (b), (g); *Hunter Report*, p. 9.

3 A Report from the Commissioner of Police Bombay to the Government of Bombay (1919) Concerning Political Developments before and during 1919, J. C. Curry Papers: Govt. of Bombay, Home Dept. Special File No. 521-1A of 1919, *Source Material for a History of the Freedom Movement in India, Vol. 2*, p. 378.

4 Weekly report of D.C.I., 10 March 1919, Proceeding No. 149 of Home Pol., B, April 1919, Nos. 148–52; A Report from the Commissioner of Police Bombay to the Government of Bombay (1919) Concerning Political Developments before and during 1919, J. C. Curry Papers. A hartal is a day of mourning marked by the cessation of business.

5 Gandhi gave the number as 600; press report of speech by him, 14 March 1919, S.N. No. 6458. The Governor of Bombay estimated 800; Sir G. Lloyd to E. S. Montagu, 18 March 1919, I.O.L., Montagu Papers, Mss. EUR. D. 523 (24).

6 J. Dwarkadas to A. Besant, 27 February 1919, Besant Papers.

leaders, including B. Chakravarti and Fazlul Haq, sent a wire on 4 March to Annie Besant, Gandhi, Pandit Malaviya and N. C. Kelkar, supporting the principle of passive resistance, on 16 March a conference held under the auspices of the Bengal P.C.C. merely set up a committee to consider practical ways of implementing the vow.

In Bihar the matter was postponed until a provincial conference met, and in the U.P. the municipal elections then in progress absorbed most local political energy. In Allahabad, the hub of U.P. Congress activity, opinion was divided, and Motilal Nehru for one could not see how gaol-going could put pressure on the government to withdraw the bills, and was frankly horrified at the thought of any of his family going to prison. In the Punjab there were no known signatures to the vow, people were mostly interested in local and economic problems, and only in the larger towns like Lahore and Amritsar was there any feeling about the bills.[1] *The Tribune* considered satyagraha in some depth but refused to make any judgement on it:

> Yet let us not judge a movement hastily at the head of which stands that remarkable man who, in a life more eventful than that of most men, has never yet championed a wrong cause or championed any cause without carrying it to victory...When such a man launches upon such a campaign for his country, the proper attitude for those who, like ourselves, whole-heartedly support the principle of the campaign and have their doubts only about its policy, is that of suspension of judgement, of "wait and see."[2]

So far Gandhi's supporters were Home Rulers and younger men in the two areas of the Bombay Presidency where he had had a chance to build up a following through local satyagrahas. Some of them were genuinely captivated by the Mahatma's novelty, his idealism and his concern for the underprivileged: most of them had little to lose and much to gain by putting themselves in the political limelight. Elsewhere the established politicians had their eyes on the power which the reforms promised, however much they criticized them as inadequate. Although passive resistance was in theory an ideal way out of their impasse over the Rowlatt legislation, they were torn between understandable reluctance to risk imprisonment at such a critical time and a desire to put pressure on the raj. Gandhi appears, however, to have over-estimated their support. He felt fairly sure of Bombay, Madras, Bihar and Sind,[3] and was alleged to have told Abdul Bari 'that he had agents in every city and that the passive resistance idea would

[1] For provincial reactions, see Fortnightly reports from the provinces for second half of March 1919, Home Pol., Deposit, April 1919, No. 49. For further details on Bengal, see Bengal leaders' telegram to A. Besant and others, 4 March 1919, Besant Papers; *The Tribune*, 19 March 1919. For Motilal Nehru's reaction, see J. Nehru, *An Autobiography*, pp. 41–2.

[2] *The Tribune*, 6 March 1919.

[3] Gandhi, *An Autobiography*, p. 383.

spread to the servants of the officials and the army. Hindu Muslim unity would be complete and the government would be paralysed.'[1]

The government calculated Gandhi's support rather differently and approached the situation with cautious optimism. However, officials felt that he was sufficiently powerful to be an asset to them if he could be converted into a collaborator, as they had done at the time of the war conferences the previous year: so the Viceroy saw Gandhi on 5 March. Nothing came of their meeting, because Gandhi had published his satyagraha manifesto before going to Delhi.[2] He sent a final appeal to J. L. Maffey, the Viceroy's Private Secretary, on 12 March, but Maffey replied by urging him not to throw dust in people's eyes, and to remember that as a leader with a 'magnetic personality' he had a responsibility for the stability of the state.[3] Chelmsford comforted himself with the fact that Mrs Besant was reluctant to follow him, and that fifteen non-official Indian members of his Council, though opposed to the Rowlatt Act, were firmly against unconstitutional tactics. He told Montagu,

> I think he is trying to frighten us, and I propose to call his "bluff". In any case no other course is open to us. The fact is he has got passive resistance on the brain and cannot suppress it any longer. We can congratulate ourselves that he has not chosen his ground better. I am quite happy in defending my present position.[4]

Chelmsford judged correctly that Gandhi was not on firm ground. He faced opposition on several fronts from established political leaders. Among his opponents were the group of non-official Indian members of the Imperial Legislative Council Chelmsford had mentioned: on 2 March they signed a manifesto stating,

> While strongly condemning the Rowlatt Bills as drastic and unnecessary and while we think we must oppose them to the end, we disapprove of the passive resistance movement started as a protest against them and dissociate ourselves from it in the best interests of the country, especially in view of the reforms proposals which are about to be laid before Parliament.[5]

The group included Sir D. E. Wacha, Surendranath Bannerjee, T. B. Sapru, M. M. Shafi, Sir Fazalbhoy Currimbhoy and Srinivasa Sastri. As Sastri explained to a member of the S.I.S., their reasons for opposing satyagraha were that it would hinder the reforms, that in any case Council

1 Delhi Police Abstract, 1919, par. 321, quoted in Home Pol., Deposit, April 1921, No. 67.

2 5 March 1919, Diary of G. S. Khaparde, Khaparde Papers; Chelmsford to E. S. Montagu, 12 March 1919, Mss. EUR. D. 523 (8).

3 Gandhi to J. L. Maffey, 12 March 1919, S.N. No. 6452; J. L. Maffey to Gandhi, 13 March 1919, S.N. No. 6456.

4 Chelmsford to E. S. Montagu, 20 March 1919, Mss. EUR. E. 264 (5); see also Chelmsford to E. S. Montagu, 12 March 1919, Mss. EUR. D. 523 (8).

5 *The Tribune*, 4 March 1919.

modifications had taken the sting out of the Rowlatt Act, and that satyagraha was not a suitable weapon because no ordinary citizen could civilly disobey the Act but would have to disobey other laws instead.[1] The signatories of the 2 March manifesto insisted that they had no personal animus against Gandhi. Sastri told Gandhi of his 'utmost personal regard' and 'feeling of reverence' towards him, while Sapru said that 'he had the highest respect for Mr. Gandhi.'[2]

However, some of the opposition to Gandhi had a personal and bitter twist. G. S. Khaparde, when asked to help in the movement, poured scorn on Gandhi's attitude to western civilization and scientific inventions and said that he did not believe in satyagraha. As a Marathi-speaking follower of Tilak he looked askance at Gandhi's assertion of leadership, and 'remarked that Gandhi would say one thing to-day and another thing tomorrow. He had no faith in the Guzrathi [sic] signatories to the *Satyagraha* vow. He said that one stripe with a whip was sufficient to deter them from their determination. He doubted the genuineness of the signatures to the vow.'[3] Mrs Besant made trouble for Gandhi throughout, because she believed he was stealing away her followers. Jamnadas Dwarkadas's eagerness to go off in pursuit of the Mahatma was a danger signal for her own popularity in Bombay, but eventually she allowed him and others in her following to sign the pledge, and decided to sign herself, provided that she could form her own satyagraha committee and need not bow to the wishes of Gandhi's committee.[4] There was little else she could do if she wished to remain in the political limelight and keep her following, but even so she visited Bombay in Gandhi's absence and tried to wean her men from satyagraha.[5] After the Rowlatt Act was passed she condemned satyagraha on the grounds that there was nothing in the Act to resist civilly (as Sastri had also pointed out), and that to break laws at the dictate of others was exceedingly dangerous. Such views caused extreme embarrassment to those of her henchmen who had signed the pledge. Sir P. Subramania Iyer, for example, declined to be Vice-President of the satyagraha

[1] V. S. S. Sastri to S. G. Vaze, 3 March 1919, S.P., Correspondence File, 1919, Letters to & from Sastri, No. 300. Sir D. E. Wacha had already tried to dissuade Gandhi from satyagraha in a letter of 1 March 1919, S.N. No. 6453.

[2] V. S. S. Sastri to Gandhi, 8 March 1919, S.N. No. 6447; speech by T. P. Sapru at meeting on 24 March 1919 at which the U.P. Liberal Association was inaugurated, *The Tribune*, 27 March 1919.

[3] Fortnightly report from Bombay for second half of March 1919, Home Pol., Deposit, April 1919, No. 49.

[4] A. Besant to P. K. Telang, telegram, 1 March 1919, S.N. No. 6442. Gandhi allowed her this concession; P. K. Telang to A. Besant, telegram, probably 1 March 1919, S.N. No. 6443.

[5] Mahadev Desai to N. Parikh, 8 March 1919, S.N. No. 9167. (Gujarati translated by Dr R. A. Modi at Harijan Ashram, Ahmedabad.) Mahadev Desai had thought that Annie Besant had little option but to join the movement; Mahadev Desai to N. Parikh, 2 March 1919, S.N. No. 11907.

organization because Annie Besant thought it a 'party proceeding'. He told Gandhi, 'My long relation with her makes it my duty not to array myself against her in what she takes to be a faction opposed to her.'[1]

It is hard to discover the opinions of educated Indians who, though part of the political nation, were not active politicians. The Madras government judged that, though there was much unease and misunderstanding about the purpose of the Rowlatt legislation, the principle of Gandhi's satyagraha was never clearly understood or closely followed. An Indian correspondent of the C.I.D., who may well have been biassed particularly when gauging opinions, reported that many educated Indians thought satyagraha futile as a weapon, some thought it amusing, while others feared that it would soon become active resistance. Gandhi, though respected for his character and simple life, was openly being called a crank and was judged to have blundered in joining with Home Rulers of the type of Horniman and Jamnadas Dwarkadas.[2] But Gandhi was not deflected by scepticism or opposition. He had taken a pledge and, as he had demonstrated in Kaira and Ahmedabad a satyagrahi's pledge was, in his terminology, sacred.

The second phase of the satyagraha – its inauguration – began with Gandhi's decision that hartal would be the best form of protest. At first he could see no way out of the difficulty raised by Annie Besant and Srinivasa Sastri, that civil disobedience in this case was bound to be artificial, because the Rowlatt Act did not touch the ordinary citizen. Gandhi was no slick politician who bore the cares of leadership lightly, and on his own confession he spent sleepless nights agonizing over his political decisions. Eventually a solution to this problem came to him early one morning 'in that twilight condition between sleep and consciousness'. As he told Rajagopalachariar, '*Satyagraha* is a process of self-purification, and ours is a sacred fight, and it seems to me to be in the fitness of things that it should be commenced with an act of self-purification. Let all the people of India therefore, suspend their business on that day and observe the day as one of fasting and prayer.'[3] He suggested this programme combined with public meetings for Sunday, 6 April in the press, and then wired to the Satyagraha Sabha in Bombay, hoping for their agreement – an order of

[1] Sir P. Subramania Iyer to Gandhi, 23 March 1919, S.N. No. 6465. Mrs Besant's argument about the impossibility of civilly disobeying the Rowlatt Act is in *New India*, 21 March 1919, though this article was not signed by her. Her views when interviewed by the press are reported in *The Pioneer*, 18 April 1919, Proceeding No. 273 of Home Pol., B, May 1919, Nos. 268–73.

[2] *Report on the Administration of the Madras Presidency for the year 1918–19* (Madras, 1920), p. ix; Weekly report of D.C.I., 24 March 1919, Proceeding No. 151 of Home Pol., B, April 1919, Nos. 148–52.

[3] Gandhi, *An Autobiography*, p. 383. Gandhi referred to his sleepless nights in a letter to the press on the satyagraha pledge, 26 February 1919, *C.W.*, vol. 15, p. 120.

events which showed his determination to steer the movement his way.[1]

Srinivasa Sastri saw Gandhi just after he had made this decision, and marvelled at this most unconventional politician at work.

> Poor Gandhi!...He goes on his course unruffled – straight & single-eyed tho' circumspect & cool to a degree. He has some converts everywhere but not many...Do you know? Gandhi has become a sort of censor of newspaper articles on the Satyagraha side, & insists on 'no abuse' & all charity in criticism & 'love your enemies' & all that sort of thing. The effect is visible in the *Hindu*, & the speeches of Satyamurti & Co. It is here [Madras] recognised as a moral miracle.[2]

The extent of the hartal varied considerably between regions, and between town and countryside. In Delhi, owing to a mix-up in communications, it was observed early, on 30 March. Many shops closed, and when station officials failed to eject a crowd which went to the station to stop sweet sellers doing business, the police and army were summoned and had to fire, then and later, and ten people were killed. Most shops opened on Monday, 31 March, and by Tuesday afternoon all shops were open.[3] Gandhi doubted whether the official version of these events was true, but he hastened to tell his compatriots through the press that if any Delhi people had indulged in violence this was inconsistent with the satyagraha pledge. At the same time he shot off telegrams to leading politicians expressing the hope that this 'tragedy' would steel the hearts of satyagrahis and convert the waverers to the cause.[4]

The rest of India observed hartal on 6 April. Annie Besant paid a flying visit to Bombay on 3 April to persuade Jamnadas Dwarkadas and others to withdraw from satyagraha, but as soon as she left they fell again under Gandhi's influence and rejoined the movement. On the scheduled day about four-fifths of the shops shut in Bombay city, few victorias and taxis were running, but theatres stayed open, despite several threats to managers, and destruction by mobs of notices about performances. The police admitted that the whole effect was a strategic success for Gandhi, even though

[1] Gandhi to the press, 23 March 1919, *ibid.* pp. 145–6; Gandhi to Satyagraha Sabha, Bombay, telegram, 25 March 1919, *ibid.* p. 150. This order of events had a parallel in 1920 when Gandhi inaugurated non-cooperation without waiting for Congress approval. See below, pp. 251–2.

[2] V. S. S. Sastri to S. G. Vaze, 1 April 1919, S.P., Correspondence File, 1919, Letters to & from Sastri, No. 314.

[3] Secretary to Govt. of India, Home Dept., to Secretary of State, telegram, 31 March 1919, Proceeding No. 141 of Home Pol., B, May 1919, Nos. 141–7; Chief Commissioner, Delhi, to Govt. of India, Home Dept., telegram, 7 April 1919, Proceeding No. 146, *ibid.*

[4] Gandhi to the press, 3 April 1919, *C.W.*, vol. 15, pp. 174–6; examples of Gandhi's telegrams to politicians, all on 3 April, are Gandhi to Kasturi Ranga Iyengar, S.N. No. 6496, Gandhi to V. S. S. Sastri, S.N. No. 6493, Gandhi to M. M. Malaviya, S.N. No. 6495.

fear of damage rather than adherence to satyagraha probably prompted some of the shop keepers.[1]

By contrast, in C.P. Gandhi had no hold over ordinary people as he had in Bombay, neither did he have the firm support of any group of politicians. As a result 6 April fell flat in most of the province. In the Marathi-speaking districts loyalty to Tilak as the apostle of Maharashtrian nationalism prevented the politicians from following this upstart Gujarati Bania. The sole exception was Wamanrao Joshi, a Brahmin from Amraoti, who accepted Gandhi's leadership and ideology early in 1919 and was a highly successful local subcontractor for him, as G. S. Khaparde noted in Amraoti on 6 April. 'All the people in the town fasted today, closed their shops and did no business. The weekly market was also practically deserted.' In the Hindi-speaking districts, notoriously backward in the politics of nationalism, the only hartal occurred at Chhindwara where the Ali brothers were interned.[2]

Further south in Madras Gandhi had little personal influence, and the support only of the politicians for whom Kasturi Ranga Iyengar and his paper, *The Hindu*, were the spokesmen. Mrs Besant's faction opposed him, as did the non-Brahmins who were more concerned with extracting protection from the raj under the Montagu–Chelmsford Reforms. Consequently little notice was taken of 6 April, except in Madras city where the shops closed and 100,000 attended a meeting on the beach, after considerable preparation in the form of meetings, posters and handbills.[3]

In Bengal, though it was singled out as one of the areas whose political traditions made the Rowlatt legislation necessary, only a minority of districts saw any observance of 6 April. The main centres of observance were Dacca, with a meeting of 1,000, and Calcutta, where some shops closed and there was a meeting of 10,000, organized by C. R. Das and B. Chakravarti. They were willing to act as Gandhi's local organizers, but not to the extent of arranging occasions of 'self-purification'.[4]

1 A Report from the Commissioner of Police Bombay to the Government of Bombay (1919) Concerning Political Developments before and during 1919, J. C. Curry Papers; Bombay Police Abstract, 1919, par. 555 (a).

2 Fortnightly report from C.P. for first half of April 1919, Home Pol., Deposit, July 1919, No. 46; 6 April 1919, Diary of G. S. Khaparde, Khaparde Papers; D. E. U. Baker, 'Politics In A Bilingual Province: The Central Provinces And Berar, India, 1919–1939' (Ph.D. thesis, Australian National University, 1969), pp. 39–48.

3 Fortnightly report from Madras, 20 April 1919, Home Pol., Deposit, July 1919, No. 46; Irschick, *Politics And Social Conflict In South India*, pp. 134–5. There was little observance of 6 April in Hyderabad, Mysore and Coorg, Fortnightly reports from those areas, 15 April 1919, Home Pol., Deposit, July 1919, No. 46.

4 Fortnightly report from Bengal, 22 April 1919, *ibid.* Lady Jenkins, wife of a former Chief Justice of the Calcutta High Court, commented how little excitement there was in Calcutta compared with Bombay. Das and Chakravarti told the Governor of Bengal that the idea of hartal had been dropped in Bengal. Zetland, '*Essayez*' (London, 1956), pp. 137–8.

Across the border in Bihar hartal was confined to large towns, Patna, Muzaffarpur, Chapra, Monghyr and Gaya. Hasan Imam's great personal influence in Patna made the celebrations successful there, and he was important in persuading other local politicians, Mazharul Haq, S. Sinha, P. N. Sinha and Rajendra Prasad, to decide (as late as 4 April) to take part. Despite Gandhi's satyagraha in Champaran, and despite his trust in Bihar, it was not at all clear that the loyalty he had built up on a local issue would hold firm when he extended his activities to all-India concerns. Not until the government took action against Gandhi did the Patna politicians align themselves firmly behind him in his all-India campaign – Hasan Imam and Haq by taking the satyagraha pledge and Rajendra Prasad by opening a registration centre at his house.[1]

U.P.'s celebration of 6 April was also predominantly urban. The news of the Delhi disturbances the previous Sunday excited the whole province, and in nearly all large towns demonstrations were held, meetings were well attended, shops shut and public transport came to a standstill. Hindus and Muslims both attended and addressed meetings – in a province notorious for communal strife. The celebrations were well organized, partly through caste panchayats, and partly through wholesale dealers in Delhi, who refused to deal with smaller traders in the U.P. unless they participated in the movement.[2] However, public demonstrations were not a reliable index of willingness to follow Gandhi further in satyagraha. Sita Ram in Meerut, for example, judged that about 20,000 people had attended a meeting there on 6 April, but he did not know of anybody in Meerut who had signed the satyagraha pledge or intended to break laws in accordance with it.[3] Delhi merchants also exerted pressure on the southern Punjab, and their efforts were reinforced by those of travelling preachers sent from the capital. In the Punjab, as in U.P., hartal was almost universal in all the large towns.[4] Further north, in Jammu, Kashmir and the North-West Frontier Province, there was no support for satyagraha. But even on the frontier Gandhi was known, and the administration reported that 'most educated Indians here, both Hindus and Muhammadans, evidently feel strongly in favour of Mr. Gandhi.'[5]

1 Fortnightly report from Bihar and Orissa, 18 April 1919, Home Pol., Deposit, July 1919, No. 46.

2 Fortnightly report from U.P., 18 April 1919, *ibid.*; Fortnightly report from U.P., 2 May 1919, Home Pol., Deposit, July 1919, No. 47.

3 Speech by Sita Ram at meeting on 16 April 1919 in Meerut Town Hall between C. L. Alexander, Meerut District Magistrate, and twenty-five to thirty people who had convened a meeting on 6 April 1919 to protest against the Rowlatt Act; typed report of meeting, Sita Ram Papers, File No. 29 B.

4 Fortnightly report from Punjab for second half of April 1919, Home Pol., Deposit, July 1919, No. 47; L. F. Rushbrook Williams, *India in 1919* (Calcutta, 1920), p. 34.

5 Fortnightly reports from Jammu & Kashmir, 17 April 1919, and N.-W Frontier Province, 18 April 1919, Home Pol., Deposit, July 1919, No. 46.

However successful the hartal as a way of popularizing Gandhi's campaign and spreading political awareness through a traditional form of protest, it was not civil disobedience: and Gandhi could not avoid the problem of how to offer civil disobedience against the Rowlatt Act. On 7 April the committee envisaged in the satyagraha pledge, headed by Gandhi, issued public advice to satyagrahis to disobey the laws dealing with prohibited literature and the registration of newspapers.[1] These particular laws were selected because disobedience to them was possible for individuals, was unlikely to lead to violence, and because the books and newspapers illegally read would be educative. Four books which had been banned by the Bombay government in 1910 for containing seditious matter, including *Hind Swaraj*, were chosen for sale.[2] Volunteers, with Gandhi among them, began to distribute them in Bombay on the evening of 6 April, and on 7 April Gandhi began an unregistered news sheet, *Satyagrahi*, urging readers to copy and circulate it.[3]

After Gandhi had announced the plans for civil disobedience to the Bombay Commissioner of Police, the Government of India instructed all local governments that should Gandhi or others be guilty of a clear breach of the law they should be arrested and prosecuted. However, the Bombay government thought that the institution of proceedings against Gandhi for his illegal newspaper would take too long to be of use; so instead, when Gandhi left Bombay on 8 April to promote satyagraha in Delhi and Amritsar, the central government authorized his restriction in the Bombay Presidency, after consultation with the governments of Delhi and the Punjab, which both feared that his entry into their territory would involve his arrest and precipitate violence among the public. Consequently on 9 April Gandhi was removed from the train in which he was travelling and sent back to Bombay, where he was set free.[4] Chelmsford was convinced that his government must be firm over civil disobedience, but on the day Gandhi was 'arrested' he commented to Montagu,

> Dear me, what a d...d nuisance these saintly fanatics are! Gandhi is incapable of hurting a fly and is as honest as the day, but he enters quite lightheartedly on a course of action which is the negation of all government and may lead to much hardship to people who are ignorant and easily led astray.[5]

1 The principal law to be disobeyed was the Indian Press Act, 1910, which operated within the terms laid down in the Press and Registration of Books Act, 1867.

2 Statement on laws for civil disobedience, 7 April 1919, *The Bombay Chronicle*, 8 April 1919, *C.W.*, vol. 15, pp. 192–4.

3 First edition of *Satyagrahi*, 7 April 1919, published in *The Bombay Chronicle*, 9 April 1919, *ibid.* pp. 190–1; Gandhi, *An Autobiography*, p. 385.

4 *Hunter Report*, pp. 60–1; file relating to Gandhi's restriction in Bombay, Home Pol., A, May 1919, Nos. 455–72. Action was taken against Gandhi under Rule 3 of the Defence of India (consolidation) Rules, 1915.

5 Chelmsford to E. S. Montagu, 9 April 1919, Mss. EUR. D. 523 (8).

Far from avoiding trouble, as the government had hoped, by restricting the area of Gandhi's activities it precipitated events which generated such bitterness that satyagraha became Congress policy a year later. When news of Gandhi's 'arrest' became public on 10 April there was unrest in Bombay which culminated the next day in closure of shops, stone-throwing and interference with transport, until the cavalry, summoned to control the thronging people, charged the crowd. In Ahmedabad news of Gandhi's 'arrest' led to mob violence, killing, and the burning of the jail, telegraph office and Collector's offices; and martial law had to be enforced. Further disturbances occurred at Nadiad on 11/12 April and at Viramgam on 12 April.[1]

The worst occurrences were in the Punjab, and Amritsar in particular, where the news about Gandhi coincided with the arrest of two Punjabi politicians, Drs Kitchlew and Satyapal. At Amritsar on 10 April mob violence, burning and looting ensued, and four Europeans were murdered. The civil authorities lost control of the city, and in a state of *de facto* martial law General Dyer's troops dispersed with gunfire a crowd of about 10,000 gathered in a walled-in open space called Jallianwalla Bagh.[2] The appalling casualties on this occasion, when the official count of deaths alone totalled nearly 400, and the administration of martial law, which was afterwards officially declared in the Punjab, became notorious throughout India when they were revealed by the official and Congress enquiries of 1919–20.[3]

However, from mid-April satyagraha against the Rowlatt Act lost momentum. The course of this final phase was determined by Gandhi's reaction to the April violence, and his subsequent standing with the government and the Indian public. When Gandhi heard what had happened in his own town and in Gujarat he went there in person. Deeply distressed at what he discovered, he admitted publicly to a 'Himalayan miscalculation' in offering civil disobedience to people insufficiently prepared by the discipline of satyagraha to practise it.[4] He wrote to J. L. Maffey:

[1] Account of disorders in Bombay in Govt. of Bombay, Home Dept., Special File No. 521, Part 1 of 1919, *Source Material for a History of the Freedom Movement in India, Vol. 2*, pp. 746–9; account of rioting in Ahmedabad, G. E. Chatfield, Ahmedabad District Magistrate, to Secretary to Govt. of Bombay, Political Dept., Bombay Govt. File No. 48613/1919, Appendix IX, *ibid.* pp. 756–61; account of disturbances in Nadiad and Viramgam, *Hunter Report*, pp. 15–17.

[2] Summary of disturbances in Punjab, Secretary to Govt. of India, Home Dept., to all local govts. and administrations, telegram, 11 April 1919, Proceeding No. 154 of Home Pol., B, May 1919, Nos. 148–78; announcement of Jallianwalla Bagh incident, Chief Secretary, Govt. of Punjab, to Secretary, Govt. of India, Home Dept., telegram, 14 April 1919, Proceeding No. 159, *ibid.*; for a detailed description of the situation in Amritsar on 10 April, see R. Furneaux, *Massacre At Amritsar* (London, 1963), pp. 33–78.

[3] For the findings of the two enquiries, see below, pp. 239–41.

[4] Gandhi, *An Autobiography*, pp. 391–2.

in the place I have made my abode I find utter lawlessness bordering almost on Bolshevism. Englishmen and women have found it necessary to leave their bungalows and to confine themselves to a few well guarded houses. It is a matter of the deepest humiliation and regret for me. I see that I over-calculated the measure of permeation of Satyagraha amongst the people. I underrated the power of hatred and illwill. My faith in Satyagraha remains undiminished, but I am only a poor creature just as liable to err as any other. I am correcting the error. I have somewhat retraced my steps for the time being. Until I feel convinced that my co-workers can regulate and restrain crowds and keep them peaceful, I propose to refrain from seeking to enter Delhi or the other parts of the Punjab. My Satyagraha, therefore, will, at the present moment, be directed against my own countrymen.[1]

For fear of adding to a disturbed situation he refused to discuss in the press the causes of discontent, which he thought were the root of the violence and had not been sufficiently tempered by the satyagrahi's spirit of restraint – Muslim fears about the future of Islam, public distrust of the reforms and resentment at the Rowlatt Act.[2]

Once back in Bombay Presidency he used his personal influence to soothe the crowds, underwent a three-day penitential fast, and on 18 April suspended the civil disobedience part of the satyagraha programme.[3] However, he insisted that 'really operative part movement namely preaching practice of truth non-violence continues', preaching which reached the public mainly through satyagraha leaflets published in Bombay by Shankarlal Banker.[4] At this point Gandhi also acquired *Young India* and *Navajivan*, an English and a Gujarati paper, which he used specifically for 'educating the reading public in *Satyagraha*'.[5] Once again Gandhi's distinctive mixture of a singular ideal and good political tactics was visible. For him the method of action, satyagraha, was as important as the end in view, because of the effect he hoped it would have on its exponents: undeterred by the temporary failure of civil disobedience, he pressed on with preaching satyagraha in its wider sense in the hope of regenerating his compatriots. On a purely tactical level such preaching was also a way of keeping his ideas before the public, of keeping the movement going while more offensive tactics were temporarily impossible.

1 Gandhi to J. L. Maffey, 14 April 1919, Home Pol., A, May 1919, Nos. 455–72.

2 Gandhi to Sir S. Reed, 15 April 1919, *C.W.*, vol. 15, pp. 227–31.

3 Gandhi's press statement on suspension of civil disobedience, 18 April 1919, *The Hindu*, 21 April 1919, *ibid.* pp. 243–5.

4 Gandhi to G. A. Natesan, telegram, 18 April 1919, *ibid.* p. 243. Satyagraha Leaflet No. 6, 'Satyagraha: Its Significance', was issued on 25 April 1919, for example, *ibid.* pp. 248–50.

5 Gandhi, *An Autobiography*, p. 395. Umar Sobhani and Shankarlal Banker controlled *Young India*; Indulal Yajnik, an associate of Sobhani and Banker, who had helped in the Kaira satyagraha, controlled *Navajivan*.

Satyagraha continued in this form, though with decreasing vitality,[1] throughout May. On 21 May Gandhi moved towards injecting new life into the movement by inviting co-workers to a conference on satyagraha.[2] At the conference on 28 May Gandhi put before the satyagrahis a new issue which he felt they should consider, though it was not covered by the satyagraha pledge – the issue of the Punjab. He suggested that should the government not appoint a commission of enquiry into the Punjab disturbances, the administration of martial law and the sentences imposed by the martial law tribunals, civil disobedience should be resumed, but only by individual Bombay satyagrahis, in order to avoid violence. All present agreed, except Jamnadas Dwarkadas, who thought that violence would break out if Gandhi or any prominent satyagrahi was arrested. But Hasan Imam sent a letter saying that he thought civil disobedience was unwise, and Swami Shraddhanand (also known as Mahatma Munshiram) wrote to announce his withdrawal from the movement.[3]

Despite the assurance of some support at the conference, Gandhi felt isolated, and told an old friend from South African days that he was still having to

> plough the lonely furrow... Strange as it may appear, I feel lonelier here than in South Africa. This does not mean that I am without co-workers. But between the majority of them and me, there is not that perfect correspondence which used to exist in South Africa. I do not enjoy the same sense of security which you all gave me there. I do not know the people here; nor they, me.[4]

On 12 June Gandhi asked the Satyagraha Sabha's Executive Committee to consider the renewal of civil disobedience in July. He felt that the conditions which had demanded its suspension in April no longer existed.

> People know what is expected of them. The Government are fully prepared on their own showing against all emergencies. A movement like satyagraha, designed as it is to work a moral revolution in society so far as the method of attaining reforms are concerned, cannot be stopped for the vague fear of unscrupulous or ignorant persons misusing it.

As a precaution against such misuse he proposed that he should determine the time, place and participants.[5] Six days later he informed the Viceroy that unless circumstances altered civil disobedience would be resumed in

[1] Gandhi, *An Autobiography*, p. 392.

[2] Gandhi to co-workers, 21 May 1919, S.N. No. 6618. This was sent to Vallabhbhai Patel, Hasan Imam, Swami Shraddhanand, among others. Hasan Imam and Shraddhanand did not attend.

[3] Notes on satyagraha conference held on 28 May, 30 May 1919, *C.W.*, vol. 15, pp. 332–3. For further details on the views of Dwarkadas, Imam and Shraddhanand, see below, pp. 183–4.

[4] Gandhi to S. Schlesin, 2 June 1919, *C.W.*, vol. 15, p. 341.

[5] Gandhi to Secretaries of Satyagraha Committee, 12 June 1919, *ibid.* pp. 364–5.

July, and he reiterated this in a wire to the Secretary of State.[1] The desire to avoid violence prompted Gandhi's decision to offer civil disobedience first, alone. He also issued detailed instructions to Bombay satyagrahis that if he were arrested there should be absolute peace and merely preaching of satyagraha for a month, followed by civil disobedience by selected leaders, probably against press and income tax laws and externment and internment orders.[2]

In spite of these preparations, Gandhi evidently hoped that he could come to some sort of agreement with the government. On 1 July he told the Bombay Commissioner of Police that he intended to break the orders restraining him within the Bombay Presidency by crossing the Bombay border at some point, but said that if the government wished him to postpone civil disobedience for a stated time he would do so, and if the government showed signs of relaxing its attitude on the Rowlatt legislation he would postpone civil disobedience indefinitely.[3] The Governor of Bombay was now Sir George Lloyd, in place of Willingdon who had crossed swords with Gandhi over Kaira and the war conference. He took Gandhi's hint: as he said later, 'I felt convinced that he really desired to postpone his campaign and possibly to give it up altogether, but he felt pledged to carry on simply because he had said he was going to do so. If we could only give him a peg on which he might hang an altered decision I thought he might take it.'[4] After a two-hour interview with the Governor on 12 July, Gandhi decided that there was a hope that the Rowlatt Act might be withdrawn, and he said that he would postpone civil disobedience if the Viceroy so wished.[5] Chelmsford quickly announced through a warning of the consequences of civil disobediences that this was his wish, and on 21 July Gandhi told the press that he had decided to suspend civil disobedience, though such resistance could not be avoided permanently if the Rowlatt Act remained on the statute book.[6]

Gandhi's activities presented the government with an extremely awkward policy decision. It was bound to adopt a hard line towards one who openly advocated disobedience to its laws:[7] but it also needed a measure of

1 Gandhi to S. R. Hignell, Private Secretary to the Viceroy, 18 June 1919, *ibid.* pp. 377–8; Gandhi to E. S. Montagu, 27 June 1919, S.N. No. 6674.

2 Gandhi to S. R. Hignell, 28 June 1919, S.N. No. 6697; Gandhi's instructions for satyagrahis, 30 June 1919, *C.W.*, vol. 15, pp. 412–16.

3 Bombay Police Abstract, 1919, par. 901.

4 Sir G. Lloyd to E. S. Montagu, 24 July 1919, Mss. EUR. D. 523 (24).

5 Gandhi to Chhaganlal Gandhi, 13 July 1919, S.N. No. 6743; Gandhi's conversation with guests on 14 July in Bombay, recorded in Bombay Police Abstract, 1919, par. 970 (a).

6 Chelmsford's warning to Gandhi in Political Secretary to Govt. of Bombay to Gandhi, 20 July 1919, S.N. No. 6763; Gandhi's letter to the press announcing suspension of civil disobedience, 21 July 1919, *Young India*, 23 July 1919, *C.W.*, vol. 15, pp. 468–71.

7 Sir William Vincent put this to Surendranath Bannerjee in a letter, 13 April 1919,

political tranquillity while the reforms were under discussion. It not only lacked the physical force to subdue a large outbreak of disorder, but it was also unwilling to use force just when the Rowlatt bills had cast doubts on its intention to allow responsible government. Consequently the most important assumption of government policy towards Gandhi was that it must avoid making him a martyr. When Bombay considered deporting him, the Government of India promised its consent only if this course was unavoidable. In the Viceroy's words, 'Of one thing I am certain – that we must endeavour by all means to avoid having to deport Gandhi, and in this Lloyd agrees with me. Interned he would be a rallying cry to the disaffected; out he may prove of great assistance to us.'[1] Chelmsford had learnt his lesson from Annie Besant's internment, and this case was the more delicate because Gandhi was no 'mere agitating politician'.[2]

As Chelmsford had indicated, government policy was also based on the hope that it might enlist Gandhi as a collaborator in peace-keeping. If it had to bow to Gandhi's public reputation in order to avoid violence it might be able to trade on that reputation to keep the peace. Officials recognized that Gandhi had done his best to calm the crowds in Bombay and Ahmedabad in April, and even the police noted that he had done his utmost to prevent outbreaks when the Government of Bombay deported B. G. Horniman later in April.[3] J. L. Maffey, whose letters to Gandhi were friendly and at times teasing, congratulated him on his calming influence, adding the P.S., 'Don't do too much fasting! You are not strong enough yet and I am sure yours is an influence which we shall all want at full horse-power.' A fortnight later he wrote, 'Can we look to you for help? I believe you could be of immense assistance in stabilising Indian opinion. I am writing this of my own initiative though I shall show it to the Viceroy.'[4]

Lloyd, as Governor of Bombay, bore the brunt of this policy of restraint. 'The proper place for a saint is heaven, not the Bombay Presidency and he is paradoxically trying to make it a hell.'[5] Lloyd was tied by the fact that he had very few troops at his disposal, and so he developed his own tactic of

Home Pol., B, May 1919, Nos. 141–7. 'Not only is he himself primarily responsible for the trouble that has occurred, but has now, by his open defiance of the law, put himself entirely beyond the pale. No one disputes Mr. Gandhi's sincerity and we all regret his wrong-headedness. But I think you will admit that now he has crossed the boundary it is quite impossible to treat with him.'

1 Chelmsford to E. S. Montagu, 16 April 1919, Mss. EUR. D. 523 (8). For the question of deporting Gandhi, see Secretary to Govt. of India, Home Dept., to Chief Secretary to Govt. of Bombay, Political Dept., telegram, 12 April 1919, Proceeding No. 619 of Home Pol., A, May 1919, Nos. 619–40 & K.-W.

2 Chelmsford to His Majesty the King, 21 May 1919, Mss. EUR. E. 264 (1).

3 E. S. Montagu to Chelmsford, 22 April 1919, Mss. EUR. E. 264 (5); Bombay Police Abstract, 1919, par. 598 (a).

4 J. L. Maffey to Gandhi, 20 April 1919, 7 May 1919, S.N. Nos. 6551 & 6593.

5 Sir G. Lloyd to E. S. Montagu, 23 May 1919, Mss. EUR. D. 523 (24).

disregarding Gandhi while dealing with his henchmen, which had the merit of avoiding outbreaks in sympathy with Gandhi, while making Gandhi unpopular. But he was feeling his way in the dark, not knowing what the Mahatma was really up to.[1] However, by mid-June he thought that his tactic was proving successful, and as satyagraha lost popularity both Lloyd and Chelmsford became convinced that Gandhi wanted a face-saving way of extricating himself from an impossible situation to which he was bound by oath – hence their joint action in July.[2]

But when it came to the question of Gandhi's future, central and local governments were wary. No local government wanted Gandhi within its jurisdiction. Moreover, Delhi and Whitehall disagreed on the question whether Gandhi was likely to be a tranquillizing influence and whether he could be trusted not to resume civil disobedience.[3] By September the Government in Delhi was less reluctant to free Gandhi, as he seemed to have no immediate plans for civil disobedience, and in view of the impending visit of Lord Hunter at the head of an official enquiry into affairs in the Punjab. Consequently, after consulting local governments it notified Gandhi that his restriction in Bombay would end on 15 October.[4]

The Rowlatt satyagraha radically altered Gandhi's standing with the government. It also provoked a strong reaction from the Indian public; whichever way the Mahatma moved – to resume or suspend civil disobedience – sections of the public criticized him. The first public reaction was one of horror at the April violence, and criticism of the satyagraha which preceded it. Some of this came from quite ordinary people, outside the ranks of the politicians.[5] Among the politicians the 'Moderates', predictably, were loudest in their protests, since mass violence, whether it was produced by the actions of Bengali terrorists or by a peace-loving Mahatma, threatened the delicately balanced structure of politics which they had created. Sir Dinshaw Wacha put their case.

1 *Idem.*; for evidence that the government had no idea of Gandhi's intentions, see Sir G. Lloyd to Chelmsford, some time in June 1919, and note by Sir W. Vincent, 20 June 1919, in Home Pol., A, August 1919, Nos. 261–72 & K.-W.

2 Sir G. Lloyd to E. S. Montagu, 12 June 1919, 24 July 1919, Mss. EUR. D. 523 (24); Chelmsford to E. S. Montagu, 18 July 1919, Mss. EUR. E. 264 (5).

3 Secretary of State to Viceroy, telegrams, 12 & 15 August 1919, Viceroy to Secretary of State, telegrams, 14 & 22 August 1919, Home Pol., A, August 1919, Nos. 261–72 & K.-W.

4 Govt. of India to all provincial administrations, telegram, 8 September 1919, Viceroy's Private Secretary to Gandhi, telegram, 3 October 1919, Home Pol., A, October 1919, Nos. 426–40.

5 For example, J. W. Petavel, Principal of Maharajah Cossimbazar's Polytechnic Institute, Calcutta, to Gandhi, 13 April 1919, S.N. No. 6529. Petavel wrote, 'Mankind being what it is, let us not stir up people's passions with talk about soul force or passive resistance which, however well meant, is inciting them in the end to defiance of the law and to *murder* finally.'

> Remember also that owing to the incipient *rebellion* prevailing in the country at this hour thanks to the grave mischief Ghandi has consciously or unconsciously created by his fantastic propaganda, utterly illogical, utterly unconcerned, & utterly devoid of an atom of political sagacity, the Reform Bill is more likely to be a *shadow* only of what we expect, if not liable to be wholly abandoned.[1]

Srinivasa Sastri said privately of Gandhi, 'even *he* can't be allowed, however unwittingly, to injure India'; while Willingdon from Madras commented that even Mrs Besant 'seems to have become violently pro-Government and I shall (figuratively?) be soon taking her to my bosom.'[2] The Madras Liberal League, which condemned the actions of the mobs and implored Gandhi to abandon satyagraha, was only one of many political groups which fired off anti-satyagraha salvoes.[3] Friends and associates of Gandhi in his home territory added their persuasion. Ambalal Sarabhai went from Ahmedabad to Bombay to try to put pressure on Gandhi to abandon civil disobedience permanently, and, more surprisingly, B. G. Horniman, one of Gandhi's staunchest associates and Vice-President of the Executive Committee of the Satyagraha Sabha, urged that all satyagrahi activity should be suspended temporarily, because the movement had been 'utilised and corrupted by unscrupulous elements, with objects totally opposed to our own, and calculated to defeat our ideals, resulting in the recent deplorable revolutionary outbreaks'.[4]

Aggrieved satyagrahis who felt abandoned by Gandhi's suspension of civil disobedience peppered him with complaints from the opposite point of view. Such hard-liners were comparatively few in number, and were mostly in Bombay. Late in April they were reported to be visiting the satyagraha office in Bombay with enquiries about Gandhi's plans. They blamed him for stopping satyagraha just when it had assumed enough momentum to be productive, and argued that nothing could be achieved without bloodshed. Such hostility grew when Gandhi refused to permit demonstrations against Horniman's deportation, and Gandhi said that he had received a number of letters protesting against his inaction, some of which threatened him with poison and murder.[5] As ominous as the potential violence of frustrated satyagrahis for Gandhi's long term plans for true Swaraj was the feeling of some Muslims that Gandhi had exploited their

[1] Sir D. E. Wacha to G. A. Natesan, 12 April 1919, G. A. Natesan Papers.

[2] V. S. S. Sastri to S. G. Vaze, 17 April 1919, S.P., Correspondence File, 1919 Letters to & from Sastri, No. 322; Willingdon to Chelmsford, 23 April 1919, Mss. EUR. F. 93 (2).

[3] Resolution passed at general meeting of Madras Liberal League, 18 April 1919, in First Annual Report of the Madras Liberal League, 1919, Besant Papers.

[4] Report from Commissioner of Northern Division of Bombay Presidency, in Bombay Police Abstract, 1919, *Source Material for a History of the Freedom Movement in India, Vol. 2*, p. 777; B. G. Horniman to Executive Committee of Satyagraha Sabha, 17 April 1919, S.N. No. 6545.

[5] Bombay Police Abstract, 1919, par. 574 (e), 598 (a), 625 (m).

religious sentiments, and that the Hindus 'having induced some of their co-religionists in India to compromise themselves in rebellion and outrage' had 'proved unprofitable allies.'[1]

After Gandhi's second suspension of civil disobedience satyagrahi critics became more vehement, and at a Bombay meeting of about 200 of them on 26 July he was mercilessly cross-examined on his decision.[2] One anonymous correspondent, who signed himself XYZ, called Gandhi 'disappointing as a leader', and said, 'I fall at your feet to resume the vow. Or else leave your leadership.'[3] In Bombay the Mahatma was publicly and unfavourably compared with Tilak, who had suffered 'martyrdom' in jail, and even in the cloth market people were known to be calling him a murderer.[4]

However, much more serious for the fate of the Rowlatt satyagraha and for Gandhi's leadership was the apathy displayed throughout the subcontinent after the first flush of enthusiasm. The hartal of 6 April had been the high point of the movement, and after the April violence and the leader's vacillations support for it disintegrated. The government had gambled on the fact that Gandhi had insufficient popular support to make civil disobedience a viable weapon against the raj, and its gamble paid off.

Even in Bombay Presidency Gandhi lost his hold. He had considered Umar Sobhani, Shankarlal Banker, Horniman and Jamnadas Dwarkadas as the main props of satyagraha in Bombay city.[5] But the government removed Horniman, and Dwarkadas yielded to renewed pressure from Annie Besant. His was the sole dissenting voice at Gandhi's satyagraha conference on 28 May, and the following day, after an interview with Gandhi, he resigned from the Satyagraha Sabha on the grounds that the resumption of civil disobedience and its extension to the Punjab would precipitate violence even greater than that which had already occurred.[6] By mid-June a hundred satyagrahis were reported to have resigned, and twelve members of the Sabha's Executive Committee were said to have notified their intention of resigning.[7] The Bombay Inspector General of Police judged rightly that the politicians would desert Gandhi, but he was convinced that Gandhi had 'undoubtedly obtained a hold on the imagination of the mass in Gujarat'. Against his conviction must be weighed the concrete evidence

1 Fortnightly report from Bombay, 30 April/4 May 1919, Home Pol., Deposit, July 1919, No. 47.

2 Bombay Police Commissioner's note in File No. 3001/4/19 of 1935, *Source Material for a History of the Freedom Movement in India, Vol. 2*, pp. 788–9.

3 XYZ to Gandhi, probably July 1919, S.N. No. 6773.

4 Bombay Police Abstract, 1919, par. 1063 (b).

5 Report by Bombay Police Commissioner of an interview with Gandhi on 27 April, *ibid.* par. 598 (a).

6 Weekly report of D.C.I., 9 June 1919, Proceeding No. 702 of Home Pol., B, June 1919, Nos. 701–4; Bombay Police Abstract, 1919, par. 791 (a). Jamnadas Dwarkadas's explanation of his resignation was published in *Young India*, 4 June 1919, Bombay Police Abstract, 1919, par. 791 (b).

7 Bombay Police Abstract, 1919, par. 826 (a), 853 (a).

that by the end of June the Surat satyagraha office had closed down and Nadiad people were fighting shy of political movements – half-heartedness in two of the places Gandhi had chosen as centres for satyagraha if he were arrested.[1] The loyalty Gandhi had generated could not yet be relied on to hold firm for a campaign on an all-India rather than a local issue. Yet his appeal was deep in his home region, even if it was still the primitive appeal of a regional hero.[2] It held potential for his future as a continental leader, if he could transform it into a conscious political following by making the Gujaratis feel that his style of politics promised profits for them and their region.

However, to the south, in the Marathi-speaking parts of the Presidency, Gandhi had no such popular appeal, nor were the local leaders willing to organize satyagraha for him. Tilak was for Maharashtra what Gandhi was becoming for Gujarat, and his local henchmen had no intention of letting this Gujarati Bania gain a foothold in the territory whose politics they, the Maharashtrian Brahmins, had dominated.[3] The same was true of Marathi-speaking C.P., where Khaparde's adherence to Tilak's style of politics blocked the way for Gandhi's satyagraha.[4] Predictably, in Madras, where the politicians had developed a successful political mode geared to their aspirations, Gandhi found few who would organize satyagraha for him. At least one who would have been prepared to do this withdrew, a casualty of the personal vendetta Annie Besant was carrying on against Gandhi. He was Sir P. Subramania Iyer, who opted out of the law-breaking part of satyagraha, although he had taken the pledge, rather than break with Annie Besant and the Theosophists.[5]

The disintegration of satyagraha was more marked in those parts of north India where Gandhi's campaign had earlier made some headway. In Delhi, which had produced about 150 signatures to the pledge and had

1 L. Robertson, Inspector-General of Police, Bombay Presidency, to Sir Charles Cleveland, Director of Central Intelligence, 26 May 1919, Home Pol., A, August 1919, Nos. 261–72; Fortnightly report from Bombay, 30 June 1919, Home Pol., Deposit, August 1919, No. 51. For Gandhi's selection of Surat and Nadiad as satyagraha centres if he were arrested, see Gandhi's instructions for satyagrahis, 30 June 1919, *C.W.*, vol. 15, pp. 412–16.

2 Gandhi's appeal in Gujarat was 'sub-political' in terms of nationalist politics, but it was rooted in the Gujaratis' aspirations for power, and as such might be exploited at a more sophisticated political level. An example of it was an agitation by village leaders against the sale of milk outside their own villages, which began in Kaira district as part of Gandhi's programme for the improvement of the Gujarati physique. Fortnightly report from Baroda, 2 December 1919, Home Pol., Deposit, January 1920, No. 5.

3 Bombay Police Abstract, 1919, par. 574 (o), (p); Fortnightly report from Bombay, 30 April/4 May 1919, Home Pol., Deposit, July 1919, No. 47.

4 Fortnightly report from C.P. for second half of April 1919, Home Pol., Deposit, July 1919, No. 47.

5 Sir P. Subramania Iyer to Gandhi, 19 May 1919, S.N. No. 6605.

exerted pressure on the U.P. and Punjab to observe hartal, the local Satyagraha Sabha collapsed at the end of May, after its two main leaders, M. A. Ansari and Swami Shraddhanand, had decided to withdraw because they considered satyagraha to be impractical in view of the violence it precipitated. Ansari called the Sabha's leading members together, and probably to avert a general recantation they abolished the Sabha and burnt the lists of satyagrahis and the papers on which they had signed the pledge.[1] In the ill-fated Punjab there were signs that although Gandhi's name had been a rallying-cry in the violent outbreaks there was also vast ignorance of him. Some of the witnesses before the Martial Law Commissioners in May claimed not to know 'whether Gandhi is a man or a thing', though it is possible that this was a panic stricken lie from people frightened of coming under suspicion. Other Punjabis were reported to look on Gandhi as a trouble-maker for their province, who should be firmly squashed by the government.[2]

In neighbouring U.P., despite the widespread hartal in the towns in April, support for satyagraha soon died away. By mid-June the Lucknow Satyagraha Sabha had been practically dissolved, and in Allahabad the movement petered out because Sundar Lal, Gandhi's main local organizer, was prosecuted and no prominent politicians were willing to take up the cause.[3] Rajendra Prasad, comparing notes with Sundar Lal at the end of May, commented that nothing was being done in Bihar to forward satyagraha. He and Hasan Imam were both unable to attend Gandhi's satyagrahis' conference on 28 May at such short notice, and they both thought that civil disobedience should be permanently suspended, because of the possibilities of violence inherent in it. A month later, when Gandhi was proposing to resume civil disobedience, he asked Prasad for the names of really staunch satyagrahis in Bihar, and Prasad replied that he could only vouch for himself and that very few, if any, satyagrahis in Patna would give the unquestioning obedience which Gandhi demanded.[4]

The Bengalis were equally hesitant to give satyagraha practical effect. At a provincial conference held simultaneously with a meeting of the Bengal

[1] Fortnightly report from Delhi, 4 June 1919, Home Pol., Deposit, July 1919, No. 49; Swami Shraddhanand's letter of withdrawal to Gandhi, 3 May 1919, S.N. No. 6583.

[2] Fortnightly report from Punjab for second half of May 1919, Home Pol., Deposit, July 1919, No. 49; Weekly report of D.C.I., 21 July 1919, Proceeding No. 318 of Home Pol., B, August 1919, Nos. 315–19.

[3] Fortnightly report from U.P. for second half of June 1919, Home Pol., Deposit, August 1919, No. 51. For a case study of Allahabad, where the Rowlatt satyagraha made very little impact on local politics, see Bayly, 'The Development Of Political Organisation In The Allahabad Locality, 1880–1925', pp. 338–41.

[4] Fortnightly report from Bihar and Orissa, 1 June 1919, Home Pol., Deposit, July 1919, No. 49; Hasan Imam to Gandhi, 25 May 1919, S.N. No. 6626; Fortnightly report from Bihar and Orissa, 1 July 1919, Home Pol., Deposit, August 1919, No. 51.

Muslim League on 19/20/21 April, C. R. Das tried to rush through a resolution in favour of the principle and practice of civil disobedience. B. C. Pal abandoned Das and said that Gandhi was always changing his mind and that he could not follow him in disobedience to laws other than the Rowlatt Act; and Fazlul Haq led the opposition with a protestation that it would be extremely dangerous to ask the illiterate masses to sign the satyagraha pledge. Eventually a compromise was reached, whereby the conference expressed full approval of Gandhian satyagraha, but declined the responsibility of putting the approval into practice.[1]

The Rowlatt satyagraha, as a political campaign on the lines which its author conceived, was a manifest failure. It did not obtain its object, the repeal of the Rowlatt Act. It erupted into violence, though its essence was intended to be non-violence. It petered out miserably in the summer months of 1919 instead of becoming the constructive campaign laying the foundations of true Swaraj which Gandhi had envisaged. Nonetheless, as Gandhi's first essay in all-India leadership it was remarkably instructive to those who could read it correctly, since it showed both the strengths and the weaknesses of the Mahatma in politics.

For a brief time Gandhi engineered an agitation whose reverberations were felt throughout the subcontinent, from the North-West Frontier to Madras, from Sind to Bengal. But the power behind that agitation was neither antagonism to the Rowlatt legislation nor loyalty to a new leader, but local discontents, which found a focus and a means of expression in Gandhi's call for hartal. In every place where hartal was well observed and Gandhi's propaganda welcomed it seems that the tinder of unrest had been drying for months and Gandhi's campaign was merely the spark which started the conflagration.

In the U.P. the local government isolated as the root causes of unrest the ignorance and fear of the educated about the Rowlatt legislation, Muslim fears about the fate of Turkey and Islam's holy places during the war, high prices of food and cloth, and the shortage of daily essentials like kerosene. The U.P. politician, T. B. Sapru, confirmed this diagnosis, 'The "Satyagrah" is only a cover for general discontent in the case of many people – but there it is & it has to be reckoned with.'[2] A senior police official made a similar calculation of the real strengths behind the Rowlatt satyagraha in the Punjab, singling out for mention the growing discontent of the educated at foreign rule sharpened by the ideology of the Arya Samaj, fears of the wealthy because of war-time taxation on excess profits, unrest among

[1] Weekly report of D.C.I., 5 May 1919, Proceeding No. 494 of Home Pol., B, June 1919, Nos. 494–7.

[2] T. B. Sapru to V. S. S. Sastri, 8 April 1919, S.P., Correspondence File, 1919, Letters to & from Sastri, No. 318; Fortnightly report from U.P., 18 April 1919, Home Pol., Deposit, July 1919, No. 46.

the labouring people because of high prices and the scarcity of necessities of life, and Muslim fears for the international future of Islam.[1]

Where case studies are available of particular places they reinforce such generalizations on the provincial scale. In Lahore, for example, local grievances had been generated over a period of time which produced a potentially revolutionary situation in the city, but they had nothing to do with the Rowlatt Act. The more prosperous, educated townsmen had taken little notice of Congress politics before the second decade of the century, but under the paternalistic regime of Sir Michael O'Dwyer as Lieutenant-Governor of the Punjab they had become seriously concerned about their influence in public life, while many of them had also suffered considerably from the financial crisis which hit Lahore in 1913 when many of the city's banks crashed. The smaller tradesmen were squeezed by rising prices during the war as they struggled, under pressure from social convention, to ape the life style of wealthier inhabitants of Lahore, although their incomes were much smaller. Rising prices also hit the city's artisan and labouring classes; between 1917 and 1919 prices of food grains rose 100%, and though the workers' wages rose during the period they never kept pace with the soaring prices. A majority of the workers were Muslims, and their distress was given an ideological dimension by their fears for Turkey, which were spread through Zafar Ali Khan's Pan-Islamic paper, *Zamindar*. In 1919 all the main social groups in Lahore had distinct causes for unrest unconnected with the Rowlatt legislation, but they all found expression in the Rowlatt satyagraha and caused an eruption which neither the traditionally influential men of the city nor the new type of politician could control.[2]

However, discontent and strain in public life was not confined to those areas which responded to Gandhi's satyagraha. Economic distress was visible everywhere, as the whole country was caught in the war-time price spiral, which was intensified by the failure of the 1918–19 monsoon; and government measures could only attempt to palliate, not control, economic trends of such dimensions.[3] Papers were full of complaints about the failure of government controls on prices, and the fortnightly reports from the provinces produced a monotonous record of local hardship and ill health, as the world-wide influenza epidemic also scourged the country.

From C.P., for example, late in 1918 a report, which might have come from anywhere in India, described a situation of such tension that it was evident that disorder was very near the surface of public life.

[1] Deputy Inspector-General of Police, C.I.D., to all Superintendents of Police in the Punjab, 6 May 1919, quoted in Weekly report of D.C.I., 12 May 1919, Proceeding No. 495 of Home Pol., B, June 1919, Nos. 494–7.

[2] Study of the Rowlatt satyagraha in Lahore by R. Kumar in R. Kumar (ed.), *Essays on Gandhian Politics. The Rowlatt Satyagraha of 1919* (Oxford, 1971), pp. 236–97: this volume contains case studies of Delhi, Bombay and Ahmedabad, and C.P. and Berar.

[3] Rushbrook Williams, *India in 1919*, pp. 63–4.

> [In several districts] the price of the staple food grains now stands at 4 to 5 seers per rupee, – a price which has never been previously reached in modern times, even in the worst famine year. As yet there have been few overt manifestations of discontent, though a feeling of unrest and disquiet is prevalent. Petty crime, involving theft of food grain, is rising in all parts of the Province, and a small grain riot in Malkapur in the Buldana district is regarded by the Inspector General of Police as the precursor of further disturbances unless prices fall.[1]

Yet C.P. did not follow Gandhi into satyagraha. Despite manifest local distress the province was virtually unmoved by his call, like Madras, Marathi-speaking Bombay, and Bengal, though none of these were free from stress and strain. The reason was the critical fact that local leaders did not exploit existing discontent and channel it into the Rowlatt satyagraha. By contrast, in Lahore Gandhi's name, his ideas and plans were used by local men – Gokul Chand Narang, Duni Chand and Rambhaj Dutt Choudhry, all lawyers and Arya Samajists. In Allahabad satyagraha found local organizers in Sundar Lal and people on the fringes of the city's political life.

Only in parts of Bombay Presidency did Gandhi have genuine popular support and a real organizational base, and even this collapsed in the summer of 1919. Elsewhere in India the success of his satyagraha depended on local conditions and the support of local political leaders: where such a network of subcontractors did not exist Gandhi was unable to kindle and organize the agitation himself. Eventually the politicians failed him in every province, because they stood to lose if satyagraha precipitated violence. Whatever their discontents at the extent of the forthcoming reforms, whatever their dislike of the Rowlatt Act, in the last resort it was in their interests that the reforms should go through in peace, so that they could tighten their grip on the reins of power.

The Rowlatt satyagraha showed Gandhi as an all-India leader of immense potential. His personality, his ideology, his novel approach to politics, and his technique of satyagraha enabled his campaign to become the focus for multifarious local grievances and gave him access to the power they generated. But if he was to realize his potential he had to lead and be the master mind of his campaigns, instead of a figurehead for local struggles. To do so he had to create a strong, organized following and thereby circumvent the entrenched political leaders, or alternatively make it worth their while to ally with him as disciplined subcontractors.

The Rowlatt satyagraha did not merely demonstrate Gandhi's strengths and weaknesses as an all-India leader. The issue which precipitated it also tipped the balance in Gandhi's mind, deciding him that the political relationship between the raj and his compatriots must occupy his attention

[1] Fortnightly report from C.P., 16 October 1918, Home Pol., Deposit, November 1918, No. 23.

more deeply than it had to date. The modern style of politics impinged so widely on India's life that he realized that, if he was to right 'wrongs' and show his country the way to Swaraj, he must play a larger part in them than he had so far. To be a part-time protagonist in the political arena was not enough if he was to forward his ideals, nor was it safe in his view to leave political decisions in the hands of the existing leadership. He said this in July 1919,[1] and demonstrated it at the Amritsar Congress in 1919. Looking back he wrote,

> I must regard my participation in Congress proceedings at Amritsar as my real entrance into the Congress politics. My attendance at the previous Congresses was nothing more perhaps than a renewal of allegiance to the Congress. I never felt on these occasions that I had any other work cut out for me except that of a mere private, nor did I desire more.[2]

The Royal Proclamation of December 1919, which accompanied the Reform Act and called for a new era of cooperation between rulers and ruled, raised in Gandhi a last flicker of hope that the British in India would be true to the ideals he believed them to hold, a hope which was the foundation of the loyalty he retained towards the raj. He called the combination of the reforms and the proclamation 'an earnest of the intention of the British people to do justice to India', but he warned that Indians must not 'sit with folded hands and...still expect to get what we want. Under the British constitution no one gets anything without a hard fight for it.'[3] He proposed that Congress should not call the reforms disappointing, but should respond to the proclamation, thanking Montagu for his work and calling on Indians to cooperate in working the reforms despite their inadequacy. Jinnah, P. B. Sitaramayya and Pandit Malaviya were among those who supported him, in opposition to C. R. Das, Tilak, Hasrat Mohani, Rambhaj Dutt Choudhry and others who wished to condemn the reforms and demand full responsible government. Eventually Congress reached a compromise whereby it called the reforms disappointing, but thanked Montagu and promised cooperation in the working of the scheme.[4]

1 See above, p. 160.

2 Gandhi, *An Autobiography*, p. 405.

3 *Young India*, 31 December 1919. For the text of the Royal Proclamation, see *Statement exhibiting the Moral And Material Progress And Condition of India During The Year 1919* (London, 1920), Cmd. 950, Appendix V, pp. 269–71.

4 Typed copy of proceedings of 34th Session of the Indian National Congress at Amritsar in December 1919, S.N. No. 7042; Tilak's attitude to the reforms and his demand for responsible government, *Report of the Thirty Fourth Session of the Indian National Congress held at Amritsar on the 27th, 29th, 30th, 31st December 1919 and 1st January 1920* (Amritsar, 1922), p. 118; Gandhi's original amendment to the Das–Tilak resolution on the reforms, A.I.C.C. Files, 1919, No. 1, Part V; Gandhi's speech on reforms resolution on 1 January 1920, *C.W.*, vol. 16, pp. 364–7.

The significance of this episode lay not in Gandhi's precise attitude towards the reforms, but in his declaration, made and recognized, that he had exchanged political isolation for a claim to all-India political leadership. He told the politicians assembled at Amritsar what he would do if they refused to thank Montagu and decided to obstruct the reforms.

> I shall challenge that position, and I shall go across from one end of India to the other and say we shall fail in our culture, we shall fall from our position if we do not do our duty that culture demands, if we do not respond to the hand that has been extended to us.[1]

Whereas in August 1918 he had refused to pit himself against the leading politicians,[2] now he opposed them in their own citadel, the Congress; and they listened to him. Gandhi's emergence and recognition as a potential all-India leader were occasioned in the intervening months by the Rowlatt satyagraha. His claim to a new status in politics was reinforced by his decision to champion the Khilafat and Punjab 'wrongs'.

[1] Gandhi's speech on reforms resolution on 1 January 1920, *ibid.* p. 366. Gandhi had little interest in the details of the Reforms Act. He was far more concerned to produce a mental revolution in his compatriots which would bring in true Swaraj, and to this end he urged on them swadeshi. *Young India*, 10 December 1919.

[2] See above, pp. 150–1.

CHAPTER 6

KHILAFAT

During the Rowlatt satyagraha Gandhi relied in certain areas on networks of loyalty built up during his satyagrahas on local issues, while in places where he had few personal links he depended on the cooperation of men who did command local support. More often than not these leaders failed him because satyagraha threatened their basic local interests. By mid-1919 Gandhi had no reliable group of subcontractors, but during that year he embarked on a campaign involving an alliance which promised to provide him with just such a group. His campaign was in support of the Muslim movement to defend the Khalifah after Turkey's defeat in the war: and it was another example of the Mahatma's compulsion to right what he saw as a 'wrong' – in this instance inflicted by the imperial government on Indian Muslims.

After his return to India Gandhi had deliberately created links with the Indian Muslim community, trying to put into practice his conviction, born of his South African experience, that Muslims and Hindus were members of one nation, whose unity was a precondition of what he considered to be true Home Rule. He had contacted Muslim leaders and spoken at Muslim League meetings. In the Champaran satyagraha one of his firmest friends among the Bihari politicians was Mazharul Haq, a Muslim who before the war had been noted for his Pan-Islamic sympathies.[1] In Gujarat he appeared to have attracted the loyalty of the Bohora Muslims.[2] The first sign of an overt all-India political alliance with a section of the Muslim community was Gandhi's championship of the interned Ali brothers; and by the December meeting of the Muslim League in 1918 this championship had earned him the status of spokesman and hero of the Muslims who entertained Pan-Islamic sympathies.[3]

That same session of the League marked the transformation of pro-Turkish sympathy in India into a deliberate campaign to safeguard the Khalifah's status after his defeat. After the meeting the League's President sent a telegram to the Viceroy telling him of its resolutions. These in-

1 Mazharul Haq's Pan-Islamist activities and his friendship with the Ali brothers are noted in History Sheet, 1 May 1915, Appendix II of Proceeding No. 408 of Home Pol., A, July 1917, Nos. 408–10.

2 Gujarat's Bohora Muslims were reported to support the plan for the First Gujarat Political Conference because Gandhi consented to preside over it. Bombay Police Abstract, 1917, par. 1041.

3 See above, pp. 151–7.

cluded a protest against the occupation of Muslim sanctuaries by British troops, a reminder that the British government had promised that the choice of a Khalifah was for Muslims to make, and a plea that the British government should do all it could to ensure that in the post-war settlement the Khalifah kept control of the Muslim sanctuaries and the Jazirat-ul-Arab.[1] But India's Pan-Islamists faced two ways: they were as concerned for their own power in India as they were for the Khalifah's power abroad. Consequently the League couched its claims for the Khilafat firmly in the context of the status of Indian Muslims, stating that the collapse of Muslim powers was bound to have an adverse effect on the political importance of Muslims in India and would strain their loyalty to the raj. The Viceroy sent back a conciliatory reply, saying that the British government had no intention of interfering with the Muslim choice of a Khalifah, that when British forces occupied Muslim sanctuaries every care was taken to ensure their sanctity, and that Britain's representatives at the Peace Conference would give consideration to the deep feelings of the Muslims.[2]

However the fate of the Khalifah and the Muslim sanctuaries was not in the hands of the Government of India. It could only act as adviser to the Imperial government in London, which created British policy towards Turkey and had to weigh up its European commitments and needs as well as the feelings of its Indian subjects. The tension between London and Delhi over Turkish policy was evident throughout the war. As early as November 1914 the Viceroy, Lord Hardinge, was embarrassed by the pronouncements of his colleagues in London. He said,

> I am always protesting against the indiscretions of our Ministers in regard to Turkey, which add greatly to my anxieties in regard to Indian Mahomedans – a consideration which appears to carry no weight at all with the Cabinet. Why should Asquith of all people at the Guildhall Banquet proclaim that the Turkish Empire will be wiped out in Europe and Asia? It is an easy development to foresee, and in my opinion very desirable to achieve, but why say so? All our Moslems are very sensitive to Turkey, which they feel to be the last great Mahomedan Power in existence, and I am quite sure that they will be greatly perturbed over Asquith's statement.[3]

1 President of Muslim League to Private Secretary to Viceroy, telegram, 2 January 1919, Proceeding No. 251 of Home Pol., A, March 1919, Nos. 251–9. The Jazirat-ul-Arab was the area bounded by the Mediterranean, the Red Sea, the Indian Ocean, the Persian Gulf and the Rivers Tigris and Euphrates. It included Arabia, Mesopotamia, Syria and Palestine. The main Muslim sanctuaries (Mecca, Medina and Jerusalem) were in the Jazirat-ul-Arab. Five lesser sanctuaries (Hajaf, Karbela, Sammara, Kazimain and Baghdad) were in Mesopotamia.

2 Secretary to Govt. of India, Home Dept., to Secretary to All-India Muslim League, telegram, 15 February 1919, Proceeding No. 254 of Home Pol., A, March, Nos. 251–9.

3 Hardinge to Sir V. Chirol, 12 November 1914, Hardinge Mss. (93).

By 1914 the British government had already calculated that it was no longer worth propping up 'the sick man of Europe', and, once involved in war with Turkey, it was subject to pressure from its allies who wanted a slice of the Turkish cake.[1] In 1919 British policy emerged as a plan to remove from the Turkish Empire any European territory, and to lop off all the Arab portions of the Empire and place them under Allied Mandates.[2] Caught between such a policy in London and the protests of its Muslim subjects, the Indian government could do little but wait for the peace treaty, trying to soothe with one hand in India and with the other to press its views on the government in Britain. In May 1919, soon after his conciliatory telegram to the Muslim League, the Viceroy cabled the Secretary of State for India, explaining his difficulties with the Muslims and asking for more information about British policy towards Turkey. In the view of his government it was essential that the Sultan should remain an independent sovereign in Constantinople, with some sort of suzerainty over the Holy Places if not over Arabia, Mesopotamia and Palestine, and that whatever the ultimate peace terms the British government must be able to show that it had done its best for Turkey.[3]

The peace terms were published in May 1920 and the treaty was signed in Sèvres three months later. In the uneasy interval between the end of the war and the treaty, Pan-Islamic ideals and pro-Turkish sympathy in India developed into a definite threefold claim. The personal centre of Islam, the Khalifah, should retain his empire with sufficient temporal power to defend the faith; the geographical centre of Islam, the Jazirat-ul-Arab, should remain under Muslim sovereignty according to the Prophet's dying injunction; the Khalifah should remain warden of the Muslim sanctuaries.[4] Leaders of the Khilafat movement insisted that these claims were part of their religious faith, and they invoked the 1858 Royal Proclamation grant-

[1] For Britain's changing policy towards Turkey before 1914 see Cunningham, 'The Wrong Horse?', Hourani (ed.), *St. Anthony's Papers. Number 17. Middle Eastern Affairs. Number Four*, pp. 56–76. In 1915 Great Britain, France, Russia and Italy agreed by secret treaties to partition the Turkish Empire into four spheres of influence. See Gopal Krishna, 'The Khilafat Movement In India: The First Phase (September 1919–August 1920)', *Journal Of The Royal Asiatic Society* (1968, Parts 1 & 2), pp. 37–8.

[2] Memorandum by A. J. Balfour for Lloyd George, 26 June 1919, E. L. Woodward and R. Butler (ed.), *Documents On British Foreign Policy 1919–1939 First Series Volume IV 1919* (London, 1952), pp. 301–3.

[3] Viceroy (Home Dept.) to Secretary of State for India, telegram, 18 May 1919, Proceeding No. 529 of Home Pol., A, May 1919, Nos. 524–32. The Government of India had already taken the precaution of advising local governments to summon leading Muslims and prepare them gently for the probable dismemberment of the Turkish Empire. Secretary to Govt. of India to all local govts. and administrations, 3 May 1919, Proceeding No. 363 of Home Pol., A, May 1919, Nos. 363–8.

[4] For example, Mahomed Ali made this threefold claim in Paris on 21 March 1920, A. Iqbal (ed.), *Select Writings And Speeches Of Maulana Mohamed Ali. Volume II* (2nd edition, Lahore, 1963), pp. 3–9.

ing religious liberty to Indian subjects of the Crown, claiming that if this liberty was denied them their loyalty to the Crown would be jeopardized.[1]

They also invoked three 'pledges' by western statesmen to justify their demands. One was Asquith's Guildhall speech of 10 November 1914 which had so embarrassed Hardinge. Despite its anti-Turkish tone it contained the specific statement that there would be no crusade against Muslim belief, and this was interpreted as a pledge to regard Muslim feeling about the Khilafat.[2] Another pledge often cited was one of President Wilson's Fourteen Points which contained the statement, 'The Turkish portions of the present Ottoman Empire should be assured a secure sovereignty,' though it continued, 'but the other nationalities which are now under Turkish rule should be assured an undoubted security of life and an absolutely unmolested opportunity of autonomous development.'[3] The third pledge was Lloyd George's declaration of 5 January 1918 that the Allies would not challenge the maintenance of the Turkish Empire in lands of Turkish race with a capital at Constantinople.[4]

Gandhi accepted the threefold Khilafat claim, partly because it involved religious belief for Muslims, but also on the grounds of secular justice in fulfilment of pledges publicly given.[5] He maintained that his 'sense of moral responsibilities' made him take up the Khilafat question: it was a 'wrong' he could not countenance because it would mean being party to a

1 Speech by Mahomed Ali in London, 22 April 1920, *ibid.* p. 36; A. Iqbal (ed.), *My Life A Fragment. An Autobiographical Sketch of Maulana Mohamed Ali* (reprint of 1942 edition, Lahore, 1946), pp. 183–4. Mohamed Ali's interpretation of the Sultan's position is clear from a letter he wrote about the Arab Revolt to Chintamini on 1 July 1916, Ali Papers: '...their action is not only *criminal* but is also *sinful.* They are rebels and something more: they come within an ace of being *renegades* as well. For the Sultan of Turkey is something more than the ruler of the Ottomans. He is to a population as large as that of India, that is to a fifth of God's creation among mankind, the vicegerent of God himself, an Emperor and Pope in one, and combining in himself as the successor or Caliph of our Prophet...the twofold function which is the logical sequence of the most rational abhorrence that Islam has for any lacerating separation between things temporal and things spiritual, things sacred and things profane, things worldly and things other-worldly. You must remember Islam is not only a religion in the ordinary sense, but also a theocracy, a Government, though it be the Government of God Himself.'

2 *Young India*, 12 May 1920, *C.W.*, vol. 17, p. 412.

3 Point Twelve of Wilson's Fourteen Points in an address to Congress stating the U.S. war aims and peace terms, 8 January 1918, *The Messages And Papers Of Woodrow Wilson. Volume 1* (New York, 1924), p. 470. Cited in *Navajivan*, 7 September 1919, *C.W.*, vol. 16, pp. 104–5.

4 Lloyd George's speech was reported in *The Bombay Chronicle*, 8 January 1918; it was cited in *Young India*, 12 May 1920, *C.W.*, vol. 17, pp. 412–13. Lloyd George sometimes maintained privately that his speech was not a pledge but merely an offer to get Turkey out of the war, but he was not entirely consistent in his attitude and on other occasions agreed that it was a pledge. E. S. Montagu to Sir G. Lloyd, 14 April 1920, Mss. EUR. D. 523 (22).

5 *Navajivan*, 29 February 1920, *C.W.*, vol. 17, p. 59.

broken pledge.[1] At the same time he saw that the Khilafat movement was a remarkable opportunity for promoting several causes about which he felt deeply. He was quite open about this, as he had been to the Ali brothers when he began his campaign against their internment.

> I hope by my "alliance" with the Mahomedans to achieve a threefold end – to obtain justice in the face of odds with the method of Satyagrah[a] and to show its efficacy over all other methods, to secure Mahomedan friendship for the Hindus and thereby internal peace also, and last but not least to transform ill-will into affection for the British and their constitution which in spite of its imperfections has weathered many a storm.[2]

The preeminence of satyagraha as a method of resolving conflict, Hindu–Muslim unity as a prerequisite for India's future peace and true Swaraj, and the necessity of a right relationship between the rulers and the ruled, based on the justice implicit in the British constitution though not always apparent in practice, were beliefs Gandhi had matured in South Africa and pursued since his return to India. He had only participated in Indian politics in so far as he could put these beliefs into practice and gain public credence for them. The Alis' internment was an occasion for promoting Hindu–Muslim unity and a right relationship with the raj. Mrs Besant's internment was an opportunity for both promoting satyagraha and expressing deep misgivings about the way the raj treated India's leaders and their aspirations, a combination which recurred on a larger scale in the Rowlatt satyagraha. All three instances were also 'wrongs' to Gandhi. Now there occurred a 'wrong' far greater in magnitude, an opportunity for Gandhi to pursue the three aims together. It propelled him into the political arena and led him to try to assume control of the Khilafat movement.

(I) THE KHILAFAT MOVEMENT UNTIL DECEMBER 1919

The first phase of the Khilafat movement lasted until December 1919, by which time the widespread sympathy for Turkey and the Sultan which was its impetus had received institutional expression in a Central Khilafat Committee. The leaders of the Committee were a middle group within the Muslim community, mainly prosperous Bombay merchants who sympathized neither with the more conservative Muslims who had lost control of the League, nor with the more extreme Pan-Islamists. Consequently the official temper of the movement until the end of 1919 was calculated moderation.

The rising tide of pro-Turkish feeling was not stemmed by Chelmsford's conciliatory reply to the resolutions of the 1918 session of the Muslim League, and sporadic meetings were held throughout India to

[1] *Young India*, 28 April 1920.

[2] *Young India*, 5 May 1920. For Gandhi's aims in championing the Ali brothers, see above, pp. 151–2.

voice Muslim fears. As the Director of Central Intelligence reported in March,

> The reports of meetings which have reached me from the provinces do not show that there has been much violent oratory, and the newspaper comments are on the whole temperate, although there is now and then a threatening note. There can be no doubt, however, that the feelings of Indian Muhammadans towards Government are very bitter and the situation requires careful watching.[1]

So far there was no concerted plan of action, but a public meeting of Muslims in Bombay on 19 March took the first step towards such a plan by electing a Bombay Khilafat Committee, with Mian Mohamed Chotani, a leading Memon and a rich timber merchant, as its President.[2] When this Committee met early in May it could not decide whether to convene a conference or send a memorial to the Viceroy, and so it formed a sub-committee to consider the question.[3]

Meanwhile Gandhi pursued a separate line by cementing an alliance with Abdul Bari of Ferangi Mahal, the Ali brothers' religious director. Some time early in March 1919 Gandhi and Bari met in Lucknow and from their meeting there emerged an understanding that Hindus would work for the Khilafat cause, while Muslims would contribute to communal harmony by trying to stop their slaughter of cows, a religious ritual which was a perennial flash-point between the two communities.[4] On 14 March Bari published in *Akhuwat*, a new Muslim paper in Lucknow, a rambling account of his interview with Gandhi, and said that he not only supported satyagraha against the Rowlatt bills, but also envisaged the possibility of satyagraha if the demands of Muslims in relation to the Khilafat and the

[1] Weekly report of D.C.I., 17 March 1919, Proceeding No. 150 of Home Pol., B, April 1919, Nos. 148–52.

[2] Fortnightly report from Bombay for second half of June 1919, Home Pol., Deposit, August 1919, No. 51. Sir George Lloyd later commented about Chotani, 'He speaks next to no English, is very uncouth and illiterate...He is merely a religious fanatic whose prominence is due to the wealth he had and which the Khilafat people wished to tap.' Sir G. Lloyd to Chelmsford, 13 February 1921, Mss. EUR. E. 264 (26).

[3] The sub-committee consisted of Chotani, M. M. Khandwani, Sir Fazalbhoy Currimbhoy, Sulleman Cassim Mitha (who had opposed Jinnah and the Lucknow Pact), F. M. Yusuf, S. D. Kanji, M. H. Labji, K. Kabiruddin, B. A. Koor, H. E. Poonawalla, H. A. Y. Isphahani, A. H. S. Khatri, M. T. Kaderbhoy and Maulvis Abdul Rauf and Rafiuddin Ahmed. History of the Freedom Movement Unit Bombay, File No. 4044/M/I.

[4] Weekly report of D.C.I., 29 September 1919, Proceeding No. 457 of Home Pol., B, September 1919, Nos. 454–7. On 24 November 1919 at the Delhi Khilafat Conference Gandhi stated that the Khilafat was a Hindu question because it was a Muslim question, and that there should be no question of exchanging Hindu cooperation in the Khilafat movement for the Muslims' abandonment of cow slaughter. Bombay Police Abstract, 1920, par. 168 (h).

Muslim sanctuaries were not conceded.[1] Gandhi kept in close touch with Bari throughout the summer on the question of the best tactics by which to obtain the Ali brothers' release, and simultaneously he urged Bari to hold fast to a communal alliance on the basis of satyagraha to obtain a favourable position for the Khalifah under the peace terms.

> The time for joint and firm action on our part is now. There will be deep disappointment and resentment after. But it will be to no purpose, everything is possible now, nothing *after* the publication of the terms...In the dignity of Satyagrah[a] lies the future of Islam, the future of India and parenthetically the future of the Ali brothers.[2]

However, in spite of Bari's published support for possible satyagraha on the Khilafat issue, correspondence which passed between him and Gandhi in the summer of 1919 showed that he was not a completely committed supporter of Gandhi's method and feared that it might produce a repetition of the violence which had occurred in the Punjab and even cause loss to the Muslim community.[3]

The Muslim League meanwhile despatched to London a deputation consisting of M. A. Jinnah and G. M. Bhurgri from Bombay, Hasan Imam from Bihar and Yakub Hasan from Madras. They laid before the Prime Minister a memorandum setting out Indian Muslim concern over the post-war fate of the Turkish Sultan.[4] Yakub Hasan at least realized that mere memorials were likely to be ineffective, and on his advice the Bombay Khilafat Committee began to organize an intensive agitation throughout India, entering into close cooperation with the more extreme Pan-Islamists in northern India for this purpose. In the summer of 1919 their combined influence was still local, and the government reckoned that only specific towns in the northern and central parts of the subcontinent were seriously affected – Bombay, Delhi, Aligarh, Lucknow, Patna and Calcutta.[5]

The next major step in the Khilafat movement after the founding of the Bombay Khilafat Committee was an all-India Khilafat Conference on 21 September in Lucknow, in which Bombay and Lucknow leaders cooperated. Gandhi did not attend, but on 18 September he addressed a

1 Weekly report of D.C.I., 17 March 1919, Proceeding No. 150 of Home Pol., B, April 1919, Nos. 148–52.

2 Gandhi to A. Bari, 27 August 1919, reported by Secret Censor, 30 August 1919, Home Pol., A, October 1919, Nos. 426–40. (The same letter with slightly different wording appears in the Abdul Bari Papers, Ferangi Mahal, Lucknow. I owe this reference to Mrs Gail Graham.) For Gandhi's correspondence with Bari on the Alis' release see above, p. 156.

3 A. Bari to Gandhi, 10 May 1919, 3 September 1919, S.N. Nos. 6603 & 6844.

4 Memorandum submitted by All-India Muslim League Deputation to the Prime Minister in London, *The Bombay Chronicle*, 30 September 1919.

5 Note by W. S. Marris, 1 May 1919, Home Pol., A, May 1919, Nos. 363–8; Fortnightly report from Bombay for second half of August 1919, Home Pol., Deposit, October 1919, No. 44.

Khilafat meeting in Bombay of about ten thousand Muslims. He urged them to make their voice heard on the Khilafat issue, but was reported to have told his audience that they were not sufficiently concerned about the matter and that the proceedings of the meeting reminded him of a play. His point was underlined by the fact that in Bombay the non-Muslim press, rather than Muslim papers, were busy rousing opinion on the Khilafat issue.[1] When the Lucknow conference convened there was a similar lack of enthusiasm among the mass of Muslims and Hindus, although the meeting itself had a good attendance, including three to four hundred delegates from outside the U.P. More disturbing than lack of public interest was the fact that the divisions which had split the Muslim League in 1918 now threatened the infant Khilafat organization. On this occasion the rift occurred over the appointment of a president, with Abdul Bari on the one hand, supported by his personal clique and some of the Muslim League officials, and on the other the Rajah of Mahmudabad and his more moderate faction. The multitude of resolutions also made the conference less hard-hitting than it might have been, because they swamped the main resolution which declared that the Sultan of Turkey's temporal power was indissolubly linked with his spiritual position as Khalifah and should not be limited.[2] The main positive result of the conference was a decision to observe 17 October as Khilafat Day.

Gandhi took up this suggestion and widened it, along lines familiar from the Rowlatt satyagraha, by urging in the press that Hindus should unite with Muslims in fasting and hartal on that day. He appealed to Hindu leaders to cooperate with his proposal if they agreed with him.[3] It is difficult to judge how favourable the circumstances were for Gandhi's proposal for joint communal action, because only scant evidence remains from which to gauge the reactions of Hindus and Muslims to the prospect of collaborating with each other on an issue specifically concerned with Muslim faith. Both communities were divided on the issue, just as they were on the details of constitutional reform. Some Pan-Islamists were so eager to gain the cooperation of the most active Hindu leaders that on 4 April the citizens of Delhi had been treated to the remarkable spectacle of Swami Shraddhanand, an Arya Samajist committed to the reconversion of Muslims to Hinduism, preaching by Muslim invitation on communal unity in the Jumma Masjid! However, from Calcutta there came Muslim objections to the presence of Hindus in mosques as 'unseemly and inadmissible'.[4]

1 Fortnightly report from Bombay, 1 October 1919, Home Pol., Deposit, November 1919, No. 15.

2 Fortnightly report from U.P., 30 September 1919, *ibid.*

3 *The Bombay Chronicle*, 13 October 1919; circular letter from Gandhi, 10 October 1919, *C.W.*, vol. 16, pp. 228–9 (this was sent, for example, to Motilal and Jawaharlal Nehru, Kasturi Ranga Iyengar, Rajagopalachariar and Rajendra Prasad).

4 Weekly report of D.C.I., 5 May 1919, Proceeding No. 494 of Home Pol., B, June 1919, Nos. 494–7.

From the Hindu side it was clear that as early as January 1918 Tilak and his men had seen that they might reap a rich harvest of mass agitation if they cooperated with the Pan-Islamists.[1] But Motilal Nehru, in a province where Pan-Islamists were at their most extreme, was more hesitant to start on this path and confided to his son his exasperation at the attitude of Sir Harcourt Butler, who had succeeded Meston as Lieutenant-Governor of the U.P. and appeared to be goading them where they preferred not to go.

> Butler has been silly enough to proscribe in this Province Ansari's speech as President of the Reception Committee of the last Moslem League. I am afraid there will not be much to choose between him and O'Dwyer in the near future. His last act not only is an open insult to Muslim feeling but puts Hindu Nationalists in an awkward position. Pan-Islamism or Pan Hinduism does not enter into the programme of the Indian Nationalist but he cannot sit tight when the right of speech is interfered with in an arbitrary manner... There are many things nearer home than the question of the Khaliphate which we have to attend to.[2]

Here was one influential Congressman at least who was aware of the contradictions inherent in the communal alliance Gandhi was proposing.

Gandhi's letters to the press and to other leaders asking them to exert their influence were a major part of the organization of Khilafat Day. He appealed that people should keep indoors and that there should be no processions or public meetings, and that millhands and others involved in essential services should stay at work so that there should be no disorder or violence.[3] Otherwise the main forms of publicity were posters and pamphlets which appeared throughout the country.[4] Bombay, where the satyagraha and Home Rule organizations cooperated with the Khilafat Committee, was the driving force behind the plan, and without the persistence and the purses of the Bombay men observance of 17 October might well have lapsed completely. As the Bombay government reported:

> Telegrams noticed in the censorship disclose the remarkable amount of organization and expense entailed in engineering the so-called 'spontaneous expression of Muhammadan opinion' and the reluctance of up-country centres to find the small outlay involved in organizing the move-

[1] Tilak met Dr Ansari in Calcutta and said that mass agitation was very important but was only possible if politics and religion were mixed. Weekly report of D.C.I., 26 January 1918, Proceeding No. 490 of Home Pol., B, January 1918, Nos. 487–90.

[2] Motilal Nehru to Jawaharlal Nehru, 16 February 1919, Nehru Memorial Museum and Library, Nehru Papers. For Ansari's speech at the 1918 Muslim League see above, p. 157

[3] Circular letter from Gandhi to Hindu leaders, 10 October 1919, *C.W.*, vol. 16, pp. 228–9; Gandhi to A. Bari, undated, *ibid.* pp. 229–30.

[4] Bombay Police Abstract, 1919, par. 1365 (a); Fortnightly report from Madras, 3 November 1919, Home Pol., Deposit, November 1919, No. 16; Fortnightly report from Bengal for second half of October 1919, *ibid.*

ment locally. Even Calcutta has drawn on Bombay for about six to eight hundred rupees and the total bill is being practically footed by the President of the Caliphate Committee, Bombay, personally.[1]

The observance of Khilafat Day is a good index of the spread of the Khilafat movement, the depth of its penetration among different groups of Muslims, and its reception among Hindus. It also shows the extent to which Gandhi had begun to create and tap a network of organization and loyalty by his espousal of a Muslim cause as opposed to the Rowlatt bills, on which issue his subcontractors had failed him. In the North-West Frontier Province, Assam, and Ajmer–Merwara with Rajputana, areas untouched by institutional politics, there was little activity on 17 October. On the North-West Frontier several important people had received telegrams from the secretaries of the Bombay Khilafat Committee asking the Hindus and Muslims to unite in observing the day, but the recipients professed not to know who the senders were. By contrast in Bangalore, which was almost as moribund by the standards of nationalist politics, the Muslim League acted on the instructions of the Bombay Khilafat Committee and organized a meeting which was attended by 3–4,000 people. It also engineered the closure of butchers' businesses and some Hindu shops.[2] The Central Provinces had the benefit of the political experience of the Maratha Brahmins, who in the southern districts tried to make the day a success. But most Muslims chose to hold aloof and not make any alliance with the Hindus, even though Gandhi's exhortations reached them in reinforcement of the local Hindu overtures.[3]

In the three Presidencies with their traditions of political agitation Khilafat Day was observed more widely. In Bombay city hartal was partial though the municipal markets, the share market, the cotton market and two mills closed, practically no meat was available and most victorias stopped plying for hire. However, in neighbourhoods like the Javeri Bazaar, where people lived who had once been Gandhi's firm supporters, business went on as usual and there was nothing like the spirit which had been behind the hartals of April 1919. In the mofussil observance was entirely urban, but attendances at Khilafat meetings were small and the

[1] Fortnightly report from Bombay, 16 October 1919, Home Pol., Deposit, November 1919, No. 14.

[2] Fortnightly reports for second half of October 1919 from Assam, North-West Frontier Province, Rajputana with Ajmer-Merwara, and Mysore, Home Pol., Deposit, November 1919, No. 16.

[3] Fortnightly report from C.P. for second half of October 1919, *ibid.* A later report from Nimar district showed that Gandhi's local adherents, led by a Hindu pleader, met with a severe rebuff from local Muslims when they tried to hold a joint Khilafat meeting. The Muslims were reported to have asked what idol worshippers had to do with the succession to the Prophet. Fortnightly report from C.P. for second half of November 1919, Home Pol., Deposit, January 1920, No. 5.

only places where hartal was observed to any extent were Ahmedabad, Kaira town, Godhra, Broach, Ahmednagar and Surat. In general Muslims were apathetic and Gandhi, aided by local Home Rule Leaguers and leaders left over from the Rowlatt satyagraha, was responsible for what observance occurred. In Kaira town, for example, most of the Hindus shut their shops while Muslims went on working, and in Shikarpur and Surat Muslims actively opposed demonstrations in company with Hindus.[1] Taking the Presidency as a whole it was clear that there were not enough Muslims to make the Khilafat Day observances very widespread and that Muslims on balance felt little sympathy for the suggestion. The only network of subcontractors on which Gandhi could call were the Home Rule Leaguers and the satyagraha leaders who had failed him earlier in the year.

In Madras Home Rule Leaguers and Congressmen had been instrumental in organizing a local Khilafat Committee during 1919 and they had considerable success in their alliance with local Muslims. Not only did the Urdu-speaking Muslims respond to the cry of the Khalifah in danger, but for the first time Tamil-speaking Muslims also began to take an interest in politics, prompted mainly by their war-time grievances against the raj for its restrictions on the tanning industry in which many of them were engaged. However Muslims were only a very small minority in the Presidency, and when it came to Khilafat Day there was no general hartal though fasting and prayers were common. In Trichinopoly Hindus not Muslims actually organized the observances. In Madras city there was a meeting on the beach of about 20,000, of whom many were Hindus.[2]

In Bengal by contrast Muslims were a majority community, but the Hindu politicians had no political contact with them and in 1919 there was only limited support for the Khilafat movement from Bengali Muslim politicians. The leading Bengali Pan-Islamist, A. K. Azad, was still in internment when Khilafat Day took place. On that day shops closed in some mofussil towns and there were meetings in most districts. In Calcutta most Muslim shops closed, as did a considerable number owned by Hindus and Marwari traders. Some of the latter were probably prompted by fears of violence or looting, but there were no outbreaks of any kind and no attempts to force the closure of shops or prevent people from using trams. The major observance was a public meeting presided over by Fazlul Haq and attended by over 10,000, most of whom were illiterate Muslims – an

1 Fortnightly report from Bombay, 1 November 1919, Home Pol., Deposit, November 1919, No. 16; Bombay Police Abstract, 1919, par. 1397 (b), (c), (d), (f), 1465 (f).

2 Fortnightly report from Madras, 3 November 1919, Home Pol., Deposit, November 1919, No. 16. For the background to the Madras Muslims' interest in the Khilafat movement and the emergence of the Tamil Muslims into institutional politics see McPherson, 'The Political Development of the Urdu- and Tamil-speaking Muslims of the Madras Presidency 1901 to 1937', pp. 94–7, 110, 115.

indication of the potential of the Khilafat movement in Bengal if leadership emerged which could mobilize such people.[1]

Punjab, like Bengal, had a Muslim majority; but the whole province lacked political experience and organization and the Khilafat movement had not produced any change in this situation. The province virtually ignored Khilafat Day. Some Hindus would have been willing to join in observance if Muslims had led the way, but in some places like Hoshiarpur the Muslims refused pointblank, while in Lahore and Amritsar Muslims who generally closed their shops for part of Friday kept open for fear of being misunderstood.[2] In neighbouring Delhi hartal was organized by a local committee. It exempted sweet and food sellers, thereby causing a rift between them and other shopkeepers, with the result that though about four-fifths of shops seemed shut many stayed open late the previous evening or traded behind closed doors.[3]

To the east of Delhi in U.P. and Bihar was the homeland of the most vociferous Pan-Islamists. However among the majority of Muslims in those provinces there was only a distinct unease and little active observance of Khilafat Day. In spite of the Pan-Islamists' efforts, the encouragement of some Hindu politicians, and the widespread use of Gandhi's name, hartal was a failure outside the cities of Lucknow, Cawnpore, Allahabad and Agra.[4] In Bihar only one-third of the districts organized any observance of the day, though there were serious attempts at Gaya, Bhagalpur and Monghyr, and at Darbhanga where the organizers had considerable success and business was almost completely suspended. In Patna preliminary meetings to arrange a programme for Khilafat Day were poorly attended and on the day itself few shops closed and many Muslim dealers refused to associate themselves with the movement.[5]

Observance of 17 October as Khilafat Day showed that by no means all Muslims were touched by the Khilafat movement, and that many of them were reluctant to join hands with Hindus on an issue related to their religious belief. So far the Khilafat movement had provided Gandhi with no new network of subcontractors, and he was forced to rely on people he had used before, whose effectiveness for him was compromised by their positions in their localities. Divergent interests in the localities hampered the

[1] Fortnightly report from Bengal for second half of October 1919, Home Pol., Deposit, November 1919, No. 16.

[2] Fortnightly report from Punjab for second half of October 1919, *ibid*; Weekly report of D.C.I., 27 October 1919, Proceeding No. 363 of Home Pol., B, October 1919, Nos. 360–3.

[3] Fortnightly report from Delhi, 1 November 1919, Home Pol., Deposit, November 1919, No. 16.

[4] Fortnightly report from U.P., 31 October 1919, *ibid*. This report suggested that even Abdul Bari was not wholeheartedly behind the idea of hartal because he feared it might lead to violence and jeopardize his own position as a leader.

[5] Fortnightly report from Bihar and Orissa, 1 November 1919, *ibid*.

spread of the movement just as they had wrecked the Rowlatt satyagraha, and they soon began to divide the Khilafat leadership itself.

Until November 1919 the Bombay Khilafat Committee controlled the campaign, and on 11 November it changed its name to the Central Khilafat Committee of India.[1] But by the end of the month its hold over the movement seemed precarious. At an all-India Khilafat Conference in Delhi on 23/24 November, convened by the Delhi Khilafat Committee and presided over by Fazlul Haq, delegates from the U.P. tried to wrest control from the Bombay men, and only Gandhi's influence stopped them.[2] The U.P., with Delhi, Rajputana and Sind, provided the majority of the delegates, U.P.'s contingent being led by Syed Hassan Raza Ali, Syed Zahur Ahmad, Abdul Bari and Hasrat Mohani. The temper of the meeting was also determined by the presence of a large number of ulema.[3] Provincial and personal rivalries were evident from the start, when elections to the subjects committee were held. Once these were out of the way it became clear that the delegates were determined to take a tougher line than the Bombay Committee had so far proposed. At the meeting on 23 November, at which Gandhi was the only Hindu present, resolutions were passed thanking Gandhi and the Hindus for their sympathy over the Khilafat, resolving to boycott the celebrations to mark the end of the war, progressively to boycott British goods, to send a deputation to England and if necessary to America, and suggesting that if the government disregarded their wishes on the Khilafat issue they might resort to non-cooperation. A sub-committee was appointed to look into the whole question of non-cooperation.

This meeting was a moment of great importance for the Khilafat movement, for Indian politics and for Gandhi's career, though it received little public notice. For the first time Gandhi envisaged total withdrawal of cooperation from the government, and for the first time he used the word 'non-cooperation' though on that occasion he was thinking aloud and had not worked out the implications of his suggestion.[4] Gandhi opposed the resolution to boycott British goods because he felt it meant inflicting economic injury and punishment, which was against his principles as a satyagrahi. Hasrat Mohani, who had proposed the resolution, argued

[1] Bamford, *Histories of the Non-Co-operation and Khilafat Movements*, pp. 144–5. A complete list of members of the Bombay Khilafat Committee is not available but those present at this meeting on 11 November were: M. M. Chotani, M. A. M. Khan, B. A. Koor, K. A. H. Siddick, R. Ahmed, C. A. Peerbhai, N. M. Latif, A. K. I. Fazla, H. A. Y. Isphahani, A. Rauf, M. A. Juma, H. A. Doothvala, M. H. Ismail, R. M. Chinoy, H. Poonawalla, Bombay Police Abstract, 1919, par. 1497 (b).

[2] Accounts of the Conference on 23/24 November are in Bamford, *op. cit.* pp. 144–5; Bombay Police Abstract, 1920, par. 168 (h); Fortnightly report from Delhi, 2 December 1919, Home Pol., Deposit, January 1920, No. 5.

[3] Fortnightly report from Bombay, 3/11 December 1919, Home Pol., Deposit, January 1920, No. 5.

[4] Gandhi, *An Autobiography*, pp. 401–2.

against him that Muslims were not satyagrahis and that economic boycott was a legitimate form of political protest, and urged that the issue should be decided on its merits, not on personalities.[1]

The following day Gandhi faced further opposition before the public meeting opened, over which he was to preside. This time his main opponents were Swami Shraddhandand, Hasrat Mohani and Shankarlal Banker, who wanted to link the Khilafat question with the actions taken under martial law by officials in the Punjab.

> Thus only, they urged, could Hindu co-operation be ensured. Gandhi maintained his veto. The opposition then said that the principle of deciding by a majority vote had been admitted at the meeting on the 23rd and should apply to this question as well. Gandhi replied by a categorical statement of his intention to resign the whole campaign if any attempt was made to call for votes or even if any amendment to his decision was suggested. This threat cowed his opponents into submission.[2]

Hasrat Mohani's fear of the power of Gandhi's personality was well justified. The extent of Gandhi's power was shown when on 24 November at the meeting open to Hindus the resolutions of the previous day which he had opposed were not pressed, and the only resolutions passed thanked him and the Hindus for their sympathy and proposed a boycott of the peace celebrations. Gandhi's influence, carried to the point of dictatorship, saved the Bombay leaders from the more extreme elements in the Khilafat movement. Nonetheless they were disturbed at the lengths to which the meeting on 23 November had gone, and decided to shelve the suggestion of boycott of British goods and non-cooperation by circulating both ideas to every local Khilafat Committee, where presumably they hoped they would be lost in protracted discussion.[3]

Before the Delhi meeting Gandhi had supported the idea of boycotting the peace celebrations if the Khilafat question was not satisfactorily settled, and he continued his publicity campaign to this end in early December.[4] However, there was no time for widespread organization of a boycott and the idea went against the natural wish of ordinary people to enjoy shows of fireworks and other celebrations after the privations of the war. As a result the celebrations went on, though there was no great enthusiasm for them. Local administrations reported the extent of the boycott. There was no bunting or illumination in the central parts of Bombay city, for example, and in Ahmedabad Gandhi 'persuaded' the municipality to withdraw its financial backing for the celebrations. There was a boycott by Muslims in

[1] *The Bombay Chronicle*, 29 November 1919.

[2] Bombay Police Abstract, 1920, par. 168 (h). Gandhi argued that the Punjab was a local matter and to mix this up with the Khilafat question would be 'a serious indiscretion'. Gandhi, *An Autobiography*, pp. 399–400.

[3] Fortnightly report from Bombay, 3/11 December 1919, Home Pol., Deposit, January 1920, No. 5.

[4] For example, *Young India*, 5 November 1919, 3 December 1919.

Chittagong, Muslim industrialists in Titagarh (Bengal), some Muslims in Ranchi and lawyers in Patna, Sunni Muslims in larger U.P. towns, some Punjab townspeople, and some Muslims in Coorg and Bangalore. Delhi city had no celebrations, but Delhi's civil lines did.[1] Although there was no general boycott, C.I.D. officials in retrospect reckoned that 'in most places it caused a serious curtailment of the programme of celebrations and gave great prominence to the Khilafat question throughout India.' They also noted that Hindus were often responsible where the boycott was successful.[2]

In the wake of this attempted boycott the Bombay Khilafat Committee met on 22 and 25 December to consider the resolutions on boycott of British goods and non-cooperation which were circulated after the Delhi Conference. They decided that a boycott was impracticable for their community. Over three-quarters of Bombay's Muslim merchants dealt in British goods and a boycott would ruin them and probably split the whole community. Non-cooperation, too, they felt would only make the position of Muslims in India worse, losing for them any hope of attaining the position to which they felt entitled by their numbers and history. To make sure that their fears were felt outside their Presidency, they urged that the sub-committee appointed at Delhi to consider non-cooperation should be enlarged to represent Muslim commercial opinion.[3]

The discussions of the Bombay men showed plainly the nature of the Khilafat leadership in the first phase of the movement. Concerned they might be over the future of the Khalifah, but they were prepared to agitate only in ways which did not threaten their material interests. Already they had been challenged by Muslims from areas where the community had few commercial vested interests to protect. Their future hold over the movement depended on whether Gandhi would in future be prepared to act as a shield for them, whether their financial backing remained essential to other regions, and whether Muslims from other areas with different local interests entered the movement to swing the balance of power in favour of the men from northern India.

(II) DECEMBER 1919 TO MID-MAY 1920

The release of the Ali brothers and A. K. Azad at the end of December

1 Fortnightly reports from provinces for December 1919, Home Pol., Deposit, January 1920, Nos. 44 & 45.

2 Weekly report of D.C.I., 12 April 1920, Home Pol., Deposit, April 1920, No. 103. In the U.P. some Muslims appear to have rejected the idea of boycotting the peace celebrations because they wanted to assert that the Khilafat movement was religious, not political, and because they were suspicious of the Hindus' interest in their cause. Fortnightly report from U.P. for second half of December 1919, Home Pol., Deposit, January 1920, No. 45.

3 Bombay Police Abstract, 1920, par. 27 (a); Fortnightly report from Bombay for second half of December 1919, Home Pol., Deposit, January 1920, No. 45.

1919 inaugurated the second phase of the Khilafat agitation. The three immediately joined forces with the U.P. leaders and by the middle of May 1920 this combination had wrested control of the movement from the Bombay men, although Bombay remained the seat of the Central Khilafat Committee of India. As the leadership slipped from a predominantly merchant group into the hands of journalists and preachers the movement made more headway in small towns and villages, wherever there was an unsophisticated working or peasant Muslim population, who were susceptible to religious exhortation through local mosques and vernacular papers but barely touched by the deliberations of the wealthy and the educated in Bombay.

A Khilafat Conference was convened in Amritsar at the end of December 1919 when Congress and Muslim League were in session there, and it sent a deputation of Hindus and Muslims to put before the Viceroy the threefold Khilafat claim. Chelmsford replied that he sympathized with Muslim feeling and that their claims were being pressed in London and at the Paris Peace Conference by himself, E. S. Montagu, two Indian representatives, Lord Sinha and the Maharajah of Bikaner, and an Indian Muslim deputation. However, he warned them that the Peace Conference would probably not recognize the Sultan's full sovereignty over the lands he had possessed before the war, since Turkey could not 'expect, any more than any other Power which drew the sword in the cause of Germany, wholly to escape the consequences of her action.' The deputation made a rejoinder to this, merely restating their claims and demanding the fulfilment of 'pledges' made by Asquith and Lloyd George.[1] Gandhi signed the deputation's address but he disapproved of its vague and wordy drafting and apologized to the Viceroy's Private Secretary, explaining that he had not seen it in time to change it.[2] Relying on his hold over the Khilafat leaders, he reprimanded them for not producing a clear statement of their minimum demands. Jawaharlal Nehru later commented, 'This argument was a novel one in political or other circles in India. We were used to vague exaggerations and flowery language, and always there was an idea of a bargain in our minds. Gandhiji, however, carried his point'.[3] The Mahatma had made it clear that he was determined to change those conventions of institutional politics which he considered wrong, wherever he had the power to do so.

After the Amritsar Conference the U.P. Khilafat leaders and their liberated allies, the Alis and A. K. Azad, began to organize support for their claims among Muslims and Hindus. Tours, meetings and speeches

[1] Khilafat Deputation to Viceroy, 19 January 1920; Viceroy's reply to Khilafat Deputation, 19 January 1920; description of Khilafat Deputation's rejoinder given in Viceroy (Home Dept.) to Secretary of State, telegram, 28 January 1920; Home Pol., A, February 1920, Nos. 413–16 & K.-W.

[2] Gandhi to J. L. Maffey, 18 January 1920, *C.W.*, vol. 16, pp. 489–90.

[3] Quoted in D. Norman (ed.), *Nehru. The First Sixty Years. Volume 1* (London, 1965), p. 60.

followed in great numbers, quickening the whole tempo of the movement, compared with its first phase, which had ended in December. Late in January the Alis attended a welcome meeting in Bombay organized by the Home Rule League and the Bombay National Union, at which Tilak pledged Hindu help on the Khilafat issue.[1] In February Abdul Bari and Shaukat Ali toured Gujarat together preaching the sanctity of the Khilafat and Hindu–Muslim unity; later they were joined by Azad for a tour of Sind.[2] Meanwhile on 1 February Mahomed Ali left India as leader of a Khilafat deputation to Europe, and once again Bombay men, and Chotani in particular, gave the only solid financial backing.[3]

The next major policy discussion occurred at the third All-India Khilafat Conference on 15/16/17 February in Bombay. G. M. Bhurgri of Bombay presided, and 175 delegates attended, sent by thirty-three local Khilafat Committees. However, many prominent politicians, both Hindus and Muslims, were absent, among them Dr Ansari, Hasan Imam, Fazlul Haq, Mrs Besant, M. M. Malaviya, C. R. Das, Tilak and Gandhi himself. About 2,500 people attended the public sessions, but the real business was done in the subjects committee, where Bombay had a majority. Bombay city provided seventeen of the members and Bombay Presidency five, compared with eleven each from Sind and the U.P., six from Bengal, Bihar and Orissa together, two from Berar and one from Ajmer. On 16 and 17 February battle was joined in the subjects committee between the more restrained (most of the Bombay delegates led by M. M. Chotani and G. M. Bhurgri) and the more extreme (most of the rest led by delegates from Sind). Eventually the crucial questions of boycott of British goods, withdrawal of cooperation from the government and Muslim service in the army were shelved, pending news from Mahomed Ali in Europe. The only resolution passed was one which called on the British government to withdraw troops from the Arabian peninsula.[4]

No definite line of action emerged from this meeting but Gandhi, seeing signs of restlessness among some Muslims, produced his own plan on 7 March 1920. Insisting that there should be no violence, no boycott

[1] History of the Freedom Movement Unit, Bombay, File No. 4044/M/1. However, the Bombay Tilakites stayed away from many other local Khilafat meetings, Bombay Police Abstract, 1920, par. 453 (f).

[2] Bombay Police Abstract, 1920, par. 301 (d), (e), (f); 413 (b).

[3] Fortnightly report from Bombay 17/13 February 1920, Home Pol., Deposit, July 1920, No. 88. At the February All-India Khilafat Conference in Bombay Bombay men promised Rs. 11 lakhs to Khilafat funds, of which Chotani's own subscription was Rs. 25,000. Sind promised Rs. 5 lakhs, Bengal Rs. 5 lakhs, and U.P. Rs. 4 lakhs. Acting Commissioner of Police, Bombay, to Secretary, Govt. of Bombay, Special Dept., 26 February 1920, Home Pol., Deposit, July 1920, No. 89.

[4] Acting Commissioner of Police, Bombay, to Secretary, Govt. of Bombay, Special Dept., 26 February 1920, Home Pol., Deposit, July 1920, No. 89.

of British goods, and no mixing up of other questions like Egypt with the Khilafat issue, he suggested that 19 March should be observed as Khilafat Day with a hartal, and that if their demands were not met they should resort to non-cooperation.[1] In promoting the idea of another Khilafat Day he was backing a resolution passed by a Bengal Khilafat Conference, held on 28 February under the presidency of A. K. Azad.[2] That gathering's principles and plans for the Khilafat movement differed considerably from Gandhi's, however. When in his 7 March manifesto he opposed boycott of British goods and the combination of the Khilafat with other issues he was registering his protest against some of its other suggestions, and simultaneously seeking to ensure that the more extreme leaders did not capture the initiative. Officials of the raj saw this Bengal Conference as the culmination of the stream of fiery speeches let loose by the release of the Alis and A. K. Azad. Its extreme tendencies in comparison with Bombay Khilafat meetings had been clear when it passed a resolution that Muslims should abandon their loyalty to the British and assist the Khalifah if his pre-war dominions were not kept intact, and when Abdul Bari made a speech which was almost a declaration of jihad, or holy war, and spoke of soaking Christians in kerosene and burning them alive.[3]

The Bombay leaders became alarmed at this outburst in Bengal and the growing threat to their position of dominance in the movement. The only gesture of conciliation the more extreme leaders were prepared to make towards them was their silencing of Abdul Bari. However, the Bombay men still carried considerable weight because of their financial resources and because they still had the benefit of Gandhi's alliance. So far he was only willing to discuss the possibility of non-cooperation, not to lead it. When the Central Khilafat Committee met in Bombay from 11 to 14 March to discuss future policy Gandhi was clearly apprehensive about outbreaks of violence, and he suggested strongly that the ground should be prepared thoroughly before non-cooperation was attempted. As a result the meeting decided that no action should be taken at the time apart from propaganda, though it decided that when further action became necessary it should take the form of non-cooperation, according to a plan drawn up by a committee of which Gandhi was the principal member. This plan suggested several stages of non-cooperation, starting with the relinquishing of titles and honours, followed by the resignation of council members, the withdrawal of private servants and government employees, including

1 Gandhi's manifesto, 7 March 1920, *Young India*, 10 March 1920, *C.W.*, vol. 17, pp. 73–6.

2 Gandhi to Bengal Khilafat Committee, undated telegram, *The Bombay Chronicle*, 11 March 1920, *ibid.* p. 77.

3 Weekly report of D.C.I., 12 April 1920, Home Pol., Deposit, April 1920, No. 103; Viceroy (Home Dept.) to Secretary of State, telegram, 3 March 1920. Home Pol., Deposit, July 1920, No. 89.

the police, the withdrawal of Muslims from the army, and culminating in a refusal to pay taxes.[1]

Fear of violence as a side effect of his satyagraha campaigns was very near the surface of Gandhi's mind after the debacle of the Rowlatt satyagraha, and his caution attracted many Hindus who had similar fears. The Bengali paper, *Nayak*, for example, welcomed Gandhi's repudiation of the Bengal Khilafat Conference resolution in favour of boycott of British goods, and later affirmed, 'We are in favour of the agitation for the preservation of the Caliphate, and if the agitation is carried on on the lines of Mahatma Gandhi's *satyagraha* we will always support it.'[2] However, memories were still vivid of the violence and repression which passive resistance had precipitated at the time of the partition of Bengal, and, despite the Bengal Khilafat Conference, there was considerable hostility in the Presidency to the idea of hartal on 19 March. *Bangali* in its issue of 19 March reminded its readers of their previous experience of passive resistance, and *Nayak* thought Gandhi was courting violence by his idea of hartal, in spite of its earlier support for Gandhian satyagraha.

> So the game that was begun at the time of the partition of Bengal and the swadeshi movement is being played anew on a small scale. The subjects are sure to lose in this game and must suffer loss and indignity. The Hindus of Bengal have acquired sufficient experience in the matter and hence we advise the Moslems not to walk into the trap. We are earthen pots, so if we fall foul of steel vessels we are sure to go to pieces... It is no time now to trust to luck and risk anything.[3]

Gandhi nonetheless continued to encourage the observance of 19 March, urging enquirers to follow the instructions given in his manifesto of 7 March.[4] The main instruments of organization seem to have been local committees, which mushroomed all over India for the purpose. It is impossible to discover the exact number of such committees, but the activities of the Delhi one were recorded in detail and are an example of the organization at its most efficient.

> Early in March the local Khilafat Committee began arranging for the Khilafat hartal to be observed on the 19th March. It wrote to Mr. Gandhi

[1] Bombay Police Abstract, 1920, par. 646 (n); Home Pol., A, September 1920, Nos. 100–3.

[2] *Nayak*, 8 March 1920, Bengal N.N., No. 11 of 1920; *Nayak*, 16 March 1920, Bengal N.N., No. 13 of 1920.

[3] *Nayak*, 16 March 1920, Bengal N.N., No. 13 of 1920; *Bangali*, 19 March 1920, *ibid.*

[4] For example, Girdhari Lal wired from Amritsar to ask if Amritsar should observe hartal and if Hindus should support the Khilafat movement. Gandhi replied that Hindus should help and act according to his manifesto. Girdhari Lal to Gandhi, telegram, 16 March 1920, S.N. No. 7138; Gandhi to Girdhari Lal, telegram, 16 March 1920, S.N. No. 7138*a*.

> asking him to instruct the Hindus to co-operate and meanwhile bargained with the local Hindu leaders offering to show interest in the hartal for the 30th March, the anniversary of the riots in 1919, in exchange for Hindu participation in the Khilafat day. At the same time the Committee put pressure on the leading gentlemen of its own community by demanding from them under threat of social boycott an immediate declaration in writing that the expulsion of the Turks from Constantinople would in fact cause them acute personal sorrow. These demands were conveyed to the recipients by uniformed members of the three Muhammadan volunteer corps – the Muslim League, the Khilafat and the Askar-i-Islamia – who were instructed to remain on the premises until a definite reply was vouchsafed. Several of the notables so addressed hurried in their perturbation to the authorities for advice...On the 19th a very complete hartal was observed. Muslim League and other Muhammadan volunteers were posted in most of the bazars and were insistent and almost aggressive in discouraging the collection of even the smallest crowd.[1]

In Calcutta some shops shut but there was not complete hartal and most Hindu leaders held aloof.[2] Taking the country as a whole, however, there was a fairly complete stoppage of business and hundreds of well-attended Khilafat meetings. The effects were far greater than those produced by the attempted organization of the boycott of peace celebrations three months earlier.[3]

Meanwhile discussion of non-cooperation began in earnest among Muslim and Hindu leaders. On 22 March ten Hindu leaders and fifteen Muslims met in Delhi; among them were Gandhi, Lajpat Rai, M. M. Malaviya, Tilak and G. S. Khaparde, Dr Ansari, A. K. Azad, Abdul Bari, Hakim Ajmal Khan and Shaukat Ali. Their main concern was united action in the future by both communities. Pandit Malaviya voiced Hindu anxiety when he said he had no proof that the Muslim public would support boycott and non-cooperation. A. K. Azad replied that he had toured Bengal and was sure that Muslims in smaller towns and villages would follow his call, and Gandhi backed him up by saying that he, too, was convinced of Muslim support. Azad and Gandhi pulled together again when challenged by Abdul Bari on the subject of non-violence. Both of them were adamant that this was not the time for a holy war. Finally a committee, composed of Gandhi, Lajpat Rai, Ajmal Khan, Shaukat Ali and Azad, was established to draw up a programme of work if the Muslims' minimum demands were not met.[4] At least some of the Hindu politicians

[1] Notes on activities of Volunteer Associations in Delhi, Home Pol., Deposit, April 1921, No. 67.

[2] Chief Secretary, Govt. of Bengal, to Secretary, Govt. of India, Home Dept., 26 November 1921, Home Pol., 1921, No. 415.

[3] Weekly report of D.C.I., 12 April 1920, Home Pol., Deposit, April 1920, No. 103.

[4] Report by an intelligence officer, 23 March 1920, Home Pol., Deposit, April 1920, No. 4.

felt that the discussion was vague and unpractical, and the plans for the future impolitic. In the words of Khaparde, 'Gandhi trotted out his Satyagraha hobby so I left with Tilak.'[1]

During the discussion on 22 March it was apparent that Gandhi faced opposition from his own community and from different elements within the Muslim leadership of the Khilafat agitation. What disturbed him more than overt opposition was his suspicion that those Muslims who did support his idea of non-cooperation were prompted by political calculation, not by faith in satyagraha. As he wrote to one of them,

> My talk with Hajrat Mohani has left me much disturbed. According to him nobody believes in non-cooperation. But it has been taken up merely to conciliate me. Now in a matter so important as this there should be no question of conciliation and I would not have anything simply for my conciliation. Moreover non-cooperation to be successful has got to be taken up most enthusiastically by all and no great cause has ever prospered if it has been handled without faith in it.[2]

Tension between Gandhi's ideal of satyagraha and the Khilafat leaders' adoption of it as a political technique remained a constant feature of the Khilafat movement as long as the Muslims needed Gandhi as a guarantee of Hindu support. Gandhi himself created this tension, despite his laments about Muslim motives, by making non-violence the precondition of his support for the movement.[3] Meetings below the highest level of leadership make it clear that among the rank and file of Muslims caught up in the agitation, and particularly among the ulema, there was no commitment to the ideal of non-violence.[4] Dr Ansari had long discussions with Muslims in northern India, on the basis of which he judged that if Gandhi launched a programme of non-cooperation there would be little support for those parts of it which touched people's material interests, resignation from jobs in particular; and he thought that among the Khilafat leaders closest to

[1] 22 March 1920, Diary of G. S. Khaparde, Khaparde Papers.

[2] Gandhi to T. Razmia, 27 March 1920, S.N. No. 9857.

[3] Looking back at this time, Jawaharlal Nehru wrote, 'There were long talks with the Moulvies and the Ulemas, and nonviolence and noncooperation were discussed, especially nonviolence. Gandhiji told them that he was theirs to command, but on the definite understanding that they accepted nonviolence with all its implications. There was to be no weakening on that, no temporizing, no mental reservations. It was not easy for the Moulvies to grasp this idea, but they agreed, making it clear that they did so as a policy only and not as a creed, for their religion did not prohibit the use of violence in a righteous cause.' Quoted in Norman (ed.), *Nehru. The First Sixty Years. Volume 1*, p. 60.

[4] For example, a Khilafat Workers' Conference in Delhi on 18/19 March 1920, attended by about 500 delegates mainly from U.P. and Punjab, who were of little social standing, was the occasion for violent anti-government speeches and a declaration that delegates would carry out the resolutions of the Calcutta Khilafat Conference. C.I.D. note on political agitation in Delhi, Home Pol., Deposit, April 1921, No. 61.

Gandhi only he, M. H. Kidwai, A. K. Azad, Abdul Bari and Shaukat Ali would undoubtedly follow Gandhi into non-cooperation.[1]

Apart from the hesitations of his Muslim allies Gandhi also faced opposition from Hindu politicians. Most of them professed sympathy with Muslims at the prospect of their Khalifah being shorn of his power: but they feared the outbreak of violence more. Fears which flickered in anticipation of hartal on 19 March were now fanned to life by the suggestion of non-cooperation. Srinivasa Sastri was full of misgivings at Gandhi's alliance with the Ali brothers, and predicted that Gandhi could no more control the Muslims if they took to violence than he had been able to in 1919.[2] A correspondent of *The Bengalee* felt that the threat of extreme tactics would 'inflame the public mind', and appealed to 'the better mind of the Muslim community to assert itself and to give a right lead to the agitation which now appears to be fast getting out of hand.'[3] The paper feared that the disloyalty to the British generated by the agitation might wreck the reform scheme.[4] Annie Besant, too, saw the prospect of non-cooperation as a threat to the closed world of institutional politics and wrote, 'Under present circumstances many of us are placed in a very painful position. We will no more follow Mr. Gandhi in his present course than we would follow him last year, for his present policy is even more dangerous than that of 1919, which ended so disastrously.'[5]

When similar fears appeared among the Bombay merchants in the heart of the Khilafat camp the more extreme among the leaders, particularly those from Sind, U.P. and Bengal, led by Abdul Bari and Shaukat Ali, tried to move the next Central Khilafat Committee meeting away from Bombay lest the non-cooperation programme should be diluted.[6] Although they did not succeed in changing the place of the meeting on 12 May they successfully steered it into confirmation of non-cooperation as already defined. A sub-committee was appointed to work out a detailed plan for starting it; the members were M. M. Chotani, Gandhi, Shaukat Ali, A. K. Azad, A. H. S. Khatri and another Mahomed Ali (not Shaukat's brother).[7]

After this meeting several members of the Central Khilafat Committee resigned – Ghulam Husain, Rahimtullah Chinoy, Sir Fazalbhoy Currimbhoy (Vice-President and Honorary Treasurer) and Badruddin Abdullah

1 M. A. Ansari to Gandhi, 1 April 1920, S.N. No. 7143.

2 V. S. S. Sastri to Gandhi, 1 February 1920, S.N. No. 7096; Sastri to Sir P.S. Sivaswami Aiyer, 13 April 1920, Jagadisan (ed.), *Letters Of V. S. Srinivasa Sastri*, pp. 64–5.

3 *The Bengalee*, 18 April 1920.

4 *The Bengalee*, 9 May 1920, Bengal N.N., No. 19 of 1920.

5 *New India*, 15 April 1920, S.N. No. 7157.

6 Note by Commissioner of Police, Bombay, Home Pol., A, February 1921, Nos. 341–54 & K.-W.

7 Bombay Police Abstract, 1920, par. 807 (q).

Koor (Honorary Secretary).[1] Sir Fazalbhoy resigned ostensibly because he was going to London, but Husain and Koor resigned because they felt that non-cooperation was unconstitutional and dangerous. Koor stated in his letter of resignation that he feared non-cooperation would precipitate violence; more important, he believed that if Muslims resigned their government appointments it would lower their status in the country without forcing the government to change its policy, and would only give further opportunities to Hindus and Sikhs who would rush to fill the gaps left by Muslim resignations. In his view non-payment of taxes would mean confiscation of Muslim property which other communities would then acquire, and once again Muslims would be the poorer.[2]

Gandhi's position in the spectrum of the Khilafat leadership had clearly changed by May 1920, compared with early March 1920. By May he was no longer prepared to act as a shield for the Bombay moderates against the stronger policies of the leaders from northern India. The reasons behind this shift of position can only be conjectured. It seems most probable that, having made an emphatic stand against violence and boycott, Gandhi realized that he must produce a viable counter-plan in order to retain Muslim support. On 19 April at a Khilafat Workers' Conference in Delhi there had been considerable restlessness among delegates from Sind, Punjab and Bengal at Gandhi's moderation in alliance with Chotani;[3] and by the end of the month intelligence officers assessing the situation reckoned that Gandhi's position as a moderating influence on the Khilafat movement was precarious.

> The association of Gandhi with any movement is a great asset, because his name is one to conjure with among the ignorant masses. Hence Shaukat Ali and his disciples claim Gandhi as their *guru* and profess to be guided entirely by his advice...Gandhi himself, in dealing with the *Khilafat* problem, has two conditions to fulfil: he has to retain Muhammadan loyalty to his own leadership, and he has to find a programme for practice which squares with his own policy and fulfils the Islamic zeal of his extremist friends. The last condition is the most urgent and has driven him to what may be described as a minimum programme, the minimum, that is which the extremists can accept as an appropriate outlet for their fanaticism...His scheme is obviously comprehensive and easily stretched into something far more than passive resistance. Using the glamour of Gandhi's name and their own weapon of religious fanaticism, the most ardent and

[1] *Ibid.* par 807 (q), 843 (s). Sir Fazalbhoy Currimbhoy had taken fright at the thought of satyagraha in March 1919. See above, p. 168.

[2] B. A. Koor to M. M. Chotani, 12 May 1920, Home Pol., Deposit, June 1920, No. 112.

[3] Weekly report of D.C.I., 3 May 1920, Home Pol., Deposit, June 1920, No. 78. Further evidence of 'extreme' Muslim distrust of Gandhi and his motives is in Weekly report of D.C.I., 26 April 1920, Home Pol., Deposit, April 1920, No. 103; Weekly report of D.C.I., 24 May 1920, Home Pol., Deposit, June 1920, No. 78.

revolutionary Pan-Islamist can work at this scheme, knowing that from passive to active resistance is but a step. Gandhi, in order to lead, has to follow; at most, he can but hope to be a brake on progress.[1]

As the balance of power within the Khilafat leadership changed, local support for the movement deepened and widened. No precise assessment is possible of the extent of popular participation. It was in the interests of leaders to stress the support they could rouse, and even the evidence of about seventy local Khilafat Committees at the beginning of 1920 may only indicate the presence of one or two vigorous agitators in each locality, rather than a genuine mass support.[2] However, officials of the raj were increasingly concerned at the spread of the movement, particularly when even a place as politically quiescent as Bangalore sent two delegates to a Bombay Khilafat Conference![3] The critical areas were U.P., Bengal and Sind. All were regions where the local power structure gave a foothold to the ulema and the journalists who were the more extreme Khilafat leaders, and where local conditions provided them with an audience susceptible to their type of leadership.

U.P., though a Muslim minority province, was fertile ground for the seeds of Khilafat propaganda since local memories of Muslim power before the British raj died hard. Those Muslims who did not belong to the group of aristocrats and older educated men who played the gentle politics of collaboration were younger educated men searching for new forms of political expression, small landowners and urban artisans already disturbed by Pan-Islamic propaganda and the economic hardships which accompanied the war. Such groups were open to the exhortation of vernacular journalists and local preachers, though the educated alone had been touched by the network of political influence created by Congressmen in Allahabad. As the journalists and their allies among the local ulema took up the Khilafat cause their agitation drew in large numbers and reached down in society to men outside the scope of existing politics. Clear evidence of this was a Khilafat Conference held at Cawnpore on 4/5 April 1920 under the auspices of the U.P. Ulema Association and attended by about 6,000 people, mostly Muslims 'of the poorer classes'. Abdul Bari and Salamatulla of Ferangi Mahal were the fieriest speakers, referring to war between Islam and Christianity and complete independence for India if the Peace Conference did not grant the Khilafat claims. Such excitement was generated

[1] Weekly report of D.C.I., 10 May 1920, Home Pol., Deposit, June 1920, No. 78.

[2] Sixty-nine local Khilafat Committees were listed in Appendix II of The Constitution of the Central Khilafat Committee of India, Bombay, printed in 1920, H.F.R.M., File No. 4044/M/II.

[3] 'Hitherto, and particularly throughout the war, the Muhammadans have been conspicuous for their loyalty and have not concerned themselves with politics. But the release of the Ali brothers and the mischievous activities of Mr. Gandhi and his followers are having their effect, even so far south as Bangalore.' Fortnightly report from Mysore, 16 February 1920, Home Pol., Deposit, July 1920, No. 88.

by this gathering that Abdul Bari himself later issued a proclamation advising patience and caution, and intelligence officers judged U.P. to be 'the hot bed of the agitation'.[1]

Just a month earlier the Viceroy had described Bengal as 'the storm centre of the Khilafat agitation'.[2] A majority of the Presidency's population were Muslim peasants who were completely untouched by politics as practised by the *bhadralok*; but during the Khilafat agitation they were a willing audience for the new Muslim leadership which emerged under A. K. Azad, aided and abetted by Abdul Bari and Shaukat Ali, who were imported from the U.P. The resolutions of the Calcutta Khilafat Conference were an indication of the temper of feeling in the Presidency on the Khilafat issue. They were also an instrument for broadening support for the movement, as the leaders arranged for them to be put to local meetings throughout the Presidency. The Calcutta men alone could not create a mass agitation and, as in the U.P. the ulema became the local leaders of the movement, so in Bengal the provincial leaders deliberately established links with Muslims who wielded local influence, and through them carried on an intensive propaganda campaign.[3]

Sind, like Bengal, had a large peasant Muslim population previously unaffected by politics. In that most backward part of the Bombay Presidency participation in institutional politics was confined to members of the Hindu Amil trading caste, some of whom had joined Mrs Besant's Home Rule League. The area was controlled by great landowners, many of whom actively opposed the aspirations of educated Indians for political power,[4] and the government relied on the collaboration of such men for the

1 Weekly report of D.C.I., 12 April 1920, Home Pol., Deposit, April 1920, No. 103. Further evidence of the spread and depth of the Khilafat agitation in the U.P. is in Bayly, 'The Development Of Political Organisation In The Allahabad Locality, 1880–1925', pp. 342–51. Bayly notes the appearance of preachers hired by local Khilafat Committees to spread the Khilafat agitation in small towns: such men were often weavers and petty traders.

2 Viceroy to Secretary of State, telegram, 17 March 1920, Home Pol., Deposit, July 1920, No. 90.

3 Viceroy to Secretary of State, telegram, 12 March 1920, Fortnightly report from Bengal for first half of March 1920, Home Pol., Deposit, July 1920, No. 90.

4 In July 1917 a meeting of the Zamindars' Anjuman Islam at Mehar in Larkana district 'held a meeting at which a resolution was passed placing on record their profound pleasure at the attitude of the Madras Government in interning Mrs. Besant and her lieutenants, and their abhorrence of the protest meetings and of the strong speeches made in furtherance of self-government. The meeting also laid down that the Sind Muhammadans were opposed to the demands of educated Indians for Home Rule on the ground that education had not yet been diffused so widely among them as to render them fit for such demands and considered that Sind was not in need of Home Rule by which the interests of the Muhammadan community was [sic] bound to suffer.' Fortnightly report from Bombay, 3 August 1917, Home Pol., Deposit, August 1917, No. 3. For Amil participation in Mrs Besant's Home Rule League see above, p. 27.

stability of the area, particularly as the local C.I.D. was short-staffed and more than ordinarily unpopular. Even before the Khilafat movement local officials were uneasy lest a Pan-Islamic agitation should attract peasants and zamindars and undermine the authority of the government. Sind was particularly vulnerable to such agitation, because its traditional Muslim leaders, known as Pirs, retained great influence, though not the temporal power they had before the British took over the administration. Many of the Pirs were known to have been involved in fanatical Muslim movements like that of the Wahabis, and between 1896 and 1914 all of them had been under government surveillance in connection with a local wave of crime and unrest. Moreover, the presence of various Muslim shrines, and the fact that Karachi was a port for Persia meant more potential foci for Pan-Islamic agitation.[1]

Official unease was justified. The Khilafat leadership tried to secure the alliance of local mullahs and Pirs, who would spread Khilafat propaganda at village level with the weight of their religious authority;[2] and the Second Special Sind Provincial Khilafat Conference (6/7/8 February 1920) demonstrated the superb success of this tactic. Attendance ranged from 15,000 on the first day to 4,000 on the third day, and the main speakers were mullahs, not local educated men.

> The purely religious cry of "Allah-ho-Akbar" was often heard and was regarded as an indication by the more ignorant Zamindars and cultivators present that their religion was being attacked. There is hardly any doubt that the majority of the Mullas in Sind has been won over by the agitators and are now beating the "drum ecclesiastic". Most of these Mullas are uneducated men and some are fanatically inclined, but their combined influence would probably be great. Nor does it appear likely that the Pirs of Sind, who have greater influence, will show any lack of eagerness in the cause of Islam for fear of losing prestige, even though the offerings of their disciples are likely to be diverted to the Sultan's cause.[3]

By the end of March 1920 the Sind C.I.D. was completely swamped by the tide of the Khilafat agitation as meetings were held nearly every day throughout the area. The Khilafat and the doctrine of disloyalty to the British were the fashion, and any unsympathetic mullah or Pir risked lapsing into obscurity.[4] At the beginning of April the Government of

[1] File containing report on Sind by C. R. Cleveland of Govt. of India, Home Dept. (12 June 1916), report by V. Vivian (5 June 1916), report from office of the Commissioner in Sind (15 July 1916), Home Pol., A, September 1916, Nos. 193–4 & K.-W.

[2] Report from Commissioner in Sind, 3 February 1920, quoted in Fortnightly report from Bombay, 17/21 February 1920, Home Pol., Deposit, July 1920, No. 88.

[3] Fortnightly report from Bombay, 1/9 March 1920, Home Pol., Deposit, July 1920, No. 89.

[4] Report of Civil Intelligence Officer, Karachi Brigade, 1 April 1920, Home Pol., A, May 1920, No. 342 & K.-W.

Bombay received emergency powers to deal with Sind in view of the Khilafat agitation.[1]

By May 1920 the Khilafat movement had spilled over into a completely different level of politics by comparison with its range in 1919. Not all Muslims joined the movement, but in certain areas where local conditions were favourable the religious appeal of the extreme leadership of the ulema and the vernacular journalists reached people outside the circle of the literate Hindu politicians. The weight of these areas was then felt in the counsels of the central Khilafat leadership, and the men from Bombay were ousted by leaders from U.P., Bengal and Sind who found their plans too moderate.

Bombay's dominance had rested partly on its control of the purse strings. It alone had found the cash in the first stage of the movement, but as support for the movement deepened and widened there was a greater financial reservoir on which to draw. Evidence about the Khilafat funds is skimpy, but it seems clear that subscriptions were coming in which loosened the financial hold of the Bombay leadership. At the Second Special Sind Provincial Conference, for example, Rs. 8,000 were collected; and from Bombay Presidency it was reported to be the fashion for such lowly folk as tea shop owners and hotel keepers to assign their takings on certain days to the Central Khilafat Fund. The Ali Brothers' Purse Fund, amounting to a lakh of rupees, was also added to the Fund and lessened the importance of large contributors like Chotani.[2] Deprived, too, of the weight of Gandhi's support, the Bombay men had during the second phase of the Khilafat movement lost all the bulwarks of their influence which had enabled them to control the movement before the release of the Ali brothers and A. K. Azad.

(III) MID-MAY TO 1 AUGUST 1920

The third phase of the Khilafat movement lasted from mid-May to 1 August 1920, when it merged with the agitation over the Punjab into a single movement of non-cooperation. During this phase Gandhi and his allies (who could be labelled 'non-violent extremists') held the balance of power among the Khilafat leaders. Their position was reinforced by the publication on 14 May of the proposed allied peace treaty with Turkey.

1 Secretary, Govt. of India, Home Dept., to Secretary. Govt. of Bombay, Judicial Dept., telegram, 8 April 1920, Proceeding No. 128 of Home Pol., B, May 1920, Nos. 124–8.

2 Fortnightly report from Bombay, 1/9 March 1920, Home Pol., Deposit, July 1920, No. 89; Weekly letter of Commissioner of Police, Bombay, 17–18 May 1920, Home Pol., Deposit, June 1920, No. 112. The total receipts of the Central Khilafat Committee in 1920 were Rs. 6,43,766–1–4. *The Bombay Chronicle*, 1 February 1922, Bamford, *Histories of the Non-Co-operation and Khilafat Movements*, p. 190.

Under its terms the Sultan would keep Constantinople as the capital of the Turkish state, but would lose Eastern Thrace to Greece, while Armenia, Syria, Mesopotamia and Palestine were to become independent states. This meant that two of the three claims made by Indian Khilafat leaders were not granted: the Jazirat-ul-Arab would not remain under Muslim sovereignty, and the Khalifah would not remain warden of the Muslim sanctuaries.[1]

Contemporaries disagreed whether these terms were a blow to essential elements of Muslim faith. Mahomed Ali insisted that they were,[2] but it was reported that Shaukat Ali admitted privately that they were not, and that the Khilafat agitation was a tactic by which he could gain support for his own political ambitions.[3] Whatever the precise significance of the treaty terms to Muslims, the Government of India felt acutely embarrassed by the necessities of European politics. Montagu called it 'a monstrous Peace', but having done everything he could to ensure that Indian Muslim feeling was known in Europe he was willing to back the Indian administration in controlling Muslim agitation.[4]

Gandhi reacted to the peace proposals with a press statement describing them as 'a staggering blow to the Indian Mussulmans'; and he advocated non-cooperation as the only way to secure justice and avoid violence.[5] However, he was determined to keep strict control over non-cooperation through a central organization, and he criticized individuals who renounced positions and titles on their own responsibility.[6]

Meanwhile the Central Khilafat Committee was still split on the propriety and the form of non-cooperation. M. M. Chotani was reported to have moved away from his original moderate position, partly because of a letter he had received from M. H. Kidwai complaining that the Committee was too timid and threatening to secede if the plan of non-cooperation was diluted.[7] Whether or not Chotani hoped to salvage some position of leader-

[1] Jerusalem would be under the Palestine government, and Mecca and Medina would be controlled by the King of Hedjaz. The terms of the treaty are in *Parliamentary Papers. Treaty Series No. 11 (1920)*, Cmd. 964.

[2] M. Ali to President of the Turkish Peace Delegation, 17 July 1920, Ali Papers.

[3] Report by a District Magistrate of a talk with G. M. Bhurgri on 9 December 1920, when Bhurgri recounted what Shaukat Ali had told him. Bombay Police Abstract, 1921, par. 9 (10).

[4] E. S. Montagu to Willingdon, 20 May 1920, Mss. EUR. D. 523 (16).

[5] Gandhi's press statement on Turkish peace terms, *The Bombay Chronicle*, 18 May 1920, *C.W.*, vol. 17, pp. 426–7.

[6] *Gujarati*, 23 May 1920, *ibid.* p. 446. Yakub Hasan, the Madras Khilafat leader, resigned from the Madras Legislative Council on 20 May, and afterwards told Shaukat Ali that he could not understand why Gandhi thought such a step premature. Y. Hasan to S. Ali, 23 May 1920, Home Pol., A, November 1920, Nos. 19–31.

[7] Viceroy (Home Dept.) to Secretary of State, telegram, 20 May 1920, Home Pol., Deposit, July 1920, No. 95. Part of Kidwai's letter to Chotani is given in Bamford, *Histories of the Non-Co-operation and Khilafat Movements*, pp. 192–3.

ship by his change of position, he took up a hard line in a letter to Mahomed Ali who was still in Europe. 'The Central Khilafat Committee have now finally decided to vigorously take up the movement of Non Co-operation in the event of an adverse decision. India stands firmly by her demands, and no compromise is now possible unless the demands are acceded to.'[1] Despite his new attitude Chotani still hoped to keep the Khilafat organization in Bombay's control, and he argued with Shaukat Ali and his supporters, who planned to hold the next major meeting in northern India: but his opponents won on 24 May when it was decided to hold the next meeting in Allahabad.[2]

However, a manifesto issued by Chotani for the Central Khilafat Committee on 28 May showed that there was still some formidable opposition within the Committee to the more extreme leadership. The manifesto marked a distinct dilution of the policy adopted at the Committee's meeting on 12 May. Having stated the Khilafat claims, it declared that the signatories did not 'desire to take hasty steps which may result in violence or unnecessary embarrassment to the Government', and that they proposed for the present only surrender of honorary offices and titles and civil employment under the government, reserving opinion on the other stages of non-cooperation which had been approved by the Committee. More interesting was their deference to the wishes of Gandhi by abandoning boycott of British goods in favour of swadeshi, and their stated concern for Hindu feeling, coupled with the denial that Muslims wished to introduce a Muslim power into India or had any aim other than the service of their religion and their country.[3]

The relationship between the Khilafat movement and the Hindu politicians became a crucial issue once non-cooperation was a practical possibility after the publication of the peace terms. Muslim leaders for their part needed Hindu cooperation if they were to exert real pressure on the British, and in order to ensure that Muslims alone would not suffer from resignation of posts and lose to other communities the few places they had in the country's administration. Hindu politicians saw opportunity for an alliance through which they could exert more pressure on the raj, but they also recognized the potential for violence in non-cooperation and needed some way of keeping violence in check.

The aspirations and fears of both groups were demonstrated at Allahabad when the Central Khilafat Committee met on 1/2/3 June, and in special sessions conferred with an influential group of Hindu leaders. Among the

1 M. M. Chotani to M. Ali, 14 May 1920, Ali Papers.

2 Bombay Police Abstract, 1920, par. 843 (s).

3 Manifesto issued by M. M. Chotani for the Central Khilafat Committee, 28 May 1920, Home Pol., A, November 1920, Nos. 19–31. Even this restricted plan of non-cooperation was accompanied by the resignation of Mirza Ali Mohammed Khan, Secretary of the Central Khilafat Committee, from office and membership of the Committee. M. A. M. Khan to M. M. Chotani, 28 May 1920, *ibid.*

Hindus present were Gandhi himself, Pandit Malaviya, Motilal Nehru, T. B. Sapru, S. Satyamurti, B. C. Pal, Rajagopalachariar and Lajpat Rai. C. R. Das did not attend, neither did Tilak and many of his followers. Of the latter group Joseph Baptista declined on the grounds that it was no use advising the Muslims because their feelings on the Khilafat issue were so strong, and that he did not believe in 'Ghandism', but could see no way of opposing it.

> I do not believe in Ghandism. He may be a saint. A saint will make a good guide for the kingdom of Heaven, but not for the Empire of India. His influence on the *Khilafat* Committee is too great. I anticipate nothing but Himalayan miscalculations from Gandhi. But he has immense influence in India and I will not venture to put myself in opposition to him.[1]

At the first session of the Central Khilafat Committee on 1 June Gandhi found difficulty in convincing the Muslims of Hindu sincerity. He had to announce that a majority of the A.I.C.C. considered non-cooperation impracticable and were not prepared to support the Muslims fully at the moment, though the A.I.C.C. had decided to hold a Special Congress at Calcutta to discuss the question. When this news was broken Abdul Bari jumped up and in an aggressive tone reminded Gandhi that he had pledged himself to support Muslims through thick and thin if they followed his advice. Gandhi pacified Bari with the assurance that this was still his personal view and that he was sorry that he did not carry sufficient weight in the A.I.C.C. to bring it round to his opinion.[2]

The next day the Committee reaffirmed four stages of non-cooperation as its policy, and to give practical effect to this appointed a sub-committee whose principal members were Gandhi, the Ali brothers, A. K. Azad, Hasrat Mohani and Saifuddin Kitchlew. Gandhi described this as the Martial Law Committee of the Khilafat movement, and was reported to have used the word 'dictator' to describe what should be his own position on it. There was a good deal of hostility to Gandhi's arbitrary manner, but in the end nobody dared oppose him.[3] According to a police report, 'Shaukat Ali said that the Mahommedans were quite prepared to leave themselves entirely under the guidance of Gandhi. There was a dead silence and people did not dare to speak one way or the other as if they did not approve of placing themselves blindly in the hands of Gandhi.'[4]

[1] J. Baptista to M. M. Chotani, 27 May 1920, *ibid.*

[2] Report from Commissioner of Police, Bombay, Home Pol., B, July 1920, No. 109. The A.I.C.C., meeting in Benares on 30 & 31 May, had decided to postpone a decision on non-cooperation until the Special Congress. A.I.C.C. to V. J. Patel, telegram, 3 June 1920, A.I.C.C. Files, 1920, No. 12.

[3] Viceroy (Home Dept.) to Secretary of State, telegram, 11 June 1920, Home Pol., Deposit, July 1920, No. 96; Sir G. Lloyd to E. S. Montagu, 25 June 1920, Mss. EUR. D. 523 (25). Later Gandhi called himself merely an 'adviser' on the sub-committee, *Young India*, 23 June 1920, *C.W.*, vol. 17, pp. 505–8.

[4] Report from Commissioner of Police, Bombay, Home Pol., B, July 1920, No. 109.

In the joint meeting of Hindu and Muslim leaders the same day Gandhi had no such walk-over, and the proceedings were very lively. The main disagreement was caused by Hasrat Mohani who, supported by Shaukat Ali, A. K. Azad and Zafar Ali Khan, said that Muslims would join any foreign Muslim army which invaded India to drive out the British. As war was in progress between India and Afghanistan this was no idle threat. Lajpat Rai voiced Hindu fears in a speech insisting that in the Punjab at least Hindu–Muslim unity would only last as long as it did not endanger India's political development, and that at the least sign of danger it would disintegrate. During this meeting Khilafat leaders failed to extract a promise of complete support in non-cooperation from the Congress politicians. Only B. C. Pal and S. Satyamurti were willing to go the whole way with them. T. B. Sapru, Mrs Besant, Motilal Nehru and Pandit Malaviya were not convinced that non-cooperation was either necessary or practicable, and they wanted to leave the decision to the Special Congress.[1]

In spite of Gandhi's failure to secure a complete communal alliance for non-cooperation, at the Allahabad meetings it was clear that he had acquired a very powerful place in institutional politics by playing the role of link-man between the two communities. To the Khilafat leaders he was the only guarantor of Hindu support and they accepted him as virtual dictator of their movement in return for a Congress promise to discuss non-cooperation at the forthcoming session. The Congress leaders were forced to rely on him as their only means of securing a Muslim alliance and avoiding violence, because he was the only leader who appeared to have the Khilafat men under some sort of control. This uneasy alliance between Congress and Khilafat men was based on a calculation of mutual advantage, and Gandhi was the lynch pin of the whole structure. He appears to have realized both the delicacy and the strength of his position, and refused to jeopardize his hold on the political situation by going to England to discuss the Khilafat question with the Secretary of State.[2]

After the Allahabad meetings a representation was sent from the office of the Central Khilafat Committee to the Viceroy, asking him to champion the Khilafat cause to the point of resigning if the peace terms were not acceptable to Indian Muslims and consistent with the 'pledges' of British Ministers. It warned Chelmsford that unless the peace terms were revised Muslims would resort to non-cooperation from 1 August and would ask Hindus to join them.[3] This document was signed by 82 Muslims (2 from Delhi, 11

1 *Ibid.*; Bombay Police Abstract, 1920, par. 932 (i).

2 'But I feel that I at least must devote for the time being my exclusive attention to the Khilafat question. I flatter myself with the belief that mine is the greatest contribution to the preservation of the public peace in India.' Gandhi to S. R. Hignell, Private Secretary to the Viceroy, 12 June 1920, enclosed in letter from Chelmsford to E. S. Montagu, 23 June 1920, Mss. EUR. D. 523 (10).

3 Muslim representation to the Viceroy, 22 June 1920, Home Pol., A, November 1920, Nos. 19–31.

from U.P., 8 from Bombay, 3 from Bengal, 10 from Bihar and Orissa, 3 from Punjab, 44 from Madras and 1 from Edinburgh), of whom the majority were merchants, lawyers and maulvis. Of the Madras signatories 22 came from Trichinopoly: many of them could not be identified by local officials, while those who could were shop keepers or men of less importance. The representation showed not just the spread of feeling about the Khilafat throughout the subcontinent, but also its penetration among men who had previously not participated in institutional politics.[1]

Gandhi sent a simultaneous letter to the Viceroy explaining that he was advising Muslims to adopt non-cooperation because it was the only form of non-violent direct action open to them. For himself he had not lost faith in the British constitution, but he felt that the peace terms were a 'wrong' which undermined Muslim and Hindu trust of the British, and that only by combating it and trying to rectify it could he retain his own loyalty.[2] He followed this up with an appeal to Hindus and Muslims to prepare for non-cooperation from 1 August.[3] Through the first half of 1920 talk of non-cooperation rarely left the realm of generalization, and the establishment of a succession of committees to consider plans absolved Gandhi and the Khilafat leaders of the necessity of committing themselves to specific action, while the A.I.C.C. had shelved the whole issue until September. However, the approach of the first elections under the Montagu–Chelmsford Reforms raised a question which needed a definite answer – whether non-cooperation should include boycott of the reformed councils. Council boycott had been accepted as part of non-cooperation by the Central Khilafat Committee in mid-March 1920, but nothing had been said about it after that date. In May Gandhi envisaged people voting in the elections for candidates who supported swadeshi, the use of vernacular languages in the country's administration, the redistribution of provinces on a linguistic basis and Hindu–Muslim unity, and who promised to do all they could to help Muslims 'in their trouble'.[4] Not until the end of June did he come out clearly against participation in the elections, with a press statement supporting Lajpat Rai's declaration that he would not stand for election.[5] In so doing Gandhi almost haphazardly reorientated

[1] Note by H. McPherson, 26 June 1920, Note by C. W. Gwynne, 28 September 1920, *ibid.* (I owe this reference to K. McPherson.)

[2] Gandhi to Viceroy, 22 June 1920, *ibid.*

[3] *Navajivan*, 27 June 1920, *C.W.*, vol. 17, pp. 514–15.

[4] *Navajivan*, 16 May 1920, *ibid.* pp. 416–18. As late as 13 June 1920 Mahadev Desai, Gandhi's private secretary, wrote to Sita Ram, 'If you read between the lines, you will see that the advice to abstain from standing for election is given only to those who are active, whole-time workers. These surely can serve the country better by remaining out than going in the Councils. There are however many who may be endowed with the necessary qualifications for serving on the Councils, but who may not afford to give all of their time to national work. They may surely stand.' Sita Ram Papers, File No. 29 A.

[5] *The Bombay Chronicle*, 30 June 1920, *C.W.*, vol. 17, pp. 521–2. Gandhi advised

the whole discussion of non-cooperation. By throwing the emphasis on a way of denying collaboration to the raj which could not be shelved for long and which touched all potential voters and candidates, he forced the members of the political nation to take a definite stand in relation to him, to non-cooperation and the raj.

The Government of India reacted to Gandhi's ultimatum by investigating the possibility of prosecuting him for promoting non-cooperation in four stages accepted by the Khilafat Committee – resignation of titles and honorary posts, resignation of posts in the civil service, resignation of police and soldiers, and finally refusal to pay taxes. It also wondered whether it would be possible to prosecute Shaukat Ali for promoting non-cooperation and inciting Muslims to leave the police and the army. Its legal advisers noted that Gandhi had been particularly careful in the wording of his public statements and they thought that a prosecution was not advisable in either case until the second or third stage of non-cooperation, when the government would have a watertight case. A majority of the Home Department agreed that they would wait until such a prosecution was possible rather than acting against Gandhi under special or emergency laws, which would only rouse a storm of opposition.[1] Officials could do nothing to stop Gandhi's call for council boycott. Such a call was neither illegal nor subversive, and they could only wait and see, hoping that the reformed councils were a large enough carrot to attract candidates and voters in sufficient numbers to prevent the elections from becoming a farce.

Anxiety about non-cooperation was not confined to government circles, and Gandhi admitted that he had received a flood of advice and criticism, including some anonymous letters, on the Khilafat issue: some people thought him too hasty, others condemned his caution.[2] Reactions to the proposal to non-cooperate on the Khilafat issue, gathered from each province, show how divided opinion was among the politically aware of both communities.

council boycott as a protest against the Khilafat and Punjab 'wrongs'; he also thought it would save money if there were no election campaigns, and he believed that it would be a good opportunity to explain the situation to the voters.

Dr R. Gordon argues that Lajpat Rai's suggestion of council boycott was the reaction of a politician who judged that he stood little chance of election under the election rules published in the second week of June. However, there is clear evidence that Gandhi and the Khilafat Committee accepted this tactic in March. But this does not detract from Gordon's thesis that it became an attractive tactic to some politicians once the election rules were published. See R. A. Gordon, 'Aspects in the history of the Indian National Congress, with special reference to the Swarajya Party, 1919–1927' (D.Phil. thesis, Oxford, 1970), pp. 35–6.

1 File containing request for legal opinion; the legal opinion; and the notes of the subsequent discussion in the Home Department, Home Pol., A, September 1920, Nos. 100–3. The policy was set out formally in a letter from the Govt. of India to all local govts., 4 September 1920, *ibid.*

2 *Young India*, 2 June 1920, *C.W.*, vol. 17, p. 474.

Bengal was comparatively calm, in marked contrast to its excitement earlier in the year. The danger was the activities of outside agitators, because most local leaders were now nervous how near to violence the Khilafat agitation had brought them. Such was Bengal's inaction that the Central Khilafat Committee demanded an explanation of how the money allocated for propaganda in the Presidency was being spent.[1] Gandhi's stance as an apostle of communal unity and his backing of A. K. Azad annoyed the overtly communal of Bengal's Muslim leaders like Nawab Ali Chaudhuri, and threatened many of the *bhadralok* into opposition as they saw the possibility that their dominance in Presidency politics might be undermined or swept away by violent outbreaks.[2] *The Bengalee*'s main fear was of violence once non-cooperation was open to 'ordinary human material... that falls far short of the high moral and spiritual level of Mahatma Gandhi.' *The Amrita Bazar Patrika* seized on the fact that if forward-looking *bhadralok* politicians stood aside in the forthcoming elections to the new councils 'the only result... will be to fill the Councils with a tribe of timid, little-souled people who will think of themselves first and of their country last or not at all.' *Nayak*, representing the less prosperous among the *bhadralok*, described itself as 'very hostile to the non-co-operation movement' because it would lead to violence, and because in the last resort their material prosperity depended on collaboration with the British who not only ruled the country but also controlled industry and trade.[3]

In neighbouring Bihar and Orissa the Khilafat movement was confined to the Bihar area, where Mazharul Haq and Q. A. Sobhani persuaded a group of maulanas to continue the agitation until the end of the year, under the guidance of the Central Khilafat Committee. However, many prominent public men were holding aloof and it was rumoured that Hasan Imam had severed his connection with the Provincial Khilafat Committee. By mid-July that Committee reported that in their province only ten to twelve Hindus and Muslims were prepared actually to non-cooperate.[4]

In the U.P. only the poorer, urban Muslims were seriously disturbed, and educated Muslims appeared reluctant to support non-cooperation to the extent of resigning remunerative positions, not merely because of the loss involved but also because of a lurking fear that Hindus, having pushed them into a tight corner, would promptly benefit from it and abandon them. In July the secretary of the Meerut Khilafat Committee thought that only

[1] Ronaldshay to E. S. Montagu, 23 June 1920, Mss. EUR. D. 523 (31); Fortnightly report from Bengal for second half of May 1920, Home Pol., Deposit, July 1920, No. 95.

[2] Broomfield, *Elite Conflict in a Plural Society*, pp. 156–7.

[3] *The Bengalee*, 10 June 1920; *The Amrita Bazar Patrika*, 2 July 1920, Bengal E.N., No. 27 of 1920; *Nayak*, 9 June 1920, Bengal N.N., No. 25 of 1920.

[4] Fortnightly report from Bihar and Orissa, 3 June 1920, Home Pol., Deposit, July 1920, No. 95; Bombay Police Abstract, 1920, par. 1043 (v).

two lawyers in the U.P. would resign their practices while public opinion opposed the boycott of schools and colleges, except for mission establishments.[1] Across the spectrum of local Hindu politicians there was similar hesitancy. T. B. Sapru, Motilal Nehru and Pandit Malaviya had made their position clear at the Allahabad meeting on 2 June. The Governor of Bombay thought that Malaviya was so frightened that he worked on him, hoping that politicians of his kind would attempt to quieten the situation in Sind.[2] Another U.P. 'Moderate', Sita Ram, told a Muslim friend that though he sympathized with Muslims over the peace terms and revered Gandhi he believed that 'non-cooperation in our present circumstances is futile and even perhaps frought [sic] with certain risks.'[3]

In the Punjab there was hardly any support for non-cooperation. The Muslim peasant majority seem to have taken little notice of the Khilafat agitation, while the few Hindu politicians of that 'backward' province opposed the idea of boycotting the new councils and wished to postpone the whole issue until the Special Congress. Only Lajpat Rai supported council boycott and he attracted a very forcible reply from *The Tribune* in consequence:[4] soon afterwards even he modified his opposition to council entry.[5]

Sind, like Punjab, had a large Muslim peasant population, but there the reaction to the Khilafat movement was welcoming and widespread because Sindhi Pirs and mullahs led the agitation. They formed a layer of subcontractors necessary for the creation of a mass agitation, which was lacking in the Punjab. In the summer of 1920 there continued a rash of village Khilafat meetings addressed by local mullahs, right outside the control of the Central Khilafat Committee or the Sind Provincial Khilafat Committee. However, by the end of August there had been no riots and the local administration had not taken emergency executive action. In the opinion of the Governor of Bombay this was due to the continuing loyalty of the Sind zamindars.[6]

1 Fortnightly report from U.P., 31 May 1920, Home Pol., Deposit, July 1920, No. 95; Bombay Police Abstract, 1920, par. 1043 (v).

2 Sir G. Lloyd to E. S. Montagu, 23 July 1920, Mss. EUR. D. 523 (25).

3 Sita Ram to 'Qaziji', 1 August 1920, Sita Ram Papers, File No. 29 B.

4 Bombay Police Abstract, 1920, par. 1043 (v); Chelmsford to E. S. Montagu, 30 June 1920, Mss. EUR. D. 523 (10).

5 Lajpat Rai felt that he would be more useful to his country outside the council and he hoped that other Congressmen would feel the same, but he promised not to oppose them if they decided in favour of council entry at the Special Congress. Lajpat Rai to editor, 1 July 1920, *The Tribune*, 3 July 1920, V. C. Joshi (ed.), *Lala Lajpat Rai Writings And Speeches Volume Two 1920–1928* (Delhi, 1966), pp. 11–17.

6 Fortnightly report from Bombay, 16 May 1920, Home Pol., Deposit, July 1920, No. 94; Sir G. Lloyd to E. S. Montagu, 27 August 1920, Mss. EUR. D. 523 (25). There is some evidence of Muslim opposition to the Khilafat movement in Sind. Some Muslims from Hyderabad said in June 1920 that there had been no

Elsewhere in the Bombay Presidency the Muslims were a small minority, but wealthy and influential compared with the Sind peasantry. Consequently they had vested interests to defend and this determined their attitude to the Khilafat agitation once it had reached the point of putting non-cooperation into practice. In Ahmedabad some local Muslims met Shaukat Ali and Gandhi on 16 May but gave them a chilly reception. They donated only Rs. 5,000 to the Khilafat cause, where a lakh had been expected from them, and told Gandhi that if they took to non-cooperation the Hindus would only snap up all the positions vacated by Muslims. In Bombay city the Muslim traders refused to jeopardize their trade by boycott, as their men on the Central Khilafat Committee had indicated. Moreover, the High Priest of the wealthy Shia Bohora sect in the city refused to let his followers contribute to the Khilafat Fund, partly because this would mean assistance to Sunni Muslims and partly because it would imply disloyalty to the British. Further south in Poona district Turkey seemed to excite little interest among Muslims, and the District Magistrate predicted that their local leaders would not encourage non-cooperation.[1]

Many Bombay Hindus took their cue from local Muslim hesitations. Jamnadas Dwarkadas, for example, in an article for *The Bombay Chronicle*, said it was strange that Bombay Muslims of such standing as M. A. Jinnah and G. M. Bhurgri had not come out in favour of non-cooperation, and that the Muslim League had not given its support either. He asked that Muslim opinion should be reasonably united before the whole country was asked to join the Muslims, though he personally opposed non-cooperation because it probably would not affect the peace terms, would undoubtedly be difficult to organize, would swell the ranks of the unemployed and would harm the people by depriving them of lawyers' protection and filling the councils with unsuitable people. Like *The Bengalee*, Dwarkadas contrasted Gandhi with ordinary people.

> If this had concerned Mr. Gandhi as an individual very few in the world would have had the right to advise him. Because I may assert with a fair amount of accuracy that Mr. Gandhi personally as a saint and a martyr is one of the few triumphs of humanity. But may I point out with equal candour that Mr. Gandhi is making the error of a personal experience as being a workable achievement for the untutored who in their enthusiasm subscribe to the formula? Apart from the company of pledged though undisciplined workers, who invite suffering, we have to reckon with the existence of the large and indeterminate body of camp-followers less amenable to restraints than others.[2]

Khilafat for many years and that it was contrary to Islam to discuss religious questions with Hindus. Bombay Police Abstract, 1920, par. 932 (o).

1 Fortnightly report from Bombay, 1 June 1920, Home Pol., Deposit, July 1920, No. 95; Bombay Police Abstract, 1920, par. 807 (q), 985 (z), 1043 (v).

2 *The Bombay Chronicle*, 7 June 1920. In the same edition an appeal against non-cooperation appeared over the signatures of Jamnadas Dwarkadas, Kanji

In Tilak country round Poona Brahmins gave no welcome to non-cooperation, being, in the words of one District Magistrate, 'much too cute to quarrel with their bread and butter.' The local political circle was currently revolving round allegations about certain Tilak Funds, which touched its members far more deeply than the trials of the Sultan.[1] N. C. Kelkar, Tilak's henchman, privately expressed the hesitations of the Poona politicians and the ambiguity they felt in their relation to the Khilafat movement when he was asked about his attitude to Gandhi.

> The Nationalist party in Poona is not favourably disposed towards Mr. Gandhi's non-co-operation movement. Personally I have got regard for Mr. Gandhi; but I view [sic] his movement will end in people's self-deception and disappointment. I think there is an apparent sincerety [sic] in the conduct of Mr. Gandhi and my belief is that he is playing the game in order to please the Muhammadans and indirectly to throw cold water on the ideas of the Muhammadans about violence and revenge. To speak the truth the Indian Muhammadans ought to have no sympathy for Turkey and the agitation in this part of the country is only superficial... As for our party, we will wait till the decision of the Special Congress be out, and if the special Congress will enjoin upon us to stick to the non-co-operation movement, myself and my party will not stand for election...On 1st August, the declared Hartal day – we will hold meetings, and many shops will be closed at Poona, but we have no heart in the movement... We have to keep up some appearance to please Mr. Gandhi, and his Muhammadan friends. My personal belief is that this is a Pan-Islamic question and the Hindus have no right to join the Muhammadans, and as long as the Indian Muhammadans have one eye towards Turkey and the other to the British Government, their loyalty towards the latter is shaky and they are not fit to be friends of the Hindus.[2]

Further south in the Central Provinces Muslims appeared as reluctant as the Bombay Muslims to sacrifice their vested interests and to submit to Gandhi's dictation. Before the meetings at Allahabad in early June Nagpur Muslim leaders told the Central Khilafat Committee that they were not prepared to accept the full programme of non-cooperation, and said that if it was forced on them they would demand a guarantee of five lakhs of rupees for the relief of sufferers. Later they refused to sound out public feeling on the question of non-cooperation and announced that they would take part in the forthcoming elections.[3] Their overt rejection of

Dwarkadas, Sir Narayan Chandarvarkar, Gokuldas Parekh and other Bombay leaders.

1 Bombay Police Abstract, 1920, par. 985 (z).

2 Report dated 22 July 1920 by G. Madurkar of Intelligence Dept. of a conversation he had with N. C. Kelkar in Poona; appended note by E. K. Deshpandi, 27 July 1920, stated that Kelkar's views were the same as Tilak's. Home Pol., Deposit, August 1920, No. 35. (I owe this reference to Dr D. Baker.)

3 Fortnightly report from C.P. for second half of May 1920, Home Pol., Deposit, July 1920, No. 95; Report by Bombay Commissioner of Police on Khilafat situation up to 20 July 1920, Home Pol., A, November 1920, Nos. 19–31.

Gandhi's leadership is the more remarkable since Nagpur was the scene of Gandhi's great Congress victory in December that year.

In Madras the Khilafat movement had secured a real following among the Muslim minority, not only in the ranks of the Muslim politicians but also deeper in society among people previously untouched by politics, as the signatures to the June memorial to the Viceroy showed. However, there were some local Muslim leaders who opposed the idea of non-cooperation as harmful to the long-term interests of their community and likely to provoke disorder, and they resigned from the Presidency's Muslim League as a result. The largest Muslim landholder in Madras, the Prince of Arcot, set himself against the whole Khilafat movement, as did the Chief Presidency Magistrate who was also a Muslim.[1] Local enthusiasm tended to fluctuate in relation to the presence of outside leaders like Shaukat Ali, or the absence of local men like Yakub Hasan at Allahabad in early June; while the Madras Khilafat leadership was permanently weakened by a personal feud between two members of the Madras Khilafat Committee, Hasan and Abdul Sharar.[2] Moreover the leaders were reluctant to follow Gandhi into council boycott because they realized that non-Khilafat Muslims would walk into the seats reserved for Muslims in the Madras Legislative Council.[3] The Khilafat movement received little non-Brahmin support. Among other Hindu politicians Rajagopalachariar and Kasturi Ranga Iyengar played a major part in its local organization, but many local 'Moderates' like Annie Besant, Sir P. S. Sivaswami Aiyer and C. P. Ramaswami Aiyer were against it. However, the opponents of non-cooperation had a rough time when the Madras Provincial Congress met early in July, and the supporters of non-cooperation managed to secure the passage of a resolution in favour of it.[4]

The chequered pattern of reaction to non-cooperation on the Khilafat issue in Madras was not peculiar to that Presidency. In no part of India were either Hindus or Muslims completely in favour of or opposed to the plan, and in no province was there a division of opinion along purely communal lines. Different groups in both communities reacted according to their different ideologies and vested interests, and it was impossible to tell how non-cooperation would fare as practical politics until its inaugura-

[1] Fortnightly report from Madras, 17 June 1920, Home Pol., Deposit, July 1920, No. 96. Among those who resigned from the Presidency League were Khuddas Badsha, Mir Asad Ali Khan and Mir Abbas Khan; McPherson, 'The Political Development of the Urdu- and Tamil-speaking Muslims of the Madras Presidency 1901 to 1937', pp. 123–4.

[2] Fortnightly report from Madras, 17 May 1920, Home Pol., Deposit, July 1920, No. 94; Fortnightly report from Madras, 17 June 1920, Home Pol., Deposit, July 1920, No. 96.

[3] Y. Hasan to S. Ali, 2 July 1920, Bombay Police Abstract, 1920, par. 1012 (o).

[4] Fortnightly report from Madras, 17 May 1920, Home Pol., Deposit, July 1920, No. 94; Willingdon to E. S. Montagu, 7 July 1920, Mss. EUR. D. 523 (20); Y. Hasan to S. Ali, 2 July 1920, Bombay Police Abstract, 1920, par. 1012 (o).

tion on 1 August and more particularly its consideration at the Special Session of Congress in September.

The Khilafat movement from early 1919 until the inauguration of non-cooperation on 1 August 1920 was the context of Gandhi's rapid emergence as an all-India political leader who was markedly different from the politicians who had previously dominated India's political world. During the Rowlatt satyagraha Gandhi had advised specific and limited types of civil disobedience by a picked group of satyagrahis: by mid-1920 his participation in the Khilafat movement had led him to try to organize a mass movement of political protest, taking the form of withdrawal of cooperation from the government. This new departure was the complete antithesis of the limited politics of the Congress and older Muslim League leaders. It presumed the participation in politics of far greater numbers from a much wider social, religious and geographical range than before. It also undermined the basic assumption on which conventional politics rested, namely that the aims of the tiny fraction of the Indian population who made up the political nation were most likely to be reached by judicious cooperation with the raj.

The real issue which Gandhi's plans for non-cooperation presented to the country was the choice between the limited politics of the past and a transformed politics in the future, whose shape had not been worked out and whose potential could not be foreseen. Some politicians were aware that a choice of fundamental importance was being placed before them. Many more were concerned only with the immediate issue, which was the threat to jobs and council places which non-cooperation presented; and in reacting to Gandhi they calculated not the long-term possibilities but the present advantages or disadvantages to be gained from joining him.

Gandhi's plans for a restricted form of satyagraha against the Rowlatt bills had failed. He was only likely to succeed in his far larger plans for satyagraha on the Khilafat question if he had in the intervening months created or gained access to networks of power which would not fail him as in 1919. It might be presumed that the Muslim community, roused by the threat to the Khalifah, would provide just such a network. But the Khilafat movement reflected the deep divisions within the Muslim community. Although Gandhi claimed to speak for all Muslims their community was not a cohesive one. It was divided by sect, caste and region, and as its nature varied in different parts of India so did its interests and its politics, and consequently it was almost impossible to find an issue which would concern and unite all Muslims. From such a divided community Gandhi had by mid-1920 gained support only where the Khilafat agitation did not clash with local Muslim interests. Some of the politically minded Muslims of Madras and Bombay were prepared to follow him, provided that his plans did not jeopardize their material interests, whether trading profits or the chance to win a place in the new councils: whenever his campaign seemed threatening they shelved the objectionable parts. Gandhi had barely touched the more old-fashioned members of the Muslim elites of northern India, who were committed to the politics of collaboration. But those who saw little point in such politics, the Pan-Islamic journalists with their allies among the ulema, were Gandhi's most ardent adherents. They were precisely the leaders most likely to give him access to a new reservoir of support and power beyond the existing political nation, because they reduced political issues to the level of the tea shop, the market place and the mosque. If Gandhi could control them they were a group of subcontractors with tremendous potential, because in the network of mullahs they had a host of local men to spread their message and act as intermediaries with the Muslim masses.

Gandhi's Muslim support was significant not solely in its direct effects – the numbers of people who could be induced to observe hartal on a particular day, to attend a Khilafat meeting, or sign a petition to the Viceroy. It was as important for its repercussions on Gandhi's personal standing in institutional politics. Congress leaders ignored the Khilafat agitation as long as they could and let the plum fall into Gandhi's hands: by so doing they unwittingly gave him a strategic position in their own political world. Once he had extended his range of supporters to areas and groups previously unconcerned with institutional politics he was able to bring their influence to play at the level of institutional politics and so acquire personal influence at that level, because he was the crucial link between two communities whose leaders both needed and feared each other. After the Rowlatt satyagraha Gandhi's standing in Congress had risen considerably, but the leadership of the Khilafat agitation gave him real power among Hindu and Muslim politicians, enabling him to exert leverage on both because he was the guarantor of the hopes and fears of both.

However, the mechanism by which Gandhi had gathered widespread Muslim support was also a potential boomerang. Religious appeals of a primitive kind carried the risk of triggering a violent reaction, despite Gandhi's efforts to ensure that the Khilafat agitation was non-violent. The possibility of violence meant that Gandhi could not rely entirely on the cooperation of his Muslim subcontractors, and it also threatened the stability of the communal alliance so shakily built at Allahabad in June 1920. Gandhi's chance of neutralizing the fears of the Hindus and swinging them into a working communal alliance – thereby making non-cooperation such a success that Muslims would feel less need to resort to violence – lay in championing a Hindu cause to match the Khilafat. The Punjab issue provided the missing ingredient.

CHAPTER 7

THE PUNJAB: COUNTERPOISE TO THE KHILAFAT

During the Rowlatt satyagraha in April 1919 mob violence erupted in parts of the Punjab. Army officers, faced simultaneously with an external threat from the forces of Afghanistan, put down the internal disturbances with extreme severity, and many of the harsher orders given under martial law and the tragic incident at Amritsar, where a crowd was dispersed with raking gunfire, became notorious throughout India. Official and unofficial enquiries into these events precipitated a political confrontation between the raj and the politicians. Beneath the passions and prejudices thus aroused the issue at stake was the nature of British rule and the foundations on which it should be built – an issue particularly critical at the time because the activities of the Punjab military authorities in 1919 seemed to deny the assumptions the Montagu–Chelmsford Reforms had made in 1918 about the guiding principles of British rule.

This was the background to Gandhi's political activities in 1919–20 although his immediate concerns were the Ali brothers, the Rowlatt bills and the Khilafat. In November 1919 he refused to link the Punjab and Khilafat issues:[1] but in June 1920, after the publication of the report of the official enquiry into the Punjab incidents, he reversed this decision and became supreme advocate of the two causes, as the apparent failure of constitutional political protest on both issues played into his hands.

The Punjab crisis added greatly to Gandhi's personal power in Indian politics, pushing him more swiftly towards the assertion of all-India leadership than the Khilafat agitation alone could have done. However the combination of the two was fortuitous. Both Khilafat and Punjab had been sources of simmering discontent, but became political flashpoints almost simultaneously because of government action, in the one case the publication of the proposed Treaty of Sèvres, in the other the publication of the Hunter Report. There is no evidence that Gandhi deliberately restrained himself on the Punjab issue to launch it as a well-timed Hindu counterpoise to Muslim concern for the Khilafat. Government policy, not Gandhi's personal calculation, precipitated a double crisis by convincing Gandhi that the Punjab as well as the Khilafat was an insupportable 'wrong' which could not be righted by conventional political methods.

The development of the Government of India's attitude towards events in the Punjab showed the tensions present in an administration which

[1] See above, p. 203.

demanded the cooperation of officials in Delhi and Whitehall, each subject to different pressures. From his sanctum in the India Office before April 1919 Montagu prophetically criticized the so-called paternalism for which the Punjab government was famous.

> I have always thought O'Dwyer's success in the Punjab so cheap a success ... He sat hard on all, and often on quite legitimate political work. He put a ring fence round the Punjab and refused to allow into it political leaders. He used all the powers that the war gave him and he made a great success of it. But if that sort of thing went on, as education and knowledge of the world increased in the Punjab, so certainly would you find that the Punjab became one of the most inflammable Provinces of India.[1]

The April violence convinced him that 'our old friend, firm government, the idol of the Club smoking room, has produced its invariable and inevitable harvest.'[2]

The harassed Viceroy defended O'Dwyer's type of government as suitable for the Punjab because that province had a tradition of stern rule, and because the Lieutenant-Governor could isolate his territory and had enough military force at his disposal for this type of action in contrast to other provincial administrations.[3] However during the period of martial law he protested against certain orders and would not allow public executions, although he refused to overrule his subordinates publicly and so weaken their authority in an abnormally grave situation which 'looked like a recurrence of the troubles of 1857'.[4]

Within a month of the imposition of martial law allegations of brutality were made, and Montagu put to his council the question of an enquiry into the situation. His aim was not only to do justice for the past but also to

[1] E. S. Montagu to Chelmsford, 8 March 1919, Mss. EUR. D. 523 (3).

[2] E. S. Montagu to Chelmsford, 1 May 1919, *ibid.*

[3] Chelmsford to E. S. Montagu, 30 April 1919, Mss. EUR. E. 264 (5). Not all officials on the spot agreed with Chelmsford's defence of O'Dwyer's government. Sir Harcourt Butler, Lieutenant-Governor of the U.P., commented: 'I may have to go down to the plains again, if this rioting spreads. So far my people have kept quiet & they have not been dragooned as O'Dwyer has dragooned the Punjab... O'D has sown the wind & reaped the whirlwind. For some time past it has been evident that the Punjab was utterly out of touch with the educated classes. We shall see what the end will be. The Punjab is, no doubt, different from other provinces; but I can't think that even there it is possible long to ignore a growing educated class altogether. They have few big landlords there to counteract them.' Sir H. Butler to his mother, 14 April 1919, Mss. EUR. F. 116 (11). For O'Dwyer's own defence of his government of the Punjab, see M. O'Dwyer, *India As I Knew It 1885–1925* (London, 1925), particularly pp. 232–62.

[4] Chelmsford to E. S. Montagu, 4 September 1919, Mss. EUR. D. 523 (9). For example, Chelmsford protested against Dyer's order that Indians should crawl on all fours down the Amritsar street where a European woman had been attacked, and the order was cancelled.

prevent any repetition of such events in the future by O'Dwyer's successor, Sir Edward Maclagan.[1] The prospect of an enquiry produced considerable apprehension among officials in India. Sir Harcourt Butler, for example, feared that an enquiry would only stir up racial feeling. He would have preferred a general clemency, excluding those who had taken to violence, as the best way of soothing racial tension and getting the reforms off to a good start.[2] However, Chelmsford accepted Montagu's decision to hold an enquiry, and assured him that his government had 'no intention of asking the Committee of Enquiry to whitewash anybody or anything'.[3] He announced this decision in a speech to the Imperial Legislative Council on 3 September, and the Committee was formally constituted on 14 October, headed by Lord Hunter, a former Solicitor-General for Scotland.[4] Meanwhile the Government of India protected its officials with an Indemnity Bill which received the Viceroy's assent on 25 September. This provided that nobody could sue an official for acts done under martial law, provided that the official had acted in good faith and with a reasonable belief that his actions were necessary for maintaining law and order; nor could anyone imprisoned under martial law sue for wrongful imprisonment or gain release by *habeas corpus* proceedings.[5]

Gandhi's initial reaction to these events in the Punjab was horror at the violence which erupted, though men using his name had apparently incited violence in some places.[6] He responded to government action with silence. While even V. S. Srinivasa Sastri condemned some of the actions taken under martial law as 'barbarous' Gandhi refused to comment, on the grounds that he had inadequate evidence.[7] He realized that this silence

[1] E. S. Montagu to Chelmsford, 1 May 1919, 11 June 1919, Mss. EUR. E. 264 (5).

[2] Sir H. Butler to Chelmsford, 25 July 1919, Mss. EUR. F. 116 (49).

[3] Chelmsford to E. S. Montagu, 25 September 1919, Mss. EUR. D. 523 (9). Later Montagu claimed 'direct responsibility' for the Punjab enquiry. At the time he had no idea that it would reveal anything that would embarrass the government. E. S. Montagu to Sir G. Lloyd, 9 September 1920, Mss. EUR. D. 523 (22).

[4] *Hunter Report*, p. iii.

[5] The Home Member, Sir William Vincent, considered such legislation 'inevitable after a period of martial law, which is in its nature an extra legal proceeding, if officers called on to discharge onerous and difficult duties in a time of emergency are to receive reasonable protection.' Statement of objects of and reasons for Indemnity Bill, signed by Vincent, 13 September 1919, and copy of the Act, Home Pol., A, November 1919, Nos. 288–95.

[6] In the few places where the rural population of the Punjab took to violence its origin seems to have been people from Lahore, Amritsar, the area round Delhi, and Udaipur, calling themselves 'Gandhi's men'. Sir M. O'Dwyer to Chelmsford, 21 April 1919, Home Pol., B, 1919, Nos. 148–78.

[7] Gandhi to J. L. Maffey, 16 May 1919, S.N. No. 6615; Gandhi to S. R. Hignell, 30 May 1919, *C.W.*, vol. 15, p. 334. V. S. S. Sastri's views appeared in *The Indian Review*, May 1919, S.P., File containing extracts from *The Indian Review*, 1915–1946, No. 32.

caused misunderstanding among his friends but he committed himself in public only when he felt sure that 'a manifest and cruel wrong' had occurred. The occasion was the conviction of Kalinath Roy, editor of *The Tribune*, by a martial law tribunal for his writing on the violence which had exploded in Delhi during the Rowlatt satyagraha and for his criticism of a speech by Sir Michael O'Dwyer. In mid-June Gandhi maintained that Roy was innocent and had been subject to a grave miscarriage of justice.[1] Through August and September he continued to comment on convictions by martial law tribunals which he considered unjust. Championship of 'wrongs' had become his personal mode of entry into politics. There is nothing to indicate that Gandhi did not sincerely believe that these Punjab cases were 'wrongs', though the Bombay government thought he was deliberately taking them up to regain public support which had waned after the Rowlatt satyagraha.[2]

On the Punjab issue Gandhi repeated the tactics he had employed in Champaran and Kaira. Simultaneously with his criticisms on specific cases he campaigned for a government enquiry into the causes of the violence, the way martial law had been administered and the sentences passed by the martial law tribunals. He broached the subject of an enquiry at his satyagrahis' meeting in Bombay on 28 May, indicating that satyagraha would be the remedy if an enquiry was not held. Two days later he made a formal request to the government for an enquiry.[3] When Chelmsford announced the appointment of the Hunter Committee three months later Gandhi was sanguine and conciliatory. Despite criticism of the personnel of the Committee from some sections of the press and disappointment that it was not a Royal Commission, Gandhi urged Indians to trust it and to bring evidence before it, citing Champaran as a case where an enquiry had done justice because the people put their case before it. In his opinion, 'where Englishmen have not formed preconceived notions or where they have not gone, as all of us sometimes do go, mad over some things, they dispense fearless justice and expose wrong even though the perpetrators may be their own people.'[4]

On the subject of the Indemnity Bill Gandhi was equally conciliatory. Before it was published he accepted that every government, even a Swaraj

[1] *Young India*, 11 June 1919, *C.W.*, vol. 15, pp. 336–9. Gandhi had meanwhile protested privately to the Government of India about the exclusion of outside counsel from the Punjab by the military authorities. Gandhi to Private Secretary to the Viceroy, 15 May 1919, S.N. No. 6613.

[2] Fortnightly report from Bombay, 16/19 June 1919, Home Pol., Deposit, August 1919, No. 50. Examples of Gandhi's later comments on martial law cases are in *Young India*, 20 August 1919, 24 September 1919, *C.W.*, vol. 16, pp. 45–8, 165–6.

[3] Note on a conference of satyagrahis, Bombay, 28 May 1919, *C.W.*, vol. 15, pp. 332–3; Gandhi to S. R. Hignell, 30 May 1919, *ibid.* pp. 334–5.

[4] *Young India*, 10 September 1919, *C.W.*, vol. 16, pp. 113–15.

government, needed to protect itself and its officials: after its publication he argued that it contained nothing objectionable and did not prevent the government from taking action against offending officials.[1] In taking this stand Gandhi flew in the face of much Indian opinion about the Bill. His attitude came as an unpleasant surprise to most of the politicians, who had great difficulty in explaining it away. As one Congressman put it privately,

> it may be stated that Mr. Gandhi's queer opinion regarding the harmlessness of this Bill has not found support among other Indians. It is a great pity that he should hold such a view about this manifestly unjust measure and no wonder that, as the saying goes, Sir William Vincent "quotes the scripture for his purpose."[2]

In contrast to Gandhi, Madan Mohan Malaviya lashed out in the Imperial Legislative Council at the impropriety of passing an Indemnity Bill concerning actions which were to be the subject of an enquiry.[3]

At this point Malaviya rather than Gandhi was representative of Congress opinion on the Punjab question. The A.I.C.C. met in Allahabad on 8 June and, having welcomed the government's promise of an enquiry, appointed its own sub-committee to arrange for an enquiry into occurrences in the Punjab, to take any legal proceedings necessary and to collect funds for this purpose. The sub-committee's members were Malaviya, Motilal Nehru, Rashbehary Ghosh, Syed Hasan Imam, B. Chakravarti, C. R. Das, Kasturi Ranga Iyengar, Umar Sobhani and Gokarannath Misra.[4] Gandhi was not coopted until mid-October, and Malaviya and Nehru took charge of the proceedings by going to the Punjab on 25 June 1919.[5]

Their preliminary investigations riled the local government and demonstrated the passions which the whole matter raised on both sides. The Punjab administration complained that Malaviya and Nehru were biassed from the start, taking evidence from friends and relatives of those convicted and accused under martial law, and deliberately avoiding consideration of officials' evidence. It reported that the Jallianwalla Bagh

1 *Navajivan*, 14 September 1919, *Young India*, 20 September 1919, *ibid.* pp. 140–1, 153–5.

2 Gokarannath Misra to V. J. Patel, 1 October 1919, A.I.C.C. Files 1919, No. 3, Part III. Evidence of the politicians' reaction to Gandhi's attitude towards the Indemnity Bill is in Fortnightly report from U.P., 30 September 1919, Home Pol., Deposit, November 1919, No. 15; Fortnightly report from Bihar and Orissa, 3 October 1919, *ibid*; Bombay Police Abstract, 1919, par. 1365 (a), 1430.

3 Speech by M. M. Malaviya in Imperial Legislative Council, 24 September 1919, *The Bombay Chronicle*, 16 October 1919.

4 Printed report of proceedings of A.I.C.C. meeting, Allahabad, 8 June 1919, Jayakar Papers, File No. 478.

5 Statement signed by M. M. Malaviya and Motilal Nehru as Chairman and Vice-Chairman respectively of the Punjab Inquiry Sub-committee of A.I.C.C., 17 November 1919, *The Amrita Bazar Patrika*, 19 November 1919, *C.W.*, vol. 16, pp. 546–50. M. M. Malaviya sent Gandhi a telegram on 18 October 1919, telling him of his cooption, S.N. No. 6947.

was naturally inspected and some shoes, bullets and other curios were collected. In due course the chairman of the municipal board received a letter from Madan Mohan Malaviya informing him that there were still bodies floating in the well in the garden and that the stench was unbearable. Expert divers were accordingly sent down and with much difficulty they retrieved an earthenware pot, dropped from a Persian wheel, and a bundle of looted cloth from the National Bank.[1]

Motilal Nehru gave his son this version of the visit:

> It was a truely gruesome sight. In spite of the lapse of nearly 2½ months after the incident there were more than one corpses to be seen floating in the well in a highly decomposed state. We spent some time there & examined the whole place very carefully.[2]

Who were the more accurate observers is impossible to tell, but the two versions show the conflict that was emerging between the raj and the politicians, and the strength of feeling on which a politician might draw if he took his stand on the Punjab issue.

While Malaviya and Nehru were investigating, the Hunter Committee was appointed. The Congress sub-committee laid down three conditions for its cooperation with the official enquiry. Firstly, the tribunal appointed to revise martial law sentences should inspire public confidence, and to this end one judge should come from outside the Punjab. Secondly, counsel must be admitted to the enquiry with the right of cross-examination. Thirdly, prominent leaders then in jail should be released for the period of the enquiry so that they could give evidence.[3] The first condition was fulfilled by the appointment of Mr Justice Mullick of the Patna High Court.[4] The second condition was fulfilled by the Hunter Committee's decision to allow counsel to appear and cross-examine if previously given permission.[5] However, the third condition produced a situation of deadlock. The Punjab government, after consulting the Government of India, decided not to release prisoners during the enquiry; but when the Hunter Committee faced the threat that the Congress group would not cooperate it tried to arrange a compromise lest the public effect of its report should be weakened because Congress representatives had not given evidence. Gandhi was summoned to see the Lieutenant-Governor and they arranged

[1] Fortnightly report from Punjab for first half of July 1919, Home Pol., Deposit, August 1919, No. 54.

[2] Motilal Nehru to Jawaharlal Nehru, 30 June 1919, Nehru Papers.

[3] Statement signed by M. M. Malaviya and Motilal Nehru as Chairman and Vice-Chairman respectively of Punjab Inquiry Sub-committee of A.I.C.C., 17 November 1919, *The Amrita Bazar Patrika*, 19 November 1919, *C.W.*, vol. 16, pp. 546–50.

[4] The A.I.C.C. sub-committee was informed of this on 10 November, *Navajivan*, 23 November 1919, *C.W.*, vol. 16, p. 300.

[5] Viceroy (Home Dept.) to Secretary of State, telegram, 9 November 1919, Proceeding No. 471 of Home Pol., A, February 1920, Nos. 465–81 & K.-W.

that six leaders should be freed on parole to give evidence. When the sub-committee realized that this concession was only for the days on which the leaders were to give evidence it held to its refusal to cooperate.[1]

It is clear that by the time this decision was made Gandhi's position within the Congress group had changed markedly from his position in June. Then he had been an embarrassment to them: now he was a member of the sub-committee and an extremely influential one at that. He rather than Malaviya, the chairman of the sub-committee, called on the Lieutenant-Governor; he rather than Malaviya told the government of the sub-committee's decision. His attitude was no longer more conciliatory than that of the other Congressmen, and there is even some evidence that he was instrumental in pushing the sub-committee into its final decision.[2]

Once the Congress sub-committee had refused to cooperate with the Hunter Committee it had to do something positive instead; and on 14 November it appointed its own team of investigators – Motilal Nehru, Fazlul Haq, C. R. Das, Abbas Tyabji and Gandhi, with K. Santanam as secretary. Fazlul Haq was soon called away on business and was replaced by M. R. Jayakar from Bombay. Their enquiries and preparation of a report lasted from 17 November 1919 to 25 March 1920. Most of the work was done by the investigators in person. They held large public meetings, inviting the public to make statements before them, and in all they examined about 1,700 witnesses.[3]

According to Jayakar the whole process lacked 'method and order',[4] and when the report was prepared for publication he was beside himself at the inefficiency of the arrangements.

> I have emerged out of this publication business a much wiser man. The way in which the whole evidence was dumped upon me by the Lahore Office – in the crudest English, bad typing, incorrect and illegible spelling, misspelt names, perplexing blanks, incoherent references, and contradictory alterations, was a lesson in itself...However, I am not sorry, for having gone through the experience, for it has revealed, what colossal improvement must be made in our methods – neatness, accuracy, des-

1 Sir E. Maclagan to Sir W. Vincent, 15 November 1919, *ibid*; Gandhi to Private Secretary to Lieutenant-Governor of Punjab, 15 November 1919, *The Leader*, 19 November 1919, *C.W.*, vol. 16, pp. 294–5.

2 For the suggestion that Gandhi forced the sub-committee's hand by threatening to resign if it cooperated with the Hunter Committee, see H. F. Owen, 'The Leadership of The Indian National Movement. 1914–20' (Ph.D. thesis, Australian National University, 1965), pp. 433–4. Owen bases this suggestion on Swami Shraddhanand, *Inside Congress* (Bombay, 1946), pp. 109–10, C. F. Andrews to R. Tagore, 3 & 16 November 1919, C. F. Andrews Papers, and *Young India*, 19 November 1919.

3 Gandhi, C. R. Das, Abbas Tyabji and M. R. Jayakar to Motilal Nehru, 20 February 1920, *C.W.*, vol. 17, pp. 39–41.

4 13 December 1919, Diary of M. R. Jayakar, Jayakar Papers.

patch, steadfastness, devotion, and kindred other qualities, before our public work can come up to the proper standard.[1]

Jayakar even began the work of binding the report at home with the help of graduate volunteers, but in the end the work was handed over to a commercial press.[2]

The amateurishness of the Congress enquiry seems to have given Gandhi the opportunity to consolidate the position he had gained in the Congress group late in 1919. Evidence from within the group shows that during the months when their report was being prepared power swung to Gandhi and he, rather than the investigation team as a limb of Congress, came to control the handling of the Punjab issue. At first their work was supervised by C. R. Das,[3] but by the end of December 1919 Gandhi had become the key man. He drafted the report on the incidents at Amritsar, and his draft passed a meeting of the investigators despite opposition from C. R. Das who would have preferred a more pugnacious approach.[4] In January 1920 Gandhi was the arbiter of what statements should be published, and Jayakar told the investigators' secretary that 'there are some others which have yet to be put into shape by Mr. Gandhi and finally passed by him before they can be handed over to you for getting ready for the press.'[5]

Finally C. R. Das, Motilal Nehru and Abbas Tyabji dropped out, leaving Gandhi and Jayakar to do the remaining work on the report.[6] Of these two Gandhi was the dominant partner. For example, in March he told Jayakar that he discounted C. R. Das's summary of evidence to prove that Dyer had laid a deliberate trap in Jallianwalla Bagh, though he added that Jayakar must not yield to his decision if he did not think it right.

> In any event the summary before me leaves me not only unconvinced but a discussion along the lines suggested can only mar a report which in my opinion is otherwise convincing. The facts marshalled by Mr. Das appear to me like so many loose pebbles which will not hang together. I want them like bricks cohering and making a roadway for you to walk to your goal. Much as I would like to discuss the suggested theory as such in our report, I cannot do it unless I have *prima facie* evidence warranting a discussion.[7]

[1] M. R. Jayakar to Jawaharlal Nehru, 18 March 1920, Jayakar Papers, Correspondence File No. 476, Punjab Inquiry I.

[2] 3 April 1920, Diary of M. R. Jayakar, Jayakar Papers. Jayakar estimated that the total cost of printing and binding the Congress report was Rs. 45,614.11.11, paid for out of the Punjab Relief Fund. M. R. Jayakar to Dr Parsharam, 1 March 1921, Jayakar Papers, Correspondence File No. 477, Punjab Inquiry II.

[3] 13 December 1919, Diary of M. R. Jayakar, Jayakar Papers.

[4] 22 and 23 December 1919, *ibid.*

[5] M. R. Jayakar to K. Santanam, 5 January 1920, Jayakar Papers, Correspondence File No. 476, Punjab Inquiry I.

[6] M. R. Jayakar, *The Story Of My Life. Volume One. 1873–1922* (Bombay, 1958), p. 329.

[7] Gandhi to M. R. Jayakar, hand-written note received by Jayakar on 11 March 1920, Jayakar Papers, Correspondence File No. 476, Punjab Inquiry I.

Not surprisingly the theory of a deliberate trap was omitted from the Congress report. Motilal Nehru also acknowledged Gandhi's dominance when he arranged a meeting of the A.I.C.C. and the Congress investigators to discuss the Congress report. According to him Gandhi was 'the one person in whose hands the whole matter rests', and he thought that 'to hold the meetings without him will be to play Hamlet without the Prince of Denmark.'[1]

This shift in power to Gandhi on the Punjab issue within the Congress leadership between the end of 1919 and March 1920 was critical for Gandhi's future as a political leader. Before December 1919 his role in Congress had been ambivalent, and when he found that he differed from Congress leaders he withdrew from the conflict rather than challenge them in their own political territory. In December 1919 in Congress he had for the first time made a stand for his own views.[2] Immediately after that session he established himself within the Congress organization as an indispensable leader by his work on the Congress report.

More significant still, he established himself on an issue which was of considerable importance to the politicians. In their eyes the issue presented by martial law in the Punjab was not just injustice inflicted on their compatriots, but whether these actions betrayed a government attitude to India which would make the forthcoming reforms worthless. Much of the private correspondence of the politicians at the end of 1919 was shot through with the fear that the government's action in the Punjab vitiated the reforms, and that without a statutory declaration of rights to prevent a repetition of such actions Indians would never be free and equal citizens with the white subjects of the Crown, whatever reforms might be conceded.[3] By making himself indispensable to the politicians on an issue which

[1] Motilal Nehru to Gokarannath Misra, 9/10 March 1920, 12 March 1920, A.I.C.C. Files, 1920, No. 8. In the letter of 12 March Nehru mentioned that Gandhi might not be able to travel to Allahabad because of ill health. The A.I.C.C. meeting was postponed until 30/31 May when Gandhi could attend. F. C. R. Robinson suggests that Gandhi feigned this illness and was playing for time so that the A.I.C.C. should meet after the publication of the Hunter Report. He cites as evidence Gandhi's activities in Ahmedabad and Bombay during April and May. (For these, see *C.W.*, vol. 17, pp. 592–4.) However, from Gandhi's correspondence during this period it seems that he was not strong enough to undertake many activities or to travel far. See Gandhi to M. Parekh, 30 April 1920, Gandhi to S. Chowdhrani, 1 May 1920, Gandhi to Maganlal Gandhi, 4 May 1920, *C.W.*, vol. 17, pp. 362–4, 365–6, 385–8. For Robinson's argument, see his 'The Politics Of U.P. Muslims 1906–1922', pp. 377–9.

[2] For Gandhi's earlier role in Congress and his stand in 1919, see above, pp. 150–1, 188–9.

[3] Examples of politicians linking the Punjab question and the reforms are: Vijiaraghavachariar to Swami Shraddhanand, 27 November 1919, Jawaharlal Nehru Papers, File No. V-36; Motilal Nehru to Sir P. S. Sivaswami Aiyer, 12 December 1919, Motilal Nehru Papers, File No. A-7. The same line of reasoning appeared in the Congress Report On The Punjab Disorders, *C.W.*, vol. 17, p. 288.

really mattered to them, Gandhi altered his standing in Congress and increased the purchase he had over the direction of Congress policy.

The Congress report on the Punjab was published on 25 March 1920, nearly two months before the Hunter Report, a greater gap than originally anticipated by the Congress investigators. They wished to publish first not merely to put forward their version and views but also to pave the way for a probable minority report by the Indian members of the Hunter Committee.[1] The plan of the report was chronological, beginning with a short survey of the history and administration of the Punjab, continuing with details about O'Dwyer's government, the Rowlatt bills and the satyagraha against them, and culminating in an investigation of martial law in 1919.[2] It was designed to answer three main questions: What were the causes of the April violence? Was the introduction of martial law justified? Were the actions taken under martial law to be accepted or condemned?

The investigators considered that there was great unease in the Punjab before April 1919, due to O'Dwyer's suppression of political opinion, his distrust of educated Indians and his methods of recruitment and collection for the war loan. In their opinion his 'utterly unjustifiable' externment of Gandhi from the province and the deportation of the Punjabi politicians, Drs Kitchlew and Satyapal, 'lighted the material he had made inflammable.' Eventually the 'unwise firing at Amritsar strained the temper of the people to the breaking point. The crowd became mad, and, in its fury, committed arson, murder and pillage, and spent its fury in three hours. The other places...caught the infection from and copied Amritsar'.[3] They considered that neither satyagraha nor hartal precipitated the violence, and that on the contrary satyagraha was a restraining influence without which events might have been infinitely worse. Gandhi's earlier admission to a 'Himalayan miscalculation' in launching satyagraha clearly embarrassed the Congress authors, so they distinguished between preaching satyagraha, which they thought restraining, and preaching civil disobedience, which might lead to violence; but they said the latter had barely penetrated the Punjab, therefore it could not have caused violence.

The investigators considered that the introduction of martial law was unjustified, that in every case it was proclaimed after order had been restored and that even if it was thought necessary for state security it was unduly prolonged. About actions taken under martial law they were extremely severe, condemning most of the military orders as unnecessary

[1] M. R. Jayakar to K. Santanam, 1 February 1920, Jayakar Papers, Correspondence File No. 476, Punjab Inquiry I.

[2] Congress Report On The Punjab Disorders, *C.W.*, vol. 17, pp. 114–292. (This report was published in two volumes, the first containing the report, the second containing the evidence. Only the first volume is given in *C.W.*)

[3] *Ibid.* p. 286.

and cruel, particularly the Jallianwalla Bagh 'massacre' – 'a calculated piece of inhumanity towards utterly innocent and unarmed men, including children, and unparallelled for its ferocity in the history of modern British administration.'[1] They judged that tribunals and summary courts caused widespread miscarriage of justice and were used to harm innocent people.

In conclusion the investigators discussed what measures should now be taken. This was outside the scope of Hunter's enquiry, but the Congressmen went into the question because they thought it was essential that official misdeeds as well as the people's violence should be punished if rulers and ruled were to approach the reforms 'with clean hands and clean minds' to make them work.[2] They called for the repeal of the Rowlatt Act, the refund of fines imposed by martial law tribunals and summary courts, the refund or remission of indemnities imposed on several cities, and the removal of punitive police. They hoped that actions by minor officials would be investigated and that senior officers who were clearly to blame, like Dyer and O'Dwyer, would be dismissed from responsible office under the Crown. Even the Viceroy came under their condemnation: his recall was demanded on grounds of passive collusion with the Punjab government rather than wilful neglect of the people's interests.

The Hunter Report was presented to the Government of India on 8 March 1920 and published on 28 May. It touched on the Delhi and Bombay disturbances, but concentrated on events leading up to and during martial law in the Punjab. Discussing the origin of the violence the Hunter Committee agreed with the Congress investigators that the Punjab was disturbed before April 1919, but it discounted the war loan and recruitment as contributory factors, stressing instead high post-war prices, intense Muslim feeling about the Khilafat, growing political awareness unhappily coinciding with increased local government power under the Defence of India Act, and the agitation against the Rowlatt legislation. It agreed with the Congress report that the specific cause of violence was the news of Gandhi's arrest and the deportation of the two Punjabi politicians; but unlike the Congress report it criticized satyagraha as tending to undermine law and order.

> We have no hesitation in saying that both in the Punjab and elsewhere a familiarity and sympathy with disobedience to laws was engendered among large numbers of people by Mr. Gandhi's movement, and the law-abiding instincts which stand between society and outbreaks of violence were undermined at a time when their full strength was required.[3]

[1] *Ibid.* p. 291.

[2] *Ibid.* p. 288.

[3] *Hunter Report*, p. 61. It is outside the scope of this work to consider the relative merits of the Congress and Hunter Reports, even if it were possible at this distance in time. The point here is to show the issues on which the reports differed because these differences and the Government of India's reaction to them were one of the planks of Gandhi's appeal for non-cooperation.

On the justification of martial law the two reports disagreed totally. The Hunter Committee judged that events in the Punjab amounted to a state of open rebellion and justified the introduction of martial law. It was more prone to criticize the duration of martial law, but concluded that local officers 'did not prolong it beyond the time during which to the best of their judgement it was necessary for the maintenance and restoration of order in the province.'[1] The Committee's review of actions taken under martial law, though not wholly condemnatory like the parallel section of the Congress report, was severely critical. Its members thought that too many people had been arrested and never tried even after lengthy detention, that the local government had been unwise to press some of the cases, that some of the political leaders like Kitchlew and Satyapal should have appeared before ordinary courts, and that outside counsel should have been allowed into the Punjab. The Committee also condemned specific orders like Dyer's 'crawling order' as injudicious and serving only to annoy the civilian population; but though it considered that there had been too many floggings and that none of these should have been public, it judged that allegations of cruelty in administering punishments were unfounded. After considering the Jallianwalla Bagh episode the Committee decided that Dyer should have given an order to the crowd to disperse before firing, and that he had committed a grave error in firing for so long.[2]

Despite such serious criticisms the Hunter Committee divided on racial lines, a minority report being signed by Jagat Narayan, Sir C. H. Setalvad and Sultan Ahmed. The minority considered both the introduction and the duration of martial law unjustifiable, and thought that certain actions warranted severer criticisms than the majority had given, particularly the Jallianwalla Bagh firing, Dyer's 'crawling order', the floggings, the exclusion of outside counsel and the arrests which had never resulted in trials. In general they commented that the martial law orders had gone beyond the mere maintenance of law and order and 'were designed and were used for punitive purposes'.[3]

The Viceroy and the Secretary of State realized that detailed discussion of the Hunter Committee's reports and the production of a joint opinion was impossible by telegram, particularly since there was some divergence

[1] *Hunter Report*, p. 75.

[2] *Ibid.* p. 30. The Hunter Committee accepted the figure of about 379 killed at Jallianwalla Bagh, which was given by the Punjab government and reported in Viceroy (Home Dept.) to Secretary of State, telegram, 5 March 1920, Proceeding No. 317 of Home Pol., A, April 1920, Nos. 317–18. *Hunter Report*, p. 29. This was in contrast to the Congress statement that '1,000 is by no means an exaggerated calculation.' Congress Report On The Punjab Disorders, *C.W.*, vol. 17, p. 174.

[3] *Hunter Report*, p. 118. (The minority report was published with the majority report.)

of opinion between the administrations in Delhi and Whitehall. In order to pronounce government policy they therefore adopted the procedure of a Government of India Despatch and a reply from the Secretary of State.

The Government of India accepted and endorsed the findings of the majority report of the Hunter Committee, though it regretted that the civil authorities had handed over to the military authorities before a proclamation of martial law, thereby throwing all responsibility on military personnel who received no guidance on how to act. It also condemned General Dyer more severely than the majority report, mentioning particularly his failure to warn the crowd before firing, his continued firing after the crowd had begun to disperse and his lack of assistance to the wounded.

> the deliberate conclusion at which we have arrived is that General Dyer exceeded the reasonable requirements of the case and showed a misconception of his duty which resulted in a lamentable and unnecessary loss of life. Although we are constrained to this decision, we are convinced that General Dyer acted honestly in the belief that he was doing what was right and we think that in the result his action at the time checked the spread of the disturbances to an extent which it is difficult now to estimate.[1]

Montagu went even further in his condemnation of Dyer, dissociating his administration from Dyer's belief that in the circumstances it was his duty to create a show rather than use as little force as possible to suppress civil disorder;[2] and he blamed O'Dwyer for approving Dyer's action. He made additional criticisms of the martial law administration, parts of which in his view were calculated to humiliate Indians as a race, and suggested that the military should not have been given so wide a jurisdiction as to include those not responsible for violence.[3] The practical result of the Hunter Committee's report was Dyer's resignation of his command at the direction of the Commander-in-Chief, and the official censure of several lesser officials. Later Montagu regretted 'more than anything else' that they had dealt comparatively leniently with O'Dwyer because of Chelmsford's anxieties about the situation and O'Dwyer's war-time

[1] Despatch No. 2. Home Dept. of Govt. of India. Political. to Secretary of State for India, 3 May 1920, Proceeding No. 162 of Home Pol., A, June 1920, Nos. 126–64 & K.-W.s.

[2] General Dyer reported his action to the General Staff, 16th Division, 25 August 1919: 'I fired and continued to fire till the crowd dispersed, and I considered that this is this least amount of firing which would produce the necessary moral and widespread effect that it was my duty to produce if I was to justify my action... *It was no longer a question of merely dispersing the crowd*, but one of producing a sufficient moral effect, from a military point of view, not only on those present, but more specially throughout the Punjab. There could be no question of undue severity.' Quoted in *Hunter Report*, p. 112. (Italics in *Hunter Report*.) Dyer's justification of his action, dated 3 July 1920, is in *Disturbances In The Punjab. Statement By Brig.-General R. E. H. Dyer, C.B.* (London, 1920), Cmd. 771.

[3] Despatch No. 108. Public. Secretary of State to Government of India, 26 May 1920, Proceeding No. 163 of Home Pol., A, June 1920, Nos. 126–64 & K.-W.s.

services. During 1920 Montagu came closer to the viewpoint of the Indian politicians that official action in the Punjab betrayed an attitude guaranteed to wreck the reforms, and he lamented to Chelmsford that he had laid himself 'open to the charge of not dealing justly with a man who is undoubtedly the idol of those who are determined to oppose the policy on which you and I are united.'[1]

When the facts about martial law in the Punjab became public, particularly Dyer's policy of making a show at the cost of Indian lives, the Government of India was caught on its own hook. What it had initiated as an enquiry into events in one province developed into a discussion of the nature and future of British rule, with particular emphasis on the reality or illusion of racial equality under the raj – an issue guaranteed to rouse passion and prejudice. Public opinion divided sharply when the Hunter Report was published. In India the English-owned press backed the majority report, and with varying shades of enthusiasm supported Dyer's action: while Indian-owned papers practically all condemned O'Dwyer and Dyer, called the majority report an attempt at whitewashing, and sympathized with the minority report.[2]

In England the division of opinion was as clear and bitter. J. L. Maffey attended the House of Commons debate on the subject and reported, 'There was plenty of excitement in the air and the old true-blue "service" section rallied in force, determined to make more noise than their numbers justified, not very clear or caring greatly about the facts and greatly prejudiced by "personal" considerations.' According to Maffey the issues this group thought were at stake were 'Is it English to break a man who tried to do his duty?' and 'Is a British General to be downed at the bidding of a crooked Jew?' E. S. Montagu, the Jew in question, did nothing to mitigate the prejudice against him by his attitude in the debate, when he maintained that the question before the House was whether India should be ruled by 'terrorism, Prussianism, racial humiliation' or 'partnership'.

> There were lots of sound men in the House inclined to support Dyer on such knowledge as they had, and it was a terribly bad opening gambit from Montagu to class them inferentially as supporters of frightfulness. He did not attempt to explain the case against Dyer, the procedure that had been followed, the reasons for delay in passing judgement and so on. It dealt in windy and unconvincing rhodomontades which merely infuriated men whom he might have convinced. He has never been popular with the conservative element in the House. But from the moment he began to speak I could feel antipathy to him sweeping all over the House.[3]

[1] E. S. Montagu to Chelmsford, 11 August 1920, Mss. EUR. D. 523 (4).

[2] Viceroy (Home Dept.) to Secretary of State, telegram, 3 June 1920, Home Pol., A, July 1920, No. 8 & K.-W.

[3] J. L. Maffey to Chelmsford, 10 July 1920, Mss. EUR. E. 264 (16). For the Common's debate on the Punjab disturbances and Lord Hunter's Committee on 8 July 1920 see *The Parliamentary Debates, 5th Series, Volume 131, House of*

In spite of this a majority of the Commons condemned Dyer's action, but after the Lords' debate 129 peers supported Dyer and only 86 voted against him. A public appeal launched by the *Morning Post* collected within a month £26,317 to mark public support for Dyer.[1] Not surprisingly this evidence of support for Dyer in England rebounded on India, increasing racial tension, making Indian politicians even more doubtful whether Britain intended to treat Indians as equals and work the reforms as a real step on the path to responsible government.[2]

On the tide of this controversy Gandhi launched himself as the champion of Indian self-respect. On 9 June 1920 he condemned the Hunter Report and the two government despatches on it as 'an attempt to condone official lawlessness' and 'page after page of thinly disguised official whitewash.' In his opinion, 'A scandal of this magnitude cannot be tolerated by the nation, if it is to preserve its self-respect and become a free partner in the Empire.'[3] At a meeting in Bombay on 26 June he supported a resolution demanding the impeachment of O'Dwyer and his fellow-officers, a demand which had first been made by the A.I.C.C. in session on 30/31 May.[4]

Later Gandhi explained that he himself preferred the recommendations of the Congress report on the Punjab to the idea of impeachment, but he was prepared to go with the majority on a matter which did not affect his conscience.[5] Just as on the Khilafat issue Gandhi was pushed forward by some of his extremer allies, so on the Punjab question he was constrained to go beyond his personal preference by the strength of feeling the question roused. Over the Punjab even Motilal Nehru let fly. Having read summaries of the Hunter Report and the government despatches he wrote to his son, 'My blood is boiling over since I read the summaries you have sent. We must hold a Special Congress now and raise a veritable hell for the rascals.'[6]

Gandhi's own remedy for the Punjab 'wrong' was satyagraha in the form of non-cooperation with the government. In early June he wrote,

> India has the choice before her now. If then the acts of the Punjab

Commons, cols. 1705–1814. For the Lords' debate on the Punjab disturbances and the case of General Dyer on 19/20 July 1920 see *The Parliamentary Debates, 5th Series, Volume 41, House of Lords*, pp. 222–378.

1 For support in England for Dyer see Furneaux, *Massacre At Amritsar*, pp. 142–3, 156–60.

2 This was put very forcibly by Lala Lajpat Rai in his Presidential Address at the Calcutta Congress, 4 September 1920, Joshi (ed.), *Lala Lajpat Rai Writings And Speeches Volume Two 1920–1928*, pp. 31–2.

3 *Young India*, 9 June 1920, *C.W.*, vol. 17, p. 482.

4 Speech by Gandhi at Bombay meeting organized by the Home Rule League and the National Union, 26 June 1920, *Navajivan*, 4 July 1920, *ibid.* pp. 513–14. The A.I.C.C.'s demand for impeachment is reported in Viceroy (Home Dept.) to Secretary of State, telegram, 3 June 1920, Home Pol., A, July 1920, No. 8 & K.-W.

5 *Young India*, 14 July 1920, *C.W.*, vol. 18, pp. 43–5.

6 Motilal Nehru to Jawaharlal Nehru, 27 July 1920, Nehru Papers.

Government be an insufferable wrong, if the report of Lord Hunter's Committee and the two despatches be a greater wrong by reason of their grievous condonation of these acts, it is clear that we must refuse to submit to this official violence. Appeal to the Parliament by all means if necessary, but if the Parliament fails us and if we are worthy to call ourselves a nation, we must refuse to uphold the Government by withdrawing co-operation from it.[1]

On 30 June he linked the Punjab and Khilafat as twin humiliating signs that Indian feelings counted for little in the British Empire, and therefore as twin reasons for resorting to non-cooperation, including boycott of the reformed councils, to regain Indian self-respect. This came three days after his public call for non-cooperation on the Khilafat issue, and reversed the decision he had taken in November 1919 not to mix the two issues.[2]

The Hunter Report and the government's reaction to it swept away Gandhi's earlier restraint on the Punjab question by convincing him that it was an intolerable 'wrong' which could not be remedied through conventional political channels. The government quite unwittingly presented him with an issue having India-wide appeal on which he felt he could and should take a moral stand, precisely at the time when an all-India issue would provide a convenient counterpoise to the specifically Muslim issue of the Khilafat. However, in spite of this conjunction of circumstances, the Khilafat leaders' support and Congress denunciation of the Hunter Report, Gandhi had no guarantee that events would go his way at the Special Congress, till which time most Hindu politicians had reserved judgement on non-cooperation. Undoubtedly by taking up the Punjab question, with its implication that the British were not intending to devolve power to Indian hands, Gandhi appeared to be championing the politicians' basic interests. However his non-cooperation was in itself a challenge to those interests, because it threatened their jobs and their hopes of increased power in the new councils; and many of the politicians hesitated to follow one who seemed to undermine with one hand what he supported with the other.

Tilak for one believed that the whole question of the Punjab had been tackled in the wrong way, and lamented to V. J. Patel, who was in England, that the politicians had lost an opportunity to tighten their grip on public life.

I entirely agree with you that we should have made this a lever to work up the British people for the reforms in the constitution of the country. I express[ed] my opinion freely at the Benares meeting of the Congress Committee, but they did not seem to take up the idea seriously. Madan

[1] *Young India*, 9 June 1920, *C.W.*, vol. 17, p. 483.

[2] *The Bombay Chronicle*, 30 June 1920, *ibid.* p. 522. For Gandhi's appeal for non-cooperation on the Khilafat issue on 27 June see above, p. 221; for his November 1919 refusal to mix the two questions see above, p. 203.

Mohan, you know, what he is. Gandhi is engaged in his supposed work for noncooperation...I do not think we can do much here unless Madan Mohan and Gandhi are prepared to help us. They are the men on the Punjab Committee who should have taken up the work in right earnest. Not only they would not do it but they do not much value foreign agitation as you know. Moderates are what you know. So the best opportunity to impress the British public and foreign nations with the abominable despotism of the bureaucracy is being or shall I say, has been lost.[1]

Tilak's frustration in the face of Gandhi's stand on the Punjab showed the weight Gandhi carried in nationalist politics by mid-1920. Gandhi's fight against the Punjab and Khilafat 'wrongs' in the first half of 1920 had so positioned him that the independence and authority he had claimed at the Amritsar Congress of 1919 were now political reality. The Khilafat and Punjab issues had both been simmering sources of political discontent, but they boiled over to make a double political crisis in the same month, May 1920, with the publication of the Turkish treaty terms and the Hunter Report. This juxtaposition, over which Gandhi had no control, was immensely significant for his personal career because it put him in a situation where he both wanted and had some chance of acquiring control of the policies adopted by nationalist politicians in their relations with the raj.

The Punjab and Khilafat 'wrongs' together resolved the ambiguity in Gandhi's attitude to the British raj and prompted him to resort to non-cooperation with the rulers. Before June 1920 Gandhi had opposed the British only on specific occasions, when he felt they were committing 'wrongs' which denied what he understood to be the ideals of the British consititution. In June 1920 he still believed that the British constitution was the best available, but the combination of the peace terms and the Hunter Report convinced him that the present representatives of the British in India had no intention of enacting the ideals of that constitution.[2]

Looking back over the past six months he explained his changed attitude,

When at Amritsar last year I pleaded...for co-operation with the Government and for response to the wishes expressed in the Royal Proclamation, I did so because I honestly believed that a new era was about to begin, and that the old spirit of fear, distrust and consequent terrorism was about to give place to the new spirit of respect, trust and goodwill. I sincerely believed that the Mussulman sentiment would be placated and that the officers that had misbehaved during the martial law regime in the Punjab would be at least dismissed and the people would be otherwise made to feel that a Government that had always been found

[1] B. G. Tilak to V. J. Patel, 26 June 1920, A.I.C.C. Files, 1920, No. 9.

[2] Gandhi to C. F. Andrews, 20 June 1920, *C.W.*, vol. 17, p. 500. Gandhi announced his belief in 'the inherent superiority of the British Constitution to all others at present in vogue' in a letter to the Viceroy, 22 June 1920; for this see above, p. 221.

quick (and rightly) to punish popular excesses would not fail to punish its agents' misdeeds. But to my amazement and dismay, I have discovered that the present representatives of the Empire have become dishonest and unscrupulous. They have no real regard for the wishes of the people of India and they count Indian honour as of little consequence.

I can no longer retain affection for a Government so evilly manned as it is now-a-days.[1]

As a result of this change of heart Gandhi moved from advising satyagraha in specific cases to suggesting total non-cooperation with the rulers, with the intention 'so far to paralyse the Government, as to compel justice from it.'[2] This meant that he needed to gain and exert as much political power as possible in order both to organize non-cooperation on a continental scale and to persuade other leaders to adopt his suggestion.

The Punjab issue also added momentum to Gandhi's emergence as a political leader by providing circumstances in which he became a key man in the institutions of politics. During his earlier satyagrahas he had worked as a freelance, assisted by groups of helpers who congregated round him either informally or under the banner of his Satyagraha Sabha. The Home Rule League organization had cooperated with him on specific occasions, but he had not controlled it. Now for the first time he inserted himself into the actual organizations of all-India politics by his actions on the Congress sub-committee of enquiry into the Punjab, and, as Tilak pointed out, made himself indispensable to Congress politicians on this topic. Gandhi's work in the Khilafat movement reinforced his importance in what was to him a new area of activity and increased the leverage he exerted in institutional politics.[3]

Striking evidence of his new position in the institutions of politics was his acceptance in April 1920 of office as President of the All-India Home Rule League in the place of Annie Besant. As he himself acknowledged,

It is a distinct departure from the even tenor of my life for me to belong to an organization that is purely and frankly political...Some friends whom I consulted told me that I should not join any political organization and that if I did, I would lose the position of splendid isolation I enjoy at present. I confess that this caution had considerable weight with me. At the same time I felt that if I was accepted by the League as I was, I should be wrong in not identifying myself with an organization that I could utilize for the advancement of the causes in which I had specialized and of the methods which experience has shown me are attended with quicker and better results than those that are usually adopted.

1 *Young India*, 28 July 1920, *C.W.*, vol. 18, p. 89.

2 *Young India*, 28 July 1920, *ibid.* p. 88. Gandhi said that no other people responded to 'soul-force' as quickly as the British, and that this was the basis of his satyagraha campaigns. *Navajivan*, 30 May 1920, *C.W.*, vol. 17, p. 468.

3 For this increased leverage because of the Khilafat movement see above, pp. 220, 229.

The 'causes' he listed as his own specialities were swadeshi, Hindu–Muslim unity 'with special reference to the Khilafat', Hindustani as the national language and the redistribution of provinces on linguistic lines, these being the path to self-government and to him infinitely more important than the reforms. The methods he advocated were truth and non-violence though he did not expect the League necessarily to follow him into civil disobedience.[1] There is virtually no evidence about Gandhi's election as President;[2] but it seems fair to assume that the reputation and influence he had gained through his work on the Khilafat and the Punjab gave him sufficient stature to be a candidate.

The Punjab 'wrong' also helped to push Gandhi towards dominance among the politicians by giving him an all-India and inter-communal cause to balance the Muslim cause of the Khilafat. It was a 'wrong' which Hindu politicians felt deeply because it betrayed an official attitude which threatened to nullify all their hopes for increased power under the reforms. If this were joined to the Khilafat as the reason for non-cooperation there was a possibility that they might be willing to work with the Khilafat men and follow Gandhi's leadership. At a deeper level events in the Punjab threw the politicians back on Gandhi because they laid bare the limitations of conventional politics. The political mode evolved by India's educated was viable and profitable provided that the raj and the politicians needed each other and were prepared to collaborate with each other. The Punjab demonstrated the impotence of the politicians when the rulers took their stand on force rather than collaboration: and just as the techniques of the politicians failed to stop the passage of the Rowlatt Act so they failed in the face of martial law and the government's subsequent attitude to it.

The failure of limited politics gave Gandhi his chance to attain leadership in the politics of Indian nationalism. What he had to show in the second part of 1920 was whether he had an alternative political mode which would prove more effective and would quell the scepticism and fear of politicians like Tilak. Yet in spite of Gandhi's growing stature in nationalist politics he retained many of the quirks and singular characteristics which had struck the politicians time and again since his return to India. He was still prompted by the ideals which had made him establish his *ashram*, though circumstances now made him feel he must pursue those ideals in politics: he was still the returning exile in search of *moksha* or deliverance from worldly attachments, though now he saw his path to deliverance in the

1 *Young India*, 28 April 1920, *C.W.*, vol. 17, pp. 347–9. Gandhi consulted Srinivasa Sastri before making this decision, and told him that at his age he could not change his views and could only join an organization to affect its policy, not to be affected by it. Gandhi to V. S. S. Sastri, 18 March 1920, *ibid.* pp. 96–8.

2 Motilal Nehru appears to have been behind the actual invitation to Gandhi, and spent some time persuading C. R. Das that this was a wise course; Das was fearful that this would conflict with Tilak's League. Motilal Nehru to Jawaharlal Nehru, 13 March 1920, Nehru Papers.

wider service of the community and the state. In his own words to Maganlal Gandhi,

> If I had not joined the Khilafat movement, I think, I would have lost everything. In joining it I have followed what I especially regard as my dharma. I am trying through this movement to show the real nature of non-violence. I am uniting Hindus and Muslims. I am coming to know one and all and, if non-co-operation goes well, a great power based on brute force will have to submit to a simple-looking thing...I cannot leave any field in which I have cultivated some strength. My *moksha* lies through them. If I refuse to work in these fields, I shall not succeed in giving anything through the Ashram either.[1]

Gandhi the politician was still the agent of Gandhi the idealist, although the Mahatma had moved into new fields of political action. Moreover he still continued his religious and philanthropic work among people right outside the ranks of the political nation. At the height of his campaigns on the Khilafat and the Punjab, for example, he was concerned with dacoities in the Matar taluka of Kaira, urging people to give him information and promising to help them with their local problem if he could.[2] Such a range of concern and contact distinguished Gandhi's public activities from those of most other major political leaders and held the possibilities of far-reaching political change if Gandhi succeeded in attaining control of the policies adopted by the politicians.

[1] Gandhi to Maganlal Gandhi, 4 May 1920, *C.W.*, vol. 17, pp. 386–7.
[2] *Navajivan*, 30 May 1920, *ibid.* p. 473.

CHAPTER 8

NON-COOPERATION, 1920: CRISIS FOR THE POLITICIANS

The Gandhi who returned to India in 1915 was an enigma to his compatriots. To many he was a Mahatma, to some a figure of fun. He had gained a reputation for saintliness, but simultaneously in South Africa he had become a successful politician. On his return he was not an open threat to India's political elite whose interests were focussed in institutional politics where its leaders and officials of the raj worked and sparred together in a fine balance. However, by mid-1920 that balance had been destroyed. The Khilafat and Punjab issues had shown up the impotence of elitist politics when the rulers stood firm. Economic change, war-time hardship and constitutional reform had increased the number of the politically aware, with the result that the political elite now found itself one group among many, surrounded by new recruits to institutional politics who might become allies but might prove to be opponents if their interests differed from those of the established politicians.

Faced with such a situation the politicians vacillated, not knowing how to adapt their principles and techniques to the changed circumstances of politics.[1] Their dilemma was made worse by the loss of their foremost leaders. G. K. Gokhale and Sir Pherozeshah Mehta died in 1915, Annie Besant seemed a tiresome old woman once the glamour of her internment had faded, Surendranath Bannerjee was being pushed by Bengali politics into the raj's train, and on 1 August 1920, the very day non-cooperation began, B. G. Tilak died. Events conspired to remove the leaders who might have taken the initiative in guiding the political elite, and thus opened the door to Gandhi, a new leader with a new style of politics. However it was not certain that Gandhi could produce a viable political alternative. Non-cooperation sounded splendid in theory as a way of paralysing the government and exerting Indian strength; but it had yet to be tested in practice and Gandhi had no way of knowing whether those who held government posts, sat in legislative councils and learnt in government schools would respond to his call. In its total concept non-cooperation was the antithesis of politics as practised by the western educated, but in its initial stages it depended for its success on their cooperation while challenging their material interests.

[1] For example, Annie Besant's hesitation in the face of political demands from low castes, and Congressmen's fears at the implications of the Khilafat movement: see above, pp. 129–30, 220, 226.

Gandhi's intentions in mid-1920 are clear. Before that date he had participated in politics only on occasions and issues when he felt he could forward his own principles and hopes for India.[1] Now that events had combined to give him power in institutional politics he was determined to use it, not just to right the Punjab and Khilafat 'wrongs' but also to restructure Indian political life on the lines laid down in *Hind Swaraj*. The means to both ends was satyagraha, in this instance in the form of non-cooperation. This was implicit, for example, in Gandhi's defence of non-cooperation by lawyers, a side effect of which would be their greater opportunity to devote time to politics.

> The lawyers today lead public opinion and conduct all political activity. This they do during the few leisure hours they get for their tennis and billiards. I do not expect that by dividing their leisure hours between billiards and politics lawyers will bring us substantially near Swaraj. I want at least the public workers to be whole timers and when that happy day comes, I promise a different outlook before the country.[2]

Behind Gandhi's wish to reorientate political life lay a consuming ideology, what Gandhi called the search for truth – for himself and his countrymen. This he explained to a critic who complained that although he had the reputation of a saint the politician in him seemed to be guiding his decisions. Though Gandhi disclaimed sainthood he affirmed,

> that the politician in me has never dominated a single decision of mine, and if I seem to take part in politics, it is only because politics encircle us today like the coil of a snake from which one cannot get out, no matter how much one tries. I wish therefore to wrestle with the snake.[3]

(I) 1 AUGUST 1920 UNTIL THE SPECIAL CONGRESS

The reluctance of Hindu politicians to commit themselves to non-cooperation before discussion of it at the Special Congress in September made Gandhi act on his own authority. Despite an appeal to desist by Madan Mohan Malaviya, he launched his programme of non-cooperation on 1 August, explaining that for him non-cooperation was a matter of conscience which could not wait on Congress deliberations.

> The Congress is after all the mouth-piece of the nation. And when one has a policy or a programme which one would like to see adopted, but on which one wants to cultivate public opinion, one naturally asks the Congress to discuss it and form an opinion. But when one has an unshakable faith in a particular policy or action, it would be folly to wait for the Congress pronouncements. On the contrary one must act and demonstrate its efficacy so as to command acceptance by the nation.[4]

[1] See above, pp. 140–59, 164, 193–4, 232–3.
[2] Gandhi to N. C. Sinha, 14 May 1920, S.N. No. 7249 A.
[3] *Young India*, 12 May 1920.
[4] *Young India*, 4 August 1920.

Gandhi's action not only had the effect he desired of demonstrating his policy: it also forced Congressmen's hands by making it difficult for them to refuse to ratify non-cooperation at the Special Congress without going back on what was already happening and thus appearing hesitant in the struggle with the raj.

Instructions for observance of 1 August were published by the non-cooperation sub-committee of the Central Khilafat Committee, the 'Martial Law Committee' of the Khilafat movement created at the Allahabad meeting in June. The signatories urged people to pray, fast and hold meetings approving of non-cooperation, but not to hold processions or commit civil disobedience, and advised holders of titles and honorary posts to resign them on that day. On 1 August Gandhi himself returned his Zulu and Boer War medals and his Kaiser-i-Hind gold medal to the Viceroy with the explanation that the Khilafat and Punjab 'wrongs' had estranged him from the raj and convinced him that a new type of politics was necessary in India. 'In my humble opinion,' he wrote, 'the ordinary method of agitating by way of petitions, deputations and the like, is no remedy for moving to repentence [sic] a Government, so hopelessly indifferent to the welfare of its charge as the Government of India has proved to be.'[1] He saw that India was too weak to offer violent resistance to the raj, and that many of his compatriots were unwilling to resort to terrorism: therefore he was offering them a peaceful form of resistance, what amounted to non-violent terrorism, as a means of compelling the raj 'to retrace its steps and undo the wrongs committed.'[2]

1 August 1920 was a Sunday, the public day of rest, whereas previous hartals organized by Gandhi on the Khilafat issue had occurred on Fridays, observed by Muslims as a partial holiday. Provincial governments reported that instances of non-cooperation were few, meetings were held only in the larger towns, and active support for hartal was confined to certain districts in Sind, Gujarat and the Punjab.[3] The net result was no advance, and in places even a reverse, by comparison with the earlier hartals Gandhi had organized. Nevertheless, his programme had percolated throughout India. His call was heard from the North-West Frontier to Madras, from Sind to Assam, with the implication that throughout India there was a network of intermediate leaders who were prepared on occasion to publicize Gandhi's views and sometimes to organize his campaigns in their own localities.

The hartal provided further evidence that Gandhi had broken through at the level of genuine all-India politics, whereas previously political

1 Instructions for 1 August, *Young India*, 21 July 1920, *The Bombay Chronicle*, 22 July 1920, *C.W.*, vol. 18, pp. 78–9. For the establishment of the 'Martial Law Committee' see above, p. 219.
2 Gandhi to the Viceroy, 2 August 1920, Home Pol., Deposit, August 1920, No. 38.
3 For a survey of the regional observance of 1 August, see Appendix to this chapter.

organization and propaganda had been the preserve of elite groups in specific localities. Greater numbers heard Gandhi's call for hartal than were reached by the Home Rule Leagues, the established politicians' limited attempt to stretch out beyond their existing political range. More striking was the fact that the areas where hartal was observed most fully, Sind, Gujarat, Punjab, and to a lesser extent U.P. and Bihar, would all have been (and often were) described as backward according to the canons of nationalist politics even five years before.

It was easy for existing political leaders to secure a minimal observance of 1 August in order to keep up appearances and placate Gandhi and his Muslim allies.[1] Meetings and resolutions were within their range and they organized such observances in the Presidencies. Such tactics also did little harm to their local standing. But the plan of non-cooperation was a threat to their positions, particularly by Gandhi's emphasis from the end of June on boycott of councils. The object of the political elite was power and prestige, and the elections scheduled for November 1920 under the Montagu–Chelmsford Reforms promised more power than ever before to the successful. But now they were being asked by a new and unpredictable leader to withdraw from the contest for council seats. Having seen the extent of Gandhi's appeal on 1 August the politicians conferred and re-aligned, having to decide whether to fight the new current and risk being washed away, or allow themselves to be carried by it to unknown and possibly dangerous waters. Although the intricacies of these discussions are known only for some provinces, it is clear that in each area local groups were weighing up the situation, balancing the power of their local rivals, their chances of election in November, and the possible gains and losses involved in alliance with Gandhi.

In the U.P., for example, the earliest supporters of non-cooperation were Muslims, the 'young Muhammadan party' rather than the old-fashioned Muslim politicians who had held their own through the reservation of special seats for their community and were determined not to lose the opportunities the reforms offered. Hindu opinion was divided on the question – if the local press was any indication of their feeling. Editors had to weigh up the disadvantage of suggesting a policy which would lose their community seats in the legislative council against the undoubted advantage in terms of circulation if they pursued an 'advanced' political line which attracted younger educated readers. Eventually *The Leader* came out as anti-non-cooperation, opposed by *The Independent*, and the rest of the press lined up behind them.[2] A further complication in the calculations of the Hindu politicians was the strength of the large landholders of the U.P. and

[1] For N. C. Kelkar's acknowledgement of this, see above, p. 226.

[2] *Report on the Administration of the United Provinces of Agra and Oudh 1919–1920* (Allahabad, 1921), pp. xxiv–xxv; *Report on the Administration of the United Provinces of Agra and Oudh 1920–21* (Allahabad, 1922), pp. xiv–xv.

their determination not to abandon their tradition of profitable collaboration with the provincial government through the legislative council. They would probably do well in the elections because of their traditional ties of authority and obligation with the new voters, and beside their well-worn channels of influence in the countryside the politicians could only pit the network of the Khilafat movement and their appeal to the urban educated.

Hindu disquiet and disorganization was evident in the correspondence of Motilal Nehru. In June 1920 he thought that he and Malaviya ought to begin to organize support for themselves as candidates for the November elections, as it would be too late if they waited until the Special Congress. He did not believe that Congress as an organization would bind itself to council boycott, and predicted that Congressmen would be left to follow their own inclinations.[1] In July he was still undecided on the issue, though his son found it hard to resist the power of Gandhi's personal appeal. As Motilal said,

> So far as your following the request of Gandhiji is concerned there is nothing to be said. That is more or less a matter of sentiment of a kind which does not enter into my composition. On the merits of the question however I am by no means sure that even Gandhiji will stick to his programme to the bitter end. Left to himself he certainly would. But this is a matter in which he has to depend upon others and those others will sooner or later drop off. There can be no manner of doubt as to this. The question is a very difficult one and I am free to confess that I have arrived at no definite conclusion. My sympathies are all for the principle of non-cooperation but I am by no means sure as to the form which it should take in practice...I do not agree with Gandhiji to boycott the Councils generally throughout India. I am inclined to think that it will give the cause immense strength, without sacrificing the principle of non-cooperation, to get our people to return us & then refuse to sit in the Council or to obstruct its business.[2]

Eventually on 22 August the U.P.'s P.C.C. took the plunge and approved of the principle of non-cooperation and recommended relinquishment of titles and honorary posts (except where elected by the people), the substitution of arbitration courts for government courts wherever possible, gradual boycott of government schools and colleges, boycott of British goods, boycott of government loans and official functions, and – critically – boycott of the legislative councils.[3]

Bombay had far longer political experience than the U.P. and its old traditions died hard. However, the Presidency's politicians were divided into many different camps and their confusion was made worse by the

[1] Motilal Nehru to Jawaharlal Nehru, 16 June 1920, Nehru Papers.

[2] Motilal Nehru to Jawaharlal Nehru, 5 July 1920, Nehru Papers.

[3] Report of resolutions passed on 22 August 1920 by U.P. P.C.C., A.I.C.C. Files, 1920, No. 13, Part II.

death of Tilak, who might have acted as a focus for some of them. As one contemporary remarked, 'What about the living? The confusion of parties & factions & opinions will be, I suppose, now worse than ever.'[1] By 15 August they had realigned, and on that day the Bombay P.C.C. approved the principle of non-cooperation but left the actual details to the Special Congress to decide. The voting was 36 for and 21 against, the opposition, led by Jamnadas Dwarkadas, consisting mainly of Mrs Besant's followers, while the majority included Gandhi's men, Bombay followers of Tilak and those labour leaders who did not follow Mrs Besant.[2] The following day a leading Bombay 'Moderate', Sir Narayan Chandarvarkar, appealed to Gandhi not to behave like an autocrat over the question of non-cooperation and to see that if this tactic did succeed in bringing down the raj it would merely result in caste strife. However, even he felt he could not condemn Gandhi outright and admitted,

> We do not take the full measure of this man by merely describing him as a saintly character, as a hero, and as a great personality. He is more – a prophet, India's awakened and still awakening Soul is speaking unto us through him and warning us against the dangers of materialism.[3]

Bombay followers of Tilak appear to have calculated that it was better for them to align with Gandhi than to risk absorption into the ranks of Annie Besant's local faction. In the Marathi-speaking parts of the Presidency they were the dominant political group and had to decide whether to fight for the independence of their area as a political entity with its own ideology in the face of Gandhi's 'Gujarati politics'. Their dislike and fear of Gandhian politics was evident:[4] and they believed that it was rank folly to boycott the new councils, thereby cutting themselves off from the fountainhead of political power. In N. C. Kelkar's words,

> we will not be able to correct Government by remaining outside the Council. There are some, who say that we should enter the council and refuse to take the oath of loyalty. But this is foolishness. It is no use to play with the Government by refusing to take oaths and to again try for election. The best way would be to see that the Nationalists join in a body, and send a large number of their party to the council, so that such elected men might prevent Government from passing any measures unpalatable to the Nationalist party and force Government's hands to pass certain resolutions for which they have been agitating.[5]

1 G. S. Bhate to M. R. Jayakar, 20 August 1920, Jayakar Papers, Chronological Correspondence File No. 11, No. 106.
2 Letter from Bombay P.C.C. to A.I.C.C., 16 August 1920, A.I.C.C. Files, 1920, No. 13, Part II; Bombay Police Abstract, 1920, par. 1184 (1).
3 *The Times of India*, 16 August 1920.
4 19 August 1920, Diary of G. S. Khaparde, Khaparde Papers.
5 Report dated 22 July 1920 by G. Madurkar of Intelligence Dept. of a conversation he had with N. C. Kelkar, Home Pol., Deposit, August 1920, No. 35. (I owe this reference to Dr D. Baker.)

On 24 August Tilak's followers met in Poona under Kelkar's leadership and decided not to oppose Gandhian non-cooperation actively, but to wait until Vithalbhai Patel could be consulted on his return from England before making a definite policy decision. Their dislike of non-cooperation appeared to have been tempered by advice from the dying Tilak, who warned them that Gandhi was a political power and they should not oppose him lightly because by so doing they risked their leadership in the politics of western India.[1]

The desire to retain local political supremacy was a key consideration for all political groups as they decided their attitude to non-cooperation. B. S. Moonje told the Poona meeting of Tilak's men that this consideration was uppermost in the minds of politicians from C.P. and Berar who were anxious to go ahead politically and not lag behind in any new move.[2] However, C.P. was divided into the politically advanced Marathi region and the backward Hindi region. This caused distinct ambivalence in the province's reaction to non-cooperation, because the Hindi-speakers had hoped that the new councils would give them an opportunity to voice their views and redress the political balance in the province, which had hitherto been in favour of the Marathi-speaking men. In April 1920, for example, one Hindi leader had exhorted Hindi-speakers to organize for the November elections in these terms.

> Loud complaints are made by the Hindi speaking people that their interests are sadly neglected. It is for you now to organise and make your voice heard through your ministers in the council...You have been neglected so far because you have not cried aloud or hit at all. You must now organise and convene district, tahsil and village conferences, pass resolutions and send them up to the government for compliance...[3]

On 22 and 25 August the C.P. P.C.C. met and decided that non-cooperation was the only effective and legitimate method of agitation left, though it excluded council boycott and only recommended boycott of British goods as a first stage, leaving other stages to be decided as necessary by the A.I.C.C.[4]

1 Bombay Police Abstract, 1920, par. 1211. G. S. Khaparde believed 'that Lok Tilak opposed Non-cooperation and told Gandhi not to press it on his death bed. As I was not there at the time I could not say it from personal knowledge but I am very credibly informed that it was so.' 16 August 1920, Diary of G. S. Khaparde, Khaparde Papers. Gandhi maintained that just before he died Tilak was sceptical about non-cooperation but said he would support Gandhi if Gandhi could muster popular support. Reminiscences of Tilak by Gandhi, some time in 1924, S.N. No. 8689 A.

2 Bombay Police Abstract, 1920, par. 1211.

3 Sir Hari Singh Gour in *Hitavada*, 10 April 1920, quoted in Baker, 'Politics In A Bilingual Province: The Central Provinces And Berar, India, 1919–1939', p. 49.

4 Letter from C.P. P.C.C. to A.I.C.C., 28 August 1920, A.I.C.C. Files, 1920, No. 13, Part II.

Bengal also wished to modify non-cooperation as suggested by Gandhi. The P.C.C. met on 15 August and decided that non-cooperation was the only weapon left to them but that each province should work out the practical details in the light of its particular circumstances. It disagreed with the idea of council boycott and wanted to return large numbers of men to the councils who would be ready to resort to non-cooperation in the council chamber.[1] Surendranath Bannerjee began to hawk round an anti-non-cooperation manifesto at the end of August.[2] His opposition was only to be expected, because he led the group of Bengali politicians who had backed the reform scheme and staked all their hopes for political power on its success: but the decision of the P.C.C. indicated that all *bhadralok* politicians were banking on success in the November elections and saw Gandhi's non-cooperation as a threat to their hold on the Presidency's political life. Caught between their fear and their assessment of Gandhi as a political power, the politicians decided to run with the hare and hunt with the hounds. As one local paper commented,

> The Committee have indulged in craftiness to an extreme extent...Mr. Gandhi is preaching non-co-operation all over the country. And if at such a time Bengal declares itself against it, it will forfeit the friendship of the Extremists. Hence the committee have accepted the principle of non-cooperation in their speeches, while in reality they have struck at its very roots.[3]

The Bengalee thought that 'the older provinces which have been longest in public life...are all against non-cooperation';[4] and the fate of Gandhi's plans for non-cooperation in Madras substantiated this claim. Madras Congressmen faced not only the demands of the non-Brahmins for more power in the Presidency's public life but also their organization, the Justice Party, bent on seizing such power under the reforms. Consequently for the Congressmen the proposal to boycott the council elections amounted to throwing in the sponge, and they all opposed it, despite their local divisions. Annie Besant accused Gandhi of being unrealistic and dangerous, and condemned non-cooperation as revolutionary: her programme was cooperation with the government in everything constructive to hasten Home Rule, and this included using 'every scrap of power which the Reform Act gives'.[5] The anti-Theosophist 'Moderates', led by C. P. Ramaswami Aiyer and including local members of the Servants of India Society, opposed non-cooperation as much, but hesitated to go into alliance with her because, in Srinivasa Sastri's words, 'of the personal antipathy

[1] Resolutions passed at Bengal P.C.C. meeting on 15 August 1920, A.I.C.C. Files, 1920, No. 13, Part II.

[2] 24 August 1920, Diary of G. S. Khaparde, Khaparde Papers.

[3] *Sanjivani*, 19 August 1920, Bengal N.N., No. 35 of 1920.

[4] *The Bengalee*, 3 August 1920.

[5] *The Looker On*, 4 September 1920; *The Theosophist*, August 1920.

to her and the general nervousness about being hustled by her and let into inconvenient situations.'[1]

The 'Nationalists' of Madras, led by Kasturi Ranga Iyengar and S. Satyamurti, also opposed boycott of councils, courts and schools, and through the columns of *The Hindu* carried on a running battle against the small group of Gandhi's Hindu followers led by Rajagopalachariar.[2] Like their counterparts in Bengal the 'Nationalists' of Madras were caught in a tight corner. They opposed the elements of non-cooperation which threatened their local position, yet they did not want to fight Gandhi so completely as to forego the local power that alliance with him could give – hence the ambiguity of Kasturi Ranga Iyengar's personal stand as an opponent of council boycott yet as a prominent local organizer of the Khilafat movement.

Gandhi and Shaukat Ali toured Madras from 10 to 26 August before the Special Congress to counteract this local hostility; but Gandhi admitted that he was disappointed with the results.[3] None of Annie Besant's party or the non-Theosophist 'Moderates' were present to welcome them to Madras, and the latter, with C. P. Ramaswami Aiyer as spokesman, openly criticized non-cooperation as impracticable at an informal meeting on 13 August. At the same meeting the 'Nationalist' Satyamurti said that his party had no intention of boycotting the council elections and letting the 'Moderates' step in. At another informal conference in Trichinopoly on 17 August, attended by about 80 leading Muslims and others (half the number invited), similar criticisms were made, and local politicians decided to draw up a more practical scheme of non-cooperation, much against the will of Gandhi and Shaukat Ali.[4] The Madras P.C.C. met three times to discuss the issue – on 5, 15 and 24 August – and the outcome was approval of a policy of non-cooperation but rejection of Gandhi's programme.[5]

By contrast Gujarat and Bihar, two 'backward' areas without established political traditions where Gandhi had built up a local reputation and a network of subcontractors, swung powerfully into all-India politics for the first time solidly in support of him. Gujarat held a provincial conference independently of the Bombay P.C.C., and before it met Gandhi tried to influence its executive committee by urging two of his local henchmen, Indulal Yajnik and Vallabhbhai Patel, to see that it resolved for non-cooperation.[6] At its meeting on 11 July at Nadiad (in Kaira district) the

[1] V. S. S. Sastri to S. G. Vaze, 15 July 1920, S.P., Correspondence File, 1919, Letters to & from Sastri, No. 337.

[2] Irschick, *Politics And Social Conflict In South India*, p. 194.

[3] *Navajivan*, 29 August 1920, *C.W.*, vol. 18, pp. 209–13.

[4] Bombay Police Abstract, 1920, par. 1238 (1).

[5] Letter from Madras P.C.C. to A.I.C.C., 26 August 1920, A.I.C.C. Files, 1920, No. 13, Part II.

[6] Gandhi to Indulal Yajnik, undated letter read out to executive committee, *The Bombay Chronicle*, 16 July 1920, *C.W.*, vol. 18, p. 26; Gandhi to Vallabhbhai

executive committee complied with Gandhi's wishes, and decided that it was derogatory to national self-respect to cooperate with the government by sitting in legislative councils or taking part in council elections until the government dealt justly with the Khilafat and Punjab questions.[1] The provincial conference was held in Ahmedabad on 27/28/29 August, and the resolution on non-cooperation, which Gandhi moved in person, was passed.[2]

Satyagraha in Kaira and Ahmedabad had paid off on the grand scale: Gujarat gave Gandhi full support in the face of opposition from other parts of India before Congress had discussed non-cooperation. In so doing it lived up to Vallabhbhai Patel's claim two years before that Gujarat could no longer be counted as a politically backward area. He agreed that a decade earlier Gujarat had with some justification been criticized as 'unmoving and unchanging, cold and indifferent towards the national movement'.

> Absorbed in her own commercial occupations, and without the guidance of real leaders, she remained for a time unaffected by the changes and upheavals that were taking place all around her in the country...Indeed, slow as she was to move in the field of politics and of social reform, she has made up for it with a vengeance, for to-day, slow-moving Gujarat is in the forefront of the national movement.[3]

Similarly Bihar, the scene of Gandhi's satyagraha for Champaran's peasants, also swung into all-India politics behind Gandhi and non-cooperation. On 31 July its P.C.C. approved of the principle of non-cooperation and appointed a committee, which included Mazharul Haq and Rajendra Prasad, to consider Gandhi's programme.[4] In the last week of August the province held a conference at Bhagalpur, at which Rajendra Prasad, Gandhi's chief Bihari subcontractor, presided, just as Vallabhbhai Patel, Gandhi's chief man in Gujarat, had chaired the reception committee of the Gujarat conference. Some Bihari leaders were opposed to non-cooperation and many were doubtful, but the conference resolved in favour of non-cooperation with certain reservations about the details of the stages as so far proposed. The passage of this resolution was secured by the

Patel, 9 July 1920, *ibid.* pp. 26–7. Yajnik and Patel had been Gandhi's principal helpers in the Kaira satyagraha; see above, p. 105.

[1] Resolutions passed at Gujarat Rajkiya Mandal meeting, 11 July 1920, A.I.C.C. Files, 1920, No. 3, Part II.

[2] Resolutions passed by the 4th Gujarat Political Conference, *Young India*, 1 September 1920; speech by Gandhi on non-cooperation on 28 August 1920 at Gujarat Political Conference, *Gujarati*, 5 September 1920, *C.W.*, vol. 18, pp. 200–3.

[3] Speech by V. J. Patel as President of Gujarat Political Conference, *The Bombay Chronicle*, 18 November 1918.

[4] Letter from Bihar and Orissa P.C.C. to A.I.C.C., 9 August 1920, A.I.C.C. Files, 1920, No. 13, Part II.

bloc vote of about 180 peasant delegates, this being the first local conference where delegates came mainly from outside the professional classes.

Such an extension of the political nation involved consideration of questions which affected the wider groups now involved in politics; and a curious result of this at the Bihar conference was the passage of a resolution urging the government to relieve distress caused by high food prices – which was of course completely incompatible with the principle of non-cooperation with the government![1] Political awareness had deepened in Bihari society and extended in range beyond urban areas since 1917, when Gandhi had encountered political ignorance and lethargy in the countryside. The change was partly due to satyagraha in Champaran, and partly to the Khilafat movement in which Gandhi's subcontractors had been at work to break out of the confines of elitist politics.[2]

Of the other areas for which details of discussions on non-cooperation are not available the Andhra and Punjab P.C.C.s approved of non-cooperation but deferred a decision on Gandhi's programme until the Special Congress. The Sind P.C.C. approved the principle and the programme, with the exception of withdrawal from the army and police, but considered that the ground should first be prepared by propaganda.[3] Delhi recommended its own scheme of non-cooperation, including a parallel government for all civil matters.[4]

Provincial decisions on Gandhi's plan of non-cooperation before the Special Congress must be seen in the context of local politics and local power structures, as men in each area weighed up the options open to them. Opposition to Gandhi's plan was most marked in the three Presidencies where there existed well-established elites who owed their influence largely to western education, government posts and local councils, all of which were threatened by non-cooperation. In most other provinces the politicians feared non-cooperation sufficiently to hesitate or whittle down the programme, the notable exceptions being Gujarat, Bihar and Sind, areas 'new' to institutional politics where Gandhi's supporters had little

1 Fortnightly report from Bihar and Orissa for first half of September 1920, Home Pol., Deposit, September 1920, No. 70; Rajendra Prasad, *Mahatma Gandhi And Bihar. Some Reminiscences*, pp. 39–40.

2 For example, during Shaukat Ali's tour of Bihar in the spring of 1920 Mazharul Haq convened a meeting on 24 April which was attended by about 10,000. *Searchlight*, 29 April 1920, noted 'the presence of people from the moffussil, who had rushed to Patna at a very short notice.' Another feature of the meeting was the presence of a large number of maulvis. Home Pol., A, September 1920, Nos. 100–3.

3 Letter from Andhra P.C.C. to A.I.C.C., 26 August 1920, letter from Punjab P.C.C. to A.I.C.C., 9 August 1920, A.I.C.C. Files, 1920, No. 13, Part II; undated letter from Sind P.C.C. to A.I.C.C., A.I.C.C. Files, 1920, No. 13, Part I.

4 Sitaramayya, *The History Of The Indian National Congress. Volume 1 (1885–1935)*, p. 200.

to lose from non-cooperation and much to gain by being in the van of a new political agitation.

Taking India as a whole, however, the politicians decided that they had not enough evidence on which to make a final decision about non-cooperation. So far it was not clear how important it would be locally to be Gandhi's man, and whether this would outweigh the loss involved in boycotting the elections. Therefore the majority of them played for time and postponed their decisions until the Special Congress. This meant that the Calcutta session would be particularly critical, as politicians consulted and aligned among themselves, assessing the position, trying to see which way the wind was blowing. It meant, too, that there was a likelihood of a landslide for or against Gandhi in the course of the session, as the politicians searched for a consensus on the most profitable course of action rather than splitting Congress further and weakening it in its relations with the raj.

While the politicians conferred the government held back. Officials, like the politicians, had to base their policy on an assessment of Gandhi's power and the disadvantages of being his declared enemy. The Madras government thought that it was worth stamping on Gandhi, and asked the Government of India for permission to extern him during his projected tour of the Presidency.[1] As the Governor, Lord Willingdon, said, 'The G. of I. think they are going to kill this agitation by kindness. They won't. I know Gandhi well & have hitherto looked upon him as a selfless & high-minded man, & with all his peculiarities a loyal citizen. But I can't think so any longer. He is out for our blood.'[2] Taking an all-India viewpoint, the Government of India weighed up the situation differently. It refused the request from Madras in the belief that an externment 'might only have the effect of advertising and stimulating the movement which so far has received no widespread support in spite of its promoter's frantic efforts, and...is almost certain to be dead failure if left to itself.'[3] When the tour passed off peacefully Willingdon admitted that perhaps his 'more militant ideas were wrong.'[4]

The Home Department of the Government of India in discussing a policy towards Gandhi decided that it must avoid increasing his power by giving him 'the crown of martyrdom',[5] and on 4 September a letter was sent to all

[1] Chief Secretary, Govt. of Madras, to Secretary, Govt. of India, Home Dept., telegram, 6 August 1920, Proceeding No. 127 of Home Pol., A, August 1920, Nos. 127–8.

[2] Willingdon to E. S. Montagu, 8 August 1920, Mss. EUR. D. 523 (20).

[3] Secretary, Govt. of India, Home Dept., to Chief Secretary, Govt. of Madras, telegram, 8 August 1920, Proceeding No. 128 of Home Pol., A, August 1920, Nos. 127–8. Madras was reminded that it could prosecute Gandhi under the criminal law if his speeches warranted it.

[4] Willingdon to E. S. Montagu, 22 August 1920, Mss. EUR. D. 523 (20).

[5] Note by C. W. Gwynne, Deputy Secretary, Home Dept., 4 August 1920, with which the other members of the Home Dept. agreed in a discussion on 11 August 1920, Home Pol., Deposit, August 1920, No. 38.

local governments explaining the policy of inaction. It stated that the Government of India believed that India would reject non-cooperation as foolish unless government interference with the leaders made martyrs of them, and cited the legal opinion it had obtained that prosecution of Gandhi at this stage was inadvisable. However, it said that the Government was prepared to risk an early prosecution if this became necessary and had asked Bombay to prepare a case for the prosecution of the whole non-cooperation sub-committee of the Central Khilafat Committee. It also stressed that despite an all-India policy of inaction local governments should prosecute any leaders who incited people to violence within their territories, and that association with the apostle of non-violence should not shield Gandhi's co-workers.[1] As Chelmsford said,

> it is the small people who speak in the villages who do the mischief, and they have no wish to be made martyrs. They value their comfort too highly, and if we can only by our action convince these people that they are on the wrong side, I think we are in a fair way to combat the movement.[2]

By catching Gandhi's subcontractors he hoped to prove that it was not worth their while being Gandhi's men locally, and so to detach the layer of men who were both the strength and weakness of Gandhi's leadership. Montagu supported Chelmsford's tactics, fearing most of all that if the government acted against Gandhi himself he would 'hunger strike and die in prison, and then I don't know where we should be.'[3] The Government of India, like the politicians, had realized that Gandhi was a new political phenomenon requiring a nicely calculated response.

(II) THE CALCUTTA SPECIAL CONGRESS

The Special Congress was held in September 1920 in Calcutta, the cradle of elitist politics and the home of some of Gandhi's most obdurate opponents. When Gandhi went to Calcutta to challenge the politicians he had to do so on the home territory of some of the most skilled political organizers in India; later he commented, 'my plight was pitiable indeed. I was absolutely at sea as to who would support the resolution and who would oppose it...I only saw an imposing phalanx of veteran warriors assembled for the fray'.[4]

1 Government of India to all local governments, 4 September 1920, Home Pol., A, September 1920, Nos. 100–3. For the legal opinion see above, p. 222. For a discussion of government policy see D. A. Low, 'The Government of India and the First Non-cooperation Movement – 1920–1922', *The Journal Of Asian Studies*, XXV, 2 (February 1966), 241–59.

2 Chelmsford to J. L. Maffey, 9 September 1920, Mss. EUR. E. 264 (16).

3 E. S. Montagu to Chelmsford, 9 September 1920, Mss. EUR. E. 264 (6).

4 Gandhi, *An Autobiography*, p. 416.

The 'veteran warriors' began to draw up the opposing ranks before the session began. Tilak's former henchman, G. S. Khaparde, linked up with the Bengalis, Motilal Ghose, B. C. Pal and B. Chakravarti, and on 1 September they decided to oppose Gandhi's programme of non-cooperation.[1] Motilal Nehru organized another opposition group and, while meeting M. A. Jinnah at Howrah station off the Congress special train from Bombay, apparently suggested that he and Jinnah with C. R. Das, Pandit Malaviya and Annie Besant should combine to defeat Gandhi's proposal to boycott the councils.[2] An informal conference of leaders took place on 3 September in Calcutta at which the majority opposed Gandhi's programme though they favoured the principle of non-cooperation.[3] Despite such opposition there were rumours that Gandhi would bring off something dramatic by guile or good management: Surendranath Bannerjee for one believed that the Mahatma would pack the Congress, and in the circumstances he decided he could do no good attending the session.[4]

The swing towards Gandhi began in the elections to the subjects committee on Sunday, 5 September. These were fought on the issue of non-cooperation and in every provincial bloc Gandhi's men were elected. In the Madras election for example Gandhi's supporters captured all the seats, defeating every one of the group led by Kasturi Ranga Iyengar as President of the Madras P.C.C., in spite of their careful organization. Nearly half the Madras members of the subjects committee were Muslims who were attending Congress to press the Khilafat question.[5] *The Bengalee* called the subjects committee 'a packed body' and complained 'that those who wished to be elected for the Subjects Committee had to declare themselves "ab-initio" as pledged to all that Mr. Gandhi has so far preached without the authority of the Congress.'[6]

Lala Lajpat Rai as President had formally opened Congress the previous day. Departing from the tradition of Congress Presidents, he deliberately refrained from expressing his own views on non-cooperation and said he felt it was his duty to act as impartial ring-master, since the country was so divided on the issue.[7] The struggle really began on 5 September in the subjects committee.

[1] 1 September 1920, Diary of G. S. Khaparde, Khaparde Papers.

[2] Dwarkadas, *Gandhiji Through My Diary Leaves. 1915–1948*, pp. 24–5.

[3] 3 September 1920, Diary of M. R. Jayakar, Jayakar Papers.

[4] Ronaldshay to E. S. Montagu, 1 September 1920, Mss. EUR. D. 523 (31).

[5] *The Times of India*, 6 September 1920. A train placarded as the Khilafat Special took 200 delegates from Madras to Calcutta; most of them were Muslims from Bangalore, Trichinopoly and places in North Arcot district. Fortnightly report from Madras for first half of September 1920, Home Pol., Deposit, September 1920, No. 70. (I owe this reference to K. McPherson.)

[6] *The Bengalee*, 7 September 1920.

[7] Lajpat Rai's Presidential Address to Calcutta Congress, 4 September 1920, Joshi (ed.), *Lala Lajpat Rai Writings And Speeches Volume Two 1920–1928*, pp. 22–66. For Lajpat Rai's personal views see above, pp. 221, 224.

Gandhi proposed his non-cooperation resolution with an expression of 'utter distrust of the bureaucracy' and a denunciation of the reforms as 'a dangerous trap which concealed gilded chains that enslaved the country.' His resolution advised a boycott of the elections to the reformed councils, boycott of foreign goods, refusal to serve in Mesopotamia or attend government functions, gradual boycott of government schools, colleges and courts, and surrender of titles and honorary offices. Various amendments were at once suggested, including one by C. Vijiaraghavachariar and Motilal Nehru who, with C. R. Das, wanted the demand for Swaraj to be incorporated into the resolution: to this Gandhi agreed. The inclusion of boycott of foreign goods was also a concession to the wishes of Gandhi's opponents. He himself supported swadeshi but opposed bare boycott on the grounds that it implied punishment of the opponent rather than the ideal of the satyagrahi, and was in this case impracticable unless the whole country resorted to it. Nevertheless he included it in his resolution, as he said later, because he could not reject it as a matter of conscience.[1] In spite of these concessions G. S. Khaparde reported that Gandhi was 'endeavouring to dominate the situation', claiming to be Congress's chief adviser yet refusing to be bound by the majority's wishes.[2]

The subjects committee continued to discuss non-cooperation for two more days. In the words of one eye-witness on 6 September Gandhi was 'unusually firm & obdurate', relying on the support of Muslims 'and other stalwarts who don't care for Congress or Swaraj and Gujerati rank & file, too faithful to be discriminating.'[3] Another contemporary confirmed this impression that by the time the subjects committee met, Gandhi, far from lamenting his weakness had realized his strength and was determined to hold out for his plan against any sort of compromise.

> it would not probably be much beyond the truth to state that the whole rank and file of the Congress now assembled, would go in for the non-

[1] Report of subjects committee meeting on 5 September 1920, *The Hindu*, 6 September 1920, *C.W.*, vol. 18, pp. 282–3; Gandhi's non-cooperation resolution, 5 September 1920, *Young India*, 15 September 1920, *ibid.* pp. 230–1; Gandhi *An Autobiography*, p. 416. For Gandhi's reasons for including the boycott of foreign goods in his resolution, and for his personal opposition to such boycott, see speech by Gandhi on the non-cooperation resolution in Congress, 8 September 1920, *Young India*, 15 September 1920, *C.W.*, vol. 18, pp. 248–9, and article in *Young India*, 25 August 1920, *ibid.* pp. 198–9.

[2] 5 September 1920, Diary of G. S. Khaparde, Khaparde Papers.

[3] 6 September 1920, Diary of M. R. Jayakar, Jayakar Papers. In the original diary Jayakar used the shortened form 'Mhdns' which normally means Mohammedans. In the typed transcripts of the diary, also in the N.A.I., this is transcribed as Madan Mohan Malaviya, which seems impossible in view of Malaviya's stated opposition to Gandhi's non-cooperation at the Special Congress (see *The Bombay Chronicle*, 15 September 1920). When quoting from his diary in his autobiography Jayakar reworded the phrase to read, 'leaders to whom loyalty to Gandhi and his Non-Co-operation appeared to be of more value than the unity of Congress.' Jayakar, *The Story Of My Life. Volume 1. 1873–1922*, p. 390.

co-operation programme of Mr. Gandhi... Under such circumstances it is doubtful if even Mr. Gandhi would be obeyed if he were to come to a compromise on the question of his non-co-operation programme. The continued sittings of the Subjects Committee are a sure index of the difficulty that is being felt by those who are pressing for the modification of the non-co-operation programme. This difficulty is undoubtedly being accentuated by the presence of the Khilafat party. This group is strong and numerous, both in the body of the Congress and in the Subjects Committee.[1]

On 7 September B. C. Pal proposed an amendment accepting the principle of non-cooperation, but recommending immediate adoption of the uncontroversial points of Gandhi's programme and consideration of the other parts. He suggested that there should be a committee to devise a non-cooperation programme suitable to the various provinces and a mission to England to demand complete Swaraj. Gandhi rejected this as a matter of conscience and practical expediency, but accommodated himself to his opponents by reaffirming that his resolution should include a demand for Swaraj. He had already agreed that withdrawal of students and lawyers should be gradual, as this was happening in practice.[2] After prolonged and heated discussions, during which Shaukat Ali apparently 'threatened to lay violent hands upon Jinnah for disagreeing with him and was only prevented from doing so by the physical intervention of other delegates',[3] the subjects committee voted on non-cooperation on 7 September. Gandhi's proposal was carried by a majority of twelve: 144 voted for it, 132 against, and a few remained neutral. Among Gandhi's supporters were Motilal Nehru, Saifuddin Kitchlew, Jitendralal Bannerjee, Shaukat Ali, Yakub Hasan and Dr Ansari; while his opponents included Pandit Malaviya, Annie Besant, M. A. Jinnah, H. Kunsru and Jamnadas Dwarkadas.[4]

The reassessments of position and realignments which must have taken place in the committee to produce this result are not known in detail; but G. S. Khaparde clearly felt that the conversion of Motilal Nehru into a Gandhian supporter on 7 September was a critical point in the process, for it was followed by 'Many minor defections' and he feared 'a deep laid plan behind it all.'[5] What transformed Motilal Nehru's pre-Calcutta opposition into support for Gandhi's non-cooperation is a matter of conjecture, but it seems likely that having weighed up Gandhi's manifest support both in committee and among the rank and file of delegates he

[1] *Herald*, 9 September 1920, Bengal E.N., No. 37 of 1920.

[2] 7 September 1920, Diary of M. R. Jayakar, Jayakar Papers; report of Gandhi's speech at subjects committee meeting on 7 September 1920, *The Hindu*, 8 September 1920, *C.W.*, vol. 18, pp. 233–5.

[3] Ronaldshay to E. S. Montagu, 22 September 1920, Mss. EUR. D. 523 (31).

[4] *The Times of India*, 9 September 1920.

[5] 7 September 1920, Diary of G. S. Khaparde, Khaparde Papers.

decided that cooperation with Gandhi was the wisest political tactic. If he flew in the face of popular opinion he risked not only his position in Congress and in the U.P. but also threatened to split Congress and so weaken its hand against the raj. He would also divide his family because Jawaharlal was a firm adherent of Gandhi's.

Fazlul Haq from Bengal was almost certainly converted to Gandhi's side by considerations of influence in local politics. In the subjects committee his suggestion of a *via media* had been howled down, but eventually he voted for Gandhi's resolution after a clash with Shaukat Ali, who carried considerable weight through the Khilafat network among the Muslim peasants of Bengal. In the words of the Bengal administration, 'He may have been helped to this decision by the overt threats of his former associates, that they would stump the country for the purpose of vilifying his reputation and ruining his professoinally [sic] and socially.'[1]

Although Gandhi won by only a small margin in the subjects committee, it was commonly assumed that he would have an overwhelming majority in open Congress.[2] The open session debated non-cooperation on 8 September and C. R. Das, M. A. Jinnah and B. C. Pal spoke against Gandhi's resolution, Pal moving his amendment which had been defeated in committee.[3] However the tide was flowing in Gandhi's favour. When Annie Besant got up to speak she was 'howled down',[4] and Congress carried Gandhi's resolution on 9 September. Reports of actual voting figures vary, but roughly half the registered delegates did not vote, and of those who did Gandhi's majority was about 1,000.[5]

Gandhi had brought off a considerable *coup d'etat*, contrary to the intentions of most established political leaders before the session began. To understand the crisis Gandhi created for their style of politics it is crucial to uncover the roots of his power. One reason for his majority in open Congress was clearly good tactics. Because of the strength of his supporters in the subjects committee only his resolution and B. C. Pal's amendment emerged from committee on the issue of non-cooperation to be voted on in

1 Fortnightly report from Bengal for first half of September 1920, Home Pol., Deposit, September 1920, No. 70.

2 *The Times of India*, 9 September 1920.

3 8 September 1920, Diary of M. R. Jayakar, Jayakar Papers; 8 September 1920, Diary of G. S. Khaparde, Khaparde Papers.

4 Ronaldshay to E. S. Montagu, 22 September 1920, Mss. EUR. D. 523 (31).

5 *The Bombay Chronicle*, 10 September 1920, reported that there were 5,814 registered delegates, of whom 2,773 took part in the voting. *The Bengalee*, 10 September 1920, reported 5,873 registered delegates of whom 2,735 took part in the voting. Lord Ronaldshay reported that Gandhi won by 1,826 votes to 884; Ronaldshay to E. S. Montagu, 22 September 1920, Mss. EUR. D. 523 (31). *The Bombay Chronicle*, 10 September 1920, reported 1,826 votes for Gandhi and 804 against, and *The Indian Social Reformer*, 12 September 1920, agreed with these figures, article inset in Mss. EUR. D. 523 (20). *Young India*, 15 September 1920, reported 1,855 for Gandhi and 873 against.

open Congress, thus leaving no way in which those who disapproved totally of non-cooperation could vote to register their opposition.[1] This would account for the abstention of nearly half the possible voters, if opponents of any form of non-cooperation felt unable to vote on two variants of it. The ballot provoked an outcry that such a massive abstention invalidated the vote, making it completely unrepresentative of provincial feeling.[2]

However, good management alone does not account for Gandhi's success. He clearly had substantial groups of supporters who rallied to him on voting day despite the opposition of the Presidency politicians to his programme. The identity of those who voted for Gandhi is hard to trace because the evidence is fragmentary and often coloured by recrimination. Allegations of packing were made, for example by the Governor of Bengal and by Kasturi Ranga Iyengar's paper, *The Hindu*:[3] but two of Gandhi's opponents who could have made capital out of such a charge – the 'Moderate' paper, *The Indian Social Reformer*, and N. C. Kelkar – discounted it.[4] What is certain is that both sides attempted to rally support in Calcutta.[5] At the time there were rumours that delegates' badges were being sold at Rs. 10 to any who applied;[6] and later it was alleged that Umar Sobhani and Shankarlal Banker gathered in from the Calcutta streets over 100 supporters of non-cooperation on ballot day.[7] Under the existing Congress constitution there was no limit to the number of delegates, and such last minute recruitment was a common phenomenon, adding particular importance to the siting of the session.

A large group of Gandhi's supporters seem to have been businessmen, particularly Marwari merchants, who formed a substantial community in Calcutta. *The Bengalee* reported that the way Bengal voted in Congress was 'determined by the votes of Marwari and Hindustani communities, who are here on purposes of business', and *The Bombay Chronicle* noted

[1] The Governor of Bengal noted that Calcutta's English papers were flooded with complaints on this score. Ronaldshay to E. S. Montagu, 22 September 1920, Mss. EUR. D. 523 (31).

[2] See for example *The Leader*, 12 September 1920, and *The Bengalee*, 10 September 1920.

[3] Ronaldshay to E. S. Montagu, 15 September 1920, Mss. EUR. D. 523 (31); *The Hindu's* allegations are noted in *The Indian Social Reformer*, 12 September 1920, inset in Mss. EUR. D. 523 (20).

[4] Article by N. C. Kelkar in *The Bombay Chronicle*, 21 September 1920; *The Indian Social Reformer*, 12 September 1920, inset in Mss. EUR. D. 523 (20).

[5] *The Times of India*, 9 September 1920.

[6] Ronaldshay to E. S. Montagu, 22 September 1920, Mss. EUR. D. 523 (31); *Raiyat*, 18 September 1920, Bengal N.N., No. 40 of 1920.

[7] Dwarkadas, *Gandhiji Through My Diary Leaves. 1915–1948*, p. 25. B. R. Ambedkar recorded that 'The late Mr. Tairsee once told me that a large majority of the delegates were no others than the taxi drivers of Calcutta who were paid to vote for the non-co-operation resolution.' Quoted in K. B. Sayeed, *Pakistan. The Formative Phase. 1857–1948* (2nd edition, London, 1968), p. 49.

that the Bombay vote in Gandhi's favour was swelled by 'some piece-goods merchants, whose faces are more familiar to those in Calcutta than those who have come from Bombay.' Later the Bengal administration agreed that the Marwaris had been among Gandhi's strongest supporters in the Calcutta Congress.[1]

This alliance between highly successful business communities and the ascetic Mahatma was a continuing phenomenon of Gandhi's political leadership. Visible in 1917 when the Bihari Marwaris welcomed Gandhi to Champaran, clear in Bombay in 1919 when the cloth merchants followed him in the Rowlatt satyagraha, in 1920 businessmen's support enabled Gandhi to further his plans for the transformation of Indian public life both with their votes in Congress and with cash donations.[2] But not all businessmen supported Gandhi. In the words of one,

> Personally I think Gandhi has made a great blunder by pressing his non-cooperation on the Congress with such a sharp difference of opinion even amongst the lawyers and politicians. The commercial community was, of course, in no way represented at the Congress and it is correct to say that they do not share the view that non-cooperation is feasible or even desirable.[3]

Despite this disclaimer, however, contemporary evidence makes it plain that a strong group of businessmen did contribute to Gandhi's success at Calcutta.

Another solid bloc of support for Gandhi were the Muslims who attended Congress to press the Khilafat cause and to ensure that the Hindu leaders did not slide out of a definite commitment to non-cooperation, as they had at Allahabad in June. Muslim strength in the subjects committee

1 *The Bengalee*, 10 September 1920; *The Bombay Chronicle*, 10 September 1920; Fortnightly report from Bengal for second half of November 1920, Home Pol., Deposit, January 1921, No. 33. In this report the Bengal administration suggested that the Marwaris supported non-cooperation in the hope that Muslims would in return stop killing cows. Religious orthodoxy was probably a powerful strand in their attraction to Gandhi. As the Governor of Bengal noted later, 'The Marwaris are great supporters of Gandhi and are consequently inclined to support his policy of non-cooperation. They are very orthodox and very emotional and easily carried away by a man like Gandhi who promises them the disappearance of Western civilization and a return to the golden days of Hindu supremacy in the land.' Ronaldshay to E. S. Montagu, 6 January 1921, Mss. EUR. D. 523 (32).

2 For example in June 1920 Bombay and Calcutta Marwaris subscribed Rs. 50,000 at a meeting in Bombay for five years of propaganda to spread Hindi in Madras Presidency. *Young India*, 16 June 1920, *C.W.*, vol. 17, pp. 490–1.

3 P. Thakurdas to 'Sir Henry', 14 September 1920, Nehru Memorial Museum and Library, Purshotamdas Thakurdas Papers, File No. 24, P3, 1920–2. Thakurdas was willing to complain to the government over war-time trading difficulties, but this unease did not push him into non-cooperation. See Letter of complaint about Excess Profits Tax Bill signed by Thakurdas and others to the Secretary, Govt. of India, Finance Dept., 4 February 1919, *The Bombay Chronicle*, 8 February 1919.

is clear from the evidence of the Madras election, from M. R. Jayakar's and *Herald's* comments on Muslim solidarity behind Gandhi, and from the string of prominent Khilafat leaders who voted for Gandhi's resolution on 7 September. In open Congress Muslim influence was equally apparent. *The Bombay Chronicle* noted in passing 'the Khilafat adorers of Mahatma Gandhi', and reported that of the 217 Bombay delegates who voted for Gandhi on 9 September 43 were Muslims led by M. M. Chotani who were simultaneously delegates to a Khilafat Conference.[1] The Governor of Madras thought 'that the Muslims were so strong at the Congress that they swamped the rest'.[2] His assessment was probably coloured by his Presidency's delegation to Calcutta but similar complaints came from other parts of India. A member of the C.P. P.C.C. printed an appeal to the nation to consider whether the Calcutta vote was representative of national opinion, and called on the Congress President to declare how many of the votes were cast by Muslims.[3]

In Bombay Joseph Baptista and G. S. Khaparde complained that Gandhi had used in Congress 'the Sword of Damocles wielded by the Khilafat Committee'. They were reported to be

> very bitter against Gandhi and *Khilafatists* in outmanoeuvering them and flooding the Congress and Subjects Committee with their adherents: all the more so as Gandhi adopted the very tactics which they themselves utilized to oust the Moderates from the Congress. Baptista has not minced matters; in an interview he gave a representative of the *Bombay Chronicle*, he practically accuses Gandhi of handing over the Congress, a Hindu preserve, to the Muhammadans, not hesitating to over-ride even the constitution of the Congress in his determination to play in the full Muhammadan hand.[4]

Although there is no official report of the Calcutta Congress or of the distribution of delegates by religion, these contemporary comments leave little doubt that Gandhi's Calcutta victory and claim to Congress leadership was partly the fruit of his alliance with those of the Muslim community who were interested in the Khilafat cause. Their emergence in Congress as a political force to be reckoned with was a new departure in the relationship of the Congress and the Muslim community.[5]

When Gandhi's support is analysed by region it is striking that several

[1] *The Bombay Chronicle*, 9 September 1920, 10 September 1920.

[2] Willingdon to E. S. Montagu, 15 September 1920, Mss. EUR. D. 523 (20).

[3] Printed appeal to nation by M. D. Lavangia, member of C.P. P.C.C., 27 September 1920, A.I.C.C. Files, 1920, No. 3, Part II.

[4] Fortnightly report from Bombay for first half of September 1920, Home Pol., Deposit, September 1920, No. 70.

[5] For early Muslim reluctance to take part in Congress politics see above, pp. 20, 29–30. After the Lucknow Pact the Muslim League and Congress met simultaneously and passed similar resolutions, but comparatively few Muslims were delegates to Congress. In 1919 only 314 Muslims were Congress delegates, 4.9% of the total. Gopal Krishna, 'The Development of the Indian National Congress as

areas which had previously been backward in nationalist politics and had exerted little influence in Congress deliberations contributed significantly to the triumph of his non-cooperation resolution, particularly U.P., Bihar and the Punjab.[1] These provinces had all come within Gandhi's orbit in the years 1919–20, though the Presidency politicians had barely touched them in the three previous decades since the foundation of Congress. The U.P. was the home of the most virulent Khilafat leaders and of the Nehrus, of whom the father and son were both converts to Gandhi's side by the end of the Calcutta session.[2] Bihar was the scene of Gandhi's first Indian satyagraha and its loyalty to his non-cooperation had been demonstrated at its provincial conference before the Special Congress met. The Punjab was the subject of Gandhi's satyagraha propaganda from mid-1920 and some contemporaries expected the province's delegates to vote for Gandhi's non-cooperation as a matter of course.[3] *The Bombay Chronicle*

Table 5

Voting by province on non-cooperation at the Calcutta Congress, 1920

Province	*Number of votes for Gandhi's resolution*	*Number of votes for B. C. Pal's amendment*
Bombay	243	93
Madras	161	135
Bengal	551	395
U.P.	259	28
Punjab	254	92
Andhra	59	12
Sind	36	16
Delhi	59	9
Bihar	184	28
Burma	14	4
C.P.	30	33
Berar	5	28
	1855	873

Source: Young India, 15 September 1920.

a Mass Organization, 1918–1923', *The Journal Of Asian Studies*, XXV, 3 (May 1966), 421.

1 See Table 5.

2 After Calcutta Motilal Nehru ran down his thriving legal practice and changed his family's style of life from costly western luxury to a simplicity more in keeping with the Mahatma. Motilal Nehru to Gandhi, 17 September 1920, S.N. No. 7255; B.R. Nanda, *The Nehrus: Motilal and Jawaharlal* (London, 1962), pp. 184–6.

3 *The Bengalee*, 12 August 1920, Bengal E.N., No. 33 of 1920: Surendranath Bannerjee's fears that Bengal would be 'swamped by delegates from the Punjab and other parts of India' was noted by Ronaldshay in a letter to E. S. Montagu, 1 September 1920, Mss. EUR. D. 523 (31).

referred to Gandhi's 'Gujerat and Punjab followers' at Calcutta;[1] and though Gujarat registered no separate vote at Congress, being part of the Bombay Presidency, as Gandhi's home region, committed to his non-cooperation before the Special Congress, it sent a strong contingent to swell support for him within the Bombay delegation. Among its representatives were some of the inmates of the Ahmedabad *ashram*, and 'a number of Guzrati ladies', including Anasuya Sarabhai, the millowner's sister who had cooperated with Gandhi in the Kaira, Ahmedabad and Rowlatt satyagrahas.[2] Several other 'backward' areas which had seen the Presidency politicians as an overt threat to their progress and independent expression also voted for Gandhi at Calcutta, though their actual numbers were small beside U.P., Punjab and Bihar. Chief among these were Sind and Andhra: the latter, with its own Telugu-speaking province, produced a far larger proportion of its total vote for Gandhi than did Tamil-speaking Madras.[3]

Whether Gandhi's adherents are analysed by region, religion or occupation, it is clear that many of them were new to institutional politics. Gandhi triumphed at Calcutta with his plans for abandoning the assumptions and conventions of the political elite by relying on support from outside their ranks. The existence of latent sources of political power was evident when Montagu and Chelmsford launched their reform proposals in India; but at Calcutta in 1920 for the first time a leader tapped some of those latent sources to gain power at the apex of institutional politics. Gandhi's ideology and political style, created in South Africa, his Indian satyagrahas and his championship of the Khilafat and Punjab causes had so positioned him that he could mobilize supporters from groups and areas with which the established politicians had little connection. Consequently his non-cooperation resolution precipitated a crisis for the politicians as they found the evidence they needed to decide the question they had left open in August – whether it was worth defending their vested interests in their customary way, or whether it would pay to take the political leap in the dark and become Gandhi's men.

1 *The Bombay Chronicle*, 9 September 1920.

2 *The Bombay Chronicle*, 10 September 1920. 682 delegates attended from Bombay of whom 322 voted. A few, including Jamnadas Dwarkadas, opposed any kind of non-cooperation. 93 voted for Pal's amendment, including Kelkar and the followers of Tilak, Vithalbhai Patel, Joseph Baptista, M. A. Jinnah and M. R. Jayakar.

3 For the fear of the established political elite displayed by Sind and Andhra during Montagu's visit and earlier see above, p. 34, 128. Sind and Andhra were given their own Congress provinces in 1917, Sitaramayya, *The History Of The Indian National Congress. Volume 1 (1885–1935)*, pp. 147–8. A discussion of the emergence of once backward regions into nationalist politics and the threat this produced to the Presidency leaders is in J. H. Broomfield, 'The Regional Elites: A Theory of Modern Indian History', *The Indian Economic And Social History Review*, III, 3 (September 1966), 279–91.

(III) NON-COOPERATION – CALCUTTA TO NAGPUR

Although the Calcutta vote was a signal success for Gandhi and non-cooperation the matter did not rest there. Almost at once there was public discussion whether a vote taken in such circumstances was binding on the defeated minority, and several prominent politicians, including Srinivasa Sastri and Lajpat Rai, urged that it was not.[1] Battle was joined again in the sub-committee of the A.I.C.C. which had been appointed on 9 September to draft instructions for non-cooperation. Its members were Gandhi, Motilal Nehru and Vithalbhai Patel, who as a Bombay delegate had voted against Gandhi at Calcutta. Gandhi took the Calcutta vote to mean adoption of all stages of his plan, including boycott of councils, schools, courts and the army, and the report of the sub-committee was geared to this. In what amounted to a dissenting minute Patel insisted that Congress had not accepted the whole plan. He advised only boycott of councils and foreign goods (which Gandhi noted as an unfortunate interpolation), and vigorously opposed immediate or total withdrawal from schools and courts.[2]

The A.I.C.C. met to discuss the report on 2 October, though only 35 out of the 177 members attended. At this meeting controversy continued over the sub-committee's report, centering on the boycott of schools and courts and the interpolation of the word 'gradual' in the Congress resolution. The main issue at the Congress meeting had been council boycott: but now the representatives of the western educated were engaged in conflict about the fundamentals of their existence as an elite in Indian society. In a sense the decision to boycott the councils had been a simple though painful one. It demanded the boycott of only one election, admitting the hope of council entry in the future, whereas the boycott of schools and courts, unless hedged around with the precautionary word 'gradual', cut at the roots of the elite's position in society. If council boycott was akin to surgery, school and court boycott was a continuing therapy – or, for those who did not share Gandhi's hopes for the future of India, a continuing strangulation of those who had taken the lead in modern political life rather than a single reluctant act of self-denial.

Motilal Nehru and Shaukat Ali were Gandhi's main supporters, opposed by Joseph Baptista and S. Satyamurti, while some of Gandhi's opponents, like Jinnah and Jamnadas Dwarkadas, were present but took

[1] Report of speech by V. S. S. Sastri, *The Indian Review*, September 1920, S.P., File containing extracts from *The Indian Review* 1915–1946, No. 44; Lala Lajpat Rai's views were given in *Bande Mataram*, 19 September 1920, Punjab Native Newspaper Report, cited in Argov, *Moderates And Extremists In the Indian Nationalist Movement 1883–1920*, p. 167.

[2] Typed report of draft instructions for non-cooperation much altered in Gandhi's writing, signed by Gandhi, Motilal Nehru and Vithalbhai Patel, 22 September 1920, accompanied by Patel's minute of dissent, S.N. No. 7266.

no part in the proceedings. Eventually the substance of Gandhi's report was adopted, though his criticisms of boycott of foreign goods as an unfortunate interpolation was expunged and instructions were issued that school and court boycott should be gradual. However, the A.I.C.C. statement to the press merely gave the instructions, not drawing attention to these differences, and consequently the result was popularly seen as another personal triumph for Gandhi.[1]

After this meeting Jamnadas Dwarkadas and Mavjee Govindjee Seth, both from Bombay, and others resigned from the A.I.C.C. as a protest against the adoption of non-cooperation. As Dwarkadas put it,

> believing, as I do, that the movement will either fizzle out and make the Congress ridiculous or that if it is prolonged for some time it will inevitably bring disaster to the country, I refuse to share any responsibility for it, directly or indirectly... I believe that want of discrimination and enthusiasm for a highly respected...and admittedly unique personality have led them [Congress delegates] into the acceptance of "non-co-operation" but I feel sure that its practice will prove to them the unwisdom of their step, and experience alone will bring about disillusionment which the words of old and trusted leaders have failed to achieve.[2]

Annie Besant did not resign from the A.I.C.C., though she announced that she would not attend any of its meetings until the Nagpur Congress.[3] In the intervening weeks she condemned non-cooperation as a 'channel of hatred' that menaced 'the very existence of India', and summoned all Theosophists to range themselves against the threat of anarchy on the side of ordered and progressive freedom.[4] She was not the only political leader to take a hard line. Srinivasa Sastri made an outspoken attack on non-cooperation and Gandhi as 'an impractical person having extremely fanciful notions of life';[5] while the veteran Sir D. E. Wacha inveighed against 'the pernicious doctrine of noncooperation'. As he wrote to the Madras politician, G. A. Natesan,

[1] Fortnightly report from Bombay for first half of October 1920, Home Pol., Deposit, December 1920, No. 59; Bombay Police Abstract, 1920, par. 1359 (41). For the instructions as eventually passed see Bamford, *Histories of the Non-Co-operation and Khilafat Movements*, pp. 220–2.

[2] J. Dwarkadas to Motilal Nehru, 5 October 1920, A.I.C.C. Files, 1920, No. 7. For other letters of resignation from the A.I.C.C. see Mavjee Govindjee Seth to General Secretary of A.I.C.C., 5 October 1920, A.I.C.C. Files, 1920, No. 3, Part II; undated letter with torn signature, probably Mr Pranjpe of Cawnpore, to President of A.I.C.C., A.I.C.C. Files, 1920, No. 7; undated letter from Hatti Sankar Ram, Anantpur Dist., to Secretary of A.I.C.C., A.I.C.C. Files, 1920, No. 15 Part I.

[3] Account of A.I.C.C. meeting at Calcutta, 9 September 1920, *The Bombay Chronicle*, 14 September 1920, *C.W.*, vol. 18, p. 257.

[4] *The Theosophist*, November 1920 and December 1920, *Annie Besant Builder Of New India* (Adyar, 1942), pp. 151–3, 153–4.

[5] Newspaper report of speech by V. S. S. Sastri on 2 October 1920 at Sivagunga, dated 6 October 1920, S.N. No. 9870.

> Pherozeshah [Mehta ?] & I never gave Ghandi credit for even an iota of political sagacity and political circumspection. The man is full of overweening conceit & personal ambition and the vast unthinking multitude, let alone the so called "leaders" of the hour, and the lip "patriots", seem to be quite mad... in following like a flock of sheep, this unsafe shepherd who is bringing the country on the very brink of chaos & anarchy. And your people were for a time so *enthused* & worshipped him as if he were a mortal god on earth. Time, time, time, will be the avenger of the wrongs this madman is now inflicting on the poor country in his mad & arrogant career.[1]

It was not surprising that such Liberal or 'Moderate' leaders opposed Gandhian non-cooperation and its directive to boycott the new councils. They had supported the Montagu–Chelmsford scheme of reform, despite its omissions, as the greatest prize yet of their limited political methods and here was Gandhi, an upstart leader, suggesting that they should abandon their election campaigns and make nonsense of all their work of past years. As one contemporary commented, 'To reduce politics to reductio ad absurdum a Gandhi was needed.'[2]

Opposition to council boycott was not, however, confined to 'Moderates'; it appeared wherever men calculated that they stood to profit from the opportunities provided by the reforms. In western India, for example, Tilak's ex-follower, G. S. Khaparde, who refused to stand down from the elections, groused privately about 'this wretched non-cooperation' and published a memorandum denouncing boycott as providing no training-ground for 'political-mindedness'.[3] Bombay leaders of a very different political tradition, such as Sir D. E. Wacha, Sir Narayan Chandarvarkar, Gokuldas Parekh and K. Natrajan, launched a counter-non-cooperation movement which included pamphlets on cooperation, and pre-election tours in the Deccan and Gujarat in the wake of Gandhi and Shaukat Ali to persuade voters that only cooperation with the government through the elections would win Swaraj.[4] In December the Bombay 'Moderates' joined leaders of a similar outlook in Madras under the banner of the National Liberal Federation to denounce non-cooperation on the grounds that it withdrew able men from the councils.[5] Madras Presidency showed

1 Sir D. E. Wacha to G. A. Natesan, 6 October 1920, G. A. Natesan Papers.

2 G. S. Bhate to M. R. Jayakar, 10 October 1920, Jayakar Papers, Chronological Correspondence File No. 11, No. 158. Jayakar described the baffled feelings of many of the old leaders at the overthrow of their old political methods implicit in non-cooperation in *The Story Of My Life. Volume 1. 1873–1922*, pp. 370–1.

3 3 October 1920, Diary of G. S. Khaparde, Khaparde Papers; Sitaramayya, *The History Of The Indian National Congress. Volume 1. (1885–1935)*, p. 205.

4 Report of meeting to launch counter-non-cooperation movement in Bombay, *The Times of India*, 11 October 1920; pamphlet on cooperation, *The Times of India*, 21 October 1920; account of pre-election tours, Fortnightly report from Bombay, 16–24 November 1920, Home Pol., Deposit, December 1920, No. 74.

5 *The Bombay Chronicle*, 30 December 1920; *The Times of India*, 30 December 1920.

particularly clearly how Gandhi's opponents came from all the political groups which hoped to profit from council entry. Annie Besant said that boycott would deprive India of her best councillors; the 'Nationalist' paper, *The Hindu*, opposed Gandhi on this issue; and the Justice Party disregarded the Congress fiat and organized for the polls.[1]

Like the Madras non-Brahmins there were some Muslim leaders who, despite the Khilafat movement, believed that council entry was the best political tactic for their community. Fazl-i-Husain in the Punjab took this line, as did Nawab Ali Chaudhuri in Bengal who argued

> that non-co-operation will not in any way help us in overcoming the present downtrodden condition to which the Mussalmans have fallen. On the other hand, if we can cautiously utilize the responsibilities to which we have been entrusted under the Reforms, I doubt not that we will be able to improve our condition by degrees and develop our various resources which will ultimately help in attaining our end in view.[2]

Political traditions and calculations in favour of council entry were not the only grounds of opposition to Gandhi and non-cooperation. Non-cooperation as envisaged would affect a far wider spectrum than those who stood in the November elections: it threatened the whole life style and security of the western educated and led to reservations about its wisdom even among Gandhi's political adherents. Chief among such reservations was the fear that non-cooperation would precipitate violence, as in 1919. Bombay Liberals used this argument; so did the National Liberal Federation.[3] Annie Besant echoed the Bengali 'Moderates' when she condemned non-cooperation as implying revolution; the Bengalis for their part harked back to their own passive resistance movement with its attendant violence and refused to play 'that game' again.[4] Others thought that Gandhi's Muslim alliance over the Khilafat was a specific threat to peace. Among them were Fazlul Haq and other Bengali Muslims who complained of Shaukat Ali's tactics and threats of violence towards his opponents, and communicated their fears to Bengali Hindus.[5] The Bihari, Hasan Imam, thought that the Alis' fanatical influence over the younger generation of Muslims should be curbed, and told Gandhi,

1 Report of Annie Besant's views in *The Times of India*, 5 November 1920; Irschick, *Politics And Social Conflict In South India*, pp. 182, 196–7.

2 *The Bengalee*, 31 October 1920, Bengal E.P., No. 43 of 1920. For Fazl-i-Husain's opposition to non-cooperation, see Husain, *Fazl-i-Husain. A Political Biography*, p. 106.

3 Report of meeting to launch counter-non-cooperation movement in Bombay, *The Times of India*, 11 October 1920; report of meeting of National Liberal Federation, *The Bombay Chronicle*, 30 December 1920.

4 *Bangali*, 11 September 1920, Bengal N.N., No. 38 of 1920; *New India*, 23 December 1920, *Annie Besant Builder Of New India*, pp. 112–13.

5 Mahadev Desai to S. Ali, 21 September 1920, quoting part of a letter Desai had received from Calcutta, Bombay Police Abstract, 1920, par. 1339.

> Your own programme has no element of violence in it but I cannot believe that your programme will be followed by the people. I have long seen the danger of violence coming as a sequence to Non-cooperation and in this I am confirmed by what has been admitted to me by some of your staunchest supporters in this movement. To mention only one name Shaukat Ali talks of violence and Afghan invasion quite freely.[1]

Hasan Imam reluctantly called himself an opponent of non-cooperation but some of Gandhi's closest Muslim friends were as dubious about his association with the Ali brothers. In the words of Abbas Tyabji, who had presided at the Gujarat conference which voted for non-cooperation before Calcutta, 'Whatever opinion you & the Khilafat Committee may have of the Ali Brothers many of us take them to be splendid *agitators* & very little more. They certainly are not the type of men in whom we would have much faith were they placed to rule over us.'[2]

Twin to the fear of violence was fear that successful non-cooperation would produce social chaos as people resigned government jobs, lawyers abandoned the courts and students left their desks. Srinivasa Sastri predicted two generations of chaos, while Jinnah maintained that Gandhi's appeal to 'the inexperienced youth and the ignorant and the illiterate' meant 'complete disorganization and chaos'.[3] Even Gandhi's supporters were uneasy on this point, and Mian Mohamed Chotani made a public appeal that political leaders should take constructive steps to deal with the results of non-cooperation. This followed his experience in the Khilafat Office which had been flooded with requests for financial aid from people who had resigned from their schools and their professions.[4] Gandhi, like Chotani, received numerous appeals for help from non-cooperators, one of whom asked whether he realized that non-cooperation might only produce chaos.[5]

Fears of violence and social dislocation were natural reactions from an educated elite whose members were bent on maintaining their position. Their apprehensions that Gandhi was hustling them further than they wished found another focus in their criticisms of his autocratic method. Such criticisms came to a head over his dealings with the Home Rule League, of which he had been President since April. The League had helped him informally in previous satyagrahas, but now as its President he

1 Hasan Imam to Gandhi, 12 December 1920, S.N. No. 7379. See also Hasan Imam to Sir E. Gait, 2 October 1920, enclosed in letter from Chelmsford to E. S. Montagu, 17 November 1920, Mss. EUR. E. 264 (6).

2 A. Tyabji to Gandhi, 8 October 1920, S.N. No. 7296.

3 Newspaper report of speech given by V. S. S. Sastri on 2 October 1920 at Sivagunga, dated 6 October 1920, S.N. No. 9870; M. A. Jinnah to Gandhi, undated, quoted in H. Bolitho, *Jinnah* (London, 1954), p. 84.

4 Appeal by M. M. Chotani, 17 December 1920, Jayakar Papers, Chronological Correspondence File No. 11, No. 197.

5 V. B. Alur to Gandhi, 5 October 1920, S.N. No. 7300.

was determined to make it a regular part of his satyagraha machinery. A general meeting of the League was held in Bombay on 3 October, but only 61 members attended out of a total of 600 in Bombay alone and about 6,000 throughout India. Nevertheless, the meeting went ahead and by 42 votes to 19 changed the League's name to Swarajya Sabha (Hindi for Home Rule League) and altered its constitution so that its aim became the securing of Swaraj by peaceful and effective action.

Jinnah argued that a majority of 23 in a meeting of 61 could not bind 6,000 members; and afterwards he resigned in company with eighteen others, including M. R. Jayakar and the Dwarkadas brothers, complaining that procedure had been irregular and that the new constitution omitted any reference to the British connection and envisaged unconstitutional activity.[1] Gandhi publicly refuted these criticisms,[2] but he could not silence opposition to his dictatorial methods. His friend, Abbas Tyabji, had to tell him another unpleasant truth: '...many of my friends consider yr [sic] action autocratic & point out the danger of placing the whole movement under an autocrat who holds himself above all rules of procedure! Excuse me for writing thus bluntly. It is only fair to yourself & myself that I should speak unreservedly & straight.'[3]

Although disquiet shading into overt opposition to Gandhi's plans was a continuing feature of the weeks between the Calcutta Congress and the regular session held at Nagpur in December, obdurate opponents were in a minority among the major political leaders. Most important groups of politicians were gravely embarrassed by the Congress decision, but Congress had for so long been a mouthpiece of the national movement that many of them felt that they could not oppose its resolutions without losing their influence in its deliberations and appearing retrograde and half-hearted in the struggle with the raj. G. S. Khaparde noted that many of his friends thought non-cooperation was 'foolish and suicidal and yet they do not like to dissent publicly from Gandhi's view & programme because Congress, they say, has adopted it.'[4] Such men realized that they must adjust to the new situation if they wished to retain political influence in Congress because the Calcutta vote had made it plain that Gandhi could outmanoeuvre and outvote them in Congress if they maintained consistent opposition to him. Consequently in the Presidencies the groups which had hitherto stood out as the most advanced or nationalist bowed to Gandhi, at least in the matter of council boycott.

1 Fortnightly report from Bombay for first half of October 1920, Home Pol., Deposit, December 1920, No. 59; mass letter of resignation from Swarajya Sabha, 27 October 1920, quoted in Jayakar, *The Story Of My Life. Volume 1. 1873–1922*, p. 405.

2 Gandhi to M. A. Jinnah, 25 October 1920, *The Bombay Chronicle*, 26 October 1920, and *The Times of India*, 27 October 1920.

3 A. Tyabji to Gandhi, 8 October 1920, S.N. No. 7296.

4 29 September 1920, Diary of G. S. Khaparde, Khaparde Papers.

In Madras Kasturi Ranga Iyengar and S. Satyamurti offered their resignations to the local P.C.C. on their return from Calcutta, but later withdrew them at the request of the P.C.C. and other politicians, including the Bengali, Motilal Ghose, who wished to keep his paper, *The Amrita Bazar Patrika*, in line with Iyengar's paper, *The Hindu*. Despite the verbal battle which *The Hindu* kept up against council boycott Iyengar and Satyamurti eventually withdrew from the election, leaving only Srinivasa Iyengar of their group to maintain adamant opposition and win a seat on the legislative council.[1] As *The Hindu* commented, 'Successful politics consists in judicious though not slavish subordination of the individual to the general will. Majorities are not always in the right; but it is politically convenient... to assume that they generally are.'[2] In Bengal *The Amrita Bazar Patrika* had already begun to veer towards council boycott,[3] and the main bloc of Bengali 'Extremists' led by C. R. Das and B. Chakravarti announced their decision to bow to the majority decision and withdraw from the elections.[4] In western India N. C. Kelkar led Tilak's former followers in a similar decision, trimming their sails to the Gandhian wind which blew from Calcutta.

> In this matter Mr. Gandhi has won and we have lost. We regret the decision as depriving the Nationalists, for at least three years more, of the use of an effective lever of constitutional agitation inside constituted official bodies; but we feel that, notwithstanding our regret, we must loyally abide by the decision of the Congress.[5]

In this group the most prominent deviant was G. S. Khaparde who insisted on standing for election despite a barrage of requests from his friends to stand down.[6]

At first sight the decision of the nationalist groups in the Presidencies to support Gandhi, at least in council boycott, appears curious. What better way could there be to safeguard their political position than to ignore the Congress fiat and, like Khaparde, prove Gandhi's plans ill-considered and unworkable by winning the elections? The reasoning behind the decision taken by Kelkar, Das, Kasturi Ranga Iyengar and their associates lay

1 Willingdon to E. S. Montagu, 15 September 1920, Mss. EUR. D. 523 (20); V. K. Narasimhan, *Kasturi Ranga Iyengar* (Delhi, 1963), pp. 190–3; Irschick, *Politics And Social Conflict In South India*, pp. 194–7.

2 Narasimhan, *op. cit.* p. 191.

3 *The Amrita Bazar Patrika*, 14 September 1920, Bengal E.N., No. 37 of 1920.

4 Manifesto published by Bengal Nationalists announcing their withdrawal from the elections though they still opposed the Calcutta non-cooperation resolution, *Servant*, 15 September 1920, *ibid.*

5 Article on non-cooperation by N. C. Kelkar, *The Bombay Chronicle*, 21 September 1920.

6 8, 20, 21 and 23 October 1920, Diary of G. S. Khaparde, Khaparde Papers. On 23 October, for example, Khaparde received a letter from Poona signed by about fifty people asking him to withdraw.

partly in their wish to remain in the van of Congress opinion; and after Calcutta it was plain that they could only do this by acceptance of Gandhi's plans. But the full force of the dilemma in which Gandhi placed them is comprehensible only from the spread of support for non-cooperation in the localities. If Gandhi was attracting wide support in 'old' areas with established political traditions and leaders as well as in areas 'new' to institutional politics, he could not only oust the Presidency leaders in Congress but also undermine them on their home ground, threatening them with defeat in the elections if they stood and the loss of local positions of leadership.

Most of the precise evidence for the extent of non-cooperation naturally concerns the elections, and other manifestations of non-cooperation are less well documented. The A.I.C.C.'s various registers of non-cooperators recorded that during 1920 44 lawyers suspended their practices, 46 Honorary Magistrates gave up their positions, 19 men gave up seats on local boards and committees, 14 members of municipalities gave up their seats, 61 holders of medals and titles returned them, about 120 holders of government and teaching posts resigned and 18 arbitration courts were set up.[1] However, these figures are sketchy and ill-authenticated, and as many of these forms of non-cooperation were accompanied by the saving word 'gradual' in the Congress plan they are not a precise index of support for non-cooperation in the country. Only the patchy evidence left by contemporary observers remains to fill in the picture: nevertheless it indicates that Gandhian non-cooperation was gaining support both in areas which were veterans and novices in Congress politics.

In Bengal, as in Madras, there seemed to be very little enthusiasm for non-cooperation.[2] Abul Kalam Azad engineered a student strike at the Calcutta Madrassa, but when the government closed the classes and asked parents what they wanted to do with their sons only three wrote to withdraw them and the majority of students returned immediately.[3] By early December parents were keeping their children in schools and colleges, and when Gandhi, A. K. Azad and the Alis toured the Presidency they raised little enthusiasm. It was even doubted whether the Marwaris contributed enough to cover the cost of the tour, badly hit as they were by the post-war readjustment of the coinage. Fazlul Haq dared to come out openly against boycott of the courts, compared with his submission to Gandhi and his allies at Calcutta. The Bengal government took this to mean that in Haq's 'view this line is now safe; non-co-operation in practice may be said to be dead in Bengal. Gandhi is regarded with veneration and any abuse of him

[1] Handwritten registers of non-cooperators, A.I.C.C. Files, 1920, No. 5.

[2] *Report on the Administration Of Bengal 1920–21* (Calcutta, 1922), p. iii; *Report on the Administration of the Madras Presidency for the year 1919–20* (Madras, 1921), p. ix.

[3] Ronaldshay to E. S. Montagu, 18 November 1920, Mss. EUR. D. 523 (31).

would not be allowed, but his non-co-operation programme is regarded almost with the tolerance extended to children's games.'[1]

However there is evidence that in the oldest Presidency non-cooperation was taking root among groups who had been untouched by *bhadralok* pioneers of nationalist politics, and were unlikely to produce statistics for non-cooperation in terms of withdrawal of lawyers, title-holders or council members. Among them were the poorer Hindus for whom *Nayak* spoke when it denounced *bhadralok* nationalism as 'a diplomatic manoeuvre to deceive the ruling class and to earn celebrity' by the 'Babus of Calcutta and the mofassil, including the Moderates and the Extremists, the democrats and the aristocrats.'[2] The same paper commented after Calcutta, 'Congress has at last become the property of businessmen, shopkeepers, agriculturalists and the people at large. It is they who constitute the present Congress and they are the guardians and protectors of non-co-operation, which will be spread and circulated by them.' It was no use, explained *Nayak*, to expect the *bhadralok*, 'the big Babus', to counteract non-cooperation: they could not converse with lesser folk who could not understand their English and anglicized Bengali even had they been willing to go into the villages to explain their politics.[3]

The Muslims of Bengal, similarly outside the political range of 'the big Babus', were also deeply stirred by Gandhian non-cooperation, because the Mahatma had Muslim preachers as an intermediary layer of mobilizers for his cause.[4] Such unsophisticated groups might have little understanding of the implications of non-cooperation;[5] but their mobilization for political action by Gandhi's men threatened the status and traditions of the *bhadralok* elite, and posed *bhadralok* politicians with the immediate possibility that if they stood for election they might see their constituents melting away into the villages rather than coming to the polls.

In Bombay Presidency the only recorded examples of non-cooperation after Calcutta were the withdrawal of thirty-seven out of 500 students at Gujarat College, Ahmedabad, and the boycott of courts by half a dozen pleaders – of these four never practised in the first place and two were elderly men merely anticipating their retirement by a short period.[6]

[1] Fortnightly report from Bengal for first half of December 1920, Home Pol., Deposit, February 1921, No. 35. For the post-war manipulation of the rupee and the loss to Indian merchants who ordered British goods at the old rate of exchange but had to pay for them at the new rate, see V. Chirol, *India Old And New* (London, 1921), pp. 263–7.

[2] *Nayak*, 9 March 1920, Bengal N.N., No. 12 of 1920.

[3] *Nayak*, 12 October 1920, Bengal N.N., No. 43 of 1920.

[4] *Ibid*; *Bangali*, 6 October 1920, Bengal N.N., No. 42 of 1920.

[5] 'Many of them do not understand what non-co-operation means...They know that Gandhi is a saint preaching this principle for India's welfare. That is enough for them.' *Bangali*, 6 October 1920, Bengal N.N., No. 42 of 1920.

[6] Sir G. Lloyd to E. S. Montagu, 22 October 1920, Mss. EUR. D. 523 (25);

Despite these minute figures there was a groundswell of support for non-cooperation apparent to observers, which indicated that Gandhi had reached both 'new' groups in parts of the Presidency where nationalist politics were of long standing and whole areas which were previously backward in such politics. The strength of support for Gandhi was determined by a combination of local influences – Gandhi's personal reputation, the power and caste structure of the area and the attitude of local leaders – which varied from place to place, sometimes providing Gandhi with a web of subcontractors, sometimes not. In certain places the support of merchant communities was clear: Shankarlal Banker reported this from Bombay, and the Ahmednagar District Magistrate noted 'a tendency among the wealthy Guzerathi and Marwadi merchants to indulge in' non-cooperation, 'Possibly...due to the fact that Gandhi is a Gujarati Bania – quite as much as to any real liking for the movement.'[1] At village level there was often a conflict of interests. In the Poona area, for example, the village leaders and officials, talatis, patels, shroffs and the like, were reported to be responding to non-cooperation and organizing their villages to stay away from the polls; while at the same time some Marathas were becoming convinced that non-cooperation was another Brahmin tactic to retain power, and were determined to resist attempts to hinder Maratha voters.[2]

However in Gujarat, that whole tract of the Presidency which had been notorious for its political lethargy, non-cooperation caught on and penetrated deeply into society, largely because Gandhi had local educated followers who tramped the countryside preaching his doctrines. Purshotamdas Thakurdas lamented to a Surat friend, 'It is a pity that meak [sic] Gujarat should be the first one to be in the throes of the movement.'[3] He received the reply:

> I am convinced that unless prominent leaders like your goodself and others address the masses & explain the real inwardness of Mr. Gandhi's movement, these unfortunate people will get more & more entangled in his dangerous doctrines...These people cannot think for themselves and unless you do their thinking and explain to them to what the movement is leading us...these people feel that the only man who feels for the masses is Mahatma Gandhi & he is the true Saviour of India. Thus they blindly follow him.[4]

The net result of the non-cooperation campaign in Bombay Presidency caused despondency among G. S. Khaparde's friends who in early Novem-

Fortnightly report from Bombay, 30 September to 7 October 1920, Home Pol., Deposit, December 1920, No. 84.

[1] S. Banker to Gandhi, 25 September 1920, S.N. No. 7275; Bombay Police Abstract, 1920, par. 1430 (26).

[2] Bombay Police Abstract, 1920, par. 1471 (15), 1491 (21).

[3] P. Thakurdas to C. Gandhi, 16 October 1920, Purshotamdas Thakurdas Papers, File No. 24, P2, 1920–22.

[4] C. Gandhi to P. Thakurdas, 20 October 1920, *ibid.*

ber 'sat talking about the folly of Bombay in not giving a hearing to Mrs. Besant.' In their view, 'The non-cooperators appear to have lost their head.'[1] Such support for Gandhi might produce few resignations of titles or offices, but it was a powerful deterrent to former 'Extremist' leaders who wished to stand for election and knew they would risk their constituents' abstention from the polls even if they were not howled down during their campaigns.

In other 'backward' areas besides Gujarat Gandhi and non-cooperation attracted wide support: the most striking examples were the Punjab and Hindi-speaking C.P.[2] In the latter, as in parts of Bombay, Gandhi's campaign drew in new participants in politics because he had a powerful group of intermediate followers who organized their area in support of him. Chief of these among the small group of western educated men was Ravi Shankar Shukla, a lawyer from Raipur who belonged to the locally powerful Kanya Kubja Brahmin caste. Gandhi's non-cooperation offered him a chance to make a name in politics and to exert the influence of the Hindi-speakers against the Marathi-speakers of C.P., whose longer political traditions and loyalty to Tilak made them suspicious of non-cooperation. When Shukla decided to withdraw from the elections he was followed by his political associates, E. Raghavendra Rao, a Naidu lawyer, Thakur Chedilal, a Rajput lawyer, and G. S. Gupta, a Bania pleader: their cumulative example converted older men like Pandit B. D. Shukul who did not want to face public scorn if they stood for election though their natural inclination was to continue in council politics.[3] By opting for council boycott the C.P. politicians resolved the ambiguity in their attitude to Gandhi before and during the Calcutta Congress. Another major subcontractor in Gandhi's service in Hindi-speaking C.P. was the Marwari merchant, Jamnalal Bajaj, who campaigned for Gandhi in the C.P. towns and particularly among the members of his own community.[4]

By the beginning of December Gandhi's subcontractors had done their work well, and Hindi C.P., once so politically backward, presented the spectacle of new groups entering nationalist politics for the first time, ousting any of the western educated who refused to follow Gandhi's plans.

1 5 November 1920, Diary of G. S. Khaparde, Khaparde Papers.

2 Although Gujarat, Punjab and Hindi-speaking C.P. were the most dramatic examples of 'new' areas participating in politics in non-cooperation there is evidence of similar mobilization in Bihar and in Assam. For Assam, see Printed report of 5th Session of Surma Valley Conference held at Sylhet on 19/20/21 September 1920, A.I.C.C. Files, 1920, No. 11, Part I; Fortnightly report from Assam for first half of October 1920, Home Pol., Deposit, December 1920, No. 59. For Bihar, see Fortnightly report from Bihar and Orissa for first half of December 1920, Home Pol., Deposit, February 1921, No. 35.

3 Baker, 'Politics In A Bilingual Province: The Central Provinces And Berar, India, 1919–1939', p. 53.

4 Circular by J. Bajaj to fellow Marwaris, *The Bombay Chronicle*, 6 October 1920, quoted in *ibid.* pp. 61–2.

> The class most affected is perhaps the Marwari traders and shopkeepers. A curious situation has arisen in regard to the political position of the pleaders. In many places they are opposed to the programme of non-co-operation, and in all have refused to resign practice, with the result that they are vilified by the non-co-operators and have lost much of their political power over the masses. The movement is led by irresponsible mob orators of no status, who collect crowds by the violence of their abuse of the Government in their speeches.[1]

However, the result of non-cooperation in C.P. in actual resignations was limited:[2] but as in Bombay this was not a true gauge of provincial feeling because it did not register the wide support of people whose jobs and status gave them no opportunity to participate in the initial stages of non-cooperation by resignations or withdrawals.

Punjab was an area as new to nationalist politics as Hindi C.P. Only three years before it had considered participation in such politics an aberration akin to heresy,[3] but now some of its major educational institutions, Khalsa College, Amritsar, Islamia College and Muslim High School, Lahore, were badly affected by non-cooperation, though the other parts of the programme received little attention.[4] Supporters of non-cooperation included members of the Punjab Muslim League and Hindus who felt they could not oppose Gandhi in view of the fact that non-cooperation was in part a protest on behalf of their province.[5] Gandhi's greatest success, however, was in converting the Sikh League to his cause in October 1920, which gave him access to a network of subcontractors in some parts of the province. The way for this had been prepared by a growing accumulation of Sikh grievances against the government, which ranged from a dislike of government control of the Khalsa College and of government-approved

[1] Fortnightly report from C.P. for first half of December 1920, Home Pol., Deposit, February 1921, No. 35. This was in marked contrast to the Marathi-speaking districts of C.P., where Gandhi's programme was received coolly, and what support there was was engineered by Wamanrao Joshi who declared himself a disciple of Gandhi and an opponent of Tilak's methods. See 30 September 1920, 15 November 1920, Diary of G. S. Khaparde, Khaparde Papers; *Report on the Administration of the Central Provinces And Berar for the year 1920–21* (Nagpur, 1922), p. xviii.

[2] There were few resignations of posts or titles or withdrawals from legal practice, and though there was a wave of unrest in colleges and schools few students left. *Report on the Administration of the Central Provinces & Berar for the year 1919–20* (Nagpur, 1921), p. xv.

[3] See above, p. 20.

[4] *Report on the Administration of the Punjab and its Dependencies for 1920–21* (Lahore, 1922), p. 3.

[5] Govandhardas of Lahore was one who felt he could not stand for council election in these circumstances. 22 September 1920, Diary of G. S. Khaparde, Khaparde Papers. The Punjab Muslim League adopted the principle of non-cooperation on 5 October 1920 although it did not endorse the Congress programme. Husain, *Fazl-i-Husain. A Political Biography*, p. 106.

managers of the Golden Temple at Amritsar, to a belief that under the Montagu–Chelmsford Reforms Sikhs were not getting the representation their importance and war-time services warranted. Gandhi and the Ali brothers addressed the October meeting of the League with Punjabi politicians, and in many of the speeches 'made by persons such as Dr. Kitchlew and Mr. Ram Bhaj Dutt, subtly flattering references were made to the Sikhs as men of action and to the results that might be expected to accrue if they resolved to lend their support to non-co-operation.'[1] This meeting was followed by violent gatherings in favour of non-cooperation, particularly in Jullundur and Hoshiarpur districts where there were many Sikhs who had returned from abroad. Such was the intensity of feeling which non-cooperation aroused that the government applied the Seditious Meetings Act to the districts of Lahore, Amritsar, Sheikhupura and Jullundur, and to the towns of Lahore and Amritsar.[2]

Patchy as the evidence is of the regional reception of non-cooperation after Calcutta, it shows that however small the number of withdrawals from schools and courts, and resignations of titles and posts, non-cooperation found favour among aspirants to politics and among many who were unlikely to have the opportunity to become statistics in a non-cooperation register. Such people were new to politics and came both from politically backward provinces and from regions and groups within the Presidencies which had previously provided few members of the political elite. Their presence in politics during and after the Calcutta Congress forced the 'Extremists' among the established political leaders to look to their own positions, and helped to persuade them that it was politically suicidal not to be Gandhi's men at least on the immediate issue of council boycott.

In contrast to this patchy regional picture, there is more evidence about the November elections, as this was the form of non-cooperation which immediately concerned the government, and for which precise and reliable statistics could be gathered. The elections passed off peacefully and successfully, according to the government, since in only six cases out of 637 was an election impossible because there was no candidate, while throughout India only fourteen successful candidates were officially considered 'unsuitable' – like the tailor and small shopkeeper reported from C.P.[3] However the polls varied wildly in strength. Variations clearly reflected in many places the strength or weakness of local non-cooperators, although the fact that this was the first election under the reformed franchise

[1] Letter on Sikh unrest in the Punjab from C. M. King, Officiating Chief Secretary to the Punjab Govt., to Secretary to Govt. of India, Home Dept., 26 March 1921, Mss. EUR. E. 264 (39).

[2] *Report on the Administration of the Punjab and its Dependencies for 1920–21*, p. 3.

[3] House of Commons Paper, No. 202 of 1921, *Statement exhibiting the Moral and Material Progress and Condition of India during the year 1920. Fifty-sixth number* (London, 1921), pp. 65–6; file containing provincial reports on suitability of candidates elected in 1920, Home Pol., A, January 1921, Nos. 61–9 & K.-W.

meant that there was no standard against which the 1920 polls could be measured.

Of the provinces Madras had the highest poll – over 50% in Chingleput, Bellary and Madras city itself, where the efforts of parading bands of students with non-cooperation posters had little effect. In the southern districts heavy floods made voting difficult. Feeling about the Khilafat seriously reduced the Muslim poll – to 8.4% in urban areas and 14.0% in the countryside: but among Hindus only one or two coastal Telugu districts were affected by non-cooperation.[1] The key to the strength of the Madras poll was the organization of the Justice Party which stoutly resisted council boycott and carried sixty-three out of the ninety-eight elected seats to the legislative council.[2]

By contrast elections threatened to be difficult right from the start in C.P., where non-cooperation surprised officials of the raj by its widespread hold.[3] Eventually seven constituencies had no candidates, and thirty-three out of fifty-two constituencies had no contested election. Where contests occurred diverse sorts of pressures, including intimidation, were put on voters and candidates, and the poll was in the region of 22%, with little variation between town and country, Hindu and Muslim.[4] In Bombay Presidency the poll was higher, averaging nearly 31.5% in Hindu constituencies though it dropped to 8% in Bombay city and 4.4% among urban Muslims.[5] However in Sholapur city it was known that the local non-cooperators pocketed their principles at the last moment and rallied their partisans to vote against the cooperating candidate.[6]

To the north in the Punjab the towns were very badly hit by non-cooperation – only 8.5% of urban voters, both Hindu and Muslim, went to the polls. The rural poll was heavier – 38% among the Hindus and 44% among the Muslims, while 26% of Sikh voters turned out. There were some cases of intimidation, reported as particularly serious in Lahore, where the poll dropped to 5%.[7] From Delhi came a detailed description of the kind of intimidation non-cooperators could produce.

1 *Report on the Administration of the Madras Presidency for the year 1919–20*, p. x; Viceroy (Home Dept.) to Secretary of State, telegram, 5 December 1920, Home Pol., Deposit, January 1921, No. 33; *Return Showing the Results of Elections In India* (London, 1921), Cmd. 1261, p. 1. (Percentage polls given from this source for the provinces are for elections to the local legislative councils.)

2 Irschick, *Politics And Social Conflict In South India*, p. 178.

3 Willingdon to E. S. Montagu, 3 November 1920, Mss. EUR. F. 93 (4).

4 *Report on the Administration of the Central Provinces And Berar for the year 1920–21*, pp. vi–vii; *Return Showing the Results of Elections In India*, p. 2.

5 *Return Showing the Results of Elections In India*, p. 1; Viceroy (Home Dept.) to Secretary of State, telegram, 5 December 1920, Home Pol., Deposit, January 1921, No. 33. The rural Muslim vote in Bombay Presidency reached the surprisingly high level of 59.9%.

6 *The Times of India*, 1 December 1920.

7 Memorandum enclosed in letter from Sir E. Maclagan to Reading, 4 January 1922,

on the 5th, the day before the election to the council, Shankar Lal demanded a rigid social boycott of candidates and voters. Asaf Ali declared that such people were on the side of the devil and must expect to suffer the natural consequences. On the 6th all the polling stations were picketted by volunteers on horse and foot with numerous flags who did everything except use physical force to discourage intending voters. In the evening at a public meeting Arif Hasuri called for the social boycott of Mr. Nur Ahmad one of the candidates who was described as a national enemy and Asaf Ali demanded the professional boycott of Mr. Raj Narain a lawyer who had stood for election. Mr. Nur Ahmad was later unable to perform the marriage ceremony of his child until he had apologised to Hakim Ajmal Khan.[1]

In Assam the voting pattern was diametrically opposite to that in the Punjab: Assam's urban vote was nearly 50%, compared with a rural vote of 24.7% for Hindus and 19.2% for Muslims.[2] This reflected the jungly nature of the Assam countryside rather than any strong tendencies among rural folk to support council boycott. Further south in Bengal the Governor was surprised at the strength of non-cooperation in his Presidency, as displayed by the number of candidates who withdrew from the elections after the Calcutta Congress. At election time the Hindu vote was fairly high – 40% in the towns and only slightly less in the countryside. However, the Bengali Muslim vote was only 16.1% in the towns and 26.6% in the rural areas – a reflection both of Muslim backwardness in modern styles of politics and of the success among them of Gandhi's subcontractors.[3] The attraction of non-cooperation for rural voters, whose interests the *bhadralok* had barely considered in previous elections on a smaller franchise, was lessened by the desire of such new participants in politics to defend themselves through the councils against their landlords. In February 1920 two Calcutta papers, *Viswamitra* and *Nayak*, reported and encouraged anti-zamindar organization among the raiyats in anticipation of the elections; and though some of the old landlord families retained their influence in the November elections ten of the successful Muslim candidates for rural constituencies represented 'the agricultural interest'.[4]

Landlord–tenant relations also complicated the elections in Bihar and

I.O.L., Reading Papers, Mss. EUR. E. 238 (24); Viceroy (Home Dept.) to Secretary of State, telegram, 5 December 1920, Home Pol., Deposit, January 1921, No. 33; Chirol, *India Old And New*, pp. 208–9. Chirol attributed the comparatively high Muslim rural vote to the remaining influence of old conservative families.

1 C.I.D. note on political agitation in Delhi, with special reference to Volunteers, Home Pol., Deposit, April 1921, No. 67.

2 *Return Showing the Results of Elections In India*, p. 2.

3 Ronaldshay to E. S. Montagu, 22 September 1920, Mss. EUR. D. 523 (31); *Return Showing the Results of Elections In India*, p. 1.

4 *Viswamitra*, 18 February 1920, *Nayak*, 17 February 1920, Bengal N.N., No. 9 of 1920; Broomfield, *Elite Conflict in a Plural Society*, p. 176.

U.P., adding a distorting factor to the straight issue of council boycott and partially compromising the politicians' allegiance to the Congress decision. U.P. landlords had bestirred themselves early in the year, fearing that the politicians might oust them from what they considered their rightful predominance in the provincial legislative council. In return some of the local politicians began a judicious cultivation of peasant loyalty, throwing their weight behind the current peasant agitation in the province, the Kisan Sabha movement, with an eye to the forthcoming elections.[1] How completely the politicians dropped this tactic when they accepted council boycott, or how far they merely left intermediary leaders to continue the anti-landlord campaign while they stood aside, or indeed how far they were able to control such a peasant movement, is not clear. The provincial poll averaged 33%, the highest figure being 64%: but overall the Muslim vote was lighter than the Hindu vote, and the urban vote was significantly lighter than the rural vote.[2] Gandhi was in Allahabad and Partabgarh at election time and his presence made the vote drop there: in the village of Soraon, in a district where Gandhi had spoken the day before the election, there were no voters at all. However, in Jhansi town in spite of Gandhi the local non-cooperators sacrificed their principles and voted in an unsuccessful attempt to defeat Y. Chintamini, Secretary of the National Liberal Federation.[3] U.P. landlords got their council majority as a result of these elections, but the local administration commented that 'elections in some Oudh districts prove clearly that where candidates take up the cause of the tenants they can beat all but the very most powerful landlords opposed to them.'[4] It was apparent that the reforms were rousing the quiescent to political awareness and organization, though ironically because of council boycott Gandhi was not able to exploit their potential in November 1920.

In neighbouring Bihar, Home Rulers had in 1919 listened to peasant complaints against their landlords and had attempted to interest them in Kisan Sabhas like those in the U.P.[5] The local anti-landlord leader was a Swami Bidyanand, who seemed to have modelled himself on Gandhi and was stirring up peasants with a view to the forthcoming elections, particu-

[1] Fortnightly report from U.P., 3 January 1920, Home Pol., Deposit, January 1920, No. 45; Fortnightly report from U.P., 16 February 1920, Home Pol., Deposit, July 1920, No. 88.

[2] *Report on the Administration of the United Provinces of Agra and Oudh 1919–1920*, p. xxv; *Return Showing the Results of Elections In India*, p. 1. The Muslim urban vote was 9%, compared with a Hindu urban vote of 14%: the Muslim rural vote was 28%, compared with a Hindu rural vote of 35%.

[3] Fortnightly report from U.P., 17 December 1920, Home Pol., Deposit, February 1921, No. 35; Chirol, *India Old And New*, pp. 201–2.

[4] Fortnightly report from U.P., 17 December 1920, Home Pol., Deposit, February 1921, No. 35.

[5] Fortnightly report from Bihar and Orissa for second half of August 1919, Home Pol., Deposit, October 1919, No. 44; Fortnightly report from Bihar and Orissa, 18 October 1919, Home Pol., Deposit, November 1919, No. 14.

larly in the districts of Darbhanga and Bhagalpur. The Bihar administration thought he was allied to the local politicians, but it is impossible to discover how close this alliance was, or what happened to it when Biharis adopted council boycott. During the elections Bidyanand was alleged to have used Gandhi's name to attract votes for Kisan Sabha candidates, but Gandhi publicly disclaimed any connection with or approval of the Swami. However, in the four contests where raiyat candidates participated they won, with particularly sweeping victories in North Darbhanga and North Bhagalpur under the Swami's leadership.[1]

Despite the way the issue of landlord–tenant relations compromised the allegiance of some parts of Bihar to Gandhi's programme, the election returns bore the marks of non-cooperation and the Khilafat agitation. As in the U.P. the towns were affected more than the countryside and the Muslims more than the Hindus. 27.3% of the Hindu electorate and 12.1% of the Muslim electorate went to the polls in the towns: the Hindu rural poll was 41.8% compared with 28.2% for the Muslims. In Tirhut, the Division including Champaran, only 13% of the electorate voted, compared with a far higher poll in Orissa and Chota Nagpur, where Gandhi and non-cooperation were little known.[2]

During the weeks between the Calcutta and Nagpur Congresses the officials of the raj as well as the politicians laid their political bets on the basis of what they could see of non-cooperation. In spite of pressure from some papers in Britain and from some of its own officials,[3] the Government of India maintained its policy of inaction. It reiterated this publicly on 6 November and appealed to all citizens to work against attempts to stir up the young and ignorant.[4] As Chelmsford had explained, the government still believed that people at large would not adopt non-cooperation, and that it therefore stood to lose more than it would gain by stamping on Gandhi.

> we have yet to see this victory in the Congress translated into practice...I cannot myself see that we are a penny the worse for all the talking and the

1 Fortnightly report from Bihar and Orissa for second half of October 1919, Home Pol., Deposit, November 1919, No. 16; Fortnightly report from Bihar and Orissa for second half of December 1919, Home Pol., Deposit, January 1920, No. 45; Fortnightly report from Bihar and Orissa, 4 March 1920, Home Pol., Deposit, July 1920, No. 89; Fortnightly report from Bihar and Orissa, 29 December 1920, Home Pol., Deposit, February 1921, No. 35; *Report on the Administration of Bihar And Orissa 1920–1921* (Patna, 1922), p. ii.

2 *Report Showing the Results of Elections In India*, p. 2; *Bihar And Orissa in 1921* (Patna, 1922), p. 14.

3 *The Daily Telegraph* demanded 'more rigorous measures of repression', for example, quoted in *The Statesman*, 31 December 1920. Sir Reginald Craddock, Lt.-Governor of Burma, was among the officials who advocated a stronger line. Low, *J.A.S.*, xxv, 2 (1966), 244.

4 Resolution of Govt. of India, Home Dept., 6 November 1920, Proceeding No. 274 of Home Pol., A, November 1920, Nos. 273–4.

> voting on this question of non-co-operation. It is true that people take a gloomy view of the situation, but I cannot get myself to a state of mind in which I can conceive that non-co-operation is a practical policy. On the other hand, there is no doubt that the policy of Gandhi & Co. is consolidating the moderate party, the leaders of which have come out quite rapidly and denounced it. As it seems to me, we have to sit still and take care that we do not make any mistake through which we shall drive the moderates away from us and into the arms of the extremists.[1]

The Home Member had weighed up the risk of violence if the government acted against the risk of general subversion if it did nothing, and had concluded that if it had been a question of prosecuting a man like Shaukat Ali he would not have hesitated, 'but Gandhi is now, to many Hindus and Muhammadans, a semi-divine person' and one against whom they should not act 'except in the direst extremity.' His view was reinforced by the legal opinion that even if Gandhi were prosecuted the sentence would not be severe.[2]

Moreover as elections approached the government had another incentive to hold back – the old theory of conciliating the 'Moderates', now re-christened as saving the reforms. Montagu and Chelmsford were convinced that the only stable foundation for British rule in India was a working alliance between the raj and a substantial proportion of Indian public men on the lines laid down in their reform scheme, and understandably after three years of negotiation and committee work they were determined to save their brain-child from Gandhi's attack. By a policy of tactful restraint they hoped to salvage a remnant of collaboration from public men who disliked non-cooperation and would be prepared to work the reforms.[3]

(IV) THE NAGPUR CONGRESS

After a spasm of exertion at election time Indian politicians subsided into comparative inactivity: as Sir George Lloyd reported early in December, 'The situation politically may be described as stagnant; all are waiting for Nagpur, where I am afraid Gandhi will win simply because he will pack the Congress and the Moderates are too idle to do the same.'[4] However, it was no foregone conclusion that the policies adopted at Calcutta would be confirmed at Nagpur, even though council boycott, which had raised the fiercest opposition to Gandhi, was a dead issue once the elections were over.

From the politicians' point of view the choices open to them were be-

[1] Chelmsford to E. S. Montagu, 6 October 1920, Mss. EUR. E. 264 (6).

[2] Note by Sir W. H. Vincent, 19 October 1920, and opinion of the Advocate-General, Bombay, 19 November 1920, Home Pol., A, December 1920, Nos. 210–16 & K.-W.

[3] E. S. Montagu to Chelmsford, 7 October 1920, Mss. EUR. E. 264 (6); Chelmsford to E. S. Montagu, 19 October 1920, Mss. EUR. D. 523 (11).

[4] Sir G. Lloyd to E. S. Montagu, Mss. EUR. D. 523 (25).

coming increasingly difficult. In a sense it had been comparatively easy for them to abstain from the elections. Gandhi's following posed problems for them if they attempted to campaign, and they knew that whatever happened in 1920 the councils would be waiting for them when the next elections came round. But at Nagpur the issue before them was the rest of Gandhi's non-cooperation plan, including the boycott of government jobs, courts and educational institutions. This, if given immediate effect, would cut at the roots of their position and power in the subcontinent. Consequently although a majority of politicians had acquiesced in the Calcutta decision and given council boycott considerable success during the elections, they arrived at Nagpur armed with powerful arguments of self-interest in opposition to the next stages of non-cooperation.

C. R. Das voiced their arguments when he visited Nagpur during the first three days of December to unfold to local leaders a plan which, according to him, had the approval of Lajpat Rai, Pandit Malaviya and B. C. Pal. Although they agreed that non-cooperation was the only weapon left in a constitutional struggle for Swaraj, they criticized some of the details of Gandhi's plan as purely negative, particularly the proposal to boycott schools and courts. They acknowledged that the educational system needed a radical overhaul 'to foster the sense of nationality and patriotism', but until adequate alternative facilities were available they opposed the wholesale withdrawal of students. With a similar ambivalence they denounced the existing administration of justice as 'injurious both morally and economically', but argued, 'we recognise that the Law Courts cannot be completely boycotted at present and therefore the lawyers as a body cannot reasonably be called upon to withdraw from practice until the full programme is put into force.'

By hedging around the critical parts of non-cooperation with such provisos Das and his allies demonstrated their concern for their vested interests as members of India's western educated, professional elite. However, the reverse side of their plan was the proposal to carry political organization to the masses, indicating that they realized that a new era had dawned in Indian politics. Both the rules and the participants in the political game had been changed by the coincidence of the Montagu–Chelmsford Reforms introducing an extended franchise and the emergence of Gandhi, a new leader bent on reaching supporters outside the existing political nation. Das's plan suggested the reorganization of Congress to represent all classes of people, particularly the newly enfranchised, by means of a network of district organizations, and proposed a national fund and a controlling action committee which would ensure that Congress was an efficient, active body as well as an association for deliberation.[1] Clearly Das

[1] B. S. Moonje to V. J. Patel, 5 December 1920, enclosing C. R. Das's statement, undated but discussed at Nagpur from 1 to 3 December, A.I.C.C. Files, 1920, No. 2.

and his friends had realized that the days were over when elitist politics were viable. If the western educated hoped to retain power they must adopt the techniques of Gandhi: they must go out at least to the new voters if not to the real 'masses', the illiterate and poor in town and village, and capture their loyalty, they must create a political organization which they could hold with deep-rooted support and use to enact their policies throughout the subcontinent.

The fate of non-cooperation, however, lay in the hands of the 14,582 delegates assembled at Nagpur – the largest number ever to attend a Congress session and twice the number present at Amritsar in 1919.[1] The temper of the session was determined partly by the decision of some total opponents of non-cooperation to stay away. Some attended the conference of the National Liberal Federation in Madras, a small and rather depressing gathering according to Srinivasa Sastri, where Annie Besant moved a resolution explaining the Federation's 'emphatic disapproval' of non-cooperation.[2] Others, like S. B. Dhumal from Nasik, went to Nagpur but left when the elections to the subjects committee made it plain that men of their views would not get a hearing.[3]

The Governor of Bombay had feared that Gandhi would pack the Nagpur Congress. What constitutes packing in such circumstances is debatable, but there clearly occurred a considerable amount of careful organization and manoeuvring as before any session, and this was not confined to Gandhi's henchmen. In Bengal, for example, by early December there were two distinct camps, each trying to outmanoeuvre the other. Gandhi's men, organized by Jitendralal Bannerjee in league with the Central Khilafat Committee, tried to whip up 'whole-hogger' delegates in support of Gandhi, while the Bengal Khilafat Committee sanctioned Rs. 10,000 for their expenses at Nagpur as well as Rs. 6,000 for a special Congress train to take them there. On the other side C. R. Das, B. C. Pal and B. Chakravarti made strenuous efforts to rally Bengali delegates of their viewpoint, while Das approached Pandit Malaviya, M. A. Jinnah and Jamnadas Dwarkadas so that they could take similar steps. It was estimated that Das paid Rs. 36,000 out of his own pocket to pay for 250 delegates from Bengal and Assam.[4]

In Bombay Presidency similar preparations were made, though here Gandhi's men seem to have taken the initiative. From Sind two Pirs, Ghulam Mujadid and Mahbub Shah, announced their intention of attend-

[1] Krishna, *J.A.S.*, xxv, 3 (1966), 418.

[2] *The Times of India*, 1 January 1921; 29 December 1920, Diary of V. S. S. Sastri, S.I.S., Madras.

[3] Bombay Police Abstract, 1921, par. 37 (15).

[4] Fortnightly report from Bengal for first half of December 1920, Home Pol., Deposit, February 1921, No. 35; Fortnightly report from Bengal for second half of December 1920, Home Pol., Deposit, February 1921, No. 77; Sitaramayya, *The History Of The Indian National Congress. Volume 1. (1885–1935)*, p. 206.

ing Congress, the latter apparently having received a letter from Gandhi pressing him to go to Nagpur. From Gujarat Ahmedabad alone sent 250 delegates. Further south Nasik nominated twenty-eight delegates and Yeola seventeen, prompting the police comment that there had been a great effort to fill Congress with 'inarticulate' delegates who would vote for Gandhi but had no interest in politics and merely wanted a holiday and an entertaining show. Of those who went from Nasik some were merely servants of delegates but counted as further delegates, while others had been subject to pressure to attend because they had business connections in Nagpur.[1]

C.P. as host area to Congress was predictably the scene of much organization. Since the Calcutta vote C.P. had changed its allegiance so completely to Gandhi that early in November G. S. Khaparde lamented that people 'were out of hand & can think of nothing but non-cooperation.'[2] Meanwhile Gandhi ensured that this local feeling would bear fruit for him at Nagpur. He directed Jamnalal Bajaj to accept the chair of the Congress reception committee;[3] and planned a tour of C.P. and Berar in December, the object of which was 'said to be to secure local support for the non-cooperation movement at the forthcoming Congress, so as to avoid if possible the expense of bringing a large number of delegates from other parts of India.'[4] After the tour he was reported to have had spectacular success in the one area from which a majority of delegates had opposed his non-cooperation at Calcutta.

> To-day there is none so moderate as to urge the mere acceptance of responsible government in this province. Mr. Gandhi has been devoting special attention to bring [sic] the erring sheep into the fold of non-co-operation, and it is said that he has succeeded beyond even his own expectations in converting the Central Provinces to not merely the principle and policy of non-co-operation, but into aggressive "whole-hoggers".[5]

Details of pre-Congress manoeuvres in other provinces are not so obvious, but organization by Gandhi and his subcontractors in western India was critical for his success at the Nagpur session, because 79.04% of the delegates came from C.P., Berar and Bombay.[6] The evidence, though patchy, makes it clear that areas previously backward in the politics of nationalism, particularly C.P. and Gujarat, contributed a large proportion of the western Indian delegates, and, as at Calcutta, they were joined by other groups who before 1920 had sent few delegates to Congress. For

1 Bombay Police Abstract, 1921, par. 9 (47), (48), 37 (15), 63 (7).

2 9 November 1920, Diary of G. S. Khaparde, Khaparde Papers. For C.P.'s vote at Calcutta, see above, p. 270.

3 Gandhi to J. Bajaj, 27 September 1920, *C.W.*, vol. 18, p. 296.

4 Fortnightly report for C.P. for second half of November 1920, Home Pol., Deposit, January 1921, No. 33.

5 *The Times of India*, 27 December 1920.

6 Krishna, *J.A.S.*, XXV, 3 (1966), 418.

example, the Bombay police noticed the large number of Marwari delegates who were attracted to Nagpur both by Gandhi's personality and the hope of expressing their anger against the government for the post-war readjustment of the exchange rate of the rupee. They also reported the view of Abdul Ghani, a member of the Central Khilafat Committee, who insisted that without the Muslim support of the Central Khilafat Committee Gandhi might well 'have been thrown over' at Nagpur. *The Bengalee* confirmed this impression with its insinuations that Gandhi's supporters from Bengal were not Bengalis at all but Marwaris and Muslims.[1]

Contemporary observers were struck by the fact that many of the delegates could by no stretch of the imagination be called members of the western educated elite, who had previously controlled politics and formed the small group of the politically aware. The Secretary to the Government of India's Home Department, for one, was convinced that a new era was dawning in political leadership and participation.

> As regards the class of persons attending, whilst many of the prominent politicians were present, the Bengal contingent included hundreds of ex-detenus and the intelligentsia, which dominated earlier Congresses, seems to have been swamped in a mass of semi-educated persons swept up from all parts of India...it would be wrong to overlook the fact which this Congress clearly brings out, namely, that the extremists have at their disposal many thousands of men who are available for propaganda amongst the masses of the most unscrupulous, reckless, and dangerous character.[2]

Against this background Congress met from 26 to 31 December. In the elections to the subjects committee, held on the first day, Gandhi's supporters made a clean sweep or gained a large majority in every provincial bloc except Bengal. In the Bengal camp two attempts to hold an election proved abortive: negotiations degenerated into a free fight between Jitendralal Bannerjee's men and the followers of C. R. Das, after which their camp was left strewn with benches used in the fracas.[3] Gandhi addressed the warring factions and implored his supporters not to be violent and even to allow the election of Das's men if Das would declare that the election had been fair. Eventually the dispute was decided in favour of Das's faction.[4]

[1] Bombay Police Abstract, 1921, par. 223, 399 (50); *The Bengalee*, 30 December 1920, Bengal E.P., No. 1 of 1921. 7.2% of the delegates to Nagpur were Muslims; Krishna, *J.A.S.*, xxv, 3 (1966), p. 421.

[2] Note by S. P. O'Donnell, 14 January 1921, Home Pol., Deposit, January 1921 No. 3 & K.-W.

[3] *The Times of India*, 28 December 1920. The Bengal government commented that these 'violent scenes may be ascribed largely to the fact that C. R. Das's supporters included some 300 *ex*-detenus and *ex*-convicts of the Dacca Anushilan Samiti under the leadership of Srish Chandra Chatterji.' Fortnightly report from Bengal for first half of January 1921, Home Pol., Deposit, April 1921, No. 41.

[4] Speech by Gandhi to Bengal delegates, 26 December 1920, *The Amrita Bazar Patrika*, 30 December 1920, *C.W.*, vol. 19, pp. 158–9; *The Times of India*, 29 December 1920.

C. Vijiaraghavachariar from Madras opened Congress with his presidential speech on 26 December. According to press reports he described the principle of non-cooperation as 'sacred', but sharply criticized the boycott of government schools when there were not enough national ones to replace them and the boycott of the very courts which upheld freedom through the rule of law. Such plans, he thought, were 'an unintentional and even unconscious proposal to rebarbarise the people of India, by no means a very auspicious preparation to establish and maintain the democratic form of responsible government which we all have so dear at heart.' However, the version he communicated to the press was not what he actually said in Congress, and it appears that as a result of Gandhi's insistence he watered down some of his criticisms on the day.[1] This was a striking tribute to Gandhi's power in Congress. As *The Bombay Chronicle* commented, 'There is no manner of doubt about it that this is a Gandhi Congress': there might be varying shades of opposition to the Mahatma but the general opinion among delegates was that Gandhi would have his way.[2]

A swing to Gandhi among the major leaders became clear on 27 December when N. C. Kelkar, spokesman of the Maharashtrian 'Nationalists', accepted Gandhi's programme, after he agreed to include in it a request to merchants to withdraw gradually from foreign trade. It was also rumoured that C. R. Das had asked for time to consider a compromise with Gandhi.[3] The topic under discussion in the subjects committee on 27 December was the Congress creed. Jinnah, Das, B. C. Pal and Pandit Malaviya led the party in favour of retaining in the creed mention of a connection with Britain, while in extreme opposition to them the Ali brothers tried to push through proposals for 'complete independence' and a 'republic'. Differences were so sharp that the discussion continued until late in the evening, but eventually a compromise formula was agreed which represented a triumph for Gandhi over both wings of the opposition to him. The suggested creed read, 'The object of the Indian National Congress is the attainment of Swarajya by the people of India by all legitimate and peaceful means.'[4]

1 Report of Vijiaraghavachariar's speech, *The Times of India*, 27 December 1920; Sir Frank Sly, Chief Commissioner of C.P., to Chelmsford, 1 January 1921, Mss. EUR. E. 264 (26).

2 *The Bombay Chronicle*, 27 December 1920.

3 *The Times of India*, 28 December 1920.

4 Fortnightly report from C.P. for second half of December 1920, Home Pol., Deposit, February 1921, No. 77; *The Bombay Chronicle*, 29 December 1920. Although the clearest opposition to Gandhi at Nagpur came from those who felt that non-cooperation was going too far, there is some evidence that Gandhi also had to fend off those who wished to resort to violence. It was reported that in secret meetings at Nagpur Gandhi opposed violence as suggested by Hasrat Mohani and Swami Shraddhanand. Viceroy (Home Dept.) to Secretary of State, telegram, 15 January 1921, Home Pol., Deposit, February 1921, No. 77.

The following day, 28 December, the creed was discussed in open Congress. Gandhi proposed the new formula, supported by Lajpat Rai and B. C. Pal. This chameleon change by the Punjabi and Bengali leaders surprised G. S. Khaparde completely.[1] Before Congress Lajpat Rai had supported C. R. Das's plan for opposition to Gandhi and had maintained this stand in the subjects committee: now he was openly supporting Gandhi beside one of Das's foremost henchmen from Bengal. Judging from later events at Nagpur, Pal's alliance with Gandhi was an indication of the political calculations the Bengalis were being forced to make. It was later said that Lajpat Rai was forced into this position by the Punjabi delegates who urged him to support Gandhi or imperil his position of provincial leadership.[2] Whether this happened or not his speech made it plain that he found Gandhi's compromise formula acceptable: to him it meant that India would stay in the British Empire provided she could do so on her own terms and not 'at the dictation of anybody or by fear.'[3] When Gandhi spoke on the new creed he affirmed that he did not wish to end India's connection with Britain if that connection could help India's development, and that he would only reject it if it was 'inconsistent with our national self-respect'. Jinnah was Gandhi's main opponent on this issue and insisted that the new creed implied a bid for complete independence, whatever Gandhi said to the contrary.[4] However the audience made it plain that they disliked Jinnah's attitude, and two days later the delegates voted almost solidly in favour of the new creed.[5]

On 29 December rumours were current that Gandhi and C. R. Das were about to reach a compromise on the critical question of the non-cooperation programme.[6] The subjects committee meeting which began that day continued until 1 o'clock the next morning before a compromise agreement could be reached: and such was the excitement generated by these discussions that delegates started arriving at 2.0 a.m. on 30 December in order to get a vantage point for the open session that day.[7] When the session opened

1 28 December 1920, Diary of G. S. Khaparde, Khaparde Papers.

2 Obituary for Lajpat Rai, *Statesman*, 18 November 1928, cited in Argov, *Moderates And Extremists In The Indian Nationalist Movement 1883–1920*, p. 167. I have found no contemporary evidence of Punjabi delegates forcing Lajpat Rai's hand. M. R. Jayakar later commented that Rai was prompted 'by the fruitlessness of continued opposition.' Jayakar, *The Story Of My Life. Volume 1. 1873–1922*, p. 376.

3 Speech by Lajpat Rai seconding resolution on change in Congress creed at Nagpur Joshi (ed.), *Lala Lajpat Rai Writings And Speeches Volume Two 1920–1928*, pp. 72–9.

4 For the speeches made by Gandhi and Jinnah on the creed see *Report of The Thirty-Fifth Session of The Indian National Congress held at Nagpur, on the 26th, 28th, 30th and 31st December, 1920* (Nagpur, 1925), pp. 47, 56.

5 28 December 1920, Diary of G. S. Khaparde, Khaparde Papers; *Young India*, 5 January 1921, *C.W.*, vol. 19, p. 198.

6 *The Bombay Chronicle*, 30 December 1920.

7 *The Bombay Chronicle*, 1 January 1921.

the alliance later known as the Das–Gandhi pact was clear for all to see, when Das moved the resolution reaffirming the Calcutta non-cooperation resolution. It was seconded by Gandhi and supported by B. C. Pal, Lajpat Rai, Kasturi Ranga Iyengar, Jitendralal Bannerjee, Saifuddin Kitchlew, Hakim Ajmal Khan and Mahomed Ali among others – a motley crew of Gandhi's Hindu supporters, the Khilafat leaders and Gandhi's former Hindu opponents.[1]

The resolution differed from the resolution Gandhi had drafted earlier by spelling out the precise steps towards boycott of schools and courts to be taken by the public. Whereas Gandhi's draft had specifically proposed the removal of the word 'gradual' in relation to court and school boycott, on which much of the discussion had focussed since Calcutta, the resolution as accepted bypassed the controversial word. But in effect it went some way to safeguarding the interests of the western educated by stressing the importance of providing alternative national institutions, by calling on parents to make the decision about withdrawal of children under sixteen and on students over sixteen to withdraw only if prompted by their consciences, and by calling on lawyers only 'to make greater efforts to suspend their practice'. The Congress resolution also added to Gandhi's draft proposals for non-cooperation the call for an organization down to village level, for a band of national workers and for a Tilak Memorial Swaraj Fund to finance the new workers and organization. These additions echoed Das's plan to go out to the newly enfranchised as well as Gandhi's long-held conviction that politics must be the concern of those outside the circle of the western educated if true Swaraj was to be attained.[2]

Despite the hours of debate in the subjects committee, Gandhi made no concessions of principle or major modifications in the practice of non-cooperation to win over Das, Pal, Lajpat Rai and Kasturi Ranga Iyengar. Nevertheless Lajpat Rai supported the resolution, declaring that it was more comprehensive and practical than the Calcutta resolution, while Kasturi Ranga Iyengar said that Madras Nationalists now supported non-cooperation as it had been given a workable plan, particularly in its emphasis on national education.[3] Evidently there were sufficient safeguards in the plan to soothe the fears of the timid: but contemporaries thought that it was consideration of tactics rather than the content of the resolution which prompted a leader of C. R. Das's stature to ally with Gandhi. The Governor of Bengal reported to the Viceroy:

1 *Report of 35th I.N.C.*, pp. 70–85.

2 Gandhi's draft resolution for private circulation, undated, *C.W.*, vol. 19, pp. 182–5; Congress resolution on non-cooperation as passed on 30 December 1920, *ibid.* pp. 576–8. Both resolutions envisaged a gradual boycott of foreign goods and called for the encouragement of hand-spinning and hand-weaving.

3 Lajpat Rai's speech in Congress supporting the non-cooperation resolution, Joshi (ed.), *op. cit.* pp. 67–71; Narasimhan, *Kasturi Ranga Iyengar*, p. 194.

It has been suggested to me...that the *volte face* of Mr. C. R. Das who went to the Congress at Nagpur with the intention of opposing the application of the non-co-operation programme to students and lawyers, but who came away from it an ardent convert to Mr. Gandhi's views is to be explained on the grounds that Gandhi himself was able to persuade Das that he had now practically won the battle and that he (Das) had better throw in his lot with him while there was yet time.[1]

M. R. Jayakar later drew a similar conclusion, though he put it in gentler terms. According to him Das disliked Gandhi's doctrines but recognized the danger if Gandhi acquired 'unhampered hold' over the youth of Bengal. Assessing the situation at the end of 1920, 'He soon saw that it was a glorious opportunity to lead and direct the young men of his Province in seeming accord with the new doctrine, but with freedom later to modify it to suit his conception of a popular movement.'[2]

In the face of this potent and unexpected alliance many of Gandhi's prominent opponents like Khaparde and B. S. Moonje sat silent. Only Pandit Malaviya, unable to attend because he was ill, protested by sending a message, which was read out in Congress, opposing both the new creed and the non-cooperation resolution. At the end of the debate the delegates voted by province, and all provincial blocs approved of the non-cooperation resolution unanimously, the exceptions being Sind and U.P., each of which had one dissenting voice.[3]

On the final day of the Congress session delegates approved a new constitution for Congress, which had been prepared by a committee appointed on 2 January 1920 by the A.I.C.C.[4] This constitution, so calmly accepted by way of postscript after the heated discussions on the creed and non-cooperation, was a landmark in the direction, composition and structure of institutional politics. Unmistakably it bore the marks of Gandhi's hand. His influence would have been clear even without the complaint of A. Rangaswami Iyengar that it was not a proper report of the committee's ideas, but merely a bundle of draft alterations to the existing constitution which amounted to Gandhi's minority view.[5]

[1] Ronaldshay to Chelmsford, 25 January 1921, Mss. EUR. E. 264 (26).

[2] Jayakar, *op. cit.* p. 374. Das's biographer says that Das and Gandhi promised each other 'freedom of propaganda in his own sphere' and that this was the basis of their pact. P. C. Ray, *Life And Times Of C. R. Das* (London, 1927), p. 159.

[3] *Report of 35th I.N.C.*, p. 83; Jayaker, *op. cit.* p. 421.

[4] Congress constitution adopted at Nagpur, *C.W.*, vol. 19, pp. 190–8. Information about the appointment of the committee is in a letter drafted by Gandhi from the committee to the A.I.C.C., 25 September 1920, *C.W.*, vol. 18, pp. 288–90. The members of the committee according to Gandhi were N. C. Kelkar and I. B. Sen. Gandhi, *An Autobiography*, p. 407.

[5] Undated minute of dissent appended by A. Rangaswami Iyengar to report on revision of Congress constitution, Annie Besant Papers. Iyengar said that the committee had never met. Gandhi said the committee consulted by correspondence and produced a unanimous report. Gandhi, *An Autobiography*, p. 407.

As a preliminary the Nagpur Congress decided to abandon the British Committee of Congress in London and its paper, *India*.[1] This cleared the ground for the new constitution by marking the end of a style of politics wholly dependent on petition and by declaring publicly that henceforth Indian leaders would rely more on their own actions within India than on the response of the imperial authorities to their petitions and complaints. It was a development akin to the change in Gandhi's own political style when he abandoned conventional political methods for satyagraha. Although this decision was in line with Gandhi's personal attitude,[2] it also reflected the fears of many politicians while the reforms were under discussion that the British Committee was too moderate to be anything but a drag on their activities. It also voiced the disillusion some of them felt about the value of foreign propaganda as a tactic for remedying Indian grievances. As Motilal Nehru wrote early in 1920, even a deputation to England of Gandhi, Malaviya and Das multiplied four times over would only be 'as so many drops in the ocean'. 'Our destiny lies in our own hands and we must work it out in our own country. If we can only quicken our own nation to life the rest will follow as surely as day follows night.'[3]

Motilal Nehru, like C. R. Das before Nagpur, realized that successful political activity in the future would mean mobilizing and controlling a wider range of Indians than before. This was the object of the machinery constructed by the new Congress constitution. It set up a working committee of fifteen to be a permanent Congress executive, in contrast to the loose and ineffective A.I.C.C. of earlier years, which had had a membership of nearly 200.[4] By enlarging the A.I.C.C. to at least 350 members and relegating it to a secondary place beneath a small group of men who could act as the Congress spearhead, the Congress turned itself into an active organization, instead of a shambling federation of local groups who met annually for discussion. The creation of the working committee repeated what Gandhi had done in the Gujarat Political Conference and the Khilafat movement: it bore the stamp of his leadership which placed a premium on single-minded action and a central control which verged on dictatorship.

The second major innovation in the new constitution was the creation of a mechanism to broaden the base of Congress support – the reorganization

1 29 December 1920, Diary of G. S. Khaparde, Khaparde Papers.

2 For Gandhi's attitude to petitions to England in relation to the Punjab and Khilafat issues see above, pp. 244–5.

3 Motilal Nehru to Girdhari Lal, 11 March 1920, Motilal Nehru Papers, File No. G-8. For expressions of disquiet about the moderation of the British Committee of Congress over the reforms, see Weekly report of D.C.I., 7 December 1918, Proceeding No. 93 of Home Pol., B, January 1919, Nos. 93–5; unsigned report entitled 'How We Get On II', enclosed in letter of Tilak from England, 20 March 1919, Khaparde Papers.

4 In 1918 the A.I.C.C. had 181 members. Krishna, *J.A.S.*, xxv, 3 (1966), 415. Krishna's article is an important examination of the changes which occurred in Congress partly as a result of the changes in the constitution.

of Congress circles on the basis of language areas, and the extension of Congress organization to subdivisional and taluka level. Congress had taken tentative steps towards the linguistic redistribution of its circles in 1917 when it had become obvious that it risked the hostility of 'backward' areas like Sind and Andhra if it did not recognize them in its structure. Gandhi had also asserted that the acceptance of linguistic areas as natural units of political activity was one of his major concerns.[1] It was in his interests to press this principle, because when Congress adopted it it opened its doors to areas which had previously wielded little influence in Congress as they were overpowered by the strength of the Presidencies but which were the precise areas from which his main support came.

Gandhi also insisted, despite the opinions of the other members of the drafting committee, that the number of delegates should be fixed in proportion to the population of each province.[2] This was a further safeguard against swamping of sessions by one area, as in former years when the Presidency men dominated Congress: it meant that in the future control of Congress would go either to a continental alliance of regional leaders or to a politician who could muster an all-India following. The extension of Congress organization down to district level brought nationalist politics within the range of literate peasants, small town traders and lawyers in all parts of India. For the first time power in Congress through voting rights came within the reach of men whose outlook and interests differed from those of the men who composed and controlled Congress in its first forty years: and these new Congressmen were precisely the people who had responded to Gandhi in person in Bihar and Gujarat, and to his network of subcontractors in other parts of the subcontinent.

Gandhi's plans for the reorganization of Congress were accepted partly because of his support among the Congress rank and file at Nagpur, and partly because they crystallized and enacted the growing conviction of some other leaders that they must abandon the politics of limitation. For men like C. R. Das a broadly based and well-organized Congress was a way of reaching the newly enfranchised under the Montagu–Chelmsford Reforms, and of establishing links of influence and patronage between the political leaders and groups who had previously been outside the ranks of those whom the educated could mobilize with their limited goals and techniques, but who now were involved in the political process and could not be ignored by men who aspired to political leadership. This may well

[1] For Congress recognition of the principle of linguistic circles as the highest level of its local organization in 1917, see Sitaramayya, *op. cit.* p. 148. Gandhi's encouragement of the distribution of provinces on a linguistic basis was one of the major interests he emphasized when he accepted the Presidency of the Home Rule League. See above, p. 248.

[2] Gandhi to N. C. Kelkar, 2 July 1920, *C.W.*, vol. 18, p. 3; letter drafted by Gandhi from Congress drafting committee to Chairman of A.I.C.C., 25 September 1920, *ibid.* p. 289.

have been a further incentive for Das, Lajpat Rai and Kasturi Ranga Iyengar to throw in their lot with Gandhi at Nagpur, in the belief that it was best to be on the same side as India's most successful political mobilizer.

However, the immediate effects of the reorganization of Congress promised to be the strengthening of Gandhi's personal position in Congress by giving acknowledged places to the people on whom he already relied for his power. Not surprisingly contemporaries saw the Nagpur session as a massive personal triumph for the man who five years before had returned from South Africa as a peripheral contender in the arena of Indian politics. In the words of C.P.'s Chief Commissioner,

> The outstanding feature of the Congress has been the personal domination of Gandhi over all political leaders and followers alike. He has carried through the policy that he had decided for this Congress without any material modification. All opposition to his views has been overcome without difficulty, owing to his strong hold over the bulk of delegates and visitors, with whom his word is law.[1]

August to December 1920 deserve to be called months of crisis for the established political leadership. They witnessed the triumph of a new leader at the Calcutta and Nagpur sessions of Congress, and with him the adoption of political aims and techniques which threatened not only the political style and power of the established politicians but also the position in public life of the western educated whose spokesmen the politicians were.

Dramatic assertions of leadership in Congress were not unknown before 1920. They had occurred, as at Surat in 1907, when a group of leaders manoeuvred the session to a place conveniently loyal to them and by assembling large numbers of local delegates outnumbered their opponents, who retired temporarily defeated to lick their wounds before returning to the fray in succeeding sessions. The Calcutta and Nagpur Congresses were significantly different. The Calcutta session was held in the heart of enemy territory as far as Gandhi was concerned, and Nagpur was a place where even two months earlier Gandhi's opponents were expected to exert strong influence.[2] Moreover Gandhi's opponents in Congress, once defeated, did not depart to nurse their grievances in anticipation of further battle. At Calcutta it is true that most of them acquiesced only in the decision to boycott the new councils, but at Nagpur, apart from a tiny minority, they actually ranged themselves with Gandhi halfway through the session and contributed to his success.

Nevertheless if 1920 was unlike 1907 in these respects, nor was it the occasion of a great conversion of the politicians to Gandhian ideals and

1 Sir F. Sly to Chelmsford, 1 January 1921, Mss. EUR. E. 264 (26).
2 Chelmsford to E. S. Montagu, 27 October 1920, Mss. EUR. E. 264 (6).

methods; many of them continued to have doubts about Gandhi's wisdom while some later abandoned non-cooperation. To understand what prompted the politicians in 1920 and to see the significance of the alliances which emerged at Calcutta and Nagpur it is necessary to look at the structure of nationalist politics. When the negotiations and votes in Congress are placed in this wider context it becomes plain that they were a defensive reaction by men faced with an acute threat to their public position.

The crisis which Gandhi's assertion of leadership precipitated in the politicians' world was both an internal and an external one. Their politics were organized through local and personal groupings which formed shifting local and continental alliances among themselves as they jockeyed for position in provincial and all-India politics. There were no political parties on western lines with firm discipline, funds, recruiting mechanisms or agreed ideologies to unite politicians within or across regions. Consequently in any crisis of policy or vacuum of leadership the political structure tended to disintegrate temporarily until a powerful leader or group emerged to provide an attractive band-waggon. This was precisely the position in late 1920. Government policy on the Punjab and the Khilafat issues had shown up the poverty of the politicians' accustomed tactics and consequently the more 'extreme' groups in each area could not contest the elections without appearing to go back on their stand on these two issues and possibly obscuring the differences between them and their local rivals who had taken a safer line and were organizing for council entry. Moreover Tilak's death on 1 August removed the one leader who might have rallied the politicians and formulated a policy for them.

The result was total disarray among the politicians who opposed Gandhi. G. S. Khaparde made this clear when he noted how C. R. Das's non-cooperation plan was received at Nagpur early in December. 'In my opinion it does not go far enough...Kelkar appears undecided and others uncertain. Jamnalal objects to the manifesto & our Nagpur friends do not know what to do, though Dr. Moonje appears to entertain views similar to mine.'[1] Gandhi alone offered a clear, active policy and no other leader or combination of leaders appeared strong enough to challenge him: divisions and lack of organization among the politicians played into his hands. As M. R. Jayakar remembered,

> In each Province, there were...one or two leading men who would have liked to oppose the advance of the new ideas, but they were all isolated. One group did not know what was passing in the mind of a similar group in another Province. Gandhi was becoming popular too rapidly to allow these groups to meet together and consider a common course of action.[2]

Jayakar's reminiscences hint that the crisis produced by Gandhi's claim

[1] 2 December 1920, Diary of G. S. Khaparde, Khaparde Papers.

[2] Jayakar, *op. cit.* p. 375.

to leadership had its source outside the existing political nation, though it was made worse by the disintegration and aimlessness of that nation at the point when Gandhi made his claim: the Mahatma 'was becoming popular too rapidly'. Earlier politicians had succeeded because their aims and influence were so limited. Their loose political structure had been adequate because the numbers involved were so small and the participants so similar in background and aspirations.[1] However Gandhi challenged all the assumptions of this style of politics and broke his way into its closed shop by relying on supporters from groups and areas which had had virtually no voice in institutional politics before 1920. The details of voting at Calcutta and Nagpur demonstrate this: his strength was based on areas which were backward by the canons of Presidency politics, not only whole provinces like Bihar, U.P. and C.P., but also areas within the Presidencies like Gujarat. His followers were, with local variations, Muslims, merchants, and prosperous cultivators, English-speakers who had had little say in Congress because their areas were politically backward, and vernacular literates whose political potential the Congress leaders had only begun to grasp when the reforms were mooted.

The influence of such supporters lay not solely in the number of votes they provided for Gandhi in Congress. As stones thrown into water spread ripples in expanding circles, so the influence of these new forces behind Gandhi spread far wider than the point of their initial impact at Calcutta and Nagpur. They threw out of balance the established political structure not only by threatening to outvote existing leaders in Congress but also by presenting them with a drastic limitation of their room to manoeuvre, to make alliances and rouse support, and by so doing threatened their local and all-India positions. In each of the Presidencies the new forces impinged on a fragmented political world. The Presidencies were houses divided against themselves and when a storm blew up outside their walls they fell – to Gandhi.

In Bengal there were three major political groups – Gandhi's men under Jitendralal Bannerjee, who had influence if not control over the Muslim peasantry via the Khilafat organization and a certain following among the younger *bhadralok* and less prosperous Hindus, C. R. Das's men, and Surendranath Bannerjee's followers, who had opted to work the reforms. Das realized that Gandhi could defeat him in open Congress and could probably undermine him in Bengal: but alliance with Surendranath was impossibly retrograde and consequently the only hope for the future seemed to be alliance with Gandhi.

In Bombay Presidency former followers of Tilak found Gandhi challenging their local position of political dominance by pitting against Poona Brahmins the strength of mercantile groups in Bombay city and the mofussil, and the weight of newly active Gujarat. Simultaneously he was

[1] See above, pp. 19–23.

threatening their all-India influence by his position in the Khilafat movement and the support he could rally through its network. They, too, saw only impossible allies in other local political groups – in their case the discontented non-Brahmins and 'Moderates' of Sir Narayan Chandarvarkar's hue.

In Madras the 'Nationalists' led by Kasturi Ranga Iyengar and S. Satyamurti were in a weak position not so much because Gandhi had undermined their local strength but because the Presidency's political community was so divided. They had to choose between Gandhi and his small band of local men who could defeat them in Congress, the Besant–Theosophist combine, the non-Theosophist 'Moderates' and the non-Brahmins. If they allied with any of the non-Gandhian groups they made a nonsense of their past politics, though submission to Gandhi also threatened their identity and political style. In all three Presidencies those of the established politicians who had claimed to be most advanced or extreme opted for Gandhi – Kelkar's men, followed by C. R. Das and finally by Iyengar. All had stood down from the elections reluctantly, but at Nagpur they ratified the rest of the non-cooperation plan.

Because the political elite was so fragmented no group could stand alone and retain its local power, let alone its all-India influence; and political tradition and practice prevented the groups from uniting to oppose Gandhi. Moreover, they stood little chance of retaining political dominance in the old style as the range of participants in politics widened under Gandhi's banner. Gandhi appeared to be the most powerful of possible allies and also the most dangerous of opponents to those who were determined to retain local leadership; consequently they acknowledged him as leader because he was the only possible mediator between their old style of limited politics and the new forces ranged behind him which promised to be threatening unless they could be canalized and controlled.

Gandhi for his part needed the Presidency leaders: he might be able to defeat them in open Congress, where he could muster all-India support, but they were a necessary part of his network of subcontractors if non-cooperation was to succeed in the Presidencies among the western educated with traditions of political activity. According to B. S. Moonje, Gandhi conceded 'Provincial autonomy so far as it agreed with the fundamentals of his Non-co-operation' – a gesture of conciliation which served to bind his former opponents closer to him in an alliance of mutual need. Moonje probably voiced the opinion of most of them when he wrote to Jayakar:

> The only programme before us now is that of breaking certain immoral laws of the Govt. and of proving to the world and convincing the Govt. that we mean serious business this time and that we are prepared for any and all kinds of personal sacrifices that the Govt. may prefer to inflict on us. If we shrink back this time from this ordeal, not only we but the whole Maharashtra shall loose [sic] its name...The time is ripe for us all now,

> reserving the right to ourselves to express our differences amongst ourselves whenever a proper occasion arrives, to close up our ranks and offer a united front to the Government under the guidance of the only man – Mahatma Gandhi – who can be somewhat of a leader to us, under the present circumstances. How we wish the great Lokmanya was amongst us to guide us through skillfully.[1]

Put in less flamboyant language, they had made the best of a bad job. In each Presidency the most advanced politicians acknowledged the realities of Gandhi's power and bowed to him at Nagpur, hoping thereby to salvage their positions in the crisis he had produced in their political world.

1 B. S. Moonje to M. R. Jayakar, 5 January 1921, Jayakar Papers, Chronological Correspondence File No. 12, No. 2.

APPENDIX

Regional Survey of the extent of observance of 1 August 1920

The following survey is taken from a file containing reports from local governments on how 1 August 1920 was observed; Home Pol., B, August 1920, Nos. 338–67 & K.-W.

Bombay Presidency reported little enthusiasm except in parts of Gujarat and Sind. There were slight disturbances in Karachi and Bombay city, a hartal in Bombay city similar to the last one but probably helped by the news of Tilak's death, partial hartal in Hyderabad, but almost complete hartal in the districts of Ahmedabad, Kaira, Karachi and Larkhana. (Ahmedabad and Kaira were of course the districts where Gandhi was best known because of his satyagrahas in 1918, while Karachi and Larkhana were in Sind, notorious for its welcome to the Khilafat agitation.) The Central and Southern Divisions of the Presidency, where Tilak's men held local political power, showed little sympathy for the idea of hartal except in Sholapur, where mourning for Tilak probably caused the partial hartal. C.P. reported no resignations or other signs that the non-cooperation programme was being enacted. There was a partial hartal in Jubbulpore, capital of the Hindi-speaking part of the province, but people in the Marathi-speaking districts closer to Bombay only stopped business when they heard of Tilak's death.

Further south, Coorg had no hartal or other forms of non-cooperation. In Bangalore city the market and most shops closed, 2,000 Muslims held a meeting and one municipal commissioner resigned: but in the civil and military station Hindus opposed hartal and Muslims were indifferent. In Madras Presidency there were no instances of non-cooperation, though a meeting held on the Madras beach, attended by about 10,000, of whom half were Hindus, passed a resolution in favour of it. In the mofussil there were some meetings and half-hearted hartal.

Bengal reported that Hindus were little affected by plans for non-cooperation and Muslims only partially. Hartal was a practical failure, and even in Calcutta only a few shops closed though 6,000 people turned out to a meeting. The only manifestations of non-cooperation were the return of a recruit's certificate, one refusal to attend a darbar, and a refusal to attend the Governor's garden party. To the north Assam reported slight observance of hartal but no instances of non-cooperation. On this occasion there was little to choose between the secluded, 'backward' area and the oldest Presidency with its long political tradition!

Bihar and Orissa reported that only Patna and the other towns of Bihar were affected. In urban areas there were meetings and fairly successful hartals, but there was no great enthusiasm anywhere, Patna's meeting of 1,000 being the largest. There were, however, three resignations – one title-holder, one honorary magistrate, and one member of the local legislative council. Neighbouring U.P. reported no examples of non-cooperation and commented that this was the worst supported hartal so far. It was non-existent in the rural areas, and only partial in district headquarter towns and a few smaller ones, though there were some quite large meetings. Punjab reported no instances of non-cooperation, few meetings, but a wide observance of hartal in the central districts of the province. Complete hartal was kept, for example, in Lahore, Amritsar, Ludhiana, Multan, Sargodha, the Simla bazaar and Rohtak and other places. It was the more outlying districts like Mianwali which did not observe the day. Surprisingly on the North-West Frontier, as secluded and 'backward' as Assam in politics, there was complete hartal in four places and partial hartal in others. All the teachers of the district board school in Peshawar resigned, as did twelve constables in Kohat.

CHAPTER 9

NON-COOPERATION, 1921–2: THE TEST OF GANDHI'S POLITICAL POWER

By the beginning of 1921 Gandhi had captured the Congress citadel, and India's politically aware, including the officials of the raj, were agog to see whether his victory was ephemeral and what he would do with his new-found power. Gandhi made no secret of his aim. He believed that India could attain Swaraj within a year if its people followed his plan of non-cooperation. He had said so at Calcutta in September 1920: he reiterated his belief in February 1921, though on that occasion he took care to insist that the essential preconditions were the spirit of non-violence, Hindu-Muslim unity, the abolition of untouchability, the establishment of the Congress organization in every village and a spinning-wheel in every home.[1] Such provisos showed that even when Gandhi gained control of the key institution of Indian nationalism he was just as far from desiring straightforward political Home Rule for Indians as he had been when he wrote *Hind Swaraj*, or erupted into Indian politics in 1917.

The precise nature of the Swaraj at which he aimed in 1921 was not clear to contemporaries, although he said that it was 'parliamentary swaraj in accordance with the wishes of the people of India' and not Swaraj as depicted in *Hind Swaraj*.[2] Lord Reading, who succeeded Chelmsford as Viceroy in April, could get no precise definition out of the Mahatma; and as Jawaharlal Nehru remembered,

> about our goal there was an entire absence of clear thinking. It seems surprising now, how completely we ignored the theoretical aspects, the philosophy of our movement as well as the definite objective that we should have. Of course we all grew eloquent about Swaraj, but each of us probably interpreted the word in his or her own way...Gandhiji was delightfully vague on the subject, and he did not encourage clear thinking about it either.[3]

Despite this vagueness about the ultimate goal, Gandhi was clear about the means. His political sense showed him that British rule was based on the

[1] *Young India*, 22 September 1920, *C.W.*, vol. 18, pp. 270–3; *Young India*, 23 February 1921, *C.W.*, vol. 19, pp. 383–5.

[2] *Young India*, 26 January 1921, *C.W.*, vol. 19, pp. 277–8.

[3] Nehru, *An Autobiography*, p. 76. Reading reported after interviews with Gandhi on 13/14 May 1921, 'All I could gather was that when Indians had regained their self-respect and had pursued a policy of non-co-operation with the Government and had refrained from violence they would have attained Swaraj.' Viceroy to Secretary of State, telegram, 14 May 1921, Mss. EUR. E. 238 (10).

active collaboration of some Indians and the acquiescence of the rest, and that if Indians were to force the British into a position where they could no longer inflict intolerable 'wrongs' on their Indian subjects then those subjects must undermine the foundation of their rule. Non-cooperation was the means he offered, consciously presenting it as the antithesis of collaboration.[1]

The Viceroy met Gandhi in May 1921 and painted a striking picture of this non-violent revolutionary.

> There is nothing striking about his appearance. He came to visit me in a white *dhoti* and cap, woven on a spinning-wheel, with bare feet and legs, and my first impression on seeing him ushered into my room was that there was nothing to arrest attention in his appearance, and that I should have passed him by in the street without a second look at him. When he talks the impression is different. He is direct and expresses himself well in excellent English with a fine appreciation of the value of the words he uses. There is no hesitation about him and there is a ring of sincerity in all that he utters, save when discussing some political questions. His religious views are, I believe, genuinely held and he is convinced to a point almost bordering on fanaticism that non-violence and love will give India its independence and enable it to withstand the British Government. His religious and moral views are admirable...but I confess that I find it difficult to understand his practice of them in politics. To put it quite briefly, he is like the rest of us, when engaged in a political movement he wishes to gather all under his umbrella and to reform them and bring them to his views. He has consequently to accept many with whom he is not in accord, and has to do his best to keep the combination together.[2]

Reading's political analysis was correct: Gandhi's following was a diverse one. Apart from a small group of loyal henchmen like Rajendra Prasad, Vallabhbhai Patel and the less known Jawaharlal Nehru, Gandhi's power in Congress rested on three main bases – newly mobilized groups and areas which had not previously participated in the politics of nationalism; an unstable alliance with sections of the Muslim community, which helped to push new areas into politics and provided him with allies in the ranks of the politicians; and the unwilling consent of some sections of the existing political elite, particularly in the Presidencies, who calculated that he was their best bet because of his other sources of power. Gandhi had broken open the old world of limited politics by opening it to the latent forces of power whose pressures it had seldom registered: he had gained influence by exploiting the latent because he was able to campaign on new issues, using new techniques.

The accuracy of this hypothesis of the nature of Gandhi's power can be tested by an analysis of the non-cooperation movement as it developed through 1921 until March 1922. If those were the three bases of his

[1] *Young India*, 12 January 1921, *C.W.*, vol. 19, p. 219.
[2] Reading to Montagu, 19 May 1921, Mss. EUR. E. 238 (3).

strength at Nagpur they should be visible in the working out of the policies adopted at Nagpur. By tracing them, their relationship with each other and with Gandhi we should see not only the source of Gandhi's political power but also its extent and stability, and as a result the reasons for the success or failure of non-cooperation.

Non-cooperation failed in that India had not gained Swaraj at the end of 1921. Moreover by March 1922 the leader of non-cooperation was in gaol, having called off civil disobedience after an outbreak of violence in the U.P.; and his movement, far from undermining the foundations of the raj, lay in ruins leaving the British masters of the field.[1] Nevertheless in the months between Nagpur and Gandhi's imprisonment certain aspects of non-cooperation had remarkable success in some areas, though computed over all its success was as patchy as it was temporary.

The resignation of titles was the part of the Congress plan which had least effect. By the end of January 1921, out of 5,186 Indian title-holders counted the August before only 24 had resigned, 8 of them in C.P., 5 in Bombay and 4 in the U.P.[2] The government historian of non-cooperation commented, 'those honoured were not the type of persons to be carried away by Non-Co-operation agitation'; but one Rai Sahib, the Delhi barrister Piare Lal, was frightened into resignation after being heckled at a public meeting in November 1920, though he continued to use the initials R. S. on his writing paper.[3] The Viceroy reported that resignation from government service was also 'infinitesimable and, as I understand, such resignations as have taken place are really not more than in normal times.' However, by March 1921 about 87 Honorary Magistrates had resigned, 40 of them in Madras; and when pressure from Gandhi to resign posts was strongest, in October and November 1921 after the arrest of the Ali brothers, 37 Muslim police resigned in the U.P. and 40 Muslim police in Bengal, while 17 resignations in Bombay were directly attributable to the arrest of the Alis and to 'political propaganda'.[4] Government servants who

1 As this chapter is an investigation of Gandhi's power neither a chronological account of the non-cooperation movement nor a comprehensive survey of politics is given. For a chronological account of the movement see Sitaramayya, *The History Of The Indian National Congress. Volume 1 (1885–1935)*, pp. 210–41, and, more briefly, a chapter by H. F. Owen in S. Ray (ed.), *Gandhi, India and the World* (Melbourne, 1970), pp. 171–87. An account by an assistant to Gandhi is R. B. Gregg's abridged and edited version of Krishnadas, *Seven Months With Mahatma Gandhi Being An Inside View Of The Non-Co-operation Movement Of 1921–22* (Ahmedabad, 1951). A summary of the evolution of Congress policy is given at the end of this chapter.

2 Home Pol., B, March 1921, Nos. 223–38.

3 Bamford, *Histories of the Non-Co-operation and Khilafat Movements*, p. 109; Home Public, 1924, No. 953 (I owe this reference to Dr D. Baker).

4 Reading to His Majesty the King, 3 November 1921, Mss. E. 238 (1); Home Pol., A, May 1921, No. 348; Appendix IV of Home Pol., 1921, No. 303.

did not resign often found their position made extremely difficult by the passive hostility of the public, and in the U.P. they were often actively hindered.[1] More serious were the efforts made by politicians and preachers to undermine the loyalty of Indian troops, and the social harassment suffered by some Indian soldiers and their families, though the net result in actual resignations from the army was not great.[2]

The boycott of government law courts was more successful. By the beginning of March 1921, just over 180 lawyers of different kinds had resigned, 33 of them in C.P., 43 in U.P. and 43 in Bihar and Orissa. There were some spectacular resignations of great lawyers like Motilal Nehru and C. R. Das, but many of the others only resigned for a couple of months and then returned to practice. Some who called themselves non-cooperators never gave up their practices, as in the case of B. Sita Ram from the U.P.; and others, like G. R. Wakhale from C.P., gave up their practices and found that political work paid them better![3]

The reverse side of boycott's coin was the establishment of local panchayat courts to deal with cases which would have gone before government courts. In Bihar and Orissa these gained so much popularity that in some places hundreds of cases were withdrawn from government courts in a day.[4] Elsewhere the courts which sprang up collapsed quickly because social boycott and violence were the only sanctions at their disposal, and because they often dispensed a queer kind of justice. In Bengal, for example,

> One of the most amazing decisions was that of a court which found an accused guilty of abducting a married woman but fined the husband Rs. 12 before consenting to order the return of the woman. The husband was obliged to borrow the money, and the court then ordered the woman to be kept by the lender until the debt was paid.[5]

Statistics for the boycott of schools and colleges were far more impressive than for boycott of courts or resignations from government service. During 1921 and 1922 the growth of Indian education suffered a noticeable setback, which was most marked in colleges and secondary schools and was due to non-cooperation rather than economic causes (see Table 6).

[1] Bombay Police Abstract, 1921, par. 206 (64); C. E. Wild, Opium Agent, U.P., to T. Sloan, Deputy Secretary to U.P. Govt., 6 June 1921, Sita Ram Papers, File No. 18/2.

[2] Between 27 May 1920 and 21 July 1921 100 cases of tampering with the loyalty of troops were reported, Home Pol., 1921, No. 322. Instances of social pressure, including the case of 250 soldiers' wives praying in a regimental gurdwara not to be sent back to their villages because of social harassment, are in Home Pol., 1922, No. 584.

[3] Home Pol., A, May 1921, Nos. 335–65; for individual cases see Home Public, 1924, No. 953.

[4] Weekly report of D.C.I., 25 January 1921, Home Pol., Deposit, January 1921, No. 75; Bamford, *op. cit.* p. 25.

[5] Govt. of India policy letter to all local govts. and administrations, 7 May 1929, Home Pol., 1929, No. 179.

Table 6
The progress of education in India, 1919–23

Year	Arts Colleges		Secondary Schools						Primary Schools	
							Total			
	Institutions	Scholars	High Schools	Scholars	Middle Schools	Scholars	Institutions	Scholars	Institutions	Scholars
1919–20	150	52,482	2,113	632,032	6,595	649,778	8,708	1,281,810	155,844	6,133,521
1920–21	160	48,170	2,184	600,583	6,739	653,942	8,923	1,254,525	159,345	6,327,973
1921–22	167	45,933	2,248	594,910	6,739	644,614	8,987	1,239,524	160,072	6,310,451
1922	170	47,632	2,246	595,402	6,731	643,839	8,977	1,239,241	159,889	6,304,457
1923	174	52,639	2,312	632,943	6,732	698,462	9,044	1,331,405	162,015	6,600,116

Source: Bamford, *Histories of the Non-Co-operation and Khilafat Movements*, p. 103.

Numerous 'national' institutions were opened (see Table 7); but there is little reliable information on their duration or the quality of education they imparted. In Bengal the personal effect of C. R. Das on the volatile Calcutta student population when he returned from Nagpur was dramatic; and at the end of January 1921 virtually all the Calcutta colleges closed rather than keep up the unequal struggle against non-cooperation. Outside Calcutta almost all Bengal's colleges and numerous schools were affected.[1] By the end of February 1921 the students were gradually coming back to their desks, but though the boycott at its height was merely a temporary burst of fireworks it burnt a permanent mark across Bengal's educational progress for two years.[2]

Table 7

National schools and colleges, 1921–2

Province	Institutions	Scholars
Madras	92*	5,072*
Bombay	189	17,100
Bengal	190	14,819
U.P.	137*	8,476*
Punjab	69	8,046
Bihar+Orissa	442	17,330
C.P.	86*	6,338*
Assam	38	1,908
N.W.F.P.	4*	120*
Minor administrations	10	1,255

* = Opened until 31 July 1921.

Source: Bamford, *Histories of the Non-Co-operation and Khilafat Movements*, p. 104.

In other provinces too the educational boycott was short-lived, and in Bombay, for example, the situation was fairly normal after April 1921. Evidently the pull of a western education was as strong as ever, whatever denunciations Gandhi might launch against it. Literacy meant profit, power and prestige; and Indians were no more willing to forego these than they had been after the partition of Bengal.[3]

[1] *Report on the Administration Of Bengal 1920–21*, p. xix.

[2] Chelmsford to E. S. Montagu, 23 February 1921, Mss. EUR. E. 264 (6). In 1920–1 the total number of educational institutions in Bengal rose from 52,879 to 53,968, but fell in 1921–2 to 53,767. In 1920–1 the total number of pupils fell from 1,953,909 to 1,945,145 and in 1921–2 to 1,890,454. *Report on the Administration Of Bengal 1920–21*, p. 128; *Report on the Administration Of Bengal 1921–22* (Calcutta, 1923), p. 289.

[3] *Bombay 1921–22. A Review of the Administration of the Presidency* (Bombay, 1923), pp. 166–8. In Bihar the national schools declined in popularity during 1922, and by the end of that year two of the six high schools which had been

Finance linked the educational boycott to the question whether non-cooperators should follow through their boycott of the legislative councils perfectly logically and boycott elections to municipal councils, too. If they did so they cut themselves off from the bodies which controlled the finance of local schools and could be used to starve government schools of funds, or to insist on their 'nationalization'. It appears that after the Nagpur Congress Gandhi and most other political leaders decided that non-cooperators should try to capture the municipalities and use them for their own ends, though in Delhi at least the local non-cooperators felt that this was denying the logic of non-cooperation.[1] Control of the municipalities was possession of real power in the local sphere of Indian public life. Municipal councillors had control over appointments, contracts and public works; and for non-cooperators below the level of all-India politician the opportunities the municipalities offered were as hard to forego as the profits of a western education. Consequently in the spring of 1921 they contested the local elections and in some places had spectacular success. They captured the Surat municipality, winning 37 out of 40 seats; they gained 7 out of 12 seats in one Bihar municipality, and had an easy win in the Lahore municipal elections. In Karachi, however, non-cooperators only won 9 out of 45 seats. One of the main planks in non-cooperators' electoral campaigns was the 'nationalization' of local government schools, and in Nadiad and Ahmedabad the municipalities actually refused the government grant to local primary schools.[2]

Later in 1921, particularly from early April until the end of June, Gandhi and the A.I.C.C. switched the emphasis of non-cooperation from boycott of schools and courts to swadeshi and called for the introduction of two million *charkhas*, or spinning-wheels, into India. Presumably they realized that the boycott of schools and courts was unlikely to elicit any more response and chose this as a way of keeping up the momentum of non-cooperation.[3] It is impossible to discover the number of spinning-wheels brought into action, but statistics for imported cloth show a drastic

nationalized applied for renewal of government recognition. *Bihar And Orissa in 1922* (Patna, 1923), p. 113.

1 Weekly report of D.C.I., 1 February 1921, Home Pol., Deposit, March 1921, No. 90; Viceroy (Home Dept.) to Secretary of State, telegram, 30 April 1921, Mss. EUR. E. 238 (10).

2 Viceroy (Home Dept.) to Secretary of State, telegrams, 10 & 22 May 1921, Mss EUR. E. 238 (10); Fortnightly report from Bombay, 18–21 February 1921, Home Pol., Deposit, June 1921, No. 12; Fortnightly report from Bombay, 19–24 March 1921, Home Pol., Deposit, June 1921, No. 65.

3 Resolution 1 at Bezwada A.I.C.C. meeting, 31 March 1921, *The Hindu*, 1 April 1921, *C.W.*, vol. 19, p. 496. According to Gandhi the reason for this switch was that however many students and lawyers had actually withdrawn from schools and courts, 'the Congress had achieved the real objects of propaganda, namely, the demolition of prestige of these institutions of the bureaucratic Government of this country.' *The Hindu*, 1 April 1921, *ibid.* p. 494.

drop. Total imports of cloth decreased in value from Rs. 102 crores in 1920–1 to Rs. 57 crores in 1921–2.

The government attributed this partly to the reduced purchasing power of India in general at this time and to the difficulties encountered by merchants as a result of the fall in the exchange rate: but it could not deny that at least part of the reason lay in the swadeshi campaign. Further proof of this was the increase in imports of cotton twist and yarn from 47 million lbs. in 1920–1 to 57 million lbs. in 1921–2, particularly in the class of yarn most suitable for handlooms. Indian mills also expanded their production of yarn in this class. The effect of the swadeshi movement was felt throughout India, but Bengal, Bombay, Madras and the U.P. bore the brunt of it.[1] However, where boycott of foreign cloth cut across the economic interests of Indian merchants, Gandhi's appeals had little permanent effect, and even the Marwaris of Bengal who had become notorious for their support of the Mahatma refused to pledge themselves never to trade in foreign cloth. The Marwari Chamber of Commerce, meeting in Calcutta on 5 September 1921, only bound its members not to enter into foreign contracts until the end of the year, and it seems that they were forced into this small self-denying ordinance by the threat of their Oriya employees to strike unless they stopped dealing in foreign cloth.[2]

If intimidation and picketing made some dealers at least temporary swadeshi merchants others were not slow to cash in on the new fashion; and the Secretary of the Poona District Congress Committee, for example, was inundated with letters from drapers, tailors and general merchants who introduced themselves as *khadi*-sellers.[3] The call to spin and weave by hand also had material advantages for the unemployed who took the opportunity to implore Gandhi for work.[4] But many of those who took to the *charkha* did so out of deference to the Mahatma and the practice he required from his associates. The most striking aspects of the whole swadeshi

1 Bainford, *op. cit.* pp. 100–1; L. F. Rushbrook Williams, *India In 1922–23* (Calcutta, 1923), pp. 120–1. It should be noted that many of the Bombay mills never used foreign yarn in the first place, while many of those who gave up its use had only used it for the borders of expensive *dhotis*. In Cawnpore none of the big foreign cloth dealers joined the movement and the firms which promised not to order foreign cloth were almost all dealers in Indian mill goods. Bombay P.C.C. Annual Report to 31 October 1921, Appendix A, Jayakar Papers, File No. 478; Fortnightly report from U.P., 17 August 1921, Home Pol., 1921, No. 18.

2 Fortnightly report from Bengal for first half of September 1921, Home Pol., 1921, No. 18. Some of the Marwaris who signed the pledge not to order foreign cloth had broken it by early October, Fortnightly report from Bengal for first half of October 1921, *ibid.*

3 For examples, see Nehru Memorial Museum and Library, Poona D.C.C. records, File No. 15. *Khadi* is hand-spun cloth.

4 S. G. Paregaonker, President of Sangamner Weavers' meeting, to Gandhi, 23 December 1920, Poona D.C.C. records, File No. 11; M. Hissamuddin to Secretary of Poona D.C.C., postcard, 3 December 1921, Poona D.C.C. records, File No. 12.

campaign were not only the large bonfires of foreign cloth which took place throughout India,[1] but also the way *khadi* became a virtual uniform for nationalist politicians.

Another all-India manifestation of non-cooperation was the curious appearance of a temperance movement, not planned or anticipated by Gandhi or Congress, though both encouraged it once it had caught on.[2] The real roots of the movement were probably a combination of the antipathy of orthodox Hindus and Muslims to alcoholic drink, the inducement of claiming greater ritual purity to backward castes which abandoned alcohol as part of a campaign of sanskritization, and the undoubted shortage of money after the war. But temperance also meant less excise revenue: and although Gandhi maintained that 'the deprivation to the Government of the drink revenue is of the least importance in the campaign',[3] non-cooperators realized the potential of temperance as a political weapon. At a political conference in Bilaspur a resolution stated openly that people should give up excisable articles in order to cripple the government financially and paralyse the administration.[4]

C.P. was one of the provinces earliest hit by the temperance movement, the auctions of liquor licences in January and February 1921 were so badly affected that in several places they had to be abandoned. Taken over all, Punjab, Bihar and Orissa and Bombay suffered particularly, losing from their excise revenue in the financial year 1921–2 33, 10 and 6 lakhs of rupees respectively; while in February 1922 the Governor of Madras commented, 'Our position is really desperate. We have a 65 lakhs deficit

[1] For a description of a bonfire where Motilal Nehru burnt his foreign ties among other clothes, see Krishnadas, *Seven Months With Mahatma Gandhi*, pp. 15–16. For Gandhi's argument that foreign cloth was dirt and therefore should be burnt rather than given to the poor, see *Navajivan*, 17 July 1921, *C.W.*, vol. 20, pp. 381–2.

[2] *Young India*, 12 January 1921, *C.W.*, vol. 19, p. 222; Resolution 4 at Bezwada A.I.C.C. meeting, 31 March 1921, *The Hindu*, 1 April 1921, *ibid.* p. 497. The council of the Bombay P.C.C. took up the anti-liquor campaign early in June 1921, and on 27 June 1921 created a Vigilance Committee to organize it. It divided Bombay city into 15 sections, each with a captain, and about 1,500 volunteers picketed 840 liquor shops. Bombay P.C.C. Annual Report to 31 October 1921, Jayakar Papers, File No. 478.

[3] *Young India*, 8 June 1921, *C.W.*, vol. 20, p. 190.

[4] Viceroy (Home Dept.) to Secretary of State, telegram, 8 April 1921, Mss. EUR. E. 238 (10). It was also clear in Bihar that many temperance preachers were using it as a political weapon rather than as an instrument of social reform. Villagers were told that if they abstained now they would have a big reward when Swaraj was attained because they would be free to manufacture their own liquor. Some were told that they need only abstain from government-licensed liquor, and in one case from Monghyr the Collector reported that 'the accused who were Santals stated in their confessions [when prosecuted for illicit distillation] that the *Gandhiwalas* had told them they might make liquor for themselves now-a-days'. *Report On The Administration Of The Excise Department In The Province Of Bihar And Orissa For The Year 1920–21* (Patna, 1921), p. 10.

this year mainly due to the Gandhi propaganda with regard to excise'.[1] Although Gandhi insisted that only 'legitimate, courteous means' should be used to persuade people to give up drink, intimidation and social ostracism were rife. In Gaya, for example, when the servant of a liquor seller died nobody would assist with the burial for twenty-four hours; and in Monghyr a midwife refused to attend a woman until her husband gave up drink![2]

Where social intimidation and picketing took place it was often the work of the so-called Volunteer groups. Many of these had existed well before 1920, often in the form of *seva samitis* or social service organizations; but after the Nagpur Congress both Congress and Khilafat leaders added to their numbers to form a task force for the local organization of non-cooperation.[3] According to a conservative government estimate in August 1921 there were 345 Volunteer corps in existence with 15,186 members, and 404 *seva samitis* with 15,269 members: Bombay Presidency and Bengal contributed nearly half this number.[4] Although some Volunteers received some drilling and pseudo-military training, most local governments believed that their danger lay not in this but in the fact that most of them were merely undisciplined mobs of rowdies who could be called out to enforce non-cooperation but over whom the real political leaders had virtually no control.

Bengal in particular emphasized this danger, following the systematic recruitment of Volunteers from among the low-paid Muslim millworkers of Calcutta by Muhammad Osman of Monghyr, who joined Calcutta's Khilafat Office as its paid head preacher in April 1921. The Officiating Chief Secretary to the Government of Bengal described in some detail the activities of the local Volunteers.

> Reference has already been made to the change in status of the men enlisted in this way. They are now distinctly of a lower class than at first, and are backed by the riffraff of the town, recruited on a payment of a daily wage to do whatever work is demanded of them. These tasks vary from time to time. The collection of funds is a frequent duty, as also figuring at meetings and demonstrations in support of so-called "leaders," but latterly their activities have taken on a more sinister aspect. Ever since

[1] Govt. of India policy letter to all local govts. and administrations, 7 May 1929, Home Pol., 1929, No. 179; Bamford, *op. cit.* pp. 108–9; Willingdon to E. S. Montagu, 11 February 1922, Mss. EUR. F. 93 (4).

[2] *Navajivan*, 8 May 1921, *C.W.*, vol. 20, pp. 74–5; Govt. of India policy letter to all local govts. and administrations, 7 May 1929, Home Pol., 1929, No. 179.

[3] For a description of the Volunteer movement with particular case histories, see Govt. of India policy letter to all local govts. and administrations, 7 May 1929, Home Pol., 1929, No. 179.

[4] Home Pol., 1922, No. 327, Part IV. In Bengal some ex-revolutionaries appeared to be reviving their organization under the cloak of non-cooperation, and 400 Volunteers were enrolled by Purna Das, a former state prisoner. Weekly report of D.C.I., 25 April 1921, Home Pol., Deposit, June 1921, No. 54.

the pressing of the foreign boycott campaign these men have been conspicuous in picketing cloth shops and, in a lesser degree, liquor-vendors; their methods are those of threat and intimidation, and complaints against them are numerous, though it is difficult to get anyone to come forward in public. Another recent turn of demonstration has been interference with taxi-cabs and passers-by in the streets, while on the occasion of the recent trial of certain Khilafat workers, there were scandalous organised demonstrations at the court house and jail characterised by the presence of uniformed volunteers, and degenerating into a minor riot in Dalhousie Square. But perhaps most serious is the latest direct attempt to intimidate and seduce the police, in which these volunteers figure prominently, and which has been successful so far to the extent of bringing about some 50 resignations. The police both privately and on duty are being frankly terrorized.[1]

The last straw for the Government of India when faced with such reports was the highly successful hartal which Gandhi called for 17 November to mark the arrival in India of the Prince of Wales, and in which the Volunteers played no little part. In Calcutta the British temporarily lost control and in Bombay violence broke out on a large scale. As a result local governments were permitted to take far more drastic steps against non-cooperators than had hitherto been permitted. Many of them took the opportunity to proscribe the Volunteer corps in their provinces.[2] However, this by no means stopped their enrolment, and in January 1922 Bombay Presidency had about 125 corps with numbers ranging from under 10 to over 100, while in the U.P. in January the P.C.C. estimated that there were about 80,000 Volunteers.[3]

What statistical evidence remains of the all-India response to the various parts of the non-cooperation plan demonstrates that for the time being the old closed shop of limited politics had been thrown wide open. Far greater numbers than before were participating in an overt political campaign, using a far wider range of techniques than earlier politicians had ever used simultaneously, although they had experimented with some of them singly: and, moreover, the participants came from all parts of India. The 'new' areas which carried weight at Calcutta and Nagpur were well to the

[1] Officiating Chief Secretary to Govt. of Bengal, to Secretary to Govt. of India, Home Dept., 17 November 1921, Home Pol., 1921, No. 398. For a summary of the views of other local governments on the Volunteer movement see Home Pol., 1922, No. 327, Part I.

[2] Note by S. P. O'Donnell, 2 December 1921, summarizing Govt. of India policy towards Volunteers, Home Pol., 1921, No. 415; Low, *J.A.S.*, xxv, 2 (1966), 247–8. For the success of the 17 November hartal, see Fortnightly reports from the provinces for November 1921, Home Pol., 1921, No. 18.

[3] List of all Volunteer corps in the Bombay Presidency with dates of formation, leaders, numbers etc., Supplement to Bombay Police Abstract, 1922, 4 February 1922; Secretary to U.P. P.C.C. to General Secretary of A.I.C.C., 20 January 1922, A.I.C.C. Files, No. 3, Part II of 1922.

fore in non-cooperation, joined by provinces like Assam which were more backward still by the former standards of institutional politics.[1] 'New' social groups, too, gave certain aspects of non-cooperation particular success; for significantly it was those aspects like temperance, swadeshi and Volunteering which received most support, rather than the boycotts which touched the material interests of the western educated.

The political nation as it had existed before Gandhi's eruption into politics was still reluctant to support him when it hurt their pockets or their prestige, and he had to turn to wider social groups for solid support for non-cooperation. The precondition of support for non-cooperation from those outside the ranks of the political nation was the involvement of intermediate layers of leadership beneath the politicians who responded to Gandhi's appeal and were both willing and able to organize their localities or their personal followings in support of his campaign. During 1921–2 Gandhi's subcontractors included barristers out to create a following, village leaders pursuing the goals of parish politics, communities aiming at integration and power, maulvis hoping to defend their faith and increase their reputations, and even roaming *sadhus*, prompted by diverse mixtures of religious sincerity, antipathy to the British and self-advertisement.[2]

1 Some indication of the spread of the response to non-cooperation is the following list of convictions by province for offences arising from the Khilafat and non-cooperation movements. It is not a very satisfactory index of response because it only covers parts of the movements which, like Volunteering, seditious speeches and contravention of excise regulations, laid people open to prosecution.

Province	*Number of convictions* (1921 to mid-1922)
Madras	617
Bombay	1,041
Bengal	9,163
U.P.	2,772
Punjab	1,374
Bihar and Orissa	414
C.P.	344
Assam	721
N.W.F.P.	68
Coorg	12
Delhi	186

Source: C. W. Gwynne, Deputy Secretary to Govt. of India, to Sir William Duke, Under-Secretary of State for India, 8 February 1923, Home Pol., 1922, No. 28.

Bengal's figure is swollen by the number of Volunteers in the Presidency. For Assam's response to non-cooperation see below, pp. 324–6.

2 For the activities of *sadhus* (Hindu holy men) as preachers of non-cooperation, see note by Madras C.I.D., 6 October 1921, note by Bengal C.I.D., enclosed in letter from Bengal Govt. to Govt. of India, Home Dept., 9 July 1921, and letter from U.P. Govt., Home Dept., to Govt. of India, Home Dept., 15 November 1921, Home Pol., 1922, No. 118. Gandhi appears to have enlisted about 100 *sadhus* in the non-cooperation cause at Nagpur on 28 December 1920; he thought

Gandhi's reliance on new areas and groups of followers was nowhere clearer than in the places which prepared for civil disobedience after Gandhi and the Congress Working Committee at last agreed, on 5 November 1921, that it was appropriate to resort to civil disobedience by refusing to pay taxes. Only in Gujarat did Gandhi agree to try the experiment, realizing the danger inherent in a step which in his words amounted to 'civil revolution which...would mean an end of Government authority in that particular area and open defiance of Government and its laws.'[1] The Gujarat P.C.C., meeting on 13 November, was assured by representatives from Kaira and Surat districts that their talukas of Anand and Bardoli were ready for civil disobedience. The police noted tremendous preparations in both places. In the Anand taluka of Kaira by the end of November over 1,500 signatures to a civil disobedience pledge had been collected, and over thirty police patels had promised to resign. Anand was a taluka where the Patidars clustered thickly and had been prominent in the 1918 satyagraha; and now, in 1921, most of the signatories were Patidars. The leaders (including women from Ahmedabad and M. K. Pandya, famous from 1918) tried not very successfully to convert the lower castes to non-cooperation, lest they should step into the patels' shoes which the Patidars intended to vacate.

In Bardoli about 300 people had signed the civil disobedience pledge; but the taluka was evidently not sufficiently equipped with *khadi* to fulfil one of the A.I.C.C.'s conditions for civil disobedience, and hastily imported a large quantity so that Gandhi should think that the taluka was ready.[2] Civil disobedience was in fact postponed because of the riots in Bombay which accompanied the hartal of 17 November, but Bardoli was the chosen place when Gandhi decided to take the plunge in February 1922.[3] Between three and four thousand people attended the conference of the taluka held on 29 January to discuss civil disobedience; and according

their role was particularly important in preventing recruiting. Note by Bengal C.I.D., enclosed in letter from Bengal Govt. to Govt. of India, Home Dept., 9 July 1921, *ibid.*

An interesting report on *sadhus* in U.P. in 1919 shows how the way was open for Gandhi's activities among them. *Sadhus* were reported to be discontented because of police shadowing and because of their new habit of reading the vernacular press, which had given them a surprising interest in politics even in remote places. Weekly report of D.C.I., 19 May 1919, Proceeding No. 496 of Home Pol., B, June 1919, Nos. 494–7.

[1] Speech by Gandhi at A.I.C.C. meeting in Delhi on 4 November 1921, *The Hindu*, 7 November 1921, *C.W.*, vol. 21, p. 396. The A.I.C.C. permitted each province to undertake civil disobedience in the manner considered most appropriate by its P.C.C., under certain strict conditions designed to maintain discipline and non-violence; for the text of the A.I.C.C. resolution see *Young India*, 10 November 1921, *ibid.* pp. 412–13.

[2] Bombay Police Abstract, 1921, par. 1263 (6), (7), (9), (12); 1324 (9); 1366 (10).

[3] Gandhi to the Viceroy, 1 February 1922, Home Pol., 1922, No. 89, Part I, Serial No. I, K.-W.

to Gandhi those most committed to civil disobedience in Bardoli, as in Anand, were not the old political nation but prosperous, rural folk. 'The people who have taken an interest in and joined this struggle are the so-called respectable classes, and especially the *Patidars* among them.'[1]

The other area which resorted to non-payment of taxes in 1922 (with Gandhi's very doubtful blessing)[2] was the Guntur district of 'backward' Andhra. The heart of the movement to postpone payment of taxes was Peddanandipad firka in Bapatla taluka, where a majority of village officials resigned. Here were people like the Patidars of Gujarat, influential in village life but not part of the political nation in relation to the institutional politics of nationalism. They took up civil disobedience even more dramatically than Gandhi would have wished, while the delta talukas of Guntur which were more westernized seemed likely to fall behind, on the admission of the President of the Andhra P.C.C.[3] Two years later Andhra, this new area to take part in politics, whose backwardness had made it fear for its integrity in the face of Tamil domination, had so come to the fore that Srinivasa Sastri could speak of 'Andhra country, where extremism and non-co-operation have long found firm lodgement.'[4]

Expansion of political activity on such a scale implied an enormous increase in the funds available for political work. In 1918 the total sum available to the A.I.C.C. had been Rs. 7,234.12.9. This had risen to Rs. 29,469.15.0. in 1919 and Rs. 43,873.4.9. in 1920; but between 1921 and 1923 the A.I.C.C.'s total funds exceeded Rs. 13 million.[5] Rs. 10,000,000 of this was collected between April and June 1921, after an appeal by the A.I.C.C. on 31 March for a crore of rupees for the Tilak Swaraj Fund by 30 June.[6] Previously backward areas were among the largest contributors (*see* Table 8). Bombay Presidency showed in microcosm how the balance of influence in politics had swung away from old to new areas as Gandhi took control and launched the Congress appeal for funds. By mid-July the

1 *Navajivan*, 5 February 1922, *C.W.*, vol. 22, p. 334. For the Bardoli conference of 29 January 1922, see *Young India*, 2 February 1922, *ibid.* pp. 295–7, and Bombay Police Abstract, 1922, par. 193 (11).

2 Gandhi did not think that Andhra was ready for civil disobedience but he felt he could not interfere if Andhra men thought that the conditions for civil disobedience decided by the A.I.C.C. in Delhi in November had been satisfied. Gandhi to K. Venkatappayya, President of Andhra P.C.C., 17 January 1922, *The Hindu*, 21 January 1922, Gandhi to Venkatappayya, telegram, 20 January 1922, *The Hindu*, 23 January 1922, *C.W.*, vol. 22, pp. 211–12, 228.

3 *The Hindu*, 25 January 1922, Home Pol., 1922, No. 529.

4 V. S. S. Sastri to editor of *The Leader*, 3 April 1924, Jagadisan (ed.), *Letters Of Srinivasa Sastri*, p. 118.

5 Krishna, *J.A.S.*, xxv, 3 (1966), 425, 427. The balance sheet of the A.I.C.C. for 1919 is available in A.I.C.C. Files, 1919, No. 1, Part V.

6 Resolution 1 at Bezwada A.I.C.C. meeting, 31 March 1921, *The Hindu*, 1 April 1921, *C.W.*, vol. 19, p. 496. The collection of the sum was announced in *Navajivan*, 3 July 1921, *C.W.*, vol. 20, p. 315.

Presidency had contributed Rs. 57½ lakhs, of which Bombay city contributed Rs. 37½ lakhs, Gujarat 15, Maharashtra 3 and Sind 2.[1]

Money was collected by temporarily unemployed lecturers, 'national' schoolboys and others whom the local Congress organizations could rope in, from groups who in previous decades would probably never have heard of Congress – like the Fyzabad tenants in the U.P., who were told that if they subscribed Gandhi would bring Swaraj in a few months, when tenants would be free from ejection and the landless would have land without rent.[2] Gandhi's Marwari supporters also contributed munificently to non-cooperation funds – a lakh of rupees in Bengal in January 1921, for example, and two lakhs from one individual Marwari, the faithful Jamnalal Bajaj, during 1921–2 specifically for the support of non-cooperating lawyers.[3] Other individual merchants and business associations gave similar sums: some of these donors were quite unknown in political life, like the jute millowner of Ellore who gave considerable sums to non-cooperators and to the Ellore 'national' school, but was described by officials as 'a man

Table 8

Distribution of collections for Tilak Swaraj Fund from January 1921 to 30 June 1922

Province	Rupees
Bombay Presidency and City	3,170,049
U.P.	596,228
Central India	26,800
Madras	538,069
Delhi	39,964
Bihar + Orissa	483,419
Sind	112,530
N.W.F.P.	8,480
Bengal	1,800,000
Rajputana	44,558
Assam	86,563
C.P.	264,500
Punjab	856,000

Source: Statement of Tilak Swaraj Fund Collections compiled from C.I.D. reports, published accounts, etc., with warning attached that the figures are sketchy because of the material available and the unsatisfactory way the funds were kept. Home Pol., 1922, No. 741.

1 Fortnightly report from Bombay for first half of July 1921, Home Pol., No. 18.

2 Fortnightly report from U.P., 7 May 1921, Home Pol., Deposit, June 1921, No. 13.

3 Fortnightly report from Bengal for second half of January 1921, Home Pol., Deposit, April 1921, No. 42; Sitaramayya, *op. cit.* pp. 212, 242.

of colourless character who has not taken a prominent part in public life outside his own town of Ellore and knows little English.'[1] Such instances show how deeply non-cooperation bit into social groups outside the ranks of the western educated. Added to these funds were those collected specially for the Khilafat agitation. By June 1922 Rs. 1,960,278 had been donated to the Khilafat Fund, quite apart from the money raised for Angora and Smyrna.[2] Evidently Gandhi could depend on Muslim purses as well as votes in Congress.

The end of limited politics and the eruption of the latent into a political campaign is all the clearer when the focus is changed from all-India analysis of the effects of non-cooperation as adopted by Congress to an investigation of regional details. There emerges a fascinating patchwork of local variations as non-cooperation took on local colour and became an element and an instrument in the power structure of each locality, entangled in local circumstances to a degree which Gandhi and Congress could never have envisaged. Gandhi saw non-cooperation as a way of involving the whole spectrum of Indian society in a political movement. His vision was achieved on a scale far beyond that of the Rowlatt satyagraha, because for the first time he made contact with groups of subcontractors who found in the techniques he offered ways of defending or promoting their local interests. The result was no monolithic political movement. Instead, non-cooperation became a chameleon campaign, taking colour from its surroundings as it was shaped in each locality by the particular forces at work and the strains and stresses of the local power structure. Every province, indeed every district, in India would provide evidence of this, but a few examples will show not only how a continental campaign took on a variety of local faces but also how it was precisely this flexibility which attracted men outside the old political nation, whether in the Presidencies or in the backward political areas.

Jungly Assam was one of India's most backward provinces in terms of nationalist politics before 1921: but in June 1921 one of Assam's ministers, Syed Abdul Majid, visited his home district, Sylhet, and said that there was a change 'such as I would never have believed if I had not seen with my eyes open'. He reported that there were

> on the average ten paid preachers in each sub-division who preach disloyalty broadcast in the interior, realize subscriptions and organize village committees who also raise money and settle disputes. Besides these there are hundreds of honorary workers whose duties are just as those of the paid preachers. They have been able to spread a network of organization

1 Description of Mothey Gangarazan of Ellore, Home Public, 1924, No. 953; for a list of prominent mercantile contributors, see Krishna, *J.A.S.*, xxv, 3 (1966), 426.

2 Home Pol., 1922, No. 741. Any attempt to give details of Khilafat finances is hazardous because there was later a scandal about the way M. M. Chotani handled the funds, and the figures are therefore suspect.

throughout the district and are creating hatred of Government and Europeans.[1]

About twelve men, half of them Hindus and half Muslims, including some non-Bengali Muslims specially sent by the Congress–Khilafat organization, appear to have been the prime movers of the agitation.[2] The non-Bengali emissaries of the non-cooperation cause were probably a concession to the antipathy of the Assamese to all outsiders and to Bengalis in particular, who dominated so many of the trades and professions in Assam by virtue of their superior education. However, in 1921–2 outsiders succeeded dramatically because in non-cooperation they offered to people in Assam a means of voicing and attempting to remedy their peculiar local grievances.

Their first success was among another group of immigrants, the workers in the tea gardens. Badly hit by a post-war depression in tea which stopped them adding overtime to their standard wage, coolies listened to the message of non-cooperation and decided to use the weapon against their planter employers. By mid-May 1921 between six and seven thousand had left the gardens and begun the journey to their homes in Bihar and the U.P. They took a month to reach their destinations because Bengali non-cooperators promptly exploited their plight by engineering steamer and rail strikes to hold them up and embarrass the government.[3] Gandhi knew nothing of what was said and done in his name in the Assam tea gardens, nor could he control it; and he deplored the steamer strike as political, though ostensibly it was one of sympathy with the tea garden coolies.[4]

Beneath the temporary strain in provincial life produced by the depression in tea was a deeper stress – the antipathy of some Bengalis, the educated Assamese and the mass of the Assamese population to the planting community, which was as influential as its counterpart in Bihar. From the beginning of non-cooperation the campaign was extended in Assam to include non-cooperation against European planters and merchants.[5] As

[1] Fortnightly report from Assam, 19 June 1921, Home Pol., Deposit, June 1921 No. 46. For a description of the backwardness of Assam in the politics of the western educated see Sir William Marris to Reading, 2 December 1921, Mss. EUR. E. 238 (23).

[2] Ronaldshay to E. S. Montagu, 18 May 1921, Mss. EUR. D. 523 (32); Sir W. Marris to Sir W. Vincent, 14 June 1921, Mss. EUR. E. 238 (23); Fortnightly report from Assam, 1 December 1921, Home Pol., 1921, No. 18.

[3] Ronaldshay to E. S. Montagu, 1 June 1921, Mss. EUR. D. 523 (32); Viceroy to Secretary of State, telegram, 21 June 1921, Mss. EUR. E. 238 (10); for the Bengali part of the affair see Broomfield, *Elite Conflict in a Plural Society*, pp. 214–19.

[4] *Young India*, 8 June 1921, *Young India*, 15 June 1921, *C.W.*, vol. 20, pp. 182–3, 225–8.

[5] Printed report of 5th Session of Surma Valley Conference, Sylhet, 19/20/21 September 1920, A.I.C.C. Files, 1920, No. 11, Part I.

non-cooperation proceeded anti-planter feeling continued to generate support for it and to give it peculiar local twists. In Gandhi's name, for example, many illiterate Assamese were involved in the boycott of local markets which were fixed at auction by the government. Although the few educated Congressmen of the province intended this as a means of cutting off government revenue,[1] it caught on because villagers could display through it their hostility to the planters, and a vague, millenarian hope that when Gandhi ruled things would be cheaper and taxes would be abolished.[2]

To the south in Bihar non-cooperation took its local shape from the strains in provincial public life, just as in Assam. Here a prominent local issue was the right to graze cattle on waste lands, hotly disputed by planters and peasants, although the Champaran enquiry had attempted to settle the friction between them. As a result, although this had nothing to do with all-India politics, Champaran and Muzaffarpur were by the end of 1921 the storm centres of non-cooperation in Bihar: and on 1 November a mob of several thousand burnt a sugar factory in Champaran and additional police and cavalry were sent to hold the area.[3]

Across the border once-quiescent U.P. became one of the Government of India's nightmares during 1921. The reason was the entanglement of non-cooperation with the Kisan Sabha movement, a peasant uprising against landlords who were exploiting old dues in an attempt to make their estates pay. Although this Kisan movement originated in parochial grievances long before non-cooperation, politicians led by Motilal and Jawaharlal Nehru deliberately exploited it to create a local following for their all-India campaign.[4] Once again Gandhi found that local circumstances distorted non-cooperation out of all recognition though he personally attempted to keep it true to his blueprint. On a tour of U.P. in February 1921 he 'held aloof

1 Assam P.C.C. to A.I.C.C., received 25 January 1922, A.I.C.C. Files, 1922, No. 3 Part III.

2 Assam Home Dept. to Secretary to Govt. of India, Home Dept., 20 January 1922, enclosing note on how people of Kamrup district understood Swaraj; Home Pol., 1922, No. 525. For a description of market boycott see Chief Secretary to Assam Govt. to Secretary to Govt. of India, Home Dept., 27 January 1922, Home Pol., 1922, No. 534.

3 File dealing with disturbances in Champaran, Home Pol., 1921, No. 357; File dealing with disturbances in Tirhut Division, Home Pol., 1921, No. 441.

4 For a description of the Kisan Sabha movement and its connections with non-cooperation, see *Report on the Administration of the United Provinces of Agra and Oudh. 1921–1922* (Allahabad, 1923), pp. xiv–xix; P. D. Reeves, 'The Politics of Order', *The Journal Of Asian Studies*, xxv, 2 (February 1966), 261–74; Bayly, 'Political Organisation In The Allahabad Locality, 1880–1925', pp. 360–84. Bayly points out that the usefulness of the Kisan Sabha movement to the non-cooperation politicians was limited in the Allahabad area because it was directed against the small Muslim zamindars who supported the Khilafat cause and non-cooperation; if the politicians had allowed the Kisans their head they would have been alienating a powerful local source of support for non-cooperation. *ibid.* p. 158.

from wilder elements and...conspicuously avoided the Kisan Sabhas', and exhorted peasants to be non-violent and not to withold taxes from the government or rent from their landlords.[1] Another local twist was given to non-cooperation by hillmen's dislike of forest regulations: and by July 1921 the U.P. government was convinced that non-cooperators were behind the destruction of 250,000 of the 400,000 acres of forest in the Kumaon Division. As Sir Harcourt Butler remarked from his summer capital, 'We have nearly been turned out of N[aini] Tal. The hill-sides all round have been ablaze. Incendiary fires. The forest dept are unpopular & there is a spirit of lawlessness abroad.'[2]

In previously 'backward' Punjab non-cooperation also took a firm hold but in a form peculiar to the province because, as in the U.P., it became a weapon in a local struggle whose roots were anterior to and quite different from non-cooperation as planned centrally by Gandhi and Congress. Here the struggle was the Sikh movement for control and reform of their shrines which were in the hands of Santanists, or unorthodox Sikhs, whose customs and beliefs were nearer to those of their Hindu neighbours than of the reformers in their community. Since the government was bound to protect the property rights of the Santanist guardians of the shrines the reform movement became by implication anti-government. It was led by the Shiromani Gurdwara Parbandhak Committee and enforced by the Akali Dal. The members of this quasi-military organization marched the Punjab from late 1920, but they grew in numbers and organization after the tragedy at Nankana Gurdwara on 20 February 1921, when a group of Akalis tried to seize the gurdwara and were massacred by the priest in charge and his followers.[3]

As with the U.P. Kisans, Gandhi gave only guarded approval to such potentially violent subcontractors.[4] However throughout 1921 his non-

[1] Viceroy to Secretary of State, telegram, 6 March 1921, Mss. EUR. E. 264 (14); Gandhi's instructions to U.P. peasants, *Young India*, 9 March 1921, *C.W.*, vol. 19, pp. 419–20.

[2] Sir H. Butler to his mother, 26 May 1921, Mss. EUR. F. 116 (12); Viceroy (Home Dept.) to Secretary of State, telegram, 10 July 1921, Mss. EUR. E. 238 (10). Forest fires and other attacks on forest administration were a feature of non-cooperation in Madras, too; *Report on the Administration of the Madras Presidency for the year 1921–22* (Madras, 1923), pp. 180–4.

[3] A detailed account of the Sikh movement in 1921–2 which also analyses the Akali Dal, the Shiromani Gurdwara Parbandhak Committee and their relationship with each other is in Home Pol., 1922, No. 459/II. During 1921–2 the Sikh League, which had adopted non-cooperation in October 1920, was comparatively quiescent, and the control of the reform movement passed to these other bodies.

[4] Gandhi sympathized with the Sikh reform movement but begged the Sikhs not to resort to violence, and, after the Nankana tragedy, not to resort to government courts for the punishment of the murderers. See his speech at Sikh conference, 25 February 1921, *Navajivan*, 17 April 1921, his speech at Nankana, 3 March 1921, *Young India*, 16 March 1921, and his message to Lahore Sikhs, 4 March 1921, *Young India*, 16 March 1921, *C.W.*, vol. 19, pp. 386, 396–8, 399–402.

cooperation tactic found increasing favour among the more extreme Sikhs. In April according to the Punjab government the Sikh movement was 'becoming more and more political and a less reforming one,' and was 'now almost entirely directed by avowed non-co-operators.' On 10/11 May those in favour of non-cooperation controlled a meeting of the Gurdwara Committee and pushed through a resolution in favour of general non-cooperation with the raj and passive resistance to any executive opposition to Sikh reform – a resolution which was confirmed on 28 August by a newly elected Committee purged of most Sikh opponents of non-cooperation. By November the Punjab reported that 'the closest possible connection exists between Khilafat and Congress Committees and various Sikh organisations.'[1] However, this 'closest possible connection' jeopardized non-cooperation as Gandhi saw it, since its provincial exponents were not workers dedicated to non-violence but Akalis in black turbans carrying large *kirpans*, the steel daggers which were a mark of their faith.

The Sikhs, like the Andhra men, were on the periphery of the political nation and feared the devolution of power to that nation through a mechanism in which numerical majorities mattered: yet they leapt at non-cooperation because it posed no threat but was a technique through which they could forward their particular interests. Similarly in the Presidencies groups shut out of elitist politics entered the non-cooperation movement precisely because it could be moulded to suit their parochial needs.

In Bengal, for example, C. R. Das and his men deliberately cashed in on particularist grievances to gather support, mindful of the dangers of isolation which faced an earlier generation of Bengali politicians, and able now to remedy their defect because they had the alliance of the Khilafat organization to forge links with the countryside.[2] Late in June Ronaldshay reported, 'An intensive propaganda has been carried on in the villages by non-cooperation agents of all descriptions and a great deal of unrest has been produced. The things that are said and done in Gandhi's name would make that gentleman shudder, if ever he heard a fraction of them.'[3] Midnapore district was one area where the politicians had great success in reaching out to the countryside. Das's chief local henchman, the Namasudra barrister, B. N. Sasmal, seized on villagers' fears that the new Union Boards, intended as a measure of rural self-government, would merely

[1] Viceroy (Home Dept.) to Secretary of State, telegram, 20 April 1921, Mss. EUR. E. 238 (10); Report on the Akali Dal and the Shiromani Gurdwara Parbandhak Committee, Home Pol., 1922, No. 459/II; Viceroy (Home Dept.) to Secretary of State, telegram, 9 November 1921, Mss. EUR. E. 238 (10).

[2] For the importance of the mosques in village propaganda see Chief Secretary to Govt. of Bengal to Secretary to Govt. of India, Home Dept., 19 February 1921, Home Pol., Deposit, July 1921, No. 3 & K.-W. Examples of maulvis who emerged as political leaders during the Khilafat movement (and then went on to contest the 1923 elections) are in Home Public, 1924, No. 179.

[3] Ronaldshay to E. S. Montagu, 30 June 1921, Mss. EUR. D. 523 (32).

mean increased taxation while power would remain in official hands.[1] He organized a no-tax campaign which spread so widely that in November the Bengal government was forced to withdraw the act setting up the Boards.[2]

The patchwork of aspirations and enterprises which gave non-cooperation shape and impetus at the most local level demonstrated the great variety of lesser leaders who allied with Gandhi or used his name. However, the capacity of non-cooperation to suck in all manner of local leaders and groups was not only its strength as a technique of mobilization, but also its weakness for Gandhi and the Congress leadership. Subcontractors entered the movement to defend or improve their position in their local power structure, and having served a remote apprenticeship under Gandhi they tended to become contractors in their own right for their particular groups or interests, sliding beyond the reach of any central control. As U.P. reported in June 1921, 'It is difficult to know what to do. The matter is out of the hands of the politicians and in the hands of the maulvis.'[3] By the beginning of 1922 the U.P. sent in the news that in many places non-cooperation was 'out of central control. Lower strata in many cities and town[s] under little discipline and Mahomedans in particular are sullen.' While from Bengal came the report that 'The movement...is now so decentralised that local Congress councils are the only ones that count in their own area and even their influence is uncertain in direction of restraint.'[4]

A corollary of the disintegration of central control was the likelihood of violence as non-cooperation gathered strength from local grievances. Between August and November the Government of India recorded riots, disturbances and eruptions of violence in almost every part of the subcontinent, ranging in degree from arson in government schools in Orissa in September to the Moplah Rebellion in Malabar in August, when non-cooperation propaganda galvanized the poor Muslim cultivators of the Malabar coast into insurrection against the government and murder and pillage amongst their Hindu landlords and neighbours.[5]

1 The fears of villagers about the Union Boards are described in S. C. Bhose, *The Indian Struggle 1920–1942* (New York, 1964), pp. 56–7: a good contemporary example of feeling against the Boards is in *Charu Mihir*, 15 November 1921, Bengal N.N., No. 47 of 1921.

2 For the no-tax campaign see Broomfield, *Elite Conflict in a Plural Society*, pp. 210–12; the government later admitted to a virtual collapse of the police and of tax collection in parts of Bengal, Govt. of India policy letter to all local govts. and administrations, 30 March 1929, Home Pol., 1929, No. 179.

3 Fortnightly report from U.P., 18 June 1921, Home Pol., Deposit, June 1921, No. 64.

4 Viceroy (Home Dept.) to Secretary of State, telegram, 12 February 1922, Mss. Eur. E. 238 (11).

5 Summary of outbreaks of violence between July and November 1921, in policy letter from S. P. O'Donnell, Secretary to Govt. of India, to all local govts. and administrations, 24 November 1921, Home Pol., 1921, No. 303. For details of the

In the end violence and the threat of more violence was the death of non-cooperation. It brought down on non-cooperators the heavy hand of the raj, leading to the imprisonment of many of the major leaders of the movement, including C. R. Das, the two Nehrus, Lajpat Rai and eventually Gandhi himself. Moreover, it made the Mahatma call off civil disobedience, thereby halting the forward march of non-cooperation in such a way that it fell into ruins within a few months. In February 1922 the massacre of twenty-two policemen at Chauri Chaura in the U.P. came to Gandhi as the last straw after news of a whole series of ugly incidents throughout the land, making him feel he could no longer lead such a movement and retain his integrity. In his own words to the imprisoned Jawaharlal Nehru,

> I assure you that if the thing had not been suspended we would have been leading not a non-violent struggle but essentially a violent struggle. It is undoubtedly true that non-violence is spreading like the scent of the otto [sic] of roses throughout the length and breadth of the land, but the foetid smell of violence is still powerful, and it would be unwise to ignore or underrate it. The cause will prosper by this retreat. The movement had unconsciously drifted from the right path. We have come back to our moorings.[1]

The adaptability of non-cooperation to local conditions had further repercussions as serious as the disintegration of central control. The danger which the political elite had seen as far back as the 1880s was now manifest – that in a plural society politics divides, because it is concerned with the locus of power in society. For Gandhi as for them it was no simple matter to extend the range of the politically aware because such an extension meant using or forging linkage networks with wider groups along lines of common interest: and in a plural society the interests which could be exploited in this way often clashed. As non-cooperation penetrated the localities the clash of interests, particularly of caste and community, was sharpened rather than softened by Gandhi's tactics.

Doubtful!

In the Bijapur area of Bombay, for example, the non-Brahmins opposed the boycott of schools on the grounds that it would make them more backward still in education, by contrast with the Brahmins who were urging them to adopt non-cooperation. Some Marathas in the Deccan refused to take part in the temperance campaign, arguing that if the excise revenue dropped the government would have less to spend on education.[2] For their part the higher castes disliked Gandhi's emphasis on the elevation of the

Moplah Rebellion see Bamford, *Histories of the Non-Co-operation and Khilafat Movements*, pp. 174–6: R. H. Hitchcock, *A History Of The Malabar Rebellion* (Madras, 1925): files relating to Moplah uprising, Home Pol., 1921, No. 241, Part 1A; 1922, No. 23 & K.-W., No. 241/1B: *Telegraphic information, Etc., regarding the Moplah Rebellion, 24th August to 6th December* (London, 1921), Cmd. 1552.

[1] Gandhi to J. Nehru, 19 February 1922, J. Nehru Papers, File No. G. 11, 1922 (ii).

[2] Bombay Police Abstract, 1921, par. 128 (34); 461 (18); 845 (3); 715 (7).

Depressed Classes and their inclusion in non-cooperation. In Broach taluka Patidars were reported to be much upset by Dheds who entered Patidar homes when they attended a Depressed Classes Conference, and in Panch Mahals Bania ladies felt the need to take purificatory baths after attending meetings of the Mahatma who mixed with all castes.[1] In Bihar and Orissa Brahmins and Rajputs began to feel that non-cooperation 'as directed by Gandhi involves a levelling process and obliteration of caste distinctions'; and they held a conference which decided that Vaisyas and Sudras 'should remain in their present places.'[2]

In the Punjab the extension of non-cooperation through the Sikh reform movement embittered communal relations. It antagonized Hindus, and in turn the Sikhs became suspicious that the Hindus had no intention of helping them.[3] In Bihar, as non-cooperation bit more deeply into the countryside it served not to unite Hindus and Muslims as Gandhi had hoped, but to bring to prominence the differences between them, particularly on the question of cow-killing. Despite Gandhi's specific request to local leaders to stop public discussion of cow-killing, the rift widened and seriously interfered with the recruitment of Volunteers and the collection of non-cooperation funds.[4]

Old communal antipathies sharpened in neighbouring Bengal as the non-cooperation campaign was publicized at a local level. In a Hindu picture being sold in the markets Gandhi as Krishna was painted above a Muslim flag, and one paper complained,

> The manner in which Mr. Gandhi is being worshipped in the country makes it impossible for the Moslem community to pull on with him. We are ready to work with the Hindus as their brethren; we can even forego *korbani* [cow-sacrifice] for their satisfaction, but we will never allow the holy crescent to lie low at the feet of Sri Krishna.[5]

More disquieting still for the non-cooperation leaders were the communal antagonisms generated by the Moplah Rebellion. Hindus reacted strongly to the news of Muslim violence against Hindus and the forcible conversion of some Hindus to Islam, while Muslims were put in the embarrassing position of having to denounce their co-religionists to placate their Hindu allies.[6]

[1] *Ibid.* par. 297 (70); 382 (10).

[2] Viceroy (Home Dept.) to Secretary of State, telegram, 22 May 1921, Mss. EUR. E. 238 (10).

[3] Fortnightly report from Punjab for first half of April 1921, Home Pol., Deposit, June 1921, No. 51; Fortnightly report from Punjab for first half of May 1921, Home Pol., Deposit, June 1921, No. 63.

[4] Fortnightly report from Bihar and Orissa, 5 June 1921, Home Pol., Deposit, June 1921, No. 46; Fortnightly report from Bihar and Orissa, 3 July 1921, Home Pol., Deposit, July 1921, No. 1.

[5] *Navayuga*, 16 April 1921, Bengal N.N. No. 17 of 1921.

[6] For Hindu anger and fear after the Moplah Rebellion see Bombay Police Ab-

Evidently the participation of new groups and areas in his political campaign was a liability for Gandhi as a leader as well as the foundation of his power: the weapon he had brandished in Congress in the face of the Presidency politicians was two-edged. The communal tensions which were apparent as non-cooperation drove deeper in society suggested, too, that Gandhi's Muslim alliance, which had contributed to his success at Calcutta and Nagpur, might also prove to be a shifting foundation for continuing control. Muslim involvement in non-cooperation certainly contributed to such success as the movement attained. The Khilafat cause, more than any other single factor, was the driving force behind Gandhi's campaign. Muslim preachers acted as its local organizers in Bengal, Bihar, U.P. and Bombay: as the oldest Presidency reported, 'Muhammadan feeling is becoming more and more adverse to Government, ordinary maulvis and mollahs who had formerly held aloof from politics having recently been drawn into the boycott movement.'[1] In certain places like Delhi and parts of the U.P. low paid Muslim town-dwellers were the core of the agitation.[2] Nonetheless Gandhi's Muslim alliance, both at the local level and among the upper ranks of the leaders, was an unstable one.

At the level of political leadership Gandhi's major henchmen were the Ali brothers. Although the Mahatma believed that Hindu–Muslim cooperation was essential for the integrity and future of India as a nation, they made no secret of the fact that for them the alliance with Gandhi was grounded in political calculation. In July 1921 Mahomed Ali wrote:

> You...know how confident we felt that non-violence suffices to bring the Government to its senses and how futile was the use of force on the part of a disarmed people against a Government which spent more than half the revenue of India on its Military Forces...When the Congress was adopting for the first time the Khilafat programme of non-violent non-co-operation, the essential thing was the unity of Hindu and Musulmans and even if Musulmans had been ready for violence, which they were not, they couldn't have succeeded without Hindu good-will. Hitherto the English had ruled over us by playing Hindu against Musulman, and Musulman against Hindu. This was their chief strength and our chief weakness. So

stract, 1921, par. 1171 (1); Fortnightly report from Bombay for second half of January 1922, Home Pol., 1922, No. 18. Dr B. S. Moonje thought that Hindus should organize in self-defence after the Moplah outbreak, B. S. Moonje to M. R. Jayakar, 23 June 1922, Jayakar Papers, Correspondence File No. 402. Hakim Ajmal Khan at the 1921 Congress felt constrained to say that 'no Muslim worthy of the name' would condone the Moplahs' acts; speech by H. A. Khan at Ahmedabad Congress, A.I.C.C. Files, 1921, No. 3, Part III.

1 Fortnightly report from Bengal for first half of November 1921, Home Pol., 1921, No. 18.

2 In Delhi poor urban Muslims were the most affected by the Volunteer movement. On 15 December 1921 a band of Volunteers was arrested which was composed of 29 Muslims, 5 Hindus and 3 Sikhs. Fortnightly report from Delhi, 17 December 1921, *ibid.*

long before we were free we had made up our minds to bring about a complete *entente* between Hindus and Moslems, even if the Moslems had to suffer many discomforts and process [sic], and the best man among the Hindus to deal with was Mahatma Gandhi, a peace-loving and non-violent patriot who was intensely religious without a fury of a theologian and whose honesty all could rely upon. He found us to be equally religious and equally without the fury of the theologian, and as Moslems we could not pledge ourselves to remain non-violent in all circumstances, he found that we too regarded force at present to be futile, and above all he could trust our word as much as we trusted him. Even if we ourselves wished to use force immediately, which we did not and could not, we would have lost his support and thus have lost the chance of bringing about the Hindu–Moslem *entente* and thus have lost the chance of bringing the Government to its senses.[1]

In other words the Alis were only interested in an alliance with Gandhi provided that he could carry a majority of Hindus with him, and provided that non-violence was the only viable means of exerting pressure on the raj. Should either of these conditions cease to obtain Gandhi would no longer be able to rely on them and their followers; and he had the political sense to understand this.[2] But the Mahatma was walking a political tightrope. He needed the Alis as mobilizers in order to retain sufficient all-India power to prove a profitable ally and a dangerous opponent to the doubting Hindu politicians: yet he dared not allow the Alis their heads, lest their violent language should rouse the Muslim community to violent action and alienate all shades of Hindu political opinion.

The tension in Gandhi's relations with the Alis was clear early in 1921. They had always been embarrassing allies, but when Mahomed Ali openly spoke of possible Muslim assistance to an invading Afghan force Gandhi was hard pressed to soothe the Hindus.[3] The Government of India discussed the possibility of prosecuting the Ali brothers, but the Indian members of the government, Sapru, Shafi and Sarma, believed that if this happened Gandhi would be bound to support them and then the government would have to act against him, with uncertain consequences for the peace of India: they thought that Gandhi might in fact be willing to

[1] M. Ali to Dr Abdul Ahmed Said, 23 July 1921, enclosed in letter from E. S. Montagu to Reading, 22 December 1921, Mss. EUR. E. 238 (3). M. Ali said publicly at Fyzabad on 10 February 1921 that the two brothers and Gandhi stood on the same non-violent platform, 'he for reasons of principle and we for those of policy.' Bamford, *op. cit.* p. 54.

[2] Gandhi wrote of S. Ali, 'He does believe in non-violence, though he believes equally in violence. If he cannot secure honourable terms for the Khilafat by means of non-violence, and if he finds that he can usefully lead his people on the path of violence, he will do so.' *Young India*, 2 February 1921, *C.W.*, vol. 19, p. 315.

[3] Weekly reports of D.C.I., 9 and 16 May 1921, Home Pol., Deposit, June 1921, No. 55.

negotiate with the government on the matter.[1] Thus prepared, Reading received deputations from Pandit Malaviya and C. F. Andrews, who were equally worried about the situation, and urged the Viceroy to see the Mahatma.[2]

Gandhi meanwhile conferred with some of the main non-cooperation leaders at Allahabad on 10 and 11 May, and it was plain that the Alis did not want Gandhi to see the Viceroy in case he came to some sort of compromise which would be to the detriment of the Muslim cause.[3] However on 13 and 14 May Gandhi and Reading met with a view to easing the situation, although Gandhi did not know beforehand that the government was contemplating prosecution of the Alis. Their conversations ranged widely over Gandhi's views and the political situation; but the final result was an apology extracted by Gandhi from the Alis for those parts of their speeches which appeared to incite to violence, and a promise not to advocate violence while they were associated with non-cooperation. In return for this the government decided not to prosecute them.[4]

The government's policy rested on the assumption that of the two men, Gandhi and Mahomed Ali, the latter was the more dangerous; but since he needed Gandhi as guarantor of the communal alliance he would be likely to do what Gandhi wished. Although this would put more power into Gandhi's hands, the government thought this was preferable to leaving power with Mahomed Ali, and infinitely preferable to a prosecution which would precipitate a dire conflict between Gandhi and the government.[5]

Quite what the relationship was between Gandhi and the Alis as a result is difficult to know, because both sides and the nationalist press had an interest in not washing such dirty linen as there was in public. However, the Alis took great pains to say that they had offered their statement only to Gandhi and their fellow countrymen lest there should be any mistake about their attitude towards violence, and not to the Government of India as an apology to save themselves from prosecution.[6] Meanwhile from

1 Reading to E. S. Montagu, 28 April 1921, Mss. EUR. E. 238 (3); memorandum by M. M. Shafi, 30 April 1921, enclosed in letter from M. M. Shafi to Reading, 30 April 1921, Mss. EUR. E. 238 (23).

2 Viceroy to Secretary of State, telegrams, 5 and 8 May 1921, Mss. EUR. E. 238 (10).

3 Weekly report of D.C.I., 25 May 1921, Home Pol., Deposit, June 1921, No. 55.

4 Text of Alis' apology in Viceroy to Secretary of State, telegram, 30 May 1921, Mss. EUR. E. 238 (10); text of agreed statement by Gandhi and Reading about their talks in Viceroy to Secretary of State, telegram, 2 August 1921, *ibid.* For the official communications between the Govt. of India and the U.P. Govt. on the withdrawal of the prosecution, see Home Pol., 1922, No. 112.

5 Viceroy to Secretary of State, telegram, 19 May 1921, Mss. EUR. E. 238 (10); Reading to Chelmsford, 2 July 1921, Mss. EUR. E. 238 (22); E. S. Montagu to Willingdon, 5 July 1921, Mss. EUR. F. 93 (4).

6 Speech by M. Ali at Broach, 1 June 1921, Home Pol., 1921, No. 11; M. Ali to Dr Abdul Ahmed Said, 23 July 1921, enclosed in letter from E. S. Montagu to Reading, 22 December 1921, Mss. EUR. E. 238 (3).

Bombay came reports that relations between Gandhi and the Alis were extremely strained, and that the latter were smarting under a sense of wrong and betrayal.[1] Srinivasa Sastri, in London at the time, interpreted the episode thus: 'Gandhi has had a triumph with the Ali borthers [sic] but they will try to be even with him and recover the ground they have lost with the country. In doing so they are certain to injure themselves and come to grief. I believe the incident is the beginning of the end of N.C.O.'[2]

Two months later Sastri's prediction was proved right in part. At the All-India Khilafat Conference held at Karachi from 8 to 10 July, the Alis and others supported a resolution that it was wrong for Muslims to serve in the British army. After this occasion there was no question of representatives of the raj negotiating with Gandhi, such was the overt challenge to the government's authority, and the brothers were arrested, prosecuted and gaoled.[3] This time none could have been more vehement in their defence than Gandhi. On 19 September, within days of their arrest, he proclaimed in public, 'I am sorry that I was not present at that historic conference in Karachi and had I been present there and had the conference permitted me, I should also have been one of those who would have supported that resolution.'[4] He then proceeded to organize a meeting in Bombay on 4 October, from which emerged a manifesto claiming that everybody had a right to express his opinion on the propriety of serving the government, and that in the opinion of the signatories it was 'contrary to national dignity' for any Indian to serve the raj either as a civilian or as a soldier.[5] The signatories included most of the prominent Congress and Khilafat leaders, and the manifesto was ratified by the A.I.C.C. on 5 November.

The logic of the non-cooperation campaign seems to have pushed Gandhi into this stand. Boycott of councils, schools and courts, collection of funds, swadeshi, had all been tried in succession: each aspect of non-

[1] Bombay Police Abstract, 1921, par. 523; Sir G. Lloyd to E. S. Montagu, 24 June 1921, Mss. EUR. D. 523 (26).

[2] V. S. S. Sastri to R. Suryanarayana Rao, 9 June 1921, S.P., Correspondence File, Letters to & from Sastri, No. 351.

[3] Account of Karachi Khilafat Conference, Bombay Police Abstract, 1921, par. 577 (18); extract from speech by M. Ali on 10 July 1921 in Karachi, for which he was prosecuted, Ali Papers. For the government discussions leading up to the decision to prosecute the Alis taken by the Viceroy's Council on 28 August, see Home Pol., 1922, No. 135; Sir G. Lloyd to E. S. Montagu, 23 September 1921, Mss. EUR. D. 523 (26).

[4] Speech by Gandhi at Trichinopoly, 19 September 1921, *The Hindu*, 22 September 1921, *C.W.*, vol. 21, p. 148.

[5] Manifesto, 4 October 1921, *Young India*, 6 October 1921, *ibid.* pp. 235–6. Among the signatories were Vithalbhai Patel, N. C. Kelkar and M. R. Jayakar, not because they approved of it but for fear of causing a split and weakening the movement. 4 October 1921, Diary of M. R. Jayakar, Jayakar Papers.

cooperation had attracted some support, but none had given the movement more than a temporary momentum. By the end of September a further and extremer stage was required, and the Alis provided Gandhi with the opportunity, this time couching their opposition to the government in the peaceful request for soldiers and civilians to withdraw from government service, and not in the violent suggestion that Muslims might ally with an invasion to topple the raj.

In prison the Alis ceased to be an embarrassment to Gandhi, but their removal only showed up the tensions in the Congress–Khilafat alliance at a much deeper level. Although Muslims were no more united by the Khilafat agitation behind Gandhi and Congress than in 1919 and 1920,[1] there is evidence of a growing groundswell of discontent in the community at the control of the non-cooperation movement by non-Muslims. Such discontent was voiced by a group of ulema at an All-India Khilafat Conference in Meerut on 7–10 April 1921, embarrassing Mahomed Ali who was trying to act as a bridge between the communities.[2] Late in June about fifty ulema from Bihar and Orissa conferred with A. K. Azad from Calcutta and A. K. A. Sobhani from Cawnpore: their plans to establish an ulema organization for India created, according to the local police, 'an impression among the Hindus, that the Muhammadan community is going to break away from them and the Non-co-operation Movement, and judging by the speeches delivered there appear to be some grounds for this belief.'[3]

Once the Alis were out of the way they could not stem this undercurrent of extremism. It swirled up into Muslim politics, carrying to prominence A. K. Azad, A. K. A. Sobhani and Hasrat Mohani, men on whose political calculation Gandhi could not rely, but whose alliance he needed because they were in touch with the ulema who were a potent part of his sub-contracting network. Between 21 and 24 September the Central Khilafat Committee and the Jamiat-ul-Ulema-i-Hind met at Hakim Ajmal Khan's house in Delhi and discussed the arrests which had followed the Karachi Khilafat Conference. 'Headed by the notorious Abul Kalam Azad, the divines took a very strong line and called for immediate and aggressive civil disobedience. The political faction, composed chiefly of lawyers, and

1 The Bengal Muhammadan Association, for example, hoped 'to save the Muslim community from the foolish and nauseating movement of Mr. Gandhi', Bamford, *op. cit.* p. 164. In Sind the 'essential features of Gandhi-ism' made the non-cooperation movement 'utterly repugnant to the better class Sind Muhammadan feeling', despite such Muslims' sympathy for the Khilafat cause. Commissioner in Sind to Govt. of Bombay, 13 December 1921, Mss. EUR. D. 523 (26).

2 Weekly report of D.C.I., 18 April 1921, Home Pol., Deposit, June 1921, No. 54; Bamford, *op. cit.* p. 166.

3 Deputy Inspector-General of Police, Crime & Railway, Bihar and Orissa, to Chief Secretary, Govt. of Bihar and Orissa, 2 July 1921, in file relating to Conference of Ulema held at Patna, 25/26 June 1921, Home Pol., 1921, No. 180. J. P. Gulvajani, editor of *Bharatvasi*, challenged the Alis with this in an open letter to them, 20 July 1921, Ali Papers.

certain divines jealous of Abul Kalam's ascendancy, offered great resistance to this intemperate advice.'[1]

Two weeks later at a meeting of the Congress Working Committee on 5 October Azad and Sobhani, joined by Abdul Bari, again pressed that soldiers and police should be asked to resign, while Gandhi wanted to give the government notice of this to enable it to station British troops at places where he intended to tell Indian troops to resign.[2] The more extreme Muslims began to muster their forces, determined not to be dragged back by Gandhi: as the Governor of Bombay reported,

> Of course the next fence is the Ahmedabad Congress when great pressure will be put on Gandhi to reintroduce Satyagraha: at present he is reluctant but may be driven to do it by the Moslems. The Moslems are very bitter with Gandhi for remaining free while their leaders are in gaol. Gandhi replies in effect that it isn't his fault and that he has done all that any one can do to get into gaol without success. The Moslems merely retort that they have been let in! Indeed, I am sadly afraid there is a good deal of mutual recrimination going on in the Hindu–Moslem brotherhood![3]

The showdown came in Christmas week at Ahmedabad when Congress, Muslim League and Khilafat Conference met simultaneously, and just over a tenth of the delegates to Congress were Muslim.[4] Gandhi's Muslim opponents, led by Hasrat Mohani, wanted the policy of non-violence alone dropped in favour of a policy which admitted the possibility of violence; and when it was pointed out to them that this would require a change in the Congress creed Mohani announced that he would press for such a change. They launched their attack in the A.I.C.C. on Christmas Day and on 27 December, but were defeated by 200 votes to 52 on the question of changing the creed to one demanding complete independence by all possible and proper means. On the same day, 27 December, a similar attack by Mohani in the Khilafat Conference was deflected by the President, Hakim Ajmal Khan. In open Congress the following day Mohani made another attempt to change the Congress creed, having first prepared the ground, using his authority as president of the U.P. P.C.C. to get U.P. delegates to canvass other delegates for such a change. He called on Congress to remember that Swaraj in one year, which the Mahatma had promised, had proved a mirage and that neither Punjab nor Khilafat

[1] C. A. Barron to S. P. O'Donnell, 1 October 1921, Home Pol., 1921, No. 137. The Jamiat-ul-Ulema-i-Hind had been founded in December 1919 by some U.P. ulema and had been important as an instrument of ulema organization in the Khilafat movement.

[2] Bombay Police Abstract, 1921, par. 1034 (2).

[3] Sir G. Lloyd to E. S. Montagu, 5 November 1921, Mss. EUR. D. 523 (26). The 'Young Khilafatists' likely to support A. K. Azad and Hasrat Mohani captured the Khilafat organization in Sind, for example, in the later months of 1921. Bombay Police Abstract, 1922, par. 11 (1).

[4] Krishna, *J.A.S.*, xxv, 3 (1966), 421.

questions had been settled, and said that he could not see a way out of the impasse unless Congress declared for complete independence. Gandhi in reply upbraided the assembly like a schoolmaster and told the delegates that they had not fulfilled the conditions for Swaraj and that they must recognize their limitations and be realistic in their demands. Congress finally backed Gandhi rather than Mohani, as did the subjects committee of the Muslim League on 30 December, when Mohani's resolution to change the League creed in a similar way was defeated by 36 votes to 23.

Gandhi's allies among the Muslim politicians could still manage the votes of their community behind the Mahatma, though they could not control the feelings of discontent at his leadership throughout the country. Despite his victory at Ahmedabad the groundswell of opposition was manifest, particularly among the Muslim divines. Gandhi had to parley with a group of ulema separately on the night of 26 December in order to persuade them to drop the subject of resorting to violence; and at the open meeting of the Muslim League on 30 December the mullahs and ulema were in favour of Mohani's resolution and precipitated an embarrassingly violent debate.[1]

Despite the defeat of Mohani and his ulema allies at Ahmedabad, their opposition to non-cooperation as directed by Gandhi did not end there. In January some of them began to play again with the idea of setting up an ulema organization headed by an Amir. Taking this into account with the support given to Mohani at Ahmedabad, the Commissioner of Police for Bombay assessed the position thus:

> It is clear that there is a party to whom the policy of non-violence is repugnant; it is, I understand regarded as degrading that a race that has hitherto taken a pride in its martial valour and has been respected for it should now ally itself with an unbelieving leader whose religion forbids him to take any sort of life and should moreover accept its policy from him; and there are many who argue that nothing has ever yet been achieved by non-violence.[2]

Into this ferment Gandhi dropped his bombshell of suspending civil disobedience after the Chauri Chaura violence. An All-India Khilafat

[1] Detailed reports on the meetings at Ahmedabad are in Bombay Police Abstract, 1922, par. 32, which appears to have been forwarded *in toto* in letter from Secretary to Govt. of Bombay, Home Dept. (Special), to Secretary, Govt. of India, Home Dept. (Political), 7 January 1922, Home Pol., 1921, No. 461. A more detailed report of proceedings at Congress including reports on all the speeches was forwarded in letter from Secretary to Govt. of Bombay, Home Dept. (Special), to Secretary, Govt. of India, Home Dept., 20 January 1922, *ibid.* Press reports of many of these meetings and speeches are available in *C.W.*, vol. 22. Evidence of the 27 December Khilafat Conference and the U.P. canvassing is in *Pioneer*, 30 December 1921, Home Pol., 1922, K.-W. to No. 89, Part I, Serial No. I.

[2] Comments by Commissioner of Police, Bombay, 25 January 1922, File dealing with question of electing an Amir-ul-Hind, Home Pol., 1922, No. 551.

Conference held in Delhi on 25/26 February showed how completely at a loss the Khilafat leaders were as a result. They talked of continuing non-cooperation on the Khilafat issue and organizing themselves so that decisions like that taken by Congress at Bardoli should not affect them; yet they held to the idea of a communal alliance.[1] At a meeting of the Jamiat-ul-Ulema at Ajmer in March those led by Mohani and Abdul Bari who wanted to go ahead without the Hindus were only reconciled to continuing the communal alliance by the personal intervention of Gandhi, who made an overnight dash from Ahmedabad to Ajmer, and took Mohani back to Ahmedabad with him.[2] On the evening of his return, 10 March 1922, Gandhi was arrested.

Gaol saved the Mahatma's face and preserved the illusion of his power. The outstretched hand of the raj rescued him from the embarrassment of having to admit that the Hindu–Muslim alliance which he had seen as the precondition of Swaraj was not a rock but a quicksand. The participation of Khilafat Muslims in non-cooperation had given it strength and bite to such an extent that it brought the movement to the edge of violence, and on occasion over the brink into the horror of communal strife, as in Malabar. The Muslim alliance, like the participation of other new groups and regions in politics under Gandhi's leadership, was a splendid springboard to victory in Congress; but it soon slipped from his control and was not a reliable base for a lengthy political campaign, as subcontractors became contractors for their own particular causes and chafed against the restraints of their former instructor. The Muslim politicians could only attempt to hold the alliance together and to restrain their priestly allies as long as Gandhi could assure them of Hindu support and a viable political technique. Despite their recriminations and remonstrances the Ali brothers held the alliance until they were arrested: Hakim Ajmal Khan did likewise at Ahmedabad. But after Bardoli Gandhi ceased to be able to deliver the political goods, and the alliance began to disintegrate.

The third base of Gandhi's power at Calcutta and Nagpur had been the reluctant acquiescence in his leadership of a group of existing political leaders in each Presidency who calculated that they would lose their power if they opposed him. Their calculation depended on Gandhi's mobilization and apparent control of new forces in institutional politics, and on his ability to provide them with a tactic which was a viable political alternative to council entry. In July 1921 Gandhi's successful insistence that Congress should concentrate on swadeshi before authorizing civil disobedience and should not resort to council entry showed that the Presidency politicians believed that their calculation made in December 1920 was still correct.

1 C.I.D. reports on All-India Khilafat Conference in Delhi, 25/26 February 1922, dated 27 February and 2 March 1922, Home Pol., 1922, No. 632; Bamford, *op. cit.* p. 191.

2 C.I.D. report, 20 March 1922, on an article in *Justice*, Home Pol., 1922, No. 501.

When Gandhi threatened to retire from the movement if he was overruled, they reckoned that they could not do without him and let him have his way.[1] But the tactics of dictatorship only worked while Gandhi held the keys to power which the politicians believed he held in 1920. As non-cooperation became more localized in its leadership and impetus, as the Muslim alliance grew more unstable, Gandhi lost the position he had held at the end of 1920, and so ceased to command the allegiance of the Presidency politicians.

As early as March 1921 the Bengali leader, B. C. Pal, broke away from his Nagpur alliance with Gandhi, and as President of the Bengal Provincial Conference warned the Presidency against Gandhi's autocracy and suggested that a compromise with the government might be a better way of attaining real power than the tactic of non-cooperation.[2] Pal was an isolated rebel as yet, and C. R. Das still worked on the assumption that he could best put pressure on the government and forward his own political career by working non-cooperation on lines suitable for Bengal, however deviant from the Mahatma's blueprint. Labour strikes followed the boycott of schools and colleges, despite Gandhi's disapproval of such tactics; and in November Das threw himself into the Volunteer movement, even involving his wife and other women in the campaign.

By the end of November, however, Das felt that the Mahatma was too conciliatory as a leader, however much latitude he allowed individual provinces, and when Gandhi reacted to the outbreak of violence in Bombay with a penitential fast and the declaration that he could not conduct civil disobedience while the spirit of violence was still abroad, Das was one of those who tried to force the pace at a meeting of the Congress Working Committee on November 23.[3] On 1 December the Working Committee again pressed Gandhi to resort to civil disobedience; and the Governor of Bombay reported 'that Das and his colleagues desire to get rid of Gandhi under whose dictatorship they chafe and whose tergiversations, apologies and fastings embarrass and annoy them.'[4] According to Das's recalculation of the political score, Gandhi had so lost control of the non-cooperators that he feared to launch civil disobedience, and thus could no longer provide a political tactic which promised power to the politicians. Consequently Das looked elsewhere.

Imprisoned on 10 December, he heard in gaol that the government was willing to consider a Round Table Conference in order to prevent a

1 Reading to E. S. Montagu, 4 August 1921, Mss. EUR. E. 238 (3).

2 Weekly report of D.C.I., 11 April 1921, Home Pol., Deposit, June 1921, No. 54; Broomfield, *op. cit.* pp. 228–9.

3 Fortnightly report from Bombay, 1 December 1921, Home Pol., 1921, No. 18. Gandhi's horror at the Bombay violence and its repercussions on the civil disobedience plan were published in a leaflet on 18 November 1921, *Young India*, 24 November 1921, *C.W.*, vol. 21, pp. 462–5.

4 Sir G. Lloyd to E. S. Montagu, 3 December 1921, Mss. EUR. D. 523 (26).

hartal on the day the Prince of Wales reached Calcutta, and he thought this was a spectacular opportunity to recover the political initiative and to achieve something concrete by the end of the year in which Gandhi had promised Swaraj. He recommended to Gandhi that the Viceroy's offer should be accepted, but Gandhi imposed conditions which the government could not accept, among them the release of those gaoled in connection with non-cooperation, including those who had been sentenced as a result of the Karachi Khilafat Conference. With his hopes of a settlement dashed, Das was left thoroughly disquieted at what he saw as the lost chance of a lifetime.[1] From that date he abandoned the Mahatma as a profitable ally and began to search for others who would consider afresh the possibility of council entry, a decision which was confirmed when Gandhi suspended civil disobedience at Bardoli. To Das this seemed yet another example of Gandhi's political bungling, just when civil disobedience might have been practical politics, another order to retreat when a road to power lay open.[2]

The lodestar which guided Das and his followers in their relations with Gandhi was political power. In Bengal for the first nine months of 1921 alliance with him secured them the power they coveted, particularly as they controlled the Bengal P.C.C., despite the opposition of the local Gandhians led by Jitendralal Bannerjee.[3] In Madras the position was reversed; and Gandhi's reluctant allies at Nagpur, led by Kasturi Ranga Iyengar, found themselves excluded from the Madras P.C.C. by the local Gandhians under Rajagopalachariar. Gandhi would do nothing to help them, and consequently he lost the chance of building up a permanent alliance with them on the foundations of mutual convenience which had emerged at Nagpur. Finding that they could exert no local influence while he dictated Congress policy, they bided their time, planning to reassert themselves in a reversion to council entry.[4]

Meanwhile in Bombay Presidency and the Marathi-speaking districts of C.P. the politicians who had bowed to Gandhi at Nagpur lost none of their former reservations about his leadership and techniques, and maintained a running calculation of the profits and losses involved in following in his train. One of them told Gandhi point blank that he would only

[1] This episode is described in Bhose, *The Indian Struggle 1920–1942*, pp. 67–8; the crucial telegrams between Das and Gandhi were exchanged on 19 December 1921, *C.W.*, vol. 22, p. 55 and fn. 1; government policy is analysed in Low, *J.A.S.*, xxv, 2 (1966), 249–50.

[2] Bhose, *op. cit.* pp. 73–4; Das's attitude was described by S. R. Bomanji at Congress Working Committee meeting, 17/18 March 1922 in Ahmedabad, report by T. Hussain, 20 March 1922, Home Pol., 1922, No. 501.

[3] Broomfield, *op. cit.* pp. 219–20.

[4] Gandhi's resolution at the Congress Working Committee on 31 July 1921 that the disputed Congress elections in Madras and Bengal should be left undisturbed, *C.W.*, vol. 20, p. 452. Divisions among the Madras politicians are described in Irschick, *Politics And Social Conflict In South India*, pp. 199–203.

accept non-cooperation so long as it proved capable of pushing the government into such a hole that it could be dictated to.

> If you expect me to support the non-co-operation movement exactly on your own basis and lines, I am sorry I shall not be able to do so. I do not believe in its religious character or efficacy, and regard it purely as a political instrument for gaining freedom for my mother-land and as such I use it and follow it as far as I can.[1]

Dr Moonje, when pressed by non-cooperating students, admitted that he was 'quite aghast at the idea of national regeneration by means of the spinning wheel' and only posed as a non-cooperator to prove that the Mahatma's technique was futile.[2]

The real bone of contention between Gandhi and the ex-Tilakites was not just that they found Gandhi slippery and dictatorial, but that they felt increasingly that non-cooperation was failing as a means of putting pressure on the government.[3] Far from providing them with a path to power as they had hoped at Nagpur, non-cooperation had lost them the political initiative. The editor of *Prajapaksha* was one of the first to disavow Gandhi's methods completely and suggest entering the councils, in a speech at Wardha on 14 September: but a desire for another and more productive policy prompted N. C. Kelkar and most of the other Bombay men on the Congress Working Committee who, at its meeting on 5 October, urged Gandhi to move on to civil disobedience.[4] The proposal to throw over parts of Gandhi's programme was aired publicly at a conference at Shahapur on 20/22 November, and at a conference in Akola on 2/4 December when a policy of 'obstructive cooperation' was recommended in place of Gandhi's original programme of non-cooperation. 'Obstructive cooperation' meant abandoning the boycott of schools and courts, and reverting to the old tactic of contesting council elections.[5] Gandhi's reaction was that if the majority of Maharashtrians thought this way they must act accordingly.[6]

At the Ahmedabad Congress Gandhi went out of his way to conciliate the Maharashtrians, meeting them privately on 24 December, soothing them with the promise of provincial autonomy in the enactment of non-

1 B. G. Khaparde (son of G. S. Khaparde) to Gandhi, late May 1921, Khaparde Record 1.

2 *Hitavada*, 5 February 1921, quoted in Baker, 'Politics In A Bilingual Province: The Central Provinces And Berar, India, 1919–1939', p. 79.

3 Bombay Police Abstract, 1921, par. 511 (88), 714, 1034 (2).

4 Bombay Police Abstract, 1921, par. 996, 1034 (2).

5 For the Shahapur conference, see 20, 21 November 1921, Diary of M. R. Jayakar, Jayakar Papers; Jayakar, *The Story Of My Life. Volume One. 1873–1922*, pp. 471–7. For the Akola conference, see Fortnightly report from C.P. for first half of December 1921, Home Pol., 1921, No. 18; 1, 2, 4 December 1921, Diary of M. R. Jayakar, Jayakar Papers; Jayakar, *op. cit.* pp. 481–5.

6 *Young India*, 8 December 1921, *C.W.*, vol. 21, pp. 540–2.

cooperation, and insisting in the subjects committee the next day that non-cooperators should not condemn lawyers, teachers and others who did not agree with them sufficiently to boycott schools and courts. Under pressure from Hasrat Mohani and the ulema, Gandhi probably felt bound to do all he could to draw the sting from Kelkar's bitter attack in the Working Committee on 23 December against the proposal to invest Gandhi with virtually dictatorial powers.[1] Yet Gandhi did not need to fear the Maharashtrians in Congress even if they united with men from Bengal and Madras. This was the first Congress held under the new constitution, and consequently voting power was spread throughout the subcontinent, giving weight to areas like Bihar, U.P., Andhra and the Punjab, which were unlikely to drag their heels.[2] Gandhi's hesitant allies among the Presidency politicians might block the enactment of non-cooperation in their own areas but they could not outvote the Mahatma.

At the Ahmedabad Congress delegates vested in Gandhi sole executive authority of the Congress and the powers of the A.I.C.C. Kelkar's fears about such power were confirmed when Gandhi took the decision at Bardoli to suspend civil disobedience. Tilak's heir opposed this fiercely, in the belief that the time had come for a trial of strength with the government; that if they held back now they would lose face and once more the political initiative would slip from their hands. He represented the views of Tilak's former followers who felt once again that Gandhi had failed to give them a viable political weapon: if he discounted council entry he should at least take civil disobedience the whole way. As the C.P. administration reported after Bardoli,

> This party which has inherited the policy of Tilak, has no faith in the doctrine of non-violence and fears that the new programme of social reform

[1] 24, 25 December 1921, Diary of M. R. Jayakar, Jayakar Papers; account of meetings at Ahmedabad, Bombay Police Abstract, 1922, par. 32, also forwarded in letter from Secretary to Govt. of Bombay, Home Dept. (Special), to Secretary, Govt. of India, Home Dept., (Political), 7 January 1922, Home Pol., 1921, No. 461; speech by Gandhi at subjects committee meeting, 25 December 1921, *The Hindu*, 26 December 1921, *C.W.*, vol. 22, pp. 94–5.

[2] Delegates to the 1921 Congress came from each province as follows:

Andhra	383	Rajputana	399
Kerala	33	Utkal	108
Maharashtra	263	C.P. (Marathi)	44
Karnatak	304	Assam	17
Gujarat	185	Berar	58
Bombay	17	Madras	162
Burma	56	Bengal	373
Punjab and N.W.F.P.	518	U.P.	888
Sind	63	C.P. (Hindustani)	205
Delhi	92	Bihar	558

Source: information given to Gandhi by Secretary of Congress Reception Committee, *Young India*, 12 January 1922, *C.W.*, vol. 22, pp. 166–7.

drawn up by the Working Committee will damp the political fervour of those expecting early and effective results from the campaign of civil disobedience. They consider that Gandhi should either have carried his policy of civil disobedience through to the bitter end or should have retired from the political arena.[1]

The reaction of the Presidency men only served to underline the fact that their acquiescence in Gandhi's leadership at Nagpur had been merely an alliance of mutual convenience, and not a submission. Gandhi had gained leverage in their world because of his other sources of power, but he never had power over their actions in their own regions, and when alliance with him proved unprofitable they dished his plans for non-cooperation in the areas where they alone had real control.

By mid-March 1922 the three bases on which Gandhi had built his power at Nagpur had collapsed. His very triumph in securing the passage of the non-cooperation resolution at the Nagpur Congress held the seeds of weakness, because Gandhi proved unable to control his subcontractors through a campaign although he could mobilize them for a Congress vote. By offering the programme of non-cooperation to the multifarious forces at work in Indian public life he initiated a process he could not control, which drifted towards violence, invited repression from the raj, landed in prison his most able henchmen who might have been able to steer the movement, made him hesitate to resort to the final stage of civil disobedience, and finally prompted him to call off civil disobedience entirely.

As the Muslims and the Presidency leaders saw the Mahatma struggling to retain the direction of the movement they realized that non-cooperation was not a profitable tactic through which they could pursue their own aims: it could neither guarantee a communal alliance nor secure them the power they sought. Consequently they tried to push Gandhi to more extreme tactics. After Chauri Chaura he stood firm against their pressure, alienating not only them but even his allies from outside the Presidencies, including the Nehrus and Lala Lajpat Rai. The Punjabi leader in Lahore prison castigated the Mahatma's blundering tactics, particularly his reliance on the Muslims and his decision at Bardoli, just when his followers' hopes were at their highest. He concluded his lengthy letter of complaint with the bitter words,

The fact is that no single man however able, high-minded, wise and

[1] Fortnightly report from C.P. for second half of February 1922, Home Pol., 1922, No. 18. Kelkar's opposition at Bardoli is recorded in C.I.D. report, Surat, 13 February 1922, Home Pol., 1922, No. 580-II. At the A.I.C.C. meeting in Delhi to consider the Bardoli resolutions Dr Moonje said that since the beginning of non-cooperation 'the leaders had been playing ducks and drakes with the honour and prestige of the country, and the Bardoli resolution had brought them to the lowest depth of degradation.' Krishnadas, *Seven Months With Mahatma Gandhi*, pp. 245–6.

> sagacious can lead a movement of this nature without making mistakes. Mahatmaji's over-confidence in his judgement and his impulsiveness has often landed us, his humble colleagues, in very false positions but now we are simply routed, and the only thing for us to do is to be happy in our prison cells in the consciousness that at least we have not contributed to the collapse of the movement.[1]

Caught in a downward spiral of violence and recrimination, Gandhi lost the leverage he had possessed in politics at the end of 1920. But he remained true to his satyagraha creed. Rather than lead a violent revolution or become the figurehead for outbreaks of local disorder, he called off civil disobedience, gambling his position of political leadership. He had always maintained that he participated in politics to attain certain specified ends, and not for the sake of political power itself; and when the non-cooperation movement jeopardized those ends he withdrew, unwilling to hang the idealist within him by the noose of the professional politician.

RETROSPECT

Much nationalist mythology and hagiography surrounds the first non-cooperation movement and its leader, naturally enough, since in retrospect these were the halcyon days of Indian nationalism, when the whole country seemed to move for the first time against the might of its imperial rulers and before the shadow of partition darkened the political scene. Such is the evidence now available about the movement that it is possible to examine more clinically two of the major assumptions which are often made about it – that Gandhi acquired political leadership and power because of his 'charismatic' appeal, and that satyagraha was a successful way of combating the might of the raj.

During the non-cooperation movement Gandhi's all-India leadership and appeal developed in a pattern very similar to that observed on a local scale in Bihar and Gujarat at the start of his Indian career.[2] It was no monolithic leadership or appeal, but rather should be seen in terms of three tiers of response in public life. At the top were those representatives of the western educated, like the Nehrus, C. R. Das, Lajpat Rai and N. C. Kelkar, who deliberately chose to follow in the Mahatma's train and cut

[1] Letter from Lajpat Rai to Congress Working Committee, February 1922, Joshi (ed.), *Lala Lajpat Rai Writings And Speeches Volume Two 1920–1928*, pp. 89–96. Jawaharlal Nehru's anguish at the Bardoli decision was evident from Gandhi's letter to him in gaol, 19 February 1922, J. Nehru Papers, File No. G.-11, 1922 (ii). For the anger of Muslims, Bengalis, and men from Delhi and the Punjab at the Delhi A.I.C.C. meeting and Khilafat Committee meetings to consider the Bardoli decision, see Fortnightly report from Delhi for second half of February 1922, Home Pol., 1922, No. 18.

[2] See above, ch. 3.

themselves off from their compatriots with a similar educational background, like Surendranath Bannerjee or the followers of Annie Besant, who felt that Gandhi denied all they held most valuable in politics and civilization. Among these educated followers of Gandhi some were true converts either to his ideology or to his novel methods of political advance, while others were temporary adherents, calculating when the Mahatma showed the way out of a political impasse. In 1920–2 Jawaharlal and Motilal Nehru respectively typified these two kinds of acceptance of Gandhi's leadership.[1] However, even those who were never true Gandhians in any sense felt the pull of his personality and were embarrassed by outright opposition to him.[2]

Below this tier of followers Gandhi secured support from a wide middle band in public life – men educated either in the vernacular or in English, small town lawyers, traders, money-lenders, village officials, village priests and ulema, prosperous cultivators, men typified by the Marwaris of Calcutta and Bihar, and the Patidars of Gujarat. They were the layer of subcontractors who were critical for Gandhi's leadership because they formed not only a possible network of propaganda and command but also a potential source of disaffection, if they decided that Gandhi's movement as centrally conceived in Congress did not suit their local interests. On their reaction Gandhi's power stood or fell.

The Mahatma's appeal to this group was partly ideological, as with the Marwaris, and partly political, as in the case of the Patidars. For the first time men like the Patidars found an experienced leader who was concerned with their type of politics, with their aspirations and organization for power at a local level, and promised an all-India political future which took account of their interests and did not cater solely for the interests of the western educated. The first non-cooperation movement showed that Gandhi exerted leverage in this stratum of society to a far greater extent than other Congress leaders before him. Where Tilak had been confined to western India in his deeper appeal, Gandhi's leadership spread, albeit unevenly, throughout the subcontinent. It was clearest in Gujarat and Hindi-speaking

1 Jawaharlal's attitude is described in Nehru, *An Autobiography*, pp. 76–7. Motilal made his attitude to Gandhi plain in a letter to Jawaharlal, undated, probably April 1922, Nehru Papers, and in a letter to Gandhi, 10 July 1924, Jayakar Papers, Correspondence File No. 403, No. 151. He wrote to Gandhi, 'As I have made clear to you from time to time, my agreement with you on several items of your programme is not based on the identical grounds upon which you rely and, if I have come to the same conclusions as you have, it is on purely political or economic and sometimes also moral grounds, having no reference whatever to the religious beliefs of any section of the Congress. My religion is my country, and I am prepared to serve it honestly and truthfully with all my heart and soul through thick and thin according to my own lights unaffected by all the religious dogmas in the world.'

2 See Gandhi's influence at the Delhi A.I.C.C. meeting in February 1922 when the Bardoli decisions were discussed, Krishnadas, *op. cit.* pp. 246–7.

C.P., but was evident, too, in U.P., Bihar and Andhra, as Gandhi reached down in the power structures of areas unaccustomed to elitist politics, drawing new social groups into a political campaign which made sense to them in terms of their local interests and aspirations.[1]

Beneath this wide middle sector of public life were the real 'masses' of India, the illiterate, low-paid workers and the unemployed of town and countryside. Non-cooperation as an integrated political weapon never reached this far: it was manifest only in diverse local forms, when leaders found an exploitable local grievance among such lowly folk, when agitators offered the excitement and the scanty monetary rewards of the Volunteer organization, and when caste aspirations or economic hardship fitted the call for temperance. Yet even at this level Gandhi was a name to conjure with. In March 1921 the C.I.D. watched with amazement as thousands of villagers flocked to Seohara in Bijnore district of the U.P. when they heard that Gandhi had been invited there. 'Never before has any political leader, or perhaps even a religious leader, in his own lifetime stirred the masses to their very depths throughout the country and received the homage of so many people, Hindus and Moslems alike. His influence is certainly phenomenal and quite unprecedented.'[2] *Bangali* commented in July 1921:

> Being present at the various meetings that were held at Calcutta on the 30th June, we have been struck with two things. First, that a new spirit has taken hold of the lower class people, and secondly, the majority of the people in India have accepted Mr. Gandhi as leader... What a leadership! Such a leadership in politics has never been known before.[3]

From 'the lower class people' Gandhi in fact elicited no truly political response, if that is taken to mean a willingness to plan, organize and be subject to discipline for the sake of gaining power. They reacted to him with a mixture of religious adulation and milleniary anticipation. Time and again local reports showed that Gandhi's appeal depended on a popular belief that if he came to power all distress and hardship would end. The Assamese boycotted official markets in this hope. From East Bengal came the comment, 'The people are still almost entirely concerned with the prices of food, jute and cloth. They are interested only in politics connected with the name of Gandhi as so many of them believe that *Swaraj* means cheap food and clothing.'[4] Later the Governor of Bengal was told 'that it is being widely stated in the villages that Gandhi Raj has come and that there is no longer any necessity to pay anything to any body. They [the

[1] Evidence of non-cooperation indicates that Gandhi was mobilizing support from a wider social range than the elites of once backward areas, as suggested by Broomfield, *I.E.S.H.R.*, III, 3 (1966), 279–91.

[2] Weekly report of D.C.I., 10 March 1921, Home Pol., Deposit, June 1921, No. 53.

[3] *Bangali*, 1 July 1921, Bengal N.N., No. 28 of 1921.

[4] An East Bengal district report quoted in Ronaldshay to Reading, 3 February 1922, Mss. EUR. E. 238 (24).

villagers] are consequently not only refusing to pay rent and taxes but are repudiating their debts.'[1]

The idea that Gandhi was in some sense divine took deep root throughout India during 1921–2. In May 1921 the 'idea that Gandhi is an incarnation of God' was 'being sedulously fostered and...obtaining wide credence among the masses,' in Bengal; while in Kaira about nine to ten thousand people turned out to two meetings where he was garlanded, feted and welcomed as 'a hero and demi-god', even by those who had no sympathy with non-cooperation.[2] In Gujarat 'miracle' stories about Gandhi began to spread, like the one which recounted that he was gaoled in Surat and the doors immediately flew open; in the U.P. a regular Gandhi *puja* (worship) started up at Ghazipur, and people strained to obtain a *darshan* of the Mahatma, Hindu women going as far as worshipping him, putting their babies on his lap and feet.[3]

However, such an appeal tended to be ephemeral; and the reverse side of adulation's coin was disappointment when Gandhi did not live up to popular expectation, or when he failed to secure the benefits associated with his name. In Assam, for example, the myth of the Mahatma was shattered by Gandhi in person. As one of the Indian ministers reported, probably with a certain bias, 'All were unanimous in thinking that Gandhi unseen was a far greater personage than Gandhi seen and that his visit to Sylhet has done more harm to their cause than good, and the common people's observation was that he was only a Kaya.'[4]

Gandhi clearly exercised a charismatic appeal at the lowliest levels of Indian society, but such an appeal was a fragile base for political leadership. When Gandhi's power to lead and control a political campaign is analysed in detail it is evident that he, like politicians before and after him, depended in the last resort on the strength and loyalty of subcontractors who held the reins of power in local society and could act as brokers between the centre and the periphery.

In the mythology of Indian nationalism non-cooperation holds nearly as high a place as the Mahatma's 'charismatic' leadership. It is assumed to be Gandhi's unique tactical contribution to the national struggle, a tactic

1 Ronaldshay to E. S. Montagu, 9 February 1922, Mss. EUR. D. 523 (32).

2 Ronaldshay to E. S. Montagu, 18 May 1921, *ibid*; Bombay Police Abstract, 1921, par. 424 (8).

3 Bombay Police Abstract, 1921, par. 441 (11); Fortnightly report from U.P., 19 May 1921, Home Pol., Deposit, June 1921, No. 63; Fortnightly report from U.P., 17 August 1921, Home Pol., 1921, No. 18.

4 A *Kaya* is a merchant and money-lender. In Assam *Kayas* were often Marwaris, and many of them kept tea garden shops where coolies were encouraged to buy, and where they borrowed money at a stiff rate of interest. Comment by Saiyid Abdul Majid quoted in Fortnightly report from Assam, 16 September 1921, Home Pol., 1921, No. 18. Other disappointed comments were noted from the Punjab in Weekly report of D.C.I., 24 March 1921, Home Pol., Deposit, June 1921, No. 53.

which enabled the politicians to escape from the impasse they had reached in 1920, when both the politics of terrorism and the politics of petition had proved unproductive. But again an analysis of non-cooperation casts doubts on such a simple assumption.

In theory non-cooperation was a viable political alternative to terrorism and petition, an ideal technique to use against a colonial government which consciously relied on the collaboration of its subjects for the stability of its rule and was both unwilling and unable to hold its empire by force. However, in practice it was clear that a mass movement of non-cooperation was uncontrollable. As it slipped from the grasp of the political leaders at the centre it became a series of local protest movements, and not a withdrawal of collaboration at key points in the structure of the raj. Moreover, in a plural society the diversities of interest became sharper and clearer once the movement began to impinge on the locus of power in each area, and by March 1922 enough of those interests were sufficiently threatened for the British to know that in a showdown they could find enough collaborators in India with whom to buttress their dominion.[1]

The weakness of non-cooperation in 1921–2 lay in its failure to seduce enough of the raj's important collaborators to force the government to parley with the leaders of the movement. Had it succeeded, 1922 might well have seen not Gandhi in gaol but Gandhi conferring with the representative of the Empire for constitutional advance. This possibility was a real one late in 1921. Throughout 1921 there had been a group of 'Moderate' politicians firmly opposed to Gandhi's campaign and willing to cooperate with the government by sitting in the reformed legislative councils. Srinivasa Sastri, though in London at the time, voiced their feelings when he wrote to a friend about Gandhi:

> You say "after all he is our countryman." So he is. Does it mean we should fold our hands, while he wreaks his unrelenting, disastrous will on the country? I do not agree. We must combat and counteract all we can. If Government curbs his freedom, it does not come a moment too soon. My sympathy, my support must go to Government. *I* cannot let my regard for Gandhi swallow up my love of the country.[2]

With the backing of such men the Government of India was content with its policy of restraint towards the non-cooperators. However, late in 1921

[1] The landed interest is a case in point. Note by T. B. Sapru on Gandhi's influence, 9 October 1921, Home Pol., 1921, No. 303. The government deliberately made the most of their landed collaborators through *aman sabhas* or loyalty leagues in the U.P., for example. See Reeves, *J.A.S.*, XXV, 2 (1966), 261–74.

[2] V. S. S. Sastri to R. Suryanarayana Rao, 11 October 1921, S.P., Correspondence to and from Sastri. For others who wanted to work the reforms and subscribe to the old Congress creed, see circular, 22 August 1921, signed by K. Dwarkadas inviting M. R. Jayakar to a Reforms Conference to be held on 29/30 August with Annie Besant as President, Jayakar Papers, Miscellaneous Correspondence File No. 12.

its decision to clamp down on the Volunteer movement alienated so much 'Moderate' opinion that it was forced to consider parleying with the leaders of non-cooperation for fear of losing the allies on whom it had depended. In the Viceroy's words, 'Unfortunately, large body of moderate and other opinion is either openly expressing dissatisfaction with Government policy described as repressive or is sulking in its tent. In Bengal Indian support of Government policy is now difficult to find, and even the Bengal landowners to my surprise are afraid of supporting the Government.'[1] However, Gandhi was not willing to come to terms with the government, and on 21 December Reading told a 'Moderate' delegation that a conference was therefore out of the question.[2] Gandhi's stand saved the government from the loss of the collaborators it needed. Once more the 'Moderates' felt that the Mahatma was an impossible ally and leader of India, particularly when he wrecked yet another attempt by some of them in January to secure a conference with the Viceroy; and the government believed that it could depend on their support.[3]

December 1921 demonstrated the potential strength of non-cooperation as a way of undermining a government which refused to use force; it also showed its weakness as directed by Gandhi. Unless Gandhi could unite under its banner more of the raj's critical allies, non-cooperation would be only a means of protest for a section of the population and not a technique for undermining the government. It was, as Gandhi had seen, a kind of non-violent terrorism, but like terrorism it failed as a political tactic if it was not supported by negotiation and reasoned discussion. In March 1922 Gandhi paid the price of political miscalculation. With the backing of the 'Moderates' once more secured the government decided that it could safely arrest the man who had tried to undermine it, and on 18 March the Mahatma was sentenced to six years' imprisonment.[4] The middle-aged stranger

1 Viceroy to provincial governors, telegram, 19 December 1921, Mss. EUR. E. 238 (23). *Justice*, 12 December 1921, complained of government repression though it was usually anti-Gandhi as the spokesman of Madras non-Brahmins, Home Pol., 1922, No. 155; *The Bengalee*, 11 and 13 December 1921, did likewise, Bengal E.N., No. 49 of 1921.

2 Speech by Reading in reply to 'Moderate' deputation, 21 December 1921, Mss EUR. E. 238 (50*a*). For Gandhi's attitude, see above, p. 341.

3 A conference called by Malaviya, Jinnah, M. R. Jayakar and others proved abortive because Gandhi would not give up civil disobedience. Press reports of the conference and Gandhi's speeches are in *C.W.*, vol. 22. The government reaction is in S. R. Hignell, Private Secretary to Viceroy, to Hon. Secretary of the Representative Conference, telegram, 26 January 1922, Mss. EUR. E. 238 (14), and text of government communique of 6 February 1922, Viceroy (Home Dept.) to Secretary of State, telegram, 6 February 1922, Mss. EUR. E. 238 (11). For government policy from November to January, see Low, *J.A.S.*, xxv, 2 (1966), 248–51.

4 For the timing of Gandhi's arrest, see *ibid.* pp. 253–5. The Viceroy postponed Gandhi's arrest after the Bardoli decision to suspend civil disobedience in deference to the wishes of the Indian members of his government, as in the case of the Ali brothers in 1921. He proceeded against Gandhi only when he knew he

of 1915 who had captured the Congress in 1920 and led the largest agitation against the raj which had yet occurred was lodged in gaol, leaving his followers in disarray, his opponents in control of the councils and his reluctant allies scheming to capture them at the forthcoming election, in defiance of his plan of non-cooperation.

could carry his Indian colleagues with him. Viceroy to Secretary of State, telegrams, 27 February and 1 March 1922, Mss. EUR. E. 238 (16).

Summary of the evolution of the Congress policy of non-cooperation 1921–2

31 January 1921	Working Committee met at Calcutta: framed rules for the allocation of the Tilak Swaraj Fund, and decided that Hindustani and spinning should be taught in 'National' schools.
31 March – 1 April 1921	Working Committee and A.I.C.C. met at Bezwada: decided that the time had not come for civil disobedience, but called for Rs. one crore for the Tilak Swaraj Fund, one crore of Congress members and twenty lakhs of spinning-wheels by 30 June.
15 June 1921	Working Committee met at Bombay: decided that if non-cooperators were prosecuted they should merely make a statement of fact to the court, but should not otherwise participate in court proceedings or give security if requested to.
28–30 July 1921	A.I.C.C. met at Bombay: called for boycott of foreign cloth and for manufacture of *khadi*; pending the completion of the swadeshi programme civil disobedience should be postponed. Decided that people should not associate with functions connected with the visit of the Prince of Wales.
6, 7, 8, 11 September 1921	Working Committee met at Calcutta: deplored Moplah violence and called for non-violence from all Indians.
5 October 1921	Working Committee met at Bombay: congratulated Ali brothers on their prosecution, and said that it believed that every government employee, military and civilian, should withdraw from government service. As the boycott of foreign cloth was incomplete there should be no general civil disobedience, but individuals might resort to civil disobedience if authorized by their P.C.C.
4 November 1921	Working Committee and A.I.C.C. met at Delhi: ratified 4 October manifesto following the Alis' imprisonment; authorized every province to take to civil disobedience, including non-payment of taxes, under certain conditions which included the adoption of swadeshi by each individual or a majority in each area contemplating civil disobedience.

23 November 1921	Working Committee met at Bombay: following violence in Bombay postponed the civil disobedience Gandhi was planning to start in Bardoli; called for recruitment of Volunteers pledged to non-violence.
Christmas week, 1921	Ahmedabad Congress: confirmed non-cooperation resolutions passed at Calcutta and Nagpur, decided that Congress should suspend its other activities so that people could concentrate on offering themselves for arrest by joining Volunteer organizations, and on preparing for civil disobedience; invested Gandhi with the sole executive authority of Congress.
17 January 1922	Working Committee postponed civil disobedience until end of January, pending negotiations between representatives of the 'Moderates'' conference and the government.
31 January 1922	Working Committee congratulated Bardoli on its resolve to offer civil disobedience, and advised the rest of India to wait and watch.
12 February 1922	Working Committee met at Bardoli: suspended all civil disobedience as a result of the violence at Chauri Chaura on 5 February; drew up constructive programme, which included the spread of spinning-wheels, 'National' schools and temperance.
24–25 February 1922	A.I.C.C. met at Delhi: endorsed Bardoli decisions of Working Committee, except that it permitted individual civil disobedience under the authority of P.C.C.s.

CONCLUSION

The years 1915 to 1922 were a coherent whole in the life of M. K. Gandhi. They spanned the time from his return from South Africa to his first incarceration in an Indian gaol, and witnessed his development from a little known philanthropist to India's major but most enigmatic nationalist leader. Contemporaries and later commentators have recognized that Indian politics underwent significant changes at the same time. This work, therefore, has studied the career of the leader and the political circumstances in which that career developed, seeking to understand the connection between them. It has traced and analysed the mechanics of Gandhi's rise to power and investigated what was happening in Indian politics to make this possible, asking how far the new leader was altering politics or exploiting political changes which occurred independently of his leadership.

Gandhi's recognition as a major political leader was not the result of a continuous accretion of power. His rise to influence was an erratic process, and he followed no predictable route to fame, as so many of his contemporaries had done through the law courts, legal and political associations and local administration. By early 1918 Gandhi had emerged from the comparative obscurity of his first years back in India by leading three local satyagrahas. These campaigns, though 'sub-political' by the standards of modern style Indian politics, gained him both a local following in his home territory of Gujarat and across the subcontinent in Bihar, and wide public esteem as a saintly worker and a humanitarian righter of 'wrongs'. Although these assets had political potential, none of the politicians considered that Gandhi was a serious contender for power in their world, and the debacle of the Rowlatt satyagraha seemed to confirm such an assessment of Gandhi. His first all-India satyagraha came to nothing and its violent side effects were diametrically opposed to those the peace-loving Mahatma had intended.

By the second half of 1918 his public repute was at such a low ebb as a result of this and of his recruiting campaigns that it appeared that in a few months his attempt at intervention in all-India politics had squandered the capital accumulated through slow, constructive work in the localities. Yet the Rowlatt satyagraha, despite its failure, showed that the new leader with his simple technique of passive resistance and his rallying cry of a fight to the finish against 'wrongs' inflicted by the government, was capable of mobilizing wide sections of society who felt a variety of discontents often unrelated to the question at issue, though he could neither control those he roused nor channel the energy they generated. However, by the end of 1920 this erratic leader had regained his lost ground, declared himself a committed politician, captured control of the Congress and persuaded it as a body to adopt his plan of non-cooperation, in stark contradiction of its former policies. Gandhi's dramatic assertion of dominance depended on his championship of the Khilafat and Punjab 'wrongs', which succeeded where his campaign against the Rowlatt 'wrong' had failed. It secured him an all-India following and manoeuvred the politicians into a position of weakness which played into his hands.

A new leader was able to seize power because the bonds uniting the politicians were so weak and because their range of supporters was so limited. When the foundations of Gandhi's strength are analysed it becomes evident that he relied on people who were outside the political nation as it had existed in relation to Congress politics. The members of that nation were the western educated, largely from the three Presidencies which had earliest felt and responded to the educational and administrative penetration of the West, and had evolved a political style well suited to gaining the goals to which they aspired, namely place and influence in the administration, and equality of status and opportunity with their rulers whose educational equals they now were. Gandhi's supporters in Congress by contrast were men from areas such as Gujarat, U.P., Bihar and the Punjab, merchant groups and Muslims, all of whom had been rare participants in Congress affairs, either because they lacked the necessary skills or because they had ambitions which Congress politics could seldom satisfy and fears which Congressmen could not assuage. But Gandhi's campaigns had touched them all by 1920 and in him they thought they saw a leader who could voice their aspirations and remedy their grievances in a way the western educated had not done.

Such new support not only gave Gandhi votes in Congress: it also gave him leverage among the existing politicians who saw that he was a power to be reckoned with. They were themselves so divided by regional differences and personal rivalries that they could not close up their ranks against him, and enough of them judged that support for Gandhi was the most profitable option open to them to give him control over their main political institution. However, by early 1922 Gandhi had proved himself unable to control the new forces which had brought him to power. The new participants in politics, who had acted as subcontractors for Gandhian non-cooperation in their own areas and groups, pursued personal or sectional ends through his technique of satyagraha instead of following his central plan, and as non-cooperation disintegrated Gandhi also lost the leverage he had acquired among the former political leaders. Only gaol saved him from a fall from power as ignominious as his rise to power had been startling.

Conclusion

The phenomenon of the philanthropist's emergence as a political leader forced contemporaries to wonder if Gandhi had changed radically, and the debate has continued since whether the Great Soul was transformed into a scheming worldling, whether the Mahatma and the politician coexisted uneasily in the one man, or whether the religious devotee consciously used the weapons of this world in the pursuit of higher goals. Sir Harcourt Butler at the time, for example, took the simple way out and judged Gandhi to be a politician. 'I am afraid that I cannot attribute any honest motive to that man. He is behind & above all a slim politician.'[1] Lord Reading, on the other hand, thought he was 'a religious enthusiast' who was forced further and further along the slippery path of politics until there was a clash within him between the saint and the politician:

> as his influence increased, as it undoubtedly did and very largely in consequence of what Indians regarded as his saintly character and life, he gradually found himself the leader of a political party ready, for a time at any rate, to follow him blindly...his power grew, but equally he had to meet all the difficulties of a political combination...I have always thought that he became more the politician than the holy man and in the former capacity had to say and do things which were not strictly compatible with the latter.[2]

Gandhi, however, saw no dichotomy in his life, nor any inconsistency between his old and new activities. Before 1919 he had been merely a peripheral participant in politics, venturing into that realm only when he felt he had to to forward the causes which were his life's work – the immediate service of his fellow men by righting 'wrongs' inflicted on them, and the wider service of his country by promoting his ideal of true Swaraj, when Hindus and Muslims, and high and low castes would live together in harmony, where the corruptions of modern civilization would have been purged out of society, and where the relationship of British and Indian would be one of partnership rather than subjection. From 1919 onwards the actions of the rulers and the attitudes of Indian politicians convinced him that part-time political action combined with local, constructive work was not enough if he was to continue the service he had in mind. After the Rowlatt satyagraha he saw that power on an all-India level might be within his reach and he consciously entered the ranks of the politicians, challenging them in their own citadel of Congress. His aims had not changed but the arena of his actions had broadened. Nor did Gandhi feel that he was a religious worker making temporary use of the weapons of the world. Satyagraha saved him from having to wrestle perpetually with the problem of reconciling the use of bad means for the attainment of good ends, because in it he believed he had found the perfect technique of

1 Sir H. Butler to his mother, 21 July 1921, Mss. EUR. F. 116 (12).

2 Reading to the Prime Minister, 4 May 1922, Mss. EUR. E. 238 (22).

conducting conflict. It was to him both means and end, because if properly followed it transformed its exponents into men capable of ruling themselves and searching for truth, without violating their opponents' integrity by force of any kind. On the occasions when satyagrahis abandoned his ideas for violence he stopped his campaigns rather than permit in his name the use of methods which would vitiate the goal by corrupting the protagonists.

Gandhi deliberately set out to challenge the established politicians after 1919, but how far he consciously tapped new sources of strength in an attempt to oust them is a question almost impossible to answer. There is no evidence that Gandhi had in mind any plan for a political career: he was drawn into politics when his ideals demanded that he should pursue them in this arena of public life. Neither is there any proof that he consciously went out to groups and areas beyond the political nation in a considered campaign to undermine the existing leaders and build up support for himself. Rather, the accident of his birth in Gujarat, his experience in South Africa of working among low castes, traders and Muslims, and his belief, held since the first decade of the century, that ordinary Indians were being enslaved by modern civilization through the instrument of the raj and their compatriots educated in western style, trained him naturally to turn to people the politicians had left out of account.

It is tempting to argue from Gandhi's successful reliance on new participants in politics that his rise to power was accompanied by a total transformation of Indian politics. An investigation of non-cooperation shows far greater numbers than ever before participating in a political campaign, coming from areas and groups the older politicians had barely touched, and pursuing goals very different from those of the earlier politicians, because they were as relevant to the lives of the new political participants as council places and entry into the civil service were for the western educated. An analysis of Congress after the reform of its constitution in 1920 shows a similar 'transformation'. Membership figures soared, the organization was extended almost throughout British India to all the previously backward areas, the Muslims and Sikhs received places on the A.I.C.C. reflecting more accurately their proportion of the population.[1] However, the eruption of a new leader with his allies and his policies worked no permanent transformation in the structure and goals of Indian politics or of its participants. Gaol saved Gandhi's face but limited his room to manoeuvre and regain power, and late in 1925 the Secretary of State, Lord Birkenhead, was

[1] Krishna, *J.A.S.*, xxv, 3 (1966), 413–30. Correspondence between the A.I.C.C. and P.C.C.s in January 1922 shows how widely Congress organization had spread to once backward areas. Sind had 9 district committees and subordinate to them 68 other local committees, Gujarat had 5 district committees and 38 taluka committees, Berar had 4 district committees and 100 committees at taluka level and below, while U.P. had 11 district committees, 61 tahsil committees and at least 126 committees at a lower level. A.I.C.C. Files, 1922, No. 3, Parts I, II & III.

able to write, 'Poor Gandhi has indeed perished, as pathetic a figure with his spinning wheel as the last minstrel with his harp, and not able to secure so charming an audience![1] A section of the Congress reverted to the old tactic of council entry at the next election, and the number of Congress delegates declined sharply from 4,728 at the 1921 session to 3,848 in 1922, and 1,661 in 1923.[2] Moreover, after the collapse of non-cooperation and the abolition of the Khilafat in 1924 by the Turks themselves, the Hindu-Muslim alliance disintegrated, and Muslim attendance at Congress dropped. Within two years of Gandhi's imprisonment Congress members and their policies were reminiscent of the closed-shop politics of the early Congress rather than the Gandhi-dominated sessions of 1920 and 1921.

The net result of the political ebullitions of 1920–2 was not a radical restructuring of political life, the pursuit of totally new goals or the removal from political leadership of the western educated elite of the Presidencies. Much of the old structure, geared to the old goals, remained, because it was one real avenue to power in Indian public life. Many of the Presidency leaders retained their positions, because however much Gandhi denigrated the sources of their influence they were important men in public life and had never completely lost their grip in their home regions. The difference between politics before and after non-cooperation lay not in the transformation of the political nation in relation to nationalist politics, but in the extension of the groups which formed that nation and the reorganization of Congress to accommodate the new participants and their aspirations. The doors of modern politics were opened not to the 'masses' or even to all those who had participated in non-cooperation, but to the western educated of the once backward areas and to some vernacular literates from town and countryside who had acted as subcontractors for non-cooperation or found themselves on voters' lists for the first time in 1919, and saw in nationalist politics post-Montagu and Chelmsford and post-Gandhi a means of forwarding and protecting their interests.

Such a conclusion is less dramatic than the assumption which has often been made that Gandhi's emergence as a leader was the dawn of an era of the mass politics of nationalism, as the Mahatma by his charismatic leadership harnessed the feeling of the masses to the political skill and ambition of the educated. Yet it is more realistic. This investigation of the nature of Gandhi's appeal and the extent to which charisma could elicit a political response, and of the sources and stability of Gandhi's political power, shows how difficult it was for Gandhi to make any direct political outreach to wide sections of Indian society. Public life was far more complicated than such an interpretation of the Mahatma's actions would suppose. The essence of politics was organization to exercise power in public life, and

1 Quoted in H. Montgomery Hyde, *Lord Reading. The Life of Rufus Isaacs, First Marquess of Reading* (London, 1967), p. 389.

2 Krishna, *J.A.S.*, xxv, 3 (1966), 418.

power in a diverse society such as India often involved the clash of interests. To expect even such a novel leader as Gandhi to be capable of a direct political appeal to the masses is to deny the complexities of public life and to forget the very real barriers which confined the actions of earlier politicians and convinced them that any extension of the range of their political allies was dangerous, if not impossible. Even Gandhi needed a powerful organization of his own, and failing that a strong network of subcontractors who would organize and control for him in the places where his personal writ did not run: when he had neither he was as powerless as they had been.

A realistic assessment of Gandhi's role in politics must look behind the image of the Mahatma reaching out to the masses however satisfying that is to the nationalist hagiographer, for it does not do justice to the complexities of Indian society or consider the relationship of Gandhi's leadership to changes which were occurring independently of his actions. The evidence suggests that instead of working out from an assumption that participation in modern politics must of necessity spread to increasing numbers, or from the concept of Indian nationalism, and trying to trace a progression from elite to mass involvement in the nationalist movement in which Gandhi is the key figure, an understanding of what actually happened comes only from beginning at the grass roots, from investigating the component parts of Indian public life, the relationship of the parts with each other and Gandhi's place in those relationships.

The all-India activities of those western educated Indians who formed the backbone of the early Congress and earned the name of nationalists were only one mode of political action in the subcontinent. The men who evolved such a political style did so because their education introduced them to examples of similar styles in the experience of the West and because it was able to win them many of the prizes they coveted. However, if politics in its wider sense is the aspiration to exercise power in the community and the development of techniques to achieve this end, it follows that different political modes were likely to emerge as men sought access to sources of power different from those the western style politicians aspired to control. Such different layers of political action were visible in India as people became aware that society was changing under the impact of British rule and as a result of growing contact with the West, though most of the resulting struggles for power were 'sub-political' by the standards of the nationalist politicians who specialized in the manoeuvres of councils, congresses, deputations and the press. The landholders, for example, played their type of politics through loyal collaboration with the raj combined with a customary manipulation of their tenants, while wealthy traders and urban magnates did likewise in the towns, securing the ear of the Collector while extending their influence through networks of patronage among client groups. At a lower level villagers played out their own struggles for power, using the weapons of caste, faction and village office. Such groups were outside the political nation in terms of nationalist politics and rare participants in Congress activities, because Congress was not an arena in which they could contend for the prizes which mattered to them.

Nationalist politics were only an elegant surface veneer, the most sophisticated political layer beneath which were a host of struggles for power, no less real to the contestants and no less political because the style of action evolved by western educated politicians was irrelevant to them. The educated politicians inhabited a limited political world, but they were safe within it provided it remained isolated from the struggles occurring simultaneously at other levels of public life. To reach out to those involved in other modes of politics was generally unnecessary and always difficult for them, because they had few pawns to offer which were relevant to those other political games. However, should their isolation end, through their own volition or because of external pressure, they risked an eruption of latent forces into their political calculations.

Gandhi's rise to power was made possible by events which put an end to the isolation between the different layers of politics. The war and its ramifications in public life produced a situation where various groups were no longer satisfied with the political mode to which they had been accustomed, and developed aspirations which could only be fulfilled or grievances which could only be remedied by activity in other arenas of politics. One direct effect of the war was to push up prices and dislocate the economy in most parts of India, prompting cultivators, industrial workers and businessmen to seek new means of redress, and focussing the discontent of all groups on the raj, which attempted to mitigate economic hardship by imposing unpopular restrictions on traders and businessmen, yet proved singularly incapable of holding down the spiral of prices which hurt the bulk of the population. Because the war found Britain and Turkey on opposite sides it also disturbed a large number of Muslims and made them amenable to new forms of political agitation.

But the indirect effects of the European conflict on Indian public life were the most far-reaching. By forcing the British into a tight corner where they sorely needed Indian collaborators if they were to hold their Empire the war was the occasion for a redivision of power in public life through constitutional reform. Once it became clear that considerable power was to be devolved to Indian hands through the Montagu–Chelmsford Reforms a multitude of groups who had seen little to be gained from participating in the politics of councils and congresses realized that the rewards and losses would be so great in that political arena that they could not afford to be left out. Landholders, businessmen, peasants, caste groups, religious leaders, all realized that modern style politics would impinge increasingly on their local positions as power was devolved, and that they would have to learn its ways if they were not to lose out to other groups of their fellow countrymen. The Reforms not only raised the stakes in nationalist politics: by extending the franchise they also gave leverage in such politics to once backward or uninterested people. The politicians in turn recognized that they would have to extend the range of their political allies if they were to retain power in the changing situation. Thus the war years saw the breakdown of many of the barriers between the different political arenas, making it both possible and profitable for previously latent groups to erupt into the old limited world of western style politics.

Gandhi was singularly well equipped to take advantage of such a situation of latency – by his ideology, his simple and adaptable technique of satyagraha, by his experience of working with varied groups in South Africa, and, as a stranger to Indian politics, by his freedom from those ties with any one group or area which had tended to curb the activities of earlier leaders. The eruption of participants accustomed to lower layers of politics into the modern all-India political arena was first visible when Montagu toured India. It was strikingly clear when Gandhi temporarily changed the rules of the political game in that arena by introducing non-cooperation. People from once backward groups and areas seized on non-cooperation as a means of expressing their grievances and promoting their interests, and Gandhi rose to prominence as he played the role of mediator between the various levels of political aspiration and activity. In 1920–2 he did on an all-India scale what he had done in Bihar and Gujarat in 1917 and 1918.

After March 1922 many of the new participants reverted to their former political modes. As prices dropped, as the Khilafat agitation died down, and as non-cooperation collapsed, their incentives and opportunities for new forms of political activity declined. The latent subsided into comparative quiescence, except for the few who were incorporated into the political nation. However, Gandhi by his temporary exploitation of latent forces in political life spelt out for himself and the other politicians a crucial problem which was raised by the devolution of power to Indian hands. The prospect of power was divisive in a plural society where there was no consensus about ultimate aims. Non-cooperation showed the dangers of clashes between conflicting aims when people outside the old political nation became aware of changes in the locus of power in the community and were given an opportunity to express their fears and ambitions.

The abandonment of non-cooperation and the partial return to old style politics shelved the problem temporarily, but as the British continued on the path of constitutional reform it became increasingly acute. Gandhi and the political leaders realized all too clearly that they could not just reach out to the masses with the gospel of nationalism and expect unconditional support any more than the earlier politicians could have done, because different groups interpreted the 'nation' in different ways or had other foci for their loyalty. Congress leaders tried to make nationalism a unifying ideal, promising nearly all things to nearly all men when Swaraj was obtained, hoping thereby to bind together the diverse groups with their often conflicting interests which made up society in the subcontinent. To a certain extent they succeeded, but the partition of the country and the fissiparous tendencies which have plagued both India and Pakistan since independence demonstrated that their success was neither complete nor permanent.

The Mahatma in his first years back in his native land had shown himself to be a superb mobilizer of men, a skilled mediator between different layers of political activity. But in the last resort he could not understand or satisfy the demands for power and influence which he had helped to let loose and which were the stuff of politics. The idealist created in South Africa became a political failure, ousted by the pragmatists among his compatriots from the arena of politics in which he felt bound to pursue his ideals after 1919. The wheel came full circle, and in the last months of his life the Mahatma reverted to that political isolation and practical philanthropy which had marked his earliest years as an exile returned to his homeland.

GLOSSARY

Proper names as of castes are not included in this list. In the text Indian words have not been italicized if they occur often or if they have become part of the English language as indicated by *The Shorter Oxford Dictionary.*

abwab: illegal levy
ahimsa: non-violence
anjuman: Muslim association
aryavarta: land of the Aryans
ashram: a spiritual retreat; place where a Hindu devotee or religious community lives

babu: clerk; later used with pejorative overtones to denote educated Indian
bhadralok: 'respectable folk' in Bengal, generally drawn from the three highest Hindu castes
bigha: a measurement of land; in Champaran 1.16 to 1.40 acres

crore: 10,000,000

darshan: sight or view, generally of a holy man
dharma: in Hindu thought a person's allotted role in life
dhoti: loin cloth

ghee: clarified butter
gur: unrefined sugar
gurdwara: Sikh place of worship
guru: spiritual teacher

hartal: strike, traditionally used to indicate mourning or protest

jihad: holy war

karma: in Hindu thought fate or destiny resulting from actions committed in successive states of existence
katha: fraction of a *bigha*
kaya: merchant, money-lender (Assam)
khadi: hand-spun cloth
Khalifah: successor to the Prophet as ruler of Muslims; the Sultan of Turkey. From this, *Khilafat*, used of the post-First World War movement to protect the *Khalifah*
kharif: autumn harvest
kirpan: Sikh dagger

kirtan: religious ballad or song
kisan: peasant
korbani: Muslim cow sacrifice

lakh: 100,000

ma-bap: mother and father
mahajan: banker, merchant
Mahatma: title of respect; literally 'Great Soul'
mamlatdar: chief Indian revenue official in a *taluka*; generally used in western India
maulana: title of respect given to a learned Muslim
maulvi: man learned in Muslim law and literature
maund: measurement of weight which varied from place to place; the standard *maund* was just over 82 lbs
mofussil: country districts as opposed to the principal town
moksha: salvation
mullah: Muslim theologian

panchayat: court of arbitration, from *panch* meaning five
patwari: village accountant
Pir: Muslim religious leader
puja: worship

rabi: spring harvest
raiyat: peasant
raj: rule

sabha: assembly, association
sadhu: Hindu ascetic
satyagraha: 'truth-force', 'soul-force'; Gandhian passive resistance. From this, *satyagrahi*, one who practises *satyagraha*
seer: a measurement of weight which varied widely in different parts of India; in British India the equivalent of 2.2 lbs
seva samiti: social service organization
sharabeshi: release from obligation to grow indigo by paying enhanced rent
swadeshi: produced in one's own country
Swaraj: self-rule

taluka: division of a district for land revenue purposes
tawan: release from obligation to grow indigo by payment of a lump sum
tehsil (*tahsil*): the revenue subdivision of a district
thikadar: temporary tenure-holder

ulema: pl. of *alim*: the Muslim clerisy

Vaishnava: relating to Vishnu; worshipper of Vishnu
vakil: pleader, Indian lawyer

zamindar: landholder, paying revenue direct to government
zirat: cultivated directly by tenure-holder

BIOGRAPHICAL NOTES

ALI, MAHOMED, b. 1878; son of Rampur zamindar; younger brother of Shaukat Ali; Aligarh and Lincoln College, Oxford; failed I.C.S. & Allahabad bar examinations; Opium agent, Baroda, 1904–12; Pan-Islamist journalist, founder of *Comrade* and *Hamdard*; interned, May 1915 – December 1919; Khilafat leader; interned, 1921–3; d. 1931.

ALI, SHAUKAT, b. 1873; elder brother of Mahomed Ali; Aligarh; Pan-Islamist journalist and politician; helped to found Anjuman-i-Khuddam-i-Kaaba, 1913; interned with Mahomed, 1915–19, 1921; Khilafat leader.

ANDREWS, CHARLES FREER, b. 1871; Anglican priest and one-time Fellow of Pembroke College, Cambridge; associate and friend of Rabindranath Tagore and Gandhi; d. 1940.

ANSARI, MUKHTAR AHMAD, b. 1880; Sunni from Ghazipur dist. settled in Delhi, 1910; doctor and politician; led Red Crescent Mission to Turkey, 1912–13; founded Delhi Home Rule League, 1917; Khilafat leader and later Muslim Nationalist; d. 1936.

BAJAJ, JAMNALAL, b. 1889; adopted by wealthy Marwari relation; C.P. cotton merchant and banker; gave up Rai Bahadurship and became prominent in politics under Gandhi, 1920; treasurer of I.N.C. for some years; d. 1942.

BANNERJEE, SURENDRANATH, b. 1848; B.A., Calcutta, 1868; dismissed from I.C.S., 1874; Bengali politician; editor of *The Bengalee*; founder of Indian Association, 1876; Minister in Bengal govt., 1921–3; d. 1925.

BARI, ABDUL, Lucknow Sunni who taught at Ferangi Mahal and was acknowledged religious director of various prominent U.P. Muslims, including Mahomed and Shaukat Ali; Pan-Islamist politician; led ulema attending Muslim League meeting, 1918; first President of Jamiat-ul-Ulema-i-Hind, 1919; prominent and potentially violent Khilafat leader; d. 1926.

BESANT, ANNIE, b. 1847; British theosophist; lived at Theosophical Society headquarters, Adyar, Madras; established Indian Home Rule League, 1916; editor of *New India* & *The Commonweal*; d. 1933.

BUTLER, SIR HARCOURT, b. 1869; posted to North-West Provinces, 1890; Lt.-Governor of Burma, 1915–18; Lt.-Governor of U.P., 1918–21; Governor of U.P., 1921–3; d. 1938.

CHELMSFORD, 3rd. Baron & 1st. Viscount, b. 1868; called to bar, 1893; Governor of Queensland, 1905–9; Governor of New South Wales, 1909–13; Viceroy of India, 1916–21; First Lord of Admiralty, 1924; d. 1933.

DAS, CHITTA RANJAN, b. 1870; of *bhadralok* family from Dacca district; successful Calcutta lawyer who made his name defending nationalists in 1907–8 political trials; entered politics in response to prospect of constitutional reform, 1917; allied with Gandhi, 1920, and became leader of non-cooperation in Bengal; Swarajist, 1922; d. 1925.

DESAI, MAHADEV, b. 1892; Gandhi's private secretary and close associate; d. 1942.

DYER, REGINALD (Brigadier-General), b. 1864; Commissioned to Queen's Royal Regiment, 1885; transferred to Indian army; active service, 1886–1908; commanding operations in S.E. Persia; resignation required by C.-in-C., India, after shooting at Amritsar, 1920; d. 1927.

GAIT, SIR EDWARD, b. 1863; entered I.C.S., 1882; career in Assam & Bengal; Lt.-Governor of Bihar & Orissa, 1915–20.

GOKHALE, GOPAL KRISHNA, b. 1866; Bombay university teacher and politician; founded S.I.S., 1905; member of Imperial Legislative Council, 1902–15; d. 1915.

HAQ, FAZLUL, b. 1873; Muslim lawyer and politician from Barisal; moved to Calcutta and entered politics at founding of Muslim League, 1906; member of Bengal Legislative Council, 1913–20; supporter of Lucknow Pact, 1916; minister in Bengal government, 1924; chief minister of Bengal, 1937–43.

HAQ, MAZHARUL, b. 1886; called to English bar, 1891; Bihari lawyer and politician; one of founders of Muslim League, 1906; helped to engineer Lucknow Pact, 1916; d. 1930.

HARDINGE, Baron Hardinge of Penshurst, b. 1858; joined Foreign Office, 1880; travelled extensively, holding diplomatic posts in Europe and Middle East; Permanent Under-Secretary of State for foreign affairs, 1906; Viceroy of India, 1910–16; d. 1944.

HASAN, YAKUB, b. 1875; educated Aligarh; Madras timber merchant; founder member of Madras Presidency Muslim League, 1908, & its secretary until 1921; member of Madras Khilafat Committee & Central Khilafat Committee, 1920–1; d. 1940.

HORNIMAN, B. G., b. 1873; political agitator and journalist; editor of *The Bombay Chronicle*; deported from India, April 1919 and returned, 1926; d. 1948.

IMAM, SYED HASAN, b. 1871; younger brother of Sir Ali Imam; called to English bar, 1892; Bihari lawyer and politician; President of I.N.C., 1918; d. 1933.

IYENGAR, KASTURI RANGA, b. 1859; Madras lawyer, journalist and politician; founding member of Madras Mahajana Sabha, 1884; editor of *The Hindu*, 1905–; reluctant supporter of non-cooperation; opposed formation of Swaraj party, 1923; d. 1923.

JAYAKAR, MUKUND RAMRAO, b. 1873; Bombay lawyer and politician; Swarajist; member of Bombay Legislative Council, 1923–5; member of Indian Legislative Assembly, 1926–30; d. 1959.

JINNAH, MUHAMMAD ALI, b. 1876; enrolled in Bombay High Court, 1906; supporter of Lucknow Pact, 1916; opposed Gandhi's non-cooperation and takeover of Home Rule League, 1920; leader of Muslim movement for Pakistan; Governor-General of Pakistan, 1947–8; d. 1948.

KELKAR, NARASIMHA CHINTAMAN, b. 1872; Maharashtrian journalist, politician, follower of Tilak; editor of *Mahratta*, 1896–1918; Poona municipal councillor, 1898–1924; d. 1947.

KHAN, HAKIM AJMAL, Sunni Muslim from Delhi; founder member of Muslim League, 1906; involved in 'Young Party' Muslim politics and later in Khilafat movement; d. 1925.

KHAN, SIR SYED AHMED, b. 1817; Delhi Muslim who entered service of British, 1837; educationalist and reformer; founder of Aligarh Scientific Society and the Muhammadan Anglo-Oriental College, 1875; member of Governor-General's Legislative Council, 1878–82; d. 1898.

KHAPARDE, GANESH SRIKRISHA, b. 1854; pleader from Amraoti, C.P.; follower of Tilak and opponent of Gandhi's non-cooperation; d. 1938.

KIDWAI, MUSHIR HUSAIN, b. 1878; Sunni from Lucknow; lawyer and politician; closely connected with Abdul Bari; prominent Khilafatist, but did not give up legal practice during non-cooperation.

LLOYD, SIR GEORGE (later 1st Baron Lloyd), b. 1879; Conservative M.P., 1910–18; attached to Arab Bureau, 1916–17; Governor of Bombay, 1918–23; thereafter career in Colonial Service and British Council; Secretary of State for Colonies, 1940–1; d. 1941.

MALAVIYA, MADAN MOHAN, b. 1861; U.P. lawyer and politician; member of Imperial Legislative Council, 1910–20; founded Benares Hindu University, 1916; d. 1946.

MEHTA, SIR PHEROZESHAH, b. 1848; Parsi lawyer and politician, Bombay; d. 1915.

MESTON, SIR JAMES (later 1st Baron Meston), b. 1865; entered I.C.S., 1885; Lt.-Governor of U.P., 1912–18; d. 1943.

MOHANI, FAZL-UL-HASAN HASRAT, b. 1877; Sunni settled in Cawnpore; Pan-Islamic journalist and politician; closely connected with 'extremer' ulema in Khilafat movement, and challenged Gandhi on independence issue in Congress, 1921.

MONTAGU, EDWIN SAMUEL, b. 1879; Liberal M.P., 1906–22; Parliamentary Under-Secretary of State for India, 1910–14; Secretary of State for India, June 1917–March 1922; d. 1924.

MOONJE, BALKRISHNA SHEORAM, b. 1872; eye surgeon and medical practitioner, Nagpur, C.P.; politician and leader of Hindu Mahasabha.

NEHRU, JAWAHARLAL, b. 1889; son of Motilal Nehru; U.P. barrister and politician; entered politics as supporter of Gandhi; President of Congress, 1929, 1936, 1937, 1946, 1951–4; Prime Minister of India, 1947–64; d. 1964.

NEHRU, MOTILAL, b. 1861; U.P. barrister and politician; with C.R. Das leader of Swaraj party, 1923; father of Jawaharlal Nehru; d. 1931.

O'DWYER, SIR MICHAEL, b. 1864; entered I.C.S., 1885; Lt.-Governor of Punjab, 1913–19; d. 1940.

PAL, BIPIN CHANDRA, b. 1858; Bengali journalist and politician; imprisoned for sedition, 1911; d. 1932.

PATEL, VALLABHBHAI, b. c. 1875 at Nadiad, Kaira, of Patidar family; brother of Vithalbhai Patel; Gujarati lawyer, municipal councillor and politician; joined Gandhi in Kaira satyagraha and rose to be leading Congress organizer, politician and Deputy Prime Minister of India; d. 1950.

PATEL, VITHALBHAI, b. 1870; brother of Vallabhbhai Patel; Bombay lawyer and politician; President of Indian Legislative Assembly, 1925–30; d. 1933.

PRASAD, BRAJ KISHORE, Vakil at Darbhanga; Bihari politician; member of Bihar & Orissa Legislative Council, 1912–16; cooperated with Gandhi in Champaran, 1917; gave up legal practice during non-cooperation; d. 1946.

PRASAD, RAJENDRA, b. 1884; M.A., Calcutta, 1908; Bihari lawyer and politician; joined Annie Besant's Home Rule League; cooperated with Gandhi in Champaran; rose to be prominent Congressman and first President of Indian Republic; d. 1963.

RAI, LALA LAJPAT, b. 1865; Punjabi politician and Arya Samajist; deported from India, 1907; supported Gandhi at Nagpur, 1920; d. 1928.

RAJAGOPALACHARIAR, C., b. 1879; Tamil Brahmin lawyer and politician from Salem; firm supporter of Gandhi and 'No-Changer' after 1923; first Indian Governor-General.

READING, 1st Marquess of, b. 1860; called to bar, 1887; Q.C., 1898; Liberal M.P., 1904–13; Lord Chief Justice of England, 1913–21; Viceroy of India, 1921–6; d. 1935.

RONALDSHAY, Lord (2nd Marquess of Zetland), b. 1876; M.P., 1907–16; member of Royal Commission on the Public Service in India, 1912–14; Governor of Bengal, 1917–22; d. 1961.

SAPRU, TEJ BAHADUR, b. 1875; U.P. lawyer and politician; member of U.P. Legislative Council, 1913–16; member of Imperial Legislative Council, 1915–20; Law Member of Government of India, 1920–3; d. 1949.

SASTRI, V. S. SRINIVASA, b. 1869; Madras politician; joined S.I.S., 1907; President of S.I.S., 1915–27; member of Viceroy's Legislative Council, 1916–20; represented India abroad, e.g. as first Agent of the Government of India in South Africa, 1927–9; d. 1946.

SHRADDHANAND, SWAMI (also known as Mahatma Munshiram), b. 1856; Arya Samajist; founder of Kangri Gurukul, Hardwar; politician; d. 1926.

SHUKLA, RAJ KUMAR, son of prosperous Brahmin cultivator in Champaran; money-lender and manager of Champaran lands of an Allahabad Brahmin; moved resolutions on indigo planters at Bihar Provincial Conference, 1915, and I.N.C., 1916; persuaded Gandhi to visit Champaran, 1917.

SOBHANI, AZAD, Sunni *alim* from Cawnpore; Pan-Islamic politician and prominent Khilafat leader; pressed for complete independence at Muslim League, 1921–2.

TILAK, BAL GAHANDHAR, b. 1856; Chitpavan Brahmin and leading Nationalist politician in Maharashtra; helped to found *Kesari* and *Mahratta*; deported for 6 years; rejoined Congress having been excluded by 'Moderates', 1916; d. 1920.

VINCENT, SIR WILLIAM, b. 1866; arrived in India, 1887; member of Executive Council of Bihar & Orissa, 1915–17; Home Member of Viceroy's Executive Council, 1917–23; retired, 1923.

WACHA, SIR DINSHAW EDULJI, b. 1844; Bombay politician, journalist and millowner; d. 1936.

WILLINGDON, 1st Marquess of, b. 1866; Liberal M.P., 1900–10; Governor of Bombay, 1913–18; Viceroy of India, 1931–6; d. 1941.

BIBLIOGRAPHY

UNPUBLISHED SOURCES

(i) *Private Papers*

India Office Library, London
  Papers of Sir Harcourt Butler. Mss. EUR. F. 116
  Papers of Lord Chelmsford. Mss. EUR. E. 264
  Papers of Sir James Meston. Mss. EUR. F. 136
  Papers of E. S. Montagu. Mss. EUR. D. 523
  Papers of Lord Reading. Mss. EUR. E. 238
  Papers of Lord Willingdon. Mss. EUR. F. 93
University Library, Cambridge
  Papers of Lord Hardinge
Centre of South Asian Studies, Cambridge
  Papers of J. C. Curry
Harijan Ashram, Ahmedabad
  Papers of M. K. Gandhi in the Gandhi Sabarmati Sangrahalaya Collection
National Archives of India, New Delhi
  Papers of M. R. Jayakar
  Papers of G. S. Khaparde. (A microfilm copy of these papers is also available in Cambridge, and where this has been used the reference is given to Khaparde Record.)
  Papers of V. S. S. Sastri
  Papers of Sita Ram
Nehru Memorial Museum and Library, New Delhi
  Nehru Papers (this collection comprises letters which passed between Motilal and Jawaharlal Nehru)
  Papers of J. Nehru
  Papers of M. Nehru
  Papers of G. A. Natesan
  Papers of Sri Prakasa
  Papers of Purshotamdas Thakurdas

  Files of the A.I.C.C.
  Records of the Poona District Congress Committee
  Records of the Home Rule League (Poona)

Jamia Millia Islamia, New Delhi
  Papers of M. Ali
History of the Freedom Movement Unit, Bombay
  Miscellaneous files on the Khilafat movement

Archives of the Theosophical Society, Adyar, Madras
Papers of Annie Besant
Office of the Servants of India Society, Madras
Assorted diaries of V. S. S. Sastri, including those of 1915, 1917, 1918 and 1920

(ii) *Government Papers*

National Archives of India, New Delhi
Records of the Home Department of the Government of India, filed as Home Public and Home Political. Home Political files are divided into A, B, and Deposit categories.
Bombay
Bombay Presidency Police, Secret Police, Secret Abstracts of Intelligence, 1915–22. (Most of the quotations from these abstracts which appear in this work are published in *Source Material for a History of the Freedom Movement in India. Vol. III. Mahatma Gandhi Part I: 1915–1922* (Bombay, 1965).)

PUBLISHED SOURCES

(i) *Official Publications*

Census Of India, 1911. Volume V. Bengal, Bihar And Orissa And Sikkim. Part I. Report. Calcutta, 1913.
Census Of India, 1911. Volume VII. Bombay. Part I. Report. Bombay, 1912.
Census Of India, 1921. Volume VII. Bihar And Orissa. Part I. Report. Patna, 1923.
Census Of India, 1921. Volume VII. Bihar And Orissa. Part II. Tables. Patna, 1923.
Census Of India, 1921. Volume VIII. Bombay Presidency. Part I. General Report. Bombay, 1922.
Census Of India, 1921. Volume IX. Cities Of The Bombay Presidency. Part I. Report. Poona, 1922.
Census Of India, 1921. Volume IX. Cities Of The Bombay Presidency. Part II. Tables. Bombay, 1922.
Bihar and Orissa District Gazetteers. Champaran. 1907 edition revised 1932. Patna, 1938.
Champaran. District Gazetteer. Statistics, 1900–01 – 1910–11. Patna, 1914.
Gazetteer Of The Bombay Presidency. Volume III. Kaira And Panch Mahals. Bombay, 1879.
Gazetteer Of The Bombay Presidency. Volume III-B. Kaira And Panch Mahals. Bombay, 1914.
Gazetteer Of The Bombay Presidency. Volume IV. Ahmedabad. Bombay, 1879.
Gazetteer Of The Bombay Presidency. Volume IV-B. Ahmedabad. Bombay, 1913.
Gazetteer Of The Bombay Presidency. Volume IX. Part I. Gujarat Population: Hindus. Bombay 1901.

Report on the Administration of Bengal, 1918–1919. Calcutta, 1921.
Report on the Administration Of Bengal, 1920–21. Calcutta, 1922.
Report on the Administration Of Bengal 1921–22. Calcutta, 1923.
Report On The Administration Of Bihar And Orissa 1917–1918. Patna, 1919.
Report on the Administration of Bihar And Orissa 1920–1921. Patna, 1922.
Bihar And Orissa in 1921. Patna, 1922.
Bihar And Orissa in 1922. Patna, 1923.
Bombay 1921–22. A Review of the Administration of the Presidency. Bombay, 1923.
Report on the Administration of the Central Provinces & Berar for the year 1918–19. Nagpur, 1920.
Report on the Administration of the Central Provinces & Berar for the year 1919–20. Nagpur, 1921.
Report on the Administration of the Central Provinces And Berar for the year 1920–21. Nagpur, 1922.
Report on the Administration of the Madras Presidency for the year 1918–19. Madras, 1920.
Report on the Administration of the Madras Presidency for the year 1919–20. Madras, 1921.
Report on the Administration of the Madras Presidency for the year 1921–22. Madras, 1923.
Report on the Administration of the Punjab and its Dependencies for 1920–21. Lahore, 1922.
Report on the Administration of the United Provinces Of Agra And Oudh, 1917–1918. Allahabad, 1919.
Report on the Administration of the United Provinces Of Agra And Oudh, 1918–1919. Allahabad, 1920.
Report on the Administration of the United Provinces of Agra and Oudh, 1919–1920. Allahabad, 1921.
Report on the Administration of the United Provinces of Agra and Oudh, 1920–21. Allahabad, 1922.
Report on the Administration of the United Provinces of Agra and Oudh. 1921–1922. Allahabad, 1923.
Report On The Administration Of The Excise Department In The Province Of Bihar And Orissa For The Year 1920–21. Patna, 1921.
Report On The Land Revenue Administration Of The Province Of Bihar And Orissa For The Year 1916–1917. Patna, 1917.
Land Revenue Administration Report, Part I, of The Bombay Presidency, Including Sind, – For The Year 1917–18. Bombay, 1919.
Land Revenue Administration Report, Part II, of The Bombay Presidency, Including Sind, – For The Year 1917–18. Bombay, 1919.
Report Of The Director Of Public Instruction In The Bombay Presidency 1912–13 – 1916–17. Bombay, 1917.
Rushbrook Williams, L. F. *India In The Years 1917–18*. Calcutta, 1919.
Rushbrook Williams, L. F. *India in 1919*. Calcutta, 1920.
Rushbrook Williams, L. F. *India In 1922–23*. Calcutta, 1923.
Bamford, P. C. *History of the Non-Co-operation and Khilafat Movements*. Delhi, 1925.

(ii) *Parliamentary Papers*

Report of Indigo Commission and Papers relating to that Commission, 1861 Parliamentary Papers XLIV.

Report On Indian Constitutional Reforms. London, 1918. Cd. 9109.

Addresses Presented In India To His Excellency The Viceroy And The Right Honourable The Secretary Of State For India. London, 1918. Cd. 9178.

Report Of Committee Appointed To Investigate Revolutionary Conspiracies In India. London, 1918. Cd. 9190.

Report Of The Committee Appointed By The Government Of India To Investigate Disturbances In The Punjab, Etc. London, 1920. Cd. 681.

Disturbances In The Punjab. Statement By Brig.-General R. E. H. Dyer, C.B. London, 1920. Cmd. 771.

Parliamentary Papers. Treaty Series No. 11 (1920). Cmd. 964.

Statement exhibiting the Moral And Material Progress And Condition of India During The Year 1919. London, 1920. Cmd. 950.

Statement exhibiting the Moral and Material Progress and Condition of India during the year 1920. Fifty-sixth number. London, 1921. House of Commons Paper, No. 202 of 1921.

Return Showing the Results of Elections In India. London, 1921. Cmd. 1261.

Telegraphic information, Etc., regarding the Moplah Rebellion, 24th August to 6th December. London, 1921. Cmd. 1552.

Statistical Abstract For British India 1917–18 to 1926–27. London, 1929. Cmd. 3291.

The Parliamentary Debates, 5th Series, Volume 41, House of Lords.

The Parliamentary Debates, 5th Series, Volume 97, House of Commons.

The Parliamentary Debates, 5th Series, Volume 131, House of Commons.

(iii) *Congress Reports*

Report of the Thirtieth Indian National Congress held at Bombay on the 27th, 28th and 29th December, 1915. Bombay, 1916.

Report of the Thirty-first Indian National Congress held at Lucknow on the 26th, 28th and 30th December, 1916. Allahabad, 1917.

Report of the XXXII Session of the Indian National Congress. Held at Calcutta on 26th, 28th & 29th December, 1917. Calcutta, 1918.

Report of the Thirty-third session of the Indian National Congress held at Delhi on the 26th, 28th, 29th, 30th, 31st December, 1918. Delhi, 1919.

Report of the Thirty Fourth Session of the Indian National Congress held at Amritsar on the 27th, 29th, 30th, 31st December 1919 and 1st January 1920. Amritsar, 1922.

Report of The Thirty-Fifth Session of The Indian National Congress held at Nagpur, on the 26th, 28th, 30th and 31st December, 1920. Nagpur, 1925.

(iv) *Newspapers and Journals*

(Where no reference is given beyond the title and date of the paper, either the original has been seen or a cutting from the files in the Jayakar papers.)

The Amrita Bazar Patrika. National Library, Calcutta.

The Bengalee. National Library, Calcutta.

The Bombay Chronicle. Nehru Memorial Museum and Library, New Delhi.
The Indian Review. File containing extracts in the papers of V. S. S. Sastri, National Archives of India, New Delhi.
The Looker On. 1920 Souvenir Number in the archives of the Theosophical Society, Adyar, Madras.
The Servant of India. File containing extracts in the papers of V. S. S. Sastri, National Archives of India, New Delhi.
The Social Reform Advocate. 1916 file in the office of the Servants of India Society, Madras.
The Theosophist. Copies in the archives of the Theosophical Society, Adyar, Madras.
The Tribune. Nehru Memorial Museum and Library, New Delhi.
Young India. 1919–20 files in the Harijan Ashram, Ahmedabad.

Reports on Native Newspapers from the Bombay Presidency. India Office Library.
Reports on Native Newspapers from Bengal, and Reports on English Newspapers from Bengal, National Archives of India, New Delhi.
Files of newspaper cuttings in the papers of M. R. Jayakar, National Archives of India, New Delhi.

(v) *Collections of documents, letters and other source material.*
(Autobiographies are listed under secondary works.)

Annie Besant Builder Of New India. Adyar, 1942.
Gandhi, M. K. *The Collected Works Of Mahatma Gandhi.* Delhi, in process of publication, 1958–.
Iqbal, A. (ed.) *Select Writings And Speeches Of Maulana Mohamed Ali. Volume II.* 2nd edition, Lahore, 1963.
Jagadisan, T. N. (ed.) *Letters Of The Right Honourable V. S. Srinivasa Sastri P.C., C.H., Ll.D., D.Litt.* 2nd edition, Bombay, 1963.
Joshi, V. C. (ed.) *Lala Lajpat Rai Writings And Speeches Volume Two 1920–1928.* Delhi, 1966.
Karve, D. G., and Ambekar, D. V. (ed.) *Speeches And Writings of Gopal Krishna Gokhale. Volume Three: Educational.* Poona, 1967.
Misra, B. B. (ed.) *Select Documents on Mahatma Gandhi's Movement in Champaran 1917–18.* Patna, 1963.
Nadvi, R. A. J. (ed.) *Selections From Mohammad Ali's Comrade.* Lahore, 1965.
Nehru, J. *A Bunch of Old Letters.* 2nd edition. Bombay, 1966.
Norman, D. (ed.) *Nehru. The First Sixty Years. Volume 1.* London, 1965.
Philips, C. H. (ed.) *The Evolution Of India And Pakistan 1858 to 1947 Select Documents.* London, 1962.
Source Material for a History of the Freedom Movement in India. (*Collected from Bombay Government Records.*) *Vol. II. 1885–1920.* Bombay, 1958.
Vidwans, M. D. (ed.) *Letters Of Lokamanya Tilak.* Poona, 1966.
The Messages And Papers Of Woodrow Wilson. Volume 1. New York, 1924.
Woodward, E. L. and Butler, R. (ed.) *Documents On British Foreign Policy 1919–1939 First Series Volume IV 1919.* London, 1952.

Bibliography

SECONDARY WORKS

(Only those works actually cited are listed below.)

Ahmad, A. *Islamic Modernism In India And Pakistan.* London, 1967.

Argov, D. *Moderates And Extremists In The Indian Nationalist Movement, 1883–1920.* London, 1967.

Bachelors of Arts, Two. *The Oriya Movement.* Aska, 1919.

Baker, D. E. U. 'Politics In A Bilingual Province: The Central Provinces And Berar, India, 1919–1939', Unpublished Ph.D. thesis, 1969, Australian National University.

Banerjea, S. *A Nation In Making.* Reprint of 1925 edition, Calcutta, 1963.

Barrier, N. G. 'The Punjab Disturbances of 1907: the response of the British Government in India to Agrarian unrest', *Modern Asian Studies,* I, 4 (1967).

'The Punjab Government and Communal Politics, 1870–1908', *The Journal Of Asian Studies,* XXVII, 3 (1968).

Bayly, C. A. 'The Development Of Political Organisation In The Allahabad Locality, 1880–1925', Unpublished D.Phil. thesis, 1970, Oxford.

Bhose, S. C. *The Indian Struggle 1920–1942.* New York, 1964.

Bolitho, H. *Jinnah.* London, 1954.

Bondurant, J. V. *Conquest of Violence. The Gandhian Philosophy of Conflict.* Princeton, 1958.

Broomfield, J. H. 'The Vote and the Transfer of Power: a Study of the Bengal General Election, 1912–1913', *The Journal Of Asian Studies,* XXI, 2 (1962).

'The Regional Elites: A Theory of Modern Indian History', *The Indian Economic And Social History Review,* III, 3 (1966).

Elite Conflict in a Plural Society: Twentieth-Century Bengal. Berkeley and Los Angeles, 1968.

Brown, J. M. 'Gandhi In India, 1915–20: his emergence as a leader and the transformation of politics', Unpublished Ph.D. thesis, 1968, Cambridge.

Cantwell Smith, W. *Modern Islam In India. A Social Analysis.* reprint of 1946 London edition. Lahore, 1963.

Chirol, V. 'Pan-Islamism', *The National Review,* vol. XLVII, 1906.

India Old And New. London, 1921.

Cumpston, M. 'Some early Indian Nationalists and their allies in the British Parliament, 1851–1906', *The English Historical Review,* vol. LXXVI, 1961.

Danzig, R. 'The Announcement of August 20th, 1917', *The Journal Of Asian Studies,* XXVIII, 1 (1968).

Desai, M. H. *A Righteous Struggle.* Ahmedabad, 1951.

Diwarkar, R. R. *Bihar Through The Ages.* Calcutta, 1959.

Dwarkadas, K. *Gandhiji Through My Diary Leaves. 1915–1948.* Bombay, 1950.

Enthoven, R. E. *The Tribes And Castes of Bombay,* 3 vols. Bombay, 1920–2.

Erikson, E. *Gandhi's Truth. On the Origins of Militant Nonviolence.* London, 1970.

Fischer, L. *The Life of Mahatma Gandhi.* London, 1951.

Furneaux, R. *Massacre At Amritsar.* London, 1963.

Gandhi, M. K. *An Autobiography. The Story Of My Experiments With Truth.* Paperback edition, London, 1966.

Satyagraha In South Africa. Revised 2nd edition, Ahmedabad, 1961.

Ghosh, P. C. *The Development Of The Indian National Congress. 1892–1909.* Calcutta, 1960.

Gilbert, M. *Servant of India.* London, 1966.

Gillion, K. L. *Ahmedabad. A Study in Indian Urban History.* Berkeley and Los Angeles, 1968.

Gordon, R. A. 'Aspects in the history of the Indian National Congress, with special reference to the Swarajya Party, 1919–1927', Unpublished D.Phil. thesis, 1970, Oxford.

Hancock, W. K. *Survey of British Commonwealth Affairs. Volume I. Problems of Nationality 1918–1936.* Oxford, 1937.

Four Studies Of War And Peace In This Century. Cambridge, 1961.

Smuts. The Sanguine Years 1870–1919. Cambridge, 1962.

Hardy, P. 'The 'Ulama In British India', Unpublished seminar paper, 1969, London.

Heimsath, C. H. *Indian Nationalism And Hindu Social Reform.* Princeton, 1964.

A History Of The Freedom Movement. Volume III. 1906–1936. Part I. Karachi, 1961.

Hitchcock, R. H. *A History Of The Malabar Rebellion.* Madras, 1925.

Hourani, A. (ed.) *St. Anthony's Papers. Number 17. Middle Eastern Affairs. Number Four.* Oxford, 1965.

Husain, A. *Fazl-i-Husain. A Political Biography.* Bombay, 1946.

Huttenback, R. A. 'Indians In South Africa, 1860–1914: the British Imperial Philosophy on Trial', *The English Historical Review,* vol. LXXXI, 1966.

(See also the following which was published after my book was finished: Huttenback, R. A. *Gandhi in South Africa British Imperialism and the Indian Question, 1860–1914.* Ithaca and London, 1971.)

Hyam, R. *Elgin and Churchill at the Colonial Office 1905–1908. The Watershed of the Empire–Commonwealth.* London, 1968.

Hyde, H. Montgomery, *Lord Reading. The Life of Rufus Isaacs, First Marquess of Reading.* London, 1967.

Iqbal, A. (ed.) *My Life A Fragment. An Autobiographical Sketch of Maulana Mohamed Ali.* Reprint of 1942 edition, Lahore, 1963.

Irschick, E. F. *Politics And Social Conflict In South India. The Non-Brahman Movement And Tamil Separatism, 1916–1929.* Berkeley and Los Angeles, 1969.

Jayakar, M. R. *The Story Of My Life. Volume One. 1873–1922.* Bombay, 1958.

Johnson, G. 'Indian Politics 1888–1908', Unpublished Ph.D. thesis, 1967, Cambridge.

'Maharashtrian Politics And Indian Nationalism 1880–1920', Unpublished Thirlwall Prize Essay, 1969, Cambridge.

Jones, K. W. 'Communalism in the Punjab. The Arya Samaj Contribution', *The Journal Of Asian Studies,* XXVIII, 1 (1968).

Kahin, G. M., Pauker, G. J., and Pye, L. W. 'Comparative Politics Of Non-Western Countries', *The American Political Science Review,* XLIX, 4 (1955).

Kannangara, A. P. 'Indian Millowners And Indian Nationalism Before 1914', *Past And Present*, no. 40, 1968.

Kling, B. B. *The Blue Mutiny. The Indigo Disturbances in Bengal 1859–1862.* Philadelphia, 1966.

Krishna, Gopal. 'The Development of the Indian National Congress as a Mass Organization, 1918–1923', *The Journal Of Asian Studies*, XXV, 3 (1966).

'The Khilafat Movement In India: The First Phase (September 1919–August 1920)', *Journal Of The Royal Asiatic Society*, parts 1 and 2, 1968.

Krishnadas. *Seven Months With Mahatma Gandhi Being An Inside View Of The Non-Co-operation Movement Of 1921–22*, ed. R. B. Gregg. Ahmedabad, 1951.

Kumar, R. *Western India In The Nineteenth Century. A Study in the Social History of Maharashtra.* London and Toronto, 1968.

Kumar, R. (ed.) *Essays On Gandhian Politics. The Rowlatt Satyagraha of 1919.* Oxford, 1971.

Leonard, J. G. 'Politics And Social Change In South India: A Study Of The Andhra Movement', *Journal of Commonwealth Political Studies*, V, 1 (1967).

Low, D. A. 'The Government of India and the First Non-Cooperation Movement – 1920–1922', *The Journal Of Asian Studies*, XXV, 2 (1966).

Low, D. A. (ed.) *Soundings In Modern South Asian History.* London, 1968.

McCully, B. T. *English Education And The Origins Of Indian Nationalism.* New York, 1940.

McPherson, K. 'The Political Development of the Urdu- and Tamil-speaking Muslims of the Madras Presidency 1901 to 1937', Unpublished M.A. thesis, 1968, University of Western Australia.

Mehta, J. M. *A Study Of Rural Economy Of Gujarat Containing Possibilities of Reconstruction.* Baroda, 1930.

Mishra, G. 'Socio-Economic Background of Gandhi's Champaran Movement', *The Indian Economic And Social History Review*, V, 3 (1968).

Montagu, E. S. *An Indian Diary.* London, 1930.

Mukherjee, H. and U. *The Origins Of The National Education Movement. (1905–1910).* Calcutta, 1957.

Sri Aurobindo And The New Thought In Indian Politics. Calcutta, 1964.

Mukherjee, S. N. (ed.) *St. Anthony's Papers. Number 18 South Asian Affairs Number Two.* Oxford, 1966.

Nair, K. *Blossoms In The Dust. The Human Element in Indian Development.* London, 1961.

Nanda, B. R. *Mahatma Gandhi.* Boston, 1958.

The Nehrus: Motilal and Jawaharlal. London, 1962.

Narasimhan, V. K. *Kasturi Ranga Iyengar.* Delhi, 1963.

Nehru, J. *An Autobiography.* London, 1936.

O'Dwyer, M. *India As I Knew It 1885–1925.* London, 1925.

Owen, H. F. 'The Leadership of The Indian National Movement. 1914–20', Unpublished Ph.D. thesis, 1965, Australian National University.

Palmer, M. *The History Of The Indians In Natal.* Cape Town, 1957.

Panjabi, K. L. *The Indomitable Sardar.* Bombay, 1964.

Philips, C. H. (ed.) *Politics And Society In India.* London, 1963.
Pocock, D. 'The Movement of Castes', *Man,* vol. LV, 1955.
'Inclusion And Exclusion: A Process In The Caste System Of Gujarat', *Southwestern Journal of Anthropology,* vol. 13, 1957.
Prasad, Rajendra. *Mahatma Gandhi And Bihar. Some Reminiscences.* Bombay, 1949.
Satyagraha In Champaran. 2nd. revised edition, Ahmedabad, 1949.
Qureshi, I. H. *The Muslim Community Of The Indo-Pakistan Subcontinent (610–1947).* The Hague, 1962.
Ray, P. C. *Life And Times Of C. R. Das.* London, 1927.
Ray, S. (ed.) *Gandhi, India and the World.* Melbourne, 1970.
Reed, S. *The India I Knew. 1897–1947.* London, 1952.
Reeves, P. D. 'The Politics of Order', *The Journal Of Asian Studies,* XXV, 2 (1966).
Risley, H. H. *The Tribes and Castes of Bengal. Ethnographic Glossary.* 2 vols. Calcutta, 1891.
Robinson, F. C. R. 'The Politics Of U.P. Muslims 1906–1922', Unpublished Ph.D. thesis, 1970, Cambridge.
Robinson, R., and Gallagher, J. *Africa and the Victorians. The Official Mind of Imperialism.* Paperback edition, London, 1965.
Rudolph, L. I. and S. H. 'The Political Role of India's Caste Associations', *Pacific Affairs,* XXXIII, 1 (1960).
The Modernity Of Tradition. Political Development in India. Chicago and London, 1967.
Sayeed, K. B. *Pakistan. The Formative Phase. 1857–1948.* 2nd edition, London, 1968.
Seal, A. *The Emergence Of Indian Nationalism. Competition and Collaboration in the Later Nineteenth Century.* Cambridge, 1968.
Sitaramayya, B. P. *The History Of The Indian National Congress. Volume 1 (1885–1935).* Bombay, 1935.
Soman, R. J. *Peaceful Industrial Relations. Their Science And Technique.* Ahmedabad, 1957.
Spear, P. *The Nabobs.* Revised edition, London, 1963.
Srinivas, M. N. *Social Change In Modern India.* Berkeley and Los Angeles, 1966.
Tahmankar, D. V. *Sardar Patel.* London, 1970.
Tendulkar, D. G. *Mahatma.* Vol. 1. revised edition, Delhi, 1960.
Thompson, E. and Garrat, G. T. *Rise And Fulfilment Of British Rule In India.* London, 1935.
Trevelyan, C. E. *On the education of the people of India.* London, 1838.
Waheed-uz-Zaman. *Towards Pakistan.* Lahore, 1964.
Weiner, M. *Party Building In A New Nation. The Indian National Congress.* Chicago and London, 1967.
Wolpert, S. A. *Tilak And Gokhale: Revolution and Reform in the Making of Modern India.* Berkeley and Los Angeles, 1962.
Worsley, P. *The Trumpet Shall Sound. A Study of 'Cargo' Cults in Melanesia.* 2nd edition, London, 1968.
Young, G. M. (ed.) *Macaulay. Prose And Poetry.* London, 1952.
Zetland, '*Essayez.*' London, 1956.

INDEX

Index